SPELLING CONNECTIONS

The Right Connections, The Right Results!

Author
J. Richard Gentry, Ph.D.

Spelling **and** Thinking

Spelling **and** Vocabulary

Spelling **and** Reading

Spelling **and** Writing

Make the Right Connections

These Connections

Spelling **and** Thinking

Spelling **and** Vocabulary

Spelling **and** Reading

Spelling **and** Writing

Spelling Connections helps students make the important connections for real spelling success.

Unit 14
More Letters Than Sounds

short a or short e

1.
2.
3.
4.
5.
6.
7.
8.
9.
10.

Spelling **and** Thinking

READ THE SPELLING WORDS

1. meant	*meant*	I **meant** to return the library book.
2. build	*build*	Shall we **build** a tree house?
3. flood	*flood*	The **flood** was caused by heavy rain.
4. laugh	*laugh*	I had to **laugh** at your funny story.
5. breakfast	*breakfast*	I like **breakfast** better than lunch.
6. enough	*enough*	One ball game a day is **enough** for me.
7. sweater	*sweater*	Wear a **sweater** when it is cool.
8. rough	*rough*	Sandpaper is **rough,** not smooth.
9. bread	*bread*	Do you want **bread** or crackers?
10. touch	*touch*	Silk feels soft when you **touch** it.
11. spread	*spread*	The young bird **spread** its wings.
12. tough	*tough*	Old corn can be **tough** and chewy.
13. already	*already*	The sun has **already** risen.
14. built	*built*	My grandparents **built** a log cabin.
15. ready	*ready*	I am **ready** to go to bed.
16. death	*death*	That is not a life or **death** matter.
17. young	*young*	Both **young** and old enjoyed the show.
18. instead	*instead*	Amy played the part **instead** of Sue.
19. heavy	*heavy*	Can you carry that **heavy** bundle?
20. ahead	*ahead*	I will go **ahead** and meet you there.

SORT THE SPELLING WORDS

1.–12. Write the spelling words with the **short a** or the **short e** sound. Circle the letters that spell this sound.

13.–20. Write the spelling words with the **short i** or the **short u** sound. Circle the letters that spell this sound.

REMEMBER THE SPELLING STRATEGY

Remember that some words have more vowel letters than vowel sounds.

▲ **Connections to Thinking**
Help students understand important spelling strategies.

Spelling **and** Vocabulary

Word Meanings
Write a spelling word that has the same meaning as each definition.
1. the first meal of the day
2. by this time; before
3. in place of
4. a knitted garment worn on the upper part of the body

Phonics
Change one letter at the beginning of each word to write a spelling word.
5. dread
6. guild
7. blood
8. quilt

Add one letter at the end of each word to write a spelling word.
9. mean
10. read

Antonyms
Write the spelling word that is an antonym of each word.
11. cry
12. smooth
13. tender
14. life
15. light
16. gather

USING THE Thesaurus
Write a spelling word to complete each synonym set.
17. adequate, ample, sufficient, ——
18. feel, handle, stroke, ——
19. before, forward, ——
20. juvenile, youthful, ——

♦ ♦ ♦

Thesaurus Check Be sure to check the synonyms in your **Writing Thesaurus**.

Word Meanings
1.
2.
3.
4.

Phonics
5.
6.
7.
8.
9.
10.

Antonyms
11.
12.
13.
14.
15.
16.

Using the Thesaurus
17.
18.
19.
20.

◀ **Connections to Vocabulary**
Place spelling words in a meaningful context.

Make the Right Connections

Make Spelling Work

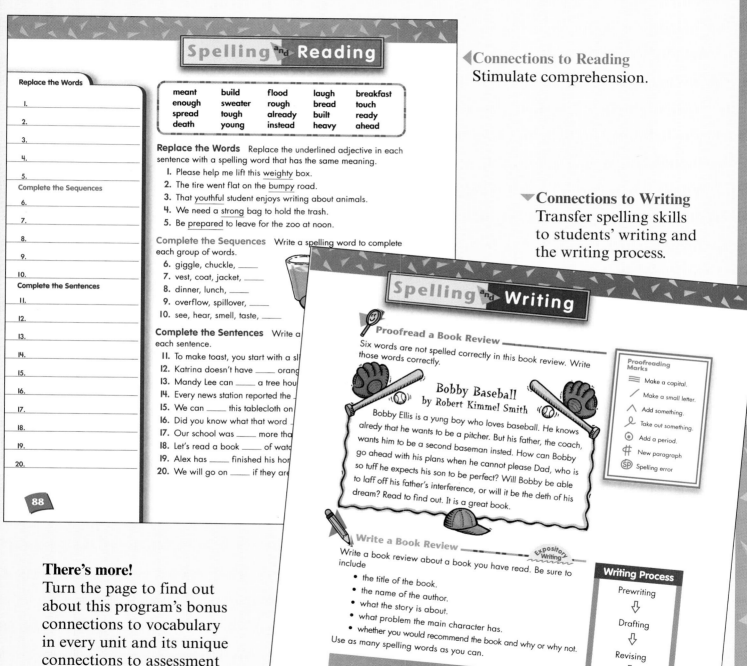

Spelling and Reading

meant	build	flood	laugh	breakfast
enough	sweater	rough	bread	touch
spread	tough	already	built	ready
death	young	instead	heavy	ahead

Replace the Words   Replace the underlined adjective in each sentence with a spelling word that has the same meaning.

1. Please help me lift this weighty box.
2. The tire went flat on the bumpy road.
3. That youthful student enjoys writing about animals.
4. We need a strong bag to hold the trash.
5. Be prepared to leave for the zoo at noon.

Complete the Sequences   Write a spelling word to complete each group of words.

6. giggle, chuckle, _____
7. vest, coat, jacket, _____
8. dinner, lunch, _____
9. overflow, spillover, _____
10. see, hear, smell, taste, _____

Complete the Sentences   Write a [spelling word to complete] each sentence.

11. To make toast, you start with a sl[ice]
12. Katrina doesn't have _____ orang[es]
13. Mandy Lee can _____ a tree hou[se]
14. Every news station reported the _____
15. We can _____ this tablecloth on
16. Did you know what that word _____
17. Our school was _____ more tha[n]
18. Let's read a book _____ of wat[ching]
19. Alex has _____ finished his hor[se]
20. We will go on _____ if they are

Replace the Words

1.
2.
3.
4.
5.

Complete the Sequences

6.
7.
8.
9.
10.

Complete the Sentences

11.
12.
13.
14.
15.
16.
17.
18.
19.
20.

88

◀ **Connections to Reading**
Stimulate comprehension.

▼ **Connections to Writing**
Transfer spelling skills to students' writing and the writing process.

Spelling and Writing

🎾 **Proofread a Book Review**

Six words are not spelled correctly in this book review. Write those words correctly.

Bobby Baseball
by Robert Kimmel Smith

Bobby Ellis is a yung boy who loves baseball. He knows alredy that he wants to be a pitcher. But his father, the coach, wants him to be a second baseman insted. How can Bobby go ahead with his plans when he cannot please Dad, who is so tuff he expects his son to be perfect? Will Bobby be able to laff off his father's interference, or will it be the deth of his dream? Read to find out. It is a great book.

Proofreading Marks

≡ Make a capital.
/ Make a small letter.
∧ Add something.
ℰ Take out something.
⊙ Add a period.
New paragraph
ⓢⓟ Spelling error

✏ **Write a Book Review** _____ *Expository Writing*

Write a book review about a book you have read. Be sure to include

• the title of the book.
• the name of the author.
• what the story is about.
• what problem the main character has.
• whether you would recommend the book and why or why not.

Use as many spelling words as you can.

Proofread Your Writing During

Writing Process

Prewriting
⇩
Drafting
⇩
Revising
⇩
Editing
⇩
Publishing

Proofread your writing for spelling errors as part of the editing stage in the writing process. Be sure to check each word carefully. Use a dictionary to check spelling if you are not sure.

89

There's more!
Turn the page to find out about this program's bonus connections to vocabulary in every unit and its unique connections to assessment and review.

Vocabulary Connections
in Every Unit!

Vocabulary study improves scores on achievement tests and learning outcomes in all the content areas. **Every** unit connects spelling and vocabulary development. And two more bonus pages in every unit ensure vocabulary growth and understanding.

▼ **Connections to Strategy Words**
Reinforce each strategy with additional words above and below grade level.

▼ **Connections to Content Words**
Help students learn the important content-area words for their grade.

Conne

Vocabulary

Unit 14 enrichment

Strategy Words

Review Words

1. _____
2. _____
3. _____
4. _____
5. _____

Preview Words

6. _____
7. _____
8. _____
9. _____
10. _____

Review Words: More Letters Than Sounds

Write a word from the box that spells each sound in the following way.

| heat | board | friend | great | weigh |

1. the **long e** sound spelled **ea**
2. the **long a** sound spelled **ea**
3. the **long a** sound spelled **eigh**
4. the **short e** sound spelled **ie**
5. the **/ô/** sound spelled **oa**

Preview Words: More Letters Than Sounds

Write words from the box by adding missing letters.

| plaid | pleasant | pleasure | subhead | sweatshirt |

6. ple _ _ _ re
7. s _ bh _ _ d
8. pl _ _ d
9. sw _ _ _ tsh _ rt
10. plea _ _ _ _ t

Conte Content Words

Health: Medicine

Write words from the box to complete the p...

| headache | discover | cause | scien... |

Modern _1._ has searched for years to ... the common cold, but scientists have only l... make cold sufferers more comfortable. Too... remedies can merely relieve your _3._ an... Doctors know that germs are the _4._ of ... but they have not found the remedy. May... become the first scientist to _5._ that re...

Health: Being Me

Write a word from the box to match ea...

| height | temper | mood | well-... |

6. a state of mind; rhymes with foo...
7. how tall someone or something ...
8. how strong someone or somethi...
9. a state of feeling good
10. one's usual state of mind; one's...

Apply the Spelling Strategy

Circle the two-letter spelling of the ... and the **long i** sound in two of the ... you wrote.

Assessment Connections
Focus Study and Review

Spelling Connections offers a new connection to assessment that jump-starts traditional review. Students apply the strategies taught in the five preceding units to new words.

▼ **New Assessment Connection**
Provides a better focus for review.

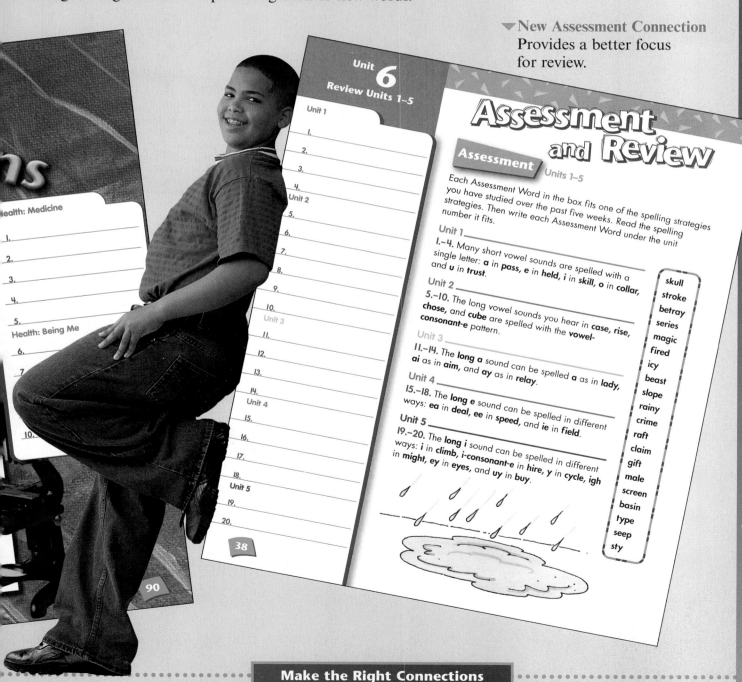

Health: Medicine

1. ____
2. ____
3. ____
4. ____
5. ____

Health: Being Me

6. ____
7. ____
10. ____

Unit 6
Review Units 1–5

Unit 1
1. ____
2. ____
3. ____
4. ____

Unit 2
5. ____
6. ____
7. ____
8. ____
9. ____
10. ____

Unit 3
11. ____
12. ____
13. ____
14. ____

Unit 4
15. ____
16. ____
17. ____
18. ____

Unit 5
19. ____
20. ____

38

Assessment and Review

Assessment Units 1–5

Each Assessment Word in the box fits one of the spelling strategies you have studied over the past five weeks. Read the spelling strategies. Then write each Assessment Word under the unit number it fits.

Unit 1 ____
1.–4. Many short vowel sounds are spelled with a single letter: **a** in **pass**, **e** in **held**, **i** in **skill**, **o** in **collar**, and **u** in **trust**.

Unit 2 ____
5.–10. The long vowel sounds you hear in **case**, **rise**, **chose**, and **cube** are spelled with the **vowel-consonant-e** pattern.

Unit 3 ____
11.–14. The **long a** sound can be spelled **a** as in **lady**, **ai** as in **aim**, and **ay** as in **relay**.

Unit 4 ____
15.–18. The **long e** sound can be spelled in different ways: **ea** in **deal**, **ee** in **speed**, and **ie** in **field**.

Unit 5 ____
19.–20. The **long i** sound can be spelled in different ways: **i** in **climb**, **i-consonant-e** in **hire**, **y** in **cycle**, **igh** in **might**, **ey** in **eyes**, and **uy** in **buy**.

skull
stroke
betray
series
magic
fired
icy
beast
slope
rainy
crime
raft
claim
gift
male
screen
basin
type
seep
sty

90

Extra Connections to

In addition to proofreading and writing in every unit, *Spelling Connections* offers a wide array of extra resources to help students transfer good spelling to their writing.

▼ **Writer's Workshops**
These bonus pages in every Assessment and Review Unit offer proofreading strategies and strategies for using the Internet and word-processing software.

Unit 6 enrichment

Grammar, Usage, and Mechanics

Possessive Nouns

A possessive noun shows ownership.
Some possessive nouns are singular. Only one person or animal is the owner.

> **Jess's** bike is old, but **Jill's** is new.
> Do not remove the **dog's** collar.

Other possessive nouns are plural. More than one person or animal are the owners.

> All the **boys'** teams are here but not the **men's** teams.
> The **horses'** hooves could be heard in the canyon as they galloped over the hill.

Practice Activity

A. Write the correct possessive form in each sentence.
  1. My (mothers'/mother's) birthday is tomorrow.
  2. One (teams'/team's) coach is late.
  3. A (pigs'/pig's) tail is curly.
  4. I knit both of my (uncles'/uncle's) hats.
  5. It was (Jakes'/Jake's) turn to feed the rabbits.

B. Change each underlined phrase to make one possessive noun.
  6. I will borrow the sweater <u>of Carlos</u>.
  7. The shoes <u>of everyone</u> need to be polished.
  8. The kennel <u>where the dogs stay</u> is very clean.
  9. Kim found the lost key <u>that belongs to your cousins</u>!
  10. The books <u>of the student</u> were piled high.

A.
  1.
  2.
  3.
  4.
  5.
B.
  6.
  7.
  8.
  9.
  10.

42

Proofreading Strategy

Read It Backwards!

Good writers always proofread their writing for spelling errors. He a strategy you can use to proofread your papers.

Instead of reading your paper from the first word to the last word, reading it from the last word to the first word. So you would read sentence **The computer was brand new** like this: **new brand was computer The**.

Does this sound like a funny thing to do? It is! But reading your pa backwards helps you think about how to spell each word instead thinking about what the whole sentence means. Try it!

Electronic Spelling

Search Engines

When you use a computer to find information in an on-line encyclopedia or on Internet, you often use search engines. These are useful tools. You type in a word or phrase, and the search engine looks for information on that topic. However, you must spell the w correctly or the search engine will report, "No matches found."

Sometimes it makes sense to type in both the singular and plural forms of a noun. Then the search engine will find both or either. I careful typing plural forms. Make sure you spell them correctly. If you type **tornaedos,** most search engines will say "No matches found for tornaedos."

Look at these plural words. Which are misspelled? Write those words correctly. Write **OK** if a word is correct.

  1. radioes   4. eyeses
  2. holidayes   5. zippers
  3. cases

Spelling Connections ▶
Software
Includes options for interactive spelling activities and games.

SPELLING CONNECTIONS support software

Spelling and Writing

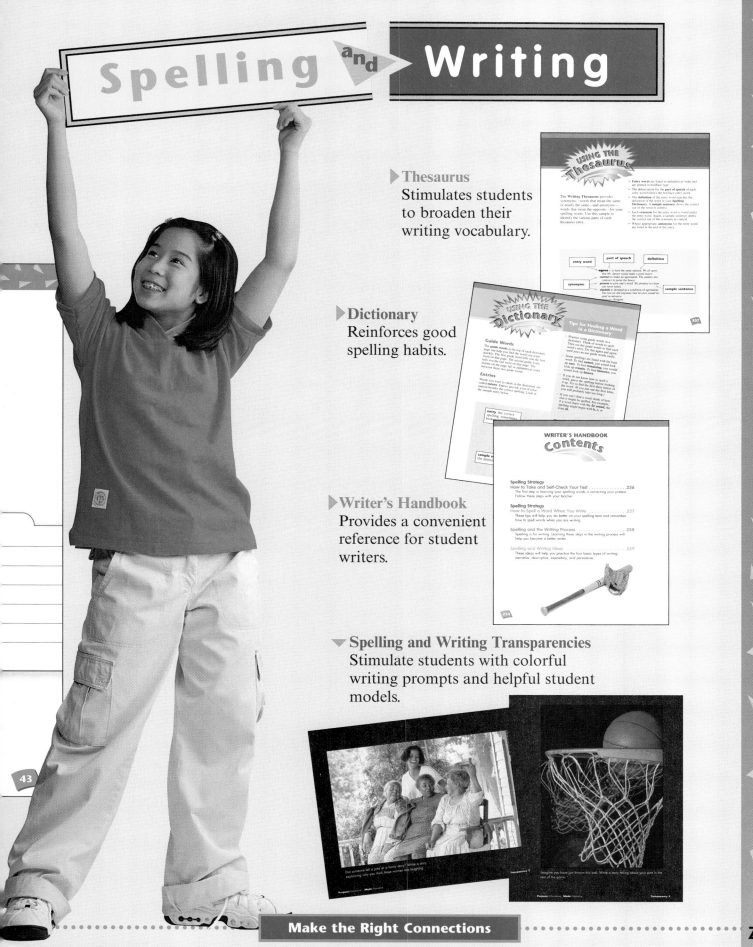

▶ **Thesaurus**
Stimulates students to broaden their writing vocabulary.

▶ **Dictionary**
Reinforces good spelling habits.

▶ **Writer's Handbook**
Provides a convenient reference for student writers.

▼ **Spelling and Writing Transparencies**
Stimulate students with colorful writing prompts and helpful student models.

Components for Spelling Success!

Student Edition
Every unit connects spelling to thinking, phonics, vocabulary, reading, and writing.

Zaner-Bloser Teacher Resource Book

SPELLING CONNECTIONS

Find These Resources Inside!

Home Study Sheets in English and Spanish!

Zaner-Bloser Teacher Edition

SPELLING CONNECTIONS

Find These Connections in Every Unit!

Spelling ➤ Thinking
Spelling ➤ Vocabulary
Spelling ➤ Reading
Spelling ➤ Writing

Home-School Connections

Standardized Tests
A Test for Every Unit!

Reteaching Activities
Practice Masters for Less Able Spellers!

Homework Masters
Extra Practice in a Game-Like Format!

Modality Checklist
Teach to Your Learners' Strengths!

Proofreading Checklist

Word Study Strategies Activities

Teacher Edition
Makes spelling easy to manage with a choice of dictation sentences, activities for different learning styles, help with language differences, and more.

Teacher Resource Book
A wide assortment of reproducibles builds flexibility into your program.

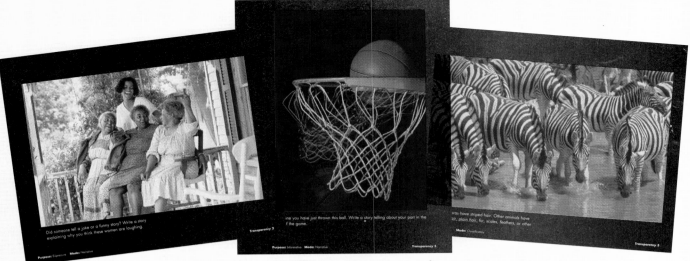

▲ **Spelling and Writing Transparencies**
Stimulate students with colorful writing
prompts and helpful student models.

◀ **Spelling Support for
Second Language
Learners**
Offers vocabulary
practice and teaching
strategies.

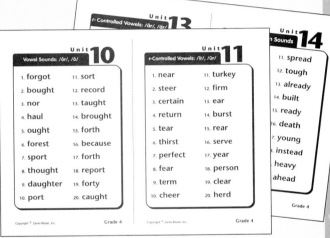

Unit 10 — Vowel Sounds: /ôr/, /ō/

1. forgot	11. sort
2. bought	12. record
3. nor	13. taught
4. haul	14. brought
5. ought	15. forth
6. forest	16. because
7. sport	17. forth
8. thought	18. report
9. daughter	19. forty
10. port	20. caught

Copyright © Zaner-Bloser, Inc.   Grade 4

Unit 11 — r-Controlled Vowels: /ir/, /ûr/

1. near	11. turkey
2. steer	12. firm
3. certain	13. ear
4. return	14. burst
5. tear	15. rear
6. thirst	16. serve
7. perfect	17. year
8. fear	18. person
9. term	19. clear
10. cheer	20. herd

Copyright © Zaner-Bloser, Inc.   Grade 4

Unit 13 — r-Controlled Vowels: /är/, /âr/

Unit 14 — n Sounds

11. spread
12. tough
13. already
14. built
15. ready
16. death
17. young
18. instead
heavy
ahead

Grade 4

▲ **Word List Transparencies**
Are available for every developmental
word list.

▶ **Proofreading Every Day Transparencies**
Develop students' proofreading skills.

◀ *Spelling Connections*
Software
Includes options for
interactive spelling
activities and games.

▲ **Audiotape**
Provides dictation
sentences for pretests and
two options for posttesting.

Assessment and Review

Spelling Connections provides a variety of opportunities to assess spelling growth throughout the year.

At the Start of the Year and the End of the Year

Two survey tests (Form A and Form B) are included at the back of this Teacher Edition. (See pages T337–T338.) The words on these tests were chosen from the basic word lists in each *Spelling Connections* Student Edition. A dictation sentence for each word is also provided.

The words on these tests appear in the order in which they appear in the program, unit by unit. However, beginning and ending units were eliminated. Thus, in Grade 1, words were chosen from Units 9 through 33, and in Grades 2 through 8, words were chosen from Units 5 through 34.

Either Form A or Form B may be administered at the beginning of the year and the other form administered at the end of the year. A comparison of these scores will help measure students' annual spelling progress.

The Pretest

The pretest is a valuable part of spelling instruction and helps students target spelling words they do not know.

To administer the pretest each week, use the **Pretest Sentences** in the Teacher Edition for each unit. Follow this procedure for each word:

1. Say the spelling word.
2. Read the context sentence aloud.
3. Say the word again.
4. Remind the students to write the word to the best of their ability.

It is important that each student self-check his or her pretest. (You may wish to use the **Word List Transparency** provided for each unit to display the word list and help the students check their pretests.) Page 256 in the Student Edition details the steps for taking and checking a pretest. You may wish to use this page as a basis for a mini-lesson to teach students correct procedures for taking and checking a pretest.

Assessment and Review

The Unit Test

Spelling Connections provides three testing options for the weekly unit test.

Option 1: One Spelling Word Per Sentence
This option can be administered in the same way as the pretest.

Option 2: Multiple Spelling Words Per Sentence
If you choose this option, ask students to write the entire sentence. In this way, you can check students' knowledge of the spelling words within a larger context. You may wish to ask the students to under-line the spelling words within the sentence.

Option 3: Standardized Test
A reproducible standardized test for each unit is provided in the *Teacher Resource Book*. This option tests students' ability to identify correct spellings within a standardized test format.

Assessment and Review Units

Every sixth unit is an **Assessment and Review Unit**. These units provide unique opportunities to measure students' understanding of targeted spelling strategies.

The first page of each **Assessment and Review Unit** presents a list of **Assessment Words** that the students have not encountered in the previous five units. These words do, however, represent the various spelling strategies the students have studied. **Assessment Words** may be used in one of two ways:

- Students may complete the **Assessment** activity on the student page. This activity challenges students to match each **Assessment Word** to a relevant spelling strategy. For example, students might match **ink** and **tank** to the spelling strategy about final conso-nant clusters.

- The **Assessment Words** may be administered as a spelling test. (Context sentences are provided in the Teacher Edition.) This pretest will help you assess how well students apply targeted spelling strategies to spell new words.

Either use helps you assess students' understanding of the spelling strategies they have encountered in the previous five units. Students can then use the **Review** activities in the remainder of the unit as reteaching tools to relearn spelling strategies they have not yet mastered.

A posttest consisting of targeted words from the **Assessment and Review Unit** completes the assessment options in each **Assessment and Review Unit**.

Spelling and Writing

The Writing Process

Spelling Connections recognizes that spelling is for writing. But while spelling may be for writing, spelling is not the first aspect of writing students should address as they work through the writing process to create a written work.

To help students understand the writing process, as well as the place of correct spelling within that process, *Spelling Connections* provides an overview of the writing process on page 258 in the Student Edition.

This overview is accompanied by a range of writing prompts within four different writing modalities: narrative, persuasive, expository, and descriptive. These writing prompts will fit nicely within your classroom's broader writing curriculum.

In addition to the information in the Writer's Handbook, each *Spelling Connections* developmental unit concludes with a proofreading activity and a related writing prompt in one of the four modalities. These activities, as well as the restatement of the steps of the writing process within each unit, allow students to implement the writing process on a regular basis.

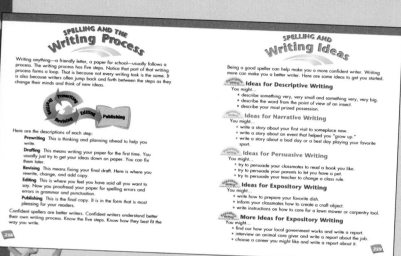

Spelling and Handwriting

Any teacher who has attempted to correct an illegible spelling test knows that handwriting and spelling are related. A child with poor handwriting may very well know how to spell words correctly, but poor handwriting may not allow him or her to communicate that knowledge on a written test. In fact, improved legibility may boost spelling test scores by as much as twenty percent!

To help students improve their handwriting, each developmental *Spelling Connections* unit includes a **One-Minute Handwriting Hint** in the Teacher Edition. Each hint relates handwriting to word features in the spelling unit (e.g., the correct joining for the letter **r** might be featured in a unit targeting **r**-controlled vowels). Each **One-Minute Handwriting Hint** can be the basis of a mini-lesson to boost your students' legibility.

Personal Spelling Journals

A personal spelling journal provides valuable assistance in helping students become confident, independent spellers. Follow these steps to help your students take advantage of this powerful learning tool.

Make the Journal

First, ask students to dedicate a spiral notebook (or a portion of a notebook) to the spelling journal. Tell them to label two consecutive pages with the letter **A,** the next two pages with **B,** and so on until they have pages for each letter of the alphabet. (They may wish to devote only a single page to letters that do not commonly begin words, such as **X.**) Tell students that they will use these pages to write words they want to learn how to spell that begin with each letter.

Find the Words

Words should be added to the journal from three basic sources: unit tests, student writing, and student reading.

- After each unit test, ask the students to write the words they missed on the test in their spelling journals.

- Explain to students that you will mark misspelled words with a green pen when you review their writing. Words marked in green should be written (spelled correctly, of course) in the spelling journal. Students should also add words that others, such as peer editors, have identified as misspelled in their writing.

- Encourage students to write words they encounter in their reading (and may wish to use in their writing) in their spelling journals.

Check the Spelling

Remind students to make sure that all words entered in the spelling journal are correctly spelled. A periodic review of each student's spelling journal can correct any errors and also offer insight into the kinds of words students add on their own.

About the Author
J. Richard Gentry, Ph.D.

Dr. Gentry has greatly influenced the way today's teachers, parents, and those interested in spelling view the subject. In addition to writing three popular books, **Spel…Is a Four-Letter Word, Teaching Kids to Spell,** and **My Kid Can't Spell!,** he has conducted workshops that have helped thousands of school districts throughout the United States adopt better practices for spelling instruction.

A popular speaker at educational conferences nationwide, Dr. Gentry has spent much of his entire, successful career finding better ways to teach spelling. In a recent interview, he explained the source of his long-standing commitment to spelling:

> *I myself am a struggling speller. I have a personal record of 252 scores of 100 on the Friday spelling test, but I've always struggled with spelling in my own writing. I know what it's like for a child who scores 100 on the Friday test, but the following week misspells those very same words in his own writing. Spelling is complex. There are many better ways to learn spelling than memorizing a list of words.*

Dr. Gentry began his career as a classroom teacher. Later, he earned his Ph.D. in Reading Education from the University of Virginia and served as professor of elementary education and reading at Western Carolina University, where he directed the reading center. As a result of his experience, he has become a well-known authority on how spelling ability develops and how it contributes to a child's writing and overall literacy development.

The Research Base for the *Spelling Connections* Word List

J. Richard Gentry, Ph.D.

Spelling research has continually documented a number of principles for teaching students to spell. *Spelling Connections* was developed to be consistent with those principles.

The Best Words Were Selected for Study

The spelling words and the way they are organized for study are vital to a good spelling program. Spelling research provides clear evidence that spelling should be taught systematically (T.D. Horn 1969), that words being studied should be presented in list form (E. Horn 1954; Strickland 1951), and that, above all else, appropriate words should be selected and presented to children only when they are developmentally ready to learn them (Henderson and Templeton 1986).

Common sense tells us a spelling program must teach the words that students actually use in their writing (E. Horn 1960; Hollingsworth 1965; T.D. Horn 1969; Graves 1981; Smith and Ingersoll 1984). A good spelling program will identify these words by using both studies of children's writings (Rinsland 1945; Smith and Ingersoll 1984) and studies that note how often particular words appear in print (Thorndike and Lorge 1944; Kucera and Francis 1967; Carroll et al. 1971; Fry et al. 1985). Other considerations should include the word's degree of difficulty, universality, permanence in English, and application to other areas of the curriculum.

Spelling Connections researchers conducted the most thorough word analysis ever done to develop the word lists in the program. Twenty-two published word lists and vocabulary studies were analyzed, enabling the author to compile details on word characteristics, including the words' frequency in children's writing, their reading level, and how well students spell them.

Also included were considerations such as whether the words have a letter or letter combination likely to cause a misspelling, the ways in which the words are commonly misspelled, and the words'

universality or permanency in the language. The result was a list of more than 7,800 words in five important categories: Basic Words, Content Words, Strategy Words, Challenge Words, and Assessment Words.

Following is a detailed summary of the word study done by *Spelling Connections* researchers:

Writing Level. The words that students learn to spell should be the same words that they use in their writing. *Spelling Connections* researchers consulted all the important recent analyses of students' written vocabulary, including Smith and Ingersoll's landmark 1984 study. In addition, the researchers compared modern lists with classic lists such as Rinsland's to determine the enduring importance, permanency, and frequency of each word in students' writing.

Reading Level. *Spelling Connections* helps students build their writing vocabularies with words they know from their reading. To find out when students might encounter a word in their reading, the researchers consulted lists of words found in children's and adults' reading material. These lists helped determine whether to include a word on the list, and if so, in which grade to place it.

Spelling Proficiency. Spelling proficiency is a measure of how difficult it is to spell a word and is based on how many students can spell the word correctly at a particular grade level. Spelling proficiency is an important clue to the grade level at which a word would best be taught. Rather than rely on obsolete data, *Spelling Connections* researchers developed their own proficiency list based on the most current word usage.

Other Criteria. Additional data helped determine how and when words should be presented for study. Gates' list of *Spelling Difficulties in 3876 Words* identified the common misspellings of many words. Several lists helped determine spelling "demons" and the most frequently misspelled words in each elementary grade. The BORN (Barbe-O'Rourke-Nault) word list was used to determine which words are no longer in common use. Twenty-two lists were consulted in selecting the words. Words were checked, rechecked, and cross-referenced before final selections were made.

The Word List Is Organized for Optimal Learning

Because spelling growth is a developmental process, the organization of words and their placement make a difference in how easily students learn to spell them. The *Spelling Connections* word list was organized according to principles set forth by linguistic, cognitive, and developmental theory.

- Early in a spelling curriculum (grades 1–2) emphasis should be placed on the *alphabetic principle,* i.e., how letters correspond to sounds.
- Later (grades 3–5), emphasis should be placed on *structural patterns, visual patterns,* and *relationships of letters* within words.
- Mature spellers should focus on how spelling is related to *meaning* and *word derivation* (Henderson and Templeton 1986) as well as *known words* (Marsh et al. 1980).

Presenting words by patterns or relationships helps students learn and retain the words (Read and Hodges 1982). The patterns should cause students to focus on word similarities rather than differences. When students *see* patterns or relationships, they find it easier to learn new information (Bloom 1956). Students can see relationships when words are grouped in a way that shows common structural characteristics or letter patterns.

Many researchers (Fitzsimmons and Loomer 1977; Frith 1980) theorize that a person's ability to spell depends upon his or her ability to perceive visual relationships between words. T.D. Horn (1969) reports that "spelling ability has long been shown to be strongly related to visual perception, discrimination, and memory." Though researchers have not specifically described *how* expert spellers perceive these visual relationships, it is clear that the ability to produce the visual form of a correctly spelled word is the key to spelling. The word lists, then, should be organized so that students are able to perceive these visual relationships.

Word lists should be organized to help students perceive the elements of meaning as well as the visual elements of words. For example, **sign, signal,** and **signature** share both meaning and visual similarities. Word lists that take into account both similarities aid analogical reasoning, which enables a person to learn new words by perceiving their similarities to known words. This strategy is especially important to the mature speller (Marsh et al. 1980). By organizing word lists according to a visual principle, *Spelling Connections* aids analogical reasoning, spelling retention, and the visualization of correct spellings.

The Program Is Based on the Developmental Characteristics of Students

Spelling is not just a matter of acquiring habits. Spelling develops (Read 1986). A large body of research on developmental spelling has provided a better understanding of the spelling process and how it is acquired (Read 1975; Gentry 1977; Henderson and Beers 1980; Read 1986). *Spelling Connections* reflects the most recent understandings of children's developing cognitive and linguistic strategies for spelling.

In *Spelling Connections,* instruction parallels children's cognitive and linguistic development. The program acknowledges that creative or invented spelling is the result of a valid thinking process and enhances early spelling development. It also enables students to apply what they have learned about spelling in their writing. The long-standing but antiquated view that spelling is simply memorization is replaced with the view that spelling is a complex cognitive process.

Learning to spell is systematic and orderly. It progresses in stages, much like learning to speak does. Several developmental stages have been identified at the early levels of spelling (Gentry 1977, 1982; Beers 1974; Henderson and Beers 1980; Read 1986).

Early on, inventive spellers create "words" by stringing together random letters (Gentry 1977). Next they recognize that letters represent sounds. They segment language by producing phonetic spelling, i.e., spelling sound by sound (Beers 1974; Read 1975; Gentry 1982). As soon as spelling is influenced by reading and formal spelling instruction, simple and concrete spelling strategies give way to complex abstract representation.

Four stages of invented spelling are illustrated in Gentry's discussion of a child who progresses from A.) *precommunicative* spelling in which invented spellings lack letter-sound correspondence, to B.) *semi-phonetic* spellings that partially map letters to sounds, to C.) *phonetic* spellings that completely map the letters to the sounds of words, to D.) *transitional* spellings that show conventions of English spelling and the influence of a visual-coding strategy (Gentry 1987).

After first or second grade, sound-by-sound spellings become secondary to a visual-coding mechanism. Spellers at the third- and fourth-grade levels take into account spelling rules and the conventions of English spelling (Henderson and Templeton 1986; Read 1986). Another developmental shift occurs around fifth or sixth grade as children spell new words by comparing them to known words (Marsh et al. 1980). At this stage, instruction must focus on word derivations, vocabulary study, and spellings related by word meaning.

The entire *Spelling Connections* program presents a curriculum that accommodates the developmental needs of students. Instruction in phonemic awareness and alphabet review early in first grade focuses on the alphabetic principle, and thus parallels student development from early phonetic segmentation and invented spellings. Later in first grade, in second grade, and continuing into third grade, *Spelling Connections* teaches phonics. It considers students' awareness of and experimentation with matching letters and sounds as students gradually construct more sophisticated spellings.

In grades three through six, attention is on the structural conventions of English spelling. Students examine prefixes, suffixes, inflectional endings, and words that are related by spelling pattern and meaning, thus focusing on comparing words and on discovering structural patterns and relationships among words.

You have now reviewed some of the important principles on which *Spelling Connections* was based. Research into spelling yields complex and fascinating results—spelling encompasses linguistics, cognition, psychology, and intriguing aspects of literacy and human development. But besides being a fascinating area of inquiry, spelling is important to schooling. *Spelling Connections* can help you achieve the goal of teaching students to spell.

Word Studies Consulted in Compiling the *Spelling Connections* Word List

The American Heritage Word Frequency Book, Carroll et al. (1971)

"The Barbe, O'Rourke, Nault (BORN) Word List," Barbe et al. (1987)

"A Basic Core for Writing," Fitzgerald (1951)

Basic Elementary Reading Vocabularies, Harris and Jacobson (1972)

A Basic Vocabulary of Elementary School Children, Rinsland (1945)

The Basic Writing Vocabulary, Horn (1927)

Canadian Word Lists and Instructional Techniques, Thomas (1974)

Computational Analysis of Present-Day American English, Kucera and Francis (1967)

"High-Frequency Word List for Grades 3 through 9," Walker (1979)

Instant Words, Fry et al. (1985)

The Living Word Vocabulary, Dale and O'Rourke (1981)

"Nault Content Words" (Grades 1–8), Nault (1988)

The New Iowa Spelling Scale, Green (1954)

"100 Words Most Often Misspelled by Children in the Elementary Grades," Johnson (1950)

Phoneme-Grapheme Correspondence as Cues to Spelling Improvement, Hanna et al. (1966)

Spelling Difficulties in 3876 Words, Gates (1937)

The Teacher's Word Book of 30,000 Words, Thorndike and Lorge (1944)

3000 Instant Words, 2d ed., Sakiey and Fry (1984)

"220 Basic Sight Words," Dolch (1939)

"2000 Commonest Words for Spelling," Dolch (1942)

Written Vocabulary of Elementary School Children, Hillerich (1978)

Written Vocabulary of Elementary School Pupils, Ages 6–14, Smith and Ingersoll (1984)

Spelling Practice Options

Games and Word Sorts

Practicing spelling words, in a focused manner, can make students more fluent spellers. But in order to remain effective, practice must be lively and engaging. A variety of practice options can help students maintain a fresh attitude toward practicing their spelling words.

Each **Assessment and Review Unit** in *Spelling Connections* includes the directions for an alternative practice option. This option is either a partner activity, which often has a game-like format, or a suggestion for sorting spelling words in a way that students have not encountered previously. Students can use these games to practice any spelling list, and the word sorts provide alternate ways of thinking about and grouping words.

The **Make Your Own Word Sort Master** in the *Teacher Resource Book* can be duplicated to allow students to physically manipulate words they are sorting.

Flip Folder

Making the Flip Folder

The **Flip Folder** can provide another way for students to practice their spelling words. To make a **Flip Folder,** simply use a standard (8½" x 11") manila file folder. Follow these steps:

- Place the file folder on a table in front of you. Turn the folder so that the edge of the folder with the tab is facing you.
- Draw two vertical lines to divide the top of the folder into three equal sections. Cut along these lines to the fold. You should have three equal flaps that remain joined to the back of the folder at the fold.
- Write "Look–Say–Cover–See" on the first flap, "Write–Check" on the middle flap, and "Rewrite" on the third flap. The folder is ready for spelling practice.

Using the Flip Folder

Duplicate the **Flip Folder Practice Master** in the back of the *Teacher Resource Book*. Each student who is using a **Flip Folder** will need a fresh copy of the **Flip Folder Practice Master** each week. Students should copy the words they wish to study in the first column of the practice sheet.

Students follow these steps to practice each word with the **Flip Folder**:

1. **Look** at the word.
   Say the word out loud.
   Cover the word.
   See (in your mind) how the word is spelled.
2. **Write** the word in the second column.
   Check your spelling by comparing what you have written with the correct spelling in the first column.
3. **Rewrite** the word in the third column.

Under your care . . .
your students receive the best possible attention everyday!

Now that you use Zaner-Bloser *Spelling Connections*, we want to be sure you get the attention you need to make your job more successful. We have many communication channels available to meet your needs: phone our Customer Service Department at 1-800-421-3018, visit our website at www.zaner-bloser.com, use the card below to write to our editors, and use the card at the bottom to join our Customer Care Club.

Zaner-Bloser cares!

If you have any questions or comments concerning Zaner-Bloser instructional materials or questions about the teaching of spelling, you may use this card to write to us. We will be happy to assist you in any way possible.

_____

_____

_____

_____

| Ms., Mr., etc. | Name | Position | Grade Level(s) |

| School | | School Address | |

| City | State | | ZIP |

( )   ( )   ( )

| School Telephone | After Hours Phone | FAX | S0447 |

Zaner-Bloser Customer Care Club

Join the Zaner-Bloser Customer Care Club and we'll make sure you stay up-to-date on current educational research and products. To enroll, return this card or call our Customer Care Club hotline at 1-800-387-2410. Upon enrollment, we'll get you started with a gift of information about teaching spelling.

✓**YES!** Enroll me in the Zaner-Bloser Customer Care Club and send me: *Twelve Strategies to Help You Grow Better Spellers* by **J. Richard Gentry, Ph.D.**

Zaner-Bloser
2200 W. Fifth Ave.
PO Box 16764
Columbus, OH
43216-6764

Visit our website:
www.zaner-bloser.com

| Ms., Mr., etc. | Name | Position | Grade Level(s) |

| School | | School Address | |

| City | State | | ZIP |

( )   ( )   ( )

| School Telephone | After Hours Phone | FAX | S0447 |

PLEASE NOTE: THIS PROGRAM IS FOR ZANER-BLOSER CUSTOMERS ONLY!

Zaner-Bloser

Customer Service: 1-800-421-3018
Customer Care Club: 1-800-387-2410
Website: www.zaner-bloser.com

BUSINESS REPLY MAIL
FIRST CLASS MAIL   PERMIT NO. 295   COLUMBUS, OH

POSTAGE WILL BE PAID BY ADDRESSEE

Zaner-Bloser

2200 W 5TH AVE
PO BOX 16764
COLUMBUS OH 43272-4176

BUSINESS REPLY MAIL
FIRST CLASS MAIL   PERMIT NO. 295   COLUMBUS, OH

POSTAGE WILL BE PAID BY ADDRESSEE

Zaner-Bloser

2200 W 5TH AVE
PO BOX 16764
COLUMBUS OH 43272-4176

Zaner-Bloser

SPELLING CONNECTIONS

J. Richard Gentry, Ph.D.

4

Series Author
J. Richard Gentry, Ph.D.

Editorial Development: Cottage Communications

Art and Production: PC&F

Photography: George C. Anderson: cover; pages 1, 4, 6, 7, 254, 255, 256, 257; The Stock Market: p. 12, © 97 mark cooper photography; p. 19, © 96 Charlies Stone; p. 25, © 91 Jim Brown; p. 37, © Ed Bock 1993; p. 48, © 96 Jose L. Pelaez; p. 49, © SuSumu Sato; p. 54, © 94 Jose L. Pelaez; p. 55, © 94 Zefa Germany; p. 66, © Kunio Owaki; p. 73, © 88 Dick Frank; p. 84, © 1994 Zefa Germany; p. 85, © 1990 Xenophon A. Beake; p. 90, © 1996 Peter Steiner; p. 102, © 93 Paolo Romani; p. 109, © 1996 Rick Gayle; p. 126, © 97 Robert Essel; p. 133, © 92 Charles Krebs; p. 138, © Charles Krebs 1992; p. 139, © 1995 ChromoSohm/Sohm; p. 144, © Ricardo B. Sanchez; p. 145, © Phillip Wallick; p. 168, © Ed Bock 1992; p. 199, © 94 Zefa Germany; p. 210, © 96 Ronnie Kaufman; p. 285 © Kennan Ward; Tony Stone Images: p. 13, © Sarah Stone; p. 18, © Gay Bumgarner; p. 24, © Joern Rynio; p. 30, © Davies & Starr Inc.; p. 31, © Tim Flach; p. 36, © Kelvin Murray; p. 60, © Tony Craddock; p. 67, © Sylvain Grandadam; p. 72, © Laurie Campbell; p. 96, © Claudia Kunin; p. 120, © Robert Shafer; p. 127, © World Perspectives; p. 132, © Myron; p. 157, © Doug Armand; p. 174, © World Perspective; p. 180, © Kevin Summers; p. 193, © Schafer & Hill; p. 205, © Will & Deni McIntyre; p. 211, © Earth Imaging; p 217, © T Davis/W Bilenduke; p. 274 © Robert Shafer; p. 276 © Ambrose Greenway; p. 280 © Dugald Bremner; p. 284 © Tim Brown; Corbis Bettmann: p. 61, ©Henry Diltz; Artville ©: p. 91, 103, 192; SUPERSTOCK ©: p. 108, p. 162, p. 169, p. 216; FPG International: p. 175, © John Terence Turner 1995; p. 181, © Margerin Studio 1987; p. 198, © Michael Nelson 1994; p. 204, © Diane Padys 1991

Illustrations: Laurel Aiello: pages 10, 21, 28, 34, 45, 51, 57, 63, 69, 81, 87, 105, 118, 123, 129, 142, 224, 229, 232, 233, 236, 238, 239, 240, 242, 244, 245, 246, 247, 248, 249, 252; Dave Blanchette: pages 9, 16, 27, 52, 58, 70, 88, 93, 94, 106, 112, 117, 124, 201, 209, 214, 215, 219, 221; Len Ebert: pages 136, 141; Tom Elliot: pages 35, 77, 97, 121, 156, 163; Ruth Flanigan: pages 11, 17, 23, 29, 47, 53, 59, 65, 71, 83, 89, 95, 101, 107, 119, 125, 131, 137, 143, 155; Rusty Fletcher: pages 203, 213, 220; Colin Fry: pages 202, 207, 219, 222; Kate Gorman: pages 172, 196; Benton Mahan: pages 38, 39, 40, 42, 74, 75, 76, 77, 110, 111, 114, 147, 148, 150, 182, 183, 184, 186; Bill Ogden: pages 64, 146, 153, 159, 178, 189, 190; Vicki Woodworth: pages 161, 166, 167, 173, 179, 191, 197

ISBN: 0-7367-0045-5

Zaner-Bloser, Inc., P.O. Box 16764, Columbus, Ohio 43216-6764 (1-800-421-3018)

Printed in the United States of America   99 00 01 02 03 QP 5 4 3 2 1

Contents

3

4

Spelling Study Strategy

Look ➡ Say ➡ Cover ➡ See ➡ Write ➡ Check

1 **Look** at the word.

2 **Say** the letters in the word. Think about how each sound is spelled.

3 **Cover** the word with your hand or close your eyes.

4 **See** the word in your mind. Spell the word to yourself.

5 **Write** the word.

6 **Check** your spelling against the spelling in the book.

7

Basic Spelling List

crust	brick
pass	felt
else	spill
skill	button
brag	held
zipper	trust
began	kept
collar	trick
drag	shell
smell	begin

Strategy Words

Review

crop	lunch
dinner	test
land	

Preview

camera	public
contest	swift
discuss	

Content Words

Science: Human Body

digest	rate
pulse	lungs
exert	

Social Studies: Islands

canal	river
inlet	England
coastal	

Individual Needs

Challenge Words

perhaps	begun
catfish	vinegar
ticket	

Alternate Word List

pass	button
zipper	held
began	trust
collar	kept
felt	begin

MATERIALS

Student Edition
Pages 8–13
Challenge Activities, p. 224

Teacher Edition
Pages T8A–T13
Challenge Activities p. T224

Other Resources
Spelling Connections Software
Unit 1 Word List Overhead
   Transparency

Teacher Resource Book
Unit 1 Home Study Master
   (English or Spanish; students
   may pretest on this sheet or use
   it for home practice.)
Unit 1 Homework Master
Unit 1 Practice Masters
Flip Folder Practice Master
Unit 1 Test Master

Visit our Web site, www.zaner-bloser.com

OBJECTIVES

Spelling and Thinking
Students will
- **read** the spelling words in list form and in context.
- **sort** the words according to short vowel sounds.
- **read** and remember this week's spelling strategy.

Spelling and Vocabulary
Students will
- **differentiate** meanings of spelling words.
- **select** and write two-syllable words with the short vowel sound in the first syllable.
- **select** and write two-syllable words with the short vowel sound in the second syllable.
- **identify** and write words that rhyme.
- **write** words in alphabetical order.

Spelling and Reading
Students will
- **complete** sentences using spelling words.
- **solve** analogies using spelling words.
- **answer** riddles by writing spelling words.

Spelling and Writing
Students will
- **proofread** a story.
- **use** the writing process to write a story.
- **proofread** their writing.

MEETING INDIVIDUAL NEEDS
Learning Styles

Visual
Write the symbols for the five short vowel sounds as headings on the chalkboard. Write each spelling word under the appropriate heading on the chalkboard. Pronounce each word and call on a student to find that word on the chalkboard, to say and spell the word aloud, and then to circle the letter that spells the short vowel sound. After all of the words have been pronounced and spelled, have the students copy the chart on paper at their desks, writing the spelling words under the appropriate headings and circling the letters that spell the short vowel sound.

Auditory
Divide the class into two teams, A and B, for a spelling bee. Assign each team an area of the chalkboard. Have the teams alternate turns. As you pronounce each spelling word, have a student identify the short vowel sound and spell the word aloud. If the word is spelled correctly, ask the student to write the word on her or his team's section of the chalkboard.

Kinesthetic
Pronounce each spelling word and ask the students to spell the word in unison. As they spell the letter making the short vowel sound, have them make a corresponding movement for that sound. For example, pronounce a word with the **short a** sound (**pass**) and have the students clap when they reach the **short a**. Repeat this procedure for the other words, having the students bend for the **short e** sound, lift (a book or imaginary item) for the **short i** sound, stomp their feet for the **short o** sound, and jump for the **short u** sound.

Language and Cultural Differences

The short vowel sounds may be difficult for some students to hear or pronounce due to regional pronunciation differences or language backgrounds that do not include these sounds or that spell them differently. Correct spelling can, however, be achieved without exact pronunciation. It is important for any students who have difficulty to know the meaning of each word. If necessary, illustrate or demonstrate the meaning for them.

Write each spelling word on the chalkboard. Pronounce each word slowly and clearly. Have the students repeat each word. Then underline the letter or letters that spell the short vowel sound /ă/, /ĕ/, /ĭ/, /ŏ/, /ŭ/ in each word. Ask the students to use the words in sentences or to tell something they know about the meanings of the words. Clarify the meanings if necessary.

MANAGING INSTRUCTION

3–5 Day Plan		Average	Below Average	Above Average
Day 1	**Day 1**	Pretest Spelling Mini-Lesson, p. T8 Spelling and Thinking, p. 8	Pretest Spelling Mini-Lesson, p. T8 Spelling and Thinking, p. 8	Pretest Spelling and Thinking, p. 8
	Day 2	Spelling and Vocabulary, p. 9	Spelling and Vocabulary, p. 9 (or) Unit 1 Practice Master, A and B	Spelling and Vocabulary, p. 9 Spelling and Reading, p. 10
Day 2	**Day 3**	Spelling and Reading, p. 10	Spelling and Reading, p. 10 (or) Unit 1 Practice Master, C and D	Challenge Activities, p. 224
	Day 4	Spelling and Writing, p. 11 Unit 1 Homework Master	Spelling and Writing, p. 11	Spelling and Writing, p. 11 Unit 1 Homework Master
Day 3	**Day 5**	Weekly Test	Weekly Test	Weekly Test
Vocabulary Connections (pages 12 and 13) may be used anytime during this unit.				

Objectives

Spelling and Thinking

Students will
- **read** the spelling words in list form and in context.
- **sort** the words according to short vowel sounds.
- **read** and remember this week's spelling strategy.

UNIT PRETEST

Use **Pretest Sentences** below. Refer to the self-checking procedures on student page 256. You may wish to use the **Unit 1 Word List Overhead Transparency** as part of the checking procedure.

TEACHING THE STRATEGY

Spelling Mini-Lesson

Write the symbols /ă/, /ĕ/, /ĭ/, /ŏ/, /ŭ/ on the chalkboard as headings. Remind the students that these are the symbols for the short vowel sounds. Ask students who have short vowel sounds in their names to identify those sounds and to write their names under the appropriate headings. For example, Tim would write his name under the symbol for **short i**.

Ask volunteers to read each spelling word and write it under the heading that matches the vowel sound in the word. Discuss the fact that the short vowel sound in each word is spelled as it sounds. Discuss any other spelling patterns students might notice. For example, several words on the list end with a double consonant (e.g., **pass**). Challenge students to think of a word that ends in a double consonant and does not have a short vowel sound spelled with the vowel. (They should be unable to find an English word that meets these criteria.)

Ask volunteers to identify which words have more than one syllable. (began, begin, zipper, collar, button)

Ask a volunteer to read **Remember the Spelling Strategy** on page 8 and draw a circle around the letters that spell the short vowel sound in the words on the chalkboard.

Order of answers may vary.

short a
1. **pass** ★
2. **brag**
3. **began** ★
4. **drag**

short e
5. **else**
6. **smell**
7. **felt** ★
8. **held** ★
9. **kept** ★
10. **shell**

short i
11. **skill**
12. **zipper** ★
13. **brick**
14. **spill**
15. **trick**
16. **begin** ★

short o
17. **collar** ★

short u
18. **crust**
19. **button** ★
20. **trust** ★

Spelling and Thinking

READ THE SPELLING WORDS

1.	crust	*crust*	Lucas cut the **crust** off his bread.
2.	pass	*pass*	I **pass** that computer store every day.
3.	else	*else*	Who **else** is coming to this party?
4.	skill	*skill*	Writing poetry is a **skill** I admire.
5.	brag	*brag*	It is rude to **brag** about your deeds.
6.	zipper	*zipper*	Maria sewed a **zipper** into her skirt.
7.	began	*began*	He was so happy he **began** to sing.
8.	collar	*collar*	Mom has a lace **collar** on her dress.
9.	drag	*drag*	We **drag** our boats into the water.
10.	smell	*smell*	Did you stop to **smell** the roses?
11.	brick	*brick*	Follow the yellow **brick** road.
12.	felt	*felt*	In the sun the sand **felt** hot.
13.	spill	*spill*	You must not **spill** your milk.
14.	button	*button*	Kwan lost a **button** from his shirt.
15.	held	*held*	I **held** the injured bird in my hand.
16.	trust	*trust*	Can I **trust** you to keep a secret?
17.	kept	*kept*	This show has **kept** me in suspense.
18.	trick	*trick*	The magician tried to **trick** us.
19.	shell	*shell*	The turtle's head was in its **shell**.
20.	begin	*begin*	Let me **begin** to tell you a story.

SORT THE SPELLING WORDS

1.–4. Write the words that have the **short a** sound spelled **a**.

5.–10. Write the words that have the **short e** sound spelled **e**.

11.–16. Write the words that have the **short i** sound spelled **i**.

17. Write the word that has the **short o** sound spelled **o**.

18.–20. Write the words that have the **short u** sound spelled **u**.

REMEMBER THE SPELLING STRATEGY

Remember that many short vowel sounds are spelled with a single letter: **a** in **pass**, **e** in **held**, **i** in **skill**, **o** in **collar**, and **u** in **trust**.

8

Pretest Sentences (See procedures on pages Z10–Z11.)

1. The earth's outer layer is called the **crust**.
2. Please **pass** the papers to me.
3. Who **else** wants to go to the zoo?
4. Keyboarding is a very useful **skill**.
5. Jimmy likes to **brag** about his mom.
6. My favorite sweater has a **zipper**.
7. After the rain, the roses **began** to bloom.
8. Lexi wore a dress with a lace **collar**.
9. Some boys and girls may **drag** their feet after gym.
10. The lilacs had a pleasant **smell**.
11. The chimney was made of **brick**.
12. The breeze **felt** cool and nice on my face.
13. The juice will not **spill** easily.
14. Please **button** your coat.
15. The drum major **held** her baton high.
16. I believe you because I **trust** you.
17. Jaime **kept** his piggy bank on his dresser.
18. Opening that door is a neat **trick**.
19. We found a beautiful **shell** on the beach.
20. It is time for the story to **begin**.

Spelling and Vocabulary

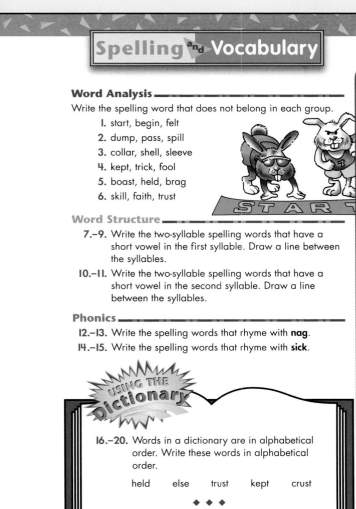

Word Analysis

Write the spelling word that does not belong in each group.

1. start, begin, felt
2. dump, pass, spill
3. collar, shell, sleeve
4. kept, trick, fool
5. boast, held, brag
6. skill, faith, trust

Word Structure

7.–9. Write the two-syllable spelling words that have a short vowel in the first syllable. Draw a line between the syllables.

10.–11. Write the two-syllable spelling words that have a short vowel in the second syllable. Draw a line between the syllables.

Phonics

12.–13. Write the spelling words that rhyme with **nag**.

14.–15. Write the spelling words that rhyme with **sick**.

USING THE Dictionary

16.–20. Words in a dictionary are in alphabetical order. Write these words in alphabetical order.

| held | else | trust | kept | crust |

◆ ◆ ◆

Dictionary Check Be sure to check the alphabetical order of the words in your **Spelling Dictionary**.

Word Analysis
1. felt
2. pass
3. shell
4. kept
5. held
6. skill

Word Structure
Order of answers may vary.
7. zip/per
8. col/lar
9. but/ton
10. be/gan*
11. be/gin*

Phonics
12. brag
13. drag
14. brick
15. trick

Using the Dictionary
16. crust
17. else
18. held
19. kept
20. trust

9

Objectives

Spelling and Vocabulary

Students will

- **differentiate** meanings of spelling words.
- **select** and write two-syllable words with the short vowel sound in the first syllable.
- **select** and write two-syllable words with the short vowel sound in the second syllable.
- **identify** and write words that rhyme.
- **write** words in alphabetical order.

Developing Oral Language Skills

A medial double consonant in words like **zipper** and **collar** can be more easily remembered if students write the word, draw a line between the two consonants, and then pronounce each syllable and listen for the repeated consonant in each syllable.

*Note: **Begin** and **began** have a short vowel sound in both syllables.

MEETING INDIVIDUAL NEEDS

Providing More Help

Write the five short vowel sounds on the chalkboard as headings. Write each spelling word on a 3" × 5" card. Shuffle the cards and place them on a table facedown. Have a student choose a card, say the word, and identify the short vowel sound. Then have the student turn over other cards to find another word with the same short vowel sound. Finally have the student remove those two cards from the table, turn the other cards facedown, and write the two words on the chalkboard under the appropriate heading for the vowel sound. Repeat until all the words are written on the chalkboard.
★ Students who need to study fewer words should use the **Alternate Word List**. This list is starred on page T8 in the Teacher Edition. The **Unit 1 Practice Masters** (*Teacher Resource Book*) provide additional practice with these words.

Unit 1 Practice Masters

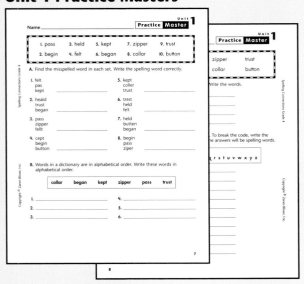

Objectives

Spelling and Reading

Students will
- **complete** sentences using spelling words.
- **solve** analogies using spelling words.
- **answer** riddles by writing spelling words.

One-Minute Handwriting Hint

Be sure the undercurve ending of the lowercase **l** swings wide to allow room for the loop and slant stroke of the second letter.

SWING WIDE

Legible handwriting can boost spelling scores by as much as 20%.

Complete the Sentences

1. begin
2. spill
3. skill
4. trick
5. trust
6. brag
7. collar
8. zipper
9. else
10. shell

Solve the Analogies

11. crust
12. drag
13. smell
14. kept
15. held

Solve the Riddles

16. button
17. pass
18. felt
19. brick
20. began

Spelling and Reading

crust	pass	else	skill	brag
zipper	began	collar	drag	smell
brick	felt	spill	button	held
trust	kept	trick	shell	begin

Complete the Sentences   Write a spelling word to complete each sentence.

1. We will _____ each sentence with a capital letter.
2. If you fill your glass too full, you may _____ your drink.
3. It takes great _____ to play professional sports.
4. The magician taught us a new _____.
5. I hope I can _____ you to keep this secret.
6. I like to _____ about my brother's paintings.
7. Because I was hot, the _____ of my shirt got wrinkled.
8. A _____ in a jacket makes it easy to open and close.
9. Did anyone _____ get the right answer to that question?
10. A turtle goes into its _____ when it is frightened.

Solve the Analogies   Write a spelling word to complete each analogy.

11. **Skin** is to **apple** as _____ is to **bread**.
12. **Stroller** is to **push** as sled is to _____.
13. **See** is to **eye** as _____ is to **nose**.
14. **Sleep** is to **slept** as **keep** is to _____.
15. **Say** is to **said** as **hold** is to _____.

Solve the Riddles   Write a spelling word for each riddle.

16. I am round and have eyes.
17. I rhyme with **glass** and mean "to go by."
18. I am the "yesterday" word of "today's" word **feel**.
19. One of the three little pigs used me to build a house.
20. I am a two-syllable word that means "started."

10

MEETING INDIVIDUAL NEEDS

Providing More Challenge

Challenge Words and **Challenge Activities** for Unit 1 appear on page 224. **Challenge Word Test Sentences** appear on page T224.

Unit 1 Challenge Activities

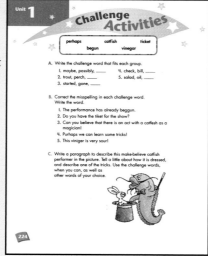

Weekly Test Options

Option 1:
One Spelling Word Per Sentence

(See procedures on pages Z10–Z11.)

1. Who **else** would like to go to town?
2. Pat **kept** skating until he got cold.
3. Mother **held** the bike while I got on.
4. Ann **felt** the strong wind hit her in the face.
5. I love the **smell** of a rose.
6. We found the **shell** in the sand.
7. We will **pass** the test.
8. It is not nice to **brag**.
9. Please do not **drag** the bags on the ground.
10. Skating is a **skill**.
11. If you hold the milk with care, it will not **spill**.
12. Our home is made of red **brick**.
13. The clown did a **trick** at the circus.
14. I **trust** that he will be on time.

Spelling and Writing

Proofread a Story

Six words are not spelled correctly in this story. Write the words correctly.

A Gift From the Beach

At the beach, I found a shel I could not pas by. It
        shell   pass

had a pink edge that looked like a colar. When I
                            collar

held
helt it in my hand, it felled smooth. I could smell
             felt

             trust
the sea on it. I trusst it will always remind me of

that happy day.

Write a Story

Narrative Writing

Write a story about an interesting place you have visited.
Include all the information the reader will need to know.
Be sure to tell the following:
- the name of the place you visited
- names of people, if any, you went with
- what you did there
- how long you stayed
- what interesting sights you saw
- what interesting things you did
- what you liked best about your visit

Use as many spelling words as you can.

Proofread Your Writing During → **Editing**

Proofread your writing for spelling errors as part of the editing
stage in the writing process. Be sure to check each word
carefully. Use a dictionary to check spelling if you are not sure.

11

Proofreading Marks

≡ Make a capital.
/ Make a small letter.
∧ Add something.
℘ Take out something.
⊙ Add a period.
⌗ New paragraph
SP Spelling error

Writing Process

Prewriting
⇩
Drafting
⇩
Revising
⇩
Editing
⇩
Publishing

15. The toast has a thick **crust**.
16. He broke the **zipper** on his coat.
17. Her dress had a pretty **collar**.
18. That **button** is loose.
19. You can't end something until you **begin** it.
20. I **began** to read that book.

Option 2:
Multiple Spelling Words Per Sentence
(See procedures on pages Z10–Z11.)

1. I **held** a large **brick** while mother **began** to work.
2. The coat with the blue **collar** has a long **zipper**.
3. The puppy likes to **drag** my shirts and chew on a **button**.
4. Who **else** can **smell** the **crust**?
5. I **trust** that you will soon **begin** to learn a **skill**.
6. Please don't **spill** the milk when you **pass** it.
7. My father likes to **brag** about the **shell** he found.
8. He **felt** that doing another **trick** would have **kept** the people happy.

Option 3:
Standardized Test
(See *Teacher Resource Book,* Unit 1.)

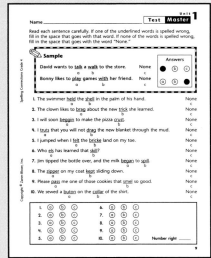

Unit 1 Test Master

Name _____ **Test Master** Unit 1

Read each sentence carefully. If one of the underlined words is spelled wrong, fill in the space that goes with that word. If none of the words is spelled wrong, fill in the space that goes with the word "None."

Sample

| David wants to take a walk to the store. | None |
| Bonny likes to play games with her friend. | None |

Answers: ● ⓑ ⓒ / ⓐ ⓑ ⓒ

1. The swimmer <u>held</u> the <u>shell</u> in the palm of his hand. None
2. The clown likes to <u>brag</u> about the new <u>trick</u> she learned. None
3. I will soon <u>beggin</u> to make the pizza <u>crust</u>. None
4. I <u>truts</u> that you will not <u>drag</u> the new blanket through the mud. None
5. I jumped when I <u>felt</u> the <u>bricke</u> land on my toe. None
6. Who <u>els</u> has learned that <u>skill</u>? None
7. Jim tipped the bottle over, and the milk <u>began</u> to <u>spill</u>. None
8. The <u>zipper</u> on my coat <u>kept</u> sliding down. None
9. Please <u>pass</u> me one of those cookies that <u>smel</u> so good. None
10. We sewed a <u>button</u> on the <u>collar</u> of the shirt. None

1. ⓐ ⓑ ⓒ   6. ⓐ ⓑ ⓒ
2. ⓐ ⓑ ⓒ   7. ⓐ ⓑ ⓒ
3. ⓐ ⓑ ⓒ   8. ⓐ ⓑ ⓒ
4. ⓐ ⓑ ⓒ   9. ⓐ ⓑ ⓒ
5. ⓐ ⓑ ⓒ   10. ⓐ ⓑ ⓒ   Number right _____

Objectives

Strategy Words

Students will

- **review** words studied previously that are related to the spelling strategy.
- **preview** unknown words that are related to the spelling strategy.

Unit 1 enrichment

Vocabulary

Remind the students that the **Strategy Words** are related to the spelling patterns they have studied in this unit. The **Review Words** are below grade level, and the **Preview Words** are above grade level. You may wish to use the following sentences to introduce the words in context.

Review Words:
Words From Grade 3

1. The corn **crop** was good this year.
2. I will invite my friend to **dinner**.
3. My parents bought some **land** in the country.
4. We ate **lunch** at noon.
5. My sister will take her spelling **test** on Friday.

Preview Words:
Words From Grade 5

6. I took many pictures with my new **camera**.
7. The boys had a **contest** on the playground.
8. We will **discuss** the Nile River during history class.
9. The girls enjoyed **public** speaking.
10. The dogs could not catch the **swift** deer.

Review Words

1. dinner
2. lunch
3. test
4. crop
5. land

Preview Words

6. swift
7. contest
8. public
9. discuss
10. camera

Strategy Words

Review Words: Short Vowel Sounds

Write a word from the box to complete each sentence. The word you write will rhyme with the underlined word.

crop	dinner	land	lunch	test

1. Each day I miss my _____, I get a little <u>thinner</u>.
2. The rabbit ate a <u>bunch</u> of carrots for its _____.
3. Our teacher chose the <u>best</u> questions for the _____.
4. That farmer couldn't <u>stop</u> bringing in his _____.
5. A pilot cannot _____ a seaplane on the <u>sand</u>.

Preview Words: Short Vowel Sounds

Synonyms are words that have the same meanings. **Antonyms** are words with opposite meanings.

camera	contest	discuss	public	swift

6. Write the word from the box that is a synonym of **fast**.
7. Write the word from the box that is a synonym of **competition**.
8. Write the word from the box that is an antonym of **private**.

Write the word from the box that could replace the underlined words in each sentence.

9. Our class will <u>talk about</u> the Civil War.
10. Bring your <u>device that takes pictures</u> on a trip.

12

Unit 1 RECAP

You may wish to assign the **Unit 1 Homework Master** (*Teacher Resource Book,* Unit 1) as a fun way to recap the spelling words.

Unit 1 Homework Master

Name _____

Homework Master Unit 1

The groups of letters below are written in code. To break the code, write the letter that comes just before each code letter. The answers will be spelling words.

a b c d e f g h i j k l m n o p q r s t u v w x y z

1. d s v t u = _____
2. f m t f = _____
3. l f q u = _____
4. i f m e = _____
5. g f m u = _____
6. t n f m m = _____
7. t i f m m = _____
8. q b t t = _____
9. c s b h = _____
10. e s b h =

11. t l j m m = _____
12. t q j m m = _____
13. c s j d l = _____
14. u s j d l = _____
15. u s v t u = _____
16. d p m m b s = _____
17. c v u u p o = _____
18. c f h j o = _____
19. c f h b o = _____

20. One word from the list isn't used in the above code. Write that word.
21. Why isn't this code good for the above word?

10

Connections

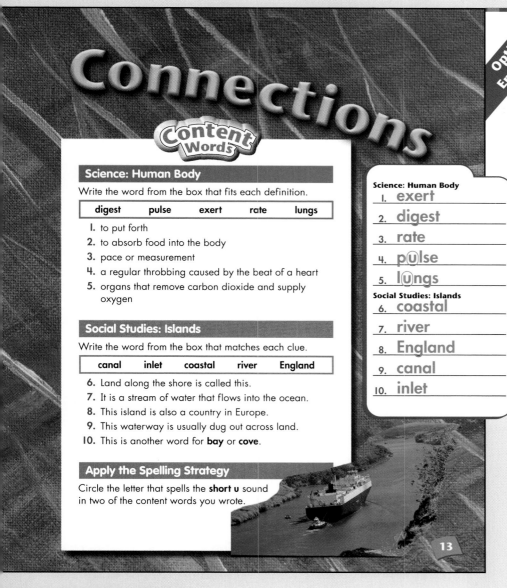

Content Words

Science: Human Body

Write the word from the box that fits each definition.

digest	pulse	exert	rate	lungs

1. to put forth
2. to absorb food into the body
3. pace or measurement
4. a regular throbbing caused by the beat of a heart
5. organs that remove carbon dioxide and supply oxygen

Social Studies: Islands

Write the word from the box that matches each clue.

canal	inlet	coastal	river	England

6. Land along the shore is called this.
7. It is a stream of water that flows into the ocean.
8. This island is also a country in Europe.
9. This waterway is usually dug out across land.
10. This is another word for **bay** or **cove**.

Apply the Spelling Strategy

Circle the letter that spells the **short u** sound in two of the content words you wrote.

13

Science: Human Body
1. exert
2. digest
3. rate
4. p(u)lse
5. l(u)ngs

Social Studies: Islands
6. coastal
7. river
8. England
9. canal
10. inlet

Unit 2 Home Study Master

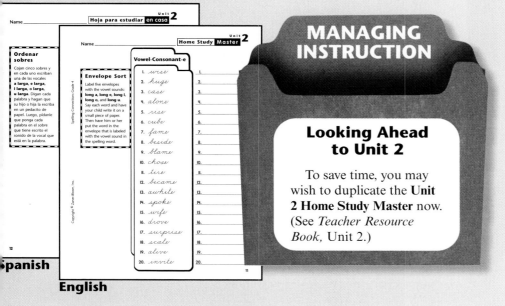

Spanish

English

Looking Ahead to Unit 2

To save time, you may wish to duplicate the **Unit 2 Home Study Master** now. (See *Teacher Resource Book,* Unit 2.)

MANAGING INSTRUCTION

Objectives

Content Words

Students will
- **expand** vocabulary with content-related words.
- **relate** the spelling strategy to words outside the basic spelling list.

Content Words

Science: Human Body

Review the meanings of these words with the students. You may wish to use these sentences to introduce these words in context.

1. It may take an hour to **digest** the food.
2. The boy took his **pulse** before running.
3. I always **exert** myself during gym.
4. His heart **rate** rose when he became frightened.
5. Her **lungs** expanded as she breathed in the fresh air.

Encourage the students to use these words in a story about staying healthy.

Social Studies: Islands

Review the meanings of these words with the students. You may wish to use these sentences to introduce these words in context.

6. The **canal** connected the two lakes.
7. The boat sailed into the **inlet**.
8. The **coastal** region is very cold in the winter.
9. We swam in the **river** while we were on our trip.
10. We will travel to **England** next summer.

Encourage the students to use these words in listing places they visited during a vacation.

Basic Spelling List

wise	tire
huge	became
case	awhile
alone	spoke
rise	wife
cube	drove
fame	surprise
beside	scale
blame	alive
chose	invite

Strategy Words

Review

close	write
face	wrote
size	

Preview

complete	locate
froze	underline
include	

Content Words

Math: Numbers

fifty	thousand
ninety	seventy
nineteen	

Health: Nutrition

dessert	spinach
sandwich	dine
diet	

Individual Needs

Challenge Words

fuse	antelope
female	otherwise
trapeze	

Alternate Word List

huge	awhile
case	wife
alone	drove
beside	surprise
became	invite

MATERIALS

Student Edition
Pages 14–19
Challenge Activities, p. 225

Teacher Edition
Pages T14A–T19
Challenge Activities, p. T225

Other Resources
Spelling Connections Software
Unit 2 Word List Overhead
  Transparency

Teacher Resource Book
Unit 2 Home Study Master
  (English or Spanish; students
  may pretest on this sheet or use
  it for home practice.)
Unit 2 Homework Master
Unit 2 Practice Masters
Flip Folder Practice Master
Unit 2 Test Master

Visit our Web site, www.zaner-bloser.com

OBJECTIVES

Spelling and Thinking
Students will
• **read** the spelling words in list
  form and in context.
• **sort vowel-consonant-e** words
  by long vowel sounds.
• **read** and remember this
  week's spelling strategy.

Spelling and Vocabulary
Students will
• **write** spelling words for
  their synonyms.
• **divide** spelling words into
  syllables.
• **substitute** letters to form
  spelling words.
• **locate** spelling words in a
  dictionary and answer questions about them.

Spelling and Reading
Students will
• **solve** analogies using spelling
  words.
• **identify** spelling words that
  can replace phrases.
• **write** spelling words to
  complete a paragraph.

Spelling and Writing
Students will
• **proofread** a friendly letter.
• **use** the writing process to
  write a friendly letter.
• **proofread** their writing.

MEETING INDIVIDUAL NEEDS
Learning Styles

 Visual

For each word, have the students draw boxes and label them **vowel-consonant-e** as shown.

Then have them write each spelling word, putting the letters that spell the **vowel-consonant-e** pattern in the proper boxes.

 Auditory

Pronounce the word **case** and ask the students what vowel sound they hear. (long a) Then pronounce each spelling word and have the students, in unison, repeat the word, identify the **long vowel** sound, and spell the word. Finally, have the students whisper each letter of the word to themselves as they write it.

 Kinesthetic

Draw twenty squares on a piece of poster board and write a spelling word in each square. Place the poster board on the floor and have the students take turns throwing a beanbag or an eraser onto the board. After each turn, have the student write on the chalkboard the word the beanbag or eraser lands on, circling the **long vowel** sound in the word.

Language and Cultural Differences

The **long vowel** sounds may be difficult for some students to hear and spell due to regional pronunciation differences. In addition, some language backgrounds may not include these sounds or may spell them differently. However, correct spelling is possible without exact pronunciation, provided the student has the opportunity to associate the word meaning with the visual sequence of the letters.

Write the vowels **a, i, o,** and **u** on the outside of separate plastic cups. Have the students write each spelling word on a slip of paper and place the word in the appropriate cup, depending on the long vowel sound heard in the word. Then call on a volunteer to take a word out of one of the cups, say the word, and make a sentence using the word. Continue until all four cups are empty.

MANAGING INSTRUCTION

3–5 Day Plan		Average	Below Average	Above Average
Day 1	**Day 1**	Pretest Spelling Mini-Lesson, p. T14 Spelling and Thinking, p. 14	Pretest Spelling Mini-Lesson, p. T14 Spelling and Thinking, p. 14	Pretest Spelling and Thinking, p. 14
	Day 2	Spelling and Vocabulary, p. 15	Spelling and Vocabulary, p. 15 (or) Unit 2 Practice Master, A and B	Spelling and Vocabulary, p. 15 Spelling and Reading, p. 16
Day 2	**Day 3**	Spelling and Reading, p. 16	Spelling and Reading, p. 16 (or) Unit 2 Practice Master, C and D	Challenge Activities, p. 225
	Day 4	Spelling and Writing, p. 17 Unit 2 Homework Master	Spelling and Writing, p. 17	Spelling and Writing, p. 17 Unit 2 Homework Master
Day 3	**Day 5**	Weekly Test	Weekly Test	Weekly Test

Vocabulary Connections (pages 18 and 19) may be used anytime during this unit.

Objectives

Spelling and Thinking
Students will
- **read** the spelling words in list form and in context.
- **sort vowel-consonant-e** words by long vowel sounds.
- **read** and remember this week's spelling strategy.

UNIT PRETEST

Use the **Pretest Sentences** below. Refer to the self-checking procedures on student page 256. You may wish to use the **Unit 2 Word List Overhead Transparency** as part of the checking procedure.

TEACHING THE STRATEGY

Spelling Mini-Lesson

Tell the students that in this lesson they will spell words that have long vowel sounds spelled by the **vowel-consonant-silent e pattern**.

Write **case, rise, chose,** and **cube** on the chalkboard. Ask a volunteer to pronounce each word and to identify the **vowel-consonant-e** in each word. Remind the students that **vowel-consonant-e** is a common pattern in English spelling and that when a final **silent e** is present, the preceding vowel will probably have a long vowel sound.

Write **became** and **alive** on the chalkboard. Ask a volunteer to identify the **vowel-consonant-e** pattern in these words. Ask students if they notice any difference between these words and **case, rise, chose,** and **cube**. (Became and alive have two syllables, but the other words have one syllable.)

Read the complete list aloud.

Spelling and Thinking

Order of answers may vary.

a-consonant-e
1. case ★
2. fame
3. blame
4. became ★
5. scale

i-consonant-e
6. wise
7. rise
8. beside ★
9. tire
10. awhile ★
11. wife ★
12. surprise ★
13. alive
14. invite ★

o-consonant-e
15. alone ★
16. chose
17. spoke
18. drove ★

u-consonant-e
19. huge ★
20. cube

READ THE SPELLING WORDS

1.	wise	*wise*	Owls are described as **wise** birds.
2.	huge	*huge*	An elephant is a **huge** animal.
3.	case	*case*	We bought a **case** of spring water.
4.	alone	*alone*	Are you **alone** or with friends?
5.	rise	*rise*	Soap bubbles **rise** in the air.
6.	cube	*cube*	A **cube** has six sides.
7.	fame	*fame*	Movie stars earn **fame** and money.
8.	beside	*beside*	Magda sits **beside** me in school.
9.	blame	*blame*	He did not **blame** us for the mistakes.
10.	chose	*chose*	They **chose** sides for the game.
11.	tire	*tire*	My bicycle **tire** is flat.
12.	became	*became*	The hiker **became** lost in the woods.
13.	awhile	*awhile*	Rest **awhile** if you are tired.
14.	spoke	*spoke*	Joy **spoke** her lines well.
15.	wife	*wife*	I met Uncle Theo's new **wife**.
16.	drove	*drove*	Mother **drove** the truck to work.
17.	surprise	*surprise*	Aunt Belle paid us a **surprise** visit.
18.	scale	*scale*	Use the **scale** to check the cat's weight.
19.	alive	*alive*	Grandfather is **alive** and well.
20.	invite	*invite*	I will **invite** you to the party.

SORT THE SPELLING WORDS

Write the spelling words that have a long vowel sound spelled the following ways:

1.–5. a-consonant-e   15.–18. o-consonant-e

6.–14. i-consonant-e   19.–20. u-consonant-e

REMEMBER THE SPELLING STRATEGY

Remember that the long vowel sounds you hear in **case, rise, chose,** and **cube** are spelled with the **vowel-consonant-e** pattern.

Pretest Sentences (See procedures on pages Z10–Z11.)

1. We become **wise** by learning from our mistakes.
2. The blue whale is a **huge** mammal.
3. Kaya put her flute into its **case**.
4. Susan is hardly ever **alone** because she has two sisters and three brothers.
5. Bread dough usually takes one or two hours to **rise**.
6. He added an ice **cube** to his juice.
7. Jamal's speeches brought him **fame**.
8. Fumiko and Amy played in the sand **beside** the water.
9. When our team loses a game, we never **blame** one player.
10. Julie liked many of the books, but she **chose** only one.
11. Mom bought a new **tire** for the car.
12. As the morning passed, the town **became** busy with activity.
13. After our tennis match, we rested **awhile**.
14. After the show, the principal **spoke** to us.
15. Mr. Crosby and his **wife** dance well together.
16. Dad **drove** his new car to the game.
17. The coat from my grandmother was a nice **surprise**.
18. My mother weighs my baby brother on a **scale**.
19. It is great to be **alive** and well.
20. I would like to **invite** you to my birthday party.

Spelling and Vocabulary

Synonyms

Words that have the same or almost the same meaning, such as **simple** and **easy,** are called **synonyms**. Write a spelling word that is a synonym for each of these words.

1. carton   3. recognition   5. smart
2. gigantic   4. accuse

Word Structure

6.–12. Write the spelling words that have two syllables. Draw a line between the syllables.

Phonics

Change one or two letters at the beginning of each of these words to write spelling words.

13. life   15. broke   17. tube
14. wire   16. tale   18. those

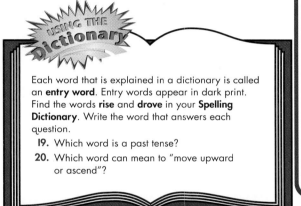

USING THE Dictionary

Each word that is explained in a dictionary is called an **entry word**. Entry words appear in dark print. Find the words **rise** and **drove** in your **Spelling Dictionary**. Write the word that answers each question.

19. Which word is a past tense?
20. Which word can mean to "move upward or ascend"?

Synonyms
1. case
2. huge
3. fame
4. blame
5. wise

Word Structure
Order of answers may vary.
6. a/lone
7. be/side
8. be/came
9. a/while
10. sur/prise
11. a/live
12. in/vite

Phonics
13. wife
14. tire
15. spoke
16. scale
17. cube
18. chose

Using the Dictionary
19. drove
20. rise

15

Objectives

Spelling and Vocabulary

Students will
- **write** spelling words for their synonyms.
- **divide** spelling words into syllables.
- **substitute** letters to form spelling words.
- **locate** spelling words in a dictionary and answer questions about them.

Developing Oral Language Skills

If there is a **silent e** at the end of the word, the vowel ahead of it will say its name. Have the children say the following sentence aloud, prolonging the long vowel sound in each word as they point to it.

<u>These wise mice made</u> us laugh at their <u>cute noses</u>.

MEETING INDIVIDUAL NEEDS

Providing More Help

Provide the students with copies of the chart below.

r	h	f	sc	w	c	bl
ame	uge	ube	ale	ise		ase

Ask volunteers to identify the **long vowel** sound in each **vowel-consonant-e** pattern. Have the students match word beginnings from the top row to **vowel-consonant-e** patterns on the bottom row to form spelling words. Have the students write the spelling words on the chalkboard. (rise, huge, fame, scale, wise, cube, case, blame)

★ Students who need to study fewer words should use the **Alternate Word List**. This list is starred on page T14 in the Teacher Edition. The **Unit 2 Practice Masters** (*Teacher Resource Book*) provide additional practice with these words.

Unit 2 Practice Masters

Practice Master 2

Name _____

| 1. case | 3. wife | 5. invite | 7. surprise | 9. alone |
| 2. became | 4. awhile | 6. beside | 8. drove | 10. huge |

A. Words that are the same or almost the same in meaning are called **synonyms**. The words **simple** and **easy** are synonyms. Write a spelling word that is a synonym for each of these words.

1. carton _____
2. ask _____
3. gigantic _____
4. singly _____
5. shock _____

B. Write the spelling word that goes with each meaning.

1. to ask someone to come somewhere or do something _____
2. grew or came to be _____
3. without anyone else _____
4. next to _____
5. a large box _____
6. the woman a man is married to _____
7. something unexpected _____
8. operated a car _____

13

14

Practice Master 2

| surprise | alone |
| drove | huge |

Objectives

Spelling and Reading

Students will
- **solve** analogies using spelling words.
- **identify** spelling words that can replace phrases.
- **write** spelling words to complete a paragraph.

One-Minute Handwriting Hint

Be sure to close the oval in the lowercase **a**. Pull the slant stroke to the baseline before you make the undercurve ending. If you do not pull the slant stroke to the baseline, the letter **a** may look like **o**.

CLOSE OVAL

Legible handwriting can boost spelling scores by as much as 20%.

Solve the Analogies
1. huge
2. rise
3. tire
4. scale
5. wise
6. became
7. cube

Substitute a Word
8. invite
9. case
10. drove
11. awhile
12. beside
13. fame

Complete the Paragraph
14. spoke
15. wife
16. surprise
17. alive
18. alone
19. chose
20. blame

Spelling and Reading

wise	huge	case	alone	rise
cube	fame	beside	blame	chose
tire	became	awhile	spoke	wife
drove	surprise	scale	alive	invite

Solve the Analogies Write a spelling word to complete each analogy.

1. **Small** is to **tiny** as _____ is to **big**.
2. **Down** is to **up** as **descend** is to _____.
3. **Skate** is to **foot** as _____ is to **car**.
4. **Ruler** is to **measure** as _____ is to **weigh**.
5. **Ignorance** is to **wisdom** as **ignorant** is to _____.
6. **Came** is to **come** as _____ is to **become**.
7. **Four** is to **six** as **square** is to _____.

Substitute a Word Sometimes authors save space by using one word that has the same meaning as two or more words. Write one spelling word for each of these phrases.

8. ask to come
9. a box for carrying something
10. went by car
11. for a short time
12. at the side of
13. the quality of being well known

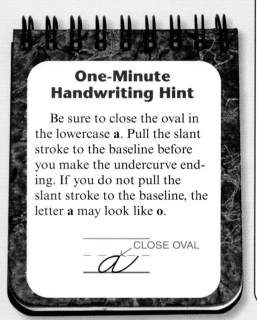

SPEED 45 LIMIT

Complete the Paragraph Write the spelling words from the box that complete the paragraph.

The detective __14.__ to the __15.__ of the missing man. "It will come as no __16.__ to learn that your husband is __17.__ and well. You __18.__ knew where he was hiding, and you __19.__ to keep it a secret. You and he must take the __20.__ for this deceit."

surprise
alone
chose
alive
blame
spoke
wife

16

MEETING INDIVIDUAL NEEDS

Providing More Challenge

Challenge Words and **Challenge Activities** for Unit 2 appear on page 225. **Challenge Word Test Sentences** appear on page T225.

Unit 2 Challenge Activities

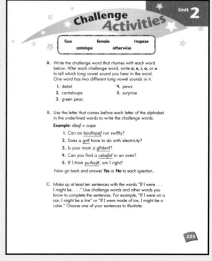

Weekly Test Options

Option 1:
One Spelling Word Per Sentence
(See procedures on pages Z10–Z11.)

1. She put her ring in a **case**.
2. She will win **fame** for her skating.
3. I can't **blame** you for wanting to go swimming.
4. He put the apples on a **scale**.
5. The sky **became** clear after the storm.
6. Please **rise** when you hear your name.
7. It is **wise** to wear boots in the rain.
8. The husband and **wife** went downtown.
9. The party was a **surprise** for my sister.
10. We put a new **tire** on the car.
11. A plant needs water to stay **alive**.
12. She will **invite** us to her home.
13. We are going to stay **awhile**.
14. Mother sat **beside** Dad at the play.
15. He **chose** to wear a blue shirt.

T16

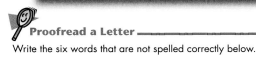

Spelling and Writing

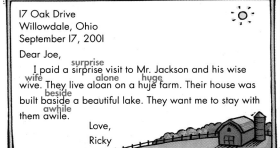

Proofread a Letter

Write the six words that are not spelled correctly below.

17 Oak Drive
Willowdale, Ohio
September 17, 2001

Dear Joe,
    I paid a sirprise ^{surprise} visit to Mr. Jackson and his wise
wive. ^{wife} They live aloan ^{alone} on a hujė ^{huge} farm. Their house was
built baside ^{beside} a beautiful lake. They want me to stay with
them awile. ^{awhile}
          Love,
          Ricky

Proofreading Marks

≡ Make a capital.
/ Make a small letter.
∧ Add something.
℘ Take out something.
⊙ Add a period.
⌗ New paragraph
🆂🅿 Spelling error

Write a Letter

Narrative Writing

Imagine that you have taken a trip. Write a letter to your family or friends. Be sure to include the following information:
- where you are
- why you went there
- what you like about the place
- how long you plan to stay
- what you plan to do after you leave
- when you will visit or call

Use as many spelling words as you can.

Writing Process

Prewriting
⇩
Drafting
⇩
Revising
⇩
Proofread Your Writing During ➔ **Editing**
⇩
Publishing

Proofread your writing for spelling errors as part of the editing stage in the writing process. Be sure to check each word carefully. Use a dictionary to check spelling if you are not sure.

17

Objectives

Spelling and Writing

Students will
- **proofread** a friendly letter.
- **use** the writing process to write a friendly letter.
- **proofread** their writing.

Using the Writing Process

Before assigning **Write a Letter,** see pages 258–259 in the Student Edition for a complete review of the writing process and additional writing assignments. You may also wish to refer to pages Z12–Z13 in the Teacher Edition.

Keeping a Spelling Journal

Encourage students to record the words they misspelled on the weekly test in a personal spelling journal. These words may be recycled for future study. Students may also wish to include words from their writing. See pages Z12–Z13 in the Teacher Edition for more information.

---

16. The child **spoke** to the clown.
17. Grandfather **drove** the new car.
18. There was an ice **cube** in the glass.
19. That **huge** animal has big paws.
20. Sometimes I like to play **alone**.

Option 2:
Multiple Spelling Words Per Sentence

1. The man **spoke** of his **wise wife** who won **fame** for a book she wrote.
2. I **chose** to read **awhile** before I went to sleep.
3. She came **alive** when she found out the party was a **surprise** for her **alone**.
4. The **huge tire** was too big to fit into the **case**.
5. She saw the moon **rise** above the trees as she **drove** home.
6. Would you weigh a **cube** of cheese on that **scale**?
7. Do not **blame** the dog for jumping **beside** us.
8. Sue **became** happy when she saw me **invite** Ed.

Option 3:
Standardized Test
(See *Teacher Resource Book,* Unit 2.)

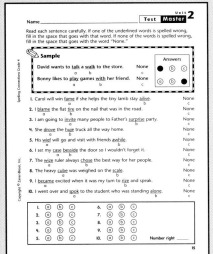

Unit 2 Test Master

T17

Objectives

Strategy Words
Students will
- **review** words studied previously that are related to the spelling strategy.
- **preview** unknown words that are related to the spelling strategy.

Remind the students that the **Strategy Words** are related to the spelling patterns they have studied in this unit. **Review Words** are below grade level, and the **Preview Words** are above grade level. You may wish to use the following sentences to introduce the words in context.

Review Words:
Words From Grade 3
1. Will you **close** the door when you come in?
2. My **face** feels cold from the wind.
3. The toddler wore a small **size** shirt.
4. I will **write** a letter to my grandparents.
5. My cousin **wrote** me a letter from camp.

Preview Words:
Words From Grade 5
6. We will **complete** our homework on time.
7. The water **froze** quickly in the cold weather.
8. He will **include** a picture with his story.
9. Can you **locate** your city on the map?
10. The words that I **underline** for you are challenge words.

Review Words
1. wrote
2. write
3. size
4. face
5. close

Preview Words
6. locate
7. complete
8. underline
9. include
10. froze

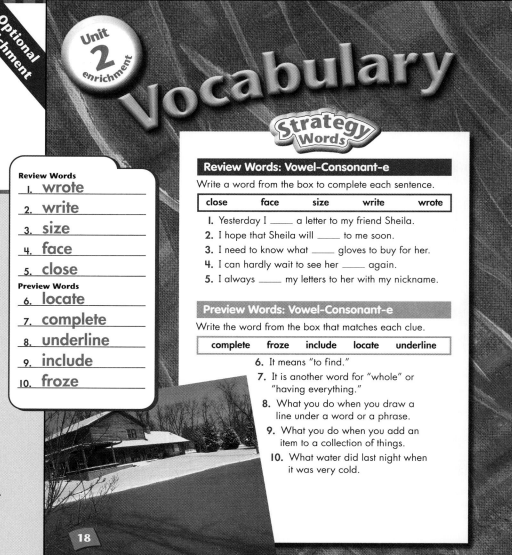

Unit 2 enrichment

Vocabulary

Strategy Words

Review Words: Vowel-Consonant-e
Write a word from the box to complete each sentence.

close	face	size	write	wrote

1. Yesterday I _____ a letter to my friend Sheila.
2. I hope that Sheila will _____ to me soon.
3. I need to know what _____ gloves to buy for her.
4. I can hardly wait to see her _____ again.
5. I always _____ my letters to her with my nickname.

Preview Words: Vowel-Consonant-e
Write the word from the box that matches each clue.

complete	froze	include	locate	underline

6. It means "to find."
7. It is another word for "whole" or "having everything."
8. What you do when you draw a line under a word or a phrase.
9. What you do when you add an item to a collection of things.
10. What water did last night when it was very cold.

18

Unit 2 RECAP

You may wish to assign the **Unit 2 Homework Master** (*Teacher Resource Book*, Unit 2) as a fun way to recap the spelling words.

Unit 2 Homework Master

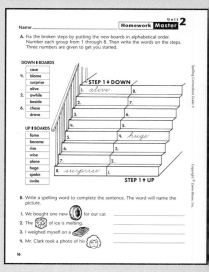

Name _____

Homework Master Unit 2

A. Fix the broken steps by putting the new boards in alphabetical order. Number each group from 1 through 8. Then write the words on the steps. Three numbers are given to get you started.

DOWN BOARDS
- case
- blame
- surprise
- alive
- awhile
- beside
- chose
- drove

UP BOARDS
- fame
- became
- rise
- wise
- alone
- huge
- spoke
- invite

STEP 1 ↓ DOWN
alive
STEP 1 ↑ UP

B. Write a spelling word to complete the sentence. The word will name the picture.
1. We bought one new _____ for our car.
2. The _____ of ice is melting.
3. I weighed myself on a _____.
4. Mr. Clark took a photo of his _____.

16

TI8

Connections

Objectives

Content Words

Students will
- **expand** vocabulary with content-related words.
- **relate** the spelling strategy to words outside the basic spelling list.

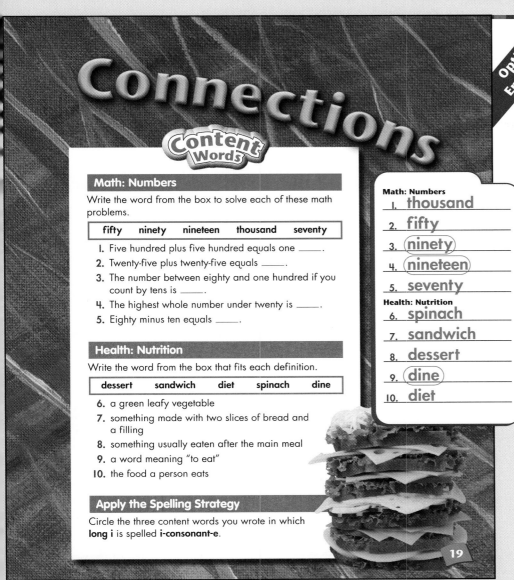

Content Words

Math: Numbers

Write the word from the box to solve each of these math problems.

fifty	ninety	nineteen	thousand	seventy

1. Five hundred plus five hundred equals one _____.
2. Twenty-five plus twenty-five equals _____.
3. The number between eighty and one hundred if you count by tens is _____.
4. The highest whole number under twenty is _____.
5. Eighty minus ten equals _____.

Health: Nutrition

Write the word from the box that fits each definition.

dessert	sandwich	diet	spinach	dine

6. a green leafy vegetable
7. something made with two slices of bread and a filling
8. something usually eaten after the main meal
9. a word meaning "to eat"
10. the food a person eats

Apply the Spelling Strategy

Circle the three content words you wrote in which **long i** is spelled **i-consonant-e**.

19

Math: Numbers
1. thousand
2. fifty
3. ninety
4. nineteen
5. seventy

Health: Nutrition
6. spinach
7. sandwich
8. dessert
9. dine
10. diet

Content Words

Math: Numbers

Review the meanings of these words with the students. You may wish to use these sentences to introduce these words in context.

1. There were **fifty** people in the store today.
2. Your grandmother is **ninety** years old.
3. My brother will be **nineteen** tomorrow.
4. I would like to save one **thousand** dollars.
5. Count out **seventy** marbles for each person.

Encourage the students to write these numbers in proper sequence.

Health: Nutrition

Review the meanings of these words with the students. You may wish to use these sentences to introduce these words in context.

6. My mother does not serve **dessert** with every meal.
7. I had a **sandwich** and an apple in my lunch.
8. My family tries to stay on a **diet** of healthy foods.
9. A **spinach** salad would be good with dinner.
10. We will **dine** with friends this evening.

Encourage the students to use these words in a story about healthy eating.

Unit 3 Home Study Master

Spanish

English

MANAGING INSTRUCTION

Looking Ahead to Unit 3

To save time, you may wish to duplicate the **Unit 3 Home Study Master** now. (See *Teacher Resource Book,* Unit 3.)

Basic Spelling List

aim	remain
holiday	favor
paper	rail
station	taste
able	trailer
crayon	lady
flavor	nation
lazy	relay
brain	fail
anyway	radio

Strategy Words

Review

away	maybe
laid	paint
mail	

Preview

explain	prepaid
grayest	reclaim
midday	

Content Words

Social Studies: Sailing

barrier	surf
scrape	sailboat
reef	

Fine Arts:
Making Models

cardboard	wire
poster	modeling
clay	

Individual Needs

Challenge Words

nickname	regain
stadium	trainer
replay	

Alternate Word List

holiday	trailer
paper	lady
station	nation
able	relay
favor	radio

MATERIALS

Student Edition
Pages 20–25
Challenge Activities, p. 226

Teacher Edition
Pages T20A–T25
Challenge Activities, p. T226

Other Resources
Spelling Connections Software
Unit 3 Word List Overhead
   Transparency

Teacher Resource Book
Unit 3 Home Study Master
   (English or Spanish; students
   may pretest on this sheet or use
   it for home practice.)
Unit 3 Homework Master
Unit 3 Practice Masters
Flip Folder Practice Master
Unit 3 Test Master

Visit our Web site, www.zaner-bloser.com

OBJECTIVES

Spelling and Thinking
Students will
• **read** the spelling words in list form and in context.
• **sort** words with the **long a** sound by spelling patterns.
• **read** and remember this week's spelling strategy.

Spelling and Vocabulary
Students will
• **select** and write two-syllable words with a **long a** sound in the second syllable.
• **select** and write two-syllable words with a **long a** sound in the first syllable.
• **divide** words into syllables.
• **write** a spelling word that matches a given clue.
• **arrange** spelling words in alphabetical order.

Spelling and Reading
Students will
• **select** and write spelling words to complete sentences.
• **solve** analogies using spelling words.

Spelling and Writing
Students will
• **proofread** a diary entry.
• **use** the writing process to write a diary entry.
• **proofread** their writing.

MEETING INDIVIDUAL NEEDS
Learning Styles

Visual

Print each spelling word four times on heavy paper. Separate the letters by cutting between them. Mix all of the letters together in a box. Divide the class into pairs of students. Two pairs may play at the same time. Taking turns as they choose each letter, have player A from each pair choose twenty letters from the box. Have each pair of students use their letters to make as many spelling words as they can in three minutes. Have player B of each pair write down the words that have been formed. Then the letters are returned to the box. Repeat this procedure until all the pairs have played.

Auditory

Have the students stand in a circle. Have one student stand inside the circle with a list of the spelling words. Have this student pick one letter of the alphabet to be the "buzz" letter. To start the game, ask her or him to say the "buzz" letter and then say a spelling word. Going clockwise, have the students spell the word, each saying one letter. When the "buzz" letter comes up, the student whose turn it is must say "buzz" instead of the letter. If a student forgets to say "buzz," but says the letter instead, he or she must sit out the next word.

Kinesthetic

For each spelling word, have the students use modeling clay to form the letter or letters that spell the **long a** sound. Next, have them trace over the clay outline with their index fingers, then say the word, and, finally, write the word on their papers.

Language and Cultural Differences

The **long a** sound may be difficult for some students to hear or pronounce because of regional pronunciation differences or because their first language is not English. For example, the Spanish language has two similar sounds, one spelled **e** and one spelled **ei** or **ey**. If a student has difficulty hearing or pronouncing a word with /ā/, first make sure the student knows the meaning of the word. If necessary, provide the meaning through pictures or by using the word in a sentence.

Write the spelling words on the chalkboard. Explain that every one of these words has the **long a** sound, but it is not always spelled the same way. Say each word clearly. Have the students repeat each word, noticing how the **long a** sound is spelled.

MANAGING INSTRUCTION

3–5 Day Plan		Average	Below Average	Above Average
Day 1	**Day 1**	Pretest Spelling Mini-Lesson, p. T20 Spelling and Thinking, p. 20	Pretest Spelling Mini-Lesson, p. T20 Spelling and Thinking, p. 20	Pretest Spelling and Thinking, p. 20
	Day 2	Spelling and Vocabulary, p. 21	Spelling and Vocabulary, p. 21 (or) Unit 3 Practice Master, A and B	Spelling and Vocabulary, p. 21 Spelling and Reading, p. 22
Day 2	**Day 3**	Spelling and Reading, p. 22	Spelling and Reading, p. 22 (or) Unit 3 Practice Master, C and D	Challenge Activities, p. 226
	Day 4	Spelling and Writing, p. 23 Unit 3 Homework Master	Spelling and Writing, p. 23	Spelling and Writing, p. 23 Unit 3 Homework Master
Day 3	**Day 5**	Weekly Test	Weekly Test	Weekly Test
Vocabulary Connections (pages 24 and 25) may be used anytime during this unit.				

Objectives

Spelling and Thinking

Students will
- **read** the spelling words in list form and in context.
- **sort** words with the **long a** sound by spelling patterns.
- **read** and remember this week's spelling strategy.

UNIT PRETEST

Use **Pretest Sentences** below. Refer to the self-checking procedures on student page 256. You may wish to use the **Unit 3 Word List Overhead Transparency** as part of the checking procedure.

TEACHING THE STRATEGY

Spelling Mini-Lesson

Write /ā/ on the chalkboard and ask a volunteer to identify the sound this symbol represents. (the long a sound)

Ask the students to brainstorm different ways to spell /ā/. Encourage them to provide an example word for each spelling pattern. Write their suggestions on the chalkboard, and circle the **long a** spelling pattern in each word.

Explain that the most common way to spell /ā/ in English is **a**. If they have not already chosen all the spelling words with this pattern, ask volunteers to identify the remaining words that spell /ā/ with **a** and to write those words on the chalkboard.

Tell students that the next most common ways to spell /ā/ are **ai** and **ay**. Ask volunteers to identify **ai** words on the spelling list and to write them on the chalkboard. Circle **ai** in each word. Finally, do the same with **ay** words; circle **ay** in each word.

Ask students to compare the position of /ā/ in words with the **ai** spelling and in words with the **ay** spelling. Guide students to the conclusion that the **ai** spelling of /ā/ never occurs at the end of an English word, but the **ay** spelling of /ā/ does often occur at the end of a word.

Conclude by reading **Remember the Spelling Strategy** on page 20.

T20

Unit 3
Long a: a, ai, ay

Spelling and Thinking

Order of answers may vary.

a
1. paper ★
2. station ★
3. able ★
4. flavor
5. lazy
6. favor ★
7. taste
8. lady ★
9. nation ★
10. radio ★

ai
11. aim
12. brain
13. remain
14. rail
15. trailer ★
16. fail

ay
17. holiday ★
18. crayon
19. anyway
20. relay ★

READ THE SPELLING WORDS

1.	aim	*aim*	Her **aim** is to become a doctor.
2.	holiday	*holiday*	Which **holiday** falls on January 1?
3.	paper	*paper*	Todd forgot to sign his **paper**.
4.	station	*station*	The radio **station** went off the air.
5.	able	*able*	Humans are **able** to travel in space.
6.	crayon	*crayon*	Blue **crayon** is good for coloring sky.
7.	flavor	*flavor*	I use toothpaste with mint **flavor**.
8.	lazy	*lazy*	Successful people are usually not **lazy**.
9.	brain	*brain*	Our **brain** controls our emotions.
10.	anyway	*anyway*	You may not win, but try **anyway**.
11.	remain	*remain*	Sleep and eat well to **remain** healthy.
12.	favor	*favor*	Do a **favor** for your friends.
13.	rail	*rail*	The **rail** for the train was made of steel.
14.	taste	*taste*	I like the sour **taste** of lemon.
15.	trailer	*trailer*	I got a **trailer** to pull my boat.
16.	lady	*lady*	A **lady** is known for her good manners.
17.	nation	*nation*	Our **nation** is a vast land.
18.	relay	*relay*	I will **relay** the good news to all.
19.	fail	*fail*	Try again if at first you **fail**.
20.	radio	*radio*	Karl is host of a **radio** talk show.

SORT THE SPELLING WORDS

1.–10. Write the words that have the **long a** sound spelled **a**.

11.–16. Write the words that have the **long a** sound spelled **ai**.

17.–20. Write the words that have the **long a** sound spelled **ay**.

REMEMBER THE SPELLING STRATEGY

Remember that the **long a** sound can be spelled **a** as in **lady**, **ai** as in **aim**, and **ay** as in **relay**.

Pretest Sentences (See procedures on pages Z10–Z11.)

1. My **aim** is to finish my homework before dinner.
2. It is almost time to celebrate a **holiday**.
3. Bob does his math homework on lined **paper**.
4. On Saturday I will go to the bus **station** to meet my aunt.
5. My little sister is now **able** to tie her shoelaces.
6. Betty likes to color with a purple **crayon**.
7. Adding carrots to stew helps give it **flavor**.
8. Yuan works very hard and is not **lazy**.
9. The human **brain** is protected by the skull.
10. Linda was tired, but she went to the store **anyway**.
11. When riding a bus, all children should **remain** in their seats.
12. When her friend needed help, Lakeisha was quick to do a **favor**.
13. The road crew put in a new **rail**.
14. Julio enjoys the **taste** of sweet cider.
15. Alan will go camping this week in his new **trailer**.
16. The woman who brings our mail is a very nice **lady**.
17. Washington, D.C., is the capital of our **nation**.
18. Please **relay** the message to Bob.
19. Dolores will not **fail** to attend class.
20. He likes to listen to the **radio**.

Spelling and Vocabulary

Word Structure

1.–2. Write the spelling words that have two syllables and have the **long a** sound in the second syllable. Draw a line between the syllables. Refer to your dictionary if you need help.

3.–12. Write the spelling words that have two syllables and have the **long a** sound in the first syllable. Draw a line between the syllables. Refer to your dictionary if you need help.

Word Meanings

Write a spelling word for each clue.

13. You use your mouth to do this to food.

14. Thanksgiving is an example.

15. It is the opposite of **pass**.

16. It is located in your skull.

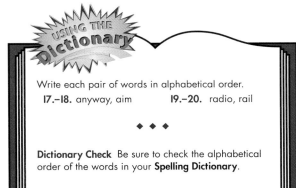

Write each pair of words in alphabetical order.

17.–18. anyway, aim   **19.–20.** radio, rail

◆ ◆ ◆

Dictionary Check Be sure to check the alphabetical order of the words in your **Spelling Dictionary**.

Order of answers may vary.

Word Structure

1. re/main
2. re/lay
3. pa/per
4. sta/tion
5. a/ble
6. cray/on
7. fla/vor
8. la/zy
9. fa/vor
10. trail/er
11. la/dy
12. na/tion

Word Meanings

13. taste
14. holiday
15. fail
16. brain

Using the Dictionary

17. aim
18. anyway
19. radio
20. rail

21

Objectives

Spelling and Vocabulary

Students will

- **select** and write two-syllable words with a **long a** sound in the second syllable.
- **select** and write two-syllable words with a **long a** sound in the first syllable.
- **divide** words into syllables.
- **write** a spelling word that matches a given clue.
- **arrange** spelling words in alphabetical order.

Developing Oral Language Skills

Write the following rhyme on the chalkboard:

> **ai** and **ay** say **a**,
> You won't **fail** these words **today**.

Ask students to chant it aloud as you point to the underlined letters.

MEETING INDIVIDUAL NEEDS

Providing More Help

Write each spelling word on a 3" × 5" card and give the cards to a student who will be the leader. Then give each of the other students three large (at least 5" × 8") blank cards. Have each student write **a** on one blank card, **ai** on another, and **ay** on the third blank card. Have the leader hold up a spelling-word card and pronounce the word. On the count of three, the other students should hold up the card that shows the **long a** spelling for the word. When all of the students have held up the proper card, have them write the spelling word on the back of the card.

★ Students who need to study fewer words should use the **Alternate Word List**. This list is starred on page T20 in the Teacher Edition. The **Unit 3 Practice Masters** (*Teacher Resource Book*) provide additional practice with these words.

Unit 3 Practice Masters

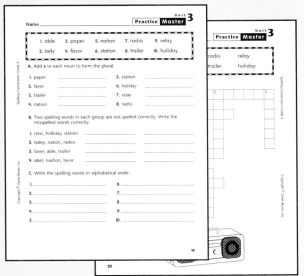

T21

Objectives

Spelling and Reading

Students will
- **select** and write spelling words to complete sentences.
- **solve** analogies using spelling words.

One-Minute Handwriting Hint

The checkstroke ending of the lowercase **o** swings right and up and then overcurves quickly to form the slant stroke of the letter **n**.

OVERCURVE

Legible handwriting can boost spelling scores by as much as 20%.

Fill in the Blanks

1. aim
2. fail
3. able
4. crayon
5. remain
6. station
7. rail
8. taste
9. trailer
10. anyway
11. radio
12. favor
13. flavor
14. relay
15. holiday

Solve the Analogies

16. paper
17. lady
18. brain
19. nation
20. lazy

Spelling and Reading

aim	holiday	paper	station	able
crayon	flavor	lazy	brain	anyway
remain	favor	rail	taste	trailer
lady	nation	relay	fail	radio

Fill in the Blanks Write the spelling word that completes each sentence.

1. If your ____ is poor, you will not hit the target.
2. I never ____ to enjoy a good book.
3. You must be strong if you are ____ to carry that heavy load.
4. I used pencil and ____ to draw and color that picture.
5. Please ____ in your seat until your name is called.
6. Jimmy and I went to the bus ____ to meet my aunt.
7. Goods are often sent by ____ or by sea.
8. Once you have had a ____ of Mother's cooking you will want more.
9. The car pulled a ____ full of furniture.
10. Dad told Jim not to open the present, but he did ____.
11. We heard a traffic report on our car's ____.
12. Do me the ____ of returning a book to the library.
13. Chocolate is my favorite ice cream ____.
14. The player will ____ the coach's message to the team.
15. Columbus Day is a ____ in some states.

Solve the Analogies Write a spelling word to complete each analogy.

16. **Paint** is to **canvas** as **pencil** is to ____.
17. **Gentleman** is to **man** as ____ is to **woman**.
18. **Heart** is to **chest** as ____ is to **head**.
19. **Country** is to ____ as **car** is to **automobile**.
20. **Slim** is to **thin** as **idle** is to ____.

22

MEETING INDIVIDUAL NEEDS

Providing More Challenge

Challenge Words and **Challenge Activities** for Unit 3 appear on page 226. **Challenge Word Test Sentences** appear on page T226.

Unit 3 Challenge Activities

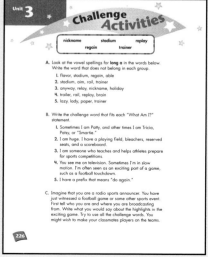

Weekly Test Options

Option 1:
One Spelling Word Per Sentence
(See procedures on pages Z10–Z11.)

1. May I have a pencil and some **paper**?
2. Please hold onto the **rail** when you walk.
3. I hear songs on the **radio**.
4. The boy was **able** to go swimming.
5. We will spend the **holiday** at home.
6. Who is swimming at the **relay** meet?
7. Hot summer days make me feel **lazy**.
8. My mother is a very nice **lady**.
9. Grandmother took the train at the **station**.
10. Many states make up our **nation**.
11. This cheese has a good **flavor**.
12. I like the **taste** of most foods.
13. Color the paper with a blue **crayon**.
14. The **brain** is a vital organ.
15. I will study for the test so I won't **fail**.

T22

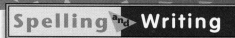

Spelling and Writing

Objectives

Spelling and Writing

Students will
- **proofread** a diary entry.
- **use** the writing process to write a diary entry.
- **proofread** their writing.

Proofread a Diary Entry

Six words are not spelled correctly in this diary entry. Write the words correctly.

October 8
Each weekend is a holliday *(holiday)* at our house. We remain at home and listen to music on our favorite raydio *(radio)* station, read the daily papur *(paper)*, and are lazey *(lazy)* without feeling guilty. I give my brane *(brain)* a rest from school, and we all relax. I did have to do some chores, but it was a great weekend enyway *(anyway)*.

Proofreading Marks

☰	Make a capital.
/	Make a small letter.
∧	Add something.
ℒ	Take out something.
⊙	Add a period.
⌗	New paragraph
SP	Spelling error

Write a Diary Entry

Narrative Writing

Write a diary entry for a real or an imagined day. Include all the information that is important. Be sure to include the following:

- the date you are writing your entry
- the date or dates you are writing about
- what you did during that time period
- what feelings you had about what happened
- what changes in your life, if any, you will make because of that experience

Writing Process

Prewriting
⇩
Drafting
⇩
Revising
⇩
Editing
⇩
Publishing

Proofread Your Writing During

Proofread your writing for spelling errors as part of the editing stage in the writing process. Be sure to check each word carefully. Use a dictionary to check spelling if you are not sure.

23

Using the Writing Process

Before assigning **Write a Diary Entry,** see pages 258–259 in the Student Edition for a complete review of the writing process and additional writing assignments. You may also wish to refer to pages Z12–Z13 in the Teacher Edition.

Keeping a Spelling Journal

Encourage students to record the words they misspelled on the weekly test in a personal spelling journal. These words may be recycled for future study. Students may also wish to include words from their writing. See pages Z12–Z13 in the Teacher Edition for more information.

---

16. I will **aim** to finish my work in two hours.
17. The horse rode in the **trailer**.
18. I asked Father if he would do me a **favor**.
19. It was cold but I went **anyway**.
20. You must **remain** in your seat on the bus.

Option 2:
Multiple Spelling Words Per Sentence
(See procedures on pages Z10–Z11.)

1. The **radio station** played **holiday** songs.
2. I **aim** to **taste** every **flavor** of jelly.
3. The **rail** fell off the side of the **trailer**.
4. He was too **lazy** to pick up the **paper** and **crayon**.
5. The people of our **nation** will be **able** to **remain** free.
6. I used my **brain** but misspelled one word **anyway**.
7. That **lady** and her children should win the swimming **relay**.
8. The **favor** I ask is that you don't **fail** the test.

Option 3:
Standardized Test
(See *Teacher Resource Book,* Unit 3.)

Unit 3 Test Master

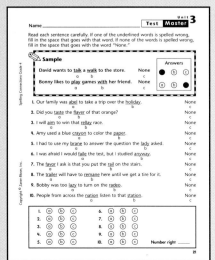

Objectives

Strategy Words

Students will
• **review** words studied previously that are related to the spelling strategy.
• **preview** unknown words that are related to the spelling strategy.

Remind the students that the **Strategy Words** are related to the spelling patterns they have studied in this unit. The **Review Words** are below grade level, and the **Preview Words** are above grade level. You may wish to use the following sentences to introduce the words in context.

Review Words:
Words From Grade 3

1. My parents will be **away** for the evening.
2. We **laid** the carpet in the living room last week.
3. Our **mail** arrives in the early afternoon.
4. Mom says **maybe** I will go to the party with you.
5. We will have someone come to **paint** our house.

Preview Words:
Words From Grade 5

6. Can you **explain** to me how you did that?
7. This is the **grayest** day we have had.
8. At **midday** we will have lunch.
9. The package will arrive **prepaid**.
10. We must **reclaim** our baggage as soon as possible.

Review Words
1. maybe
2. laid
3. mail
4. away
5. paint

Preview Words
6. grayest
7. prepaid
8. explain
9. reclaim
10. midday

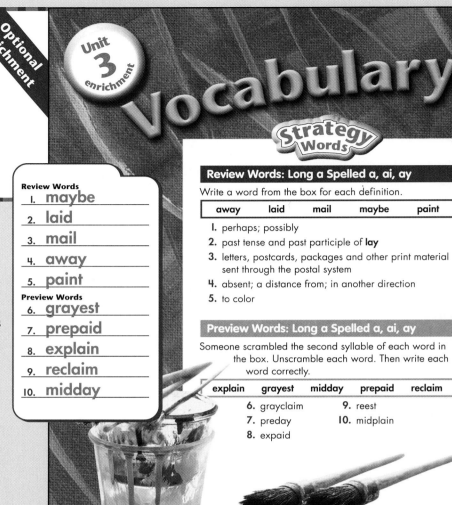

Vocabulary

Unit 3 enrichment

Strategy Words

Review Words: Long a Spelled a, ai, ay

Write a word from the box for each definition.

away	laid	mail	maybe	paint

1. perhaps; possibly
2. past tense and past participle of **lay**
3. letters, postcards, packages and other print material sent through the postal system
4. absent; a distance from; in another direction
5. to color

Preview Words: Long a Spelled a, ai, ay

Someone scrambled the second syllable of each word in the box. Unscramble each word. Then write each word correctly.

explain	grayest	midday	prepaid	reclaim

6. grayclaim
7. preday
8. expaid
9. reest
10. midplain

24

Unit 3 Homework Master

Unit 3 RECAP

You may wish to assign the **Unit 3 Homework Master** (*Teacher Resource Book,* Unit 3) as a fun way to recap the spelling words.

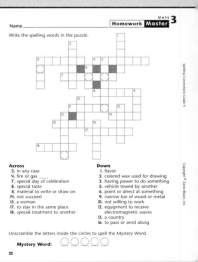

T24

Connections

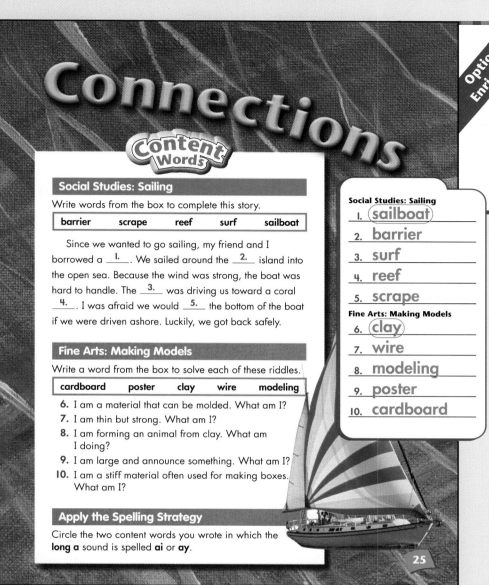

Content Words

Objectives

Content Words

Students will
- **expand** vocabulary with content-related words.
- **relate** the spelling strategy to words outside the basic spelling list.

Social Studies: Sailing

Write words from the box to complete this story.

barrier	scrape	reef	surf	sailboat

Since we wanted to go sailing, my friend and I borrowed a ___1.___. We sailed around the ___2.___ island into the open sea. Because the wind was strong, the boat was hard to handle. The ___3.___ was driving us toward a coral ___4.___. I was afraid we would ___5.___ the bottom of the boat if we were driven ashore. Luckily, we got back safely.

Fine Arts: Making Models

Write a word from the box to solve each of these riddles.

cardboard	poster	clay	wire	modeling

6. I am a material that can be molded. What am I?
7. I am thin but strong. What am I?
8. I am forming an animal from clay. What am I doing?
9. I am large and announce something. What am I?
10. I am a stiff material often used for making boxes. What am I?

Apply the Spelling Strategy

Circle the two content words you wrote in which the **long a** sound is spelled **ai** or **ay**.

Social Studies: Sailing
1. (sailboat)
2. barrier
3. surf
4. reef
5. scrape

Fine Arts: Making Models
6. (clay)
7. wire
8. modeling
9. poster
10. cardboard

25

Content Words

Social Studies: Sailing

Review the meanings of these words with the students. You may wish to use these sentences to introduce these words in context.

1. A **barrier** kept the ship from sailing through the passage.
2. He will **scrape** off the outside layer of the coconut.
3. A strip of coral under the water can be called a **reef**.
4. As we watched the ocean, we could see the incoming **surf**.
5. The **sailboat** was moving rapidly with the strong wind.

Encourage the students to use these words in a story about a visit to the ocean.

Fine Arts: Making Models

Review the meanings of these words with the students. You may wish to use these sentences to introduce these words in context.

6. You can use **cardboard** for many home and school projects.
7. We made a big **poster** to hang in the room.
8. The teacher gave us some **clay** to make our ships.
9. We used some **wire** to make a strong frame for our models.
10. The students were **modeling** good behavior.

Encourage the students to use these words in writing directions for a project.

Unit 4 Home Study Master

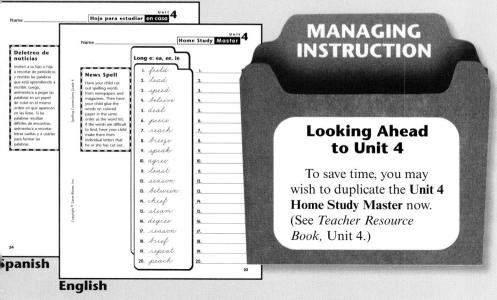

Spanish

English

MANAGING INSTRUCTION

Looking Ahead to Unit 4

To save time, you may wish to duplicate the **Unit 4 Home Study Master** now. (See *Teacher Resource Book*, Unit 4.)

Basic Spelling List

field	least
lead	season
speed	between
believe	chief
deal	steam
piece	degree
reach	reason
breeze	brief
speak	repeat
agree	peach

Strategy Words

Review

cheese	peace
leave	speech
mean	

Preview

beliefs	freedom
beneath	make-believe
decrease	

Content Words

Science: Animals

beetle	reptile
lizard	insect
grasshopper	

Health: Diseases

chicken pox	measles
itch	flu
fever	

Individual Needs

Challenge Words

wreath	breed
treason	belief
keenly	

Alternate Word List

field	speak
lead	agree
believe	between
piece	chief
reach	reason

MATERIALS

Student Edition
Pages 26–31
Challenge Activities, p. 227

Teacher Edition
Pages T26A–T31
Challenge Activities, p. T227

Other Resources
Spelling Connections Software
Unit 4 Word List Overhead
Transparency

Teacher Resource Book
Unit 4 Home Study Master
(English or Spanish; students
may pretest on this sheet or use
it for home practice.)
Unit 4 Homework Master
Unit 4 Practice Masters
Flip Folder Practice Master
Unit 4 Test Master

Visit our Web site, www.zaner-bloser.com

OBJECTIVES

Spelling and Thinking

Students will
- **read** the spelling words in list form and in context.
- **sort** the spelling words according to the **long e** sound spelled **ea, ee,** and **ie.**
- **read** and remember this week's spelling strategy.

Spelling and Vocabulary

Students will
- **read** definitions of spelling words and write the words that match those definitions.
- **write** spelling words to complete word categories.
- **identify** syllables in spelling words.
- **refer** to the **Spelling Dictionary** to verify that **lead** is a homograph and write the word.

Spelling and Reading

Students will
- **solve** analogies with spelling words.
- **identify** rhyme and write spelling words to complete sentences.
- **complete** a paragraph with spelling words.

Spelling and Writing

Students will
- **proofread** a newspaper rental ad.
- **use** the writing process to write a newspaper rental ad.
- **proofread** their writing.

MEETING INDIVIDUAL NEEDS
Learning Styles

Visual

Make a large game board, as shown below. Write a spelling pattern for the **long e** sound on each leaf (**ea, ee, ie**). Make a set of forty cards, writing each spelling word on two 3" × 5" cards. Have each student place a small marker on the tree. Ask the first player to draw a card, study the word, and then write the word on his or her paper without looking at the card.

If this player spells the word correctly, he or she may advance to the next leaf that has the form of the **long e** spelling pattern used in the word just spelled. The goal is to reach the apple from the tree.

Auditory

Divide the class into two teams. Spell a word for Team A. The first player on that team must say the word and then spell another word from the spelling list with the same **long e** spelling pattern. If the word he or she spelled is correct, that player gets to write the word on the chalkboard. Next, spell a word for Team B. The teams take turns until all of the spelling words have been written on the chalkboard.

Kinesthetic

Choose one student to be Simon for a game of "Simon Says." Have Simon call on a student to spell a spelling word while hopping for **ee** words, swinging arms for **ie** words, or running in place for **ea** words. If the student both spells the word and moves correctly, she or he becomes the new Simon.

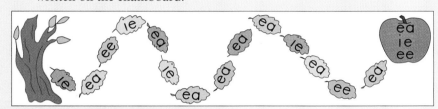

Language and Cultural Differences

The **long e** sound may be difficult for some students to hear due to differences in regional pronunciation or language backgrounds. For example, the **long e** sound in Spanish is usually spelled by the letter **i**.

Write each spelling word on the chalkboard, explaining that the **long e** sound can be spelled in different ways. Say each word clearly and have the students repeat it and tell something about its meaning. Next, underline the letters that spell the **long e** sound. Have the students fold their papers to make three columns labeled **ee, ea,** and **ie,** and ask them to write the spelling words in the appropriate columns.

MANAGING INSTRUCTION

3–5 Day Plan		Average	Below Average	Above Average
Day 1	**Day 1**	Pretest Spelling Mini-Lesson, p. T26 Spelling and Thinking, p. 26	Pretest Spelling Mini-Lesson, p. T26 Spelling and Thinking, p. 26	Pretest Spelling and Thinking, p. 26
	Day 2	Spelling and Vocabulary, p. 27	Spelling and Vocabulary, p. 27 (or) Unit 4 Practice Master, A and B	Spelling and Vocabulary, p. 27 Spelling and Reading, p. 28
Day 2	**Day 3**	Spelling and Reading, p. 28	Spelling and Reading, p. 28 (or) Unit 4 Practice Master, C and D	Challenge Activities, p. 227
	Day 4	Spelling and Writing, p. 29 Unit 4 Homework Master	Spelling and Writing, p. 29	Spelling and Writing, p. 29 Unit 4 Homework Master
Day 3	**Day 5**	Weekly Test	Weekly Test	Weekly Test
Vocabulary Connections (pages 30 and 31) may be used anytime during this unit.				

Objectives

Spelling and Thinking

Students will

- **read** the spelling words in list form and in context.
- **sort** the spelling words according to the **long e** sound spelled **ea, ee,** and **ie**.
- **read** and remember this week's spelling strategy.

UNIT PRETEST

Use **Pretest Sentences** below. Refer to the self-checking procedures on student page 256. You may wish to use the **Unit 4 Word List Overhead Transparency** as part of the checking procedure.

TEACHING THE STRATEGY

Spelling Mini-Lesson

Write /ē/ on the chalkboard as a heading. Ask students which sound this symbol represents. (long e)

Ask the students to brainstorm different words with the **long e** sound. Write their suggestions on the chalkboard. Ask volunteers to underline the **long e** spelling pattern in each word. Focus attention on words in which **long e** is spelled **ee, ea,** and **ie**. Explain that all the words on this week's list have one of these **long e** spelling patterns.

Write any words from this week's list on the chalkboard that are not already there. Ask volunteers to underline the **long e** spelling pattern in each word. You may wish to point out that when a word has the **long e** sound in the final position, /ē/ is often spelled **ee**. In some one-syllable words, however, /ē/ is spelled **ea**, as in **pea** and **tea**.

Focus students' attention on these words: **field, piece, brief, chief, believe**. Remind them that while they hear only **long e** in these words, they must remember to include **i** in the spellings.

Conclude by reading **Remember the Spelling Strategy** on page 26.

Order of answers may vary.

ea
1. lead ★
2. deal
3. reach ★
4. speak ★
5. least
6. season
7. steam
8. reason ★
9. repeat
10. peach

ee
11. speed
12. breeze
13. agree ★
14. between ★
15. degree

ie
16. field ★
17. believe ★
18. piece ★
19. chief ★
20. brief

Spelling and Thinking

READ THE SPELLING WORDS

1. field	field	The cows are grazing in the **field**.
2. lead	lead	If you **lead**, I will follow.
3. speed	speed	Do bikers **speed** on this path?
4. believe	believe	I **believe** you are telling the truth.
5. deal	deal	That **deal** was too good to be true.
6. piece	piece	We lost a **piece** of the puzzle.
7. reach	reach	Ava cannot **reach** the top shelf.
8. breeze	breeze	The **breeze** helped cool us today.
9. speak	speak	We are learning to **speak** Italian.
10. agree	agree	Yes, I **agree** with your plan.
11. least	least	It has rained for at **least** six days.
12. season	season	Summer is the **season** I like best.
13. between	between	This secret is **between** you and me.
14. chief	chief	A **chief** is head of a group.
15. steam	steam	You can **steam** these vegetables.
16. degree	degree	The temperature rose one **degree** today.
17. reason	reason	What is your **reason** for being so early?
18. brief	brief	A **brief** tale is a short story.
19. repeat	repeat	Do not **repeat** everything you hear.
20. peach	peach	The skin of a **peach** is fuzzy.

SORT THE SPELLING WORDS

1.–10. Write the words that have the **long e** sound spelled **ea**.

11.–15. Write the words that have the **long e** sound spelled **ee**.

16.–20. Write the words that have the **long e** sound spelled **ie**.

REMEMBER THE SPELLING STRATEGY

Remember that the **long e** sound can be spelled in different ways: **ea** in **deal**, **ee** in **speed**, and **ie** in **field**.

Pretest Sentences (See procedures on pages Z10–Z11.)

1. We grow hay in that **field**.
2. She will **lead** the parade down the avenue.
3. There is a limit to the **speed** you may travel.
4. I **believe** the forecaster said that the sun will shine.
5. Did we **deal** with butterflies in science class yesterday?
6. I would like a **piece** of watermelon.
7. June could not **reach** the high shelf.
8. Today we need a cool **breeze**.
9. Deandre likes to **speak** to large audiences.
10. I **agree** with your suggestion.
11. John bought the **least** expensive pen.
12. Spring is Shameka's favorite **season**.
13. The ball landed **between** the houses.
14. He is the **chief** of the fire department.
15. The **steam** rose from the hot stew.
16. The temperature outside is one **degree** above freezing.
17. He explained his **reason** for walking.
18. The senator's speech was **brief**.
19. The teacher will **repeat** the question.
20. My favorite fruit is a **peach**.

Spelling and Vocabulary

Word Meanings

Write a spelling word for each definition.

1. a fuzzy, sweet fruit
2. a leader; head of a group
3. to handle in a certain way; cope
4. gas made from water
5. to talk
6. a part
7. smallest in size or amount
8. to extend

Word Categories

Write a spelling word to complete each category.

9. area, meadow, _____
10. current, wind, _____
11. swiftness, rapidity, _____
12. short, concise, _____

Syllables

13.–19. Write the spelling words that have two syllables.
Draw a line between the syllables.

USING THE Dictionary

20. Words that have the same spellings but different origins, meanings, and sometimes pronunciations are called **homographs**. The dictionary usually has a separate entry for each homograph. Write the spelling word that is a homograph.

♦ ♦ ♦

Dictionary Check Be sure to check your answer in your **Spelling Dictionary**.

Word Meanings
1. peach
2. chief
3. deal
4. steam
5. speak
6. piece
7. least
8. reach

Word Categories
9. field
10. breeze
11. speed
12. brief

Syllables
13. be/lieve
14. a/gree
15. sea/son
16. be/tween
17. de/gree
18. rea/son
19. re/peat

Using the Dictionary
20. lead

27

Developing Oral Language Skills

Each of the spelling patterns for the **long e** sound studied in this lesson combine the letter **e** with another vowel. However, the other vowel remains silent while the letter **e** "says its name." Write several spelling words on the chalkboard and have students say them aloud as you point to the letters that spell the **long e** sound.

MEETING INDIVIDUAL NEEDS

Providing More Help

Make two cards for each spelling word. On one card, write a spelling word minus the **long e** spelling pattern; on the second card, write the letters that spell the **long e** sound. Mix the cards up and arrange them facedown on a table. Have the students take turns turning over two cards at a time. Whenever the cards make a spelling word, have the student write the word on the chalkboard, circling the **long e** spelling pattern.

★Students who need to study fewer words should use the **Alternate Word List**. This list is starred on page T26 in the Teacher Edition. The **Unit 4 Practice Masters** (*Teacher Resource Book*) provide additional practice with these words.

Unit 4 Practice Masters

Name _____

Practice Master Unit 4

| 1. lead | 3. reach | 5. agree | 7. field | 9. chief |
| 2. speak | 4. reason | 6. between | 8. piece | 10. believe |

A. A **base word** is a word to which a prefix or suffix can be added. Write the base word of each suffix form.

1. agreed _____
2. speaking _____
3. leader _____
4. reasonable _____
5. reaching _____
6. pieces _____
7. fields _____
8. believed _____

B. Write the spelling word that goes with each meaning.

1. a part of the whole _____
2. a piece of open or cleared land _____
3. fact that explains why something happens _____
4. to stretch or extend an arm _____
5. a leader _____
6. in the space that separates two things _____

25

Practice Master Unit 4

| field | chief |
| piece | believe |

...rd that belongs in each group.

...hidden in the puzzle. Circle

26

T27

Objectives

Spelling and Reading

Students will

- **solve** analogies with spelling words.
- **identify** rhyme and write spelling words to complete sentences.
- **complete** a paragraph with spelling words.

One-Minute Handwriting Hint

The undercurve beginning of the lowercase **e** must be wide to allow room for the loop and the slant stroke that follow. Keep the loop open or the letter will look like an **i**.

WIDE UNDERCURVE
e

Legible handwriting can boost spelling scores by as much as 20%.

Solve the Analogies

1. peach
2. breeze
3. speak
4. lead
5. piece
6. brief
7. steam
8. reason

Complete the Sentences

9. field
10. repeat
11. reach
12. speed
13. least
14. chief
15. deal

Complete the Paragraph

16. season
17. believe
18. agree
19. between
20. degree

Spelling and Reading

field	lead	speed	believe	deal
piece	reach	breeze	speak	agree
least	season	between	chief	steam
degree	reason	brief	repeat	peach

Solve the Analogies Write a spelling word to complete each analogy.

1. **Carrot** is to **vegetable** as _____ is to **fruit**.
2. **Huge** is to **big** as gale is to _____.
3. **Monarch** is to **ruler** as talk is to _____.
4. **Happy** is to **sad** as **follow** is to _____.
5. **Country** is to **state** as **whole** is to _____.
6. **Seek** is to **search** as _____ is to **short**.
7. **Heat** is to _____ as **cold** is to **ice**.
8. **Question** is to **ask** as _____ is to **think**.

Complete the Sentences Write a spelling word to complete each sentence. The spelling word rhymes with the underlined word.

9. The farmer's _____ will surely yield a crop.
10. You must never _____ that dangerous feat.
11. I swim at a beach that is not out of _____.
12. When biking, you need to be aware of your _____.
13. We dined at a feast with five courses at _____.
14. To appoint him a _____ is beyond my belief.
15. A five-dollar meal is a very good _____.

Complete the Paragraph Write words from the box to complete the paragraph.

My friends and I have different ideas about which _16._ is best. I _17._ summer is perfect, but Marcie does not _18._. She prefers winter while Paul is torn _19._ spring and fall. He needs a high _20._ of cool, brisk weather.

believe
agree
degree
between
season

28

MEETING INDIVIDUAL NEEDS

Providing More Challenge

Challenge Words and **Challenge Activities** for Unit 4 appear on page 227. **Challenge Word Test Sentences** appear on page T227.

Unit 4 Challenge Activities

Challenge Activities Unit 4

wreath   treason   keenly
breed   belief

A. Write the challenge words that rhyme with the words below.
1. relief   4. reason
2. creed   5. beneath
3. queenly

B. Write a challenge word to complete each sentence.
1. If you betray your country by aiding the enemy, you are guilty of _____.
2. If you have faith in something, you have a _____.
3. If your eyes are sharp, you see _____.
4. A ring made of flowers, leaves, or small branches is a _____.
5. A group of animals, such as beagles, can be called a _____.

C. List several answers to each question below. Look over your lists to see whether one of your answers suggests something you could write about. Then write a short paragraph using the word or words you selected.
1. What are some names for different breeds of dogs?
2. Where might a person put a wreath?
3. What do you feel keenly, or very strongly, about?

227

Weekly Test Options

Option 1:
One Spelling Word Per Sentence
(See procedures on pages Z10–Z11.)

1. Father got a good **deal** on the car.
2. I will **speak** to my dad.
3. Mom has to work at **least** three days this week.
4. My teacher chose me to **lead** the band.
5. She had a good **reason** for leaving early.
6. I could not **reach** my coat.
7. I ate the **peach**.
8. Which **season** of the year do you like best?
9. We will **steam** the corn.
10. He drives at a slow **speed** in town.
11. I am sure Dad will **agree** to go with me.
12. He could feel the warm **breeze**.
13. I asked her to **repeat** her name.
14. Today it is one **degree** warmer outside.
15. The bush was planted **between** two large trees.

T28

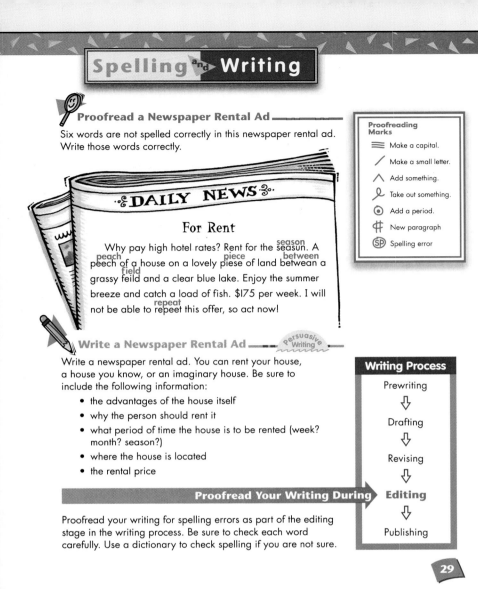

Spelling and Writing

Proofread a Newspaper Rental Ad

Six words are not spelled correctly in this newspaper rental ad. Write those words correctly.

DAILY NEWS

For Rent

Why pay high hotel rates? Rent for the **seasun** [season]. A **peech** [peach] of a house on a lovely **piese** [piece] of land **between** land **feild** [field] and a clear blue lake. Enjoy the summer breeze and catch a load of fish. $175 per week. I will not be able to **repeet** [repeat] this offer, so act now!

Proofreading Marks

≡ Make a capital.
/ Make a small letter.
∧ Add something.
℀ Take out something.
⊙ Add a period.
⌗ New paragraph.
ⓢⓟ Spelling error

Write a Newspaper Rental Ad — Persuasive Writing

Write a newspaper rental ad. You can rent your house, a house you know, or an imaginary house. Be sure to include the following information:

• the advantages of the house itself
• why the person should rent it
• what period of time the house is to be rented (week? month? season?)
• where the house is located
• the rental price

Proofread Your Writing During Editing

Proofread your writing for spelling errors as part of the editing stage in the writing process. Be sure to check each word carefully. Use a dictionary to check spelling if you are not sure.

Writing Process

Prewriting
⇩
Drafting
⇩
Revising
⇩
Editing
⇩
Publishing

29

Objectives

Spelling and Writing

Students will
• **proofread** a newspaper rental ad.
• **use** the writing process to write a newspaper rental ad.
• **proofread** their writing.

Using the Writing Process

Before assigning **Write a Newspaper Rental Ad,** see pages 258–259 in the Student Edition for a complete review of the writing process and additional writing assignments. You may also wish to refer to pages Z12–Z13 in the Teacher Edition.

Keeping a Spelling Journal

Encourage students to record the words they misspelled on the weekly test in a personal spelling journal. These words may be recycled for future study. Students may also wish to include words from their writing. See pages Z12–Z13 in the Teacher Edition for more information.

---

16. The cow ate grass in the green **field**.
17. I will have one **piece** of bread.
18. Our talk will be very **brief**.
19. Our **chief** cook won a blue ribbon.
20. I **believe** that it will not rain.

Option 2:
Multiple Spelling Words Per Sentence

(See procedures on pages Z10–Z11.)

1. Do you **agree** that the **chief** should **speak** to the children?
2. I **believe** we made a **deal** to drive at a slower **speed**.
3. The **breeze** blew **between** the trees in the **field**.
4. Please **repeat** the **reason** that you want to **lead** the parade.
5. The **season** of spring is **brief**.
6. The heat may **reach** a high **degree** in the summer.
7. Dad wanted to **steam** his shirts for at **least** ten seconds when he ironed them.
8. Mother cut the **peach** in half and gave me a **piece**.

Option 3:
Standardized Test

(See *Teacher Resource Book,* Unit 4.)

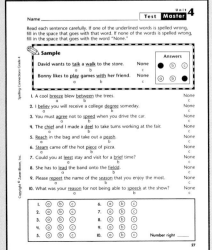

**Unit 4
Test Master**

T29

Objectives

Strategy Words

Students will
- **review** words studied previously that are related to the spelling strategy.
- **preview** unknown words that are related to the spelling strategy.

Remind the students that the **Strategy Words** relate to the spelling patterns they have studied in this unit. The **Review Words** are below grade level, and the **Preview Words** are above grade level. You may wish to use the following sentences to introduce the words in context.

Review Words:
Words From Grade 3
1. Some **cheese** would taste good on my sandwich.
2. I will **leave** here at noon.
3. I really **mean** to get my homework finished early tonight.
4. We hope for **peace** in the world.
5. The teacher will make a **speech** for the parents.

Preview Words:
Words From Grade 5
6. His **beliefs** about raising children are different from mine.
7. Look **beneath** the big leaves in the garden to find bugs.
8. We need to **decrease** the time it takes to do this work.
9. We have great **freedom** in this land.
10. My little brother likes to play **make-believe**.

Review Words
1. peace
2. leave
3. mean
4. cheese
5. speech

Preview Words
6. decrease
7. make-believe
8. beliefs
9. freedom
10. beneath

Unit 4 enrichment

Vocabulary

Strategy Words

Review Words: Long e Spelled ea, ee, ie

Write a word from the box for each clue.

cheese	leave	mean	peace	speech

1. the opposite of **war**
2. to go away
3. an antonym of **kind**
4. a solid food made from milk
5. a public talk

Preview Words: Long e Spelled ea, ee, ie

Substitute a word from the box to replace each underlined word.

beliefs	beneath	decrease	freedom	make-believe

6. The store owner has promised that he will <u>lower</u> his prices.
7. Some children have <u>imaginary</u> friends.
8. Our <u>strong opinions</u> are that we will play and win the game.
9. Be thankful for your <u>independence</u>.
10. The new subway system runs <u>under</u> all the city streets.

30

Unit 4 RECAP

You may wish to assign the **Unit 4 Homework Master** (*Teacher Resource Book,* Unit 4) as a fun way to recap the spelling words.

Unit 4 Homework Master

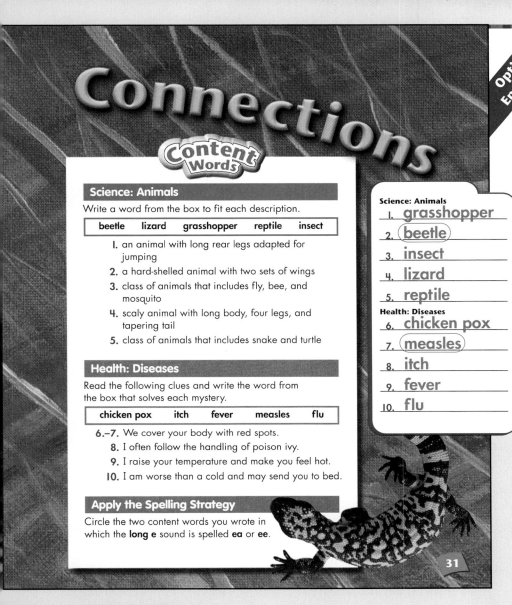

Connections

Content Words

Science: Animals

Write a word from the box to fit each description.

beetle	lizard	grasshopper	reptile	insect

1. an animal with long rear legs adapted for jumping
2. a hard-shelled animal with two sets of wings
3. class of animals that includes fly, bee, and mosquito
4. scaly animal with long body, four legs, and tapering tail
5. class of animals that includes snake and turtle

Health: Diseases

Read the following clues and write the word from the box that solves each mystery.

chicken pox	itch	fever	measles	flu

6.–7. We cover your body with red spots.
8. I often follow the handling of poison ivy.
9. I raise your temperature and make you feel hot.
10. I am worse than a cold and may send you to bed.

Apply the Spelling Strategy

Circle the two content words you wrote in which the **long e** sound is spelled **ea** or **ee**.

31

Science: Animals
1. grasshopper
2. (beetle)
3. insect
4. lizard
5. reptile

Health: Diseases
6. chicken pox
7. (measles)
8. itch
9. fever
10. flu

Objectives

Content Words

Students will
- **expand** vocabulary with content-related words.
- **relate** the spelling strategy to words outside the basic spelling list.

Content Words

Science: Animals

Review the meanings of these words with the students. You may wish to use these sentences to introduce the words in context.

1. A **beetle** crawled up the stem of a rose that I cut for my mother.
2. The **lizard** scurried along the ground.
3. My little brother caught a **grasshopper**.
4. Snakes belong to the **reptile** family.
5. My science report was about a very unusual **insect**.

Encourage the students to write a report about insects or one of the animals in the list.

Health: Diseases

Review the meanings of these words with the students. You may wish to use these sentences to introduce the words in context.

6. Many children had the **chicken pox** this year.
7. Some diseases cause rashes that **itch**.
8. The baby's high **fever** worried the parents.
9. Have you ever had the **measles**?
10. We get a shot each year to protect us from the **flu**.

Encourage the students to use these words in a story about a day at a doctor's office.

Unit 5 Home Study Master

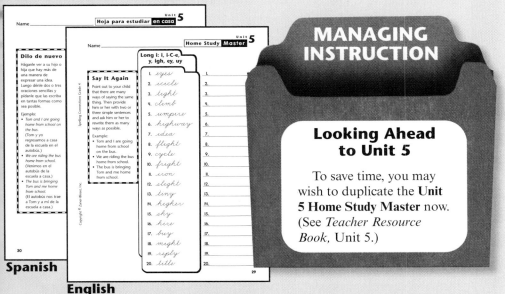

Spanish

English

MANAGING INSTRUCTION

Looking Ahead to Unit 5

To save time, you may wish to duplicate the **Unit 5 Home Study Master** now. (See *Teacher Resource Book*, Unit 5.)

Basic Spelling List

eyes	iron
icicle	slight
tight	tiny
climb	higher
umpire	shy
highway	hire
idea	buy
flight	might
cycle	reply
fright	title

Strategy Words

Review

fight	right
find	wild
price	

Preview

arrive	style
delight	supply
silent	

Content Words

Language Arts: Verbs

carried	hurried
grabbed	climbed
chased	

Language Arts: Exact Meaning

hiked	wobbled
wandered	strolled
marched	

Individual Needs

Challenge Words

dial	lightly
rely	blight
hydrant	

Alternate Word List

eyes	iron
climb	tiny
idea	shy
flight	buy
cycle	might

MATERIALS

Student Edition
Pages 32–37
Challenge Activities, p. 228

Teacher Edition
Pages T32A–T37
Challenge Activities, p. T228

Other Resources
Spelling Connections Software
Unit 5 Word List Overhead
  Transparency

Teacher Resource Book
Unit 5 Home Study Master
  (English or Spanish; students
  may pretest on this sheet or use
  it for home practice.)
Unit 5 Homework Master
Unit 5 Practice Masters
Flip Folder Practice Master
Unit 5 Test Master

Visit our Web site, www.zaner-bloser.com

OBJECTIVES

Spelling and Thinking
Students will
- **read** the spelling words in list form and in context.
- **sort** the words according to the **long i** sound spelled **i, i-consonant-e, y, igh, ey,** or **uy**.
- **read** and remember this week's spelling strategy.

Spelling and Vocabulary
Students will
- **identify** and write spelling words to replace words with similar meanings.
- **select** and write spelling words with more than one syllable.
- **divide** words into syllables.
- **identify** beginning and ending sounds.
- **read** and translate dictionary respellings of words.

Spelling and Reading
Students will
- **complete** sentences using spelling words.
- **identify** and write spelling words to solve riddles.
- **solve** analogies using spelling words.

Spelling and Writing
Students will
- **proofread** a poster.
- **use** the writing process to write a poster.
- **proofread** their writing.

MEETING INDIVIDUAL NEEDS
Learning Styles

Visual

First, ask students to write the spelling words on the chalkboard using colored chalk for just the letters that make the **long i** sound. Have them study the /ī/ spelling pattern in each word. Then have each of them draw a circle in the center of a sheet of paper and label it **uy/ey**. Next, tell each student to fold the paper in quarters and label each quarter with a **long i** spelling pattern—i.e., **i, i-consonant-e, y,** and **igh**. Finally, have each student write each spelling word correctly in one of the five sections of the paper.

Auditory

Have the students look at the completed chart described in the visual activity. Then ask them to say and spell each spelling word aloud, identify the **long i** spelling pattern aloud, and write the word.

Kinesthetic

Have the students write the spelling words on the chalkboard and study them. Ask them to pronounce each word, spell the word, and do an action according to the spelling pattern of the /ī/ as follows:

- the **long i** sound is spelled **i,** draw an **i** in the air;
- **i-consonant-e,** draw **i-C-e** in the air;
- **y,** stretch out both arms over their heads;
- **igh,** slap their thighs;
- **uy** or **ey,** cover their eyes with both hands.

Language and Cultural Differences

Some students may find it difficult to understand and frustrating that there are multiple spelling patterns for the **long i** sound. They may be particularly resistant to the **igh** pattern, which is among the most difficult patterns in English spelling.

Write each spelling word on the chalkboard, explaining that all the words have the **long i** sound and that this sound is spelled in different ways. Point out that some of the words with the **long i** sound have silent letters that are called "vowel lengtheners." (**flight, highway**)

Say each word clearly. Have the students repeat each word. In each spelling word, circle the letters that spell the **long i** sound. Next, ask the students to use the word in a sentence or to tell something about the meaning of the word. Then have them write each spelling word three times.

MANAGING INSTRUCTION

3–5 Day Plan		Average	Below Average	Above Average
Day 1	**Day 1**	Pretest Spelling Mini-Lesson, p. T32 Spelling and Thinking, p. 32	Pretest Spelling Mini-Lesson, p. T32 Spelling and Thinking, p. 32	Pretest Spelling and Thinking, p. 32
	Day 2	Spelling and Vocabulary, p. 33	Spelling and Vocabulary, p. 33 (or) Unit 5 Practice Master, A and B	Spelling and Vocabulary, p. 33 Spelling and Reading, p. 34
Day 2	**Day 3**	Spelling and Reading, p. 34	Spelling and Reading, p. 34 (or) Unit 5 Practice Master, C and D	Challenge Activities, p. 228
	Day 4	Spelling and Writing, p. 35 Unit 5 Homework Master	Spelling and Writing, p. 35	Spelling and Writing, p. 35 Unit 5 Homework Master
Day 3	**Day 5**	Weekly Test	Weekly Test	Weekly Test
Vocabulary Connections (pages 36 and 37) may be used anytime during this unit.				

Objectives

Spelling and Thinking

Students will
- **read** the spelling words in list form and in context.
- **sort** the words according to the **long i** sound spelled **i, i-conso-nant-e, y, igh, ey,** or **uy**.
- **read** and remember this week's spelling strategy.

UNIT PRETEST

Use **Pretest Sentences** below. Refer to the self-checking procedures on student page 256. You may wish to use the **Unit 5 Word List Overhead Transparency** as part of the checking procedure.

TEACHING THE STRATEGY

Spelling Mini-Lesson

Write /ī/ on the chalkboard. Ask the students which sound this symbol stands for. (long i) Tell the students that in this lesson they will spell words that have the **long i** sound.

Write **i, i-consonant-e, y, igh, ey,** and **uy** as subheadings under /ī/. Point out that the spelling words in this unit all use one of these six spelling patterns to spell the **long i** sound. Assign one spelling pattern to each of six volunteers. Ask the volunteers to come up and write all the spelling words with that pattern under the pattern on the chalkboard.

Ask the students to suppose that there are no words with the **long i** sound in the English language. Therefore, things that are now named by such words would have to have new names or be referred to by their synonyms. Ask the students to brainstorm synonyms for some of the spelling words or to create phrases that are synonyms (e.g., **frozen stick** for **icicle**). List the synonyms on the chalkboard.

Conclude by reading **Remember the Spelling Strategy** on page 32.

Unit 5
Long i: i, i-C-e, y, igh, ey, uy

Spelling and Thinking

Order of answers may vary.

i
1. icicle
2. climb ★
3. idea ★
4. iron ★
5. tiny ★
6. title

i-consonant-e
7. umpire
8. hire

y
9. reply
10. cycle ★
11. shy ★

igh
12. tight
13. highway
14. flight ★
15. fright
16. slight
17. higher
18. might ★

ey or uy
19. eyes ★
20. buy ★

32

READ THE SPELLING WORDS

1. eyes	*eyes*	Sunglasses protect our **eyes**.
2. icicle	*icicle*	An **icicle** is a hanging stick of ice.
3. tight	*tight*	My shoes are too **tight** for comfort.
4. climb	*climb*	Some bears can **climb** trees.
5. umpire	*umpire*	The **umpire** called the pitch a strike.
6. highway	*highway*	A **highway** is wider than a street.
7. idea	*idea*	Whose **idea** was it to hold this meeting?
8. flight	*flight*	In **flight**, bats scoop up insects.
9. cycle	*cycle*	The water **cycle** supports life.
10. fright	*fright*	The haunted house gave us a **fright**.
11. iron	*iron*	Steel and **iron** are strong materials.
12. slight	*slight*	A **slight** rip can be sewn easily.
13. tiny	*tiny*	A dot is a **tiny** mark.
14. higher	*higher*	Go to **higher** ground during floods.
15. shy	*shy*	A **shy** person tries to avoid notice.
16. hire	*hire*	Will the city **hire** more workers?
17. buy	*buy*	I **buy** my shoes at that store.
18. might	*might*	She was afraid they **might** be late.
19. reply	*reply*	I must **reply** to the invitation.
20. title	*title*	What is the **title** of your story?

SORT THE SPELLING WORDS

Write the words that have the **long i** sound spelled:

1.–6. **i**.   12.–18. **igh**.
7.–8. **i-consonant-e**.   19.–20. **ey or uy**.
9.–11. **y**.

REMEMBER THE SPELLING STRATEGY

Remember that the **long i** sound is spelled **i** in **climb**, **i-consonant-e** in **hire**, **y** in **cycle**, **igh** in **might**, **ey** in **eyes**, and **uy** in **buy**.

Pretest Sentences (See procedures on pages Z10–Z11.)

1. Both David and Kathy have beautiful **eyes**.
2. The dripping water froze and made an **icicle**.
3. Tom's shoes were too **tight** for comfort.
4. Dakota likes to **climb** the knotted rope at the gym.
5. An **umpire** rules on plays in a baseball game.
6. Terry drove his car on a four-lane **highway**.
7. Every invention starts as an **idea**.
8. Suzy will take an evening **flight** when she travels to Mexico.
9. This year we studied the life **cycle** of the frog.
10. When the lion suddenly appeared, Jill was filled with **fright**.
11. My dad presses his clothes with an **iron**.
12. I woke up with a **slight** headache this morning.
13. The baby is so **tiny** you can hold him in one arm.
14. The apples in the tree were **higher** than we could reach.
15. Oki does not like to sing for an audience because she is **shy**.
16. After Demarcus resigned, the boss had to **hire** a new person.
17. Tracy likes to **buy** new clothes at that store.
18. We **might** visit Pilar in her new home.
19. Usually when someone asks you a question, you should **reply**.
20. The **title** of the song is written on the cassette.

T32

Spelling and Vocabulary

Word Meanings

Replace each underlined word or group of words with a spelling word.

1. We took a <u>plane ride</u> from Denver to Seattle.
2. Because we were on a <u>close</u> schedule, we had to hurry.
3. After a <u>brief</u> delay, the plane took off.
4. I <u>could</u> have relaxed, but then I realized I had forgotten my suitcase.
5. That gave me quite a <u>scare</u>.

Word Structure

6.–15. Write the spelling words that have more than one syllable. Draw a line between syllables.

Phonics

16. Write the one-syllable word that ends with a consonant that is not sounded.
17. Write the one-syllable word that ends with a **silent e**.
18. Write the one-syllable word that starts like **ship** and ends like **try**.

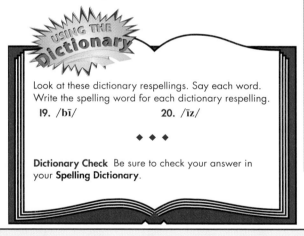

USING THE Dictionary

Look at these dictionary respellings. Say each word. Write the spelling word for each dictionary respelling.

19. /bī/   20. /īz/

♦ ♦ ♦

Dictionary Check Be sure to check your answer in your **Spelling Dictionary**.

Order of answers may vary.
Word Meanings
1. flight
2. tight
3. slight
4. might
5. fright

Word Structure
6. i/ci/cle
7. um/pire
8. high/way
9. i/de/a
10. cy/cle
11. i/ron
12. ti/ny
13. high/er
14. re/ply
15. ti/tle

Phonics
16. climb
17. hire
18. shy

Using the Dictionary
19. buy
20. eyes

33

Spelling and Vocabulary

Students will

- **identify** and write spelling words to replace words with similar meanings.
- **select** and write spelling words with more than one syllable.
- **divide** words into syllables.
- **identify** beginning and ending sounds.
- **read** and translate dictionary respellings of words.

Developing Oral Language Skills

Many words in English end with a **long i** sound. Give students a word such as **try** that ends with a **long i** sound. Challenge students to create a rhyming word by substituting letters. Caution them to keep the final **long i** spelled **y**. As students name new words, have another student write the word on the board. Possible rhymes are **fly, cry, my,** and **sly**.

MEETING INDIVIDUAL NEEDS

Providing More Help

Make five columns on the chalkboard labeled **i, y, igh, i-consonant-e, ey,** and **uy**. Write a clue for each spelling word, similar to the clues below. Designate a student to read the clues aloud. When a student guesses correctly, have that student write the word in the proper column.

I am attracted to magnets. (iron)
I am run over all day long. (highway)
I make sure you play a fair game. (umpire)
I do not like warm weather, so I leave. (icicle)
I tell you to reach up and up. (higher)

★ Students who need to study fewer words should use the **Alternate Word List**. This list is starred on page T32 in the Teacher Edition. The **Unit 5 Practice Masters** (*Teacher Resource Book*) provide additional practice with these words.

Unit 5 Practice Masters

T33

Spelling and Reading

Students will
- **complete** sentences using spelling words.
- **identify** and write spelling words to solve riddles.
- **solve** analogies using spelling words.

One-Minute Handwriting Hint

The overcurve ending of the lowercase **g** crosses at the base-line and then turns into a wide undercurve that forms the loop in the letter **h**.

CROSS AT BASELINE

Legible handwriting can boost spelling scores by as much as 20%.

Spelling and Reading

eyes	icicle	tight	climb	umpire
highway	idea	flight	cycle	fright
iron	slight	tiny	higher	shy
hire	buy	might	reply	title

Complete the Sentences Write a spelling word to complete each sentence.

1. Volunteering to help the needy is a good ____.
2. Even ____ people can learn to speak in public.
3. It is hard to follow the ball with the sun in your ____.
4. Many people have tried to ____ Mount Everest.
5. The plant is going to ____ more workers.
6. The ____ called the player out at third base.
7. What is the ____ of the book you are reading?
8. I thought her ____ to the question was excellent.
9. I want to ____ my mother a birthday present.
10. Jill thinks she ____ have a plan to raise money.

Solve the Riddles Write a spelling word to solve each riddle.

11. I am little; I rhyme with **fight**. Who am I?
12. As a verb, I press; as a metal, I am heavy. Who am I?
13. I am wide and black; cars ride on my back. Who am I?
14. I am best in the cold but drip in the heat. Who am I?

Solve the Analogies Write a spelling word to complete each analogy.

15. **Big** is to **huge** as **small** is to ____.
16. **Up** is to **down** as **loose** is to ____.
17. **Gallop** is to **horse** as ____ is to **bird**.
18. **Canoe** is to **paddle** as **bike** is to ____.
19. **Leave** is to **go** as **scare** is to ____.
20. **Empty** is to **full** as **lower** is to ____.

Complete the Sentences
1. idea
2. shy
3. eyes
4. climb
5. hire
6. umpire
7. title
8. reply
9. buy
10. might

Solve the Riddles
11. slight
12. iron
13. highway
14. icicle

Solve the Analogies
15. tiny
16. tight
17. flight
18. cycle
19. fright
20. higher

34

MEETING INDIVIDUAL NEEDS

Providing More Challenge

Challenge Words and **Challenge Activities** for Unit 5 appear on page 228. **Challenge Word Test Sentences** appear on page T228.

Unit 5 Challenge Activities

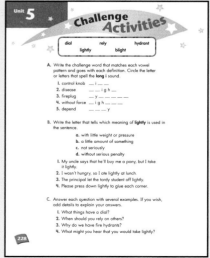

Weekly Test Options

Option 1:

One Spelling Word Per Sentence
(See procedures on pages Z10–Z11.)

1. The little bug was **tiny**.
2. An **umpire** works at a baseball game.
3. Is Don's new **cycle** a bicycle or a motorcycle?
4. Going to the game was a good **idea**.
5. Our airplane **flight** was smooth.
6. I have a **slight** cold.
7. An airplane can fly **higher** than a kite.
8. She will **iron** the shirt after it is dry.
9. Many cars travel that busy **highway**.
10. The boys will **buy** chalk.
11. I will **hire** you to work.
12. You will find the **title** on the cover.
13. I am waiting for a **reply**.
14. Mother **might** take us to see the boats.

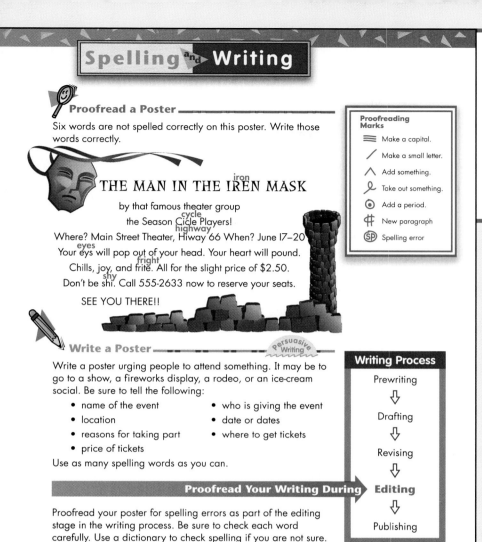

Spelling and Writing

Proofread a Poster

Six words are not spelled correctly on this poster. Write those words correctly.

THE MAN IN THE IREN MASK
(iron)

by that famous theater group
the Season Cicle Players! *(cycle)*
Where? Main Street Theater, Hiway 66 When? June 17–20 *(highway)*
Your eys will pop out of your head. Your heart will pound. *(eyes)*
Chills, joy, and frite. All for the slight price of $2.50. *(fright)*
Don't be shi. Call 555-2633 now to reserve your seats. *(shy)*

SEE YOU THERE!!

Proofreading Marks

≡ Make a capital.
/ Make a small letter.
∧ Add something.
ℒ Take out something.
⊙ Add a period.
⌗ New paragraph
SP Spelling error

Write a Poster

Persuasive Writing

Write a poster urging people to attend something. It may be to go to a show, a fireworks display, a rodeo, or an ice-cream social. Be sure to tell the following:

- name of the event
- location
- reasons for taking part
- price of tickets
- who is giving the event
- date or dates
- where to get tickets

Use as many spelling words as you can.

Proofread Your Writing During

Proofread your poster for spelling errors as part of the editing stage in the writing process. Be sure to check each word carefully. Use a dictionary to check spelling if you are not sure.

Writing Process

Prewriting
⇩
Drafting
⇩
Revising
⇩
Editing
⇩
Publishing

35

Objectives

Spelling and Writing

Students will
• **proofread** a poster.
• **use** the writing process to write a poster.
• **proofread** their writing.

Using the Writing Process

Before assigning **Write a Poster**, see pages 258–259 in the Student Edition for a complete review of the writing process and additional writing assignments. You may also wish to refer to pages Z12–Z13 in the Teacher Edition.

Keeping a Spelling Journal

Encourage students to record the words they misspelled on the weekly test in a personal spelling journal. These words may be recycled for future study. Students may also wish to include words from their writing. See pages Z12–Z13 in the Teacher Edition for more information.

---

15. Father had to **climb** the ladder.
16. The boys jumped with **fright**.
17. The **icicle** was very cold.
18. My shoes are too **tight**.
19. My **eyes** are blue.
20. My friend does not talk much because he is **shy**.

Option 2:
Multiple Spelling Words Per Sentence
(See procedures on pages Z10–Z11.)

1. They will **hire** the **umpire** to work at the game.
2. He **might** drive the **cycle** on the **highway**.
3. I did not feel **fright** as the plane began to **climb higher**.
4. We had a **slight** wait before our **flight** took off.
5. The girls were too **shy** to **reply** when I spoke to them.
6. A **tiny icicle** is hanging from the roof.
7. Mother wanted to **buy** a new **iron**.
8. Open your **eyes** so you can read the **title** of the book.
9. It is not a good **idea** to wear a belt that is too **tight**.

Option 3:
Standardized Test
(See *Teacher Resource Book,* Unit 5.)

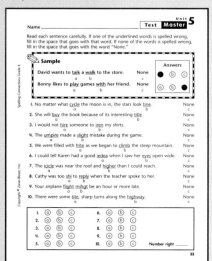

**Unit 5
Test Master**

T35

Objectives

Strategy Words

Students will
- **review** words studied previously that are related to the spelling strategy.
- **preview** unknown words that are related to the spelling strategy.

Optional Enrichment

Remind the students that the **Strategy Words** are related to the spelling patterns they have studied in this unit. The **Review Words** are below grade level, and the **Preview Words** are above grade level. You may wish to use the following sentences to introduce the words in context.

Review Words:
Words From Grade 3

1. The children did not want to **fight**.
2. You will **find** the answers in the back of the book.
3. The **price** of the toy was a little too high.
4. Try to get it **right** the first time.
5. They saw **wild** animals at the zoo.

Preview Words:
Words From Grade 5

6. The plane will **arrive** on time.
7. The child squealed with **delight** when he held the puppy.
8. The crowd was **silent** as the singer began the program.
9. That outfit will not go out of **style** for many years.
10. Who will **supply** the food for the party?

Unit 5 enrichment

Vocabulary

Strategy Words

Review Words
1. fight
2. right
3. find
4. price
5. wild

Preview Words
6. silent
7. delight
8. supply
9. arrive
10. style

Review Words: Long i Spelled i, i-C-e, y, igh, ey, uy

Write a word from the box that fits each clue.

fight	find	price	right	wild

1. This is a bad way to settle an argument.
2. This word is an antonym of **wrong**.
3. This is an antonym of **lose**.
4. This is a synonym of **cost**.
5. This rhymes with **mild**.

Preview Words: Long i Spelled i, i-C-e, y, igh, ey, uy

Write a word from the box to complete each sentence.

arrive	delight	silent	style	supply

6. The audience remained _____ during the president's speech.
7. The happy baby shook the rattle and squealed with _____.
8. I will cook the dinner if you will be good enough to _____ the food.
9. Our flight will _____ at 4:30 this afternoon at the city's new airport.
10. I like her _____ of singing.

36

Unit 5 RECAP

You may wish to assign the **Unit 5 Homework Master** (*Teacher Resource Book*, Unit 5) as a fun way to recap the spelling words.

Unit 5 Homework Master

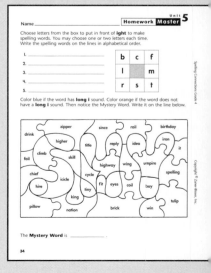

T36

Connections

Objectives

Content Words

Students will
- **expand** vocabulary with content-related words.
- **relate** the spelling strategy to words outside the basic spelling list.

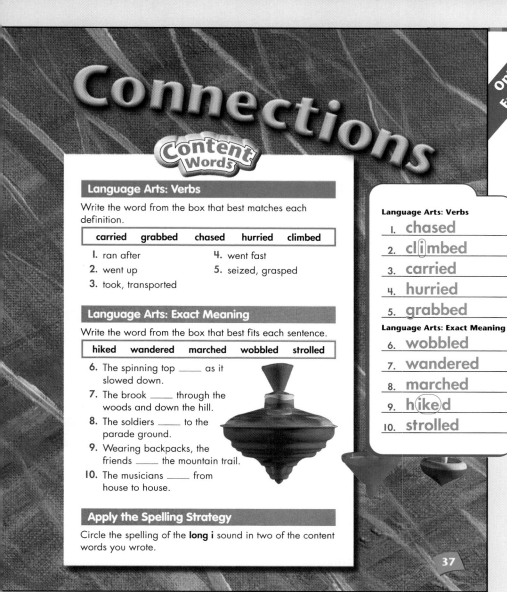

Content Words

Language Arts: Verbs

Write the word from the box that best matches each definition.

carried	grabbed	chased	hurried	climbed

1. ran after
2. went up
3. took, transported
4. went fast
5. seized, grasped

Language Arts: Exact Meaning

Write the word from the box that best fits each sentence.

hiked	wandered	marched	wobbled	strolled

6. The spinning top _____ as it slowed down.
7. The brook _____ through the woods and down the hill.
8. The soldiers _____ to the parade ground.
9. Wearing backpacks, the friends _____ the mountain trail.
10. The musicians _____ from house to house.

Apply the Spelling Strategy

Circle the spelling of the **long i** sound in two of the content words you wrote.

37

Language Arts: Verbs
1. chased
2. cl**i**mbed
3. carried
4. hurried
5. grabbed

Language Arts: Exact Meaning
6. wobbled
7. wandered
8. marched
9. h**i**ked
10. strolled

Content Words

Language Arts: Verbs

Review the meanings of these words with the students. You may wish to use these sentences to introduce the words in context.

1. We **carried** the smaller children over the mud puddles.
2. The fish **grabbed** the bait as soon as the line was dropped in the water.
3. The child **chased** after the balloon when it got away.
4. Mother **hurried** up the stairs to check on the baby.
5. The young woman **climbed** as strongly as the men.

Encourage the students to use these words in a story about the playground.

Language Arts: Exact Meaning

Review the meanings of these words with the students. You may wish to use these sentences to introduce the words in context.

6. We **hiked** through the woods and along the stream.
7. One person **wandered** off the trail and got lost for a few minutes.
8. The soldiers **marched** in single file through the narrow passage.
9. The toddler **wobbled** on unsteady legs while learning to walk.
10. As we **strolled** through the park, it began to rain.

Encourage the students to explain, or demonstrate, how the exact meanings of these words vary.

Unit 6 Home Study Master

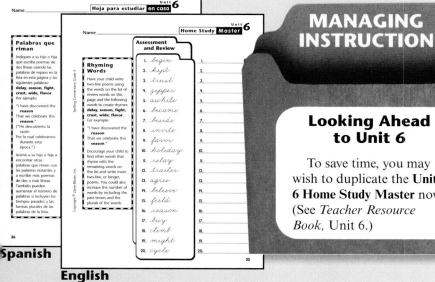

Spanish

English

MANAGING INSTRUCTION

Looking Ahead to Unit 6

To save time, you may wish to duplicate the **Unit 6 Home Study Master** now. (See *Teacher Resource Book,* Unit 6.)

Assessment Words

skull	crime
stroke	raft
betray	claim
series	gift
magic	male
fired	screen
icy	basin
beast	type
slope	seep
rainy	sty

Review Words

Unit 1

begin*	collar
kept*	held
trust*	button
zipper*	began
pass	felt

Unit 2

awhile*	drove
became*	huge
beside*	wife
invite*	surprise
case	alone

Unit 3

favor*	paper
holiday*	nation
relay*	radio
trailer*	station
able	lady

Unit 4

agree*	reach
believe*	speak
field*	lead
reason*	chief
between	piece

Unit 5

buy*	eyes
climb*	tiny
might*	idea
cycle*	iron
flight	shy

* Posttest sentences and the **Unit 6 Test Master** test these words. Students review all words listed.

MATERIALS

Student Edition
Pages 38–43

Teacher Edition
Pages T38A–T43

Other Resources
Spelling Connections Software
Spelling and Writing
Transparencies (Writing Prompt and Writing Model) for Unit 6

Teacher Resource Book
Unit 6 Home Study Master (English or Spanish; students may use this sheet for review or home practice.)
Flip Folder Practice Master
Unit 6 Test Master

Visit our Web site, www.zaner-bloser.com

OBJECTIVES

Spelling and Assessment
Students will
- **assess** their spelling success by matching new words to the spelling strategies presented in Units 1–5.
- **connect** new words to the spelling strategies in Units 1–5.
- **write** new words that relate to the spelling strategies taught in Units 1–5.

Spelling and Review
Students will
- **review** and practice the spelling strategies and words in Units 1–5.
- **learn** an alternative spelling study strategy.

Spelling and Writing
Students will
- **review** the concept of singular and plural possessive nouns.
- **compose** a descriptive piece of writing that describes a person or an animal.
- **learn** a proofreading strategy.
- **proofread** for correct plural forms when entering search terms into a search engine.

MEETING INDIVIDUAL NEEDS
Learning Styles

Visual
Print selected spelling words four times each on heavy paper. Separate the letters by cutting between them. Mix all the letters together in a box. Have pairs of students take turns choosing letters. Have Player A choose twenty letters from the box. Ask each pair of students to use their letters to make as many spelling words as they can in three minutes. Have Player B write down the words that have been formed. Then the letters are returned to the box. Repeat this procedure until all the pairs have played.

Auditory
Have students form two teams, A and B, for a spelling bee. Assign each team an area of the chalkboard. Have teams alternate turns. Select a spelling word and specify the vowel sound of the word. As you pronounce each word, have a student identify the short or the long vowel sound. The student will then spell the word aloud. If the word is spelled correctly, have the student write the word on her or his team's section of the chalkboard.

Kinesthetic
For each spelling word, have the students use modeling clay to form the letter or letters that spell the long vowel sound. Next have them trace over the clay outline with their index fingers, then say the word, and finally, write the word on their papers.

Language and Cultural Differences

Regional pronunciation differences or first-language backgrounds may present problems with both vowel and consonant sounds. For example, Spanish usually spells the **long e** sound with the letter **i** and may spell **long a** as **e, ei,** or **ey.** Students may not hear or pronounce a particular sound in the standard way. Also variant spellings of a single sound can be difficult to remember. Be aware of the individual problems. Stress the word meanings. Use pictures if necessary.

Ask the students to read along with you in their spelling books as you pronounce each spelling word. Have the students repeat each word after you. Then ask volunteers to use the words in sentences. Have other volunteers write the spelling words on the chalkboard.

MANAGING INSTRUCTION

3–5 Day Plan		Average	Below Average	Above Average
Day 1	Day 1	Assessment: Units 1–5, p. 38 (Option 1 or 2, p. T38)	Assessment: Units 1–5, p. 38 (Option 1 or 2, p. T38)	Assessment: Units 1–5, p. 38 (Option 1 or 2, p. T38)
	Day 2	Review: Units 1 and 2, p. 39	Review: Units 1 and 2, p. 39	Review: Units 1 and 2, p. 39 Review: Units 3 and 4, p. 40
Day 2	Day 3	Review: Units 3 and 4, p. 40	Review: Units 3 and 4, p. 40	Review: Unit 5, p. 41 Spelling Study Strategy, p. 41
	Day 4	Review: Unit 5, p. 41 Spelling Study Strategy, p. 41	Review: Unit 5, p. 41 Spelling Study Strategy, p. 41	Writer's Workshop, pages 42–43
Day 3	Day 5	Weekly Test, Option 1 or 2, p. T41	Weekly Test, Option 1 or 2, p. T41	Weekly Test, Option 1 or 2, p. T41

Writer's Workshop (pages 42 and 43) may be used anytime during this unit.

Objectives

Spelling and Assessment

Students will

- **assess** their spelling success by matching new words to the spelling strategies presented in Units 1–5.
- **connect** new words to the spelling strategies in Units 1–5.
- **write** new words that relate to the spelling strategies taught in Units 1–5.

Assessment and Review

Unit 1
1. skull
2. magic
3. raft
4. gift

Unit 2
5. stroke
6. fired ▲
7. slope
8. crime ▲
9. male
10. type

Unit 3
11. betray
12. rainy
13. claim
14. basin

Unit 4
15. series
16. beast
17. screen
18. seep

Unit 5
19. icy
20. sty

38

Assessment Units 1–5

Each Assessment Word in the box fits one of the spelling strategies you have studied over the past five weeks. Read the spelling strategies. Then write each Assessment Word under the unit number it fits.

Unit 1 _____

1.–4. Many short vowel sounds are spelled with a single letter: **a** in **pass**, **e** in **held**, **i** in **skill**, **o** in **collar**, and **u** in **trust**.

Unit 2 _____

5.–10. The long vowel sounds you hear in **case**, **rise**, **chose**, and **cube** are spelled with the **vowel-consonant-e** pattern.

Unit 3 _____

11.–14. The **long a** sound can be spelled **a** as in **lady**, **ai** as in **aim**, and **ay** as in **relay**.

Unit 4 _____

15.–18. The **long e** sound can be spelled in different ways: **ea** in **deal**, **ee** in **speed**, and **ie** in **field**.

Unit 5 _____

19.–20. The **long i** sound can be spelled in different ways: **i** in **climb**, **i-consonant-e** in **hire**, **y** in **cycle**, **igh** in **might**, **ey** in **eyes**, and **uy** in **buy**.

skull
stroke
betray
series
magic
fired
icy
beast
slope
rainy
crime
raft
claim
gift
male
screen
basin
type
seep
sty

ASSESSMENT: UNITS 1–5

Option 1

   Assessment Option 1 is the test that appears in the Student Edition on page 38. You may wish to have students take this test to determine their ability to recognize the spelling strategy in each unit and to match words not previously taught to that strategy. **Assessment Option 1** also serves as additional review and practice.

   ▲ Words designated with this symbol include more than one of the targeted spelling strategies. The answer key has placed them according to the most obvious spelling emphasis. However, if a student places a word in another category, and the word fits that generalization, accept that response. Remember, the objective is to place each word with any appropriate spelling generalization.

Option 2

   Assessment Option 2 is a dictation test using the sentences on page T39. This test assesses students' ability to spell words not previously taught but that are exemplars of a spelling strategy. This test more specifically assesses students' ability to apply the spelling knowledge they have learned.

   In either assessment test option, the words are identified by unit in the Teacher Edition. You may wish to index those misspelled words to review exercises that follow in this unit. Determine which units students need to review, and use additonal unit exercises found in this **Assessment and Review Unit** for reteaching the skill in a more focused way.

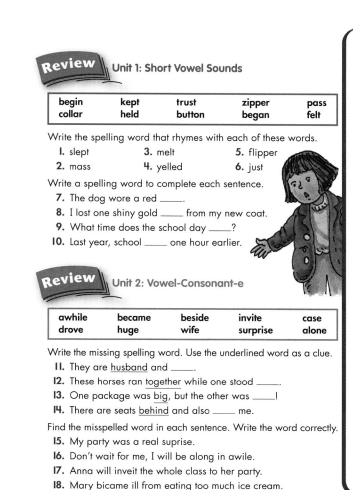

begin	kept	trust	zipper	pass
collar	held	button	began	felt

Write the spelling word that rhymes with each of these words.

1. slept   3. melt   5. flipper
2. mass   4. yelled   6. just

Write a spelling word to complete each sentence.

7. The dog wore a red _____.
8. I lost one shiny gold _____ from my new coat.
9. What time does the school day _____?
10. Last year, school _____ one hour earlier.

Review — Unit 2: Vowel-Consonant-e

awhile	became	beside	invite	case
drove	huge	wife	surprise	alone

Write the missing spelling word. Use the underlined word as a clue.

11. They are <u>husband</u> and _____.
12. These horses ran <u>together</u> while one stood _____.
13. One package was <u>big</u>, but the other was _____!
14. There are seats <u>behind</u> and also _____ me.

Find the misspelled word in each sentence. Write the word correctly.

15. My party was a real suprise.
16. Don't wait for me, I will be along in awile.
17. Anna will inveit the whole class to her party.
18. Mary bicame ill from eating too much ice cream.
19. Can the lawyer win this kase?
20. We were lost and drov three blocks out of our way.

Unit 1
1. kept
2. pass
3. felt
4. held
5. zipper
6. trust
7. collar
8. button
9. begin
10. began

Unit 2
11. wife
12. alone
13. huge
14. beside
15. surprise
16. awhile
17. invite
18. became
19. case
20. drove

39

Objectives

Spelling and Review

Students will
- **review** and practice the spelling strategy and words in Unit 1.
- **review** and practice the spelling strategy and words in Unit 2.

Assessing Progress: The Spelling Journal

If your students have been keeping a personal spelling journal, a periodical review of these journals can be a rich assessment tool. Students should include the words they misspelled from each unit spelling test. They should also be encouraged to write the words they consistently misspell in their own writing and content-area words that present a challenge. Being able to discriminate the words in their everyday writing whose spelling they need to master is a powerful spelling skill.

Pretest Sentences: Assessment Words
(See procedures on pages Z10–Z11.)

1. Ms. Chavez pointed out the **skull** on the skeleton.
2. The artist finished the painting with one great brush **stroke**.
3. Do not **betray** me by telling this secret.
4. Our team has won a **series** of three games.
5. The storm ended like **magic**, just in time for our game.
6. When the gun was **fired**, the runners began the race.
7. There is snow on the ground, and the roads are **icy**.
8. The dark shadow at first looked like a **beast**.
9. Our sled sped down the **slope** of the hill.
10. I stay inside and read a book on **rainy** days.
11. The **crime** rate has dropped for the second straight year.
12. We built a wooden **raft** to put in the river.
13. I hope someone will **claim** this lost dog.
14. I bought a Father's Day **gift** a month early.
15. We lost a black and white **male** cat named Timmy.
16. The flies entered through a rip in the **screen**.
17. Wash out the dirty gloves in this **basin**.
18. Greyhounds are my favorite **type** of dog.
19. Wrap the sandwich tightly so that the juices won't **seep** through.
20. There were several baby pigs in the **sty** in the farmyard.

Objectives

Spelling and Review

Students will
- **review** and practice the spelling strategy and words in Unit 3.
- **review** and practice the spelling strategy and words in Unit 4.

Unit 3
1. lady
2. favor
3. nation
4. station
5. holiday
6. paper
7. trailer
8. able
9. relay
10. radio

Unit 4
11. reason
12. reach
13. believe
14. between
15. field
16. piece
17. lead
18. chief
19. speak
20. agree

 Review Unit 3: Long a Spelled a, ai, ay

| favor | holiday | relay | trailer | able |
| paper | nation | radio | station | lady |

Write the spelling word that goes with each meaning.
1. another word for **woman**
2. something you ask someone to do for you
3. another word for a country under one government
4. a place to stand or an official building
5. a special kind of day
6. a sheet you write on
7. something that might be pulled by a truck or car
8. having skill or talent
9. a kind of race in which a stick might be passed from one runner to another
10. equipment that might have earphones

 Review Unit 4: Long e Spelled ea, ee, ie

| agree | believe | field | reason | between |
| reach | speak | lead | chief | piece |

Write the spelling word that completes each sentence.
11. What is your _____ for saying that?
12. You will need a stool to _____ that upper shelf.
13. I _____ that is the right answer.
14. The house stands _____ two huge old trees.
15. Tall corn grew in the farmer's _____.
16. Would you like a _____ of chocolate cake?
17. If we follow Rover, he will _____ us to the right place.
18. The _____ reason I can't go is that I have homework to do.
19. Please _____ a little more softly.
20. Do you _____ that the party was a big success?

 40

Bulletin Board Idea

Word Jobs

Review the language concepts of nouns, adjectives, and verbs. Have students make three lists of words from Units 1–5. The first list should be words that name persons, places, or things (such as **lady, umpire, eyes, brain, breeze**). The second list should be words that describe things (such as **huge, tiny, wise**). And the third list should be words that tell of activity (such as **taste, invite, speak, rise, blame**). Prepare a "Word Jobs" bulletin board. Have students make pictures to illustrate words in each category.

Mount the pictures, with their spelling word labels, in appropriate columns and label a section of the bulletin board for each group.

Word Jobs

Nouns	Adjectives	Verbs
lady	huge	taste
umpire	tiny	invite
eyes	wise	speak
brain		rise
breeze		blame

buy	climb	might	cycle	flight
eyes	tiny	idea	iron	shy

Write the spelling words for these clues.

1.–2. These words rhyme with **right**.

3. This word has three syllables.

Write the spelling word that completes each sentence.

4. Rain is part of the water _____.

5. It is fun to _____ that big old tree in our yard.

6. I have just enough money to _____ that book.

7. Most animals have two _____.

8. A very small insect is a _____ ant.

9. A tool we use to press clothes is called an _____.

10. Speak up. Don't be _____.

Unit 5
Order of answers 1 and 2 may vary.

1. might
2. flight
3. idea
4. cycle
5. climb
6. buy
7. eyes
8. tiny
9. iron
10. shy

GAME Spelling Study Strategy

Spelling Tic-Tac-Toe

Practicing spelling words can be fun if you make it into a game. Here's an idea you can try with a friend.

1. Write your spelling words in a list. Ask your friend to do the same with his spelling words. Trade spelling lists.

2. Draw a tic-tac-toe board on a piece of scrap paper. Decide who will use **X** and who will use **O**.

3. Ask your partner to call the first word on your spelling list to you. Spell it out loud. If you spell it correctly, make an **X** or an **O** (whichever you are using) on the tic-tac-toe board. If you misspell the word, ask your partner to spell it out loud for you. You miss your turn.

4. Now you call a word from your partner's spelling list.

5. Keep playing until one of you makes "tic-tac-toe." Keep starting over until you both have practiced all your spelling words.

41

Learning an Alternative Spelling Study Strategy

Students should always have a number of study strategies to draw from when it comes to learning their spelling words. **Tic-Tac-Toe** is a useful game for practicing any spelling words. Encourage students to remember this spelling study strategy and to play the game with any list they need to study and learn.

Weekly Test Options

Option 1:
One Spelling Word Per Sentence
(See procedures on pages Z10–Z11.)

1. We will spend the **holiday** at home.
2. The busy people **became** very tired.
3. Mother **might** take us to see the boats.
4. Dad and I **agree** about the idea.
5. A flag will drop to **begin** the race.
6. Please give me a good **reason**.
7. Pat got up, brushed himself off, and **kept** skating.
8. I asked Father if he would do me a **favor**.
9. The cow ate grass in the **field**.
10. Mother sat **beside** Dad at the play.
11. I **trust** that he will be on time.
12. The man drove a **cycle**.
13. He broke the **zipper** on his coat.
14. Who is swimming at the **relay** meet?
15. I **believe** that it will not rain.

16. We are going to stay **awhile**.
17. She will **invite** us to her home.
18. I told the teacher I would **buy** my lunch.
19. The horse rode in a **trailer**.
20. Father had to **climb** the ladder.

Option 2:
Standardized Test

**Unit 6
Test Master**

(See *Teacher Resource Book,* Unit 6.)

Objectives

Spelling and Writing

Students will
- **review** the concept of singular and plural possessive nouns.
- **compose** a descriptive piece of writing that describes a person or an animal. (See **Spelling and the Writing Process** below.)

Optional Enrichment

Unit **6** enrichment

WRITER'S

A
1. mother's
2. team's
3. pig's
4. uncles'
5. Jake's

B
6. Carlos's
7. everyone's
8. dogs'
9. cousins'
10. student's

Grammar, Usage, and Mechanics

Possessive Nouns

A possessive noun shows ownership.
Some possessive nouns are singular. Only one person or animal is the owner.

> **Jess's** bike is old, but **Jill's** is new.
> Do not remove the **dog's** collar.

Other possessive nouns are plural. More than one person or animal are the owners.

> All the **boys'** teams are here but not the **men's** teams.
> The **horses'** hooves could be heard in the canyon as they galloped over the hill.

Practice Activity

A. Write the correct possessive form in each sentence.
1. My (mothers'/mother's) birthday is tomorrow.
2. One (teams'/team's) coach is late.
3. A (pigs'/pig's) tail is curly.
4. I knit both of my (uncles'/uncle's) hats.
5. It was (Jakes'/Jake's) turn to feed the rabbits.

B. Change each underlined phrase to make one possessive noun.
6. I will borrow the sweater <u>of Carlos</u>.
7. The shoes <u>of everyone</u> need to be polished.
8. The kennel <u>where the dogs stay</u> is very clean.
9. Kim found the lost key <u>that belongs to your cousins</u>!
10. The books <u>of the student</u> were piled high.

42

Descriptive Writing — Spelling and the Writing Process

You may wish to use this writing assignment to help students master the writing process. For other writing ideas, see pages 258–259 in the Student Edition.

Explain that students will write a composition in which they describe a friend, family member, or pet to their classmates.

Prewriting Hint: You may wish to help students plan their writing by recommending the following graphic organizer. Have them replicate the graphic, filling in the blank circles with details about the person or pet.

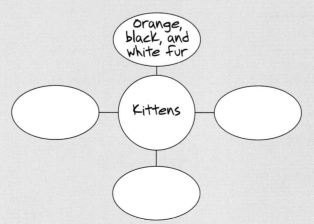

Orange, black, and white fur

Kittens

Revising Hint: Remind students that when they revise what they have written, they should look for words that paint pictures in readers' minds. Encourage them to replace general words, such as **nice,** with precise words, such as **friendly, funny,** or **braided.**

 Proofreading Strategy

Read It Backwards!

Good writers always proofread their writing for spelling errors. Here's a strategy you can use to proofread your papers.

Instead of reading your paper from the first word to the last word, try reading it from the last word to the first word. So you would read the sentence **The computer was brand new** like this: **new brand was computer The**.

Does this sound like a funny thing to do? It is! But reading your paper backwards helps you think about how to spell each word instead of thinking about what the whole sentence means. Try it!

Electronic Spelling

1. radios
2. holidays
3. OK
4. eyes
5. OK
6. OK

Electronic Spelling

Search Engines

When you use a computer to find information in an on-line encyclopedia or on the Internet, you often use search engines. These are very useful tools. You type in a word or phrase, and the search engine looks for information on that topic. However, you must spell the word correctly or the search engine will report, "No matches found."

Sometimes it makes sense to type in both the singular and plural forms of a noun. Then the search engine will find both or either. Be careful typing plural forms. Make sure you spell them correctly. If you type **tornaedos,** most search engines will say "No matches found for tornaedos."

Look at these plural words. Which are misspelled? Write those words correctly. Write **OK** if a word is correct.

1. radioes
2. holidayes
3. cases

4. eyeses
5. zippers
6. monkeys

43

Unit 7 Home Study Master

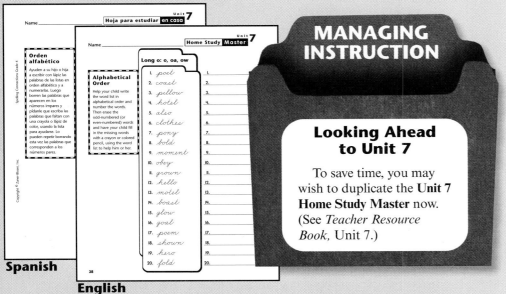

Spanish

English

MANAGING INSTRUCTION

Looking Ahead to Unit 7

To save time, you may wish to duplicate the **Unit 7 Home Study Master** now. (See *Teacher Resource Book,* Unit 7.)

Objectives

Spelling and Writing

Students will
- **learn** a proofreading strategy.
- **proofread** for correct plural forms when entering search terms into a search engine.

Using Proofreading Strategies

Students are often unaware that there are a variety of techniques they can use to proofread their own writing. Building a repertory of strategies is important to improving students' writing and editing skills.

Spelling and Technology

The advent of word processing, computer protocols, and the Internet has actually increased, not lessened, the pressure on users to be better, more aware spellers. Spell checkers, for example, create circumstances in which the ability to discriminate between an acceptable and an unacceptable spelling is a critical skill. A homophone substitution, a correct spelling of the wrong word, an inadvertent word omission—these are examples of situations in computer usage that require a deeper understanding of spelling principles and a more adroit proofreading capability. It may be worthwhile to underscore this increased need as a whole-class discussion after students finish this unit's **Electronic Spelling** activity.

Basic Spelling List

poet	grown
coast	hello
pillow	motel
hotel	boast
also	glow
clothes	goal
pony	poem
bold	shown
moment	hero
obey	fold

Strategy Words

Review
below	rainbow
nobody	soap
over	

Preview
bowl	loaves
groceries	narrow
growth	

Content Words

Social Studies: Farming
farming	visit
sowing	reaper
prairie	

Fine Arts: Stringed Instruments
cello	violin
viola	strings
harp	

Individual Needs

Challenge Words
bonus	decode
banjo	following
poach	

Alternate Word List
coast	obey
pillow	grown
also	hello
clothes	poem
moment	shown

MATERIALS

Student Edition
Pages 44–49
Challenge Activities, p. 229

Teacher Edition
Pages T44A–T49
Challenge Activities, p. T229

Other Resources
Spelling Connections Software
Unit 7 Word List Overhead
  Transparency

Teacher Resource Book
Unit 7 Home Study Master
  (English or Spanish; students
  may pretest on this sheet or use
  it for home practice.)
Unit 7 Homework Master
Unit 7 Practice Masters
Flip Folder Practice Master
Unit 7 Test Master

Visit our Web site, www.zaner-bloser.com

OBJECTIVES

Spelling and Thinking
Students will
• **read** the spelling words in list form and in context.
• **sort** the words according to the **long o** sound spelled **o, oa,** and **ow**.
• **read** and remember this week's spelling strategy.

Spelling and Vocabulary
Students will
• **identify** and write spelling words that match definitions.
• **identify** and write four-letter spelling words with one syllable.
• **identify** and write four-letter spelling words with two syllables.
• **locate** in the **Spelling Dictionary** and write parts of speech for spelling words.

Spelling and Reading
Students will
• **complete** sentences using spelling words.
• **solve** riddles using spelling words.
• **complete** a paragraph using spelling words.

Spelling and Writing
Students will
• **proofread** directions.
• **use** the writing process to write directions.
• **proofread** their writing.

MEETING INDIVIDUAL NEEDS
Learning Styles

Visual

Choose one student to be the leader. Have this student choose a spelling word and draw a blank line on the chalkboard for each letter in the word. Let the other students take turns guessing the letters that belong in the blanks. When a letter is guessed, the leader writes it in the proper blank. If a guess is incorrect, the leader draws one part of a stick figure (head, ears, body, arms, legs, hands, feet). If the players do not guess the word before all parts of the stick figure are drawn, the leader gets another chance to stump them with a different spelling word. When a player guesses a word correctly, she or he becomes the new leader.

Auditory

Have the students number their papers 1 to 20. Have them take turns selecting a spelling word and spelling it aloud, leaving out the letters that make the **long o** sound. (For example, **grown** would be spelled "**g-r**-blank-blank-**n**.") Then have a volunteer guess the word and spell it aloud with all of its letters—"**g-r-o-w-n**." Finally, have all the students write each spelling word on their papers.

Kinesthetic

Have the students work in pairs. Ask one student to start out as the "writer," facing the classroom chalkboard, and the other as the "chalkboard," facing away from the classroom chalkboard. Write a spelling word on the classroom chalkboard, and have each "writer" turn around and trace the letters of the word on the back of his or her "chalkboard." Have each "chalkboard" student write the spelling word on paper as it is traced on his or her back. Have the students in each pair reverse roles for each new word.

Language and Cultural Differences

The **long o** spelling patterns may be difficult for some students because the same sound is spelled in several different ways and because there are silent vowels in some words. These spelling patterns may be especially difficult for those students who are accustomed to a language such as Spanish, in which each vowel is spelled in a consistent way.

Write each spelling word on the chalkboard. Ask the students to make up a sentence using each word or to tell something they know about each word. Next, have a volunteer go to the chalkboard and circle the letter or letters that spell the **long o** sound in the word. Ask the student whether the word has a silent vowel. If it does, have the student point out the silent vowel to the class. Have the students copy each word on their papers, underlining the letter or letters that spell the **long o** sound.

MANAGING INSTRUCTION

3–5 Day Plan		Average	Below Average	Above Average
Day 1	**Day 1**	Pretest Spelling Mini-Lesson, p. T44 Spelling and Thinking, p. 44	Pretest Spelling Mini-Lesson, p. T44 Spelling and Thinking, p. 44	Pretest Spelling and Thinking, p. 44
	Day 2	Spelling and Vocabulary, p. 45	Spelling and Vocabulary, p. 45 (or) Unit 7 Practice Master, A and B	Spelling and Vocabulary, p. 45 Spelling and Reading, p. 46
Day 2	**Day 3**	Spelling and Reading, p. 46	Spelling and Reading, p. 46 (or) Unit 7 Practice Master, C and D	Challenge Activities, p. 229
	Day 4	Spelling and Writing, p. 47 Unit 7 Homework Master	Spelling and Writing, p. 47	Spelling and Writing, p. 47 Unit 7 Homework Master
Day 3	**Day 5**	Weekly Test	Weekly Test	Weekly Test
Vocabulary Connections (pages 48 and 49) may be used anytime during this unit.				

Objectives

Spelling and Thinking

Students will
- **read** the spelling words in list form and in context.
- **sort** the words according to the **long o** sound spelled **o, oa,** and **ow**.
- **read** and remember this week's spelling strategy.

UNIT PRETEST

Use **Pretest Sentences** below. Refer to the self-checking procedures on student page 256. You may wish to use the **Unit 7 Word List Overhead Transparency** as part of the checking procedure.

TEACHING THE STRATEGY

Spelling Mini-Lesson

Read the poem "Trot Along, Pony" by Marion Edey aloud to the students.

Trot along, pony,
　　Late in the day,
Down by the meadow
　　Is the loveliest way.

The apples are rosy
　　And ready to fall.
The branches hang over
　　By Grandfather's wall.

But the red sun is sinking
　　Away out of sight.
The chickens are settling
　　Themselves for the night.

Your stable is waiting
　　And supper will come.
So turn again, pony,
　　Turn again home.

Ask students to summarize the poem.

Write /ō/ on the board. Ask students to identify the words in the poem that have this **long o** sound. (pony, meadow, rosy, over, home) Write these words on the board. Ask a volunteer to identify the **long o** spelling pattern in each word.

Write the spelling words on the board. Ask volunteers to underline the **long o** spelling pattern in each word.

Conclude by reading **Remember the Spelling Strategy** on page 44.

T44

Spelling and Thinking

Order of answers may vary.

o
1. poet
2. hotel
3. also ★
4. clothes ★
5. pony
6. bold
7. moment ★
8. obey ★
9. hello ★
10. motel
11. poem ★
12. hero
13. fold

oa
14. coast ★
15. boast
16. goal

ow
17. pillow ★
18. grown ★
19. glow
20. shown ★

READ THE SPELLING WORDS

1.	poet	*poet*	Which **poet** wrote those lines?
2.	coast	*coast*	Along the **coast** lie sunken ships.
3.	pillow	*pillow*	A soft **pillow** cradled her head.
4.	hotel	*hotel*	The **hotel** was ten stories high.
5.	also	*also*	I can sing and **also** dance.
6.	clothes	*clothes*	My **clothes** hang in a closet.
7.	pony	*pony*	The **pony** trotted around the ring.
8.	bold	*bold*	Catching the snake was a **bold** move.
9.	moment	*moment*	In a **moment** the sun will set.
10.	obey	*obey*	Dogs can learn to **obey** commands.
11.	grown	*grown*	She has **grown** an inch this year.
12.	hello	*hello*	I say **hello** to everyone I know.
13.	motel	*motel*	A **motel** is a motor hotel.
14.	boast	*boast*	Do not **boast** of our success yet.
15.	glow	*glow*	I followed the **glow** of the lamp.
16.	goal	*goal*	The ball bounced over the **goal** line.
17.	poem	*poem*	That **poem** contains rhyming words.
18.	shown	*shown*	We were **shown** to our room.
19.	hero	*hero*	A **hero** does brave deeds.
20.	fold	*fold*	Do not **fold** or wrinkle your paper.

SORT THE SPELLING WORDS

I.–I3. Write the words with the **long o** sound spelled **o**.

I4.–I6. Write the words with the **long o** sound spelled **oa**.

I7.–20. Write the words with the **long o** sound spelled **ow**.

REMEMBER THE SPELLING STRATEGY

Remember that the **long o** sound can be spelled in different ways: **o** in pony, **oa** in goal, and **ow** in glow.

44

Pretest Sentences (See procedures on pages Z10–Z11.)

1. A person who writes a poem is called a **poet**.
2. Have you ever walked along the **coast** by the Atlantic Ocean?
3. There was a fancy, ruffled covering on the **pillow**.
4. During our vacation we stayed in a **hotel**.
5. When we go to the circus, Tito would **also** like to go.
6. Uncle Ed likes to shop for new **clothes**.
7. Lomasi rode her horse, and I rode my **pony**.
8. His handwriting was **bold** and easy to read.
9. A **moment** is a very short period of time.
10. I try to **obey** my parents' instructions.
11. Since he has **grown** three inches, Bobby is taller than his father.
12. When you first meet someone, you should say **hello**.
13. The **motel** had a lighted swimming pool.
14. I like to **boast** about how quickly my baby brother learned to talk.
15. Does the sticker on your bicycle **glow** in the dark?
16. My **goal** is to become a doctor.
17. Teresa read a **poem** that was eight lines long.
18. We were **shown** how to use the new VCR.
19. Diego became a **hero** when he saved the baby's life.
20. After the bath towels are washed, I often **fold** them.

Word Meanings

Write a spelling word for each definition.

1. a form of **grow**
2. land along the ocean
3. place offering guests rooms, meals, and other services
4. a form of **show**
5. something usually found on a bed

Syllables

Say a word to yourself and listen to the beats to determine how many syllables it has. You can also tell how many syllables a word has by the number of vowel sounds it contains. Check a dictionary to be sure.

6.–9. Write the four-letter spelling words that have one syllable.

10.–15. Write the four-letter spelling words that have two syllables.

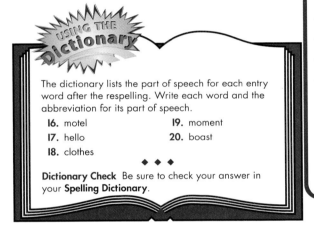

USING THE Dictionary

The dictionary lists the part of speech for each entry word after the respelling. Write each word and the abbreviation for its part of speech.

16. motel	19. moment
17. hello	20. boast
18. clothes	

◆ ◆ ◆

Dictionary Check Be sure to check your answer in your **Spelling Dictionary**.

Word Meanings
1. grown
2. coast
3. hotel
4. shown
5. pillow

Syllables
one-syllable
6. bold
7. glow
8. goal
9. fold

two syllables
10. poet
11. also
12. pony
13. obey
14. poem
15. hero

Using the Dictionary
16. motel, n.
17. hello, interj.
18. clothes, n.
19. moment, n.
20. boast, v.

45

Objectives

Spelling and Vocabulary

Students will
- **identify** and write spelling words that match definitions.
- **identify** and write four-letter spelling words with one syllable.
- **identify** and write four-letter spelling words with two syllables.
- **locate** in the **Spelling Dictionary** and write parts of speech for spelling words.

Developing Oral Language Skills

Tell students that the position of the **long o** sound can sometimes give a clue to which spelling is needed. The **long o** sound might occur at the beginning, middle, or end of a word or syllable. Have the class pronounce each spelling word as you point to the letters that spell the **long o** sound. Have them decide where the **long o** sound occurs in the word or syllable. Help them see that the **oa** spelling usually occurs in the middle of a word or syllable, as in **goal, coast,** and **boast.** The **o** spelling usually occurs at the end of a word or a syllable, as in **po/em, ho/tel,** and **he/ro.** Point out that **fold** and words that rhyme with **fold** such as **gold** and **bold** are exceptions.

MEETING INDIVIDUAL NEEDS
Providing More Help

Write the spellings of the **long o** sound (**o, oa, ow**) as headings on the chalkboard. Write each spelling word under the proper heading. Ask a student to read a word aloud and use it in a sentence. Then have the student go to the chalkboard and underline the letter or letters that spell the **long o** sound in the word. Have the students write all of the spelling words on their papers. ★ Students who need to study fewer words should use the **Alternate Word List.** This list is starred on page T44 in the Teacher's Edition. The **Unit 7 Practice Masters** (*Teacher Resource Book*) provide additional practice with these words.

Unit 7 Practice Masters

Name_____

Practice Master Unit 7

1. poem	3. also	5. moment	7. coast	9. shown
2. obey	4. hello	6. clothes	8. grown	10. pillow

A. Write the spelling words in alphabetical order.

1. _____ 6. _____
2. _____ 7. _____
3. _____ 8. _____
4. _____ 9. _____
5. _____ 10. _____

B. A spelling word is misspelled in each sentence. Write each word correctly.

1. I'm sure Nicholas would have shoan you how to saddle the pony if you had asked him.

2. Do you like to coste your bike down the hills?

3. I have grone two inches taller since last year.

4. My kitten likes to lie on my pilloaw.

5. Please put your cloze away.

6. Mrs. Martinez is alsso my sister's teacher.

40

Practice Master Unit 7

coast	shown
grown	pillow

Objectives

Spelling and Reading

Students will
- **complete** sentences using spelling words.
- **solve** riddles using spelling words.
- **complete** a paragraph using spelling words.

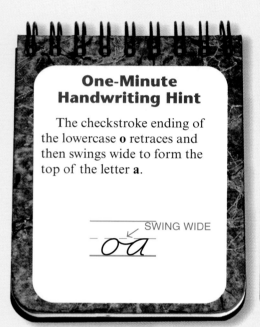

One-Minute Handwriting Hint

The checkstroke ending of the lowercase **o** retraces and then swings wide to form the top of the letter **a**.

SWING WIDE

Legible handwriting can boost spelling scores by as much as 20%.

Complete the Sentences

1. motel
2. pillow
3. grown
4. coast
5. hello
6. also
7. shown
8. poet
9. hotel
10. glow

Solve the Riddles

11. moment
12. hero
13. goal
14. poem
15. fold

Complete the Paragraph

16. clothes
17. pony
18. bold
19. obey
20. boast

46

---

poet	coast	pillow	hotel	also
clothes	pony	bold	moment	obey
grown	hello	motel	boast	glow
goal	poem	shown	hero	fold

Complete the Sentences   Write a spelling word to complete each sentence.

1. While driving to Chicago, we stopped for the night at a _____ right on the highway.
2. A _____ was at the head of the bed.
3. Mother has _____ both flowers and vegetables.
4. Many beachgoers swam and picnicked along the sandy _____.
5. Say _____ to your brother for me.
6. We play ball and _____ fly kites in the park.
7. Peter was _____ a map of the city when he was lost.
8. She is a _____, a writer, and a musician.
9. He is a doorman at a fancy _____ in New York City.
10. The _____ of fireflies lights up the night sky.

Solve the Riddles   Write a spelling word to solve each riddle.

11. I am a brief period of time. Who am I?
12. Everyone loves me because I am brave. Who am I?
13. I am something everyone wants to reach. Who am I?
14. Sometimes I rhyme, and sometimes I do not. Who am I?
15. I am something you do with paper and with clothes. Who am I?

Complete the Paragraph   Write words from the box to fill in the blanks in the story.

pony
bold
obey
boast
clothes

Children, dressed in their best _16._ , were taking turns riding a _17._ . They were having their pictures taken and felt quite _18._ when they could make the pony _19._ . I heard one boy _20._ that he was the best rider and was going to be a cowboy.

MEETING INDIVIDUAL NEEDS
Providing More Challenge

Challenge Words and **Challenge Activities** for Unit 7 appear on page 229. **Challenge Word Test Sentences** appear on page T229.

Unit 7 Challenge Activities

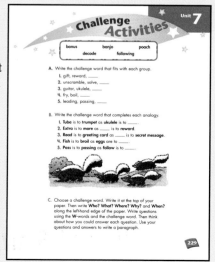

Weekly Test Options

Option 1:
One Spelling Word Per Sentence

(See procedures on pages Z10–Z11.)

1. You should try to **obey** the classroom rules.
2. The **bold** horse jumped the fence.
3. Please **fold** the shirt.
4. My father has **shown** me pictures of himself when he was young.
5. You may **also** have a peach.
6. The woman was a **hero** after she saved the puppy.
7. My friend would like to say **hello**.
8. My **goal** is to finish this game.
9. His friend lives on the **coast**.
10. Please do not brag and **boast**.
11. The bright star had a pretty **glow**.
12. A **pillow** is on every bed in our house.
13. The corn has **grown** very tall.
14. Your **clothes** look very neat.
15. Mother wrote a short **poem**.

Spelling and Writing

Objectives

Spelling and Writing

Students will
- **proofread** directions.
- **use** the writing process to write directions.
- **proofread** their writing.

Proofread Directions

Six words are not spelled correctly in these directions. Write those words correctly.

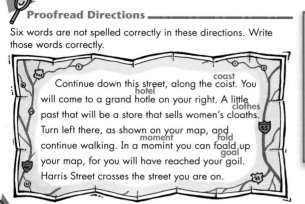

coast
Continue down this street, along the coist. You
hotel
will come to a grand hotle on your right. A little
clothes
past that will be a store that sells women's cloaths.
Turn left there, as shown on your map, and
moment   fold
continue walking. In a momint you can foald up
goal
your map, for you will have reached your goil.
Harris Street crosses the street you are on.

Proofreading Marks

≡ Make a capital.
/ Make a small letter.
∧ Add something.
ℓ Take out something.
⊙ Add a period.
⌗ New paragraph
SP Spelling error

Write Directions

Expository Writing

Write directions. Tell how to do something, get somewhere, or make, cook, or use something. Tell everything your reader will need to know. Include as needed:

- simple directions your reader can follow
- each step in order
- materials, if any, your reader will need
- how far it is to your reader's destination
- how long it will take to cook or make the item
- how hard or easy it will be to accomplish the goal

Use as many spelling words as you can.

Writing Process

Prewriting
⇩
Drafting
⇩
Revising
⇩
Editing
⇩
Publishing

Proofread Your Writing During → **Editing**

Proofread your writing for spelling errors as part of the editing stage in the writing process. Be sure to check each word carefully. Use a dictionary to check spelling if you are not sure.

47

Using the Writing Process

Before assigning **Write Directions,** see pages 258–259 in the Student Edition for a complete review of the writing process and additional writing assignments. You may also wish to refer to pages Z12–Z13 in the Teacher Edition.

Keeping a Spelling Journal

Encourage students to record the words they misspelled on the weekly test in a personal spelling journal. These words may be recycled for future study. Students may also wish to include words from their writing. See pages Z12–Z13 in the Teacher Edition for more information.

---

16. The **poet** read us a story.
17. Watch the horse and the **pony** trot down the path.
18. The **hotel** where we stayed had ten floors.
19. We stayed in a **motel** for one night.
20. I saw you on TV for a brief **moment**.

Option 2:
Multiple Spelling Words Per Sentence
(See procedures on pages Z10–Z11.)

1. Father had **shown** me how to **fold** the **clothes**.
2. The **bold** child is **also** not afraid to walk by the old cave.
3. Take a **moment** to walk in the sand along the **coast**.
4. I must say **hello** to the dog before it will **obey** me.
5. Can you see the **glow** of the sign from the **motel**?
6. The **poet** did not **boast** about the **poem** he wrote.
7. His **goal** is to become a **hero**.
8. Her **pony** has **grown** to its full size.
9. She put a **pillow** on each bed in the **hotel** room.

Option 3:
Standardized Test
(See *Teacher Resource Book,* Unit 7.)

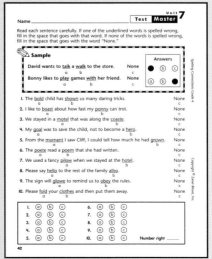

**Unit 7
Test Master**

Objectives

Strategy Words

Students will
- **review** words studied previously that are related to the spelling strategy.
- **preview** unknown words that are related to the spelling strategy.

Remind the students that the **Strategy Words** relate to the spelling patterns they have studied in this unit. The **Review Words** are below grade level, and the **Preview Words** are above grade level. You may wish to use the following sentences to introduce the words in context.

Review Words:
Words From Grade 3

1. As the plane took off, we saw the objects **below** get smaller.
2. There was **nobody** around when I arrived at the house.
3. The horses jumped **over** hurdles as they ran around the track.
4. There was a beautiful **rainbow** after the downpour.
5. Use **soap** when you wash your hands.

Preview Words:
Words From Grade 5

6. The dog licked the **bowl** clean.
7. We buy our **groceries** every Friday.
8. We keep a chart in our room to record our **growth** in height.
9. Mom made two **loaves** of sourdough bread for the picnic.
10. The hallway is very **narrow** in our school.

T48

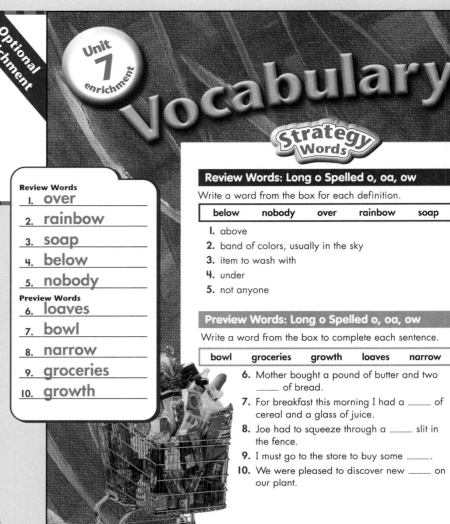

Review Words
1. over
2. rainbow
3. soap
4. below
5. nobody

Preview Words
6. loaves
7. bowl
8. narrow
9. groceries
10. growth

Unit 7 enrichment — Vocabulary

Strategy Words

Review Words: Long o Spelled o, oa, ow

Write a word from the box for each definition.

below	nobody	over	rainbow	soap

1. above
2. band of colors, usually in the sky
3. item to wash with
4. under
5. not anyone

Preview Words: Long o Spelled o, oa, ow

Write a word from the box to complete each sentence.

bowl	groceries	growth	loaves	narrow

6. Mother bought a pound of butter and two _____ of bread.
7. For breakfast this morning I had a _____ of cereal and a glass of juice.
8. Joe had to squeeze through a _____ slit in the fence.
9. I must go to the store to buy some _____.
10. We were pleased to discover new _____ on our plant.

48

Unit 7 RECAP

You may wish to assign the **Unit 7 Homework Master** (*Teacher Resource Book*, Unit 7) as a fun way to recap the spelling words.

Unit 7 Homework Master

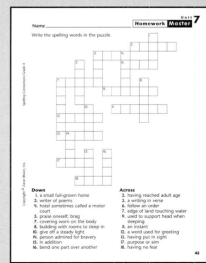

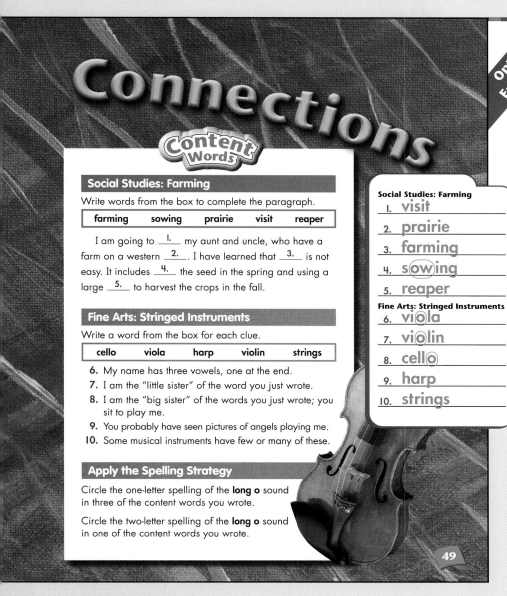

Connections

Content Words

Objectives

Content Words

Students will
- **expand** vocabulary with content-related words.
- **relate** the spelling strategy to words outside the basic spelling list.

Social Studies: Farming

Write words from the box to complete the paragraph.

farming	sowing	prairie	visit	reaper

I am going to __1.__ my aunt and uncle, who have a farm on a western __2.__. I have learned that __3.__ is not easy. It includes __4.__ the seed in the spring and using a large __5.__ to harvest the crops in the fall.

Fine Arts: Stringed Instruments

Write a word from the box for each clue.

cello	viola	harp	violin	strings

6. My name has three vowels, one at the end.
7. I am the "little sister" of the word you just wrote.
8. I am the "big sister" of the words you just wrote; you sit to play me.
9. You probably have seen pictures of angels playing me.
10. Some musical instruments have few or many of these.

Apply the Spelling Strategy

Circle the one-letter spelling of the **long o** sound in three of the content words you wrote.

Circle the two-letter spelling of the **long o** sound in one of the content words you wrote.

Social Studies: Farming
1. visit
2. prairie
3. farming
4. sowing
5. reaper

Fine Arts: Stringed Instruments
6. viola
7. violin
8. cello
9. harp
10. strings

49

Content Words

Social Studies: Farming

Review the meanings of these words with the students. You may wish to use these sentences to introduce the words in context.

1. Grandfather has been **farming** for many years.
2. He will be **sowing** the seeds for his crops in the spring.
3. The vast **prairie** land is home to many animals.
4. I will pay a **visit** to my aunt next month.
5. The **reaper** picked up the hay and baled it.

Encourage the students to use these words in a story about a farm.

Fine Arts: Stringed Instruments

Review the meanings of these words with the students. You may wish to use these sentences to introduce the words in context.

6. Two students took turns playing the **cello**.
7. The **viola** is a popular instrument in the orchestra.
8. A **harp** is a large instrument that makes a beautiful sound.
9. The conductor of the orchestra also loves to play the **violin**.
10. Many **strings** in an orchestra make it sound rich and full.

Encourage the students to use these words to write a poem about music or to make a crossword puzzle about musical instruments.

Unit 8 Home Study Master

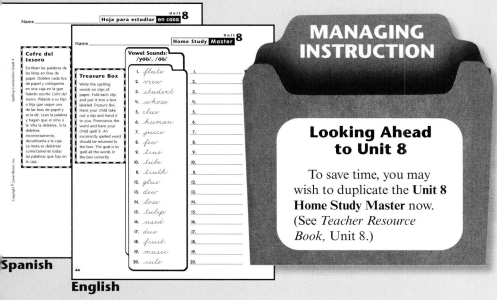

Spanish

English

MANAGING INSTRUCTION

Looking Ahead to Unit 8

To save time, you may wish to duplicate the **Unit 8 Home Study Master** now. (See *Teacher Resource Book*, Unit 8.)

Basic Spelling List

flute	truth
view	glue
student	dew
whose	lose
clue	tulip
human	used
juice	due
few	fruit
true	music
tube	rule

Strategy Words

Review
balloon	pool
drew	threw
news	

Preview
amuse	movies
beauty	suitcase
continue	

Content Words

Social Studies: Rural Life
blue jeans	waterfall
railroad	mind
matter	

Science: Birds
canary	plumage
parrot	feather
chicken	

Individual Needs

Challenge Words
menu	duties
fuel	blueberry
nephew	

Alternate Word List
whose	lose
human	used
few	fruit
true	music
tube	rule

MATERIALS

Student Edition
Pages 50–55
Challenge Activities, p. 230

Teacher Edition
Pages T50A–T55
Challenge Activities, T230

Other Resources
Spelling Connections Software
Unit 8 Word List Overhead
  Transparency

Teacher Resource Book
Unit 8 Home Study Master
  (English or Spanish; students
  may pretest on this sheet or use
  it for home practice.)
Unit 8 Homework Master
Unit 8 Practice Masters
Flip Folder Practice Master
Unit 8 Test Master

Visit our Web site, www.zaner-bloser.com

OBJECTIVES

Spelling and Thinking
Students will
- **read** the spelling words in list
  form and in context.
- **sort** the words according to
  /yo͞o/ and /o͞o/ sounds and
  spelling patterns.
- **read** and remember this
  week's spelling strategy.

Spelling and Vocabulary
Students will
- **identify** and write spelling
  words that match definitions.
- **subtract** and add letters to
  words to form spelling words.
- **use** the **Spelling Dictionary**
  to divide spelling words into
  syllables.

Spelling and Reading
Students will
- **complete** sentences using
  spelling words.
- **solve** analogies using spelling
  words.
- **complete** a paragraph using
  spelling words.

Spelling and Writing
Students will
- **proofread** a paragraph.
- **use** the writing process to
  write a paragraph.
- **proofread** their writing.

MEETING INDIVIDUAL NEEDS
Learning Styles

Visual

Draw the shape of each spelling word on the chalkboard, writing the last letter of each word inside the outline. For example, **fruit** would be

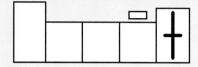

Have the students copy the shapes onto their papers. Then ask them to write the appropriate spelling word inside each shape, using colored pencil or crayon for the letters that spell /o͞o/ or /yo͞o/.

Auditory

Read the spelling words aloud in clusters, according to their spelling patterns. For example, read all of the words that have the /o͞o/ spelled **ue** together, and so on. After reading each cluster of words, have the students identify how the /o͞o/ or /yo͞o/ is spelled. Continue until the students have identified all the various spelling patterns. Then have them write each word as they say and spell it quietly to themselves.

Kinesthetic

Divide the spelling words among the students. Have them use white glue to write their words on colored construction paper. Then have them cover the words with glitter, sand, or cornmeal, remove the excess, and let the words dry.

Language and Cultural Differences

These words may be difficult for some students to spell because of the variant spelling patterns (which often include a silent vowel). This may be especially true if students are accustomed to a spelling system such as Spanish, in which each vowel is spelled in one way almost without exception.

Ask volunteers to use the words in sentences. Then write each of the spelling words on a 3" × 5" card. Shuffle the cards and lay them face down on a table. Have the students take turns choosing a card, saying the word, and identifying the letters that spell the /o͞o/ or /yo͞o/ in the word.

MANAGING INSTRUCTION

3–5 Day Plan		Average	Below Average	Above Average
Day 1	**Day 1**	Pretest Spelling Mini-Lesson, p. T50 Spelling and Thinking, p. 50	Pretest Spelling Mini-Lesson, p. T50 Spelling and Thinking, p. 50	Pretest Spelling and Thinking, p. 50
	Day 2	Spelling and Vocabulary, p. 51	Spelling and Vocabulary, p. 51 (or) Unit 8 Practice Master, A and B	Spelling and Vocabulary, p. 51 Spelling and Reading, p. 52
Day 2	**Day 3**	Spelling and Reading, p. 52	Spelling and Reading, p. 52 (or) Unit 8 Practice Master, C and D	Challenge Activities, p. 230
	Day 4	Spelling and Writing, p. 53 Unit 8 Homework Master	Spelling and Writing, p. 53	Spelling and Writing, p. 53 Unit 8 Homework Master
Day 3	**Day 5**	Weekly Test	Weekly Test	Weekly Test
Vocabulary Connections (pages 54 and 55) may be used anytime during this unit.				

Objectives

Spelling and Thinking

Students will
- **read** the spelling words in list form and in context.
- **sort** the words according to /y$\overline{oo}$/ and /$\overline{oo}$/ sounds and spelling patterns.
- **read** and remember this week's spelling strategy.

UNIT PRETEST

Use **Pretest Sentences** below. Refer to the self-checking procedures on page 256. You may wish to use the **Unit 8 Word List Overhead Transparency** as part of the checking procedure.

TEACHING THE STRATEGY

Spelling Mini-Lesson

Write each spelling word on a word strip. Distribute the strips at random to students.

Tell the students that in this lesson they will spell words that have either the vowel sound in **true** (/$\overline{oo}$/) or in **few** (/y$\overline{oo}$/). Write /$\overline{oo}$/ and /y$\overline{oo}$/ on the chalkboard as headings. Explain that these are the dictionary respellings of the two sounds.

Help them to distinguish between the two sounds by writing an example word under each respelling. Write **true** under /$\overline{oo}$/ and **few** under /y$\overline{oo}$/. Say the words aloud so the students can hear the difference in vowel sounds.

Ask the students who have the **true** word strip and the **few** word strip to come to the front and take a place under the heading on the chalkboard that matches the vowel sound in the word they have. Invite other students, at random, to come up individually, say the word on the word strip they have, and position themselves near the matching symbol on the chalkboard.

Conclude by reading **Remember the Spelling Strategy** on page 50.

Order of answers may vary.

/$\overline{oo}$/
1. fl(u)t(e)
2. wh(o)s(e) ★
3. cl(ue)
4. j(ui)ce
5. tr(ue) ★
6. t(u)b(e) ★
7. tr(u)th
8. gl(ue)
9. l(o)s(e) ★
10. fr(ui)t ★
11. r(u)l(e) ★
12. st(u)dent
13. d(ew)
14. t(u)lip
15. d(ue)

/y$\overline{oo}$/
16. v(iew)
17. h(u)man ★
18. f(ew) ★
19. (u)sed ★
20. m(u)sic ★

READ THE SPELLING WORDS

1. flute	*flute*	A **flute** is a musical instrument.
2. view	*view*	We had a clear **view** of the sea.
3. student	*student*	The **student** studied for her test.
4. whose	*whose*	I wonder **whose** shoes these are.
5. clue	*clue*	That **clue** helped solve the mystery.
6. human	*human*	We all belong to the **human** race.
7. juice	*juice*	Orange **juice** is a healthful drink.
8. few	*few*	She has **few** faults and many friends.
9. true	*true*	Is that story **true** or false?
10. tube	*tube*	That thin **tube** is a drinking straw.
11. truth	*truth*	The **truth** serves better than a lie.
12. glue	*glue*	We can **glue** the pieces together.
13. dew	*dew*	The grass sparkled with morning **dew**.
14. lose	*lose*	Whether you win or **lose**, be a good sport.
15. tulip	*tulip*	The **tulip** is a flower of spring.
16. used	*used*	My bike, though **used**, is new to me.
17. due	*due*	Yesterday's homework is **due** today.
18. fruit	*fruit*	Those **fruit** trees bear sweet pears.
19. music	*music*	I listen to **music** to relax.
20. rule	*rule*	No school **rule** should be broken.

SORT THE SPELLING WORDS

1.–15. Write the spelling words with the /$\overline{oo}$/ vowel sound. Circle the letters that spell this vowel sound.

16.–20. Write the spelling words with the /y$\overline{oo}$/ vowel sound. Circle the letters that spell this vowel sound.

REMEMBER THE SPELLING STRATEGY

Remember that the vowel sound you hear in **true** and the vowel sound you hear in **few** can be spelled in different ways.

50

Pretest Sentences (See procedures on pages Z10–Z11.)

1. Pablo knows how to play the **flute**.
2. On a clear day, the **view** is lovely.
3. Jamal is a very good **student**.
4. I saw a tree **whose** leaves were red.
5. Using the given **clue**, I found the surprise.
6. The doll looked almost **human**.
7. I enjoy the taste of orange **juice**.
8. Very **few** people came to the play.
9. The story I read was **true**.
10. Water will flow through the **tube**.
11. People will probably believe you if you always tell the **truth**.
12. Lee repaired the book cover with **glue**.
13. In the morning, the ground is sometimes wet with **dew**.
14. That dye seems to **lose** its color.
15. There is a red **tulip** in our garden.
16. Mom **used** Grandfather's car.
17. Our art project is **due** Thursday.
18. Apples are my favorite **fruit**.
19. She could hear the soft **music**.
20. Staying quiet during a fire drill is a good **rule**.

Spelling and Vocabulary

Word Meanings

Write a spelling word for each of the following definitions.

1. a scene; a range or field of sight
2. water droplets that form on cool surfaces
3. expected or scheduled
4. information that helps solve a problem
5. a sticky liquid that holds things together
6. a musical instrument

Phonics

Follow the directions to write new words.

7. toy – oy + ube = _____
8. rail – ail + ule = _____
9. useful – ful + d = _____
10. train – ain + ue = _____
11. fool – ool + ew = _____
12. jug – g + ice = _____
13. whole – le + se = _____
14. frost – ost + uit = _____
15. troop – oop + uth = _____
16. low – w + se = _____

USING THE Dictionary

Find each word in your **Spelling Dictionary**. Write the word, and draw a line between the syllables.

17. tulip
18. student
19. music
20. human

◆ ◆ ◆

Dictionary Check Be sure to check your answers in your **Spelling Dictionary**.

Word Meanings
1. view
2. dew
3. due
4. clue
5. glue
6. flute

Phonics
7. tube
8. rule
9. used
10. true
11. few
12. juice
13. whose
14. fruit
15. truth
16. lose

Using the Dictionary
17. tu/lip
18. stu/dent
19. mu/sic
20. hu/man

51

Objectives

Spelling and Vocabulary
Students will
- **identify** and write spelling words that match definitions.
- **subtract** and add letters to words to form spelling words.
- **use** the **Spelling Dictionary** to divide spelling words into syllables.

Developing Oral Language Skills

The pronunciation and meaning of the word **lose** is often confused with **loose**. Have students use the words **lose** and **loose** in oral sentences that clearly show the words' meaning and pronunciation. For example:

Try not to **lose** your book.
Don't let the dog **loose** in the park.

Write the sentences on the chalkboard and point to each word as the class repeats the sentence.

MEETING INDIVIDUAL NEEDS
Providing More Help

Write the following words on the chalkboard, omitting the lines. Have the students underline the letters that spell the vowel sound that is shared by two words in each group. (Allow for reasonable variations in pronunciation.)

1. music   human   true
2. juice   fruit   few
3. view   glue   used
4. lose   dew   music
5. flute   human   few
6. whose   student   used
7. human   due   clue
8. music   tube   rule

★Students who need to study fewer words should use the **Alternate Word List**. This list is starred on page T50 in the Teacher Edition. The **Unit 8 Practice Masters** (*Teacher Resource Book*) provide additional practice with these words.

Unit 8 Practice Masters

Name _____   Practice **Master** 8

| 1. true | 3. rule | 5. few | 7. whose | 9. human |
| 2. tube | 4. fruit | 6. lose | 8. used | 10. music |

A. Write the spelling word that is an antonym for each word.

1. false _____   3. find _____
2. many _____   4. new _____

B. Follow the directions to write the spelling words.

1. toy – oy + ube = _____
2. trust – st + e = _____
3. whole – le + se = _____
4. useful – ful + d = _____
5. frost – ost + uit = _____
6. hum + an = _____
7. rug – g + le = _____
8. lost – t + e = _____

C. Write the spelling word that belongs in each group.

1. meat, grain, vegetable, _____
2. real, correct, loyal, _____
3. direction, guide, law, _____
4. melody, harmony, tune, _____

46

Practice **Master** 8

whose   human
used   music

a letter. The words you decode are

h	i	j	k	l	m
8	9	10	11	12	13
u	v	w	x	y	z
21	22	23	24	25	26

47

Objectives

Spelling and Reading

Students will
- **complete** sentences using spelling words.
- **solve** analogies using spelling words.
- **complete** a paragraph using spelling words.

One-Minute Handwriting Hint

The lowercase **u** contains three undercurves. The last undercurve is slightly wide. The two slant strokes should be parallel. Do not loop the undercurve slant motions.

UNDERCURVES

Legible handwriting can boost spelling scores by as much as 20%.

Complete the Sentences

1. view
2. music
3. due
4. dew
5. tube
6. whose
7. rule
8. glue

Solve the Analogies

9. flute
10. tulip
11. true
12. clue
13. lose
14. human
15. few

Complete the Paragraph

16. used
17. student
18. truth
19. fruit
20. juice

Spelling and Reading

flute	view	student	whose	clue
human	juice	few	true	tube
truth	glue	dew	lose	tulip
used	due	fruit	music	rule

Complete the Sentences Write the spelling word that completes each sentence.

1. From the hill we had a great _____ of the lake.
2. Do you prefer talk shows or _____ programs on the radio?
3. My teacher said our project is _____ tomorrow.
4. In the morning _____ covered the car's windshield.
5. I squeezed the _____ of toothpaste.
6. We asked _____ book was left on the table.
7. That safety _____ will protect you from harm.
8. They used _____ to attach their pictures to paper.

Solve the Analogies Write a spelling word to solve each analogy.

9. **Strike** is to **drum** as **blow** is to _____.
10. **Animal** is to **deer** as **flower** is to _____.
11. **Huge** is to **tiny** as **false** is to _____.
12. **Puzzle** is to **piece** as **riddle** is to _____.
13. **Joy** is to **win** as **sorrow** is to _____.
14. **Coat** is to **beaver** as **skin** is to _____.
15. **More** is to **many** as **less** is to _____.

Complete the Paragraph Write the spelling word from the box that fits each blank.

An encyclopedia was _16._ by the _17._ to learn the _18._ about a healthy diet. She wanted to know if we should eat _19._ and drink _20._ at every meal or only once a day.

student
juice
truth
used
fruit

52

MEETING INDIVIDUAL NEEDS
Providing More Challenge

Challenge Words and **Challenge Activities** for Unit 8 appear on page 230. **Challenge Word Test Sentences** appear on page T230.

Unit 8 Challenge Activities

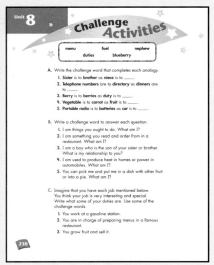

Weekly Test Options

Option 1:
One Spelling Word Per Sentence
(See procedures on pages Z10–Z11.)

1. You can fix many things with **glue**.
2. Please give me a **clue** to the riddle.
3. We will pay the bill before it is **due**.
4. Is it **true** that you have been here before?
5. She played the **flute**.
6. I know a game that has only one **rule**.
7. Do not forget to put the cap back on the **tube**.
8. A pear is a sweet **fruit**.
9. The **juice** was made from apples.
10. The people were dancing to the **music**.
11. You do not look like a **human** with that mask on your face.
12. A **tulip** grew in our yard.
13. I try to be a good **student** in school.
14. I feel good when I tell the **truth**.
15. Mother **used** the rest of the soap.
16. A **few** people had to wait.

T52

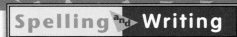

Spelling and Writing

Proofread a Paragraph

Six words are not spelled correctly in this paragraph. Write those words correctly.

>   It was a frigid day but as fine as any human
> could want. As a ~~rool~~ *rule*, I would shun the cold,
> but I am a ~~troo~~ *true* football fan. Therefore, I
> appeared when I was ~~doo~~ *due* at the stadium. The
> ~~vue~~ *view* was breathtaking. The band, sparkling with
> bright colors, was playing spirited ~~musik~~ *music*. Soon
> the teams, in splendid uniforms, trotted onto the
> springy turf. Whether my team would win or
> ~~luze~~ *lose*, this would be a day to remember.

Proofreading Marks

≡ Make a capital.
/ Make a small letter.
∧ Add something.
℘ Take out something.
⊙ Add a period.
New paragraph
ⓢⓟ Spelling error

Write a Paragraph

Descriptive Writing

Write a paragraph describing something you remember fondly. It may be a person, an interesting place, or a pleasant experience. Be sure to include

- the name of the person or place.
- the kind of experience.
- what you liked about the person, place, or experience.
- descriptive words that make the experience come alive for the reader.

Use as many spelling words as you can.

Proofread Your Writing During **Editing**

Proofread your writing for spelling errors as part of the editing stage of the writing process. Be sure to check each word carefully. Use a dictionary to check spelling if you are not sure.

Writing Process

Prewriting
⇓
Drafting
⇓
Revising
⇓
Editing
⇓
Publishing

53

Using the Writing Process

Before assigning **Write a Paragraph,** see pages 258–259 in the Student Edition for a complete review of the writing process and additional writing assignments. You may also wish to refer to pages Z12–Z13 in the Teacher Edition.

Keeping a Spelling Journal

Encourage students to record the words they misspelled on the weekly test in a personal spelling journal. These words may be recycled for future study. Students may also wish to include words from their writing. See pages Z12–Z13 in the Teacher Edition for more information.

---

17. Did you **lose** your papers?
18. Are you the boy **whose** glasses I found?
19. Sometimes **dew** is on the grass in the morning.
20. From the top of the hill there is a great **view**.

Option 2:
Multiple Spelling Words Per Sentence
(See procedures on pages Z10–Z11.)

1. It is **true** that if you change seats, you will **lose** the **view** of the circus.
2. Use **glue** to fasten the parts of the **tube** together.
3. There are a **few** drops of **dew** on the grass.
4. The girl **used** the **flute** to play **music**.
5. Please tell me **whose** paper is not **due** on Monday.
6. The **student** learned about the parts of the **human** arm.
7. Please give me a **clue** about how to grow a **tulip**.
8. The **juice** from the **fruit** had a good taste.
9. My mother made a **rule** that we always tell the **truth**.

Option 3:
Standardized Test
(See *Teacher Resource Book,* Unit 8.)

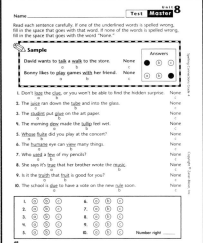

**Unit 8
Test Master**

T53

Objectives

Strategy Words

Students will

- **review** words studied previously that are related to the spelling strategy.
- **preview** unknown words that are related to the spelling strategy.

Remind the students that the **Strategy Words** relate to the spelling patterns they have studied in this unit. The **Review Words** are below grade level, and the **Preview Words** are above grade level. You may wish to use the following sentences to introduce the words in context.

Review Words:
Words From Grade 3

1. A hot air **balloon** was floating in the sky overhead.
2. We **drew** pictures in the sand.
3. The **news** is on the radio every morning when I am getting out of bed.
4. I saw several goldfish in the **pool**.
5. A little boy **threw** the ball right to me.

Preview Words:
Words From Grade 5

6. We can **amuse** ourselves while we are waiting for Dad.
7. That pink rose is a **beauty**.
8. Let us **continue** to work on our spelling lesson until noon.
9. My brother took me to two **movies** in one week.
10. Pack your **suitcase** for the trip.

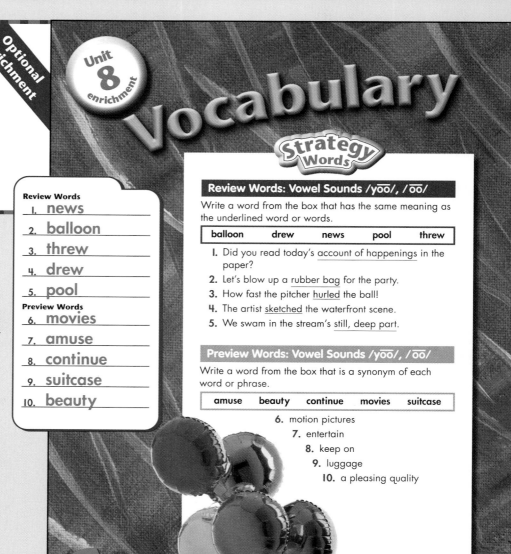

Unit 8 enrichment

Vocabulary

Strategy Words

Review Words
1. news
2. balloon
3. threw
4. drew
5. pool

Preview Words
6. movies
7. amuse
8. continue
9. suitcase
10. beauty

Review Words: Vowel Sounds /yoo/, /oo/

Write a word from the box that has the same meaning as the underlined word or words.

balloon	drew	news	pool	threw

1. Did you read today's <u>account of happenings</u> in the paper?
2. Let's blow up a <u>rubber bag</u> for the party.
3. How fast the pitcher <u>hurled</u> the ball!
4. The artist <u>sketched</u> the waterfront scene.
5. We swam in the stream's <u>still, deep part</u>.

Preview Words: Vowel Sounds /yoo/, /oo/

Write a word from the box that is a synonym of each word or phrase.

amuse	beauty	continue	movies	suitcase

6. motion pictures
7. entertain
8. keep on
9. luggage
10. a pleasing quality

54

Unit 8 RECAP

You may wish to assign the **Unit 8 Homework Master** (*Teacher Resource Book*, Unit 8) as a fun way to recap the spelling words.

Unit 8 Homework Master

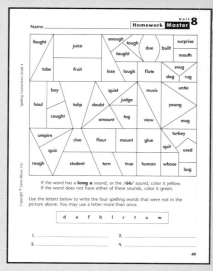

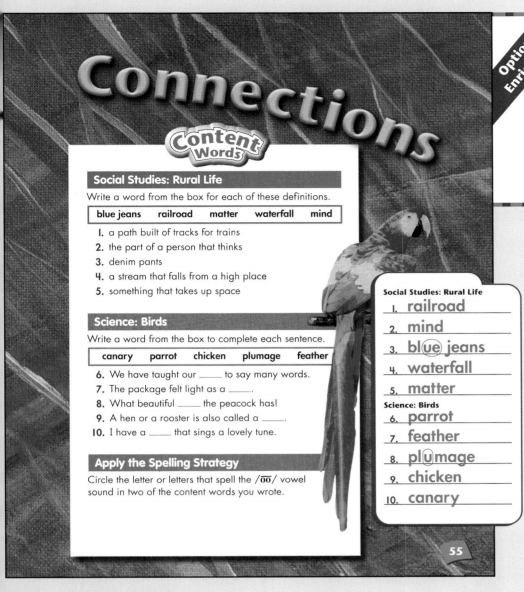

Connections

Content Words

Social Studies: Rural Life

Write a word from the box for each of these definitions.

blue jeans	railroad	matter	waterfall	mind

I. a path built of tracks for trains

2. the part of a person that thinks

3. denim pants

4. a stream that falls from a high place

5. something that takes up space

Science: Birds

Write a word from the box to complete each sentence.

canary	parrot	chicken	plumage	feather

6. We have taught our ____ to say many words.

7. The package felt light as a ____.

8. What beautiful ____ the peacock has!

9. A hen or a rooster is also called a ____.

10. I have a ____ that sings a lovely tune.

Apply the Spelling Strategy

Circle the letter or letters that spell the /o͞o/ vowel sound in two of the content words you wrote.

Social Studies: Rural Life

1. railroad
2. mind
3. bl(ue) jeans
4. waterfall
5. matter

Science: Birds

6. parrot
7. feather
8. pl(u)mage
9. chicken
10. canary

55

Optional Enrichment

Objectives

Content Words

Students will

• **expand** vocabulary with content-related words.

• **relate** the spelling strategy to words outside the basic spelling list.

Content Words

Social Studies: Rural Life

Review the meanings of these words with the students. You may wish to use these sentences to introduce the words in context.

1. I wore my **blue jeans** to work on the farm.
2. The **railroad** runs right near our barn.
3. What is the **matter** with that cow?
4. A **waterfall** is very near here.
5. Do you **mind** if we walk for a while?

Encourage the students to use these words to write a story about farm life.

Science: Birds

Review the meanings of these words with the students. You may wish to use these sentences to introduce the words in context.

6. The **canary** was singing a song for us.
7. The colors on the **parrot** were bright and beautiful.
8. My grandfather has a **chicken** farm.
9. Those birds have such colorful **plumage**.
10. That **feather** over there must have come from one of the peacocks.

Encourage the students to use these words in a paragraph about two or more birds they have seen and can describe.

Unit 9 Home Study Master

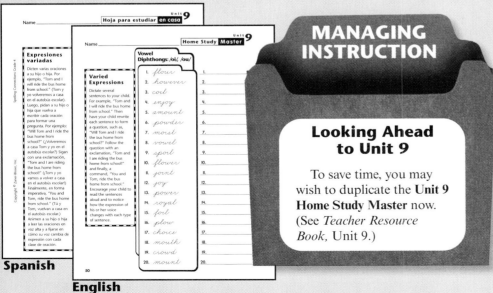

Spanish

English

MANAGING INSTRUCTION

Looking Ahead to Unit 9

To save time, you may wish to duplicate the **Unit 9 Home Study Master** now. (See *Teacher Resource Book,* Unit 9.)

Basic Spelling List

flour	joint
however	joy
coil	power
enjoy	royal
amount	foil
powder	plow
moist	choice
vowel	mouth
spoil	crowd
flower	mount

Strategy Words

Review

about	house
boil	join
found	

Preview

allowance	employ
avoid	tower
couch	

Content Words

Language Arts: Parts of Speech

adjective	verb
pronoun	noun
adverb	

Fine Arts: Singing

duet	bass
tenor	trio
solo	

Individual Needs

Challenge Words

spout	hoist
bountiful	buoyant
scowl	

Alternate Word List

however	flower
enjoy	power
amount	choice
moist	mouth
vowel	crowd

MATERIALS

Student Edition
Pages 56–61
Challenge Activities, p. 231

Teacher Edition
Pages T56A–T61
Challenge Activities, T231

Other Resources
Spelling Connections Software
Unit 9 Word List Overhead
  Transparency

Teacher Resource Book
Unit 9 Home Study Master
  (English or Spanish; students
  may pretest on this sheet or use
  it for home practice.)
Unit 9 Homework Masters
Unit 9 Practice Masters
Flip Folder Practice Master
Unit 9 Test Master

Visit our Web site, www.zaner-bloser.com

OBJECTIVES

Spelling and Thinking
Students will
- **read** the spelling words in list form and in context.
- **sort** the words according to the **/oi/** and **/ou/** sounds.
- **read** and remember this week's spelling strategy.

Spelling and Vocabulary
Students will
- **identify** and write spelling words to match definitions.
- **solve** analogies using spelling words.
- **use** the **Spelling Dictionary** to determine the part of speech of spelling words.

Spelling and Reading
Students will
- **complete** sentences using spelling words.
- **complete** a paragraph using spelling words.

Spelling and Writing
Students will
- **proofread** a newspaper ad.
- **use** the writing process to write a newspaper ad.
- **proofread** their writing.

MEETING INDIVIDUAL NEEDS
Learning Styles

 Visual

Write the diphthong in each spelling word (**ou, ow, oi, oy**) on a separate card. Tape the cards to the chalkboard. Using a piece of colored chalk, add the letters that form each spelling word that has the /**oi**/ diphthong. After each word is written, have the students say the word and write it on their papers. Repeat this procedure, using different colored chalk, with the words that contain the /**ou**/ diphthong.

 Auditory

Write on the chalkboard a series of four words, three of which are /**oi**/ spelling words. For example, write the words **coil, joy, frog,** and **foil**. Call on a student to say the three spelling words and identify the /**oi**/ diphthong. Then have all the students spell each word in unison. Use the same procedure for the words that have the /**ou**/ diphthong.

 Kinesthetic

Write the spelling words on separate strips of construction paper. Trace guidelines for cutting out the diphthongs, as shown below. Divide the word strips among the students and give them scissors. Have them cut out the outlined diphthongs and write the words.

Language and Cultural Differences

Spanish-speaking students may need extra practice to establish the sound-symbol relationships in this unit. In the Spanish language, there is a sound similar to the /**ou**/ sound in English, but it is spelled with the letters **au**. Furthermore, there is no **w** in the Spanish alphabet, except in words borrowed from other languages.

Cut out the letter **w** from sandpaper and have each student trace over the letter while saying its name aloud. Then have each student complete the activity for his or her dominant learning modality.

MANAGING INSTRUCTION

3–5 Day Plan		Average	Below Average	Above Average
Day 1	**Day 1**	Pretest Spelling Mini-Lesson, p. T56 Spelling and Thinking, p. 56	Pretest Spelling Mini-Lesson, p. T56 Spelling and Thinking, p. 56	Pretest Spelling and Thinking, p. 56
	Day 2	Spelling and Vocabulary, p. 57	Spelling and Vocabulary, p. 57 (or) Unit 9 Practice Master, A and B	Spelling and Vocabulary, p. 57 Spelling and Reading, p. 58
Day 2	**Day 3**	Spelling and Reading, p. 58	Spelling and Reading, p. 58 (or) Unit 9 Practice Master, C and D	Challenge Activities, p. 231
	Day 4	Spelling and Writing, p. 59 Unit 9 Homework Master	Spelling and Writing, p. 59	Spelling and Writing, p. 59 Unit 9 Homework Master
Day 3	**Day 5**	Weekly Test	Weekly Test	Weekly Test
Vocabulary Connections (pages 60 and 61) may be used anytime during this unit.				

Objectives

Spelling and Thinking

Students will
- **read** the spelling words in list form and in context.
- **sort** the words according to the **/oi/** and **/ou/** sounds.
- **read** and remember this week's spelling strategy.

UNIT PRETEST

Use **Pretest Sentences** below. Refer to the self-checking procedures on student page 256. You may wish to use the **Unit 9 Word List Overhead Transparency** as part of the checking procedure.

TEACHING THE STRATEGY

Spelling Mini-Lesson

Write **/oi/** and **/ou/** on the board. Remind the students that these vowel sounds, called **diphthongs,** are neither long nor short. Diphthongs seem to begin as one vowel sound, then change into another.

Ask one volunteer to write all the spelling words with the **/oi/** diphthong on the board under **/oi/**. Ask another to do the same for the words with the **/ou/** diphthong. Focus students' attention on the different spellings of each diphthong. Have them note that the **oy** spelling of the **/oi/** sound occurs at the end of a syllable or word.

Conclude by reading **Remember the Spelling Strategy** on page 56.

Order of answers may vary.

oi or oy
1. coil
2. moist ★
3. spoil
4. joint
5. foil
6. choice ★
7. enjoy ★
8. joy
9. royal

ou or ow
10. flour
11. amount ★
12. mouth ★
13. mount
14. however ★
15. powder
16. vowel ★
17. flower ★
18. power ★
19. plow
20. crowd ★

56

Unit 9
Vowel Diphthongs: /oi/, /ou/

Spelling and Thinking

READ THE SPELLING WORDS

1. flour	*flour*	Bread contains **flour** and yeast.
2. however	*however*	He is polite **however** he feels.
3. coil	*coil*	Please **coil** the hose on its reel.
4. enjoy	*enjoy*	Relax and **enjoy** the sunset.
5. amount	*amount*	The **amount** of our bill was $25.
6. powder	*powder*	We dusted the dog with flea **powder**.
7. moist	*moist*	The ground is **moist** after it rains.
8. vowel	*vowel*	Ina's name begins and ends with a **vowel**.
9. spoil	*spoil*	Do not let the rain **spoil** your fun.
10. flower	*flower*	Plant a seed to grow a **flower**.
11. joint	*joint*	Your arm bends at the elbow **joint**.
12. joy	*joy*	The hero was greeted with shouts of **joy**.
13. power	*power*	Those who rule have **power**.
14. royal	*royal*	Guards protected the **royal** family.
15. foil	*foil*	Wrap food in **foil** to keep it fresh.
16. plow	*plow*	The **plow** turned over the soil.
17. choice	*choice*	We had a **choice** of peas or beans.
18. mouth	*mouth*	How many teeth are in your **mouth**?
19. crowd	*crowd*	Follow your heart, not the **crowd**.
20. mount	*mount*	Learn to **mount** before riding a horse.

SORT THE SPELLING WORDS

1.–9. Write the spelling words in which the **/oi/** sound is spelled **oi** or **oy**.

10.–20. Write the spelling words in which the **/ou/** sound is spelled **ou** or **ow**.

REMEMBER THE SPELLING STRATEGY

Remember that the **/oi/** sound can be spelled in different ways: **oi** in **coil** or **oy** in **joy**. The **/ou/** sound can be spelled in different ways: **ou** in **mouth** or **ow** in **plow**.

Pretest Sentences (See procedures on pages Z10–Z11.)

1. Use unbleached **flour** in the recipe.
2. You may use these old magazines **however** you wish.
3. The garter snake wound itself into a **coil**.
4. During the summer we **enjoy** swimming.
5. Four dollars is the **amount** we need for our supper.
6. Light, dry snow is sometimes called **powder**.
7. Many plants grow well in **moist** soil.
8. The letter **e** is a **vowel**.
9. Some salads **spoil** quickly if they are not kept cold.
10. A red rose is a beautiful **flower**.
11. The part of the arm that allows it to bend is called the **joint**.
12. After the wedding, everyone was filled with **joy**.
13. Hoover Dam provides electric **power**.
14. There were many dukes and duchesses at the **royal** party.
15. Ashanta made decorations out of **foil**.
16. When the snow is too deep to shovel, we must **plow** it.
17. You can have your **choice** of cereal.
18. A dentist is a person who checks your teeth and **mouth**.
19. As the president spoke, a **crowd** of people gathered around.
20. You should **mount** the horse on the left side.

Spelling and Vocabulary

Word Meanings

Write a spelling word that has the same meaning as each definition below.

1. nevertheless
2. get on a horse
3. to ruin; damage
4. great strength; force
5. get pleasure from
6. selection
7. powder of ground grain
8. of kings and queens
9. total; sum
10. wind around
11. type of sound or letter

Analogies

Write a spelling word to complete each analogy.

12. **Chicken** is to **flock** as **person** is to _____.
13. **Dry** is to **arid** as _____ is to **wet**.
14. **Sneeze** is to **nose** as **yawn** is to _____.
15. **Tree** is to **leaf** as **bush** is to _____.

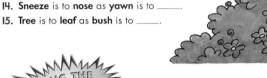

USING THE Dictionary

Read each sentence below. Write the spelling word and its part of speech. Use the **Spelling Dictionary** if you need help.

16. The candy was covered with foil.
17. Bath powder has a nice smell.
18. My shoulder joint aches.
19. The farmer will plow his fields.
20. You bring joy to everyone.

Word Meanings
1. however
2. mount
3. spoil
4. power
5. enjoy
6. choice
7. flour
8. royal
9. amount
10. coil
11. vowel

Analogies
12. crowd
13. moist
14. mouth
15. flower

Using the Dictionary
16. foil, noun
17. powder, noun
18. joint, noun
19. plow, verb
20. joy, noun

57

Developing Oral Language Skills

The second syllable in **power** and **powder** is often blurred when pronounced quickly or carelessly. As a result, the final vowel is frequently misspelled. Have students practice saying each syllable of these words as though it were a little word in order to give a clear clue to the vowel sound and spelling.

MEETING INDIVIDUAL NEEDS

Providing More Help

Play a variation of the card game "Old Maid." Make two cards for each spelling word. On one card write the spelling word, omitting the letters that spell the diphthong. On the second card write the diphthong. Four or five students can play the game. First have them shuffle and deal out all the cards. Then have them take turns drawing cards from each other in order to try to match diphthong cards with word cards.

★ Students who need to study fewer words should use the **Alternate Word List**. This list is starred on page T56 in the Teacher Edition. The **Unit 9 Practice Masters** (*Teacher Resource Book*) provide additional practice with these words.

Unit 9 Practice Masters

Name _____

Practice **Master 9**

| 1. moist | 3. enjoy | 5. amount | 7. crowd | 9. flower |
| 2. choice | 4. mouth | 6. vowel | 8. power | 10. however |

A. Write the spelling word that rhymes with each word below.

1. count _____
2. employ _____
3. voice _____
4. towel _____
5. tower _____
6. loud _____

B. Look at these symbols: ● = oi ▲ = oy ▢ = ou ♥ = ow
Write the spelling words these letters and symbols spell.

1. a m ▢ n t _____
2. c h ● c e _____
3. h ♥ e v e r _____
4. p ♥ e r _____
5. e n j ▲ _____
6. f l ♥ e r _____
7. m ● s t _____
8. c r ♥ d _____
9. m ▢ t h _____
10. v ♥ e l _____

52

Practice **Master 9**

| crowd | flower |
| power | however |

each word correctly.

1. mowth _____
2. chois _____
3. croud _____
4. vowle _____

mbled letters to make spelling words.

53

T57

Spelling and Reading

Students will
- **complete** sentences using spelling words.
- **complete** a paragraph using spelling words.

One-Minute Handwriting Hint

The checkstroke ending of the lowercase **o** swings wide and then slants down to form the overcurve of the letter **y**. The overcurve ending of the letter **y** crosses at the baseline.

SWING WIDE

Legible handwriting can boost spelling scores by as much as 20%.

Complete the Sentences

1. flour
2. flower
3. plow
4. amount
5. mouth
6. coil
7. mount
8. vowel
9. foil
10. powder
11. joint
12. spoil
13. power
14. moist

Complete the Paragraph

15. enjoy
16. however
17. crowd
18. royal
19. joy
20. choice

58

Spelling and Reading

flour	however	coil	enjoy	amount
powder	moist	vowel	spoil	flower
joint	joy	power	royal	foil
plow	choice	mouth	crowd	mount

Complete the Sentences   Write a spelling word to complete each sentence.

1. Mix water and ____ to make a thick paste.
2. The daffodils will ____ in the spring.
3. The tractor has replaced the horse and ____.
4. The reward is a large ____ of money.
5. Every tooth in his ____ sparkled.
6. His lasso was a ____ of rope.
7. The baby can ____ the stairs.
8. A consonant may be followed by a ____.
9. Bake these potatoes in aluminum ____.
10. The dry earth had turned to ____.
11. Throwing a ball can injure your shoulder ____.
12. Some foods ____ if left out of the refrigerator.
13. She was given the ____ to govern the state.
14. Air that is ____ feels warmer than air that is dry.

Complete the Paragraph   Write the spelling word that fits each blank.

I hoped to have fun. Little did I expect to ____15.____ myself as much as this, ____16.____. Following the ____17.____, we came to the changing of the queen's ____18.____ guard. It was a great ____19.____ to see the beautiful castle and all the guards. If given a ____20.____ of tourist attractions in England, you might want to choose the changing of the guard.

MEETING INDIVIDUAL NEEDS
Providing More Challenge

Challenge Words and **Challenge Activities** for Unit 9 appear on page 231. **Challenge Word Test Sentences** appear on page T231.

Unit 9 Challenge Activities

Weekly Test Options

Option 1:
One Spelling Word Per Sentence
(See procedures on pages Z10–Z11.)

1. The people came to see the **royal** couple.
2. It gives me **joy** to see other people happy.
3. The wire is in a **coil**.
4. There are many people standing in the **crowd**.
5. I need help to **mount** my horse.
6. The tulip is a pretty **flower**.
7. She wrapped the potato in **foil**.
8. The ground was **moist** after the storm.
9. They paid a large **amount** for the new ship.
10. We can make **flour** from corn.
11. Food can **spoil** if it is not in the refrigerator.
12. How many teeth are in your **mouth**?
13. Make the best **choice**.
14. We used the **plow** to turn over the soil.
15. There is at least one **vowel** sound in every word.
16. I will wait for **however** long it takes.

Spelling and Writing

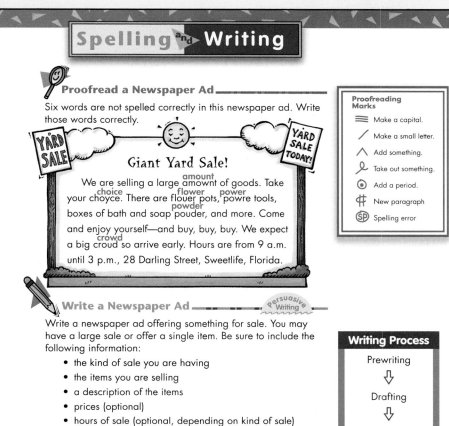

Proofread a Newspaper Ad

Six words are not spelled correctly in this newspaper ad. Write those words correctly.

Giant Yard Sale!

We are selling a large amownt of goods. Take
[amount]
your choyce. There are flouer pots, powre tools,
[choice] [flower] [power]
boxes of bath and soap pouder, and more. Come
[powder]
and enjoy yourself—and buy, buy, buy. We expect
a big crowd so arrive early. Hours are from 9 a.m.
[crowd]
until 3 p.m., 28 Darling Street, Sweetlife, Florida.

Proofreading Marks

≡ Make a capital.
/ Make a small letter.
∧ Add something.
↶ Take out something.
⊙ Add a period.
⌗ New paragraph
SP Spelling error

Write a Newspaper Ad

Persuasive Writing

Write a newspaper ad offering something for sale. You may have a large sale or offer a single item. Be sure to include the following information:

- the kind of sale you are having
- the items you are selling
- a description of the items
- prices (optional)
- hours of sale (optional, depending on kind of sale)
- a telephone number or an address

Use as many spelling words as you can.

Writing Process

Prewriting
⇩
Drafting
⇩
Revising
⇩
Editing
⇩
Publishing

Proofread Your Writing During

Proofread your writing for spelling errors as part of the editing stage in the writing process. Be sure to check each word carefully. Use a dictionary to check spelling if you are not sure.

59

17. Some chalk **powder** got on my hands.
18. I **enjoy** swimming.
19. The airplane has a lot of **power**.
20. Each of your arms and legs has a **joint**.

Option 2:
Multiple Spelling Words Per Sentence
(See procedures on pages Z10–Z11.)

1. This **powder** smells as nice as the **flower**.
2. Use the right **amount** of **flour** in the mix.
3. Take **however** much time you need to **mount** the horse.
4. The horse has the **power** to pull the **plow**.
5. We **enjoy** watching the **royal** pair.
6. Put **foil** over the buns if you want them to stay **moist**.
7. We formed a **joint** between the two pieces of **coil**.
8. You must open your **mouth** to say a **vowel**.
9. The **crowd** made the **choice** to eat now.
10. To **spoil** dinner takes all of the **joy** out of cooking.

Option 3:
Standardized Test
(See *Teacher Resource Book,* Unit 9.)

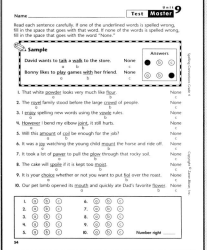

**Unit 9
Test Master**

Objectives

Strategy Words

Students will

- **review** words studied previously that are related to the spelling strategy.
- **preview** unknown words that are related to the spelling strategy.

Unit 9 enrichment

Vocabulary

Strategy Words

Remind the students that the **Strategy Words** relate to the spelling patterns they have studied in this unit. The **Review Words** are below grade level, and the **Preview Words** are above grade level. You may wish to use the following sentences to introduce the words in context.

Review Words:
Words From Grade 3

1. Please tell us **about** your weekend.
2. Do not let the stew **boil** too long.
3. I **found** the ring that I lost last week.
4. Stay in the **house** until I get home.
5. The neighbors want me to **join** them for dinner.

Preview Words:
Words From Grade 5

6. Dad gives me my **allowance** each Friday.
7. Try to **avoid** walking on the freshly mopped floor.
8. The **couch** is a comfortable place to sit.
9. The large company will **employ** many people next year.
10. We made a castle out of cardboard and put a **tower** on one side.

Review Words

1. found
2. join
3. about
4. house
5. boil

Preview Words
6. employ
7. allowance
8. tower
9. avoid
10. couch

Strategy Words

Review Words: Vowel Diphthongs /oi/, /ou/

Write a word from the box that could replace each underlined word or group of words.

about	boil	found	house	join

1. We <u>discovered</u> an injured bird.
2. I am going to <u>be a member of</u> the Boy Scouts as soon as I am old enough.
3. We studied for <u>around</u> an hour.
4. They live in the <u>dwelling</u> by the bay.
5. To make hot chocolate, heat milk in a pan but do not allow it to <u>bubble</u>.

Preview Words: Vowel Diphthongs /oi/, /ou/

Write the word from the box that is suggested by each clue below.

allowance	avoid	couch	employ	tower

6. hire for wages
7. money given on a regular basis
8. a tall, slender part of a building
9. to stay clear of
10. a sofa

60

Unit 9 RECAP

You may wish to assign the **Unit 9 Homework Master** (*Teacher Resource Book*, Unit 9) as a fun way to recap the spelling words.

Unit 9 Homework Master

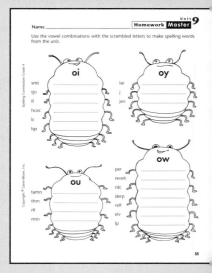

Connections

Objectives

Content Words

Students will
- **expand** vocabulary with content-related words.
- **relate** the spelling strategy to words outside the basic spelling list.

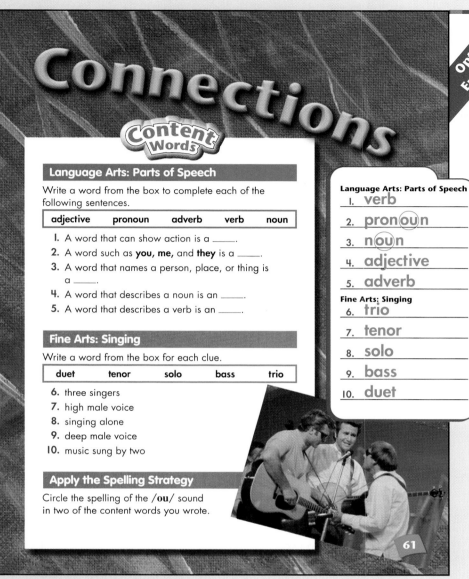

Content Words

Language Arts: Parts of Speech

Write a word from the box to complete each of the following sentences.

adjective	pronoun	adverb	verb	noun

1. A word that can show action is a _____.
2. A word such as **you, me,** and **they** is a _____.
3. A word that names a person, place, or thing is a _____.
4. A word that describes a noun is an _____.
5. A word that describes a verb is an _____.

Fine Arts: Singing

Write a word from the box for each clue.

duet	tenor	solo	bass	trio

6. three singers
7. high male voice
8. singing alone
9. deep male voice
10. music sung by two

Apply the Spelling Strategy

Circle the spelling of the /ou/ sound in two of the content words you wrote.

Language Arts: Parts of Speech
1. verb
2. pron(ou)n
3. n(ou)n
4. adjective
5. adverb

Fine Arts: Singing
6. trio
7. tenor
8. solo
9. bass
10. duet

Content Words

Language Arts: Parts of Speech

Review the meanings of these words with the students. You may wish to use these sentences to introduce the words in context.

1. An **adjective** is a describing word.
2. The **pronoun** in the sentence was not capitalized.
3. Try to find the **adverb** in each paragraph.
4. A **verb** tells about the action.
5. The **noun** in that sentence named a country.

Encourage the students to use these words to label the words in a sentence illustrating the parts of speech.

Fine Arts: Singing

Review the meanings of these words with the students. You may wish to use these sentences to introduce the words in context.

6. The girls sang a **duet**.
7. The **tenor** is usually the male lead voice in a group.
8. I sang a **solo** for my friends.
9. The **bass** voice was so deep it made the room vibrate.
10. The boys formed a singing **trio** for the local talent show.

Encourage the students to use these words in a descriptive paragraph about a concert or a music lesson.

Unit 10 Home Study Master

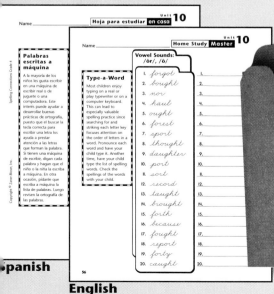

Spanish

English

MANAGING INSTRUCTION

Looking Ahead to Unit 10

To save time, you may wish to duplicate the **Unit 10 Home Study Master** now. (See *Teacher Resource Book*, Unit 10.)

Basic Spelling List

forgot	sort
bought	record
nor	taught
haul	brought
ought	forth
forest	because
sport	fought
thought	report
daughter	forty
port	caught

Strategy Words

Review

before	north
form	story
morning	

Preview

audience	important
author	launch
enormous	

Content Words

Science: Plants

blossom	pollen
petals	orchard
nectar	

Social Studies: Transportation

airport	stock
railway	depot
cargo	

Individual Needs

Challenge Words

audio	toward
naughty	dinosaur
oriole	

Alternate Word List

bought	record
nor	brought
forest	because
thought	report
sort	caught

MATERIALS

Student Edition
Pages 62–67
Challenge Activities, p. 232

Teacher Edition
Pages T62A–T67
Challenge Activities, T232

Other Resources
Spelling Connections Software
Unit 10 Word List Overhead
Transparency

Teacher Resource Book
Unit 10 Home Study Master
(English or Spanish; students
may pretest on this sheet or use
it for home practice.)
Unit 10 Homework Master
Unit 10 Practice Masters
Flip Folder Practice Master
Unit 10 Test Master

Visit our Web site, www.zaner-bloser.com

OBJECTIVES

Spelling and Thinking
Students will
- **read** the spelling words in list form and in context.
- **sort** the spelling words according to the /ôr/ and /ô/ vowel sounds.
- **read** and remember this week's spelling strategy.

Spelling and Vocabulary
Students will
- **identify** and write spelling words to match meanings.
- **choose** and write spelling words that are synonyms.
- **use** the **Spelling Dictionary** to show stressed syllables in spelling words.

Spelling and Reading
Students will
- **replace** words in sentences with spelling words.
- **write** spelling words for clues.
- **complete** a paragraph using spelling words.

Spelling and Writing
Students will
- **proofread** a story.
- **use** the writing process to write a story.
- **proofread** their writing.

MEETING INDIVIDUAL NEEDS
Learning Styles

 Visual

Have the students write the spelling words with the /ô/ sound in one column and the words with the /ôr/ sound in another column. Tell the students to use one color to circle the letters that spell the /ô/ sound and a different color to circle the letters that spell the /ôr/ sound.

 Auditory

For each word, cut a rocket shape out of construction paper. Write a spelling word on one side of the rocket and the number of letters in the word on the other side.

Place the rockets in a pile in the center of a table. Have one student choose a rocket and then pronounce and spell aloud the word on the rocket. Have this student choose another student to pronounce the same word and spell it aloud. If both students spell the word correctly, both students receive the number on the rocket as scores. Continue until all the rockets are used. The student with the highest total score is the winner.

 Kinesthetic

Have the students take turns "writing" the spelling words on a chalkboard with a flashlight as the other students watch the light and write the word at their desks. Then have them copy the words three times each.

Language and Cultural Differences

Have the students say each word aloud while listening for /ô/ and /ôr/. These sounds may be difficult for some students to hear because of regional pronunciation differences or language backgrounds that do not include these sounds. For example, since the Spanish language does not have /ô/, it may be difficult for Spanish-speaking students to identify and reproduce this sound. Have the students hold their jaws and feel the movement of their mouths as they say the spelling words aloud.

MANAGING INSTRUCTION

3–5 Day Plan		Average	Below Average	Above Average
Day 1	**Day 1**	Pretest Spelling Mini-Lesson, p. T62 Spelling and Thinking, p. 62	Pretest Spelling Mini-Lesson, p. T62 Spelling and Thinking, p. 62	Pretest Spelling and Thinking, p. 62
	Day 2	Spelling and Vocabulary, p. 63	Spelling and Vocabulary, p. 63 (or) Unit 10 Practice Master, A and B	Spelling and Vocabulary, p. 63 Spelling and Reading, p. 64
Day 2	**Day 3**	Spelling and Reading, p. 64	Spelling and Reading, p. 64 (or) Unit 10 Practice Master, C and D	Challenge Activities, p. 232
	Day 4	Spelling and Writing, p. 65 Unit 10 Homework Master	Spelling and Writing, p. 65	Spelling and Writing, p. 65 Unit 10 Homework Master
Day 3	**Day 5**	Weekly Test	Weekly Test	Weekly Test

Vocabulary Connections (pages 66 and 67) may be used anytime during this unit.

Objectives

Spelling and Thinking

Students will
- **read** the spelling words in list form and in context.
- **sort** the spelling words according to the /ôr/ and /ô/ vowel sounds.
- **read** and remember this week's spelling strategy.

UNIT PRETEST

Use **Pretest Sentences** below. Refer to the self-checking procedures on student page 256. You may wish to use the **Unit 10 Word List Overhead Transparency** as part of the checking procedure.

TEACHING THE STRATEGY

Spelling Mini-Lesson

Tell the students that in this lesson they will spell words that have either the **aw** sound or the **or** sound. Write **haul** /ô/ and **sport** /ôr/ on the chalkboard. Ask volunteers to pronounce the words. Then explain that each symbol represents the vowel sound heard in that word.

Pronounce each word and ask the students which vowel sound they hear. (You may wish to help them distinguish between /ô/ and /ôr/ by purposely overemphasizing each vowel sound.) As the students choose, ask a volunteer to write each word under **haul** /ô/ or **sport** /ôr/.

When you get to **record** you should note that the word can be pronounced in two different ways, depending on context. (rĭ kôrd´ or rĕk´ ərd) Explain that in this lesson, **record** is used as a verb. (rĭ kôrd´)

When all the spelling words are listed, ask the students what they notice about the spellings of the vowel sounds. (Point out that /ô/ can be spelled in three different ways: **au, augh,** or **ough.**) Explain that the consonants **gh** are silent but contribute to the spelling of the vowel sound.

Conclude by reading **Remember the Spelling Strategy** on page 62.

Order of answers may vary.

/ôr/
1. forgot
2. nor ★
3. forest ★
4. sport
5. port
6. sort ★
7. record ★
8. forth
9. report ★
10. forty

/ô/
11. haul
12. because ★
13. caught ★
14. daughter
15. taught
16. bought ★
17. ought
18. thought ★
19. brought ★
20. fought

READ THE SPELLING WORDS

1.	forgot	*forgot*	I almost **forgot** my friend's birthday.
2.	bought	*bought*	Wayne **bought** a new pair of shoes.
3.	nor	*nor*	Neither rain **nor** snow will bother us.
4.	haul	*haul*	A mule can **haul** heavy loads.
5.	ought	*ought*	You **ought** to eat a balanced diet.
6.	forest	*forest*	Squirrels prefer a **forest** of oak.
7.	sport	*sport*	Baseball is my favorite **sport**.
8.	thought	*thought*	We **thought** it would rain today.
9.	daughter	*daughter*	Her **daughter** is taller than she is.
10.	port	*port*	The storm kept the ship in **port**.
11.	sort	*sort*	We will **sort** the mail by date.
12.	record	*record*	I will **record** the things I did today.
13.	taught	*taught*	We **taught** our dog to do tricks.
14.	brought	*brought*	My brother **brought** a friend home.
15.	forth	*forth*	Go **forth** and do your best.
16.	because	*because*	I ran home **because** I was late.
17.	fought	*fought*	My grandfather **fought** in a war.
18.	report	*report*	Please **report** your findings.
19.	forty	*forty*	My aunt lives **forty** miles away.
20.	caught	*caught*	I **caught** six fish at the lake.

SORT THE SPELLING WORDS

1.–10. Write the spelling words in which the /ôr/ sound is spelled **or**.

11.–20. Write the spelling words in which the /ô/ sound is spelled **au, augh,** or **ough**.

REMEMBER THE SPELLING STRATEGY

The **r**-controlled vowel sound you hear in **sport** (/ôr/) is spelled **or**. The vowel sound you hear in **haul** (/ô/) can be spelled in different ways: **au** in **haul**, **augh** in **caught**, and **ough** in **ought**.

62

Pretest Sentences (See procedures on pages Z10–Z11.)

1. Dad **forgot** to give us money for lunch.
2. I **bought** a new watch.
3. The boys liked neither hiking **nor** fishing.
4. They will **haul** dirt to fill in the hole.
5. We **ought** to eat more vegetables.
6. There are many pine trees in the **forest**.
7. Basketball is my favorite **sport**.
8. She **thought** she would go for a walk.
9. Mr. and Mrs. Patel have a new **daughter**.
10. The ship's passengers will shop at the next **port**.
11. Please **sort** the clothes before you wash them.
12. Dejuan wanted to **record** his brother's speech.
13. The lifeguard **taught** me to swim.
14. They **brought** their children to the party.
15. The swing moved back and **forth**.
16. I wore no hat **because** it was warm.
17. Our ancestors **fought** for freedom.
18. Every night we watch the news **report**.
19. Of all the books, only **forty** are new.
20. Matthew ran swiftly and **caught** the ball.

Spelling and Vocabulary

Word Meanings

Write the spelling word that goes with each meaning.

1. past tense of **buy**
2. a harbor town where ships dock
3. and not; or not; not either
4. forward; into full sight
5. past tense of **bring**
6. a game, often a competition
7. an account

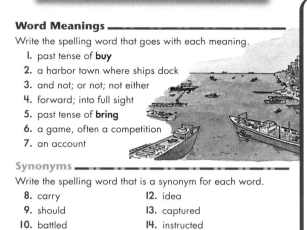

Synonyms

Write the spelling word that is a synonym for each word.

8. carry
9. should
10. battled
11. arrange
12. idea
13. captured
14. instructed

USING THE Dictionary

The dictionary identifies stressed syllables with an accent mark (′) and boldface type. Find these spelling words in your **Spelling Dictionary**. Write each one, and underline the syllable that receives the greater stress.

15. forgot
16. because
17. forest
18. daughter
19. report
20. forty

Word Meanings

1. bought
2. port
3. nor
4. forth
5. brought
6. sport
7. report

Synonyms

8. haul
9. ought
10. fought
11. sort
12. thought
13. caught
14. taught

Using the Dictionary

15. forgot
16. because
17. forest
18. daughter
19. report
20. forty

63

Objectives

Spelling and Vocabulary

Students will

- **identify** and write spelling words to match meanings.
- **choose** and write spelling words that are synonyms.
- **use** the **Spelling Dictionary** to show stressed syllables in spelling words.

Developing Oral Language Skills

Have students work in pairs. The first student asks a question that includes one of the spelling words from the spelling list. For example, the student might ask, "Do you play a **sport**?" The second student answers the question. The answer must also include a spelling word, but the spelling word must not contain the same vowel sound studied in this unit. For example, the second student might answer, "You **ought** to know I play baseball." **Sport** includes the /ôr/ sound, while **ought** includes the /ô/ sound.

MEETING INDIVIDUAL NEEDS

Providing More Help

Have the students make worksheets by drawing pictures to illustrate as many of the spelling words as they can. Tell the students to draw a blank beside each illustration. Where it is not possible to illustrate a spelling word (**nor, ought**), have the students write a sentence that includes the word, leaving a blank in place of the word. Have the students exchange their worksheets and fill in the blanks. Ask them to check each other's papers.

★ Students who need to study fewer words should use the **Alternate Word List**. This list is starred on page T62 in the Teacher Edition. The **Unit 10 Practice Masters** (*Teacher Resource Book*) provide additional practice with these words.

Unit 10 Practice Masters

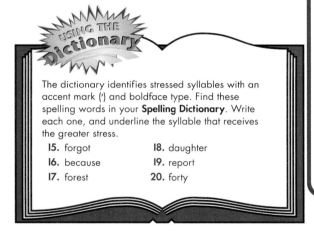

Objectives

Spelling and Reading

Students will
- **replace** words in sentences with spelling words.
- **write** spelling words for clues.
- **complete** a paragraph using spelling words.

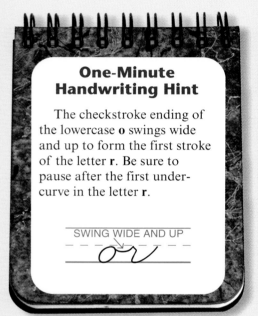

One-Minute Handwriting Hint

The checkstroke ending of the lowercase **o** swings wide and up to form the first stroke of the letter **r**. Be sure to pause after the first undercurve in the letter **r**.

SWING WIDE AND UP

Legible handwriting can boost spelling scores by as much as 20%.

Replace the Words
1. bought
2. forgot
3. brought
4. caught
5. fought
6. thought
7. taught

Use the Clues
8. port
9. daughter
10. sort
11. forty

Complete the Paragraph
12. sport
13. forest
14. report
15. record
16. ought
17. because
18. haul
19. forth
20. nor

Spelling and Reading

forgot	bought	nor	haul	ought
forest	sport	thought	daughter	port
sort	record	taught	brought	forth
because	fought	report	forty	caught

Replace the Words For each sentence, write the spelling word that is the past tense of the underlined verb.

1. Show me what you <u>buy</u> at the store.
2. I almost <u>forget</u> that today is your birthday.
3. Carlos <u>brings</u> his stamp collection to school.
4. Maria <u>catches</u> the ball for the third out.
5. Before they became friends, the two boys <u>fight</u> a lot.
6. I <u>think</u> the answer was simple.
7. Mrs. King <u>teaches</u> us how to paint with water colors.

Use the Clues Write a spelling word for each clue.

8. a good place for ships
9. a parent's female child
10. put in groups
11. twenty-eight and twelve

Complete the Paragraph Write a spelling word from the box to fill each blank in the story.

My favorite __12.__ is horseback riding. Sometimes I ride through the __13.__. When I return, I like to __14.__ my experiences to my friends and __15.__ my thoughts in my diary. A horseback rider __16.__ to carry as little as possible. That is __17.__ the more you __18.__ the harder it is for your horse. A rider should go __19.__ with a respect for nature. He or she should disturb neither animals __20.__ plants, so they will still be there for all to enjoy.

forth
ought
sport
record
forest
because
report
nor
haul

64

MEETING INDIVIDUAL NEEDS

Providing More Challenge

Challenge Words and **Challenge Activities** for Unit 10 appear on page 232. **Challenge Word Test Sentences** appear on page T232.

Unit 10 Challenge Activities

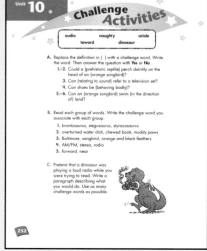

Weekly Test Options

Option 1:
One Spelling Word Per Sentence

(See procedures on pages Z10–Z11.)

1. I had no part in the play, **nor** did I want one.
2. They rode back and **forth** on the train.
3. Mother had to **sort** out my mail.
4. Robin knows much about the **sport** of golf.
5. We sat with a crowd of **forty** people.
6. The ship sailed into **port**.
7. I **forgot** to call home.
8. I **brought** my books home to study.
9. The teacher sent Gwen's parents a good **report**.
10. The teacher will **record** our test grades.
11. I **ought** to clean my room.
12. Many men and women **fought** to keep our land free.
13. He threw the ball and I **caught** it.
14. There are many oak trees in the **forest**.
15. My mother **thought** I did a fine job.
16. We will **haul** the wood in a cart.

Spelling and Writing

Proofread a Story

Six words are not spelled correctly in this story. Write those words correctly.

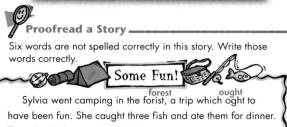

Some Fun!

Sylvia went camping in the *forist*, a trip which *oght* to [forest] [ought]

have been fun. She caught three fish and ate them for dinner.

Then she had a good night's sleep.

Her trip home, however, was not pleasant *bicause* she [because]

fergot her compass and lost her way. Then she remembered [forgot]

what her mother had *taugt* her: Moss grows on the north side [taught]

of trees. Home is south of here, she *thot*, so I should go in the [thought]

opposite direction from the moss.

She did and learned an important lesson: Before going

camping, check to see that you have all your supplies.

Proofreading Marks

≡ Make a capital.

/ Make a small letter.

∧ Add something.

℮ Take out something.

⊙ Add a period.

⌗ New paragraph.

SP Spelling error.

Write a Story

Narrative Writing

Write a story from your imagination. Include all the information your reader will want to know. Be sure to tell

- the name of the main character.
- where the main character is.
- what he or she does.
- what happens and how the story ends.

Use as many spelling words as you can.

Proofread Your Writing During

Proofread your writing for spelling errors as part of the editing stage in the writing process. Be sure to check each word carefully. Use a dictionary to check spelling if you are not sure.

Writing Process

Prewriting
⇩
Drafting
⇩
Revising
⇩
Editing
⇩
Publishing

65

Objectives

Spelling and Writing

Students will
- **proofread** a story.
- **use** the writing process to write a story.
- **proofread** their writing.

Using the Writing Process

Before assigning **Write a Story,** see pages 258–259 in the Student Edition for a complete review of the writing process and additional writing assignments. You may also wish to refer to pages Z12–Z13 in the Teacher Edition.

Keeping a Spelling Journal

Encourage students to record the words they misspelled on the weekly test in a personal spelling journal. These words may be recycled for future study. Students may also wish to include words from their writing. See pages Z12–Z13 in the Teacher Edition for more information.

---

17. The benches are dry **because** the sun came out.
18. We **bought** a box of fruit.
19. A friend **taught** me how to ride a bike.
20. Mrs. Brown has a son and a **daughter**.

Option 2:
Multiple Spelling Words Per Sentence
(See procedures on pages Z10–Z11.)

1. My teacher asked me to come **forth** and read my **report**.
2. There were **forty** ships in the **port**.
3. I have not **caught** one cold this year, **nor** do I want one!
4. I **forgot** to **haul** the dirt to my house.
5. The man had to **sort** out all of the mail that was **brought** to him.
6. We **bought** a tape **because** we wanted to **record** the sounds of the **forest**.
7. The mother knew she **ought** to read more to her **daughter**.
8. Father **fought** for what he **thought** was right.
9. We were **taught** the rules of the **sport**.

Option 3:
Standardized Test
(See *Teacher Resource Book,* Unit 10.)

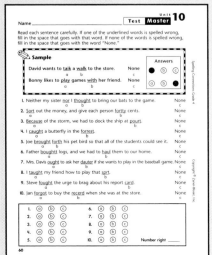

Unit 10 Test Master

T65

Objectives

Strategy Words

Students will
- **review** words studied previously that are related to the spelling strategy.
- **preview** unknown words that are related to the spelling strategy.

Remind the students that the **Strategy Words** relate to the spelling patterns they have studied in this unit. The **Review Words** are below grade level, and the **Preview Words** are above grade level. You may wish to use the following sentences to introduce the words in context.

Review Words:
Words From Grade 3

1. We will study our words **before** we take the test.
2. Let us look at the **form** for writing the business letter.
3. In the **morning** we will write a paragraph using our new words.
4. All of the desks in the classroom should be facing **north**.
5. Tell us a **story** about the beginning of our country.

Preview Words:
Words From Grade 5

6. The **audience** clapped and clapped after the performance.
7. Who is the **author** of your favorite book?
8. That is an **enormous** pile of dirt in the backyard.
9. It is **important** that you get the class notes you missed while you were away.
10. He is set to **launch** his radio-controlled boat.

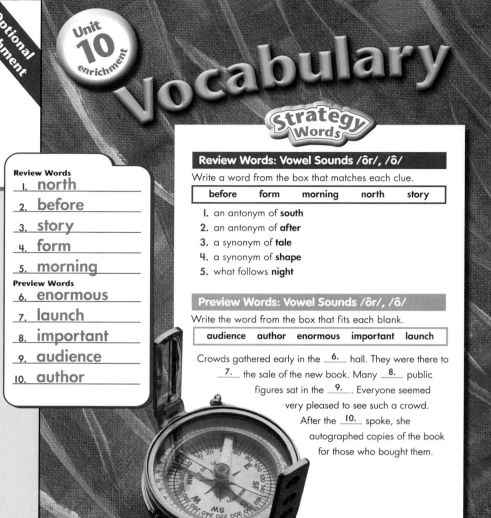

Unit 10 enrichment

Vocabulary

Strategy Words

Review Words
1. north
2. before
3. story
4. form
5. morning

Preview Words
6. enormous
7. launch
8. important
9. audience
10. author

Review Words: Vowel Sounds /ôr/, /ô/

Write a word from the box that matches each clue.

before	form	morning	north	story

1. an antonym of **south**
2. an antonym of **after**
3. a synonym of **tale**
4. a synonym of **shape**
5. what follows **night**

Preview Words: Vowel Sounds /ôr/, /ô/

Write the word from the box that fits each blank.

audience	author	enormous	important	launch

Crowds gathered early in the __6.__ hall. They were there to __7.__ the sale of the new book. Many __8.__ public figures sat in the __9.__. Everyone seemed very pleased to see such a crowd. After the __10.__ spoke, she autographed copies of the book for those who bought them.

66

Unit 10 RECAP

You may wish to assign the **Unit 10 Homework Master** (*Teacher Resource Book*, Unit 10) as a fun way to recap the spelling words.

Unit 10 Homework Master

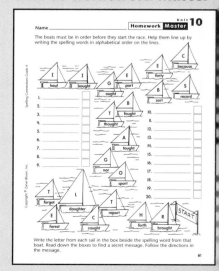

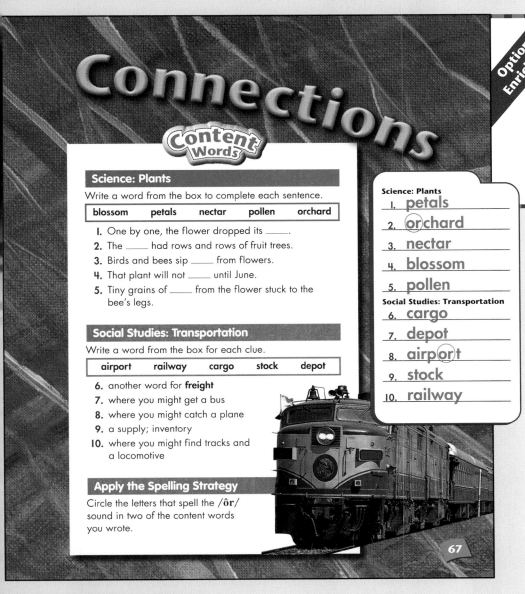

Connections

Content Words

Science: Plants

Write a word from the box to complete each sentence.

blossom	petals	nectar	pollen	orchard

1. One by one, the flower dropped its _____.
2. The _____ had rows and rows of fruit trees.
3. Birds and bees sip _____ from flowers.
4. That plant will not _____ until June.
5. Tiny grains of _____ from the flower stuck to the bee's legs.

Social Studies: Transportation

Write a word from the box for each clue.

airport	railway	cargo	stock	depot

6. another word for **freight**
7. where you might get a bus
8. where you might catch a plane
9. a supply; inventory
10. where you might find tracks and a locomotive

Apply the Spelling Strategy

Circle the letters that spell the /ôr/ sound in two of the content words you wrote.

Science: Plants
1. petals
2. or̲chard
3. nectar
4. blossom
5. pollen

Social Studies: Transportation
6. cargo
7. depot
8. airpor̲t
9. stock
10. railway

67

Unit 11 Home Study Master

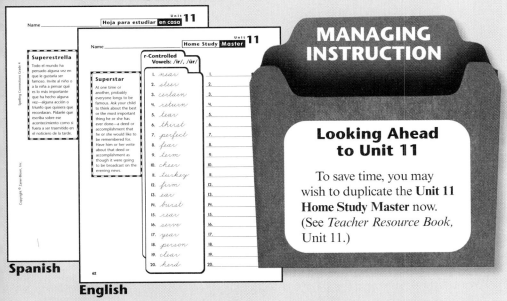

Spanish

English

Objectives

Content Words

Students will
- **expand** vocabulary with content-related words.
- **relate** the spelling strategy to words outside the basic spelling list.

Content Words

Science: Plants

Review the meanings of these words with the students. You may wish to use these sentences to introduce the words in context.

1. The flower bud will soon be a beautiful full **blossom**.
2. A rose has many **petals**.
3. Bees get **nectar** from the flowers to make honey.
4. **Pollen** is the powdery substance found in a flower.
5. Our class will make a trip to the apple **orchard** next week.

Encourage the students to use these words to label a drawing showing parts of a flower.

Social Studies: Transportation

Review the meanings of these words with the students. You may wish to use these sentences to introduce the words in context.

6. Our plane will be arriving at the **airport** soon.
7. There is an overhead **railway** system in the big city.
8. A ship can carry lots of **cargo**.
9. The crew will **stock** the cruise ship with plenty of food for the trip.
10. We will be meeting my grandparents at the bus **depot** soon.

Encourage the students to use these words in a personal narrative about a trip they took or would like to take.

MANAGING INSTRUCTION

Looking Ahead to Unit 11

To save time, you may wish to duplicate the **Unit 11 Home Study Master** now. (See *Teacher Resource Book*, Unit 11.)

Basic Spelling List

near	turkey
steer	firm
certain	ear
return	burst
tear	rear
thirst	serve
perfect	year
fear	person
term	clear
cheer	herd

Strategy Words

Review

curl	heard
dirt	herself
fur	

Preview

appear	circulate
burnt	deserve
career	

Content Words

Health: Exercise

injure	stretching
strain	risk
jogging	

Social Studies: In Court

fact	justice
jury	juror
honor	

Individual Needs

Challenge Words

terse	reindeer
burden	earrings
skirted	

Alternate Word List

near	cheer
certain	firm
return	year
tear	person
fear	clear

T68A

MATERIALS

Student Edition

Pages 68–73
Challenge Activities, p. 233

Teacher Edition

Pages T68A–T73
Challenge Activities, p. T233

Other Resources

Spelling Connections Software
Unit 11 Word List Overhead
  Transparency

Teacher Resource Book

Unit 11 Home Study Master
  (English or Spanish; students
  may pretest on this sheet or use
  it for home practice.)
Unit 11 Homework Master
Unit 11 Practice Masters
Flip Folder Practice Master
Unit 11 Test Master

Visit our Web site, www.zaner-bloser.com

OBJECTIVES

Spelling and Thinking

Students will
- **read** the spelling words in list form and in context.
- **sort** the words according to /îr/ and /ûr/ sounds and spelling patterns.
- **read** and remember this week's spelling strategy.

Spelling and Vocabulary

Students will
- **write** spelling words that match definitions.
- **identify** and write spelling words that have an **ear** spelling pattern.
- **add** and subtract letters from words to write spelling words.
- **use** the **Spelling Dictionary** to write homographs and their parts of speech.

Spelling and Reading

Students will
- **complete** sentences using spelling words.
- **write** spelling words to complete a series of meaning-related words.
- **solve** analogies using spelling words.

Spelling and Writing

Students will
- **proofread** a travel report.
- **use** the writing process to write a travel report.
- **proofread** their writing.

MEETING INDIVIDUAL NEEDS
Learning Styles

Visual

On the chalkboard, draw three columns and label them **ir, ur,** and **er**. Write each spelling word that has the /ûr/ sound on a 3" × 5" card. Use a green marker to write the letters that spell the /ûr/ sound. Pass the cards out to the students. Have each student pronounce the spelling word on his or her card and then write it in the correct column on the chalkboard. Then have the students copy the words onto paper, using a green crayon to draw a box around the letters that spell the /ûr/ sound. Repeat this procedure for the words that have the /îr/ sound, using the color red to write or mark the letters that spell the sound.

Auditory

Use the 3" × 5" cards from the visual activity. Place the cards facedown on a table. Have each student in turn choose a card, pronounce the word on the card and spell it aloud, and then replace the card on the table. When all have spelled a word, divide the group into two teams. The first player from Team A chooses a card and pronounces the word. The students on Team B then write the word on paper as they say each letter quietly to themselves. Have the teams take turns drawing cards.

Kinesthetic

Use the cards from the visual activity. Hold up a word card. If the card has the /ûr/ sound, have the students stand and turn around as they spell the word aloud. Then have them write the word on their papers. If the card has the /îr/ sound, have the students place their hands over their ears as they spell the word aloud. Then have them write the words on their papers.

Language and Cultural Differences

Some students may have difficulty spelling the **r**-controlled vowel sounds due to regional pronunciations or different language backgrounds. In some English dialects, for example, the **r** sound in some of the spelling words is only slightly pronounced or not pronounced at all. However, correct spelling can be achieved without exact pronunciation, provided that the student has the opportunity to associate the meaning of the word with the visual sequence of letters.

Say each word and write it on the chalkboard. Have a volunteer circle the letters that spell the /îr/ sound and box the letters that spell the /ûr/ sound. Have a volunteer repeat each word and use it in a sentence. Then have the students write each word three times.

MANAGING INSTRUCTION

3–5 Day Plan		Average	Below Average	Above Average
Day 1	**Day 1**	Pretest Spelling Mini-Lesson, p. T68 Spelling and Thinking, p. 68	Pretest Spelling Mini-Lesson, p. T68 Spelling and Thinking, p. 68	Pretest Spelling and Thinking, p. 68
	Day 2	Spelling and Vocabulary, p. 69	Spelling and Vocabulary, p. 69 (or) Unit 11 Practice Master, A and B	Spelling and Vocabulary, p. 69 Spelling and Reading, p. 70
Day 2	**Day 3**	Spelling and Reading, p. 70	Spelling and Reading, p. 70 (or) Unit 11 Practice Master, C and D	Challenge Activities, p. 233
	Day 4	Spelling and Writing, p. 71 Unit 11 Homework Master	Spelling and Writing, p. 71	Spelling and Writing, p. 71 Unit 11 Homework Master
Day 3	**Day 5**	Weekly Test	Weekly Test	Weekly Test

Vocabulary Connections (pages 72 and 73) may be used anytime during this unit.

Objectives

Spelling and Thinking

Students will
- **read** the spelling words in list form and in context.
- **sort** the words according to /îr/ and /ûr/ sounds and spelling patterns.
- **read** and remember this week's spelling strategy.

UNIT PRETEST

Use **Pretest Sentences** below. Refer to the self-checking procedures on student page 256. You may wish to use the **Unit 11 Word List Overhead Transparency** as part of the checking procedure.

TEACHING THE STRATEGY

Spelling Mini-Lesson

Ask the students to find the animal name on the spelling list. (turkey) Ask what kind of sound a turkey makes. (Most American students will respond "gobble-gobble.") Explain that in China a turkey sound is described as "ko-ko-ko," in Japan as "ku-ku," and in France as "cot-cot."

Ask what words Americans use to name the sound pigs are said to make. ("oink, oink") Tell them that in Poland a pig's squeal is described as "kwick-kwick," in Russia as "khru," and in Italy as "fron-fron-fron."

Explain that **turkey** includes an **r**-controlled vowel sound. Ask students to recall why some vowels are said to be **r**-controlled. (The r after the vowel affects the way we pronounce the vowel.)

Write /ûr/ on the board. Explain that this symbol represents the **r**-controlled vowel sound in **turkey**. Write /îr/ on the board. Explain that the symbol represents the vowel sound we hear in **ear**.

Ask volunteers to pronounce each spelling word and decide if the **r**-controlled vowel sounds like /ûr/ or /îr/. Write each word in the appropriate column. (Point out that in this unit, **tear** is pronounced /tîr/ and means a "drop of liquid from the eye.")

Conclude by reading **Remember the Spelling Strategy** on page 68.

T68

Order of answers may vary.

ear or eer

1. near ★
2. steer
3. tear ★
4. fear ★
5. cheer ★
6. ear
7. rear
8. year ★
9. clear ★

er

10. certain ★
11. perfect
12. term
13. serve
14. person ★
15. herd

ir or ur

16. return ★
17. thirst
18. turkey
19. firm
20. burst

READ THE SPELLING WORDS

1.	near	*near*	I was **near** enough to touch the president.
2.	steer	*steer*	He is learning to **steer** his unicycle.
3.	certain	*certain*	Are you **certain** of the answer?
4.	return	*return*	My **return** address is on the card.
5.	tear	*tear*	The child wiped a **tear** from his eye.
6.	thirst	*thirst*	The heat of the day increased our **thirst**.
7.	perfect	*perfect*	He threw a nearly **perfect** pitch.
8.	fear	*fear*	Those who **fear** failure should try anyway.
9.	term	*term*	The first school **term** is over.
10.	cheer	*cheer*	They came to **cheer** for our team.
11.	turkey	*turkey*	We will eat **turkey** on Thanksgiving.
12.	firm	*firm*	Once on **firm** ground, I was safe.
13.	ear	*ear*	I held the seashell up to my **ear**.
14.	burst	*burst*	The soap bubble **burst** in the air.
15.	rear	*rear*	We marched at the **rear** of the parade.
16.	serve	*serve*	The waiter came to **serve** our party.
17.	year	*year*	A **year** is twelve months long.
18.	person	*person*	The price was $5 per **person**.
19.	clear	*clear*	We expect **clear** and sunny weather.
20.	herd	*herd*	In the field was a **herd** of cows.

SORT THE SPELLING WORDS

1.–9. Write the spelling words that spell the /îr/ sound **ear** or **eer**.

10.–15. Write the spelling words that spell the /ûr/ sound **er**.

16.–20. Write the spelling words that spell the /ûr/ sound **ir** or **ur**.

REMEMBER THE SPELLING STRATEGY

Remember that the **r**-controlled vowel sound you hear in **near** (/îr/) can be spelled in different ways: **ear** in **near** and **eer** in **cheer**.

The **r**-controlled vowel sound you hear in **firm** (/ûr/) can be spelled in different ways: **ir** in **firm**, **er** in **herd**, or **ur** in **burst**.

Pretest Sentences (See procedures on pages Z10–Z11.)

1. It is a short walk since I live **near** the school.
2. If you want your bike to stay on the road, you must **steer** it.
3. Are you **certain** that the show begins at seven o'clock?
4. Helen has been on vacation but is due to **return** home today.
5. As I watched the sad movie, a **tear** rolled down my cheek.
6. Demarco built up a **thirst** as he ran.
7. Mike knew all the answers, so he had a **perfect** test score.
8. When the lion at the zoo roared, I was filled with **fear**.
9. The second school **term** is nearly over.
10. The boys sat together at the game to **cheer** for their team.
11. The **turkey** is a large bird.
12. When it was chilled, the jelly became **firm**.
13. I can hear better if I cup my hand around my **ear**.
14. As she read the funny story aloud, Katie **burst** into laughter.
15. If you are at the end of the line, you are in the **rear**.
16. Dad will **serve** dinner on the porch tonight.
17. On your birthday you will be another **year** older.
18. An author is a **person** who writes a book or other work.
19. We were able to see through the **clear** glass.
20. The cows stood together in a **herd**.

Spelling and Vocabulary

Word Meanings

Write a spelling word that has the same meaning as each word or phrase.

1. come back
2. a need for liquid
3. a period of time; reign
4. break open suddenly
5. offer food
6. a group of animals

Phonics

7. Write the spelling word that has only three letters.

8.–13. Write spelling words that rhyme with the word you just wrote and that spell the /îr/ sound the same way.

Word Math

Follow the directions to write spelling words.

14. certify – ify + ain = _____
15. perhaps – haps + son = _____
16. first – st + m = _____
17. perplex – plex + fect = _____
18. turban – ban + key = _____

 USING THE Dictionary

Find these homographs in your **Spelling Dictionary**. Beside each word write the number of the definition and the letter that tells what part of speech it is.

19. steer
20. cheer

◆ ◆ ◆

Dictionary Check Be sure to check the part of speech in your **Spelling Dictionary**.

Word Meanings
1. return
2. thirst
3. term
4. burst
5. serve
6. herd

Phonics
7. ear
8. near
9. tear
10. fear
11. rear
12. year
13. clear

Word Math
14. certain
15. person
16. firm
17. perfect
18. turkey

Using the Dictionary
19. steer 1, v. 2, n.
20. cheer 1, n. 2, v.

69

Developing Oral Language Skills

Do a word sort by sound. Write /îr/ and /ûr/ on a chalkboard or an overhead transparency. Then have a volunteer read the spelling word list, asking students to write each word under one of the two headings according to the sound it contains. When they have finished listing the words, ask students to repeat the words and consider the letters in each word that spell one of the target sounds. Then have volunteers circle the letters that spell the sounds.

MEETING INDIVIDUAL NEEDS

Providing More Help

Write each spelling word on a 3" × 5" card. Place all of the cards in a box or can. Then make two columns on the chalkboard labeled /îr/ and /ûr/. Write **ear** and **eer** under the /îr/ heading, and write **ir, er,** and **ur** under the /ûr/ heading. Have the students take turns choosing a card, reading the word aloud, and writing it on the chalkboard in the proper column. Then have each student circle the letters that spell the **r-**controlled vowel sound they hear in the word.

★ Students who need to study fewer words should use the **Alternate Word List**. This list is starred on page T68 in the Teacher Edition. The **Unit 11 Practice Masters** (*Teacher Resource Book*) provide additional practice with these words.

Unit 11 Practice Masters

Name _____

Practice Master Unit **11**

| 1. near | 3. year | 5. clear | 7. firm | 9. person |
| 2. tear | 4. fear | 6. cheer | 8. certain | 10. return |

A. Write the spelling word that goes with each meaning.

1. to go back, give back, or send back _____
2. a drop of liquid from the eye _____
3. a human being _____
4. to encourage by yelling _____
5. 365 days _____
6. sure _____
7. not far away _____
8. a feeling of fright _____
9. not fuzzy _____
10. hard or solid _____

B. Write the spelling word that goes with each group of words.

1. shout, yell, _____
2. day, week, month, _____
3. solid, stiff, hard, _____
4. alarm, fright, horror, _____
5. liquid, droplet, _____
6. sure, positive, definite, _____

64

Practice Master Unit **11**

| firm | person |
| certain | return |

...ch sentence.

...words hidden in the puzzle. Circle

65

T69

Spelling and Reading

Students will
- **complete** sentences using spelling words.
- **write** spelling words to complete a series of meaning-related words.
- **solve** analogies using spelling words.

One-Minute Handwriting Hint

There are two pauses in the lowercase **r**. Be sure to make a good slant-right stroke so the letter will have the correct width.

Legible handwriting can boost spelling scores by as much as 20%.

Spelling and Reading

near	steer	certain	return	tear
thirst	perfect	fear	term	cheer
turkey	firm	ear	burst	rear
serve	year	person	clear	herd

Complete the Sentences   Write two spelling words to complete each sentence.

1.–2. Whitney would like to _____ one _____ as the class president.

3.–4. Please wait _____ this bench until I _____.

5.–6. That _____ has a voice that is pleasing to the _____.

Group the Words   Write the spelling word that goes with each group.

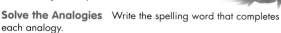

7. sparrow, crow, chicken, _____
8. shout, yell, _____
9. day, week, month, _____
10. solid, stiff, hard, _____
11. alarm, fright, horror, _____
12. drive, guide, operate, _____
13. sure, positive, definite, _____
14. correct, excellent, _____
15. liquid, droplet, _____

Complete the Sentences
1. serve
2. term
3. near
4. return
5. person
6. ear

Group the Words
7. turkey
8. cheer
9. year
10. firm
11. fear
12. steer
13. certain
14. perfect
15. tear

Solve the Analogies
16. thirst
17. burst
18. clear
19. rear
20. herd

Solve the Analogies   Write the spelling word that completes each analogy.

16. **Food** is to **hunger** as **water** is to _____.
17. **Glass** is to **break** as **balloon** is to _____.
18. **Cloudy** is to **overcast** as **sunny** is to _____.
19. **Face** is to **front** as **back** is to _____.
20. **Birds** are to **flock** as **cattle** are to _____.

70

MEETING INDIVIDUAL NEEDS
Providing More Challenge

Challenge Words and **Challenge Activities** for Unit 11 appear on page 233. **Challenge Word Test Sentences** appear on page T233.

Unit 11 Challenge Activities

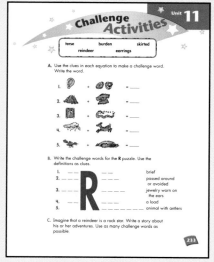

Weekly Test Options
Option 1:
One Spelling Word Per Sentence

(See procedures on pages Z10–Z11.)

1. Many animals were in the large **herd**.
2. Her voice was soft but **firm**.
3. Do you want to ride in the front or **rear** of the bus?
4. She does not hear well in her left **ear**.
5. After the fog lifted, the air became **clear**.
6. Mom will **steer** the boat.
7. I have a great **thirst** for juice.
8. She will go to school next **year**.
9. Nice music will **cheer** me up if I begin to feel sad.
10. To be afraid of something means that you **fear** it.
11. The table is **perfect**, since it doesn't have a scratch on it.
12. That doll can cry a real **tear**.
13. Your left shoe is **near** your right shoe.
14. You must **return** the tape to the same store.
15. My best friend is a nice **person**.

Spelling and Writing

Proofread a Travel Report

Six words are not spelled correctly in this travel report. Write those words correctly.

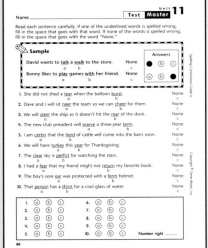

San Diego in the Fall

San Diego is a great city to visit any time of the *yeer*. My
family chose fall and was not disappointed. The weather
was bright and *cleer* in October. If you go, have no fear of
public transportation. We rode all over the city, and even to
Mexico and back, for $3 a *pearson* per day. Take a trolley,
a bus, a boat. The sightseeing is *purfect*. We hope to make
a *riturn* visit there. I am *sertain* you will want to revisit that
city also.

(corrections shown above words: year, clear, person, perfect, return, certain)

Proofreading Marks

≡	Make a capital.
/	Make a small letter.
∧	Add something.
ℒ	Take out something.
⊙	Add a period.
⌗	New paragraph
⑤Ⓟ	Spelling error

Write a Travel Report

Descriptive Writing

Write a report about a place you have visited or would like to visit. Be sure to include

- the name of the place.
- what you like about it.
- the best time to visit it.
- how to get around there.
- what to see there.

Use as many spelling words as you can.

Proofread Your Writing During

Proofread your writing for spelling errors as part of the editing stage in the writing process. Be sure to check each word carefully. Use a dictionary to check spelling if you are not sure.

Writing Process

Prewriting
⇩
Drafting
⇩
Revising
⇩
Editing
⇩
Publishing

71

Objectives

Spelling and Writing

Students will
- **proofread** a travel report.
- **use** the writing process to write a travel report.
- **proofread** their writing.

Using the Writing Process

Before assigning **Write a Travel Report** in this unit, see pages 258–259 in the Student Edition for a complete review of the writing process and additional writing assignments. You may also wish to refer to pages Z12–Z13 in the Teacher Edition.

Keeping a Spelling Journal

Encourage students to record the words they misspelled on the weekly test in a personal spelling journal. These words may be recycled for future study. Students may also wish to include words from their writing. See pages Z12–Z13 in the Teacher Edition for more information.

---

16. Mother was **certain** that you would want to go to the circus.
17. The balloon will **burst** if you stick a pin in it.
18. This school **term** will end next week.
19. One of these birds is a **turkey**.
20. Grandmother will **serve** juice to her friend.

Option 2:
Multiple Spelling Words Per Sentence
(See procedures on pages Z10–Z11.)

1. A **steer** broke away from the **herd near** our field.
2. I will **serve turkey** to the people in the **rear** of the room.
3. I have a **thirst** for a **certain** drink.
4. My teacher spoke with a **firm** voice when he told me to **return** to my seat.
5. My aunt will be the chief for a **term** of one **year**.
6. That **person** got a small cut on his **ear** when he fell.
7. A **perfect** day is when the air is **clear**.
8. I told him to **cheer** up after I saw a **tear** in his eye.
9. I **fear** he will **burst** out crying if I tell him the truth.

Option 3:
Standardized Test
(See *Teacher Resource Book,* Unit 11.)

Unit 11 Test Master

[Test Master worksheet for Unit 11 shown, with a Sample section and 10 numbered questions, plus an answer grid at the bottom.]

T71

Objectives

Strategy Words

Students will
- **review** words studied previously that are related to the spelling strategy.
- **preview** unknown words that are related to the spelling strategy.

Remind the students that the **Strategy Words** relate to the spelling patterns they have studied in this unit. The **Review Words** are below grade level, and the **Preview Words** are above grade level. You may wish to use the following sentences to introduce the words in context.

Review Words:
Words From Grade 3

1. The girl will **curl** her hair for the dance.
2. Do not get **dirt** all over your face.
3. The cloth was so soft that it felt like **fur**.
4. I **heard** a noise outside that sounded like a squirrel.
5. She told **herself** that she should always do her very best.

Preview Words:
Words From Grade 5

6. Does your cousin **appear** in the second act of the play?
7. The toast is **burnt**.
8. I would like to pursue a **career** in teaching.
9. You can **circulate** that picture around the room as I talk about it.
10. We **deserve** a good education in school, and we must work hard.

Review Words
1. fur
2. curl
3. heard
4. dirt
5. herself

Preview Words
6. appear
7. circulate
8. burnt
9. deserve
10. career

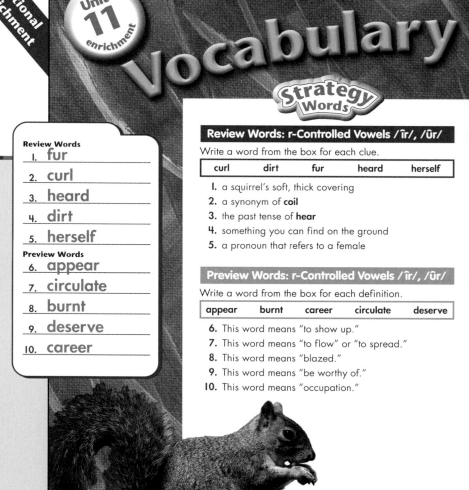

Vocabulary

Strategy Words

Review Words: r-Controlled Vowels /îr/, /ûr/

Write a word from the box for each clue.

curl	dirt	fur	heard	herself

1. a squirrel's soft, thick covering
2. a synonym of **coil**
3. the past tense of **hear**
4. something you can find on the ground
5. a pronoun that refers to a female

Preview Words: r-Controlled Vowels /îr/, /ûr/

Write a word from the box for each definition.

appear	burnt	career	circulate	deserve

6. This word means "to show up."
7. This word means "to flow" or "to spread."
8. This word means "blazed."
9. This word means "be worthy of."
10. This word means "occupation."

72

Unit **11** RECAP

You may wish to assign the **Unit 11 Homework Master** (*Teacher Resource Book*, Unit 11) as a fun way to recap the spelling words.

Unit 11 Homework Master

Connections

Objectives

Content Words

Students will
- **expand** vocabulary with content-related words.
- **relate** the spelling strategy to words outside the basic spelling list.

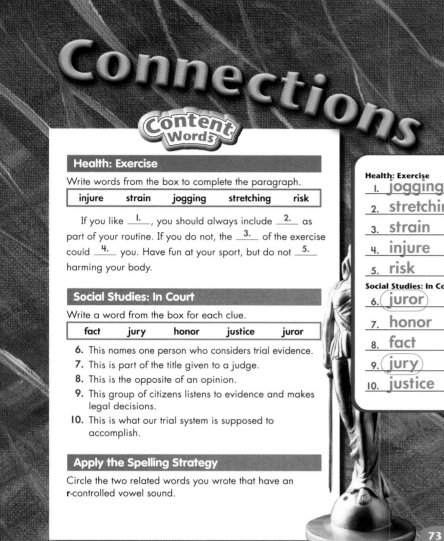

Content Words

Health: Exercise

Write words from the box to complete the paragraph.

injure	strain	jogging	stretching	risk

If you like __1.__, you should always include __2.__ as part of your routine. If you do not, the __3.__ of the exercise could __4.__ you. Have fun at your sport, but do not __5.__ harming your body.

Social Studies: In Court

Write a word from the box for each clue.

fact	jury	honor	justice	juror

6. This names one person who considers trial evidence.
7. This is part of the title given to a judge.
8. This is the opposite of an opinion.
9. This group of citizens listens to evidence and makes legal decisions.
10. This is what our trial system is supposed to accomplish.

Apply the Spelling Strategy

Circle the two related words you wrote that have an **r**-controlled vowel sound.

Health: Exercise
1. jogging
2. stretching
3. strain
4. injure
5. risk

Social Studies: In Court
6. juror
7. honor
8. fact
9. jury
10. justice

73

Health: Exercise

Review the meanings of these words with the students. You may wish to use these sentences to introduce the words in context.

1. You can **injure** yourself doing that stunt if you do not have the proper skills.
2. She might **strain** her muscles lifting those weights.
3. Many people go out **jogging** early in the morning.
4. Do your **stretching** exercises before starting to run.
5. You **risk** health problems if you do not get proper exercise.

Encourage the students to use these words in a paragraph about good health.

Social Studies: In Court

Review the meanings of these words with the students. You may wish to use these sentences to introduce the words in context.

6. Do not state anything that is not a **fact**.
7. The **jury** will determine if the accused is innocent.
8. It is a great **honor** to serve our country in some way.
9. We will watch the **justice** system at work.
10. A **juror** must listen carefully to the evidence presented.

Encourage the students to use these words to write a real or imaginary story about a courtroom scene.

Unit 12 Home Study Master

Spanish

English

MANAGING INSTRUCTION

Looking Ahead to Unit 12

To save time, you may wish to duplicate the **Unit 12 Home Study Master** now. (See *Teacher Resource Book,* Unit 12.)

Assessment Words

clothing	haunt
value	blouse
whom	ruin
pointed	mown
conserve	moan
thrown	inform
vault	tune
beard	growl
oyster	scorn
gear	fern

Review Words

Unit 7
clothes*	grown
hello*	also
moment*	poem
pillow*	obey
coast	shown

Unit 8
few*	true
lose*	fruit
used*	human
whose*	tube
music	rule

Unit 9
amount*	enjoy
choice*	mouth
flower*	power
moist*	vowel
however	crowd

Unit 10
because*	forest
brought*	record
caught*	bought
thought*	report
sort	nor

Unit 11
certain*	person
return*	firm
tear*	near
year*	fear
cheer	clear

* Posttest sentences and the **Unit 12 Test Master** test these words. Students review all words listed.

MATERIALS

Student Edition
Pages 74–79

Teacher Edition
Pages T74A–T79

Other Resources
Spelling Connections Software
Spelling and Writing
  Transparencies (Writing Prompt
  and Writing Model) for Unit 12

Teacher Resource Book
Unit 12 Home Study Master
  (English or Spanish; students
  may use this sheet for review or
  for home practice.)
Flip Folder Practice Master
Unit 12 Test Master

Visit our Web site, www.zaner-bloser.com

OBJECTIVES

Spelling and Assessment
Students will
- **assess** their spelling success by matching new words to the spelling strategies presented in Units 7–11.
- **connect** new words to the spelling strategies in Units 7–11.
- **write** new words that relate to the spelling strategies taught in Units 7–11.

Spelling and Review
Students will
- **review** and practice the spelling strategies and words in Units 7–11.
- **learn** an alternative spelling study strategy.

Spelling and Writing
Students will
- **review** the concept of common and proper nouns.
- **compose** a narrative piece of writing that tells about a time that they found something interesting or important.
- **learn** a proofreading strategy.
- **proofread** for correct compound words when using new technical language.

MEETING INDIVIDUAL NEEDS
Learning Styles

 Visual

Have a student choose a spelling word and draw a blank line on the chalkboard for each letter in the word. Let the other students take turns guessing the letters that belong in the blanks. When a letter is guessed, the first student writes it in the proper blank. If a guess is incorrect, the student draws one part of a stick figure (head, body, arms, legs, feet). If the players do not guess the word before the stick figure is drawn, the student gets another turn. When a player guesses a word correctly, she or he becomes the new leader.

 Auditory

Cut out a simple shape such as a jet plane or a rocket for each word. Write a spelling word on one side and the number of letters in the word on the other side.

Place the cut-outs in a pile in the center of a table. Have one student choose a shape and then pronounce and spell aloud the word on that shape. Have this student choose another student to pronounce the same word and spell it aloud. If both students spell the word correctly, both students score the number on the back of that shape. Continue until all the shapes are used. The student with the highest score is the winner.

 Kinesthetic

Have students take turns "writing" the spelling words on a chalkboard with a flashlight as the other students watch the light and write the word at their desks. Then have them copy the words three times each.

Language and Cultural Differences

Some students may have difficulty spelling the **r**-controlled sounds due to regional pronunciations or different language backgrounds. In some American dialects, for example, the **r** sound in some of the spelling words is only slightly pronounced or not pronounced at all. However, correct spelling can be achieved without exact pronunciation, provided that the student has the opportunity to associate the meaning of the word with the visual sequence of letters.

Say each **vowel + r** word and write it on the chalkboard. Have a volunteer circle the letters that spell the /îr/ sound and box the letters that spell the /ûr/ sound. Have a volunteer repeat each word and use it in a sentence. Then have the students write each word three times.

MANAGING INSTRUCTION

3–5 Day Plan		Average	Below Average	Above Average
Day 1	**Day 1**	Assessment: Units 7–11, p. 74 (Option 1 or 2, p. T74)	Assessment: Units 7–11, p. 74 (Option 1 or 2, p. T74)	Assessment: Units 7–11, p. 74 (Option 1 or 2, p. T74)
	Day 2	Review: Units 7 and 8, p. 75	Review: Units 7 and 8, p. 75	Review: Units 7 and 8, p. 75 Review: Units 9 and 10, p. 76
Day 2	**Day 3**	Review: Units 9 and 10, p. 76	Review: Units 9 and 10, p. 76	Review: Unit 11, p. 77 Spelling Study Strategy, p. 77
	Day 4	Review: Unit 11, p. 77 Spelling Study Strategy, p. 77	Review: Unit 11, p. 77 Spelling Study Strategy, p. 77	Writer's Workshop, pages 78–79
Day 3	**Day 5**	Weekly Test, Option 1 or 2, p. T77	Weekly Test, Option 1 or 2, p. T77	Weekly Test, Option 1 or 2, p. T77
Writer's Workshop (pages 78 and 79) may be used anytime during this unit.				

Objectives

Spelling and Assessment

Students will

• **assess** their spelling success by matching new words to the spelling strategies presented in Units 7–11.
• **connect** new words to the spelling strategies in Units 7–11.
• **write** new words that relate to the spelling strategies taught in Units 7–11.

Unit 12
Review Units 7–11

Assessment and Review

Unit 7
1. clothing
2. thrown
3. mown
4. moan

Unit 8
5. value
6. whom
7. ruin
8. tune

Unit 9
9. pointed
10. oyster
11. blouse
12. growl

Unit 10
13. vault
14. haunt
15. inform
16. scorn

Unit 11
17. conserve
18. beard
19. gear
20. fern

Assessment Units 7–11

Each Assessment Word in the box fits one of the spelling strategies you have studied over the past five weeks. Read the spelling strategies. Then write each Assessment Word under the unit number it fits.

Unit 7 _____

1.–4. The **long o** sound can be spelled in different ways: **o** in **pony**, **oa** in **goal**, and **ow** in **glow**.

Unit 8 _____

5.–8. The vowel sound you hear in **true** and the vowel sound you hear in **few** can be spelled in different ways.

Unit 9 _____

9.–12. The **/oi/** sound can be spelled in different ways: **oi** in **coil** or **oy** in **joy**. The **/ou/** sound can be spelled in different ways: **ou** in **mouth** or **ow** in **plow**.

Unit 10 _____

13.–16. The **r-controlled** vowel sound you hear in **sport** (/ôr/) is spelled **or**. The vowel sound you hear in **haul** (/ô/) can be spelled in different ways: **au** in **haul**, **augh** in **caught**, and **ough** in **ought**.

Unit 11 _____

17.–20. The **r-controlled** vowel sound you hear in **near** (/îr/) can be spelled in different ways: **ear** in **near** and **eer** in **cheer**. The **r-controlled** vowel sound you hear in **firm** (/ûr/) can be spelled in different ways: **ir** in **firm**, **er** in **herd**, or **ur** in **burst**.

clothing
value
whom
pointed
conserve
thrown
vault
beard
oyster
gear
haunt
blouse
ruin
mown
moan
inform
tune
growl
scorn
fern

74

ASSESSMENT: UNITS 7–11

Option 1

Assessment Option 1 is the test that appears in the Student Edition on page 74. You may wish to have students take this test to determine their ability to recognize the spelling strategy in each unit and to match words not previously taught to that strategy. **Assessment Option 1** also serves as additional review and practice.

Option 2

Assessment Option 2 is a dictation test using the sentences on page T75. This test assesses students' ability to spell words not previously taught but that are exemplars of a spelling strategy. This test more specifically assesses students' ability to apply the spelling knowledge they have learned.

In either assessment test option, the words are identified by unit in the Teacher Edition. You may wish to index those misspelled words to review exercises that follow in this unit. Determine which units students need to review and use additional unit exercises found in this **Assessment and Review Unit** for reteaching the skill in a more focused way.

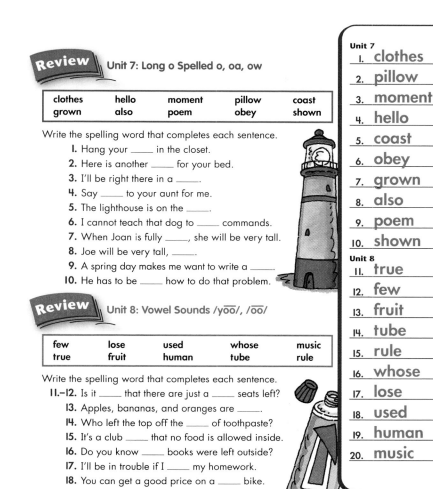

Review — Unit 7: Long o Spelled o, oa, ow

clothes	hello	moment	pillow	coast
grown	also	poem	obey	shown

Write the spelling word that completes each sentence.

1. Hang your _____ in the closet.
2. Here is another _____ for your bed.
3. I'll be right there in a _____.
4. Say _____ to your aunt for me.
5. The lighthouse is on the _____.
6. I cannot teach that dog to _____ commands.
7. When Joan is fully _____, she will be very tall.
8. Joe will be very tall, _____.
9. A spring day makes me want to write a _____.
10. He has to be _____ how to do that problem.

Review — Unit 8: Vowel Sounds /yōo/, /ōo/

few	lose	used	whose	music
true	fruit	human	tube	rule

Write the spelling word that completes each sentence.

11.–12. Is it _____ that there are just a _____ seats left?
13. Apples, bananas, and oranges are _____.
14. Who left the top off the _____ of toothpaste?
15. It's a club _____ that no food is allowed inside.
16. Do you know _____ books were left outside?
17. I'll be in trouble if I _____ my homework.
18. You can get a good price on a _____ bike.
19. All people are _____ beings.
20. We sang three songs in _____ class.

Unit 7
1. clothes
2. pillow
3. moment
4. hello
5. coast
6. obey
7. grown
8. also
9. poem
10. shown

Unit 8
11. true
12. few
13. fruit
14. tube
15. rule
16. whose
17. lose
18. used
19. human
20. music

75

Objectives

Spelling and Review

Students will
• **review** and practice the spelling strategy and words in Unit 7.
• **review** and practice the spelling strategy and words in Unit 8.

Assessing Progress: The Spelling Journal

If your students have been keeping a personal spelling journal, a periodical review of these journals can be a rich assessment tool. Students should include the words they misspelled from each unit spelling test. They also should be encouraged to write the words they consistently misspell in their own writing and content-area words that present a challenge. Being able to discriminate the words in their everyday writing whose spelling they need to master is a powerful spelling skill.

Pretest Sentences: Assessment Words
(See procedures on pages Z10–Z11.)

1. You need sturdy **clothing** for a camping trip.
2. We **value** your friendship very much.
3. To **whom** am I speaking?
4. Their guide **pointed** to the mark on the tree.
5. The hikers must **conserve** water on their journey.
6. More wood was **thrown** on the fire.
7. The money was kept in a sealed **vault**.
8. The man's **beard** was cut into a point.
9. Until our trip to the ocean, I had never seen an **oyster**.
10. Put all the camping **gear** into the back of the truck.
11. The memory of the accident seemed to **haunt** her.
12. Her **blouse** was made of silk.
13. The old stone wall had fallen into **ruin**.
14. The scent of fresh **mown** grass is nice.
15. The wind in the trees sounded like a **moan**.
16. I will **inform** you of any change in plans.
17. Each musician played a different **tune**.
18. My dog will **growl** at a stranger.
19. Her lip curled up in **scorn**.
20. The **fern** grew in the shade of the house.

Objectives

Spelling and Review

Students will

- **review** and practice the spelling strategy and words in Unit 9.
- **review** and practice the spelling strategy and words in Unit 10.

Unit 9

1. moist
2. crowd
3. vowel
4. power
5. amount
6. mouth
7. enjoy
8. choice
9. flower
10. however

Unit 10

11. nor
12. report
13. brought
14. caught
15. sort
16. because
17. thought
18. record
19. forest
20. bought

 Review Unit 9: Vowel Diphthongs /oi/, /ou/

| amount | choice | flower | moist | however |
| enjoy | mouth | power | vowel | crowd |

Write the spelling word that fits each meaning.

1. slightly damp
2. many people
3. not a consonant
4. strength or force
5. quantity or sum
6. where your teeth are
7. to have a good time
8. a selection
9. a bloom or blossom
10. anyway

Review Unit 10: Vowel Sounds /ôr/, /ô/

| because | brought | caught | thought | sort |
| forest | record | bought | report | nor |

Find each misspelled word. Write the word correctly.

11. Neither my sister nur I will be able to go to the play.
12. The weather repoort promises a fine day.
13. I brawght the book with me.
14. Mom caut five trout.
15. Please sourt the clean socks.
16. I'll be late becauze our car has a flat tire.
17. I really thout that was the right answer.
18. The teacher will recored our test grades.
19. There are tall pines in that fourist.
20. We bawte new tires for our car.

76

Bulletin Board Idea

Flowers and Forest

Use the spelling words **flower** and **forest** as the basis of a bulletin board that expands vocabulary and helps students understand categories and the differences between general and specific words.

Have students suggest the names of various flowers that they know and draw or cut out pictures to illustrate their words. Mount these on one side of the bulletin board and develop the other side using words related to a forest. Students might suggest the names of trees, birds, or plants.

| Flowers | Forest |

Daisy

Violet

Bird

Tree

Plant

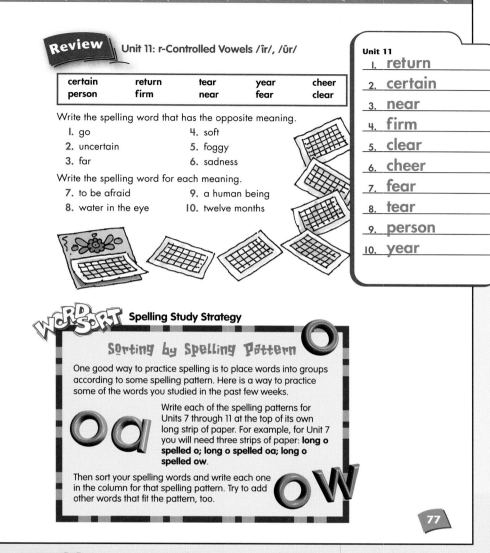

certain	return	tear	year	cheer
person	firm	near	fear	clear

Write the spelling word that has the opposite meaning.

1. go
2. uncertain
3. far
4. soft
5. foggy
6. sadness

Write the spelling word for each meaning.

7. to be afraid
8. water in the eye
9. a human being
10. twelve months

Unit 11

1. return
2. certain
3. near
4. firm
5. clear
6. cheer
7. fear
8. tear
9. person
10. year

WORD SORT

Spelling Study Strategy

Sorting by Spelling Pattern

One good way to practice spelling is to place words into groups according to some spelling pattern. Here is a way to practice some of the words you studied in the past few weeks.

Write each of the spelling patterns for Units 7 through 11 at the top of its own long strip of paper. For example, for Unit 7 you will need three strips of paper: **long o spelled o; long o spelled oa; long o spelled ow.**

Then sort your spelling words and write each one in the column for that spelling pattern. Try to add other words that fit the pattern, too.

77

Objectives

Spelling and Review

Students will
• **review** and practice the spelling strategy and words in Unit 11.
• **learn** an alternative spelling study strategy.

Learning an Alternative Spelling Study Strategy

Students should always have a number of study strategies to draw from when it comes to learning their spelling words. **Sorting by Spelling Pattern** is a useful way of studying the unit words. Encourage students to practice this spelling study strategy and to consider using it with any appropriate list they need to study and learn.

Weekly Test Options

Option 1:
One Spelling Word Per Sentence
(See procedures on pages Z10–Z11.)

1. A **few** people had to wait.
2. They paid a large **amount** for the land.
3. Make the best **choice**.
4. Did you **lose** your paper?
5. That doll can cry a real **tear**.
6. Father **used** the rest of the soap.
7. Your **clothes** look very neat.
8. You must **return** the tape to the same store.
9. Mother was **certain** that you wanted to go to the circus.
10. My father **thought** I did a fine job.
11. My friend would like to say **hello**.
12. He threw the ball and I **caught** it.
13. I saw you for a brief **moment**.
14. She will go to school next **year**.
15. I have a red **pillow** on my bed.

16. Are you the boy **whose** glasses were lost?
17. The air was unusually **moist**.
18. The tulip is a pretty spring **flower**.
19. The benches are dry **because** the sun came out.
20. I **brought** Grandmother to our house.

**Unit 12
Test Master**

(See *Teacher Resource Book,* Unit 12.)

Option 2:
Standardized Test

 **WRITER'S**

Objectives

Spelling and Writing

Students will

- **review** the concept of common and proper nouns.
- **compose** a narrative piece of writing that tells about a time that they found something interesting or important. (See **Spelling and the Writing Process** below.)

Optional Enrichment

A

1. <u>proper</u>
2. <u>common</u>
3. <u>proper</u>
4. <u>proper</u>
5. <u>common</u>

Answers for numbers 6–10 will vary. Possible answers are provided.

B

6. <u>Molly</u>
7. <u>Chicago</u>
8. <u>Washington Monument</u>
9. <u>Thanksgiving</u>
10. <u>the Beatles</u>

Grammar, Usage, and Mechanics

Common and Proper Nouns

A common noun names any person, place, or thing.

> That **student** goes to my **school**.
> The **building** is in a **city**.

A proper noun names a particular person, place, or thing. A proper noun begins with a capital letter.

> **Carl Hansen** goes to **Roosevelt School**.
> The **Empire State Building** is in **New York City**.

Practice Activity

A. What kind of noun is underlined in each sentence? Write **common** or **proper**.

1. My friend <u>Alice</u> will bring oranges.
2. Is one <u>horse</u> Black Beauty?
3. My family moved here from <u>Florida</u>.
4. The store is somewhere on <u>State Street</u>.
5. Our <u>principal</u> is Ms. Everson.

B. Write a proper noun that could replace each underlined common noun in these sentences. Be sure to begin your proper noun with a capital letter.

6. <u>She</u> lives across the street.
7. I always enjoy visiting <u>the city</u>.
8. We saw the <u>memorial</u> on our visit to Washington, D.C.
9. There is no school on <u>a holiday</u>.
10. We bought a recording of <u>my favorite singing group</u>.

78

 Narrative Writing

Spelling and the Writing Process

You may wish to use this writing assignment to help students master the writing process. For other writing ideas, see pages 258–259 in the Student Edition.

Explain that students will write a composition in which they tell their classmates about a time they found something interesting or important—an object, an animal, a person, or even an answer.

Prewriting Hint: You may wish to help students plan their writing by recommending the graphic organizer on this page. Have them replicate the graphic, filling in the blanks with details about the experience.

Who was there? me, my friend Neyda	**Where and When** did this happen? City Park, last July
What happened? 1. found a wallet 2. 3.	

Revising Hint: Remind students that when they revise what they have written they should make sure they have included enough background information so that readers will understand the people involved, the places, and what happened.

Proofreading Strategy

One Sentence at a Time!

Good writers always proofread their work for spelling errors. Here's a strategy you can use to proofread your papers.

Instead of reading your entire paper, look at one sentence at a time. Make sure that the first word starts with a capital letter. Then make sure that the last word is followed by a punctuation mark.

Looking at your paper this way helps you think about details—capital letters and punctuation—instead of ideas. It may sound strange, but it works. Try it!

Electronic Spelling

1. **artwork**
2. **screensaver**
3. **password**
4. **toolbox**
5. **laptop**
6. **keyboard**

Computer Terms

Computers have changed life in many ways. They have also changed our language. Today, we use many new words that didn't even exist fifty years ago. We also use older words in new ways. For instance, once a **notebook** was just a book that you could fill with paper. Today, a **notebook** is also a small computer.

Spell checkers may not catch these newer words, so you need to know how to spell them. Many of them are compound words—words made up of two shorter words. For example, **notebook** is made from **note** and **book**. To spell a compound word, first break it into two smaller words. Then spell each part.

One part of each compound word below is misspelled. Write the compound word correctly.

1. artwerk	4. tulebox
2. skreensaver	5. laptopp
3. passwurd	6. keybord

79

Objectives

Spelling and Writing

Students will
- **learn** a proofreading strategy.
- **proofread** for correct compound words when using new technical language.

Using Proofreading Strategies

Students are often unaware that there are a variety of techniques they can use to proofread their own writing. Building a repertory of strategies is important to improving students' writing and editing skills.

Spelling and Technology

The advent of word processing, computer protocols, and the Internet has actually increased, not lessened, the pressure on users to be better, more aware spellers. Spell checkers, for example, create circumstances in which the ability to discriminate between an acceptable and an unacceptable spelling is a critical skill. A homophone substitution, a correct spelling of the wrong word, an inadvertent word omission—these are examples of situations in computer usage that require a deeper understanding of spelling principles and a more adroit proofreading capability. It may be worthwhile to underscore this increased need as a whole-class discussion after students finish this unit's **Electronic Spelling** activity.

Unit 13 Home Study Master

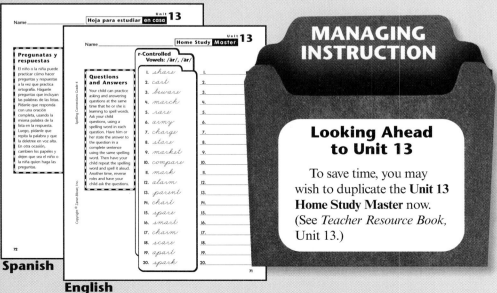

Spanish

English

MANAGING INSTRUCTION

Looking Ahead to Unit 13

To save time, you may wish to duplicate the **Unit 13 Home Study Master** now. (See *Teacher Resource Book*, Unit 13.)

Basic Spelling List

share	mark
cart	alarm
beware	parent
march	chart
rare	spare
army	smart
charge	charm
stare	scare
market	apart
compare	spark

Strategy Words

Review

bare	large
fare	partly
hare	

Preview

argue	declare
aware	pardon
carpet	

Content Words

Social Studies: Boats

barge	tugboat
skiff	schooner
ferry	

Math: Measurement

centimeter	millimeter
kilometer	kilogram
decimeter	

Individual Needs

Challenge Words

arch	glare
harness	snare
tardy	

Alternate Word List

share	mark
beware	parent
army	chart
market	scare
compare	apart

MATERIALS

Student Edition
Pages 80–85
Challenge Activities, p. 234

Teacher Edition
Pages T80A–T85
Challenge Activities, p. T234

Other Resources
Spelling Connections Software
Unit 13 Word List Overhead
  Transparency

Teacher Resource Book
Unit 13 Home Study Master
  (English or Spanish; students
  may pretest on this sheet or use
  it for home practice.)
Unit 13 Homework Master
Unit 13 Practice Masters
Flip Folder Practice Master
Unit 13 Test Master

Visit our Web site, www.zaner-bloser.com

OBJECTIVES

Spelling and Thinking
Students will
- **read** the spelling words in list form and in context.
- **sort** the spelling words according to the /är/ and /âr/ sounds and spelling patterns.
- **read** and remember this week's spelling strategy.

Spelling and Vocabulary
Students will
- **write** spelling words that match definitions.
- **write** spelling words from given clues.
- **write** spelling words in alphabetical order.

Spelling and Reading
Students will
- **complete** facts using spelling words.
- **complete** opinions using spelling words.
- **solve** analogies using spelling words.

Spelling and Writing
Students will
- **proofread** a thank-you note.
- **use** the writing process to write a thank-you note.
- **proofread** their writing.

MEETING INDIVIDUAL NEEDS
Learning Styles

Visual

Have two to four students play this game. Write each spelling word on a 3" × 5" card. Create a game board showing "Start" and "Win" spaces separated by 18 spaces. Place the cards facedown on the game board.

Give each student a marker. Have the first player draw a word card, look at it, place the card facedown on the board, and write the word on paper. If the word is written correctly, the student may advance her or his marker two spaces. If the word is misspelled, the student must write the word correctly but may not advance. In either case, the next player takes a turn.

Auditory

Use the game board and word cards from the visual activity. Have two to four students play this game. Give each a marker. Draw a word card and pronounce the word twice. Then call on the first player to spell the word aloud. If the word is spelled correctly, have the student write the word on the chalkboard and advance her or his marker two spaces. If the word is misspelled, call on another student to spell the word aloud correctly. Then have the original player write the word, correctly spelled, on the chalkboard.

Kinesthetic

Write each spelling word on a 3" × 5" card. Set up a baseball diamond in the classroom with desks. Designate one desk as home plate, one as first base, and so on. Divide the group into two teams. Have the "pitching" team draw cards from the stack and pronounce them to a "batter" from the other team. Have the batter write the word on the chalkboard. If the batter writes the word correctly, he or she may go to first base. If the word is misspelled, the batter is "out" and the word is given to the next batter. After three outs, the teams reverse roles. Continue the game until each team has batted at least three times.

Language and Cultural Differences

Some students may have difficulty spelling the **r**-controlled vowel sounds due to regional pronunciations or language backgrounds that do not include these sounds. Have the students write the words **care** and **car** as headings at the top of their papers. Then have them write each spelling word under the appropriate heading. Next have them tell you something about the meanings of the words. Clarify and expand the students' definitions. Then ask volunteers to use each word in a sentence.

MANAGING INSTRUCTION

3–5 Day Plan		Average	Below Average	Above Average
Day 1	**Day 1**	Pretest Spelling Mini-Lesson, p. T80 Spelling and Thinking, p. 80	Pretest Spelling Mini-Lesson, p. T80 Spelling and Thinking, p. 80	Pretest Spelling and Thinking, p. 80
	Day 2	Spelling and Vocabulary, p. 81	Spelling and Vocabulary, p. 81 (or) Unit 13 Practice Master, A and B	Spelling and Vocabulary, p. 81 Spelling and Reading, p. 82
Day 2	**Day 3**	Spelling and Reading, p. 82	Spelling and Reading, p. 82 (or) Unit 13 Practice Master, C and D	Challenge Activities, p. 234
	Day 4	Spelling and Writing, p. 83 Unit 13 Homework Master	Spelling and Writing, p. 83	Spelling and Writing, p. 83 Unit 13 Homework Master
Day 3	**Day 5**	Weekly Test	Weekly Test	Weekly Test
Vocabulary Connections (pages 84 and 85) may be used anytime during this unit.				

Objectives

Spelling and Thinking

Students will

- **read** the spelling words in list form and in context.
- **sort** the spelling words according to the /är/ and /âr/ sounds and spelling patterns.
- **read** and remember this week's spelling strategy.

UNIT PRETEST

Use **Pretest Sentences** below. Refer to the self-checking procedures on student page 256. You may wish to use the **Unit 13 Word List Overhead Transparency** as part of the checking procedure.

TEACHING THE STRATEGY

Spelling Mini-Lesson

Write /är/ **star** and /âr/ **mare** on the chalkboard. Ask the students if they can guess which sounds the symbols represent. (/är/ represents the r-controlled vowel sound in star, and /âr/ represents the r-controlled vowel sound in mare.)

Explain that /är/ represents the sound of the name of the letter **r**. Ask them to listen for this sound in **star** as you pronounce it. Write **cart, march, army, charge, market, mark, alarm, chart, smart, charm, apart,** and **spark** on the chalkboard under /är/. Point out that each word has the /är/ vowel sound. Ask volunteers to read them.

Pronounce **star** and **mare**. Ask the students to listen for the difference. Write **rare, share, parent, spare, stare, beware, compare,** and **scare** on the chalkboard under /âr/. Point out that each of these words has the /âr/ vowel sound. Invite volunteers to read them.

Have volunteers circle the letters that spell the **r-**controlled vowel sound in each word. Ask the students if the spelling patterns are the same. (no) Discuss the differences in spelling. (Most words with /âr/ end in silent e. The e in parent is pronounced in the second syllable.)

Conclude by reading **Remember the Spelling Strategy** on page 80.

Spelling and Thinking

Order of answers may vary.

/är/

1. cart
2. march
3. army ★
4. charge
5. market ★
6. mark ★
7. alarm
8. chart ★
9. smart
10. charm
11. apart ★
12. spark

/âr/

13. share ★
14. beware ★
15. rare
16. stare
17. compare ★
18. parent ★
19. spare
20. scare ★

READ THE SPELLING WORDS

1. share	*share*	I will do my **share** of the work.
2. cart	*cart*	The horse pulled a heavy **cart**.
3. beware	*beware*	We must **beware** of poison ivy.
4. march	*march*	Drummers will **march** in the parade.
5. rare	*rare*	A cold day in July is **rare**.
6. army	*army*	The **army** set up camp near here.
7. charge	*charge*	Put the **charge** on my bill.
8. stare	*stare*	We tried not to **stare** at the movie stars.
9. market	*market*	We bought food at the **market**.
10. compare	*compare*	Do not **compare** apples and oranges.
11. mark	*mark*	Please **mark** that date on your calendar.
12. alarm	*alarm*	That noise will **alarm** the baby.
13. parent	*parent*	Take this note to your **parent**.
14. chart	*chart*	Did you **chart** your progress?
15. spare	*spare*	Can you **spare** a pencil for me?
16. smart	*smart*	You made a **smart** play today.
17. charm	*charm*	The dancers have grace and **charm**.
18. scare	*scare*	The dark does not **scare** me.
19. apart	*apart*	He took the alarm clock **apart**.
20. spark	*spark*	Strike a **spark** to start a fire.

SORT THE SPELLING WORDS

1.–12. Write the spelling words that spell the /är/ sound **ar**.

13.–20. Write the spelling words that spell the /âr/ sound **are**.

REMEMBER THE SPELLING STRATEGY

Remember that the **r-**controlled vowel sound you hear in **cart** (/är/) is spelled **ar**. The **r-**controlled vowel sound you hear in **spare** (/âr/) is spelled **are**.

 80

Pretest Sentences (See procedures on pages Z10–Z11.)

1. Carol was kind to **share** her sandwich.
2. The pony pulled a small **cart**.
3. The word **beware** is used as a warning.
4. Everyone was asked to **march** in the parade.
5. We usually do not have steak for dinner, so this is a **rare** occasion.
6. My brother is serving his country in the **army**.
7. I am in **charge** of doing the dishes.
8. Sometimes nature's beauty causes people to **stare**.
9. My sister bought fresh vegetables at the **market**.
10. To find out which skates are better, you must **compare** them.
11. Before the race began, we had to **mark** the starting point.
12. We are to walk out of the building if we hear the **alarm**.
13. Mr. Baker is proud to be Cathy's **parent**.
14. All of our names and birthdays are listed on that **chart**.
15. We brought along a **spare** tire.
16. Kim thought Bernardo was **smart** to study.
17. A bracelet or a chain often has a **charm** attached.
18. The roar of the lion at the zoo did not **scare** me.
19. My brother fixed the toy after it came **apart**.
20. By striking stones together, we got a **spark**.

Word Meanings

Write the spelling word that matches each definition.

1. to examine two things for similarities and differences
2. a father or mother
3. to be careful of; to guard against
4. extra; more than is needed
5. a tiny piece of fire
6. intelligent
7. frighten or terrify

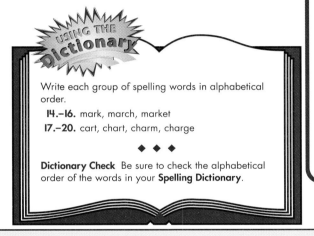

Word Clues

Write a spelling word for each clue.

8. a synonym of **uncommon**
9. a homonym of **stair**
10. an antonym of **hoard**
11. begins with a vowel and rhymes with **harm**
12. ends with a **long e** sound
13. found in the word **apartment**

USING THE Dictionary

Write each group of spelling words in alphabetical order.

14.–16. mark, march, market

17.–20. cart, chart, charm, charge

◆ ◆ ◆

Dictionary Check Be sure to check the alphabetical order of the words in your **Spelling Dictionary**.

Word Meanings
1. compare
2. parent
3. beware
4. spare
5. spark
6. smart
7. scare

Word Clues
8. rare
9. stare
10. share
11. alarm
12. army
13. apart

Using the Dictionary
14. march
15. mark
16. market
17. cart
18. charge
19. charm
20. chart

81

Objectives

Spelling and Vocabulary

Students will
- **write** spelling words that match definitions.
- **write** spelling words from given clues.
- **write** spelling words in alphabetical order.

Developing Oral Language Skills

Do a word sort by sound. Write /âr/ and /är/ on a chalkboard or an overhead transparency. Then read the spelling word list, asking students to write each word under one of the two headings according to the sound it contains. When they have finished listing the words, ask students to consider the letters in each word that spell the two sounds. Then have volunteers circle the letters that spell the sound.

MEETING INDIVIDUAL NEEDS

Providing More Help

Point out that when a spelling word has the /är/ sound heard in **cart**, the sound is spelled **ar,** but when a spelling word has the /âr/ sound heard in **rare**, the sound is spelled **are**. Put the headings **ar** and **are** on the chalkboard. Call on students to read the spelling words aloud and write the words in the proper columns, circling the **ar** or **are** letters in each word.

★ Students who need to study fewer words should use the **Alternate Word List**. This list is starred on page T80 in the Teacher Edition. The **Unit 13 Practice Masters** (*Teacher Resource Book*) provide additional practice with these words.

Unit 13 Practice Masters

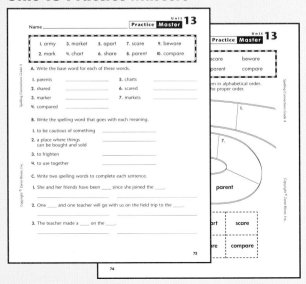

T81

Spelling and Reading

Students will
- **complete** facts using spelling words.
- **complete** opinions using spelling words.
- **solve** analogies using spelling words.

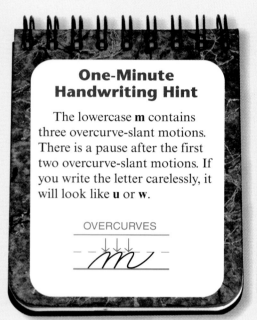

One-Minute Handwriting Hint

The lowercase **m** contains three overcurve-slant motions. There is a pause after the first two overcurve-slant motions. If you write the letter carelessly, it will look like **u** or **w**.

OVERCURVES

Legible handwriting can boost spelling scores by as much as 20%.

Spelling and Reading

share	cart	beware	march	rare
army	charge	stare	market	compare
mark	alarm	parent	chart	spare
smart	charm	scare	apart	spark

Complete the Facts Statements that can be checked and proven are facts. Write the spelling word that completes each fact.

1. A _____ is used to record a patient's progress over time.
2. The navy, marines, coast guard, and _____ are branches of our armed services.
3. You can make a _____ by striking flint on steel.
4. A _____ may have two or four wheels.
5. We can buy many different items in a _____.
6. Bands often _____ onto the football fields.
7. A smoke _____ in the house can warn us of fires.
8. Wolves are _____ in most of our states.

Complete the Opinions Statements that cannot be proven are opinions. Write the spelling word that completes each opinion.

9. Every adult wants to be a _____.
10. It is simple to take _____ all machines.
11. We should _____ of making too many friends.
12. Playing video games is a _____ way to pass time.
13. I should be in _____ of this club.
14. The most important quality a person can possess is _____.
15. It is easy to _____ brands of canned goods.

Solve the Analogies Write a spelling word to complete each analogy.

16. **Start** is to **continue** as **look** is to _____.
17. **Knife** is to **cut** as **pencil** is to _____.
18. **Selfish** is to **hoard** as **generous** is to _____.
19. **Tall** is to **stall** as **care** is to _____.
20. **Large** is to **small** as **extra** is to _____.

Complete the Facts
1. chart
2. army
3. spark
4. cart
5. market
6. march
7. alarm
8. rare

Complete the Opinions
9. parent
10. apart
11. beware
12. smart
13. charge
14. charm
15. compare

Solve the Analogies
16. stare
17. mark
18. share
19. scare
20. spare

82

MEETING INDIVIDUAL NEEDS

Providing More Challenge

Challenge Words and **Challenge Activities** for Unit 13 appear on page 234. **Challenge Word Test Sentences** appear on page T234.

Unit 13 Challenge Activities

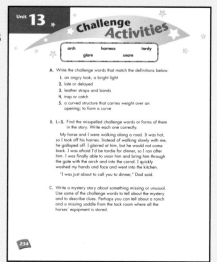

Weekly Test Options

Option 1:
One Spelling Word Per Sentence
(See procedures on pages Z10–Z11.)

1. The **alarm** will sound if there is a fire.
2. The boys have to sit **apart** from each other.
3. The band leader will begin the **march**.
4. The **spark** of fire gave us a small amount of light.
5. You should **mark** the place where you stopped reading.
6. An **army** of ants is near the bushes.
7. The **market** is a place where you can buy things.
8. Mother said I was **smart** to study every day.
9. The meat was **rare** because it was not cooked in the center.
10. The teacher is in **charge** of all the students.
11. The boss writes each name on the **chart** on the wall.
12. I **charm** my baby sister by smiling at her.
13. One **parent** of each child came to the school.
14. The word **beware** means to watch out for something.
15. We will **compare** the two cars to find out how they are the same.

Spelling and Writing

Proofread a Thank-You Note

Six words are not spelled correctly in this thank-you note. Write those words correctly.

Dear Aunt Sue and Uncle Bob,

This is just a short note to thank you for my presents and the surprise birthday party you gave me. It was nice of you to ~~shair~~ *share* your home with an army of my pals. It was ~~smert~~ *smart* to tell me I was coming to help clean out your ~~spair~~ *spare* room. I was shocked to ~~compair~~ *compare* the fun with the expected work, and that was part of the ~~chaerm~~ *charm*. It was a ~~rair~~ *rare* treat that I will never forget. Thanks for a great birthday!

Love,
Bruce

Proofreading Marks

≡ Make a capital.
/ Make a small letter.
∧ Add something.
ℒ Take out something.
⊙ Add a period.
⌗ New paragraph.
SP Spelling error

Write a Thank-You Note

Expository Writing

Write a thank-you note for a real or imagined treat. Be sure to include

- what the treat was.
- who provided it for you.
- what you liked best about it.
- how it made you feel.
- what you most appreciate about the treat giver.

Use as many spelling words as you can.

Proofread Your Writing During → Editing

Proofread your writing for spelling errors as part of the editing stage in the writing process. Be sure to check each word carefully. Use a dictionary to check spelling if you are not sure.

Writing Process

Prewriting
⇩
Drafting
⇩
Revising
⇩
Editing
⇩
Publishing

83

Objectives

Spelling and Writing

Students will
- **proofread** a thank-you note.
- **use** the writing process to write a thank-you note.
- **proofread** their writing.

Using the Writing Process

Before assigning **Write a Thank-You Note** in this unit, see pages 258–259 in the Student Edition for a complete review of the writing process and additional writing assignments. You may also wish to refer to pages Z12–Z13 in the Teacher Edition.

Keeping a Spelling Journal

Encourage students to record the words they misspelled on the weekly test in a personal spelling journal. These words may be recycled for future study. Students may also wish to include words from their writing. See pages Z12–Z13 in the Teacher Edition for more information.

---

16. Look at the sea horse, but do not stand and **stare** at it.
17. We carry a **spare** tire in our car.
18. The man put food in the **cart** at the store.
19. Do not jump out of the box and **scare** me.
20. I will cut the sandwich in half, and we will **share** it.

Option 2:
Multiple Spelling Words Per Sentence
(See procedures on pages Z10–Z11.)

1. We always need a **cart** when we go to the **market**.
2. The men in the **army** will **march** when they hear the **alarm**.
3. Please do not **stare** at my **mark** on the **chart**.
4. It is **smart** to **compare** prices of food items before you buy.
5. Mom had no money, so she had to **charge** the **spare** tire.
6. A sign that says to **beware** of the dog may **scare** people away.
7. Aunt Sara found a **rare charm** in the sand.
8. It is hard to **share** things with a friend when you live far **apart**.
9. My **parent** knew that the car needed **spark** plugs.

Option 3:
Standardized Test
(See *Teacher Resource Book,* Unit 13.)

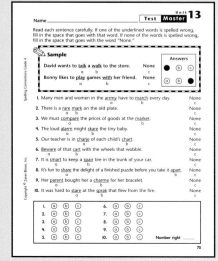

Unit 13
Test Master

Objectives

Strategy Words

Students will
- **review** words studied previously that are related to the spelling strategy.
- **preview** unknown words that are related to the spelling strategy.

Remind the students that the **Strategy Words** relate to the spelling patterns they have studied in this unit. The **Review Words** are below grade level, and the **Preview Words** are above grade level. You may wish to use the following sentences to introduce the words in context.

Review Words:
Words From Grade 3
1. The trees will soon be **bare** of their leaves.
2. We must pay a **fare** to ride the bus.
3. The **hare** was faster than the tortoise but still lost the race.
4. We will be having a **large** family gathering at Thanksgiving.
5. He was only **partly** finished with his chores.

Preview Words:
Words From Grade 5
6. Do not **argue** with your little sister.
7. Always try to be **aware** of what is going on around you.
8. We will be having the **carpet** cleaned next week.
9. It is time to **declare** your stand on this situation.
10. Please **pardon** me for being rude.

Review Words
1. hare
2. bare
3. large
4. partly
5. fare

Preview Words
6. carpet
7. pardon
8. argue
9. declare
10. aware

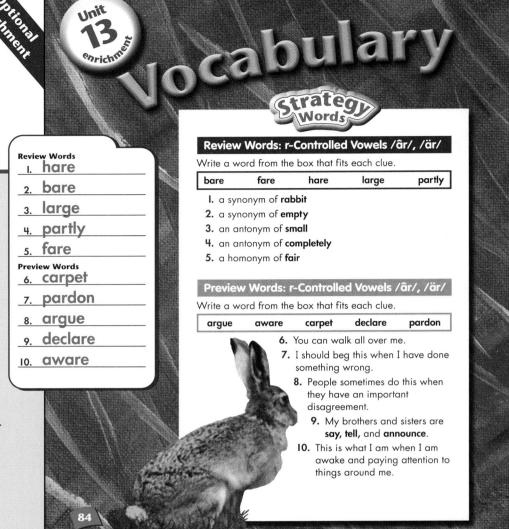

Unit 13 enrichment

Vocabulary

Strategy Words

Review Words: r-Controlled Vowels /âr/, /är/

Write a word from the box that fits each clue.

bare	fare	hare	large	partly

1. a synonym of **rabbit**
2. a synonym of **empty**
3. an antonym of **small**
4. an antonym of **completely**
5. a homonym of **fair**

Preview Words: r-Controlled Vowels /âr/, /är/

Write a word from the box that fits each clue.

argue	aware	carpet	declare	pardon

6. You can walk all over me.
7. I should beg this when I have done something wrong.
8. People sometimes do this when they have an important disagreement.
9. My brothers and sisters are **say, tell,** and **announce**.
10. This is what I am when I am awake and paying attention to things around me.

84

Unit 13 RECAP

You may wish to assign the **Unit 13 Homework Master** (*Teacher Resource Book,* Unit 13) as a fun way to recap the spelling words.

Unit 13 Homework Master

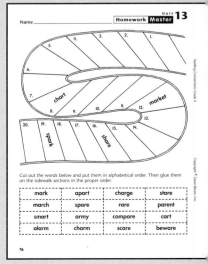

Connections

Content Words

Content Words

Students will
- **expand** vocabulary with content-related words.
- **relate** the spelling strategy to words outside the basic spelling list.

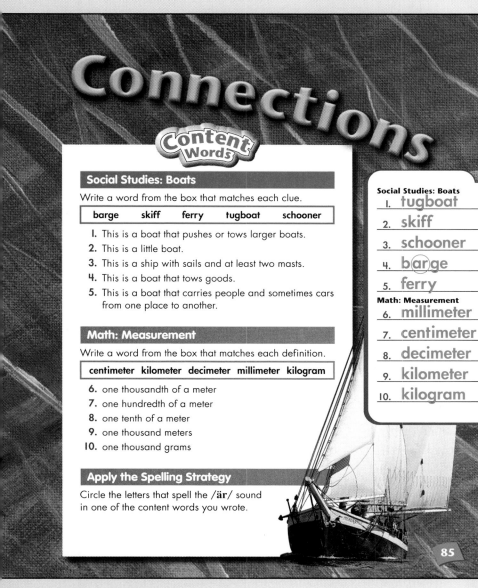

Social Studies: Boats

Write a word from the box that matches each clue.

barge	skiff	ferry	tugboat	schooner

1. This is a boat that pushes or tows larger boats.
2. This is a little boat.
3. This is a ship with sails and at least two masts.
4. This is a boat that tows goods.
5. This is a boat that carries people and sometimes cars from one place to another.

Math: Measurement

Write a word from the box that matches each definition.

centimeter	kilometer	decimeter	millimeter	kilogram

6. one thousandth of a meter
7. one hundredth of a meter
8. one tenth of a meter
9. one thousand meters
10. one thousand grams

Apply the Spelling Strategy

Circle the letters that spell the /är/ sound in one of the content words you wrote.

Social Studies: Boats
1. tugboat
2. skiff
3. schooner
4. b(ar)ge
5. ferry

Math: Measurement
6. millimeter
7. centimeter
8. decimeter
9. kilometer
10. kilogram

85

Content Words

Social Studies: Boats

Review the meanings of these words with the students. You may wish to use these sentences to introduce the words in context.

1. The **barge** coming down the river is loaded with coal.
2. The men went out in the **skiff** to do a little fishing.
3. The **ferry** had two levels loaded with cars and one level with people.
4. The little **tugboat** towed the big ship out of the harbor.
5. A **schooner** is a ship with two or more masts.

Encourage the students to use these words to start a scrapbook of boats with the name of each boat beside a picture or drawing of it.

Math: Measurement

Review the meanings of these words with the students. You may wish to use these sentences to introduce the words in context.

6. Can you find the **centimeter** mark on the meter stick?
7. A **kilometer** is slightly less than a mile.
8. A **decimeter** is one tenth of a meter.
9. A **millimeter** is a very small measurement of length.
10. One **kilogram** is a little over two pounds.

Encourage the students to make a series of signs using these words. The signs might be road signs or signs found in a grocery or hardware store.

Unit 14 Home Study Master

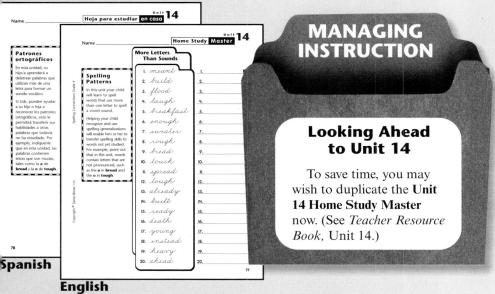

Name

Patrones ortográficos

Hoja para estudiar **en casa** **Unit 14**

En esta unidad, su hijo/a aprenderá a deletrear palabras que utilizan más de una letra para formar un sonido vocálico.

Si Uds. pueden ayudar a su hijo o hija a reconocer los patrones ortográficos, esto le permitirá transferir sus habilidades a otras palabras que todavía no ha estudiado. Por ejemplo, indíquenle que en esta unidad, las palabras contienen letras que son mudas, tales como la a de **bread** y la o de **tough**.

78

Spanish

Name

Home Study **Master** **Unit 14**

More Letters Than Sounds

Spelling Patterns

In this unit your child will learn to spell words that use more than one letter to spell a vowel sound.

Helping your child recognize and use spelling generalizations will enable him or her to transfer spelling skills to words not yet studied. For example, point out that in this unit, words contain letters that are not pronounced, such as the a in **bread** and the o in **tough**.

1. meant
2. build
3. flood
4. laugh
5. breakfast
6. enough
7. sweater
8. rough
9. bread
10. touch
11. spread
12. tough
13. already
14. built
15. ready
16. death
17. young
18. instead
19. heavy
20. ahead

1.
2.
3.
4.
5.
6.
7.
8.
9.
10.
11.
12.
13.
14.
15.
16.
17.
18.
19.
20.

77

English

Copyright © Zaner-Bloser, Inc.
Spelling Connections Grade 4

MANAGING INSTRUCTION

Looking Ahead to Unit 14

To save time, you may wish to duplicate the **Unit 14 Home Study Master** now. (See *Teacher Resource Book,* Unit 14.)

Basic Spelling List

meant	spread
build	tough
flood	already
laugh	built
breakfast	ready
enough	death
sweater	young
rough	instead
bread	heavy
touch	ahead

Strategy Words

Review

heat	great
board	weigh
friend	

Preview

plaid	subhead
pleasant	sweatshirt
pleasure	

Content Words

Health: Medicine

headache	science
discover	cure
cause	

Health: Being Me

height	well-being
temper	strength
mood	

Individual Needs

Challenge Words

wealth	biscuit
threat	tortoise
pheasant	

Alternate Word List

meant	already
build	built
breakfast	ready
enough	young
touch	instead

MATERIALS

Student Edition
Pages 86–91
Challenge Activities, p. 235

Teacher Edition
Pages T86A–T91
Challenge Activities, p. T235

Other Resources
Spelling Connections Software
Unit 14 Word List Overhead
  Transparency

Teacher Resource Book
Unit 14 Home Study Master
  (English or Spanish; students
  may pretest on this sheet or use
  it for home practice.)
Unit 14 Homework Master
Unit 14 Practice Masters
Flip Folder Practice Master
Unit 14 Test Master

Visit our Web site, www.zaner-bloser.com

OBJECTIVES

Spelling and Thinking

Students will
- **read** the spelling words in list form and in context.
- **sort** the words according to spelling patterns of vowel sounds.
- **read** and remember this week's spelling strategy.

Spelling and Vocabulary

Students will
- **write** spelling words that match definitions.
- **change** or add letters of words to form spelling words.
- **write** spelling words for antonyms.
- **use** the **Writing Thesaurus** to write spelling words that complete a series of synonyms.

Spelling and Reading

Students will
- **replace** underlined words in sentences with spelling words.
- **write** spelling words to complete a series of meaning-related words.
- **complete** sentences using spelling words.

Spelling and Writing

Students will
- **proofread** a book review.
- **use** the writing process to write a book review.
- **proofread** their writing.

MEETING INDIVIDUAL NEEDS
Learning Styles

 Visual

Give each student an appropriate grade-level magazine or newsletter. Allow the students fifteen minutes to find as many spelling words as they can. Have them highlight or circle each word and then write the words on their papers. Finally, have them underline the irregular spelling pattern in each word.

 Auditory

Have the students work in pairs. Ask them to take turns choosing a spelling word to spell aloud to their partners. The partner must then say the word. Then have both students spell the word in unison.

 Kinesthetic

Print each spelling word, in letters about 3" tall, on construction paper. Divide the words among the students. Ask them to cut out the letters and then write the word. Have the students exchange words, trace the letters of the new word with their fingers, and write the word.

Language and Cultural Differences

The silent letters and irregular spellings of sounds are parts of the English spelling system that all students must memorize for correct spelling. It is important to give students the opportunity to associate the word meaning with the visual sequence of letters used in spelling.

Make a card like this for each spelling word:

Cut each card into three pieces: the initial consonant(s), the medial vowels, and the final consonant(s). (For the words **ahead** and **enough,** the first piece will include a vowel.) Arrange the pieces randomly on a table—the initial letters in one row, the medial vowels in a second row, and the final letters in a third row. Say one of the spelling words, pronouncing it clearly. Have a student repeat the word and pronounce it correctly. Then have the student choose the letter parts that form the word, place the pieces in the correct order, and say the word. The shapes of the word pieces give added clues.

MANAGING INSTRUCTION

3–5 Day Plan		Average	Below Average	Above Average
Day 1	Day 1	Pretest Spelling Mini-Lesson, p. T86 Spelling and Thinking, p. 86	Pretest Spelling Mini-Lesson, p. T86 Spelling and Thinking, p. 86	Pretest Spelling and Thinking, p. 86
	Day 2	Spelling and Vocabulary, p. 87	Spelling and Vocabulary, p. 87 (or) Unit 14 Practice Master, A and B	Spelling and Vocabulary, p. 87 Spelling and Reading, p. 88
Day 2	Day 3	Spelling and Reading, p. 88	Spelling and Reading, p. 88 (or) Unit 14 Practice Master, C and D	Challenge Activities, p. 235
	Day 4	Spelling and Writing, p. 89 Unit 14 Homework Master	Spelling and Writing, p. 89	Spelling and Writing, p. 89 Unit 14 Homework Master
Day 3	Day 5	Weekly Test	Weekly Test	Weekly Test
Vocabulary Connections (pages 90 and 91) may be used anytime during this unit.				

Objectives

Spelling and Thinking

Students will
- **read** the spelling words in list form and in context.
- **sort** the words according to spelling patterns of vowel sounds.
- **read** and remember this week's spelling strategy.

UNIT PRETEST

Use **Pretest Sentences** below. Refer to the self-checking procedures on student page 256. You may wish to use the **Unit 14 Word List Overhead Transparency** as part of the checking procedure.

TEACHING THE STRATEGY

Spelling Mini-Lesson

Write **laugh, bread, build, touch,** and **flood** in a column on the chalkboard. Write **short a, short i, short e, short u,** and **short o** on the chalkboard. Ask volunteers to read each word and draw a line from the word to the vowel sound they hear in that word.

Discuss the fact that the short vowel sounds in these words are spelled in surprising—or irregular—ways. Ask volunteers to circle the letters that spell the short vowel sound in each word. Point out that there are more vowels in each word than vowel sounds.

Tell the students that they can use special sayings called **acrostics** to help them remember these unusual spellings. For example, to remember how to spell **laugh** and **bread,** they might write these acrostics:

Lee's	Bill and
Aunt and	Rhonda
Uncle had to	Eat
Go	Apples
Home	Daily

Encourage the students to write other acrostics for the spelling words.

Ask volunteers to read all the spelling words aloud.

Conclude by reading **Remember the Spelling Strategy** on page 86.

Order of answers may vary.

short a or short e
1. l(au)gh
2. m(ea)nt ★
3. br(ea)kfast ★
4. sw(ea)ter
5. br(ea)d
6. spr(ea)d
7. alr(ea)dy ★
8. r(ea)dy ★
9. d(ea)th
10. inst(ea)d ★
11. h(ea)vy
12. ah(ea)d

short i or short u
13. b(ui)ld ★
14. b(ui)lt ★
15. fl(oo)d
16. en(ou)gh ★
17. r(ou)gh
18. t(ou)ch ★
19. t(ou)gh
20. y(ou)ng ★

Spelling and Thinking

READ THE SPELLING WORDS

1. meant	*meant*	I **meant** to return the library book.
2. build	*build*	Shall we **build** a tree house?
3. flood	*flood*	The **flood** was caused by heavy rain.
4. laugh	*laugh*	I had to **laugh** at your funny story.
5. breakfast	*breakfast*	I like **breakfast** better than lunch.
6. enough	*enough*	One ball game a day is **enough** for me.
7. sweater	*sweater*	Wear a **sweater** when it is cool.
8. rough	*rough*	Sandpaper is **rough,** not smooth.
9. bread	*bread*	Do you want **bread** or crackers?
10. touch	*touch*	Silk feels soft when you **touch** it.
11. spread	*spread*	The young bird **spread** its wings.
12. tough	*tough*	Old corn can be **tough** and chewy.
13. already	*already*	The sun has **already** risen.
14. built	*built*	My grandparents **built** a log cabin.
15. ready	*ready*	I am **ready** to go to bed.
16. death	*death*	That is not a life or **death** matter.
17. young	*young*	Both **young** and old enjoyed the show.
18. instead	*instead*	Amy played the part **instead** of Sue.
19. heavy	*heavy*	Can you carry that **heavy** bundle?
20. ahead	*ahead*	I will go **ahead** and meet you there.

SORT THE SPELLING WORDS

1.–12. Write the spelling words with the **short a** or the **short e** sound. Circle the letters that spell this sound.

13.–20. Write the spelling words with the **short i** or the **short u** sound. Circle the letters that spell this sound.

REMEMBER THE SPELLING STRATEGY

Remember that some words have more vowel letters than vowel sounds.

86

Pretest Sentences (See procedures on pages Z10–Z11.)

1. I may have said "yes," but I **meant** to say "no."
2. Mom will use wood to **build** our table.
3. A leaky washer can **flood** a floor.
4. Circus clowns make us **laugh.**
5. The first meal of the day is **breakfast.**
6. There is **enough** yarn here to make a hat.
7. Shalonda put a **sweater** around her shoulders.
8. The bark on the tree was **rough.**
9. Ramon likes to bake whole wheat **bread.**
10. That teddy bear is soft to **touch.**
11. Julia will **spread** cream cheese on a roll.
12. Meat is hard to cut when it is **tough.**
13. I have **already** done my homework.
14. Our home was **built** last year.
15. Deangelo will be **ready** soon.
16. George Washington's **death** was in 1799.
17. My brother is too **young** to go to school.
18. I will have juice **instead** of milk.
19. The bowling ball was too **heavy** for me to use.
20. In order to win the race, Tomas must move **ahead** now.

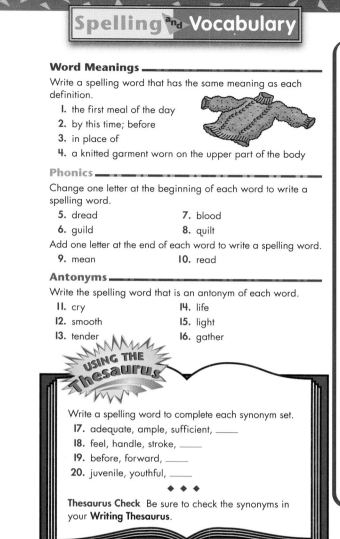

Spelling and Vocabulary

Word Meanings

Write a spelling word that has the same meaning as each definition.

1. the first meal of the day
2. by this time; before
3. in place of
4. a knitted garment worn on the upper part of the body

Phonics

Change one letter at the beginning of each word to write a spelling word.

5. dread
6. guild
7. blood
8. quilt

Add one letter at the end of each word to write a spelling word.

9. mean
10. read

Antonyms

Write the spelling word that is an antonym of each word.

11. cry
12. smooth
13. tender
14. life
15. light
16. gather

USING THE Thesaurus

Write a spelling word to complete each synonym set.

17. adequate, ample, sufficient, _____
18. feel, handle, stroke, _____
19. before, forward, _____
20. juvenile, youthful, _____

◆ ◆ ◆

Thesaurus Check Be sure to check the synonyms in your **Writing Thesaurus**.

Word Meanings
1. breakfast
2. already
3. instead
4. sweater

Phonics
5. bread
6. build
7. flood
8. built
9. meant
10. ready

Antonyms
11. laugh
12. rough
13. tough
14. death
15. heavy
16. spread

Using the Thesaurus
17. enough
18. touch
19. ahead
20. young

87

Objectives

Spelling and Vocabulary

Students will
- **write** spelling words that match definitions.
- **change** or add letters of words to form spelling words.
- **write** spelling words for antonyms.
- **use** the **Writing Thesaurus** to write spelling words that complete a series of synonyms.

Developing Oral Language Skills

Do a word sort by sound. Write **short a, short e, short i,** and **short u** on a chalkboard or an overhead transparency. Ask volunteers to say each spelling word, use it in a sentence, and write it under one of the headings according to the sound the word contains. When they have finished listing the words, ask students to consider the letters in each word that spell the sound. Then have volunteers circle the letters that spell the sound.

MEETING INDIVIDUAL NEEDS

Providing More Help

Write the vowel combinations **au, ea, ui, ou**, and **oo** on the chalkboard as headings. Then write the spelling words without their vowels on separate cards. Have the students take turns choosing the cards and deciding which vowels are missing. Then have them write the words on the chalkboard under the proper heading and circle the vowels that spell each short vowel sound.

★ Students who need to study fewer words should use the **Alternate Word List**. This list is starred on page T86 in the Teacher Edition. The **Unit 14 Practice Masters** (*Teacher Resource Book*) provide additional practice with these words.

Unit 14 Practice Masters

Name _____ **Practice Master** Unit **14**

| 1. ready | 3. meant | 5. breakfast | 7. built | 9. touch |
| 2. already | 4. instead | 6. build | 8. enough | 10. young |

A. Write the spelling word that is a synonym for each word.

1. prepared _____   4. adequate _____
2. youthful _____   5. make _____
3. feel _____   6. constructed _____

B. These words are misspelled. Write each spelling word correctly.

1. brakefast _____   5. redee _____
2. allredy _____   6. yung _____
3. ment _____   7. bilt _____
4. insted _____   8. enuf _____

C. Write the spelling word that belongs in each sentence.

1. Katrina doesn't have ____ orange paint to finish the job.
2. Mandy Lee can ____ a treehouse in the backyard. _____
3. Did you know what that word ____? _____
4. Our school was ____ over 50 years ago. _____
5. Let's read a book ____ of watching television. _____
6. Alexis has ____ finished her homework. _____
7. I ate cereal for ____. _____
8. He is too ____ to go to school. _____

79

Practice Master Unit **14**

| built | touch |
| enough | young |

...nscramble the circled letters to

...wn
... meal of the day
...nstruct, put together
...much as needed
...this time

80

T87

Objectives

Spelling and Reading

Students will
- **replace** underlined words in sentences with spelling words.
- **write** spelling words to complete a series of meaning-related words.
- **complete** sentences using spelling words.

One-Minute Handwriting Hint

Be sure to close the oval in the lowercase **d**. Pause at the top of the first undercurve; then pull the slant stroke to the baseline. Do not loop the letter.

PAUSE → 𝒹 PULL TO BASELINE

Legible handwriting can boost spelling scores by as much as 20%.

Replace the Words

1. heavy
2. rough
3. young
4. tough
5. ready

Complete the Sequences

6. laugh
7. sweater
8. breakfast
9. flood
10. touch

Complete the Sentences

11. bread
12. enough
13. build
14. death
15. spread
16. meant
17. built
18. instead
19. already
20. ahead

Spelling and Reading

meant	build	flood	laugh	breakfast
enough	sweater	rough	bread	touch
spread	tough	already	built	ready
death	young	instead	heavy	ahead

Replace the Words Replace the underlined adjective in each sentence with a spelling word that has the same meaning.

1. Please help me lift this <u>weighty</u> box.
2. The tire went flat on the <u>bumpy</u> road.
3. That <u>youthful</u> student enjoys writing about animals.
4. We need a <u>strong</u> bag to hold the trash.
5. Be <u>prepared</u> to leave for the zoo at noon.

Complete the Sequences Write a spelling word to complete each group of words.

6. giggle, chuckle, _____
7. vest, coat, jacket, _____
8. dinner, lunch, _____
9. overflow, spillover, _____
10. see, hear, smell, taste, _____

Complete the Sentences Write a spelling word to complete each sentence.

11. To make toast, you start with a slice of _____.
12. Katrina doesn't have _____ orange paint to finish the job.
13. Mandy Lee can _____ a tree house in the backyard.
14. Every news station reported the _____ of the famous author.
15. We can _____ this tablecloth on the ground for our picnic.
16. Did you know what that word _____?
17. Our school was _____ more than fifty years ago.
18. Let's read a book _____ of watching television.
19. Alex has _____ finished his homework.
20. We will go on _____ if they are late.

88

MEETING INDIVIDUAL NEEDS

Providing More Challenge

Challenge Words and **Challenge Activities** for Unit 14 appear on page 235. **Challenge Word Test Sentences** appear on page T235.

Unit 14 Challenge Activities

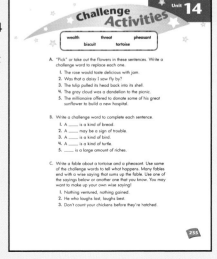

Weekly Test Options

Option 1:
One Spelling Word Per Sentence
(See procedures on pages Z10–Z11.)

1. The play was so funny that Father could not help but **laugh**.
2. I ate most of my **bread**.
3. The load of dirt should be **spread** on the garden.
4. You may leave as soon as you are **ready**.
5. I cannot believe it is **already** time to go.
6. My friend **meant** something else.
7. He was sad at the **death** of his goldfish.
8. Feel free to go **ahead** with your plan.
9. The boxes were too **heavy** to lift.
10. I put a **sweater** on over my shirt.
11. I used a red crayon **instead** of a blue one.
12. I eat **breakfast** as soon as I get up.
13. Father wants to **build** the house himself.
14. Grandfather **built** his own home.
15. The smooth stones were not **rough**.

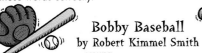

Spelling and Writing

Proofread a Book Review

Six words are not spelled correctly in this book review. Write those words correctly.

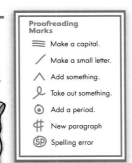

Bobby Baseball
by Robert Kimmel Smith

Bobby Ellis is a ~~yung~~ *young* boy who loves baseball. He knows ~~alredy~~ *already* that he wants to be a pitcher. But his father, the coach, wants him to be a second baseman ~~insted~~ *instead*. How can Bobby go ahead with his plans when he cannot please Dad, who is so ~~tuff~~ *tough* he expects his son to be perfect? Will Bobby be able to ~~laff~~ *laugh* off his father's interference, or will it be the ~~deth~~ *death* of his dream? Read to find out. It is a great book.

Proofreading Marks

≡ Make a capital.
/ Make a small letter.
∧ Add something.
✄ Take out something.
⊙ Add a period.
New paragraph.
ⓢⓟ Spelling error

Write a Book Review

Expository Writing

Write a book review about a book you have read. Be sure to include

- the title of the book.
- the name of the author.
- what the story is about.
- what problem the main character has.
- whether you would recommend the book and why or why not.

Use as many spelling words as you can.

Writing Process

Prewriting
⇩
Drafting
⇩
Revising
⇩
Editing
⇩
Publishing

Proofread Your Writing During Editing

Proofread your writing for spelling errors as part of the editing stage in the writing process. Be sure to check each word carefully. Use a dictionary to check spelling if you are not sure.

89

Objectives

Spelling and Writing
Students will
- **proofread** a book review.
- **use** the writing process to write a book review.
- **proofread** their writing.

Using the Writing Process

Before assigning **Write a Book Review** in this unit, see pages 258–259 in the Student Edition for a complete review of the writing process and additional writing assignments. You may also wish to refer to pages Z12–Z13 in the Teacher Edition.

Keeping a Spelling Journal

Encourage students to record the words they misspelled on the weekly test in a personal spelling journal. These words may be recycled for future study. Students may also wish to include words from their writing. See pages Z12–Z13 in the Teacher Edition for more information.

---

16. That cut of meat is **tough**.
17. We do not have **enough** people to play.
18. You must **touch** the home plate.
19. The children are at a very **young** age.
20. We once had a **flood** in our town.

Option 2:
Multiple Spelling Words Per Sentence
(See procedures on pages Z10–Z11.)

1. I **meant** to bring a **sweater instead** of a coat.
2. We **already** have **enough bread** to make sandwiches.
3. The truck took away the **heavy, rough** rocks before the workers **built** the home.
4. They may **flood** the park and **build** a rink for skating, but that would mean the **death** of the trees.
5. Please do not **touch** the **breakfast** food until we are **ready** to eat.
6. The sign up **ahead** will make you **laugh** when you read it.
7. I **spread** the dirt around that **tough young** plant.

Option 3:
Standardized Test
(See *Teacher Resource Book,* Unit 14.)

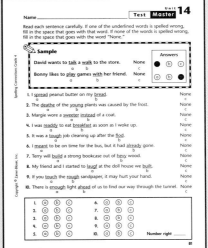

Unit 14 Test Master

T89

Vocabulary

Objectives

Strategy Words

Students will
- **review** words studied previously that are related to the spelling strategy.
- **preview** unknown words that are related to the spelling strategy.

Strategy Words

Remind the students that the **Strategy Words** relate to the spelling patterns they have studied in this unit. The **Review Words** are below grade level, and the **Preview Words** are above grade level. You may wish to use the following sentences to introduce the words in context.

Review Words:
Words From Grade 3

1. It was so cold we needed to turn on the **heat**.
2. We nailed a **board** across the hole in the fence.
3. My **friend** is coming to spend the night.
4. Today was a **great** day for being outdoors.
5. The butcher will **weigh** the meat before putting it in the freezer.

Preview Words:
Words From Grade 5

6. Susan had on a pretty **plaid** skirt with her new sweater.
7. My teacher is always **pleasant** to the students.
8. What a **pleasure** to be able to spend the day with my grandparents!
9. Under the main heading of the paragraph was a **subhead**.
10. You will need a **sweatshirt** today.

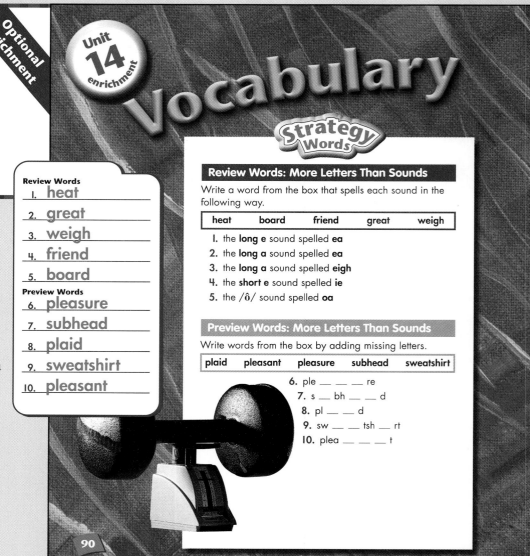

Review Words
1. heat
2. great
3. weigh
4. friend
5. board

Preview Words
6. pleasure
7. subhead
8. plaid
9. sweatshirt
10. pleasant

Strategy Words

Review Words: More Letters Than Sounds

Write a word from the box that spells each sound in the following way.

heat	board	friend	great	weigh

1. the **long e** sound spelled **ea**
2. the **long a** sound spelled **ea**
3. the **long a** sound spelled **eigh**
4. the **short e** sound spelled **ie**
5. the /ô/ sound spelled **oa**

Preview Words: More Letters Than Sounds

Write words from the box by adding missing letters.

plaid	pleasant	pleasure	subhead	sweatshirt

6. ple __ __ __ re
7. s __ bh __ __ d
8. pl __ __ d
9. sw __ __ tsh __ rt
10. plea __ __ __ t

90

Unit 14 RECAP

You may wish to assign the **Unit 14 Homework Master** (*Teacher Resource Book,* Unit 14) as a fun way to recap the spelling words.

Unit 14 Homework Master

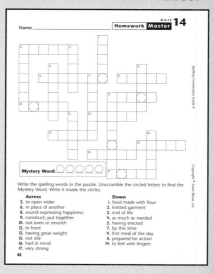

Name _____   Homework **Master** Unit **14**

Write the spelling words in the puzzle. Unscramble the circled letters to find the Mystery Word. Write it inside the circles.

Mystery Word: ○○○○○

Across
2. to open wider
6. in place of another
8. sound expressing happiness
9. construct, put together
10. not even or smooth
12. in front
13. having great weight
15. not old
16. had in mind
17. very strong

Down
1. food made with flour
2. knitted garment
3. end of life
4. as much as needed
5. having erected
7. by this time
9. first meal of the day
11. prepared for action
14. to feel with fingers

82

Connections

Content Words

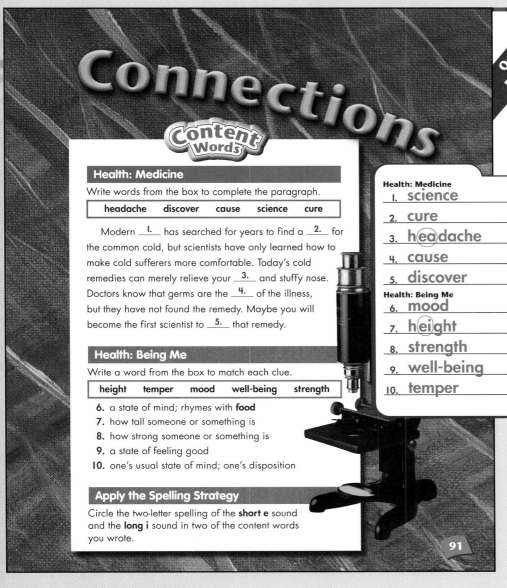

Health: Medicine

Write words from the box to complete the paragraph.

headache	discover	cause	science	cure

Modern __1.__ has searched for years to find a __2.__ for the common cold, but scientists have only learned how to make cold sufferers more comfortable. Today's cold remedies can merely relieve your __3.__ and stuffy nose. Doctors know that germs are the __4.__ of the illness, but they have not found the remedy. Maybe you will become the first scientist to __5.__ that remedy.

Health: Being Me

Write a word from the box to match each clue.

height	temper	mood	well-being	strength

6. a state of mind; rhymes with **food**
7. how tall someone or something is
8. how strong someone or something is
9. a state of feeling good
10. one's usual state of mind; one's disposition

Apply the Spelling Strategy

Circle the two-letter spelling of the **short e** sound and the **long i** sound in two of the content words you wrote.

91

Health: Medicine
1. science
2. cure
3. h(ea)dache
4. cause
5. discover

Health: Being Me
6. mood
7. h(ei)ght
8. strength
9. well-being
10. temper

Objectives

Content Words

Students will
• **expand** vocabulary with content-related words.
• **relate** the spelling strategy to words outside the basic spelling list.

Content Words

Health: Medicine

Review the meanings of these words with the students. You may wish to use these sentences to introduce the words in context.

1. My dad frequently gets a **headache** from spending so much time on the computer.
2. As we study about the human body, we will **discover** how it works.
3. What is the **cause** of your discomfort?
4. I think **science** is an exciting subject.
5. Our scientists will soon discover a **cure** for that disease.

Encourage the students to use these words in a brief story about a real or imaginary scientific discovery.

Health: Being Me

Review the meanings of these words with the students. You may wish to use these sentences to introduce the words in context.

6. We will measure your **height** at the beginning of the school year and again at the end of the year.
7. Try not to lose your **temper,** because it makes you feel bad afterward.
8. I like to be around people who are in a good **mood**.
9. The doctor is concerned about your **well-being**.
10. Eat and drink properly and get plenty of exercise so you can keep up your **strength**.

Encourage the students to use these words in a paragraph about a character in a story they have read.

Unit 15 Home Study Master

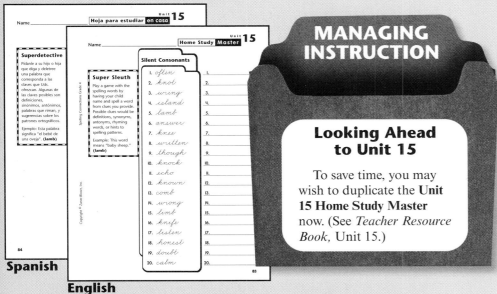

Name _____

Hoja para estudiar en casa Unit 15

Superdetective

Pídanle a su hijo o hija que diga y deletree una palabra que corresponda a las claves que Uds. ofrezcan. Algunas de las claves posibles son definiciones, sinónimos, antónimos, palabras que rimen, y sugerencias sobre los patrones ortográficos.

Ejemplo: Esta palabra significa "el bebé de una oveja". **(lamb)**

Spelling Connections Grade 4
Copyright © Zaner-Bloser, Inc.

84

Spanish

Name _____

Home Study Master Unit 15

Silent Consonants

Super Sleuth

Play a game with the spelling words by having your child name and spell a word from clues you provide. Possible clues would be definitions, synonyms, antonyms, rhyming words, or hints to spelling patterns.

Example: This word means "baby sheep." **(lamb)**

1. often
2. knot
3. wring
4. island
5. lamb
6. answer
7. knee
8. written
9. though
10. knock
11. echo
12. known
13. comb
14. wrong
15. limb
16. knife
17. listen
18. honest
19. doubt
20. calm

83

English

MANAGING INSTRUCTION

Looking Ahead to Unit 15

To save time, you may wish to duplicate the **Unit 15 Home Study Master** now. (See *Teacher Resource Book,* Unit 15.)

Basic Spelling List

often	echo
knot	known
wring	comb
island	wrong
lamb	limb
answer	knife
knee	listen
written	honest
though	doubt
knock	calm

Strategy Words

Review
half	knight
hourly	wrap
knew	

Preview
beret	knapsack
design	thorough
frighten	

Content Words

Social Studies: Crafts
crafts	weaving
sewing	knitting
handmade	

Math: Operations
answers	zero
subtraction	problem
numeral	

Individual Needs

Challenge Words
gnaw	prompt
gnat	knuckle
cough	

Alternate Word List
often	known
island	wrong
answer	listen
knee	honest
though	calm

MATERIALS

Student Edition
Pages 92–97
Challenge Activities, p. 236

Teacher Edition
Pages T92A–T97
Challenge Activities, T236

Other Resources
Spelling Connections Software
Unit 15 Word List Overhead
  Transparency

Teacher Resource Book
Unit 15 Home Study Master
  (English or Spanish; students
  may pretest on this sheet or use
  it for home practice.)
Unit 15 Homework Master
Unit 15 Practice Masters
Flip Folder Practice Master
Unit 15 Test Master

Visit our Web site, www.zaner-bloser.com

OBJECTIVES

Spelling and Thinking
Students will
- **read** the spelling words in list form and in context.
- **sort** the words according to the location of silent consonants.
- **read** and remember this week's spelling strategy.

Spelling and Vocabulary
Students will
- **write** spelling words that match definitions.
- **arrange** spelling words in alphabetical order.
- **use** the **Spelling Dictionary** to find a spelling word that can be used as a conjunction.

Spelling and Reading
Students will
- **write** spelling words for clues.
- **solve** analogies using spelling words.
- **replace** antonyms with spelling words.

Spelling and Writing
Students will
- **proofread** a letter of complaint.
- **use** the writing process to write a letter of complaint.
- **proofread** their writing.

MEETING INDIVIDUAL NEEDS
Learning Styles

Visual

Use the string-words made in the kines-thetic activity on this page. Have the students use a flash-light to trace each word with the beam of light. Have them study the words and then write them on their papers. Tell them to write the silent letters in black and the other letters in red, blue, or green.

Auditory

Write the spelling words on the chalk-board and underline the silent letters three times. Have the students chant the letters in each spelling word, emphasiz-ing the silent letters by chanting louder and slower. Then ask them to write the words on their papers as they repeat the chants softly to themselves. Ask them to circle the silent letters.

Kinesthetic

Give each student glue and a piece of yarn 30–40 inches long. Assign sev-eral words to each student. Have them write the words on construction paper with glue. Then have them place the yarn over the glue to form the spelling words.

Language and Cultural Differences

When they are learning to spell words with silent let-ters, the students must memorize the spellings. The task will be easier if the students have several opportunities to associate the meaning of each word with the visual sequence of letters used to spell it.

Write the spelling words on the chalkboard. Point to each word and pronounce it. Ask a volunteer to use the word in a sentence and define it. Then point out the silent letter in the word.

Have the students make an illustrated dictionary for the words in this unit. Allow each student to choose two words to define and illustrate. Help them with their defi-nitions. Then make a booklet by stapling their papers together.

MANAGING INSTRUCTION

3–5 Day Plan		Average	Below Average	Above Average
Day 1	**Day 1**	Pretest Spelling Mini-Lesson, p. T92 Spelling and Thinking, p. 92	Pretest Spelling Mini-Lesson, p. T92 Spelling and Thinking, p. 92	Pretest Spelling and Thinking, p. 92
	Day 2	Spelling and Vocabulary, p. 93	Spelling and Vocabulary, p. 93 (or) Unit 15 Practice Master, A and B	Spelling and Vocabulary, p. 93 Spelling and Reading, p. 94
Day 2	**Day 3**	Spelling and Reading, p. 94	Spelling and Reading, p. 94 (or) Unit 15 Practice Master, C and D	Challenge Activities, p. 236
	Day 4	Spelling and Writing, p. 95 Unit 15 Homework Master	Spelling and Writing, p. 95	Spelling and Writing, p. 95 Unit 15 Homework Master
Day 3	**Day 5**	Weekly Test	Weekly Test	Weekly Test

Vocabulary Connections (pages 96 and 97) may be used anytime during this unit.

Objectives

Spelling and Thinking

Students will

- **read** the spelling words in list form and in context.
- **sort** the words according to the location of silent consonants.
- **read** and remember this week's spelling strategy.

UNIT PRETEST

Use **Pretest Sentences** below. Refer to the self-checking procedures on student page 256. You may wish to use the **Unit 15 Word List Overhead Transparency** as part of the checking procedure.

TEACHING THE STRATEGY

Spelling Mini-Lesson

Ask the students how they would define a "silent letter." (a letter that is in a word's spelling but is not pronounced) Tell the students that all the words on this week's list have silent consonants.

Draw a simple pair of tennis shoes, or "sneakers," on the chalkboard. Write **knot, calm, doubt,** and **comb** on the chalkboard. Ask the students to identify the silent consonants in these words. (k, l, b, b) Explain to the students that they might think of the silent consonants in these words as "sneakers," because they "sneak" by without making a sound. (You might wish to draw a line from **k, l, b,** and **b** in these words to the picture of the sneakers.) Ask volunteers to read the spelling words and identify the "sneakers." (You may wish to note that while some people do pronounce /t/ in **often,** the preferred pronunciation does not include this consonant sound.) Students should note that silent consonants can come at the beginning, in the middle, or at the end of a word.

Note: Some students may identify the **w** in **known** as a silent consonant. If so, point out that the **w** is part of the spelling of the **long o** sound as taught in Unit 7. In **echo,** the **h** is considered silent since this is a relatively rare spelling of the /k/ sound found only in words from Greek.

Conclude by reading **Remember the Spelling Strategy** on page 92.

Order of answers may vary. silent consonants begin or end word

1. knot
2. wring
3. lamb
4. knee ★
5. written
6. though ★
7. knock
8. known ★
9. comb
10. wrong ★
11. limb
12. knife
13. honest ★

silent consonants in middle

14. often ★
15. island ★
16. answer ★
17. echo
18. listen ★
19. doubt
20. calm ★

92

Spelling and Thinking

READ THE SPELLING WORDS

1.	often	*often*	We **often** call our grandparents.
2.	knot	*knot*	I have a **knot** in my shoelace.
3.	wring	*wring*	We **wring** the water from our wet socks.
4.	island	*island*	You can reach the **island** by ferry.
5.	lamb	*lamb*	A **lamb** is a young sheep.
6.	answer	*answer*	Please **answer** the question.
7.	knee	*knee*	He hurt his **knee** climbing a cliff.
8.	written	*written*	They have **written** many letters.
9.	though	*though*	He could read, **though** he was not six.
10.	knock	*knock*	You should **knock** before entering.
11.	echo	*echo*	Call and you will hear an **echo**.
12.	known	*known*	Her address is not **known**.
13.	comb	*comb*	Wait until I **comb** my hair.
14.	wrong	*wrong*	No question that you ask is **wrong**.
15.	limb	*limb*	The bird sat on the **limb** of the tree.
16.	knife	*knife*	On the table were a **knife** and fork.
17.	listen	*listen*	You must **listen** to each question.
18.	honest	*honest*	Please give me an **honest** answer.
19.	doubt	*doubt*	I do not **doubt** your story.
20.	calm	*calm*	The sea was **calm** after the storm.

SORT THE SPELLING WORDS

1.–13. Write each spelling word that begins or ends with one or more silent consonants. Underline those consonants.

14.–20. Write the spelling words with one or more silent consonants within the word. Underline those consonants.

REMEMBER THE SPELLING STRATEGY

Remember that some words are spelled with silent consonants: **k** in **knot** and **s** in **island**.

Pretest Sentences (See procedures on pages Z10–Z11.)

1. I **often** walk to school.
2. The scout will practice tying a **knot**.
3. I twisted the towel to **wring** out the water.
4. Land that has water on all sides is called an **island**.
5. A baby sheep is called a **lamb**.
6. If the phone rings while I am out, please **answer** it.
7. As she climbed the stairs, Tonya hurt her **knee**.
8. Don's report was **written** in his best handwriting.
9. We had fun at the show, even **though** it snowed.
10. Before you enter the room, please **knock** on the door.
11. A dolphin finds an object by listening to an **echo**.
12. I have **known** Latoya all my life.
13. Jane held her hair in place with a **comb**.
14. Juanita had only one **wrong** answer.
15. An arm is sometimes called a **limb**.
16. Please be careful when using a **knife**.
17. Please pay attention and **listen**.
18. Most people tell the truth and are **honest**.
19. If a person does not tell the truth, you begin to **doubt** that person's word.
20. After the storm, the sea was **calm**.

Spelling and Vocabulary

Word Meanings

Write a spelling word for each definition.

1. frequently
2. quiet; peaceful
3. a young sheep
4. to be unsure
5. a reply to a question
6. a large branch of a tree
7. the joint where thigh and lower leg connect
8. to send back a sound
9. a tool with teeth; used to arrange hair

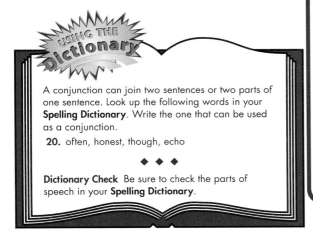

Alphabetical Order

Write each group of spelling words in alphabetical order.

10.–12. wring, wrong, written
13.–16. knot, knock, known, knife
17.–19. island, listen, honest

USING THE Dictionary

A conjunction can join two sentences or two parts of one sentence. Look up the following words in your **Spelling Dictionary**. Write the one that can be used as a conjunction.

20. often, honest, though, echo

◆ ◆ ◆

Dictionary Check Be sure to check the parts of speech in your **Spelling Dictionary**.

Word Meanings
1. often
2. calm
3. lamb
4. doubt
5. answer
6. limb
7. knee
8. echo
9. comb

Alphabetical Order
10. wring
11. written
12. wrong
13. knife
14. knock
15. knot
16. known
17. honest
18. island
19. listen

Using the Dictionary
20. though

93

Objectives

Spelling and Vocabulary

Students will
- **write** spelling words that match definitions.
- **arrange** spelling words in alphabetical order.
- **use** the **Spelling Dictionary** to find a spelling word that can be used as a conjunction.

Developing Oral Language Skills

Have volunteers read aloud the spelling words in which the first or last letter is silent. (knot, knock, knee, knife, known, wring, wrong, written, comb, lamb, limb, though) Call on students to repeat the word and identify the first and last sound they hear in each word. Then write the word on the chalkboard and ask students to underline the silent letter or letters in each word.

MEETING INDIVIDUAL NEEDS

Providing More Help

Have the students work in pairs. Have one student start out as the "writer" and the other as the "chalkboard." Ask the writer to choose a spelling word and trace the letters of that word on the back of the chalkboard, drawing one letter at a time, but drawing a straight horizontal line, rather than a letter, for the silent consonant. The chalkboard must try to guess the word and write it correctly on the classroom chalkboard. The partners then switch places for each new word.

★ Students who need to study fewer words should use the **Alternate Word List**. This list is starred on page T92 in the Teacher Edition. The **Unit 15 Practice Masters** (*Teacher Resource Book*) provide additional practice with these words.

Unit 15 Practice Masters

Name _____

Practice **Master** **Unit 15**

| 1. knee | 3. wrong | 5. island | 7. often | 9. answer |
| 2. known | 4. honest | 6. calm | 8. listen | 10. though |

A. Write the spelling words in which you find these silent letters.

1. k _____
2. w _____
3. t _____
4. h _____
5. s _____

B. Write the spelling word that goes with each meaning.

1. the joint where the thigh and the lower leg connect _____
2. a reply to a question _____
3. quiet, peaceful, not excited _____
4. try to hear _____
5. a piece of land with water all around it _____
6. many times _____
7. not correct _____
8. truthful _____

Practice **Master** **Unit 15**

| often | answer |
| listen | though |

with a spelling word that is an

...ling words. Circle and write

d	a
w	n
w	x
l	m
r	s
d	f
g	h
p	t

Objectives

Spelling and Reading

Students will
- **write** spelling words for clues.
- **solve** analogies using spelling words.
- **replace** antonyms with spelling words.

Use the Clues

1. knot
2. echo
3. comb
4. though
5. island
6. limb
7. knock
8. known
9. written

Solve the Analogies

10. lamb
11. knife
12. knee
13. wring
14. listen

Write the Antonyms

15. wrong
16. honest
17. doubt
18. answer
19. calm
20. often

One-Minute Handwriting Hint

The checkstroke ending of the lowercase **w** swings directly into the first stroke of the letter **r**. The swing-right motion should not be too low.

SWING RIGHT

Legible handwriting can boost spelling scores by as much as 20%.

Spelling and Reading

often	knot	wring	island	lamb
answer	knee	written	though	knock
echo	known	comb	wrong	limb
knife	listen	honest	doubt	calm

Use the Clues   Write a spelling word for each clue.

1. I can make your shoelaces hard to untie.
2. I am your voice sent back to you.
3. I can mean "to search carefully."
4. I rhyme with **low** and can be a conjunction.
5. I am surrounded by water.
6. I am an arm, a leg, a flipper, or a wing.
7. I am something you do on a door.
8. I am a form of the word **know**.
9. I am a form of the word **write**.

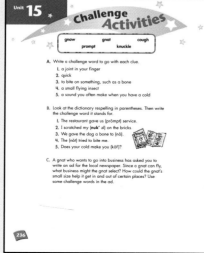

Solve the Analogies   Write the missing spelling word to complete each analogy.

10. **Cow** is to **calf** as **sheep** is to _____.
11. **Loaves** is to **loaf** as **knives** is to _____.
12. **Arm** is to **elbow** as **leg** is to _____.
13. **Not** is to **knot** as **ring** is to _____.
14. **See** is to **watch** as **hear** is to _____.

Write the Antonyms   Write the spelling word that is an antonym for each underlined word or phrase.

15. Are you sure this answer is <u>correct</u>?
16. An <u>untruthful</u> person will have many friends.
17. I <u>am sure</u> that Katera will come with us.
18. Please write the <u>question</u> on the chalkboard.
19. The sea was <u>rough</u> after the storm.
20. We <u>rarely</u> go shopping in the city.

94

MEETING INDIVIDUAL NEEDS

Providing More Challenge

Challenge Words and **Challenge Activities** for Unit 15 appear on page 236. **Challenge Word Test Sentences** appear on page T236.

Unit 15 Challenge Activities

Weekly Test Options

Option 1:
One Spelling Word Per Sentence
(See procedures on pages Z10–Z11.)

1. The hero was **known** well by all of the people.
2. I was able to hear my voice when my **echo** came back to me.
3. The sea was **calm** until the storm began.
4. Please **wring** out the wet towel and hang it up to dry.
5. Did you ever call the **wrong** person?
6. We swam to the **island** in the lake.
7. I trust you because you are **honest**.
8. The letter was **written** with a pencil.
9. The **knee** is a joint in the leg.
10. If you **knock** on the door, they will let you in.
11. The rope will be strong if you tie a good **knot** in it.
12. Slice the apples with a **knife**.
13. I do not **doubt** my friend's story.
14. The wind blew a **limb** off the tree.

Proofread a Letter

Six words are not spelled correctly in this letter of complaint. Write those words correctly.

Dear Sir or Madam:

    I have been billed the rong [wrong] amount for a pair of slacks I purchased. Since I ofen [often] shop at your store, I am sure this was an honist [honest] mistake and, since your good reputation is well known, I do not dout [doubt] that you will correct the error. The price of the slacks was $23.42, not $32.42, as charged. I would appreciate a writen anser [written answer] to this letter. Thank you.

        Sincerely,

        Thomas R. Whitman

Proofreading Marks

- ☰ Make a capital.
- / Make a small letter.
- ∧ Add something.
- ℛ Take out something.
- ⊙ Add a period.
- ⌗ New paragraph
- ⓢⓟ Spelling error

Write a Letter

Expository Writing

Write a letter of complaint about a real or imaginary problem. Be polite. Include

- the name of the person to whom you are writing.
- complete information about the problem.
- how you would like the problem to be solved.
- your name.

Use as many spelling words as you can.

Proofread Your Writing During ➤

Proofread your writing for spelling errors as part of the editing stage in the writing process. Be sure to check each word carefully. Use a dictionary to check spelling if you are not sure.

Writing Process

Prewriting
⇩
Drafting
⇩
Revising
⇩
Editing
⇩
Publishing

95

Objectives

Spelling and Writing

Students will
- **proofread** a letter of complaint.
- **use** the writing process to write a letter of complaint.
- **proofread** their writing.

Using the Writing Process

Before assigning **Write a Letter** in this unit, see pages 258–259 in the Student Edition for a complete review of the writing process and additional writing assignments. You may wish to refer to pages Z12–Z13 in the Teacher Edition.

Keeping a Spelling Journal

Encourage students to record the words they misspelled on the weekly test in a personal spelling journal. These words may be recycled for future study. Students may also wish to include words from their writing. See pages Z12–Z13 in the Teacher Edition for more information.

---

15. I would like to see you more **often**.
16. Our family went to the fair even **though** it was raining.
17. I like to **listen** to the radio.
18. A young sheep is called a **lamb**.
19. I used the **comb** for my hair.
20. Please **answer** me when I ask you something.

Option 2:
Multiple Spelling Words Per Sentence
(See procedures on pages Z10–Z11.)

1. You will hear your **echo** if you **listen**.
2. I **doubt** that my **knee** will feel better for some time.
3. Father is **known** to others as an **honest** man.
4. You did not **wring** out the **wrong** shirt.
5. My friend found a **comb** on the **island**.
6. It seems as **though** the **limb** broke off during the storm.
7. If you **knock** on the door, I will **answer** it.
8. You should stay **calm** when using a sharp **knife**.
9. The **lamb** was playing with the string with a **knot** in it.
10. I **often** send a **written** note to my grandmother.

Option 3:
Standardized Test
(See *Teacher Resource Book,* Unit 15.)

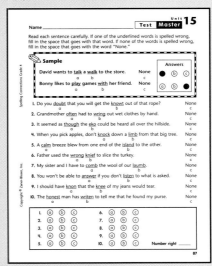

Unit 15 Test Master

Objectives

Optional Enrichment

Strategy Words

Students will
- **review** words studied previously that are related to the spelling strategy.
- **preview** unknown words that are related to the spelling strategy.

Remind the students that the **Strategy Words** relate to the spelling patterns they have studied in this unit. The **Review Words** are below grade level, and the **Preview Words** are above grade level. You may wish to use the following sentences to introduce the words in context.

Review Words:
Words From Grade 3

1. Cut the apple and give **half** to your little brother.
2. Mother was so tired because the baby was awake **hourly** during the night.
3. Since I had really studied, I **knew** I would do well on my spelling test.
4. The story told about a **knight** in shining armor.
5. We will **wrap** the birthday gifts in blue paper.

Preview Words:
Words From Grade 5

6. The Frenchman wore a **beret** with his uniform.
7. We will **design** a new outfit for you.
8. Do not **frighten** the puppy by clapping your hands near his ears.
9. He carried a sandwich and some water in his **knapsack** when he went on the hike.
10. They did a **thorough** job of cleaning the house.

Review Words
1. knew
2. hourly
3. knight
4. half
5. wrap

Preview Words
6. frighten
7. design
8. thorough
9. beret
10. knapsack

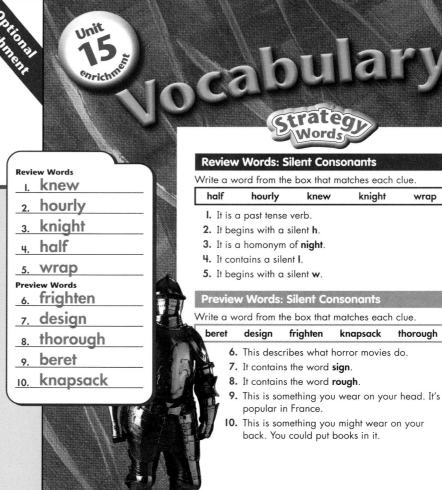

Vocabulary

Strategy Words

Review Words: Silent Consonants

Write a word from the box that matches each clue.

| half | hourly | knew | knight | wrap |

1. It is a past tense verb.
2. It begins with a silent **h**.
3. It is a homonym of **night**.
4. It contains a silent **l**.
5. It begins with a silent **w**.

Preview Words: Silent Consonants

Write a word from the box that matches each clue.

| beret | design | frighten | knapsack | thorough |

6. This describes what horror movies do.
7. It contains the word **sign**.
8. It contains the word **rough**.
9. This is something you wear on your head. It's popular in France.
10. This is something you might wear on your back. You could put books in it.

96

Unit 15 RECAP

You may wish to assign the **Unit 15 Homework Master** (*Teacher Resource Book*, Unit 15) as a fun way to recap the spelling words.

Unit 15 Homework Master

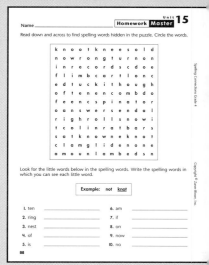

Connections

Content Words

Social Studies: Crafts

Add and subtract letters to form words from the box.

crafts	sewing	handmade	weaving	knitting

1. rafting – ing + c + s = _____
2. know – ow + it + tin + g = _____
3. h + and + making – king + de = _____
4. send – nd + win + get – et = _____
5. wear – r + v + ink – k + g = _____

Math: Operations

Write a word from the box for each clue.

answers	subtraction	numeral	zero	problem

6. I have plenty of nothing.
7. Are you taking it away?
8. Questions need these.
9. Each one of these is an example: 3, 72, 108.
10. This needs a solution.

Apply the Spelling Strategy

Circle the silent consonant that begins one of the content words you wrote. Circle the silent consonant in the second syllable in another content word you wrote.

rafting-ing+c+s

Social Studies: Crafts
1. crafts
2. knitting
3. handmade
4. sewing
5. weaving

Math: Operations
6. zero
7. subtraction
8. answers
9. numeral
10. problem

97

Objectives

Content Words

Students will
- **expand** vocabulary with content-related words.
- **relate** the spelling strategy to words outside the basic spelling list.

Content Words

Social Studies: Crafts

Review the meanings of these words with the students. You may wish to use these sentences to introduce the words in context.

1. My friend loves to do **crafts** in her spare time.
2. Grandmother always has a **sewing** project in process.
3. I like **handmade** gifts best of all.
4. There is a class in **weaving** being offered in the fall.
5. Aunt Thelma is **knitting** me a sweater.

Encourage the students to use these words in a story about early settlers in the area where they live.

Math: Operations

Review the meanings of these words with the students. You may wish to use these sentences to introduce the words in context.

6. Check your **answers** with the key when you are finished.
7. There are ten **subtraction** problems at the end of the lesson.
8. Be sure each Roman **numeral** is written neatly.
9. You will always get the same answer when you multiply anything by **zero**.
10. If you have a **problem** with any of these exercises, please tell me.

Encourage the students to use these words to write word problems for their classmates to solve.

Unit 16 Home Study Master

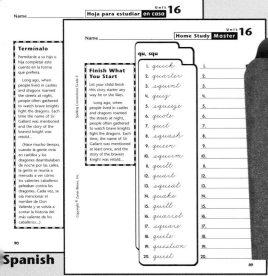

Spanish

English

MANAGING INSTRUCTION

Looking Ahead to Unit 16

To save time, you may wish to duplicate the **Unit 16 Home Study Master** now. (See *Teacher Resource Book*, Unit 16.)

Basic Spelling List

quick	quilt
quarter	quart
squint	squeal
quiz	quake
squeeze	quill
quote	quarrel
quit	square
squash	quite
queen	question
squirm	quiet

Strategy Words

Review
equal	grand
clock	stitch
fresh	

Preview
aquarium	square
quart	unequal
squirrel	

Content Words

Fine Arts: Instruments
quartet	clarinet
piccolo	bassoon
oboe	

Science: Matter
airy	solid
liquid	helium
gas	

Individual Needs

Challenge Words
quartz	squid
quaint	squirt
quiver	

Alternate Word List
quick	quilt
quarter	square
squeeze	quite
quit	question
queen	quiet

MATERIALS

Student Edition
Pages 98–103
Challenge Activities, p. 237

Teacher Edition
Pages T98A–T103
Challenge Activities, p. T237

Other Resources
Spelling Connections Software
Unit 16 Word List Overhead
Transparency

Teacher Resource Book
Unit 16 Home Study Master
(English or Spanish; students
may pretest on this sheet or use
it for home practice.)
Unit 16 Homework Master
Unit 16 Practice Masters
Flip Folder Practice Master
Unit 16 Test Master

Visit our Web site, www.zaner-bloser.com

OBJECTIVES

Spelling and Thinking
Students will
• **read** the spelling words in list
form and in context.
• **sort** the words according to
qu and **squ** spelling patterns.
• **read** and remember this
week's spelling strategy.

Spelling and Vocabulary
Students will
• **write** spelling words that
match definitions.
• **write** spelling words that
rhyme with other words.
• **use** the **Writing Thesaurus** to
write spelling words that are
synonyms for other words.

Spelling and Reading
Students will
• **answer** questions with
spelling words.
• **complete** a story using
spelling words.

Spelling and Writing
Students will
• **proofread** a diary entry.
• **use** the writing process to
write a diary entry.
• **proofread** their writing.

MEETING INDIVIDUAL NEEDS
Learning Styles

Visual

Use the illustration as an example to make two or more charts.

iet
qu	een
arter
estion
ick
it

irm
squ	ash
eeze
eal
int

Have a student slide the **qu** or **squ** strip up and down the chart. As each spelling word is formed, have the students say the word and write it on paper.

Auditory

Ask the students to choose spelling partners. Assign each partner half of the spelling words. Let the students take turns pronouncing the final letters of the spelling words (omitting the **qu** or **squ**). For example, a student would pronounce the word part **iz** from the word **quiz**. The partner would then decide whether that word part needed **qu** or **squ,** then say the word, and write it on paper. Have the students check each other's answers with the spelling list.

Kinesthetic

Make two spinners and label them as shown:

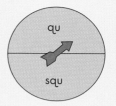 

Have a student spin the arrow on both spinners. If the arrows point to letters that form a spelling word, have the student write the spelling word.

Language and Cultural Differences

The **qu** and **squ** digraphs may be difficult for some students due to dialect or language background differences. For example, in the Spanish language, the letter **q** is always followed by a **silent u** and spells the /k/ sound heard in **keep.** Spanish-speaking students may need extra practice to establish the sound-symbol association required for this unit.

Using masking tape, form two big circles on the floor, and label each circle with the letters **qu** or **squ.** Have the students pronounce and spell each spelling word in unison. As the words are spelled, the students should identify which spelling pattern is being used and stand in the correct circle. Ask a "recorder" to write the word on the chalkboard.

MANAGING INSTRUCTION

3–5 Day Plan		Average	Below Average	Above Average
Day 1	**Day 1**	Pretest Spelling Mini-Lesson, p. T98 Spelling and Thinking, p. 98	Pretest Spelling Mini-Lesson, p. T98 Spelling and Thinking, p. 98	Pretest Spelling and Thinking, p. 98
	Day 2	Spelling and Vocabulary, p. 99	Spelling and Vocabulary, p. 99 (or) Unit 16 Practice Master, A and B	Spelling and Vocabulary, p. 99 Spelling and Reading, p. 100
Day 2	**Day 3**	Spelling and Reading, p. 100	Spelling and Reading, p. 100 (or) Unit 16 Practice Master, C and D	Challenge Activities, p. 237
	Day 4	Spelling and Writing, p. 101 Unit 16 Homework Master	Spelling and Writing, p. 101	Spelling and Writing, p. 101 Unit 16 Homework Master
Day 3	**Day 5**	Weekly Test	Weekly Test	Weekly Test
Vocabulary Connections (pages 102 and 103) may be used anytime during this unit.				

Objectives

Spelling and Thinking

Students will
- **read** the spelling words in list form and in context.
- **sort** the words according to **qu** and **squ** spelling patterns.
- **read** and remember this week's spelling strategy.

UNIT PRETEST

Use **Pretest Sentences** below. Refer to the self-checking procedures on student page 256. You may wish to use the **Unit 16 Word List Overhead Transparency** as part of the checking procedure.

TEACHING THE STRATEGY

Spelling Mini-Lesson

Tell the students that in this lesson they will spell words that have **qu** or **squ** at the beginning of the word. Write **quiz** and **squint** on the chalkboard. Ask the students what letter follows **q** in these words. (u) Point out that in English spelling, **q** is nearly always followed by **u**.

Write **/kw/** on the chalkboard. Explain that **q** and **u** work together to make the **/kw/** sound. Illustrate this fact by asking volunteers to say each spelling word aloud. Invite the students to look at each word on the spelling list as it is pronounced and listen for the **/kw/** sound. Explain that **/kw/** is the dictionary respelling for the sound represented by **qu**.

Ask the students to look up the word **quill** in their **Spelling Dictionary**. Ask a volunteer to read the definition aloud. Ask the students if they have heard this word before. (Most probably will not be familiar with **quill**.) Tell the students that many years ago books were written by hand with quill pens. Ask them how this would have made life different from life today. Ask them to imagine how their favorite book would look if it were written by hand.

Conclude by reading **Remember the Spelling Strategy** on page 98.

Order of answers may vary.

qu
1. quick ★
2. quarter ★
3. quiz
4. quote
5. quit ★
6. queen ★
7. quilt ★
8. quart
9. quake
10. quill
11. quarrel
12. quite ★
13. question ★
14. quiet ★

squ
15. squint
16. squeeze ★
17. squash
18. squirm
19. squeal
20. square ★

98

Spelling and Thinking

READ THE SPELLING WORDS

1. quick	*quick*	She is **quick** to learn her lessons.
2. quarter	*quarter*	I ate dinner at **quarter** till seven.
3. squint	*squint*	We had to **squint** in the bright light.
4. quiz	*quiz*	There will be a math **quiz** tomorrow.
5. squeeze	*squeeze*	I **squeeze** oranges for juice.
6. quote	*quote*	We would like to **quote** what you said.
7. quit	*quit*	I **quit** the game when I got tired.
8. squash	*squash*	We grew **squash** in our garden.
9. queen	*queen*	The king and **queen** rode in a carriage.
10. squirm	*squirm*	A worm will **squirm** in your hand.
11. quilt	*quilt*	A heavy **quilt** covered the bed.
12. quart	*quart*	I will buy bread and a **quart** of milk.
13. squeal	*squeal*	Children at play **squeal** with joy.
14. quake	*quake*	My cats **quake** with fear during storms.
15. quill	*quill*	A porcupine's **quill** is sharp.
16. quarrel	*quarrel*	A **quarrel** among friends is not serious.
17. square	*square*	A **square** has four sides.
18. quite	*quite*	It is not **quite** seven o'clock.
19. question	*question*	That **question** is easy to answer.
20. quiet	*quiet*	Thank-you for being **quiet** while I study.

SORT THE SPELLING WORDS

1.–14. Write the spelling words that begin with **qu**.

15.–20. Write the spelling words that begin with **squ**.

REMEMBER THE SPELLING STRATEGY

Remember that the **/kw/** sound is spelled **qu**: quiz, squint.

Pretest Sentences (See procedures on pages Z10–Z11.)

1. During the debate, Beto was **quick** to answer.
2. Twenty-five pennies equal a **quarter**.
3. The bright sun caused me to **squint**.
4. Tomorrow you will have a math **quiz**.
5. I will **squeeze** a dozen lemons to make lemonade.
6. If you are going to use someone else's words, you must **quote** them.
7. I will **quit** riding the bus to school.
8. I have a good recipe for cooking **squash**.
9. The **queen** wore a diamond crown.
10. We saw the worm **squirm** in the dirt.
11. She used bright colors in the **quilt**.
12. Two pints equal one **quart**.
13. The little pig's **squeal** was sharp.
14. Waiting for the bus in the cold made me **quake**.
15. We found a porcupine **quill**.
16. A disagreement can lead to a **quarrel**.
17. A **square** has four equal sides.
18. I was **quite** surprised to see Anne.
19. Asking to have recess for the rest of the day is a silly **question**.
20. The library is a **quiet** place.

Spelling and Vocabulary

Word Meanings
Write a spelling word for each definition.
1. a sentence that asks something
2. a coin worth twenty-five cents
3. an argument
4. to turn and twist the body
5. to look at with partly opened eyes
6. to compress; press together hard
7. a heavy bed covering
8. a rectangle with four equal sides

Rhymes
Write a spelling word that rhymes with each of these words.
9. whiz
10. wash
11. take
12. short
13. pill
14. green
15. tight
16. wit

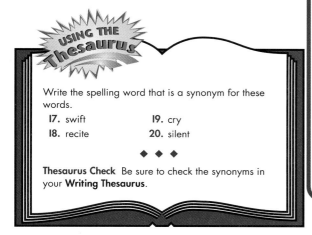

USING THE Thesaurus

Write the spelling word that is a synonym for these words.
17. swift
18. recite
19. cry
20. silent

◆ ◆ ◆

Thesaurus Check Be sure to check the synonyms in your **Writing Thesaurus**.

Word Meanings
1. question
2. quarter
3. quarrel
4. squirm
5. squint
6. squeeze
7. quilt
8. square

Rhymes
9. quiz
10. squash
11. quake
12. quart
13. quill
14. queen
15. quite
16. quit

Using the Thesaurus
17. quick
18. quote
19. squeal
20. quiet

Developing Oral Language Skills

Have students work in pairs. The first student asks a question that includes one of the words from the spelling list that begins with the /**kw**/ sound. For example, the student might ask, "Is this a **quiet** place to study?" The second student answers the question. The answer must also include a spelling word, but the spelling word must not begin with the /**kw**/ sound. For example, "No, people **squeal** past the door."

MEETING INDIVIDUAL NEEDS
Providing More Help

Tell the students that the spelling words in this unit all have the /**kw**/ sound spelled **qu**. Write each spelling word on the chalkboard with /**kw**/ in place of the **qu** spelling. Ask the students to say each word and then rewrite the word correctly.
★Students who need to study fewer words should use the **Alternate Word List**. This list is starred on page T98 in the Teacher Edition. The **Unit 16 Practice Masters** (*Teacher Resource Book*) provide additional practice with these words.

Unit 16 Practice Masters

Objectives

Spelling and Reading

Students will
- **answer** questions with spelling words.
- **complete** a story using spelling words.

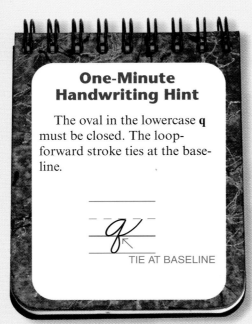

One-Minute Handwriting Hint

The oval in the lowercase **q** must be closed. The loop-forward stroke ties at the baseline.

TIE AT BASELINE

Legible handwriting can boost spelling scores by as much as 20%.

Answer the Questions

1. quarrel
2. quarter
3. square
4. quote
5. question
6. quilt
7. quake
8. squash
9. queen
10. quill

Complete the Story

11. quiet
12. quiz
13. quick
14. quart
15. squeal
16. squint
17. squeeze
18. squirm
19. quit
20. quite

---

quick	quarter	squint	quiz	squeeze
quote	quit	squash	queen	squirm
quilt	quart	squeal	quake	quill
quarrel	square	quite	question	quiet

Answer the Questions Write the spelling word that answers each question.

1. Which word means "to argue or fight"?
2. Which word means "a fourth of something"?
3. Which word refers to an open space surrounded by streets?
4. For what can quotation marks be a clue?
5. What do you answer?
6. What can keep you warm at night?
7. Which word means "to shake or vibrate"?
8. Which word names a vegetable?
9. Which is the wife of a king?
10. Which used to be part of a pen?

Complete the Story Write spelling words from the box to complete the story.

Last night it was very __11.__ in my house. I was studying for a math __12.__. I decided to take a __13.__ break for a glass of milk. As I removed the __14.__ of milk from the refrigerator, I heard a loud __15.__ outside. It was so dark, I had to __16.__ to see better. As my eyes focused, I saw our smallest piglet trying to __17.__ through a hole in the fence. He had gotten caught, so I rescued him. He surely did __18.__ around in my arms when I picked him up! He __19.__ struggling and ran when I put him down. After being stuck, he seemed __20.__ happy to be inside the fence again.

squeal
squint
squeeze
squirm
quite
quart
quick
quiz
quit
quiet

100

MEETING INDIVIDUAL NEEDS

Providing More Challenge

Challenge Words and **Challenge Activities** for Unit 16 appear on page 237. **Challenge Word Test Sentences** appear on page T237.

Unit 16 Challenge Activities

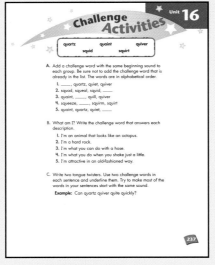

Weekly Test Options

Option 1:
One Spelling Word Per Sentence

(See procedures on pages Z10–Z11.)

1. You will hear the music if you are **quiet**.
2. The **square** has four equal sides.
3. I will finish this job and then **quit**.
4. We had a **quarrel** but then we made up.
5. To get the juice from an orange, you have to **squeeze** it.
6. I **squint** my eyes in the bright sun.
7. The **quiz** is a test to see what I know.
8. The wife of a king is called a **queen**.
9. Cover up your cold legs with a heavy **quilt**.
10. Mother gave me a **quarter** so I could buy milk.
11. You have **quite** a large glass of water.
12. Did you **quote** something I said?
13. I took a **quick** bath before dinner.
14. The pig made a loud **squeal**.
15. The answer to your **question** is "yes."

Spelling and Writing

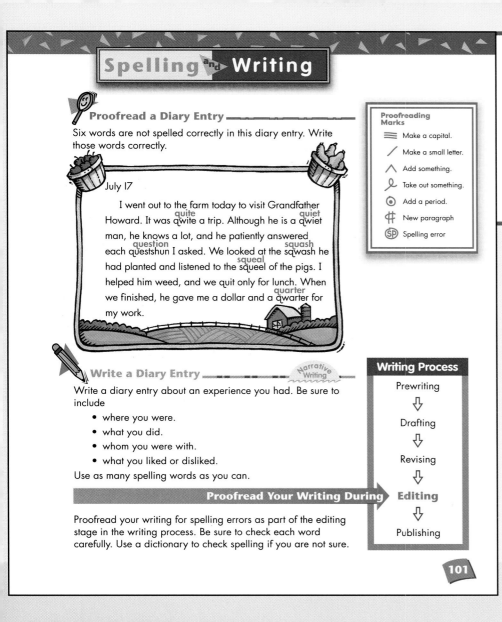

Proofread a Diary Entry

Six words are not spelled correctly in this diary entry. Write those words correctly.

> July 17
>
> I went out to the farm today to visit Grandfather Howard. It was qwite (quite) a trip. Although he is a qwiet (quiet) man, he knows a lot, and he patiently answered each questshun (question) I asked. We looked at the sqwash (squash) he had planted and listened to the squeel (squeal) of the pigs. I helped him weed, and we quit only for lunch. When we finished, he gave me a dollar and a qwarter (quarter) for my work.

Proofreading Marks

≡ Make a capital.
/ Make a small letter.
∧ Add something.
℮ Take out something.
⊙ Add a period.
⌗ New paragraph.
SP Spelling error.

Write a Diary Entry

Narrative Writing

Write a diary entry about an experience you had. Be sure to include
- where you were.
- what you did.
- whom you were with.
- what you liked or disliked.

Use as many spelling words as you can.

Proofread Your Writing During

Proofread your writing for spelling errors as part of the editing stage in the writing process. Be sure to check each word carefully. Use a dictionary to check spelling if you are not sure.

Writing Process

Prewriting
⇩
Drafting
⇩
Revising
⇩
Editing
⇩
Publishing

101

Objectives

Spelling and Writing

Students will
- **proofread** a diary entry.
- **use** the writing process to write a diary entry.
- **proofread** their writing.

Using the Writing Process

Before assigning **Write a Diary Entry,** see pages 258–259 in the Student Edition for a complete review of the writing process and additional writing assignments. You may also wish to refer to pages Z12–Z13 in the Teacher Edition for more information.

Keeping a Spelling Journal

Encourage students to record the words they misspelled on the weekly test in a personal spelling journal. These words may be recycled for future study. Students may also wish to include words from their writing. See pages Z12–Z13 in the Teacher Edition for more information.

---

16. We will have **squash** with our holiday dinner.
17. I held on tight to the pig when it began to **squirm**.
18. The president used a **quill** pen to sign the letter.
19. The jug holds a **quart** of milk.
20. The house shook from the strong **quake**.

Option 2:
Multiple Spelling Words Per Sentence
(See procedures on pages Z10–Z11.)

1. The king gave the **queen** a **square** box made of gold.
2. The long **quill** was **quite** sharp.
3. The dish held a **quart** of cooked **squash**.
4. That was a **quick** but **quiet quake** that we had last night.
5. The pigs will **squeal** and **squirm** if you **squeeze** them.
6. What **question** do you have about that great **quote**?
7. I had to **squint** until the light **quit** flashing.
8. I finished the **quiz** in a **quarter** of an hour.
9. We had a **quarrel** over who was going to use the new **quilt**.

Option 3:
Standardized Test
(See *Teacher Resource Book,* Unit 16.)

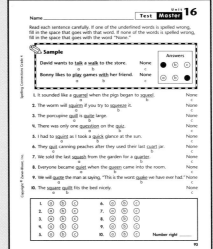

**Unit 16
Test Master**

Objectives

Strategy Words

Students will
- **review** words studied previously that are related to the spelling strategy.
- **preview** unknown words that are related to the spelling strategy.

Remind the students that the **Strategy Words** relate to the spelling patterns they have studied in this unit. The **Review Words** are below grade level, and the **Preview Words** are above grade level. You may wish to use the following sentences to introduce the words in context.

Review Words:
Words From Grade 3
1. Do ten and ten **equal** twenty?
2. Please set the alarm on the **clock** for seven in the morning.
3. We will have **fresh** vegetables with our dinner.
4. Our weather today for the picnic has been **grand**.
5. I need to **stitch** up a tear in my jeans.

Preview Words:
Words From Grade 5
6. We made a visit to the largest **aquarium** I have ever seen.
7. When we go to the store, I must get a **quart** of orange juice.
8. A **squirrel** is carrying nuts to that hole in the tree.
9. Make the large **square** blue and the small one red.
10. Those pieces of paper are of **unequal** size.

Review Words
1. clock
2. grand
3. equal
4. fresh
5. stitch

Preview Words
6. quart
7. square
8. aquarium
9. squirrel
10. unequal

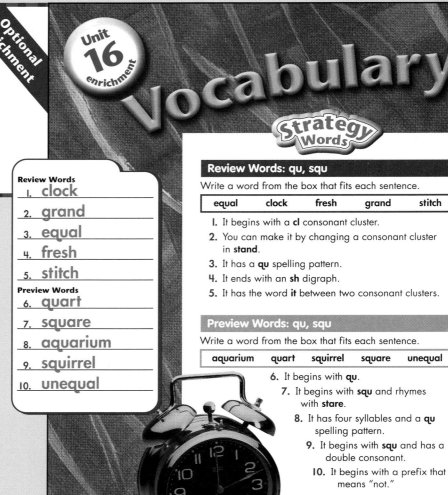

Unit 16 enrichment

Vocabulary

Strategy Words

Review Words: qu, squ

Write a word from the box that fits each sentence.

equal	clock	fresh	grand	stitch

1. It begins with a **cl** consonant cluster.
2. You can make it by changing a consonant cluster in **stand**.
3. It has a **qu** spelling pattern.
4. It ends with an **sh** digraph.
5. It has the word **it** between two consonant clusters.

Preview Words: qu, squ

Write a word from the box that fits each sentence.

aquarium	quart	squirrel	square	unequal

6. It begins with **qu**.
7. It begins with **squ** and rhymes with **stare**.
8. It has four syllables and a **qu** spelling pattern.
9. It begins with **squ** and has a double consonant.
10. It begins with a prefix that means "not."

102

Unit 16 RECAP

You may wish to assign the **Unit 16 Homework Master** (*Teacher Resource Book*, Unit 16) as a fun way to recap the spelling words.

Unit 16 Homework Master

Name _____   Homework Master Unit 16

If the word is spelled correctly, color it red. If the word is spelled incorrectly, color it blue.

sqirm		squeaze	quarel	quoot	kween
	quik				quilt
quort		quick		squeeze	
	squeal		quake		squint
quiet		quart		quit	
		quiz		squirm	question
quil	squash		quarter	quill	
		quite			queen
queit	kwit				
	qustion	skware	squeel		kwarter

Correct the misspelled words. Write them correctly on the lines.

1. sqirm _____   8. squeel _____
2. quort _____   9. kwarter _____
3. quil _____   10. kween _____
4. queit _____   11. quoot _____
5. kwit _____   12. quarel _____
6. qustion _____   13. sqeaze _____
7. skware _____   14. quik _____

94

Connections

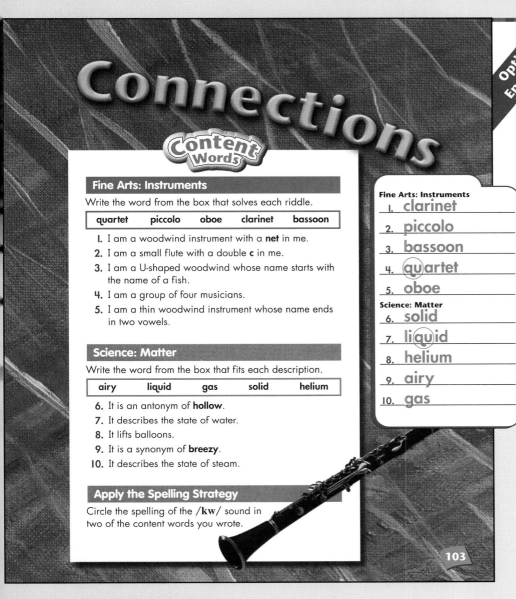

Content Words

Fine Arts: Instruments

Write the word from the box that solves each riddle.

| quartet | piccolo | oboe | clarinet | bassoon |

1. I am a woodwind instrument with a **net** in me.
2. I am a small flute with a double **c** in me.
3. I am a U-shaped woodwind whose name starts with the name of a fish.
4. I am a group of four musicians.
5. I am a thin woodwind instrument whose name ends in two vowels.

Science: Matter

Write the word from the box that fits each description.

| airy | liquid | gas | solid | helium |

6. It is an antonym of **hollow**.
7. It describes the state of water.
8. It lifts balloons.
9. It is a synonym of **breezy**.
10. It describes the state of steam.

Apply the Spelling Strategy

Circle the spelling of the /**kw**/ sound in two of the content words you wrote.

103

Fine Arts: Instruments
1. clarinet
2. piccolo
3. bassoon
4. qu)artet
5. oboe

Science: Matter
6. solid
7. li(qu)id
8. helium
9. airy
10. gas

Objectives

Content Words

Students will
- **expand** vocabulary with content-related words.
- **relate** the spelling strategy to words outside the basic spelling list.

Content Words

Fine Arts: Instruments

Review the meanings of these words with the students. You may wish to use these sentences to introduce the words in context.

1. A group of four makes a **quartet**.
2. My friend plays the **piccolo** in our school music group.
3. The **oboe** is a double-reed instrument.
4. I will show you the **clarinet** and let you hear how it sounds.
5. A **bassoon** is an interesting instrument.

Encourage the students to use these words to describe a concert they attended or heard on the radio.

Science: Matter

Review the meanings of these words with the students. You may wish to use these sentences to introduce the words in context.

6. The cloth was light and **airy**.
7. The **liquid** will turn to steam when it is heated.
8. The room filled with a sweet-smelling **gas**.
9. That is a **solid** ball of aluminum foil.
10. We filled all the balloons with **helium**.

Encourage the students to use these words to describe an experiment they have seen or done in science class.

Unit 17 Home Study Master

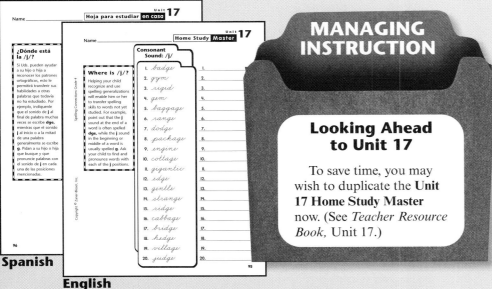

Spanish

English

MANAGING INSTRUCTION

Looking Ahead to Unit 17

To save time, you may wish to duplicate the **Unit 17 Home Study Master** now. (See *Teacher Resource Book,* Unit 17.)

Basic Spelling List

badge	gigantic
gym	edge
rigid	gentle
gem	strange
baggage	ridge
range	cabbage
dodge	bridge
package	hedge
engine	village
cottage	judge

Strategy Words

Review
age	largest
change	page
larger	

Preview
apology	imagine
average	judgment
general	

Content Words

Language Arts: Drama
outrage	wit
tour	stage
pity	

Math: Division
dividend	quotient
remainder	divisor
division	

Individual Needs

Challenge Words
gadget	beverage
gelatin	rummage
engage	

Alternate Word List
gem	edge
baggage	strange
range	bridge
dodge	village
engine	judge

MATERIALS

Student Edition
Pages 104–109
Challenge Activities, p. 238

Teacher Edition
Pages T104A–T109
Challenge Activities, p. T238

Other Resources
Spelling Connections Software
Unit 17 Word List Overhead
  Transparency

Teacher Resource Book
Unit 17 Home Study Master
  (English or Spanish; students
  may pretest on this sheet or use
  it for home practice.)
Unit 17 Homework Master
Unit 17 Practice Masters
Flip Folder Practice Master
Unit 17 Test Master

Visit our Web site, www.zaner-bloser.com

OBJECTIVES

Spelling and Thinking
Students will
- **read** the spelling words in list form and in context.
- **sort** the words according to the different spelling patterns for the **/j/** sound.
- **read** and remember this week's spelling strategy.

Spelling and Vocabulary
Students will
- **write** spelling words for clues.
- **write** spelling words by adding or changing letters in given words.
- **write** spelling words that would appear on the same dictionary page as given guide words.

Spelling and Reading
Students will
- **write** spelling words that rhyme with given words.
- **replace** words and phrases with spelling words.
- **complete** a story using spelling words.

Spelling and Writing
Students will
- **proofread** a letter of application.
- **use** the writing process to write a letter of application.
- **proofread** their writing.

MEETING INDIVIDUAL NEEDS
Learning Styles

Visual

Write the words **rigid, baggage,** and **judge** on the chalkboard. Point out that the **g** in **rigid** is followed by the vowel **i**. This pattern usually means the **g** is pronounced **/j/**. Note that the **ge** in **baggage** and **dge** in **judge** are in the final positions of the words. This pattern for **/j/** often appears at the end of a word. Have the students write all the spelling words on their papers. Then have them circle the letter or letters that spell the **/j/** sound. Finally, have them underline the vowel that follows the letter **g** when it spells the **/j/** sound.

Auditory

Have the students take turns using a tape recorder to record themselves. First, the student pronounces each spelling word, identifies the spelling of the **/j/** sound, and then spells the word. The student says, for example, **"Edge,** final **/j/** sound spelled **d-g-e; e-d-g-e."** Have the student play the tape back and write each word on paper as it is spelled.

Kinesthetic

Make a large tagboard "mat" (about 5 feet square), with five squares across and five down. Place it on the floor. Write letters in the squares as shown. Write each spelling word on a 3" × 5" card. Have the students take turns choosing a card, saying the word on it, and tossing beanbags onto the letters in sequence to spell that word. Then have them write the word on the chalkboard and underline the letter or letters that spell the **/j/** sound.

o	str	d	m	e
j	g	v	dge	p
/	l	b	u	c
a	y	ge	n	
ck	i	t	r	h

Language and Cultural Differences

The sound-symbol relationships in this unit may be difficult for some students because of regional pronunciations or language backgrounds that do not include these sounds. For example, Spanish-speaking students may have difficulty with the **/j/** sound. There is no **/j/** sound in the Spanish language, and the letter **j** spells an **/h/** sound.

Write the words **gem, gentle, range, strange,** and **package** on the chalkboard. Ask a student to go to the chalkboard, pronounce one of the words, and underline the letter or letters in it that spell the **/j/** sound. Continue until all of the words have been used.

MANAGING INSTRUCTION

3–5 Day Plan		Average	Below Average	Above Average
Day 1	**Day 1**	Pretest Spelling Mini-Lesson, p. T104 Spelling and Thinking, p. 104	Pretest Spelling Mini-Lesson, p. T104 Spelling and Thinking, p. 104	Pretest Spelling and Thinking, p. 104
	Day 2	Spelling and Vocabulary, p. 105	Spelling and Vocabulary, p.105 (or) Unit 17 Practice Master, A and B	Spelling and Vocabulary, p. 105 Spelling and Reading, p. 106
Day 2	**Day 3**	Spelling and Reading, p. 106	Spelling and Reading, p. 106 (or) Unit 17 Practice Master, C and D	Challenge Activities, p. 238
	Day 4	Spelling and Writing, p. 107 Unit 17 Homework Master	Spelling and Writing, p. 107	Spelling and Writing, p. 107 Unit 17 Homework Master
Day 3	**Day 5**	Weekly Test	Weekly Test	Weekly Test
Vocabulary Connections (pages 108 and 109) may be used anytime during this unit.				

Objectives

Spelling and Thinking

Students will
- **read** the spelling words in list form and in context.
- **sort** the words according to the different spelling patterns for the /j/ sound.
- **read** and remember this week's spelling strategy.

UNIT PRETEST

Use **Pretest Sentences** below. Refer to the self-checking procedures on student page 256. You may wish to use the **Unit 17 Word List Overhead Transparency** as part of the checking procedure.

TEACHING THE STRATEGY

Spelling Mini-Lesson

Write these sentences on the chalkboard: **Once upon a time, a cabbage, a faucet, and an egg had a race. Who do you think won?**

Invite students to think about what they know about cabbages, faucets, and eggs to answer the question. (Encourage them to be especially clever.) Discuss their ideas briefly, then provide them with this answer: "The cabbage came in ahead, the egg got beat, and the faucet is still running."

Write /j/ on the chalkboard. Ask the students to identify the word in the joke that has the /j/ sound. (cabbage) Ask the students how /j/ is spelled in cabbage. (Students will most likely reply **g**; encourage them to notice that **g** is followed by **e**.) Tell the students that in this lesson they will spell words that have the /j/ sound spelled in different ways.

Ask volunteers to read the word list and identify how /j/ is spelled in each word. Discuss the fact that when /j/ is spelled by **dg**, **dg** is nearly always followed by **e** and the spelling occurs at the end of the word (badge). When /j/ is spelled by **g**, **g** is followed by **i** (gigantic), **e** (gem), or **y** (gym). (You may wish to point out that **gym** is actually a "clipped word," or a word that was shortened from the longer word, **gymnasium**.)

Conclude by reading **Remember the Spelling Strategy** on page 104.

Spelling and Thinking

Order of answers may vary.

dge
1. **badge**
2. **dodge** ★
3. **edge** ★
4. **ridge**
5. **bridge** ★
6. **hedge**
7. **judge** ★

g followed by e, y, or i
8. **gem** ★
9. **baggage** ★
10. **range** ★
11. **package**
12. **cottage**
13. **gentle**
14. **strange** ★
15. **cabbage**
16. **village** ★
17. **gym**
18. **rigid**
19. **engine** ★
20. **gigantic**

104

READ THE SPELLING WORDS

1.	badge	*badge*	She pinned the **badge** on her uniform.
2.	gym	*gym*	In **gym** we climb ropes and play ball.
3.	rigid	*rigid*	My teacher avoids **rigid** rules.
4.	gem	*gem*	A diamond is a precious **gem**.
5.	baggage	*baggage*	He checked his **baggage** at the airport.
6.	range	*range*	Their ages **range** from six to ten.
7.	dodge	*dodge*	In this game you must **dodge** the ball.
8.	package	*package*	The **package** was delivered yesterday.
9.	engine	*engine*	Oil keeps an **engine** from overheating.
10.	cottage	*cottage*	He built a **cottage** in six months.
11.	gigantic	*gigantic*	A **gigantic** wave crashed ashore.
12.	edge	*edge*	The **edge** of a ruler is straight.
13.	gentle	*gentle*	A calf is **gentle** and friendly.
14.	strange	*strange*	That book had a **strange** plot.
15.	ridge	*ridge*	Trees grew along the rocky **ridge**.
16.	cabbage	*cabbage*	A **cabbage** has a solid, round head.
17.	bridge	*bridge*	The **bridge** spanned the stream.
18.	hedge	*hedge*	He trimmed the **hedge** to lower it.
19.	village	*village*	The band played on the **village** green.
20.	judge	*judge*	The **judge** instructed the jury.

SORT THE SPELLING WORDS

1.–7. Write the spelling words that spell the /j/ sound **dge**.

8.–20. Write the spelling words that spell the /j/ sound **g** followed by **e, y,** or **i**.

REMEMBER THE SPELLING STRATEGY

Remember that the /j/ sound can be spelled in different ways: **g** followed by **e** in **gem** and **range**, **g** followed by **y** in **gym**, and **g** followed by **i** in **gigantic**. The /j/ sound can also be spelled **dge: edge**.

Pretest Sentences (See procedures on pages Z10–Z11.)

1. The officer wore a **badge**.
2. During the winter we play basketball in the **gym**.
3. The metal rod was so **rigid** we could not bend it.
4. An emerald is a green **gem**.
5. Our **baggage** was left on the airplane.
6. A rainbow contains an entire **range** of colors.
7. Try to **dodge** the hole in the road.
8. The mail carrier brought a **package** to our house.
9. The train gets all of its power from the **engine**.
10. During vacation we stay in a small **cottage** by the lake.
11. Many dinosaurs were **gigantic** creatures.
12. The **edge** of the ruler is straight.
13. Please be **gentle** when you play with the puppy.
14. Moonlight made my room seem different and **strange**.
15. The mountain goat stood on a **ridge**.
16. One of my favorite vegetables is **cabbage**.
17. Last year I saw a covered **bridge**.
18. The **hedge** is a hiding place for the rabbits.
19. Very few people live in the small **village**.
20. The winner of the art contest will be chosen by the **judge**.

Word Meanings

Write a spelling word for each clue.

1. Take me on your trip.
2. I am very big.
3. Use me for sports.
4. I can be gift-wrapped.
5. I've got a green head.

Words and Letters

Follow the directions to write spelling words.

6. Drop one letter in **frigid**.
7. Drop one letter in **ledge**.
8. Change the first letter of **fudge**.
9. Change the first letter of **pottage**.
10. Change the last two letters of **villain**.
11. Change the last letter of **get**.
12. Add a letter at the start of **edge**.
13. Change the second letter in **budge**.
14. Add one letter to **ride**.
15. Add one letter to **bride**.
16. Drop one letter from **strangle**.

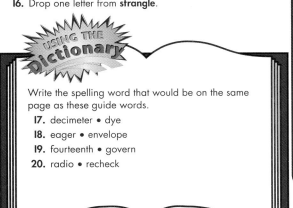

USING THE Dictionary

Write the spelling word that would be on the same page as these guide words.

17. decimeter • dye
18. eager • envelope
19. fourteenth • govern
20. radio • recheck

Word Meanings
1. baggage
2. gigantic
3. gym
4. package
5. cabbage

Words and Letters
6. rigid
7. edge
8. judge
9. cottage
10. village
11. gem
12. hedge
13. badge
14. ridge
15. bridge
16. strange

Using the Dictionary
17. dodge
18. engine
19. gentle
20. range

105

Objectives

Spelling and Vocabulary

Students will
- **write** spelling words for clues.
- **write** spelling words by adding or changing letters in given words.
- **write** spelling words that would appear on the same dictionary page as given guide words.

Developing Oral Language Skills

Do a word sort by sound. Write **beginning, middle,** and **end** on the chalkboard or on an overhead transparency. Then have volunteers read the spelling word list, asking them to place each word under one of the three headings according to where the /j/ sound occurs in the word.

When they are finished listing the words, ask students to repeat the words and to consider the letters that spell the /j/ sound in each word. Then have volunteers come to the board and circle the letters that spell the sound.

MEETING INDIVIDUAL NEEDS

Providing More Help

Post three large pieces of construction paper or oaktag. Write one of the following headings at the top of each piece: /j/ spelled **g**, /j/ spelled **ge**, /j/ spelled **dge**. Tell each student to take out a blue and a red crayon. Have the students take turns reading the spelling words aloud and writing them on the proper chart with their blue crayons. Then have them retrace the letters that spell the /j/ sound with their red crayons.

★Students who need to study fewer words should use the **Alternate Word List**. This list is starred on page T104 in the Teacher Edition. The **Unit 17 Practice Masters** (*Teacher Resource Book*) provide additional practice with these words.

Unit 17 Practice Masters

Name_____

Practice **Master** Unit **17**

| 1. gem | 3. strange | 5. baggage | 7. judge | 9. bridge |
| 2. range | 4. village | 6. edge | 8. dodge | 10. engine |

A. Write the spelling word that is the singular form of each plural noun.

1. engines _____   4. ranges _____
2. judges _____   5. gems _____
3. villages _____   6. bridges _____

B. Write a spelling word that is a synonym for each word.

1. side _____
2. luggage _____
3. suburb _____
4. unusual _____
5. sidestep _____

C. Write two spelling words to complete each sentence.

1. The story was about the ____ things that happened in a little ____.

2. The car's ____ stopped as we started to cross the ____.

3. He placed his ____ on the ____ of the platform as he got off the train.

97

Practice **Master** Unit **17**

judge   bridge
dodge   engine

i	j	k	l	m
9	10	11	12	13
v	w	x	y	z
22	23	24	25	26

98

Objectives

Spelling and Reading

Students will

- **write** spelling words that rhyme with given words.
- **replace** words and phrases with spelling words.
- **complete** a story using spelling words.

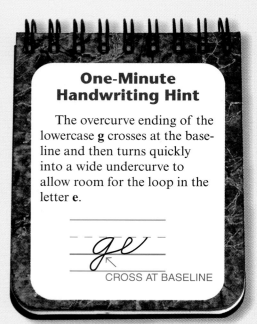

One-Minute Handwriting Hint

The overcurve ending of the lowercase **g** crosses at the base-line and then turns quickly into a wide undercurve to allow room for the loop in the letter **e**.

CROSS AT BASELINE

Legible handwriting can boost spelling scores by as much as 20%.

Find the Rhymes
1. gentle
2. gigantic
3. gym
4. engine
5. gem
6. dodge
7. range

Replace the Words
8. rigid
9. baggage
10. package
11. village
12. hedge
13. edge
14. cabbage
15. judge

Complete the Story
16. strange
17. cottage
18. ridge
19. badge
20. bridge

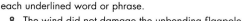

Spelling and Reading

badge	gym	rigid	gem	baggage
range	dodge	package	engine	cottage
gigantic	edge	gentle	strange	ridge
cabbage	bridge	hedge	village	judge

Find the Rhymes   Write the spelling word that rhymes with each of these words.

1. lentil
2. Atlantic
3. grim
4. bearskin
5. stem
6. lodge
7. strange

Replace the Words   Write the spelling word to replace each underlined word or phrase.

8. The wind did not damage the <u>unbending</u> flagpole.
9. All of our <u>luggage</u> was put onto the plane.
10. Did anyone deliver a <u>parcel</u> to 18 Locust Drive?
11. They live in a <u>place smaller than a town</u> in Ohio.
12. He trimmed the <u>fence of bushes</u> with his clippers.
13. She put stones around the <u>border</u> of her flower garden.
14. Sue boiled a <u>vegetable with a leafy head</u> for dinner.
15. The <u>person who presides over a court</u> wore a black robe.

Complete the Story   Write spelling words to complete the story.

Yesterday we came across a __16.__ scene. We saw a deserted __17.__ on a pine-covered mountain __18.__. No one knew who lived there. The sheriff pinned on his __19.__ and asked me to go with him. We rode across the __20.__ over the river and entered the house. There we found nothing but cobwebs— and a newspaper dated July 1, 1898.

badge
cottage
strange
ridge
bridge

106

MEETING INDIVIDUAL NEEDS
Providing More Challenge

Challenge Words and **Challenge Activities** for Unit 17 appear on page 238. **Challenge Word Test Sentences** appear on page T238.

Unit 17 Challenge Activities

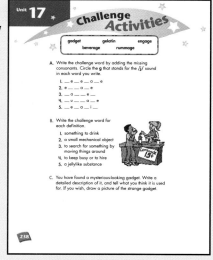

Weekly Test Options

Option 1:
One Spelling Word Per Sentence
(See procedures on pages Z10–Z11.)

1. A **village** is a very small town.
2. That **gem** is a pretty stone.
3. We cook foods that **range** from simple to fancy.
4. There is a skirt for you in the **package**.
5. The rain was not heavy but **gentle**.
6. Grandmother lives in a **cottage** near the lake.
7. The place seemed **strange** to me.
8. Do you like **cabbage** salad?
9. The Boy Scout wore a **badge** on his shirt.
10. We trimmed the **hedge** next to our house.
11. I put our **baggage** on the bus.
12. The knife has a very sharp **edge**.
13. The **judge** wore a black robe.
14. A stream runs under the **bridge**.
15. The row of hills forms a **ridge**.
16. She can **dodge** the ball by jumping to the left.

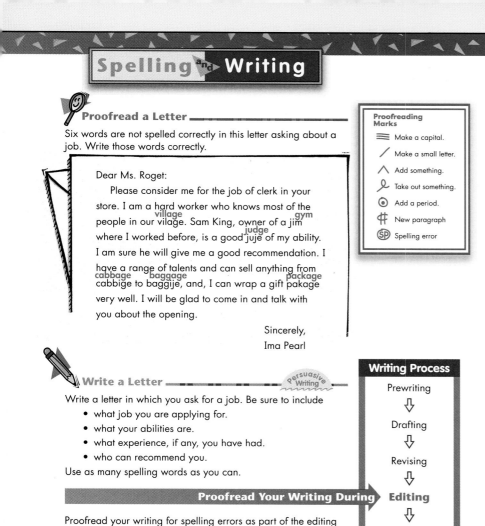

Spelling and Writing

Proofread a Letter

Six words are not spelled correctly in this letter asking about a job. Write those words correctly.

Dear Ms. Roget:

Please consider me for the job of clerk in your store. I am a hard worker who knows most of the people in our vilage. Sam King, owner of a jim where I worked before, is a good juje of my ability. I am sure he will give me a good recommendation. I have a range of talents and can sell anything from cabbige to baggije, and, I can wrap a gift pakage very well. I will be glad to come in and talk with you about the opening.

Sincerely,

Ima Pearl

village *gym* *judge* *cabbage* *baggage* *package*

Proofreading Marks

≡ Make a capital.
/ Make a small letter.
∧ Add something.
⌿ Take out something.
⊙ Add a period.
⌗ New paragraph
(SP) Spelling error

Write a Letter

Persuasive Writing

Write a letter in which you ask for a job. Be sure to include
• what job you are applying for.
• what your abilities are.
• what experience, if any, you have had.
• who can recommend you.
Use as many spelling words as you can.

Proofread Your Writing During

Proofread your writing for spelling errors as part of the editing stage in the writing process. Be sure to check each word carefully. Use a dictionary to check spelling if you are not sure.

Writing Process

Prewriting
⇩
Drafting
⇩
Revising
⇩
Editing
⇩
Publishing

107

Objectives

Spelling and Writing

Students will
• **proofread** a letter of application.
• **use** the writing process to write a letter of application.
• **proofread** their writing.

Using the Writing Process

Before assigning **Write a Letter** in this unit, see pages 258–259 in the Student Edition for a complete review of the writing process and additional writing assignments. You may also wish to refer to pages Z12–Z13 in the Teacher Edition.

Keeping a Spelling Journal

Encourage students to record the words they misspelled on the weekly test in a personal spelling journal. These words may be recycled for future study. Students may also wish to include words from their writing. See pages Z12–Z13 in the Teacher Edition for more information.

---

17. The power to run the car comes from the **engine**.
18. The **gigantic** tree is the largest one in the forest.
19. These cards are too **rigid** to bend.
20. We kick the ball around the **gym** at school.

Option 2:
Multiple Spelling Words Per Sentence
(See procedures on pages Z10–Z11.)

1. The **cottage** is near a **bridge** in the **village**.
2. The **gem** has a **rigid edge**.
3. The **judge** wore a **strange badge** on his coat.
4. There was a wide **range** of vegetables at the store, including **cabbage**.
5. The rabbit ran over the **ridge** to **dodge** the puddles.
6. I lost my **baggage** near the **hedge**.
7. There was a **gigantic engine** in the **package**.
8. A **gentle** kitten was playing in the **gym**.

Option 3:
Standardized Test
(See *Teacher Resource Book,* Unit 17.)

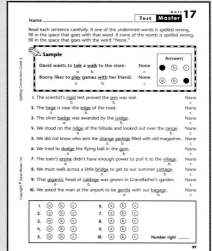

Unit 17 Test Master

Objectives

Strategy Words

Students will
- **review** words studied previously that are related to the spelling strategy.
- **preview** unknown words that are related to the spelling strategy.

Vocabulary

Remind the students that the **Strategy Words** relate to the spelling patterns they have studied in this unit. The **Review Words** are below grade level, and the **Preview Words** are above grade level. You may wish to use the following sentences to introduce the words in context.

Review Words:
Words From Grade 3

1. He is just the right **age** to enter kindergarten.
2. You need to **change** buses at the next corner.
3. They have **larger** chairs in the upper grades.
4. That is the **largest** elephant I have ever seen.
5. Turn to **page** 103 in your math book.

Preview Words:
Words From Grade 5

6. I received an **apology** from my sister last night.
7. We will **average** the ten grades to get the final result.
8. Give us a **general** overview of the chapter.
9. See if you can **imagine** what it is like to be a bird.
10. It is my **judgment** that you should return the money to your friend.

Review Words
1. larger
2. age
3. page
4. largest
5. change

Preview Words
6. judgment
7. apology
8. general
9. average
10. imagine

Strategy Words

Review Words: Consonant Sound /j/

Write the word from the box that matches each definition.

age	change	larger	largest	page

1. bigger
2. number of years old
3. sheet of paper
4. biggest
5. make different

Preview Words: Consonant Sound /j/

Write a word from the box to fit each description.

apology	average	general
	imagine	judgment

6. This word has two syllables.
7. This word has four syllables.
8. This word means "a high-ranking officer."
9. This word means "not great, not bad."
10. This word tells what fiction writers do.

108

Unit 17 Homework Master

Unit 17 RECAP

You may wish to assign the **Unit 17 Homework Master** (*Teacher Resource Book,* Unit 17) as a fun way to recap the spelling words.

Name _____

Homework Master Unit 17

Use the Morse Code to find letters for the spelling words. Write the spelling words on the lines below.

100

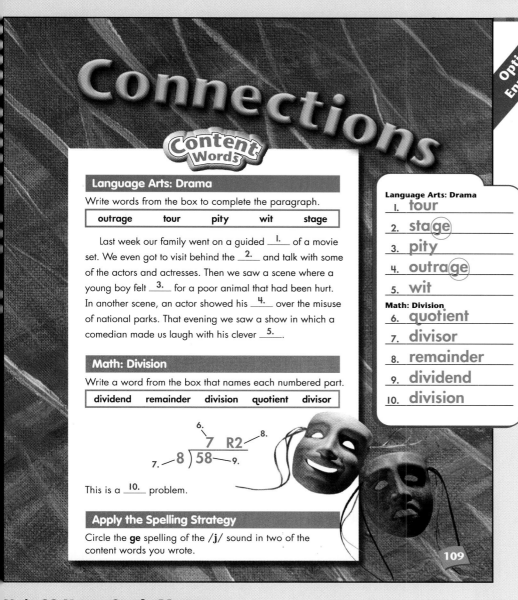

Connections

Content Words

Language Arts: Drama

Write words from the box to complete the paragraph.

outrage	tour	pity	wit	stage

Last week our family went on a guided __1.__ of a movie set. We even got to visit behind the __2.__ and talk with some of the actors and actresses. Then we saw a scene where a young boy felt __3.__ for a poor animal that had been hurt. In another scene, an actor showed his __4.__ over the misuse of national parks. That evening we saw a show in which a comedian made us laugh with his clever __5.__.

Math: Division

Write a word from the box that names each numbered part.

dividend	remainder	division	quotient	divisor

$$6. \quad 7 \text{ R2} \quad 8.$$
$$7. \quad 8)\overline{58} \quad 9.$$

This is a __10.__ problem.

Apply the Spelling Strategy

Circle the **ge** spelling of the /j/ sound in two of the content words you wrote.

109

Language Arts: Drama
1. tour
2. sta(ge)
3. pity
4. outra(ge)
5. wit

Math: Division
6. quotient
7. divisor
8. remainder
9. dividend
10. division

Objectives

Content Words

Students will
- **expand** vocabulary with content-related words.
- **relate** the spelling strategy to words outside the basic spelling list.

Language Arts: Drama

Review the meanings of these words with the students. You may wish to use these sentences to introduce the words in context.

1. We all felt **outrage** over the unfairness of the decision.
2. We will go on **tour** with our play when we have perfected the production.
3. What a **pity** that we cannot learn our lines more quickly.
4. The student had a sharp **wit**.
5. Everyone take your places on the **stage** for rehearsal.

Encourage the students to use these words to describe an actor or actress they know about.

Math: Division

Review the meanings of these words with the students. You may wish to use these sentences to introduce the words in context.

6. The **dividend** is the quantity to be divided.
7. An amount left from subtracting or dividing is the **remainder**.
8. There are twenty **division** problems for homework.
9. The answer to your division problem is called a **quotient**.
10. Your **divisor** is an even number in this problem.

Encourage the students to use these words to label the parts of their math problems.

Unit 18 Home Study Master

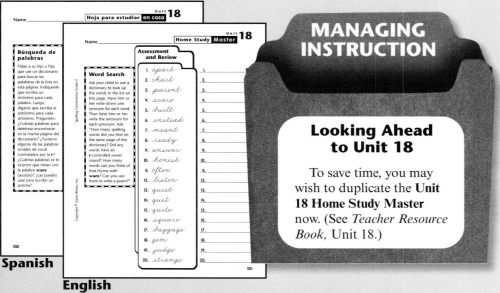

Spanish

English

MANAGING INSTRUCTION

Looking Ahead to Unit 18

To save time, you may wish to duplicate the **Unit 18 Home Study Master** now. (See *Teacher Resource Book,* Unit 18.)

Assessment Words

starch	squawk
deaf	wreck
bomb	dread
squab	carve
flare	mare
squad	steady
wage	voyage
leather	sword
fudge	queer
writer	urge

Review Words

Unit 13
apart*	compare
chart*	share
parent*	beware
scare*	mark
market	army

Unit 14
built*	young
instead*	breakfast
meant*	already
ready*	build
enough	touch

Unit 15
answer*	though
honest*	island
often*	knee
listen*	wrong
known	calm

Unit 16
quiet*	squeeze
quit*	question
quite*	queen
square*	quilt
quarter	quick

Unit 17
baggage*	edge
gem*	engine
judge*	range
strange*	dodge
village	bridge

*Posttest sentences and the **Unit 18 Test Master** test these words. Students review all words listed.

MATERIALS

Student Edition
Pages 110–115

Teacher Edition
Pages T110A–T115

Other Resources
Spelling Connections Software
Spelling and Writing
  Transparencies (Writing Prompt
  and Writing Model) for Unit 18

Teacher Resource Book
Unit 18 Home Study Master
  (English or Spanish; students
  may use this sheet for review or
  home practice.)
Flip Folder Practice Master
Unit 18 Test Master

Visit our Web site, www.zaner-bloser.com

OBJECTIVES

Spelling and Assessment
Students will
- **assess** their spelling success by matching new words to the spelling strategies presented in Units 13–17.
- **connect** new words to the spelling strategies in Units 13–17.
- **write** new words that relate to the spelling strategies taught in Units 13–17.

Spelling and Review
Students will
- **review** and practice the spelling strategies and words in Units 13–17.
- **learn** an alternative spelling study strategy.

Spelling and Writing
Students will
- **review** the concept of linking verbs.
- **compose** an essay that explains how to prepare some food.
- **learn** a proofreading strategy.
- **proofread** for correct forms of frequently confused words.

MEETING INDIVIDUAL NEEDS
Learning Styles

Visual

Give each student an appropriate grade-level magazine or newsletter. Allow students fifteen minutes to find as many spelling words as they can. Have them highlight or circle each word and then write the words on their papers. Last, have them underline any irregular spelling pattern in each word.

Auditory

Write the spelling words on the chalkboard and underline the letters that spell the sound or sounds being emphasized. Have the students chant the letters in each spelling word, emphasizing the focus letters by chanting louder and slower. Then ask students to write the words on their papers as they repeat the chants softly to themselves. Have them circle the letters illustrating the spelling strategy.

Kinesthetic

Trace the spelling words about 3" tall on construction paper. Divide the words among the students. Have them cut out the letters and then write the words. Have the students exchange words, trace the letters of the new words with their fingers, and write the words.

Language and Cultural Differences

The silent letters and irregular spellings of sounds are parts of the English spelling system that all students must memorize for correct spelling. It is important to give students the opportunity to associate the word meaning with the visual sequence of letters used in spelling.

Make a card for each spelling word. Cut each card into three pieces: the initial consonant(s), the medial vowels, and the final consonant(s).

Arrange the pieces randomly on a table—the initial letters in a first row, the medial vowels in a second row, and the final letters in a third row. Say one of the spelling words, pronouncing it clearly. Have a student repeat the word and pronounce it correctly. Then have the student choose the letter parts that form the word, place the pieces in the correct order, and say the word. The shapes of the word pieces give added clues. Continue until all of the words have been practiced.

MANAGING INSTRUCTION

3–5 Day Plan		Average	Below Average	Above Average
Day 1	Day 1	Assessment: Units 13–17, p. 110 (Option 1 or 2, p. T110)	Assessment: Units 13–17, p. 110 (Option 1 or 2, p. T110)	Assessment: Units 13–17, p. 110 (Option 1 or 2, p. T110)
	Day 2	Review: Units 13 and 14, p. 111	Review: Units 13 and 14, p. 111	Review: Units 13 and 14, p. 111 Review: Units 15 and 16, p. 112
Day 2	Day 3	Review: Units 15 and 16, p. 112	Review: Units 15 and 16, p. 112	Review: Unit 17, p. 113 Spelling Study Strategy, p. 113
	Day 4	Review: Unit 17, p. 113 Spelling Study Strategy, p. 113	Review: Unit 17, p. 113 Spelling Study Strategy, p. 113	Writer's Workshop, pages 114–115
Day 3	Day 5	Weekly Test, Option 1 or 2, p. T113	Weekly Test, Option 1 or 2, p. T113	Weekly Test, Option 1 or 2, p. T113

Writer's Workshop (pages 114 and 115) may be used anytime during this unit.

Objectives

Spelling and Assessment

Students will

- **assess** their spelling success by matching new words to the spelling strategies presented in Units 13–17.
- **connect** new words to the spelling strategies in Units 13–17.
- **write** new words that relate to the spelling strategies taught in Units 13–17.

Assessment and Review

Unit 13
1. starch
2. flare
3. carve
4. mare

Unit 14
5. deaf
6. leather
7. dread
8. steady

Unit 15
9. bomb
10. writer
11. wreck
12. sword

Unit 16
13. squab
14. squad
15. squawk
16. queer

Unit 17
17. wage
18. fudge
19. voyage
20. urge

Assessment Units 13–17

Each Assessment Word in the box fits one of the spelling strategies you have studied over the past five weeks. Read the spelling strategies. Then write each Assessment Word under the unit number it fits.

Unit 13

1.–4. The **r**-controlled vowel sound you hear in **cart** (/är/) is spelled **ar**. The **r**-controlled vowel sound you hear in **spare** (/âr/) is spelled **are**.

Unit 14

5.–8. Some words have more vowel letters than vowel sounds.

Unit 15

9.–12. Some words are spelled with silent consonants: **k** in **knot** and **s** in **island**.

Unit 16

13.–16. The /**kw**/ sound is spelled **qu**: **quiz, squint**.

Unit 17

17.–20. The /**j**/ sound can be spelled in different ways: **g** followed by **e** in **gem** and **range**, **g** followed by **y** in **gym**, and **g** followed by **i** in **gigantic**. The /**j**/ sound can also be spelled **dge**: **edge**.

starch
deaf
bomb
squab
flare
squad
wage
leather
fudge
writer
squawk
wreck
dread
carve
mare
steady
voyage
sword
queer
urge

110

ASSESSMENT: UNITS 13–17

Option 1

Assessment Option 1 is the test that appears in the Student Edition on page 110. You may wish to have students take this test to determine their ability to recognize the spelling strategy in each unit and to match words not previously taught to that strategy. **Assessment Option 1** also serves as additional review and practice.

Option 2

Assessment Option 2 is a dictation test using the sentences on page T111. This test assesses students' ability to spell words not previously taught but that are exemplars of a spelling strategy. This test more specifically assesses students' ability to apply the spelling knowledge they have learned.

In either assessment test option, the words are identified by unit in the Teacher Edition. You may wish to index those misspelled words to review exercises that follow in this unit. Determine which units students need to review and use additional unit exercises found in this **Assessment and Review Unit** for reteaching the skill in a more focused way.

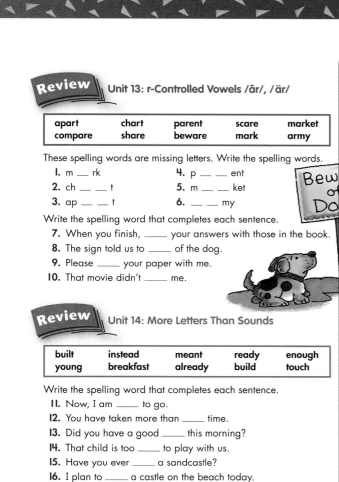

Review Unit 13: r-Controlled Vowels /âr/, /är/

apart	chart	parent	scare	market
compare	share	beware	mark	army

These spelling words are missing letters. Write the spelling words.

1. m __ rk
2. ch __ t
3. ap __ t
4. p __ __ ent
5. m __ __ ket
6. __ __ my

Write the spelling word that completes each sentence.

7. When you finish, _____ your answers with those in the book.
8. The sign told us to _____ of the dog.
9. Please _____ your paper with me.
10. That movie didn't _____ me.

Review Unit 14: More Letters Than Sounds

built	instead	meant	ready	enough
young	breakfast	already	build	touch

Write the spelling word that completes each sentence.

11. Now, I am _____ to go.
12. You have taken more than _____ time.
13. Did you have a good _____ this morning?
14. That child is too _____ to play with us.
15. Have you ever _____ a sandcastle?
16. I plan to _____ a castle on the beach today.
17. Lee wants to build a sand city _____ of a castle.
18. I'm sorry, but that was not what I _____ to say.
19. If you stretch, can you _____ the top of the door?
20. I have read that book _____.

Unit 13
1. mark
2. chart
3. apart
4. parent
5. market
6. army
7. compare
8. beware
9. share
10. scare

Unit 14
11. ready
12. enough
13. breakfast
14. young
15. built
16. build
17. instead
18. meant
19. touch
20. already

111

Objectives

Spelling and Review
Students will
- **review** and practice the spelling strategy and words in Unit 13.
- **review** and practice the spelling strategy and words in Unit 14.

Assessing Progress: The Spelling Journal

If your students have been keeping a personal spelling journal, a periodical review of these journals can be a rich assessment tool. Students should include the words they have misspelled from each unit spelling test. They should also be encouraged to write the words they consistently misspell in their own writing and content-area words that present a challenge. Being able to discriminate the words in their everyday writing whose spelling they need to master is a powerful spelling skill.

Pretest Sentences: Assessment Words
(See procedures on pages Z10–Z11.)

1. The laundry adds **starch** to Dad's good shirts.
2. The sonic boom left everyone feeling **deaf**.
3. Two people volunteered to examine the **bomb**.
4. We could hear the **squab** cooing in the old barn.
5. The captain spotted the distress **flare** in the distance.
6. Coach Weiss asked his **squad** to play their best game.
7. She will earn more than the minimum **wage**.
8. Amelia carried a new **leather** purse.
9. I love homemade **fudge**.
10. Jan hopes to be a **writer** someday.
11. There was a loud **squawk** from the frightened chicken.
12. The driver almost had a **wreck**.
13. People in the path of tornadoes have a real **dread** of bad weather.
14. Will you **carve** the turkey for dinner?
15. A **mare** is a female horse.
16. You must keep your canoe **steady** or it will tip.
17. Magellan faced many dangers during his long **voyage**.
18. King Arthur had a famous **sword**.
19. The animal in the cartoon looked very **queer**.
20. I **urge** you to study your spelling.

Objectives

Spelling and Review

Students will

- **review** and practice the spelling strategy and words in Unit 15.
- **review** and practice the spelling strategy and words in Unit 16.

Unit 15
1. answer
2. island
3. knee
4. wrong
5. listen
6. known
7. often
8. honest
9. though
10. calm

Unit 16
11. quilt
12. squeeze
13. square
14. quite
15. queen
16. quarter
17. quiet
18. question
19. quick
20. quit

 Review Unit 15: Silent Consonants

answer	honest	often	listen	known
though	island	knee	wrong	calm

Add the missing silent consonants to write the spelling words.

1. ans __ er
2. i __ land
3. __ nee
4. __ rong
5. lis __ en
6. __ nown
7. of __ en
8. __ onest
9. thou __ __
10. ca __ m

 Review Unit 16: qu, squ

quiet	quit	quite	square	quarter
squeeze	question	queen	quilt	quick

Write the spelling word that rhymes with the underlined word in each clue.

11. These flowers will <u>wilt</u>, but they'll stay fresh in the _____.
12. This doll will <u>sneeze</u> if you give her a _____.
13. The shape of the <u>fair</u> was set up in a _____.
14. That tall person has _____ a great <u>height</u>.
15. This delicious <u>bean</u> soup is fit for a _____.
16. John played the mail <u>sorter</u>, and stamps were just a _____.

Write the spelling word that has the opposite meaning of each word.

17. noisy
18. answer
19. slow
20. continue

112

Bulletin Board Idea

Words From Our Personal Spelling Journals

Have students suggest words from their personal spelling journals, drawing particularly from words chosen from their reading and content-area work. Organize these words around specific topics on a bulletin board entitled "Words From Our Personal Spelling Journals." For example, **prairie** in one column might elicit **buffalo, wheat, plains, agriculture, Illinois**. Have students select one column of words to use in a paragraph and underline their new words. Have them illustrate their writing.

Words From Our Personal Spelling Journals

Prairie	Animals	Math
prairie	plains	square
wheat	illinois	quarter
buffalo		quilt

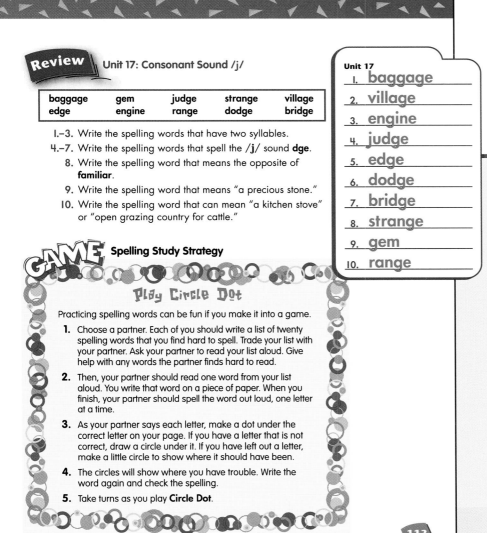

baggage	gem	judge	strange	village
edge	engine	range	dodge	bridge

1.–3. Write the spelling words that have two syllables.

4.–7. Write the spelling words that spell the /**j**/ sound **dge**.

8. Write the spelling word that means the opposite of **familiar**.

9. Write the spelling word that means "a precious stone."

10. Write the spelling word that can mean "a kitchen stove" or "open grazing country for cattle."

GAME Spelling Study Strategy

Play Circle Dot

Practicing spelling words can be fun if you make it into a game.

1. Choose a partner. Each of you should write a list of twenty spelling words that you find hard to spell. Trade your list with your partner. Ask your partner to read your list aloud. Give help with any words the partner finds hard to read.

2. Then, your partner should read one word from your list aloud. You write that word on a piece of paper. When you finish, your partner should spell the word out loud, one letter at a time.

3. As your partner says each letter, make a dot under the correct letter on your page. If you have a letter that is not correct, draw a circle under it. If you have left out a letter, make a little circle to show where it should have been.

4. The circles will show where you have trouble. Write the word again and check the spelling.

5. Take turns as you play **Circle Dot**.

113

Unit 17
1. baggage
2. village
3. engine
4. judge
5. edge
6. dodge
7. bridge
8. strange
9. gem
10. range

Objectives

Spelling and Review

Students will

• **review** and practice the spelling strategy and words in Unit 17.

• **learn** an alternative spelling study strategy.

Learning an Alternative Spelling Study Strategy

Students should always have a number of study strategies to draw from when it comes to learning their spelling words. **Circle Dot** is a useful game for practicing spelling proofreading. Encourage students to remember this spelling strategy and to play the game with any list they need to study and learn.

Weekly Test Options

Option 1:
One Spelling Word Per Sentence

(See procedures on pages Z10–Z11.)

1. My friend **meant** something else.
2. My mother took the clock **apart**.
3. I will finish this job and then **quit**.
4. I trust you because you are **honest**.
5. The place seemed **strange** to me.
6. We wrote a list of classroom jobs on the **chart**.
7. I would like to see you more **often**.
8. Grandfather **built** his own home.
9. One **parent** of each child came to the school play.
10. The **judge** wore a black robe.
11. A **square** has four equal sides.
12. I like to **listen** to the radio.
13. I used a red crayon **instead** of a black one.
14. You may leave as soon as you are **ready**.
15. You have **quite** a large glass of milk.
16. Don't jump out of the box and **scare** me.
17. I put our **baggage** on the bus.
18. Can you **answer** this important question?
19. The **gem** is a pretty rock.
20. You will hear the music if you are **quiet**.

Option 2:
Standardized Test

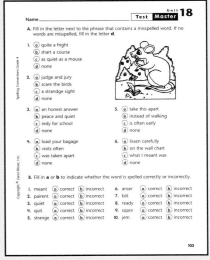

Unit 18 Test Master

(See *Teacher Resource Book*, Unit 18.)

TII3

Objectives

Spelling and Writing

Students will
- **review** the concept of linking verbs.
- **compose** an essay that explains how to prepare some food. (See **Spelling and the Writing Process** below.)

Optional Enrichment

Unit **18** enrichment

WRITER'S

A
1. was
2. seems
3. am
4. were
5. became

B
6. strange
7. calm
8. young
9. wrong
10. sweet

Grammar, Usage, and Mechanics

Linking Verbs

A linking verb links the subject with words that tell what the subject is like. For example, in the sentence, "The carpet was dirty," **was** is a linking verb. It links **carpet** and **dirty**. **Dirty** tells what the carpet is like. Linking verbs include **am, is, are, was, were, become,** and **seem**.

The swans **are** beautiful!   The football player **is** injured.

The icicles **were** cold.   The coaches **seem** proud.

Suddenly the room **became** warm.

I **am** happy.

 Practice **Activity**

A. Write the linking verb in each sentence.
   1. My school bus was late this morning.
   2. That new girl seems friendly.
   3. Today I am cold and tired.
   4. The twins were happy about the party.
   5. After the storm, the ground soon became dry again.

B. Find the linking verb in each sentence. Then write the word in each sentence that comes after the linking verb and tells what the subject is like.
   6. That picture seems strange.
   7. Everyone was calm during the storm.
   8. Last year those kittens were young.
   9. You are wrong about that!
   10. The ripe oranges tasted sweet.

114

 Expository Writing

Spelling and the Writing Process

You may wish to use this writing assignment to help students master the writing process. For other writing ideas, see pages 258–259 in the Student Edition.

Explain that students will write a composition in which they explain to a classmate how to prepare some food.

Prewriting Hint: You may wish to help students plan their writing by recommending the chart on this page. Have them replicate the chart, filling in the blanks with details and steps.

What you are making:	English muffin pizza
What you need to have:	English muffins, tomato sauce, pizza cheese
What you do first:	
What you do after that:	

Revising Hint: Remind students that when they revise what they have written, they should make sure that each step is both clear and complete.

T114

Proofreading Strategy

Work With a Partner!

Good writers always proofread their writing for spelling errors. Here's a strategy you can use to proofread your papers.

Instead of proofreading all alone, work with a partner. Ask your partner to read your work aloud. Ask the person to read slowly. While your partner reads, you look at each word and think about each sentence. Are the words spelled correctly? Does the sentence make sense?

This strategy helps you focus on spelling and meaning. Try it!

Electronic Spelling
1. here
2. eight
3. principal
4. plain
5. hour
6. its

Spell Checkers and Homophones

Many computers have spell checkers that can help you proofread. But even the best spell checker cannot do it all. You still need to think about the spelling of some words.

Sometimes you type one word and mean another. For example, do you write letters on **stationery** or **stationary**? Both words are spelled correctly because they are homophones. However, the one you write letters on contains an **e**.

A computer checked the spelling of the words in these sentences. Find the incorrect homophone the computer missed in each sentence. Write it correctly.

1. Put the boxes hear, please.
2. We have ate pencils left.
3. Our principle decides when to close school.
4. I would like plane milk with nothing in it.
5. We will leave in an our.
6. The tree has begun to lose it's leaves.

115

Objectives

Spelling and Writing

Students will
- **learn** a proofreading strategy.
- **proofread** for correct forms of frequently confused words.

Using Proofreading Strategies

Students are often unaware that there are a variety of techniques they can use to proofread their own writing. Building a repertory of strategies is important to improving students' writing and editing skills.

Spelling and Technology

The advent of word processing, computer protocols, and the Internet has actually increased, not lessened, the pressure on users to be better, more aware spellers. Spell checkers, for example, create circumstances in which the ability to discriminate between an acceptable and an unacceptable spelling is a critical skill. A homophone substitution, a correct spelling of the wrong word, an inadvertent word omission—these are examples of situations in computer usage that require a deeper understanding of spelling principles and a more adroit proofreading capability. It may be worthwhile to underscore this increased need as a whole-class discussion after students finish this unit's **Electronic Spelling** activity.

Unit 19 Home Study Master

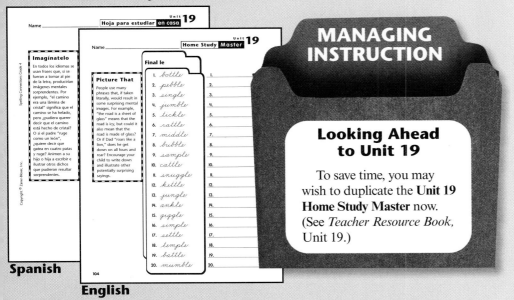

Spanish

English

MANAGING INSTRUCTION

Looking Ahead to Unit 19

To save time, you may wish to duplicate the **Unit 19 Home Study Master** now. (See *Teacher Resource Book,* Unit 19.)

Basic Spelling List

bottle	snuggle
pebble	kettle
single	jungle
jumble	ankle
tickle	giggle
rattle	simple
middle	settle
bubble	temple
sample	battle
cattle	mumble

Strategy Words

Review

circle	people
couple	uncle
maple	

Preview

bicycle	syllable
needle	triangle
principle	

Content Words

Math: Geometry

curves	width
rectangle	polygon
length	

Language Arts: Humor

pun	laughter
chuckle	witty
silly	

Individual Needs

Challenge Words

meddle	brittle
wriggle	tangle
sparkle	

Alternate Word List

bottle	cattle
single	jungle
tickle	simple
middle	settle
sample	battle

MATERIALS

Student Edition
Pages 116–121
Challenge Activities, p. 239

Teacher Edition
Pages T116A–T121
Challenge Activities, p. T239

Other Resources
Spelling Connections Software
Unit 19 Word List Overhead
Transparency

Teacher Resource Book
Unit 19 Home Study Master
(English or Spanish; students
may pretest on this sheet or use
it for home practice.)
Unit 19 Homework Master
Unit 19 Practice Masters
Flip Folder Practice Master
Unit 19 Test Master

Visit our Web site, www.zaner-bloser.com

OBJECTIVES

Spelling and Thinking
Students will
- **read** the spelling words in list form and in context.
- **sort** the words according to double and single consonants.
- **read** and remember this week's spelling strategy.

Spelling and Vocabulary
Students will
- **match** spelling words with definitions.
- **write** spelling words that rhyme with given words.
- **use** the **Writing Thesaurus** to write spelling words that are synonyms for given words.

Spelling and Reading
Students will
- **complete** sentences with spelling words.
- **write** spelling words from other forms of the words.
- **solve** analogies with spelling words.

Spelling and Writing
Students will
- **proofread** a letter.
- **use** the writing process to write a persuasive letter.
- **proofread** their writing.

MEETING INDIVIDUAL NEEDS
Learning Styles

Visual

Have the students scramble the order of the spelling words on the list and then write them as continuous word chains. Have them exchange their word chains with each other and use crayons to separate the words with slashes.

Auditory

Have the students use the spelling words to invent rhythm sentences. For example: "I'll giggle if the bottle in the middle of the kettle starts to rattle." Have them write their sentences down and read them aloud to the class.

Kinesthetic

Assign a spelling word to each student to act out or illustrate. Have the students take turns presenting their acts or illustrations to the class. Then have them spell their words using their arms or fingers to trace the letters in the air.

Language and Cultural Differences

The /l/ and /əl/ sounds spelled **le** may be difficult for some students because of regional pronunciations or language backgrounds that do not include the sound. For one thing, the **schwa** does not exist in the Spanish language. Therefore, Spanish-speaking students may need extra practice to establish the sound-symbol associations required in this unit.

Have the students write the words that end in the /l/ sound (such as **rattle**) in one color and the words that end in the /əl/ sound (such as **pebble**) in another color. Have them list the words like this:

final /l/	**final /əl/**
rattle	pebble
cattle	mumble

MANAGING INSTRUCTION

3–5 Day Plan		Average	Below Average	Above Average
Day 1	**Day 1**	Pretest Spelling Mini-Lesson, p. T116 Spelling and Thinking, p. 116	Pretest Spelling Mini-Lesson, p. T116 Spelling and Thinking, p. 116	Pretest Spelling and Thinking, p. 116
	Day 2	Spelling and Vocabulary, p. 117	Spelling and Vocabulary, p. 117 (or) Unit 19 Practice Master, A and B	Spelling and Vocabulary, p. 117 Spelling and Reading, p. 118
Day 2	**Day 3**	Spelling and Reading, p. 118	Spelling and Reading, p. 118 (or) Unit 19 Practice Master, C and D	Challenge Activities, p. 239
	Day 4	Spelling and Writing, p. 119 Unit 19 Homework Master	Spelling and Writing, p. 119	Spelling and Writing, p. 119 Unit 19 Homework Master
Day 3	**Day 5**	Weekly Test	Weekly Test	Weekly Test
Vocabulary Connections (pages 120 and 121) may be used anytime during this unit.				

Objectives

Spelling and Thinking

Students will
- **read** the spelling words in list form and in context.
- **sort** the words according to double and single consonants.
- **read** and remember this week's spelling strategy.

UNIT PRETEST

Use **Pretest Sentences** below. Refer to the self-checking procedures on student page 256. You may wish to use the **Unit 19 Word List Overhead Transparency** as part of the checking procedure.

TEACHING THE STRATEGY

Spelling Mini-Lesson

Write **le** on the board. Explain that at the end of a word, this spelling has two pronunciations, depending on the consonant sound that comes just before it.

Write **pebble** on the board. Explain that **le** is usually pronounced with the /əl/ sound, as in **pebble**. Invite the students to repeat the word aloud after you and listen for /əl/ in the second syllable. (If necessary, remind the students that /ə/ is the symbol for the schwa sound, the "uh" sound we make when we pronounce an unstressed vowel.)

Write **rattle** on the chalkboard. Explain that when a "hard" sound such as /t/ or /k/ precedes **le**, **le** is pronounced with just the /l/ sound, as in **rattle**. Invite the students to repeat the word aloud after you and listen for /l/. Point out that either pronunciation is spelled **le**.

Ask the students to look at the spelling list. Ask them if these words have anything in common besides the final **le**. (All the words have two syllables; many include double consonants.)

Ask a volunteer to define the word **fiction**. Ask the students to invent, write, and share fictional statements that use the spelling words.

Read **Remember the Spelling Strategy** on page 116.

Order of answers may vary.
double consonants

1. bot/tle ★
2. peb/ble
3. rat/tle
4. mid/dle ★
5. bub/ble
6. cat/tle ★
7. snug/gle
8. ket/tle
9. gig/gle
10. set/tle ★
11. bat/tle ★

no double consonants

12. single ★
13. (jumble)
14. tickle ★
15. sample ★
16. (jungle) ★
17. ankle
18. simple ★
19. temple
20. (mumble)

READ THE SPELLING WORDS

1. bottle	bottle	They bought a **bottle** of juice.
2. pebble	pebble	A **pebble** is smaller than a rock.
3. single	single	I have only a **single** pencil left.
4. jumble	jumble	A **jumble** of papers lay on his desk.
5. tickle	tickle	When you **tickle** me, I have to laugh.
6. rattle	rattle	Keys **rattle** when we unlock the door.
7. middle	middle	She is in **middle** school.
8. bubble	bubble	Angie blew a huge soap **bubble**.
9. sample	sample	Taste a **sample** of my cooking.
10. cattle	cattle	They raise **cattle** on the prairie.
11. snuggle	snuggle	I **snuggle** under warm blankets.
12. kettle	kettle	The hot **kettle** was whistling.
13. jungle	jungle	He photographs many **jungle** animals.
14. ankle	ankle	She wore a silver **ankle** bracelet.
15. giggle	giggle	A laugh often follows a **giggle**.
16. simple	simple	I am learning to tie **simple** knots.
17. settle	settle	They came here to **settle** the land.
18. temple	temple	We attend a **temple** on Main Street.
19. battle	battle	The **battle** was fought at sea.
20. mumble	mumble	When you **mumble**, I cannot hear you.

SORT THE SPELLING WORDS

1.–11. Write the spelling words that have double consonants. Draw a line between the syllables of each word.

12.–20. Write the words that do not have double consonants. Circle the words that have a **short u** sound in the first syllable.

REMEMBER THE SPELLING STRATEGY

Remember that the second syllable in each of this week's spelling words ends in **le**.

116

Pretest Sentences (See procedures on pages Z10–Z11.)

1. You can buy juice in a **bottle** or a can.
2. A small, smooth stone is called a **pebble**.
3. I could not see a **single** cloud in the sky.
4. When the dryer stopped, the clothes were in a **jumble**.
5. Mandy likes to **tickle** people.
6. The loud **rattle** came from the passing truck.
7. A big oak tree stood in the **middle** of our backyard.
8. That soap **bubble** contains air.
9. This delicious omelet is a **sample** of his cooking.
10. The rancher has a large herd of **cattle**.
11. My kitten and puppy **snuggle** when they sleep.
12. Grandmother cooks soup in a large iron **kettle**.
13. There are many different plants in the **jungle**.
14. Ann likes to wear **ankle** socks.
15. The monkey at the zoo made the little boy **giggle**.
16. The directions were **simple** to follow.
17. Sand in the water will **settle** to the bottom.
18. We visited an ancient **temple** during our trip to India.
19. We walked because we did not want to **battle** the traffic.
20. People cannot hear you clearly if you **mumble**.

Spelling and Vocabulary

Word Meanings

Write a spelling word for each definition.

1. a small stone
2. to touch lightly to produce laughter
3. a building for worship
4. a wild, tropical land
5. a small laugh
6. the joint that connects the leg to the foot
7. a container usually made of glass or plastic
8. a round film of liquid

Phonics

Follow the directions to write spelling words.

9.–11. Change the first letter in **tattle** to write spelling words.
12.–13. Change the first letter in **nettle** to write spelling words.
14.–15. Change the first letter in **bumble** to write spelling words.

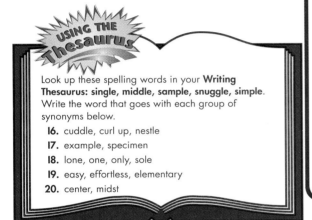

USING THE Thesaurus

Look up these spelling words in your **Writing Thesaurus: single, middle, sample, snuggle, simple.** Write the word that goes with each group of synonyms below.

16. cuddle, curl up, nestle
17. example, specimen
18. lone, one, only, sole
19. easy, effortless, elementary
20. center, midst

Word Meanings

1. pebble
2. tickle
3. temple
4. jungle
5. giggle
6. ankle
7. bottle
8. bubble

Phonics
Order of answers may vary.

9. rattle
10. cattle
11. battle
12. kettle
13. settle
14. jumble
15. mumble

Using the Thesaurus

16. snuggle
17. sample
18. single
19. simple
20. middle

117

Objectives

Spelling and Vocabulary

Students will
- **match** spelling words with definitions.
- **write** spelling words that rhyme with given words.
- **use** the **Writing Thesaurus** to write spelling words that are synonyms for given words.

Developing Oral Language Skills

Do a word sort by sound. Write **short a, short e, short i, short o, short u** on a chalkboard or an overhead transparency. Tell students that each word in the spelling list has a short vowel sound in the first syllable. Ask volunteers to read the spelling words aloud, asking students to place each word under one of the headings according to the vowel sound they hear in the first syllable. When they are finished listing the words, ask students to consider the letters in each word that spell the short vowel sound. Then have volunteers come to the board and circle the letters that spell the sound.

MEETING INDIVIDUAL NEEDS

Providing More Help

Have the students work in pairs. Have each student write the spelling words in groups of four, so that the four words run together as though they are one word. Have the partners exchange papers and draw lines to separate the spelling words. Remind the students that each spelling word ends with **le**.

★Students who need to study fewer words should use the **Alternate Word List**. This list is starred on page T116 in the Teacher Edition. The **Unit 19 Practice Masters** (*Teacher Resource Book*) provide additional practice with these words.

Unit 19 Practice Masters

Name _____
Practice Master Unit **19**

| 1. cattle | 3. bottle | 5. middle | 7. simple | 9. jungle |
| 2. battle | 4. settle | 6. single | 8. sample | 10. tickle |

A. Imagine that the spelling words can talk. Write the spelling word that would say each sentence.

1. "I am found in the center."
2. "I can hold liquids."
3. "I am another name for cows."
4. "I am easy to do."
5. "I am always alone."
6. "I can make people laugh."

B. Write a spelling word that is a synonym for each word.

1. fight _____ 5. easy _____
2. decide _____ 6. example _____
3. center _____ 7. bush _____
4. one _____ 8. cows _____

C. Write the spelling word that belongs in each sentence.

1. **Birds** are to **flock** as _____ are to **herd**.
2. **Two** is to **double** as **one** is to ____.
3. **Hard** is to **difficult** as **easy** is to ____.
4. **Deer** is to **forest** as **monkey** is to ____.
5. **Side** is to **edge** as **center** is to ____.

106

Practice Master Unit **19**

| simple | jungle |
| sample | tickle |

107

T117

Objectives

Spelling and Reading

Students will

- **complete** sentences with spelling words.
- **write** spelling words from other forms of the words.
- **solve** analogies with spelling words.

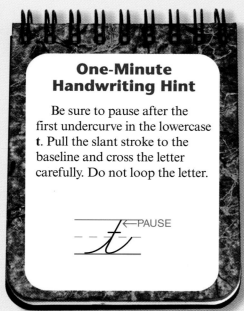

One-Minute Handwriting Hint

Be sure to pause after the first undercurve in the lowercase **t**. Pull the slant stroke to the baseline and cross the letter carefully. Do not loop the letter.

←PAUSE

Legible handwriting can boost spelling scores by as much as 20%.

Complete the Sentences

1. rattle
2. battle
3. cattle
4. settle
5. jumble
6. kettle
7. mumble

Replace the Words

8. bottle
9. bubble
10. giggle
11. snuggle
12. sample
13. tickle

Solve the Analogies

14. single
15. simple
16. pebble
17. jungle
18. temple
19. middle
20. ankle

Spelling and Reading

bottle	pebble	single	jumble	tickle
rattle	middle	bubble	sample	cattle
snuggle	kettle	jungle	ankle	giggle
simple	settle	temple	battle	mumble

Complete the Sentences   Write the spelling word that best completes each sentence.

1. The wind is making the window _____.
2. Boots and an umbrella will help us _____ the storm.
3. Do all _____ have horns and hoofs?
4. It is hard to _____ down after all that excitement.
5. All our jackets are on the bed in a _____.
6. The _____ is whistling merrily on the stove.
7. Did she _____ that she was sorry?

Replace the Words   There is one form of a spelling word in each sentence. Find that form and write the spelling word it came from.

8. The workers in the dairy are bottling milk.
9. The water will start bubbling when it boils.
10. Sarah was reading the comics and giggling.
11. Timmy enjoys snuggling up with a good book.
12. We will be sampling different fruits today.
13. The fur on my collar is tickling my chin.

Solve the Analogies   Write the spelling word that completes each analogy.

14. **Two** is to **double** as **one** is to _____.
15. **Hard** is to **difficult** as **easy** is to _____.
16. **Large** is to **boulder** as **small** is to _____.
17. **Deer** is to **forest** as **monkey** is to _____.
18. **Education** is to **school** as **religion** is to _____.
19. **Side** is to **edge** as **center** is to _____.
20. **Hand** is to **wrist** as **foot** is to _____.

118

MEETING INDIVIDUAL NEEDS

Providing More Challenge

Challenge Words and **Challenge Activities** for Unit 19 appear on page 239. **Challenge Word Test Sentences** appear on page T239.

Unit 19 Challenge Activities

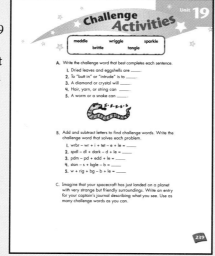

Weekly Test Options

Option 1:
One Spelling Word Per Sentence

(See procedures on pages Z10–Z11.)

1. Father broke the **bubble** I made from the soap.
2. The **kettle** on the range was hot.
3. The army fought in a **battle**.
4. The ball bounced into the **middle** of the road.
5. I like to **snuggle** up next to the kitten.
6. The child played with the soft **rattle**.
7. I found a rock and a **pebble** in the sand.
8. You two laugh and **giggle** most of the time.
9. The herd of **cattle** ran into the field.
10. I will **settle** for one piece instead of two.
11. The juice will stay fresh if you keep the cap on the **bottle**.
12. I have only a **single** pair of good shoes.
13. You will have to put the pieces back in order if you **jumble** them.
14. The teacher showed us a **sample** question.

T118

Spelling and Writing

Proofread a Letter

Six words are not spelled correctly in this letter to a newspaper editor. Write those words correctly.

Dear Editor:

I am writing to say that I am alarmed at the way our
land is disappearing. Our catle are grazing on less grass.
cattle
Our jungel animals have fewer trees. Our children are
jungle
caught in the midle with hardly any space to play. The
middle
solution seems simpel. Set aside more land for parks and
simple
wildlife refuges. A singel park can be used for both humans
single
and animals. Ask your readers to battel for open space. Let
battle
us not settle for houses, stores, and huge parking lots.

Yours truly,

Lee Jamison

Proofreading Marks

≡ Make a capital.
/ Make a small letter.
∧ Add something.
℘ Take out something.
⊙ Add a period.
⌗ New paragraph
(SP) Spelling error

Write a Letter

Persuasive Writing

Write a letter about something that concerns you. Be sure to include

- what your concerns are about.
- what you think should be done.
- the reasons for keeping or changing something.
- what the reader can do to make a difference.

Use as many spelling words as you can.

Writing Process

Prewriting
⇩
Drafting
⇩
Revising
⇩
Editing
⇩
Publishing

Proofread Your Writing During → **Editing**

Proofread your writing for spelling errors as part of the editing stage in the writing process. Be sure to check each word carefully. Use a dictionary to check spelling if you are not sure.

119

Objectives

Spelling and Writing

Students will
- **proofread** a letter.
- **use** the writing process to write a persuasive letter.
- **proofread** their writing.

Using the Writing Process

Before assigning **Write a Letter** in this unit, see pages 258–259 in the Student Edition for a complete review of the writing process and additional writing assignments. You may also wish to refer to pages Z12–Z13 in the Teacher Edition.

Keeping a Spelling Journal

Encourage students to record the words they misspelled on the weekly test in a personal spelling journal. These words may be recycled for future study. Students may also wish to include words from their writing. See pages Z12–Z13 in the Teacher Edition for more information.

15. We will see an old **temple** on our trip.
16. Father will laugh if you **tickle** him.
17. The boys gave the teacher a **simple** answer.
18. Your voice should be clear, and you should not **mumble** your words.
19. The **jungle** is home to many animals.
20. I broke my **ankle** when I was skating.

Option 2:
Multiple Spelling Words Per Sentence
(See procedures on pages Z10–Z11.)

1. The **pebble** will **settle** at the bottom of the **bottle**.
2. **Sample** the soup in the **kettle** and tell me if it is good.
3. The **battle** began in the field near the **temple**.
4. His **simple** job was to steer the **cattle** into the barn.
5. I **mumble** and **jumble** my words if I talk while I **giggle**.
6. The tiny child will **snuggle** under her cover and play with her **rattle**.
7. Animals live in the **middle** of the **jungle**.
8. Father will **tickle** my **ankle**.
9. Do you see the size of that **single bubble**?

Option 3:
Standardized Test
(See *Teacher Resource Book,* Unit 19.)

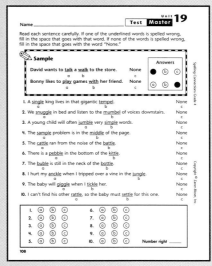

Unit 19 Test Master

Vocabulary

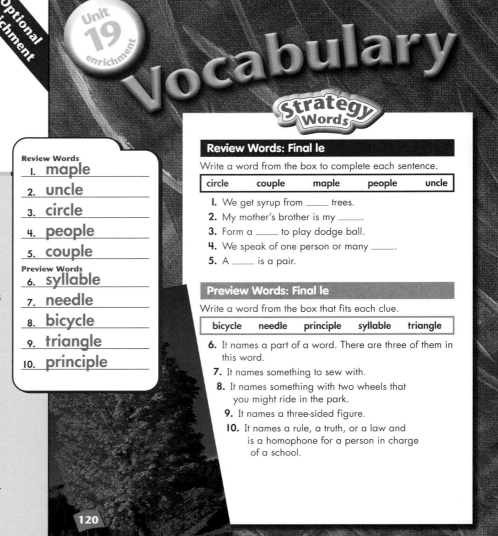

Objectives

Strategy Words

Students will
- **review** words studied previously that are related to the spelling strategy.
- **preview** unknown words that are related to the spelling strategy.

Remind the students that the **Strategy Words** are related to the spelling patterns they have studied in this unit. The **Review Words** are below grade level, and the **Preview Words** are above grade level. You may wish to use the following sentences to introduce the words in context.

Review Words:
Words From Grade 3

1. Draw a **circle** on your paper and put your name in it.
2. I will need a **couple** of volunteers for this job.
3. The **maple** tree is a beautiful color in the fall.
4. Many **people** will be at the family reunion.
5. My aunt and **uncle** will be visiting us in a few weeks.

Preview Words:
Words From Grade 5

6. Mike likes to ride his **bicycle** in the neighborhood.
7. Grandmother uses a large **needle** to make her dolls.
8. She made her decision based on **principle** rather than emotion.
9. Write a list of words with more than one **syllable**.
10. The music teacher let me play the **triangle** in the skit.

Review Words
1. maple
2. uncle
3. circle
4. people
5. couple

Preview Words
6. syllable
7. needle
8. bicycle
9. triangle
10. principle

Review Words: Final le

Write a word from the box to complete each sentence.

| circle | couple | maple | people | uncle |

1. We get syrup from _____ trees.
2. My mother's brother is my _____.
3. Form a _____ to play dodge ball.
4. We speak of one person or many _____.
5. A _____ is a pair.

Preview Words: Final le

Write a word from the box that fits each clue.

| bicycle | needle | principle | syllable | triangle |

6. It names a part of a word. There are three of them in this word.
7. It names something to sew with.
8. It names something with two wheels that you might ride in the park.
9. It names a three-sided figure.
10. It names a rule, a truth, or a law and is a homophone for a person in charge of a school.

120

Unit 19 RECAP

You may wish to assign the **Unit 19 Homework Master** (*Teacher Resource Book*, Unit 19) as a fun way to recap the spelling words.

Unit 19 Homework Master

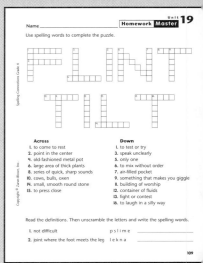

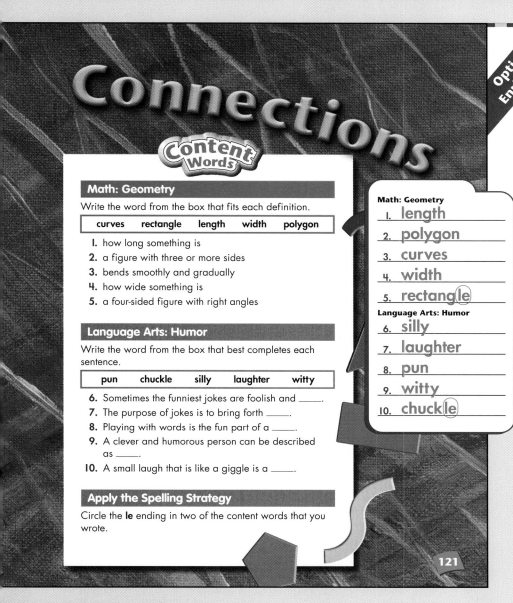

Connections

Content Words

Math: Geometry

Write the word from the box that fits each definition.

curves	rectangle	length	width	polygon

1. how long something is
2. a figure with three or more sides
3. bends smoothly and gradually
4. how wide something is
5. a four-sided figure with right angles

Language Arts: Humor

Write the word from the box that best completes each sentence.

pun	chuckle	silly	laughter	witty

6. Sometimes the funniest jokes are foolish and ____.
7. The purpose of jokes is to bring forth ____.
8. Playing with words is the fun part of a ____.
9. A clever and humorous person can be described as ____.
10. A small laugh that is like a giggle is a ____.

Apply the Spelling Strategy

Circle the **le** ending in two of the content words that you wrote.

121

Math: Geometry
1. length
2. polygon
3. curves
4. width
5. rectangle

Language Arts: Humor
6. silly
7. laughter
8. pun
9. witty
10. chuckle

Unit 20 Home Study Master

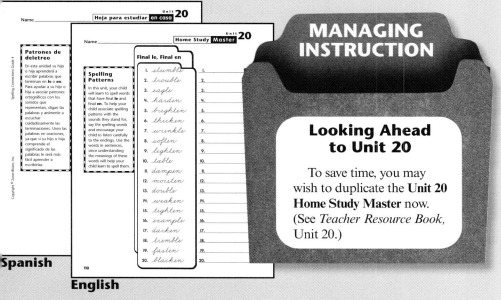

Spanish

English

MANAGING INSTRUCTION

Looking Ahead to Unit 20

To save time, you may wish to duplicate the **Unit 20 Home Study Master** now. (See *Teacher Resource Book,* Unit 20.)

Objectives

Content Words

Students will
- **expand** vocabulary with content-related words.
- **relate** the spelling strategy to words outside the basic spelling list.

Math: Geometry

Review the meanings of these words with the students. You may wish to use these sentences to introduce the words in context.

1. How many **curves** are on that one-mile stretch of highway?
2. That tablet of paper is in the shape of a **rectangle**.
3. Measure the **length** of the rope that will be used for the game.
4. We need to figure the **width** of the room so we will know how many desks will fit across the front.
5. The math lesson will be about a figure called a **polygon**.

Encourage the students to use these words to make a poster or bulletin board display of geometric figures and terms.

Language Arts: Humor

Review the meanings of these words with the students. You may wish to use these sentences to introduce the words in context.

6. A **pun** is often referred to as "a play on words."
7. My baby sister will **chuckle** every time she sees the puppy.
8. The clown was acting very **silly** at the circus.
9. We heard a great deal of **laughter** at the funny play.
10. My brother is very **witty** and keeps the family entertained.

Encourage the students to use these words to describe a television show they enjoy.

Basic Spelling List

stumble	dampen
trouble	moisten
eagle	double
harden	weaken
brighten	tighten
thicken	example
wrinkle	darken
soften	tremble
lighten	fasten
table	blacken

Strategy Words

Review
kitten	sudden
mitten	women
open	

Preview
angle	lengthen
chosen	straighten
forgotten	

Content Words

Social Studies: Time
century	twice
triple	months
decade	

Science: Astronomy
comet	planet
orbit	meteor
explode	

Individual Needs

Challenge Words
unable	wooden
whistle	woolen
beaten	

Alternate Word List
trouble	moisten
harden	double
brighten	example
lighten	darken
table	fasten

MATERIALS

Student Edition
Pages 122–127
Challenge Activities, p. 240

Teacher Edition
Pages T122A–T127
Challenge Activities, p. T240

Other Resources
Spelling Connections Software
Unit 20 Word List Overhead
Transparency

Teacher Resource Book
Unit 20 Home Study Master
(English or Spanish; students
may pretest on this sheet or use
it for home practice.)
Unit 20 Homework Master
Unit 20 Practice Masters
Flip Folder Practice Master
Unit 20 Test Master

Visit our Web site, www.zaner-bloser.com

OBJECTIVES

Spelling and Thinking
Students will
- **read** the spelling words in list form and in context.
- **sort** the words according to **le** and **en** suffixes.
- **read** and remember this week's spelling strategy.

Spelling and Vocabulary
Students will
- **write** spelling words to match definitions.
- **drop** suffixes from given words to write spelling words.
- **use** the **Spelling Dictionary** to find spelling words and label first syllables as "open" or "closed."

Spelling and Reading
Students will
- **complete** sentences using spelling words.
- **complete** a story using spelling words.

Spelling and Writing
Students will
- **proofread** a friendly letter.
- **use** the writing process to write a friendly letter.
- **proofread** their writing.

MEETING INDIVIDUAL NEEDS
Learning Styles

Visual

Have students work with a partner to construct crossword puzzles on graph paper, using as many spelling words as they can. Tell them to outline each block in which they write a letter. They should use their **Spelling Dictionaries** to write the definition for each word as a clue and give corresponding numbers to each word in the puzzle and each definition. Then tell students to make copies of their puzzles, omitting the letters in the blocks. Have the students exchange and complete the puzzles.

Auditory

Write the spelling words on the chalkboard in random order. Make cards with the following words and hold them up one at a time: **heighten, stable, crumble, crinkle, bubble, frighten, beagle, garden, slacken, harken, often, stubble, quicken, whiten, sample**. Have students say the word on the card and one of the spelling words that rhymes with that word. Then choose a student to point to the letters in the spelling word while the class spells the word out loud.

Kinesthetic

Pronounce the spelling words with the students. If a word ends with **le,** have them wink one eye. If it ends with **en,** have them slap their right knee, then their left knee. Then have the students take turns spelling words aloud. If the words end in **le,** have them wink as they spell the letters **l** and **e.** If it ends with **en,** have them slap their knees as they spell the letters **e** and **n.**

Language and Cultural Differences

The suffix **-en** in this unit may be difficult for some students to hear because of regional pronunciation differences or language backgrounds that do not include this sound. It is important for these students to hear and use each word in meaningful context so that they understand the meaning of the suffix they are being asked to spell.

Ask the students to read along with you in their spelling books as you pronounce each spelling word. Have the students repeat each word after you. Then ask volunteers to use the words in sentences.

MANAGING INSTRUCTION

3–5 Day Plan		Average	Below Average	Above Average
Day 1	**Day 1**	Pretest Spelling Mini-Lesson, p. T122 Spelling and Thinking, p. 122	Pretest Spelling Mini-Lesson, p. T122 Spelling and Thinking, p. 122	Pretest Spelling and Thinking, p. 122
	Day 2	Spelling and Vocabulary, p. 123	Spelling and Vocabulary, p. 123 (or) Unit 20 Practice Master, A and B	Spelling and Vocabulary, p. 123 Spelling and Reading, p. 124
Day 2	**Day 3**	Spelling and Reading, p. 124	Spelling and Reading, p. 124 (or) Unit 20 Practice Master, C and D	Challenge Activities, p. 240
	Day 4	Spelling and Writing, p. 125 Unit 20 Homework Master	Spelling and Writing, p. 125	Spelling and Writing, p. 125 Unit 20 Homework Master
Day 3	**Day 5**	Weekly Test	Weekly Test	Weekly Test
Vocabulary Connections (pages 126 and 127) may be used anytime during this unit.				

Objectives

Spelling and Thinking

Students will
- **read** the spelling words in list form and in context.
- **sort** the words according to **le** and **en** suffixes.
- **read** and remember this week's spelling strategy.

UNIT PRETEST

Use **Pretest Sentences** below. Refer to the self-checking procedures on student page 256. You may wish to use the **Unit 20 Word List Overhead Transparency** as part of the checking procedure.

TEACHING THE STRATEGY

Spelling Mini-Lesson

Write **-en** on the board. Explain that the **-en** ending usually means "to make" or "to become" and is often attached to adjectives.

Write **dark** and **darken** on the board. Ask a volunteer to describe the difference in meaning between the two words. (Dark means "not light." Darken means "to make dark" or "to become dark.")

Ask volunteers to use each word in a sentence. Write the sentences they create on the chalkboard. Using these sentences as examples, discuss how **-en** changes not only the meaning but also the function of the word to which it is attached. (Dark is an adjective, but darken is a verb.)

Write **damp, black,** and **moist** on the chalkboard. Ask volunteers to add **-en** to each word and write the new words. (dampen, blacken, moisten) Discuss the fact that the spelling of the base word does not change when **-en** is added.

Ask the students to read the word list aloud after you. Remind them that last week's spelling list was made up entirely of words ending in **le.**

Read **Remember the Spelling Strategy** on page 122.

Order of answers may vary.

le endings
1. eagle
2. table ★
3. stumble
4. tremble
5. wrinkle
6. double ★
7. trouble ★
8. example ★

en endings
9. dampen
10. darken ★
11. soften
12. weaken
13. harden ★
14. fasten ★
15. thicken
16. moisten ★
17. blacken
18. lighten ★
19. tighten
20. brighten ★

Unit **20**
Final le, Final en

Spelling and Thinking

READ THE SPELLING WORDS

1.	stumble	*stumble*	It is easy to **stumble** in the dark.
2.	trouble	*trouble*	When in **trouble** you need a friend.
3.	eagle	*eagle*	An **eagle** builds a huge nest.
4.	harden	*harden*	The candy will **harden** as it cools.
5.	brighten	*brighten*	Your kindness will **brighten** my day.
6.	thicken	*thicken*	Use flour to **thicken** the sauce.
7.	wrinkle	*wrinkle*	Try not to **wrinkle** your clothes.
8.	soften	*soften*	The sun will **soften** the ice.
9.	lighten	*lighten*	Two helpers will **lighten** the load.
10.	table	*table*	The children set the **table**.
11.	dampen	*dampen*	Before ironing, **dampen** the cloth.
12.	moisten	*moisten*	Please **moisten** the sponge with water.
13.	double	*double*	Twins are **double** the pleasure.
14.	weaken	*weaken*	Lack of exercise can **weaken** you.
15.	tighten	*tighten*	I must **tighten** a bolt on my bike.
16.	example	*example*	He set a good **example** for others.
17.	darken	*darken*	Rain clouds will **darken** the sky.
18.	tremble	*tremble*	The dog began to **tremble** with cold.
19.	fasten	*fasten*	Be sure to **fasten** your seat belt.
20.	blacken	*blacken*	Factory soot can **blacken** homes.

SORT THE SPELLING WORDS

1.–8. Write the words that end with **le**.
9.–20. Write the words that end with **en**.

REMEMBER THE SPELLING STRATEGY

Remember that the words on this week's list end in **le** or **en**. Final **en** usually means "to make" or "to become." The word **brighten** means "to become bright."

122

Pretest Sentences (See procedures on pages Z10–Z11.)

1. You must take care not to **stumble** on the rough ground.
2. The bear cub got into **trouble**.
3. The bald **eagle** is a symbol of the United States.
4. Put the butter in the refrigerator to **harden**.
5. The sunlight will **brighten** the room.
6. Cornstarch can be used to **thicken** gravy.
7. I will iron the **wrinkle** out of this dress.
8. It is best to **soften** clay before you work with it.
9. Removing some bricks will **lighten** the load.
10. Grandmother loves her antique oak **table**.
11. You should **dampen** the shirt before you iron it.
12. Before you wipe the table, **moisten** the sponge.
13. I had to **double** the ingredients in the recipe.
14. Add water to the lemonade to **weaken** it.
15. Mother will **tighten** the baby's shoelaces.
16. An **example** of a noun is the word *cat*.
17. Closing the shades will **darken** the room.
18. I began to **tremble** at the thought of singing a solo.
19. We should always **fasten** our seat belts.
20. Please use a marker to **blacken** the empty spaces.

T122

Spelling and Vocabulary

Word Meanings

The suffix **-en** means "to make" or "to become." Write the spelling word that goes with each meaning.

1. to make light
2. to make moist
3. to become weak
4. to become dark
5. to become hard
6. to make black
7. to make thick
8. to make damp

Word Structure

Read the following words and write the spelling word that each came from.

9. softener
10. fastener
11. brightener
12. tightener

USING THE Dictionary

Syllables ending with a vowel sound are called **open syllables**. Those ending with a consonant sound are called **closed syllables**. Find the following spelling words in your **Spelling Dictionary**. Write each word. Then write **o** if the first syllable is open or **c** if the first syllable is closed.

13. table
14. stumble
15. wrinkle
16. example
17. eagle
18. tremble
19. double
20. trouble

Word Meanings
1. lighten
2. moisten
3. weaken
4. darken
5. harden
6. blacken
7. thicken
8. dampen

Word Structure
9. soften
10. fasten
11. brighten
12. tighten

Using the Dictionary
13. table, o
14. stumble, c
15. wrinkle, c
16. example, c
17. eagle, o
18. tremble, c
19. double, o
20. trouble, o

123

Objectives

Spelling and Vocabulary

Students will
- **write** spelling words to match definitions.
- **drop** suffixes from given words to write spelling words.
- **use** the **Spelling Dictionary** to find spelling words and label first syllables as "open" or "closed."

Developing Oral Language Skills

Do a word sort by sound. Write **le** and **en** on a chalkboard or an overhead transparency. Then read the spelling word list, asking students to write each word under one of the two headings according to the ending. Then have volunteers come to the board and circle the endings.

MEETING INDIVIDUAL NEEDS

Providing More Help

Provide each student with twenty-eight cards or slips of paper. Tell the students to write one letter of the alphabet on each card. Ask them to make two cards for **t** and **e**. Lay the cards out on the desk or floor in front of them. Pronounce a spelling word and have the students arrange their letters to spell the word. Then have volunteers repeat the words and write the correct spellings on the chalkboard so all of the students can check their work.

★ Students who need to study fewer words should use the **Alternate Word List**. This list is starred on page T122 in the Teacher Edition. The **Unit 20 Practice Masters** (*Teacher Resource Book*) provide additional practice with these words.

Unit 20 Practice Masters

Name _____ Practice **Master** **Unit 20**

| 1. table | 3. trouble | 5. darken | 7. fasten | 9. lighten |
| 2. double | 4. example | 6. harden | 8. moisten | 10. brighten |

A. The suffix **-en** means "to make" or "to become." Write the spelling word that goes with each meaning.

1. to make light
2. to make moist
3. to become dark
4. to become hard
5. to make bright

B. Write the spelling words in alphabetical order.

1. _____   6. _____
2. _____   7. _____
3. _____   8. _____
4. _____   9. _____
5. _____   10. _____

C. Write the spelling word that goes with each group.

1. shine, polish, lighten, ____
2. attach, join, tie, ____
3. sample, model, ____

112

Practice **Master** **Unit 20**

fasten   lighten
moisten   brighten

a letter. The words you decode are

h	i	j	k	l	m
8	9	10	11	12	13
u	v	w	x	y	z
21	22	23	24	25	26

113

Objectives

Spelling and Reading

Students will

- **complete** sentences using spelling words.
- **complete** a story using spelling words.

One-Minute Handwriting Hint

The lowercase **n** contains two overcurves. Be sure to pause after the first overcurve-slant motion. The two slant strokes should be parallel.

OVERCURVES

Legible handwriting can boost spelling scores by as much as 20%.

Complete the Sentences

1. stumble
2. fasten
3. double
4. wrinkle
5. tighten
6. lighten
7. brighten
8. eagle
9. darken;blacken
10. blacken;darken
11. harden
12. dampen
13. weaken

Complete the Story

14. table
15. example
16. thicken
17. moisten; soften
18. soften; moisten
19. trouble
20. tremble

124

stumble	trouble	eagle	harden	brighten
thicken	wrinkle	soften	lighten	table
dampen	moisten	double	weaken	tighten
example	darken	tremble	fasten	blacken

Complete the Sentences Write the spelling word that best completes each sentence.

1. Do not _____ over the rug in the dark hallway.
2. We _____ our safety belts as soon as we get in the car.
3. This bread dough will soon _____ in size.
4. If I do not hang up this shirt, it will _____.
5. Leah's helmet strap is loose; please ask her to _____ it.
6. She took three of his books to _____ his heavy load.
7. The sun will soon _____ this cheerless, gray day.
8. We watched the magnificent _____ swoop over the hills.
9.–10. Storm clouds are about to _____ and _____ the bright sky.
11. If I don't wash this glue off my fingers, it will _____.
12. Please do not let her remarks _____ your wonderful high spirits.
13. Did the heavy rain further _____ the loose, rickety fence?

Complete the Story Write spelling words to complete the story.

Seth has often helped his neighbor, Mabel, work on projects on a __14.__ in the basement. Mabel has made useful items. For __15.__, she made a powder to help __16.__ the sparse grass in her yard. She also made a cream to __17.__ and __18.__ dry, rough skin.

Mabel's inventions were not always useful. Seth remembers when he tried a new food she had created. He knew he was in __19.__ when his mouth began to twitch and __20.__.

| thicken |
| moisten |
| trouble |
| tremble |
| example |
| soften |
| table |

MEETING INDIVIDUAL NEEDS

Providing More Challenge

Challenge Words and **Challenge Activities** for Unit 20 appear on page 240. **Challenge Word Test Sentences** appear on page T240.

Unit 20 Challenge Activities

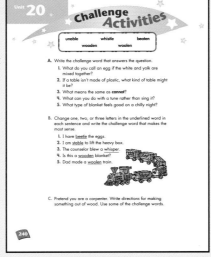

Weekly Test Options

Option 1:
One Spelling Word Per Sentence

(See procedures on pages Z10–Z11.)

1. We had no **trouble** finding your house.
2. Be careful not to **stumble** and fall over those rocks.
3. You can **soften** cheese by heating it.
4. The eggs will **harden** when you boil them.
5. Painting the walls white will **lighten** the room.
6. I will **dampen** the shirt before I iron it.
7. You can **brighten** the gym by turning on the light.
8. The **eagle** flew high into the sky.
9. Father felt his ankle **weaken** when he fell.
10. Give me an **example** of a question.
11. I will **tighten** the knot so it does not come loose.
12. Please **darken** the room so I can sleep.
13. The ground will **tremble** if we have an earthquake.
14. You can **thicken** the stew by adding more flour.
15. I would like a **double** helping of carrots.

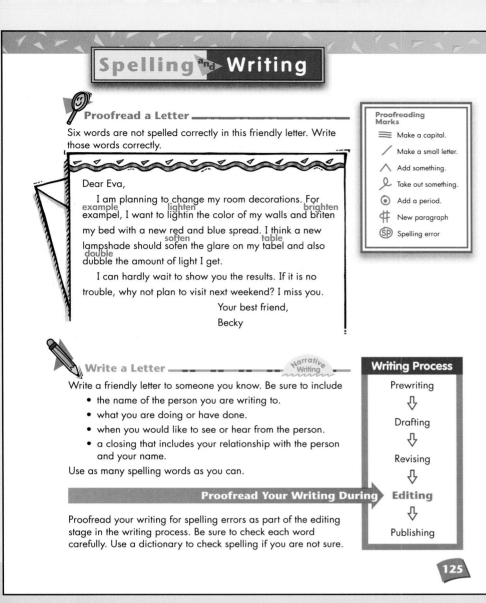

Spelling and Writing

Proofread a Letter

Six words are not spelled correctly in this friendly letter. Write those words correctly.

Dear Eva,

    I am planning to change my room decorations. For *exampel*, I want to *lightin* the color of my walls and *briten* my bed with a new red and blue spread. I think a new lampshade should *sofen* the glare on my *tabel* and also *dubble* the amount of light I get.

    I can hardly wait to show you the results. If it is no trouble, why not plan to visit next weekend? I miss you.

               Your best friend,

               Becky

(corrections shown: example, lighten, brighten, soften, table, double)

Proofreading Marks

≡ Make a capital.

/ Make a small letter.

∧ Add something.

✀ Take out something.

⊙ Add a period.

⌗ New paragraph.

(SP) Spelling error

Write a Letter — Narrative Writing

Write a friendly letter to someone you know. Be sure to include
- the name of the person you are writing to.
- what you are doing or have done.
- when you would like to see or hear from the person.
- a closing that includes your relationship with the person and your name.

Use as many spelling words as you can.

Proofread Your Writing During → Editing

Proofread your writing for spelling errors as part of the editing stage in the writing process. Be sure to check each word carefully. Use a dictionary to check spelling if you are not sure.

Writing Process

Prewriting
⇩
Drafting
⇩
Revising
⇩
Editing
⇩
Publishing

125

---

16. The sky began to **blacken** and the air became cold.
17. We set the food on the **table**.
18. Mother hopes the rain will **moisten** the dry grass.
19. The door will not open if you **fasten** the lock.
20. Please do not **wrinkle** the clothes after I iron them.

Option 2:
Multiple Spelling Words Per Sentence

(See procedures on pages Z10–Z11.)

1. Please **soften** the music and **brighten** the room.
2. **Fasten** and then **tighten** the leg of the **table**.
3. I hope you do not **darken** the room that I wanted to **lighten**.
4. Do **dampen** and **moisten** both mean the same thing?
5. We need to **blacken** the shoes of the clowns before they **stumble** into the circus ring.
6. It is no **trouble** to **wrinkle** the paper and throw it away.
7. The **eagle** will **tremble** if the branches **weaken**.
8. As the turtle grows, its shell will **thicken** and **harden**.
9. Give me an **example** of a spelling word with **double** letters.

Option 3:
Standardized Test

(See *Teacher Resource Book,* Unit 20.)

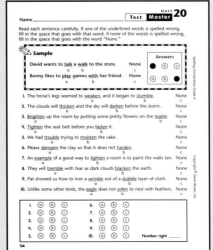

Unit 20
Test Master

TI25

Objectives

Strategy Words

Students will
- **review** words studied previously that are related to the spelling strategy.
- **preview** unknown words that are related to the spelling strategy.

Remind the students that the **Strategy Words** are related to the spelling patterns they have studied in this unit. The **Review Words** are below grade level, and the **Preview Words** are above grade level. You may wish to use the following sentences to introduce the words in context.

Review Words:
Words From Grade 3
1. The **kitten** played for hours with the ball of yarn.
2. I have lost a **mitten** from the set that Grandmother knitted for me.
3. If we **open** the window, we can get some fresh air into this room.
4. The **sudden** movement of the dog frightened the cat.
5. Many men and **women** were gathered for a meeting at the school.

Preview Words:
Words From Grade 5
6. Name a geometric figure with a right **angle**.
7. My friend was **chosen** to be the president of the class.
8. Have you **forgotten** that today is my birthday?
9. We will **lengthen** the legs on your jeans by letting out the hem.
10. Dad said we have to **straighten** our rooms before we leave.

Review Words
1. mitten
2. women
3. kitten
4. open
5. sudden

Preview Words
6. lengthen
7. forgotten
8. straighten
9. angle
10. chosen

Unit 20 Vocabulary — Strategy Words

Review Words: Final le, Final en

Write the word from the box that matches each clue.

kitten	mitten	open	sudden	women

1. something you wear
2. more than one woman
3. a young cat
4. an antonym of **close**
5. a synonym of **quick**

Preview Words: Final le, Final en

Write a word from the box to complete each sentence.

angle	chosen	forgotten	lengthen	straighten

6. I must _____ this short pair of pants in order to make them fit properly.
7. The driver has _____ the way back to town so now we are lost.
8. Please fasten the top button of your shirt and _____ your tie.
9. The road makes a sharp _____ to the right just before our house.
10. Have you _____ some heavy, warm clothes for the trip to the mountains?

126

Unit 20 RECAP

You may wish to assign the **Unit 20 Homework Master** (*Teacher Resource Book,* Unit 20) as a fun way to recap the spelling words.

Unit 20 Homework Master

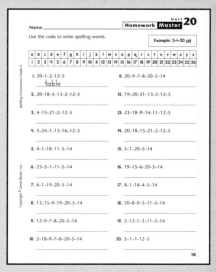

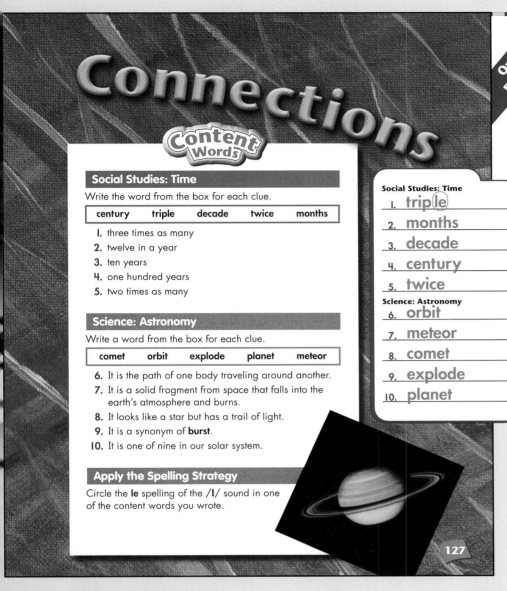

Connections

Content Words

Social Studies: Time

Write the word from the box for each clue.

century	triple	decade	twice	months

1. three times as many
2. twelve in a year
3. ten years
4. one hundred years
5. two times as many

Science: Astronomy

Write a word from the box for each clue.

comet	orbit	explode	planet	meteor

6. It is the path of one body traveling around another.
7. It is a solid fragment from space that falls into the earth's atmosphere and burns.
8. It looks like a star but has a trail of light.
9. It is a synonym of **burst**.
10. It is one of nine in our solar system.

Apply the Spelling Strategy

Circle the **le** spelling of the /l/ sound in one of the content words you wrote.

127

Social Studies: Time

1. trip(le)
2. months
3. decade
4. century
5. twice

Science: Astronomy

6. orbit
7. meteor
8. comet
9. explode
10. planet

Objectives

Content Words

Students will
• **expand** vocabulary with content-related words.
• **relate** the spelling strategy to words outside the basic spelling list.

Content Words

Social Studies: Time

Review the meanings of these words with the students. You may wish to use these sentences to introduce the words in context.

1. A **century** is a period of time lasting one hundred years.
2. The ice skater made a **triple** jump.
3. Ten years make a **decade**.
4. I rang the doorbell **twice** before anyone in the house heard me.
5. It will take two **months** for me to complete this project.

Encourage the students to use these words in a paragraph about a real or an imaginary historic event.

Science: Astronomy

Review the meanings of these words with the students. You may wish to use these sentences to introduce the words in context.

6. Did you see the **comet** cross the sky last night?
7. The spaceship will make it into **orbit** soon.
8. The balloon we are using to represent our earth will **explode** if we fill it too full of air.
9. The **planet** has many moons.
10. The scientists took pictures of the **meteor**.

Encourage the students to use these words to describe a scene from a science fiction story.

Unit 21 Home Study Master

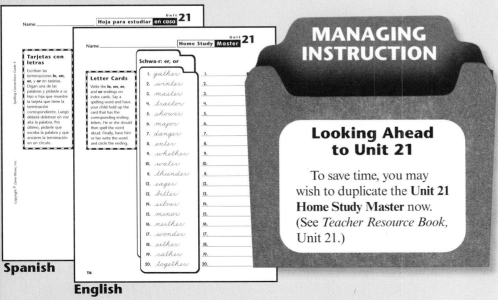

Spanish

English

MANAGING INSTRUCTION

Looking Ahead to Unit 21

To save time, you may wish to duplicate the **Unit 21 Home Study Master** now. (See *Teacher Resource Book,* Unit 21.)

Basic Spelling List

gather	thunder
winter	eager
master	bitter
tractor	silver
shower	minor
major	neither
danger	wonder
enter	either
whether	rather
water	together

Strategy Words

Review

colors	mother
father	never
later	

Preview

alligator	passenger
bother	professor
differ	

Content Words

Math: Fractions

denominator	numerator
mixed	fraction
equally	

Social Studies: Geography

altitude	timber
summit	evergreen
crag	

Individual Needs

Challenge Words

halter	razor
barber	anchor
rubber	

Alternate Word List

winter	neither
tractor	wonder
whether	either
water	rather
silver	together

MATERIALS

Student Edition

Pages 128–133
Challenge Activities, p. 241

Teacher Edition

Pages T128A–T133
Challenge Activities, p. T241

Other Resources

Spelling Connections Software
Unit 21 Word List Overhead
Transparency

Teacher Resource Book

Unit 21 Home Study Master
(English or Spanish; students
may pretest on this sheet or use
it for home practice.)
Unit 21 Homework Master
Unit 21 Practice Masters
Flip Folder Practice Master
Unit 21 Test Master

Visit our Web site, www.zaner-bloser.com

OBJECTIVES

Spelling and Thinking

Students will
- **read** the spelling words in list form and in context.
- **sort** the words according to the final **schwa-r** sound: **er** or **or**.
- **read** and remember this week's spelling strategy.

Spelling and Vocabulary

Students will
- **write** spelling words to match definitions.
- **write** spelling words that are the base words of given words.
- **use** the **Spelling Dictionary** to locate spelling words between given guide words.

Spelling and Reading

Students will
- **write** spelling words that rhyme with given words.
- **complete** sentences using spelling words.
- **solve** analogies using spelling words.

Spelling and Writing

Students will
- **proofread** a description.
- **use** the writing process to write a description of a personal experience.
- **proofread** their writing.

MEETING INDIVIDUAL NEEDS
Learning Styles

Visual
Divide the class into teams of about six members each. Pronounce a spelling word for the first team. Have the team members "huddle" for one minute to decide on the correct spelling of the word. The players must then write each letter of the word on a separate card and choose players to line up, holding one or more cards in order so that they spell the word. Players on the other teams check the spelling. A team scores five points for each correctly spelled word and loses four points for each misspelled word.

Auditory
Write each spelling word on a 3" × 5" card. Have students take turns being the "detective." Have him or her sit at a desk blindfolded, facing away from the class. Give a card to another student. Have this student sneak up behind the detective and say and spell the word in a disguised voice. Then have the group say, "Detective, you have a clue." Have the detective remove the blindfold, write the spelling word on the chalkboard, and then guess which student spelled the word.

Kinesthetic
Have the students take turns spelling the words by pacing out the shapes of the letters on the floor. Have the student first say the word and then pronounce each letter as she or he paces out its shape. Have the other students watch, listen, and write the word on their papers.

Language and Cultural Differences

The **schwa-r** sound /ər/ may be difficult for some students to hear and spell due to regional pronunciations or different language backgrounds. Moreover, all students must remember several variant spelling patterns for this one sound.

Have the students write **er** and **or** at the top of their papers to form two columns. Tell them that all of the spelling words have the **schwa-r** sound similar to that heard in the last syllable of the word **mother**. Have the students say each spelling word. Be sure the last syllable in each word is pronounced the same way. After each word is pronounced, have the students write it in the proper column on their papers. Call on the students to use the words in sentences.

MANAGING INSTRUCTION

3–5 Day Plan		Average	Below Average	Above Average
Day 1	Day 1	Pretest Spelling Mini-Lesson, p. T128 Spelling and Thinking, p. 128	Pretest Spelling Mini-Lesson, p. T128 Spelling and Thinking, p. 128	Pretest Spelling and Thinking, p. 128
	Day 2	Spelling and Vocabulary, p. 129	Spelling and Vocabulary, p. 129 (or) Unit 21 Practice Master, A and B	Spelling and Vocabulary, p. 129 Spelling and Reading, p. 130
Day 2	Day 3	Spelling and Reading, p. 130	Spelling and Reading, p. 130 (or) Unit 21 Practice Master, C and D	Challenge Activities, p. 241
	Day 4	Spelling and Writing, p. 131 Unit 21 Homework Master	Spelling and Writing, p. 131	Spelling and Writing, p. 131 Unit 21 Homework Master
Day 3	Day 5	Weekly Test	Weekly Test	Weekly Test
Vocabulary Connections (pages 132 and 133) may be used anytime during this unit.				

Objectives

Spelling and Thinking

Students will
- **read** the spelling words in list form and in context.
- **sort** the words according to the final **schwa-r** sound: **er** or **or**.
- **read** and remember this week's spelling strategy.

UNIT PRETEST

Use **Pretest Sentences** below. Refer to the self-checking procedures on student page 256. You may wish to use the **Unit 21 Word List Overhead Transparency** as part of the checking procedure.

TEACHING THE STRATEGY

Spelling Mini-Lesson

Write /ər/, **thunder,** and **tractor** on the chalkboard.

Say the words and ask the students how many syllables they hear in each word. (two) Ask which syllable is stressed (or accented) in each word and what sound is heard in the final syllable of each word. (the first syllable; /ər/) Remind the students that the schwa is the unclear vowel sound (i.e., the "uh" sound) we make when we pronounce an unstressed vowel. When the vowel is followed by **r** in a final unstressed syllable, /ər/ is produced.

Explain that any vowel letter can spell the schwa sound. Point out that on this week's list all the words end in either **or** or **er**. Read **Remember the Spelling Strategy** on page 128.

Order of answers may vary.
er

1. enter
2. water ★
3. silver ★
4. shower
5. danger
6. bitter
7. wonder ★
8. thunder
9. master
10. rather ★
11. gather
12. winter ★
13. whether ★
14. together ★
15. eager
16. either ★
17. neither ★

or

18. major
19. minor
20. tractor ★

READ THE SPELLING WORDS

1.	gather	*gather*	Let us **gather** the ripe apples.
2.	winter	*winter*	This **winter** is colder than last.
3.	master	*master*	I will **master** my fear of heights.
4.	tractor	*tractor*	The **tractor** pulled a plow.
5.	shower	*shower*	I felt cool and clean after my **shower**.
6.	major	*major*	The hail caused no **major** damage.
7.	danger	*danger*	There is no **danger** of being late.
8.	enter	*enter*	I will **enter** a drawing contest.
9.	whether	*whether*	I must decide **whether** to go or stay.
10.	water	*water*	Drink **water** when you are thirsty.
11.	thunder	*thunder*	I heard **thunder** and saw lightning.
12.	eager	*eager*	She is **eager** to see her aunt again.
13.	bitter	*bitter*	That fruit has a **bitter** taste.
14.	silver	*silver*	Kim wore **silver** earrings.
15.	minor	*minor*	That was only a **minor** mistake.
16.	neither	*neither*	She eats **neither** fish nor fowl.
17.	wonder	*wonder*	I **wonder** where I left my pen.
18.	either	*either*	We will elect **either** John or Maria.
19.	rather	*rather*	I would **rather** swim than dive.
20.	together	*together*	We can study the lesson **together**.

SORT THE SPELLING WORDS

1.–17. Write the spelling words in which the **schwa-r** sound is spelled **er**.

18.–20. Write the spelling words in which the **schwa-r** sound is spelled **or**.

REMEMBER THE SPELLING STRATEGY

Remember that the **schwa-r** sound is spelled in different ways: **er** in **water** and **or** in **major**.

128

Pretest Sentences (See procedures on pages Z10–Z11.)

1. A crowd of people will **gather** to watch the show.
2. The coldest season of the year is **winter**.
3. Before David can drive the car, he must **master** the art of parking.
4. The farmer uses a **tractor** to pull the plow.
5. This afternoon we had a brief rain **shower**.
6. The Salk vaccine was a **major** discovery in medicine.
7. Because of his skill, the lion tamer was in little **danger**.
8. Knock on the door before you **enter** the room.
9. We will go to the mountains **whether** or not it snows.
10. We should all drink lots of **water**.
11. The sound that follows a flash of lightning is called **thunder**.
12. Jeff was **eager** to go skating.
13. That lemonade had a **bitter** taste.
14. Native American jewelry is sometimes made from **silver**.
15. Repairing the window was a **minor** task.
16. I know that **neither** of the children wanted to play outside.
17. The view from the mountain filled us with **wonder**.
18. You may have **either** one or the other, but not both.
19. I could go to Monique's house, but I would **rather** stay home today.
20. We are all going swimming **together**.

Spelling and Vocabulary

Word Meanings

Write a spelling word for each definition.

1. somewhat; to a certain extent; instead
2. less important
3. having a harsh, unpleasant taste
4. to bring together in a group
5. to go into
6. excitedly wanting or expecting
7. the season between autumn and spring
8. one or the other of two
9. not one or the other

Base Words

The suffix **-ous** means "full of" or "having." Write the spelling word that is the base word for each of the following words.

10. wondrous
11. dangerous
12. thunderous

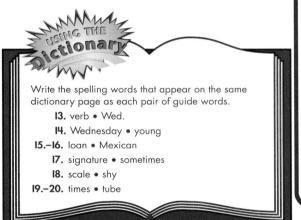

USING THE Dictionary

Write the spelling words that appear on the same dictionary page as each pair of guide words.

13. verb • Wed.
14. Wednesday • young
15.–16. loan • Mexican
17. signature • sometimes
18. scale • shy
19.–20. times • tube

Word Meanings
1. rather
2. minor
3. bitter
4. gather
5. enter
6. eager
7. winter
8. either
9. neither

Base Words
10. wonder
11. danger
12. thunder

Using the Dictionary
Order of answers 15–16 and 19–20 may vary.
13. water
14. whether
15. master
16. major
17. silver
18. shower
19. together
20. tractor

129

Objectives

Spelling and Vocabulary

Students will
- **write** spelling words to match definitions.
- **write** spelling words that are the base words of given words.
- **use** the **Spelling Dictionary** to locate spelling words between given guide words.

Developing Oral Language Skills

Do a word sort by sound. Write **closed syllable** and **open syllable** on a chalkboard or an overhead transparency. Remind students that a closed syllable ends with a consonant sound and often has a short vowel sound, but an open syllable ends with a vowel sound.

Ask volunteers to read the spelling words aloud and write each word under one of the two headings according to the type of syllable they hear in the first syllable of each word. When they are finished listing the words, ask students to consider the letter or letters in each word that spell the vowel sound in the first syllable. Then have volunteers come to the board and circle the letters that spell the vowel sound in the first syllable.

MEETING INDIVIDUAL NEEDS

Providing More Help

Tell the students that the **schwa-r** sound in each spelling word is in an unaccented syllable. Have the students copy the spelling words in large letters on construction paper. Then have them take turns reading each spelling word aloud with emphasis on the accented syllable. As the word is read, have the students trace the accented syllable with a colored crayon. Have the students circle the letters that spell the **schwa-r** sound in each word with a crayon as they repeat the words to themselves.

★Students who need to study fewer words should use the **Alternate Word List**. This list is starred on page T128 in the Teacher Edition. The **Unit 21 Practice Masters** (*Teacher Resource Book*) provide additional practice with these words.

Unit 21 Practice Masters

Name _____
Practice Master Unit 21

| 1. water | 3. silver | 5. rather | 7. together | 9. neither |
| 2. winter | 4. wonder | 6. whether | 8. either | 10. tractor |

A. Use two, or all three, of the spelling words in a sentence.

1. silver
   whether
   tractor _____

2. either
   wonder
   together _____

3. water
   winter
   rather _____

B. Write the spelling word that goes with each meaning.

1. more readily; instead _____
2. the season between autumn and spring _____
3. a large farm machine _____
4. a whitish precious metal _____
5. a clear liquid _____
6. to be curious to know _____
7. not one and not the other _____

118

Practice Master Unit 21

together   neither
either   tractor

each word below.

gather _____
either _____
actor _____

spelling words. Circle and write

r	b	n	c
t	h	e	r
c	q	i	a
f	g	t	t
n	w	h	h
p	z	e	e
o	c	r	r
r	m	p	t

119

Objectives

Spelling and Reading

Students will

- **write** spelling words that rhyme with given words.
- **complete** sentences using spelling words.
- **solve** analogies using spelling words.

One-Minute Handwriting Hint

The lowercase **w** contains three undercurves. Be sure to pause after each undercurve. Do not loop the checkstroke ending.

UNDERCURVES

Legible handwriting can boost spelling scores by as much as 20%.

Complete the Rhymes
1. wonder
2. enter
3. winter
4. shower
5. danger
6. whether

Complete the Sentences
7. together
8. master
9. eager
10. either
11. neither
12. gather
13. rather
14. silver
15. major
16. minor

Solve the Analogies
17. bitter
18. water
19. tractor
20. thunder

Spelling and Reading

gather	winter	master	tractor	shower
major	danger	enter	whether	water
thunder	eager	bitter	silver	minor
neither	wonder	either	rather	together

Complete the Rhymes   Write the spelling word that rhymes with the underlined word and completes the sentence.

1. I _____ what is <u>under</u> the blanket.
2. Use the <u>center</u> door to _____ the store.
3. Sandy got a <u>splinter</u> while chopping firewood for the _____.
4. That beautiful <u>flower</u> soaked up the rain _____.
5. The park <u>ranger</u> talked about the _____ of hiking alone.
6. I could not tell _____ the suitcase was made of plastic or <u>leather</u>.

Complete the Sentences   Write two spelling words to complete each sentence.

7.–8. If we study _____, we can help each other _____ the words.
9.–10. Shannon was not _____ to begin _____ of her two chores.
11.–12. In the story, _____ of the baby squirrels knew how to _____ nuts.
13.–14. She would _____ have a _____ dollar than a dollar bill.
15.–16. When we proofread, we correct the _____ errors as well as the _____ mistakes.

Solve the Analogies   Write a spelling word to complete each analogy.

17. **Feel** is to **rough** as **taste** is to _____.
18. **Eat** is to **food** as **drink** is to _____.
19. **Street** is to **car** as **field** is to _____.
20. **See** is to **lightning** as **hear** is to _____.

130

MEETING INDIVIDUAL NEEDS

Providing More Challenge

Challenge Words and **Challenge Activities** for Unit 21 appear on page 241. **Challenge Word Test Sentences** appear on page T241.

Unit 21 Challenge Activities

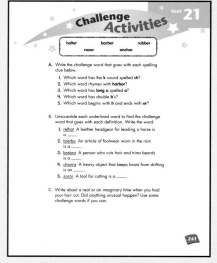

Weekly Test Options

Option 1:
One Spelling Word Per Sentence

(See procedures on pages Z10–Z11.)

1. You were the last student to **enter** the art room.
2. Beware of the **danger** ahead.
3. I **wonder** what is for lunch today.
4. Mother gave me a **silver** ring.
5. I like to drink cold **water** from a glass.
6. I would **rather** swim than play ball.
7. Dad will go fishing **whether** it rains or not.
8. The air is cold in the **winter** months.
9. We could hear loud **thunder** in the sky.
10. Do you want to take a bath or a **shower**?
11. I do not like **bitter** medicine.
12. The dog will obey its **master**.
13. Please **gather** the mail and put it in the box.
14. Mother and I will go skating **together**.
15. The weather report says a **major** storm is coming.

T130

Spelling and Writing

Proofread a Description

Six words are not spelled correctly in this description. Write those words correctly.

Reflections on a Lake

While camping in the forest, I got up early one day and wandered down to the lake. The sun was shining on the watter, turning it a beautiful silvor color. The wintir had been long. I was enjoying the warmth of spring.

As I watched the lake, I began to wunder about the fish that lived in it and the animals that drank from it. I was in no dangir from the wildlife, so I was not eger to return to camp. I would rather stay where I was.

(corrections: water, silver, winter, wonder, danger, eager)

Proofreading Marks	
≡	Make a capital.
/	Make a small letter.
∧	Add something.
ℛ	Take out something.
⊙	Add a period.
⌗	New paragraph
SP	Spelling error

Write a Description

Descriptive Writing

Write a description about something you experienced. Be sure to include
- where you were.
- the season of the year and the time of the day.
- what you saw and what you did.
- what thoughts you had.

Use as many spelling words as you can.

Proofread Your Writing During Editing

Proofread your writing for spelling errors as part of the editing stage in the writing process. Be sure to check each word carefully. Use a dictionary to check spelling if you are not sure.

Writing Process

Prewriting
⇩
Drafting
⇩
Revising
⇩
Editing
⇩
Publishing

131

Objectives

Spelling and Writing

Students will
- **proofread** a description.
- **use** the writing process to write a description of a personal experience.
- **proofread** their writing.

Using the Writing Process

Before assigning **Write a Description** in this unit, see pages 258–259 in the Student Edition for a complete review of the writing process and additional writing assignments. You may also wish to refer to pages Z12–Z13 in the Teacher Edition.

Keeping a Spelling Journal

Encourage students to record the words they misspelled on the weekly test in a personal spelling journal. These words may be recycled for future study. Students may also wish to include words from their writing. See pages Z12–Z13 in the Teacher Edition for more information.

---

16. The boy drove the **tractor** around the field.
17. Today, **neither** you nor I will be going out for lunch.
18. We were **eager** to go to the circus.
19. A **minor** fire is still enough to worry me.
20. You can **either** ride your bike or walk to school.

Option 2:
Multiple Spelling Words Per Sentence
(See procedures on pages Z10–Z11.)

1. I would **rather enter** the large **master** bedroom than the small room.
2. The **water** was not deep enough to be a **major danger**.
3. **Neither** of us would eat the **bitter** fruit.
4. We are **eager** to take a ride on the big **tractor**.
5. I **wonder** why we did not have **thunder** with that **minor** rain **shower**.
6. Can we all **gather together** and play a game?
7. We will take our trip in **either** the summer or the **winter**.
8. Do you know **whether** her bike is **silver** or gray?

Option 3:
Standardized Test
(See *Teacher Resource Book,* Unit 21.)

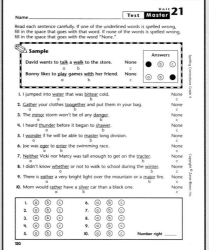

Unit 21
Test Master

T131

Vocabulary

Objectives

Strategy Words

Students will

- **review** words studied previously that are related to the spelling strategy.
- **preview** unknown words that are related to the spelling strategy.

Strategy Words

Remind the students that the **Strategy Words** are related to the spelling patterns they have studied in this unit. The **Review Words** are below grade level, and the **Preview Words** are above grade level. You may wish to use the following sentences to introduce the words in context.

Review Words:
Words From Grade 3

1. Mom's dress was made of many pretty **colors**.
2. My **father** took me fishing last weekend.
3. We were a little **later** getting home than I expected.
4. Jan's **mother** visited our classroom while we were having spelling.
5. I thought I would **never** learn to spell that hard word, but I mastered it.

Preview Words:
Words From Grade 5

6. When the **alligator** opened his mouth wide, we could see his teeth.
7. Do not **bother** your dad while he is working with the power saw.
8. How does my bike **differ** from yours?
9. A **passenger** got on the bus and sat down next to me.
10. My math **professor** in college is a neighbor of mine.

Review Words
1. never
2. father
3. later
4. colors
5. mother

Preview Words
6. professor
7. passenger
8. alligator
9. bother
10. differ

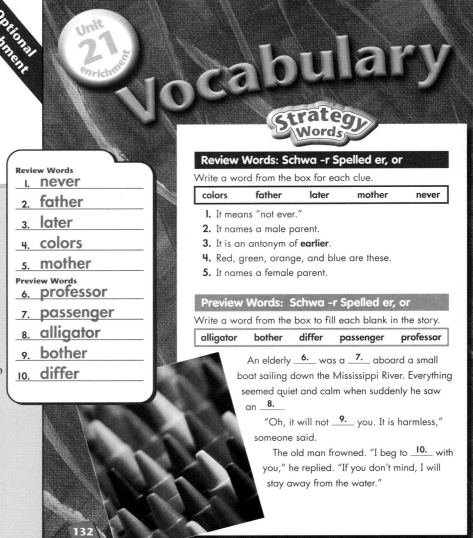

Strategy Words

Review Words: Schwa -r Spelled er, or

Write a word from the box for each clue.

colors	father	later	mother	never

1. It means "not ever."
2. It names a male parent.
3. It is an antonym of **earlier**.
4. Red, green, orange, and blue are these.
5. It names a female parent.

Preview Words: Schwa -r Spelled er, or

Write a word from the box to fill each blank in the story.

alligator	bother	differ	passenger	professor

An elderly __6.__ was a __7.__ aboard a small boat sailing down the Mississippi River. Everything seemed quiet and calm when suddenly he saw an __8.__.

"Oh, it will not __9.__ you. It is harmless," someone said.

The old man frowned. "I beg to __10.__ with you," he replied. "If you don't mind, I will stay away from the water."

132

Unit 21 Homework Master

Unit
21
RECAP

You may wish to assign the **Unit 21 Homework Master** (*Teacher Resource Book,* Unit 21) as a fun way to recap the spelling words.

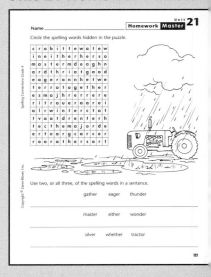

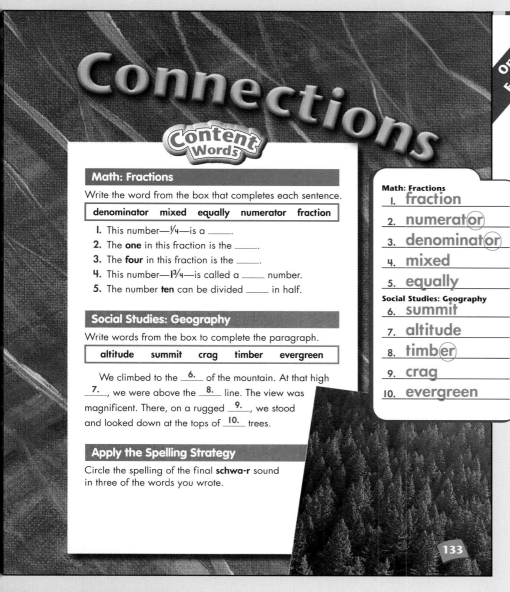

Connections

Content Words

Math: Fractions

Write the word from the box that completes each sentence.

denominator	mixed	equally	numerator	fraction

1. This number—¼—is a _____.
2. The **one** in this fraction is the _____.
3. The **four** in this fraction is the _____.
4. This number—1¾—is called a _____ number.
5. The number **ten** can be divided _____ in half.

Social Studies: Geography

Write words from the box to complete the paragraph.

altitude	summit	crag	timber	evergreen

We climbed to the __6.__ of the mountain. At that high __7.__, we were above the __8.__ line. The view was magnificent. There, on a rugged __9.__, we stood and looked down at the tops of __10.__ trees.

Apply the Spelling Strategy

Circle the spelling of the final **schwa-r** sound in three of the words you wrote.

Math: Fractions
1. fraction
2. numerat(or)
3. denominat(or)
4. mixed
5. equally

Social Studies: Geography
6. summit
7. altitude
8. timb(er)
9. crag
10. evergreen

133

Objectives

Content Words

Students will
- **expand** vocabulary with content-related words.
- **relate** the spelling strategy to words outside the basic spelling list.

Content Words

Math: Fractions

Review the meanings of these words with the students. You may wish to use these sentences to introduce the words in context.

1. Be sure to write the **denominator** in the correct place in the math problem.
2. The numbers were all **mixed** up and we had to arrange them in the proper numerical sequence.
3. Divide the supplies **equally** between the two classes.
4. Does the **numerator** go above or below the line?
5. You must reduce each **fraction** in this lesson.

Encourage the students to make up math problems using these words.

Social Studies: Geography

Review the meanings of these words with the students. You may wish to use these sentences to introduce the words in context.

6. The high **altitude** caused me to have a headache.
7. The mountain climbers wanted to reach the **summit** before nightfall.
8. A **crag** is a steep, rugged mass of rock.
9. At the top of the high mountain there was no **timber**.
10. Snow covered the branches of the **evergreen**.

Encourage the students to use these words to write a story about mountain climbing.

Unit 22 Home Study Master

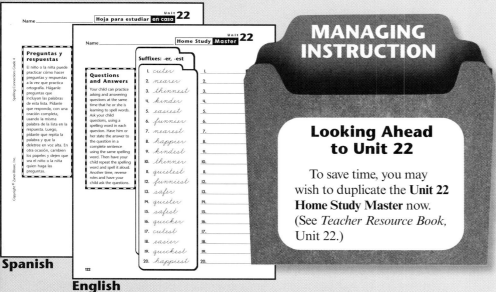

Spanish

English

MANAGING INSTRUCTION

Looking Ahead to Unit 22

To save time, you may wish to duplicate the **Unit 22 Home Study Master** now. (See *Teacher Resource Book*, Unit 22.)

Basic Spelling List

cuter	quietest
nearer	funniest
thinnest	safer
kinder	quieter
easiest	safest
funnier	quicker
nearest	cutest
happier	easier
kindest	quickest
thinner	happiest

Strategy Words

Review

closer	sharper
hotter	widest
reddest	

Preview

calmest	sunnier
slimmer	wiser
slimmest	

Content Words

Language Arts: Cities

dense	taxicab
smog	skyline
noise	

Social Studies: Ranching

auction	ranch
livestock	corral
barn	

Individual Needs

Challenge Words

bluest	heavier
healthier	heaviest
healthiest	

Alternate Word List

cuter	kindest
nearer	quietest
kinder	funniest
nearest	safest
happier	easier

MATERIALS

Student Edition
Pages 134–139
Challenge Activities, p. 242

Teacher Edition
Pages T134A–T139
Challenge Activities, p. T242

Other Resources
Spelling Connections Software
Unit 22 Word List Overhead
  Transparency

Teacher Resource Book
Unit 22 Home Study Master
  (English or Spanish; students
  may pretest on this sheet or use
  it for home practice.)
Unit 22 Homework Master
Unit 22 Practice Masters
Flip Folder Practice Master
Unit 22 Test Master

Visit our Web site, www.zaner-bloser.com

OBJECTIVES

Spelling and Thinking
Students will
• **read** the spelling words in list
  form and in context.
• **sort** the words according to
  -er and **-est** suffixes.
• **read** and remember this
  week's spelling strategy.

Spelling and Vocabulary
Students will
• **add** suffixes to base words to
  form spelling words.
• **write** the spelling word that
  does not belong in a series.
• **write** spelling words that are
  antonyms for given words.
• **use** the **Spelling Dictionary**
  to find base words of listed
  spelling words.

Spelling and Reading
Students will
• **replace** phrases with spelling
  words.
• **complete** sentences using
  spelling words.

Spelling and Writing
Students will
• **proofread** instructions.
• **use** the writing process to
  write instructions.
• **proofread** their writing.

MEETING INDIVIDUAL NEEDS
Learning Styles

Visual
Write the base words of the spelling words on the chalkboard and have the students copy them on their papers. Then have them write the **-er** and **-est** forms next to each word, using one color for **-er** words and another color for **-est** words. Last, have each student choose one base word with its **-er** and **-est** forms to illustrate.

Auditory
Write the base words of the spelling words on separate 3" × 5" cards. Have the students take turns choosing a card, reading the base word, and saying the **-er** and **-est** forms. After this is done, have the student describe the meaning of the three forms by using them in sentences. For example: "A mouse is **cute,** a kitten is **cuter,** but a puppy is **cutest** of all."

Kinesthetic
Use the base word cards from the auditory activity, plus additional cards for each of the spelling words. Shuffle the cards and arrange them faceup on a table. Have the students take turns choosing and arranging the cards so that a base word, the **-er** form, and the **-est** form are grouped together. Give the students the option of being timed to form a set number of groups. When all of the words have been grouped, have the students copy the groups on paper.

Language and Cultural Differences

The **-er** and **-est** suffixes may be difficult for some students to hear due to regional pronunciations or language background differences. For example, Spanish-speaking students may have difficulty with these suffixes because the endings are not a part of their language backgrounds. It is important to help the students grasp the concepts that these suffixes convey. For each spelling word, draw a diagram similar to this on the chalkboard to illustrate the **-er** and **-est** ending for each base word:

```
        kind
 er             est
```

Have the students pronounce the base word and the suffix. Then ask a volunteer to write the full word beside each diagram and use the word in a sentence.

MANAGING INSTRUCTION

3–5 Day Plan		Average	Below Average	Above Average
Day 1	**Day 1**	Pretest Spelling Mini-Lesson, p. T134 Spelling and Thinking, p. 134	Pretest Spelling Mini-Lesson, p. T134 Spelling and Thinking, p. 134	Pretest Spelling and Thinking, p. 134
	Day 2	Spelling and Vocabulary, p. 135	Spelling and Vocabulary, p. 135 (or) Unit 22 Practice Master, A and B	Spelling and Vocabulary, p. 135 Spelling and Reading, p. 136
Day 2	**Day 3**	Spelling and Reading, p. 136	Spelling and Reading, p. 136 (or) Unit 22 Practice Master, C and D	Challenge Activities, p. 242
	Day 4	Spelling and Writing, p. 137 Unit 22 Homework Master	Spelling and Writing, p. 137	Spelling and Writing, p. 137 Unit 22 Homework Master
Day 3	**Day 5**	Weekly Test	Weekly Test	Weekly Test
Vocabulary Connections (pages 138 and 139) may be used anytime during this unit.				

Objectives

Spelling and Thinking

Students will
- **read** the spelling words in list form and in context.
- **sort** the words according to **-er** and **-est** suffixes.
- **read** and remember this week's spelling strategy.

UNIT PRETEST

Use **Pretest Sentences** below. Refer to the self-checking procedures on student page 256. You may wish to use the **Unit 22 Word List Overhead Transparency** as part of the checking procedure.

TEACHING THE STRATEGY

Spelling Mini-Lesson

Write **near** on the chalkboard. Ask the students to identify a place that is near the school. Write the sentence, **(place #1) is near school,** substituting the place the students identify for place #1.

Then ask them to identify a place that is nearer school than place #1. Write **nearer** on the board. Substituting as needed, write the sentence, **(place #2) is nearer school than (place #1).** Point out that the **-er** ending tells us that only two places are being compared.

Write **-est** on the chalkboard. Explain that the suffix **-est** is added to words to mean "most" and is used to compare three or more things. Write **nearest** on the chalkboard, and ask the students to identify a place that is even nearer to school than place #2. Write the sentence, **(place #3) is nearest to school.** Point out that the **-est** ending tells us that at least three places are being compared.

Ask the students if the spelling of the base word **near** changed when the suffixes were added. (no) Ask them to look at the spelling list and decide if—and how—the spellings of base words changed when the suffixes were added. (Depending on the words, these changes occurred before the suffixes were added: drop final e; change final y to i; double final consonant.)

Conclude by reading **Remember the Spelling Strategy** on page 134.

TI34

Spelling and Thinking

Order of answers may vary.

-er
1. cut(er) ★
2. near(er) ★
3. kind(er) ★
4. funni(er)
5. happi(er) ★
6. thinn(er)
7. saf(er)
8. quiet(er)
9. quick(er)
10. easi(er) ★

-est
11. thinn(est)
12. easi(est)
13. near(est) ★
14. kind(est) ★
15. quiet(est) ★
16. funni(est) ★
17. saf(est) ★
18. cut(est)
19. quick(est)
20. happi(est)

134

READ THE SPELLING WORDS

1.	cuter	cuter	I think kittens are **cuter** than cats.
2.	nearer	nearer	The house is **nearer** than the store.
3.	thinnest	thinnest	That is the **thinnest** tree I ever saw!
4.	kinder	kinder	Mel seems **kinder** than Homer.
5.	easiest	easiest	Jogging is the **easiest** thing I do.
6.	funnier	funnier	That joke was **funnier** than the other.
7.	nearest	nearest	The Pells are our **nearest** neighbors.
8.	happier	happier	I could not be **happier** for you.
9.	kindest	kindest	She did the **kindest** deed of the week.
10.	thinner	thinner	My dog is **thinner** than before.
11.	quietest	quietest	Monday is the **quietest** weekday.
12.	funniest	funniest	That is the **funniest** program on TV.
13.	safer	safer	You will be **safer** wearing a helmet.
14.	quieter	quieter	Babies are **quieter** at night.
15.	safest	safest	This is the **safest** smoke alarm.
16.	quicker	quicker	The hand is **quicker** than the eye.
17.	cutest	cutest	She has the **cutest** puppy in town.
18.	easier	easier	Studying is **easier** when we are quiet.
19.	quickest	quickest	Which is the **quickest** way home?
20.	happiest	happiest	This is the **happiest** day of my life.

SORT THE SPELLING WORDS

1.–10. Write the spelling words with the **-er** suffix. Circle the suffix. Note if the spelling of the base word changes.

11.–20. Write the spelling words with the **-est** suffix. Circle the suffix. Note if the spelling of the base word changes.

REMEMBER THE SPELLING STRATEGY

Remember that suffixes such as **-er** and **-est** are added to the ends of words to make new words: **kind, kinder, kindest.**

Pretest Sentences (See procedures on pages Z10–Z11.)

1. The old doll is **cuter** than the new one.
2. The light will become brighter as you get **nearer**.
3. I had to use the **thinnest** thread to sew the seam.
4. Lamar tried to be **kinder** to his sister.
5. Riding up a hill is the **easiest** way to get to the top.
6. The short clown is **funnier** than the tall one.
7. The **nearest** town is a mile away.
8. I am **happier** now that you are here.
9. She is the **kindest** person I know.
10. He used the **thinner** wire to hang the picture.
11. The library is the **quietest** room in the school.
12. She told the **funniest** joke.
13. He was **safer** with his seat belt on.
14. He speaks softly and is **quieter** than Sharon.
15. A bank is the **safest** place to save money.
16. Marcus was **quicker** than Bob.
17. The child picked the **cutest** toy on the shelf.
18. Jogging is **easier** than running.
19. The winner of the race is the **quickest** of all.
20. That clown is the **happiest** of all.

Spelling and Vocabulary

Word Meanings

Write the correct form of the underlined word in each sentence.
1. We are the quiet of all the students in the school.
2. A whisper is quiet than a screech.
3. That was the quick fire drill of the three we had.
4. Beth is quick than the runner behind her.
5. Of all the ways to play the game, this is the safe way.

Phonics

Write the spelling word that does not belong in each group.
6. safest, funnier, nearest, quietest
7. safer, easier, kinder, cutest
8. safer, quickest, nearest, funniest

Antonyms

Write the spelling word that is the antonym of each word.
9. farther
10. thickest
11. meanest
12. hardest
13. thicker
14. saddest

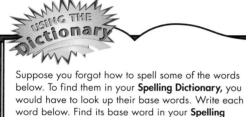

Suppose you forgot how to spell some of the words below. To find them in your **Spelling Dictionary,** you would have to look up their base words. Write each word below. Find its base word in your **Spelling Dictionary**. Circle the letters in the word you wrote that do not match the base word.
15. kinder
16. nearest
17. cuter
18. easier
19. happier
20. funniest

Word Meanings
1. quietest
2. quieter
3. quickest
4. quicker
5. safest

Phonics
6. funnier
7. cutest
8. safer

Antonyms
9. nearer
10. thinnest
11. kindest
12. easiest
13. thinner
14. happiest

Using the Dictionary
15. kind(er)
16. near(est)
17. cute(r)
18. eas(ier)
19. happ(ier)
20. funn(iest)

135

Developing Oral Language Skills

Have students work in pairs. The first student uses a spelling word ending with **-er** in a sentence. For example, the student might say, "Math is **easier** than history." The second student responds by using the same base word with the **-est** ending in a similar sentence. For example the second student might say, "Science is the **easiest** subject in school." Repeat the process until all spelling words have been used.

MEETING INDIVIDUAL NEEDS

Providing More Help

Write the following four generalizations on the chalkboard. Have the students take turns reading a spelling word aloud and telling which generalization it fits. Then have them write the spelling words and circle the base word in each.
- No change when adding the **-er** or **-est** suffix.
- Drop the final **e** when adding the **-er** or **-est** suffix.
- Double the final consonant when adding the **-er** or **-est** suffix.
- Change the final **y** to **i** when adding the **-er** or **-est** suffix.

★ Students who need to study fewer words should use the **Alternate Word List**. This list is starred on page T134 in the Teacher Edition. The **Unit 22 Practice Masters** (*Teacher Resource Book*) provide additional practice with these words.

Unit 22 Practice Masters

Name _____ **Practice Master** Unit 22

| 1. kinder | 3. nearer | 5. quietest | 7. safest | 9. happier |
| 2. kindest | 4. nearest | 6. cuter | 8. easier | 10. funniest |

A. Write the spelling word that is an antonym for each word.
1. farther _____
2. sadder _____
3. harder _____
4. meanest _____
5. loudest _____
6. farthest _____
7. meaner _____

B. Write a spelling word that goes with each meaning.
1. most funny _____
2. more happy _____
3. more cute _____
4. most quiet _____
5. more near _____
6. most kind _____
7. most safe _____
8. more easy _____

124

Practice Master Unit 22

safest   happier
easier   funniest

the word parts in Column B to

s and symbols spell.

125

Objectives

Spelling and Reading

Students will
- **replace** phrases with spelling words.
- **complete** sentences using spelling words.

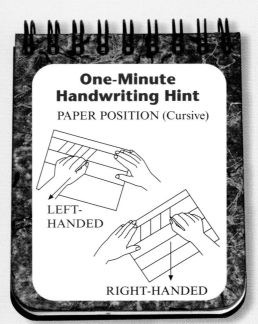

One-Minute Handwriting Hint

PAPER POSITION (Cursive)

LEFT-HANDED

RIGHT-HANDED

Legible handwriting can boost spelling scores by as much as 20%.

Replace the Words

1. cuter
2. cutest
3. kindest
4. funnier
5. thinnest
6. happier
7. nearer
8. safest
9. thinner
10. quietest

Complete the Sentences

11. safer
12. easier
13. quieter
14. happiest
15. kinder
16. nearest
17. funniest
18. quickest
19. easiest
20. quicker

---

cuter	nearer	thinnest	kinder	easiest
funnier	nearest	happier	kindest	thinner
quietest	funniest	safer	quieter	safest
quicker	cutest	easier	quickest	happiest

Replace the Words Write a spelling word to replace each underlined group of words.

1. Your cat is <u>more cute</u> than mine.
2. You drew the <u>most cute</u> picture of all.
3. You are the <u>most kind</u> person I have ever met.
4. Her comic book is <u>more funny</u> than mine.
5. Here is the <u>most thin</u> wire I could find.
6. Mrs. Crosby is <u>more happy</u> working outside the house than in it.
7. Your house is <u>more near</u> the school than mine.
8. The crosswalk is the <u>most safe</u> place to cross the street.
9. Use the <u>more thin</u> board for the sign.
10. The library is the <u>most quiet</u> room in the school.

Complete the Sentences Write a spelling word to complete each sentence.

11. Wearing a seat belt while riding in a car is _____ than riding without one.
12. I find math to be _____ than science.
13. Crickets are _____ in the daytime than at night.
14. The baby smiles and acts _____ when he is being held.
15. It would be _____ to say nothing than to say something mean.
16. The _____ library is three blocks from here.
17. That was the _____ joke I have ever heard!
18. We are in no hurry, so we do not need to go the _____ way.
19. That test was easy. In fact, it was the _____ test I ever took.
20. Sending this message by e-mail is _____ than sending a letter, which will take at least a day to arrive.

136

MEETING INDIVIDUAL NEEDS

Providing More Challenge

Challenge Words and **Challenge Activities** for Unit 22 appear on page 242. **Challenge Word Test Sentences** appear on page T242.

Unit 22 Challenge Activities

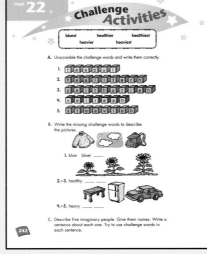

Weekly Test Options

Option 1:
One Spelling Word Per Sentence

1. This map shows a **quicker** road to the city.
2. The dog was **safer** on a leash than running loose.
3. We must all try to be **kinder** to each other.
4. It is **easier** to walk down the steps than it is to walk up.
5. I used the **thinnest** piece of rope.
6. The **happiest** teacher is one whose students do their best.
7. My mother is the **kindest** woman.
8. My little sister is the **cutest** baby.
9. I think riding the train is the **safest** way to travel.
10. Go **nearer** to the stage so you can see the show.
11. She was **thinner** than her mother.
12. The **nearest** store is closed today.
13. She was the **quickest** person to reach the finish line.
14. Father told the **funniest** joke of all.
15. His soft voice is **quieter** than my loud voice.
16. That was the **easiest** test I ever took.
17. I think the spotted puppy is **cuter** than the white one.

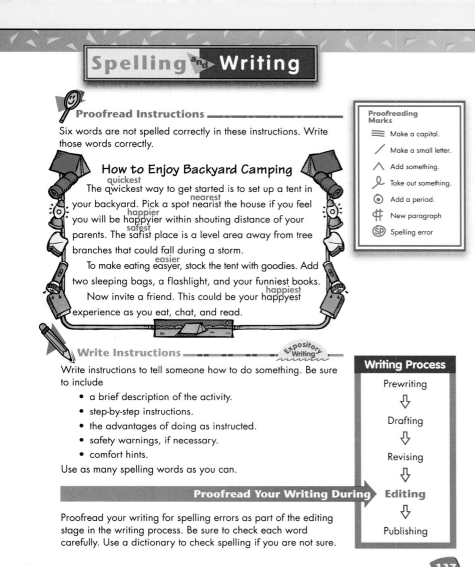

Spelling and Writing

😊 Proofread Instructions

Six words are not spelled correctly in these instructions. Write those words correctly.

How to Enjoy Backyard Camping

quickest
The qwickest way to get started is to set up a tent in
nearest
your backyard. Pick a spot nearist the house if you feel
happier
you will be happyier within shouting distance of your
safest
parents. The safist place is a level area away from tree
branches that could fall during a storm.
easier
To make eating easyer, stock the tent with goodies. Add
two sleeping bags, a flashlight, and your funniest books.
happiest
Now invite a friend. This could be your happyest
experience as you eat, chat, and read.

Proofreading Marks

≡ Make a capital.
/ Make a small letter.
∧ Add something.
↩ Take out something.
⊙ Add a period.
New paragraph
SP Spelling error

✏️ Write Instructions

Expository Writing

Write instructions to tell someone how to do something. Be sure to include

- a brief description of the activity.
- step-by-step instructions.
- the advantages of doing as instructed.
- safety warnings, if necessary.
- comfort hints.

Use as many spelling words as you can.

Writing Process

Prewriting
⇩
Drafting
⇩
Revising
⇩
Editing
⇩
Publishing

Proofread Your Writing During → **Editing**

Proofread your writing for spelling errors as part of the editing stage in the writing process. Be sure to check each word carefully. Use a dictionary to check spelling if you are not sure.

137

Using the Writing Process

Before assigning **Write Instructions,** see pages 258–259 in the Student Edition for a complete review of the writing process and additional writing assignments. You may also wish to refer to pages Z12–Z13 in the Teacher Edition.

Keeping a Spelling Journal

Encourage students to record the words they misspelled on the weekly test in a personal spelling journal. These words may be recycled for future study. Students may also wish to include words from their writing. See pages Z12–Z13 in the Teacher Edition for more information.

---

18. The man was **happier** after he had some food to eat.
19. The clowns are **funnier** each year.
20. She is the **quietest** of the three girls.

Option 2:
Multiple Spelling Words Per Sentence
(See procedures on pages Z10–Z11.)

1. The one with the **thinner** face is the **kinder** of the two boys.
2. It would be **safer** to walk **nearer** the grass than the road.
3. The **cutest** puppy is also the **quietest**.
4. That lady is the **kindest** and **funniest** person I know.
5. The **nearest** store is the **easiest** to find.
6. The work would be **easier** if the room were **quieter**.
7. The **thinnest** clown has the **happiest** face.
8. The baby gets **cuter** and **funnier** every day.
9. Find the **quickest** and **safest** way to do the job.
10. The **happier** you feel, the **quicker** you will smile.

Option 3:
Standardized Test
(See *Teacher Resource Book,* Unit 22.)

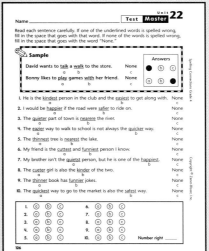

**Unit 22
Test Master**

TI37

Objectives

Strategy Words

Students will
• **review** words studied previously that are related to the spelling strategy.
• **preview** unknown words that are related to the spelling strategy.

Remind the students that the **Strategy Words** are related to the spelling patterns they have studied in this unit. The **Review Words** are below grade level, and the **Preview Words** are above grade level. You may wish to use the following sentences to introduce the words in context.

Review Words:
Words From Grade 3

1. I get excited as we get **closer** to home.
2. It is **hotter** in the south than it is in the north.
3. Those twins have the **reddest** hair I have ever seen.
4. We need a **sharper** knife to cut the meat.
5. The **widest** part of the river is also the deepest.

Preview Words:
Words From Grade 5

6. There is a saying that it is always **calmest** before the storm.
7. She looks **slimmer** in the black skirt than she does in the gray one.
8. The **slimmest** girl on the stage is also a very good dancer.
9. It is **sunnier** today than it was yesterday.
10. Mom and Dad are **wiser** than I am because they have had more experiences.

Review Words

1. widest
2. reddest
3. sharper
4. closer
5. hotter

Preview Words

6. wiser
7. calmest
8. sunnier
9. slimmer
10. slimmest

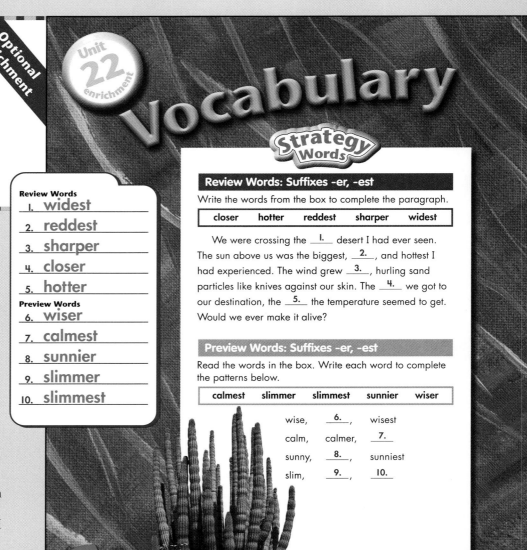

Vocabulary

Strategy Words

Review Words: Suffixes -er, -est

Write the words from the box to complete the paragraph.

closer	hotter	reddest	sharper	widest

We were crossing the __1.__ desert I had ever seen. The sun above us was the biggest, __2.__, and hottest I had experienced. The wind grew __3.__, hurling sand particles like knives against our skin. The __4.__ we got to our destination, the __5.__ the temperature seemed to get. Would we ever make it alive?

Preview Words: Suffixes -er, -est

Read the words in the box. Write each word to complete the patterns below.

calmest	slimmer	slimmest	sunnier	wiser

wise, __6.__, wisest
calm, calmer, __7.__
sunny, __8.__, sunniest
slim, __9.__, __10.__

138

Unit 22 RECAP

You may wish to assign the **Unit 22 Homework Master** (*Teacher Resource Book*, Unit 22) as a fun way to recap the spelling words.

Unit 22 Homework Master

Name _____ Homework **Master** **22**

Write spelling words with the **-er** and the **-est** suffixes to fill in the blanks. Then answer each riddle out loud. The first one is done as an example.

1. If a teacher is kinder than a farmer, and a farmer is <u>kinder</u> than a soldier, who is the <u>kindest</u>? *kinder* *kindest*
2. If the school is nearer than the library to my house, and the library is ___ than the post office to my house, which is ___?
3. If a cat is quieter than a dog, and a mouse is ___ than a cat, which is the ___?
4. If a rabbit is quicker than a fox, and a tiger is ___ than a rabbit, which is the ___?
5. If a kitten is cuter than a puppy, and a puppy is ___ than a lion cub, which is ___?
6. If a ferris wheel is safer than a rocket, and a rocket is ___ than a roller coaster, which is ___?
7. If math is easier than spelling, and spelling is ___ than science, which is ___?
8. If my sister is happier than I am right now, and I am ___ than my brother, who is ___?
9. If the clown is funnier than my dad, and my dad is ___ than I am, who is ___?
10. If the spotted dog is thinner than the black dog, and the black dog is ___ than the white dog, which dog is the ___?

127

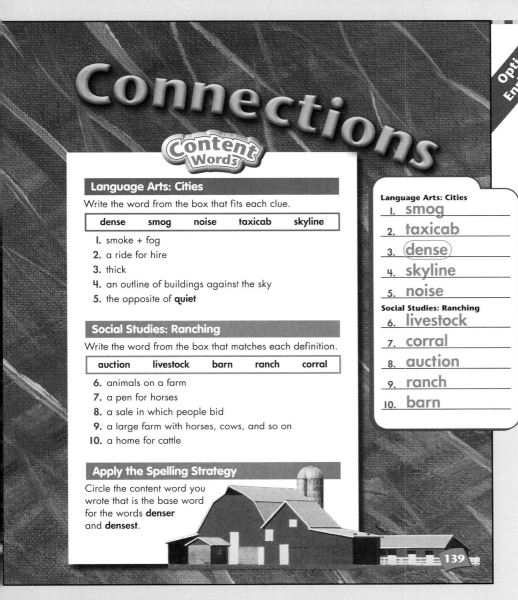

Connections

Content Words

Language Arts: Cities

Write the word from the box that fits each clue.

| dense | smog | noise | taxicab | skyline |

1. smoke + fog
2. a ride for hire
3. thick
4. an outline of buildings against the sky
5. the opposite of **quiet**

Social Studies: Ranching

Write the word from the box that matches each definition.

| auction | livestock | barn | ranch | corral |

6. animals on a farm
7. a pen for horses
8. a sale in which people bid
9. a large farm with horses, cows, and so on
10. a home for cattle

Apply the Spelling Strategy

Circle the content word you wrote that is the base word for the words **denser** and **densest**.

Language Arts: Cities
1. smog
2. taxicab
3. dense
4. skyline
5. noise

Social Studies: Ranching
6. livestock
7. corral
8. auction
9. ranch
10. barn

139

Objectives

Content Words

Students will
- **expand** vocabulary with content-related words.
- **relate** the spelling strategy to words outside the basic spelling list.

Content Words

Language Arts: Cities

Review the meanings of these words with the students. You may wish to use these sentences to introduce the words in context.

1. The fog was so **dense** this morning it was difficult to see to drive.
2. Did you know that **smog** is a combination of smoke and fog?
3. With so much **noise** in the room, it was difficult to hear what my friend was saying to me.
4. We will take a **taxicab** to the airport.
5. We could see the **skyline** as we got nearer to the city.

Encourage the students to use these words to describe a visit to a big city.

Social Studies: Ranching

Review the meanings of these words with the students. You may wish to use these sentences to introduce the words in context.

6. There will be an **auction** at my uncle's farm on Saturday.
7. The **livestock** are on display at most county fairs.
8. My grandfather's **barn** is two stories high and has lots of animal stalls.
9. We will visit a **ranch** when we go out west this summer.
10. The horses are kept in a **corral**.

Encourage the students to use these words in a real or imaginary story about a farm.

Unit 23 Home Study Master

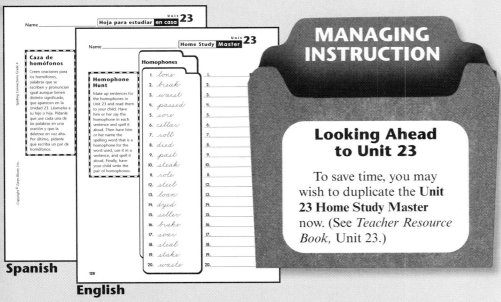

Spanish

English

MANAGING INSTRUCTION

Looking Ahead to Unit 23

To save time, you may wish to duplicate the **Unit 23 Home Study Master** now. (See *Teacher Resource Book,* Unit 23.)

Basic Spelling List

lone	role
break	steel
waist	loan
passed	dyed
sore	seller
cellar	brake
roll	soar
died	steal
past	stake
steak	waste

Strategy Words

Review

its	their
it's	they're
there	

Preview

capital	vane
capitol	vein
vain	

Content Words

Art: On Canvas

landscape	scene
print	pastel
painting	

Language Arts: Word Play

toot	sees
trap	level
loop	

Individual Needs

Challenge Words

mist	guessed
missed	aloud
guest	

Alternate Word List

break	role
waist	steel
passed	brake
roll	steal
past	waste

MATERIALS

Student Edition
Pages 140–145
Challenge Activities, p. 243

Teacher Edition
Pages T140A–T145
Challenge Activities, T243

Other Resources
Spelling Connections Software
Unit 23 Word List Overhead
Transparency

Teacher Resource Book
Unit 23 Home Study Master
(English or Spanish; students
may pretest on this sheet or use
it for home practice.)
Unit 23 Homework Master
Unit 23 Practice Masters
Flip Folder Practice Master
Unit 23 Test Master

Visit our Web site, www.zaner-bloser.com

OBJECTIVES

Spelling and Thinking
Students will
- **read** the spelling words in list form and in context.
- **sort** the spelling words according to whether they begin with a consonant cluster or a single consonant.
- **read** and remember this week's spelling strategy.

Spelling and Vocabulary
Students will
- **write** spelling words to match definitions.
- **write** homophones for given words.
- **use** the **Spelling Dictionary** to write homophones for dictionary respellings.

Spelling and Reading
Students will
- **choose** and write the correct homophones.
- **write** pairs of homophones to complete sentences.

Spelling and Writing
Students will
- **proofread** a postcard.
- **use** the writing process to write a postcard.
- **proofread** their writing.

MEETING INDIVIDUAL NEEDS
Learning Styles

Visual

Give each student ten 3" × 5" cards. Have them write the words **roll, loan, soar, died, break, stake, steal, waist, cellar,** and **past** on the cards. Then have them write the homophone of each word on the reverse side of the card. Next, ask them to underline the letters that spell the vowel sound in each word. Finally, tell them to draw a small illustration next to each word. Have them look at the word on one side of the card, write its homophone on a separate piece of paper, and then turn the card over to check the spelling of the word they wrote.

Auditory

Have the students work in pairs. Give each pair sufficient space at the chalkboard. One student of the pair says a spelling word and then writes the word and its homophone on the chalkboard, leaving blanks for the letters that spell the vowel sounds. The other student of the pair supplies the missing letters and uses each word in a sentence. Then the students reverse roles and continue working together until they have used all the spelling words.

Kinesthetic

Draw a puzzle for each homophone pair on the chalkboard.

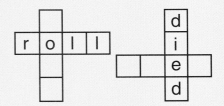

Write down the letters of one homophone in each puzzle. Divide the class into two teams. Have them "race" to fill in the puzzles. Finally, ask the students to use the words in sentences and to write the sentences.

Language and Cultural Differences

The key to helping the students spell homophones is to provide ample opportunities for associating the meaning of a word with its spelling. With homophones, the students must distinguish between two words that sound the same but have different meanings and different spellings.

Ask the students to look at the words in their spelling books as you pronounce each one. Have the students repeat each word after you and tell something about the meaning of each word. Then write the pairs of homophones on the chalkboard. Emphasize that the two words sound the same but have different spellings and meanings. Circle the letter(s) that spell the vowel sound in each word.

MANAGING INSTRUCTION

3–5 Day Plan		Average	Below Average	Above Average
Day 1	**Day 1**	Pretest Spelling Mini-Lesson, p. T140 Spelling and Thinking, p. 140	Pretest Spelling Mini-Lesson, p. T140 Spelling and Thinking, p. 140	Pretest Spelling and Thinking, p. 140
	Day 2	Spelling and Vocabulary, p. 141	Spelling and Vocabulary, p. 141 (or) Unit 23 Practice Master, A and B	Spelling and Vocabulary, p. 141 Spelling and Reading, p. 142
Day 2	**Day 3**	Spelling and Reading, p. 142	Spelling and Reading, p. 142 (or) Unit 23 Practice Master, C and D	Challenge Activities, p. 243
	Day 4	Spelling and Writing, p. 143 Unit 23 Homework Master	Spelling and Writing, p. 143	Spelling and Writing, p. 143 Unit 23 Homework Master
Day 3	**Day 5**	Weekly Test	Weekly Test	Weekly Test
Vocabulary Connections (pages 144 and 145) may be used anytime during this unit.				

Objectives

Spelling and Thinking

Students will
- **read** the spelling words in list form and in context.
- **sort** the spelling words according to whether they begin with a consonant cluster or a single consonant.
- **read** and remember this week's spelling strategy.

UNIT PRETEST

Use **Pretest Sentences** below. Refer to the self-checking procedures on student page 256. You may wish to use the **Unit 23 Word List Overhead Transparency** as part of the checking procedure.

TEACHING THE STRATEGY

Spelling Mini-Lesson

Write **cellar** and **seller** on the board; pronounce both words. Ask volunteers what they notice about these two words. (They are spelled differently but they sound the same.) You may wish to ask students to find and compare the dictionary respellings of these words to verify that they are pronounced the same way.

Explain that words that sound the same but are spelled differently are called **homophones**. (If you feel this is appropriate for your class, you may wish to note that **homophone** literally means "same sound." **Homo** means "same." **Phone** means "sound," as in **telephone**.) Explain that there are many homophones in the English language and that each one has a unique history. Tell the students that in this lesson they will study words that are homophones.

Write **stake** on the chalkboard. Ask the students to describe a stake and what it is used for. (a stick or post that can be pounded into the ground to hold a tent in place) Write this sentence on the chalkboard: "I love to have a big, juicy stake for dinner." Ask why it is important to use correct homophones in their writing. (If the wrong homophone is used, the meaning will be confused.)

Conclude by reading **Remember the Spelling Strategy** on page 140.

T140

Order of answers may vary.

consonant cluster
1. break ★
2. brake ★
3. steak
4. stake
5. steel ★
6. steal ★

single consonant
7. lone
8. loan
9. waist ★
10. waste ★
11. passed ★
12. past ★
13. sore
14. soar
15. cellar
16. seller
17. roll ★
18. role ★
19. died
20. dyed

Spelling and Thinking

READ THE SPELLING WORDS

1. lone	*lone*	There was a **lone** clerk in the store.
2. break	*break*	Lift but do not **break** the cover.
3. waist	*waist*	Around his **waist** he wore a belt.
4. passed	*passed*	We **passed** a school crossing.
5. sore	*sore*	I hiked until my feet were **sore**.
6. cellar	*cellar*	In the **cellar** was an old chest.
7. roll	*roll*	Would you like a muffin or a **roll**?
8. died	*died*	The flower **died** from lack of water.
9. past	*past*	My father drove **past** your house.
10. steak	*steak*	He likes his **steak** well-done.
11. role	*role*	What **role** did he play in the movie?
12. steel	*steel*	Aluminum is lighter than **steel**.
13. loan	*loan*	They needed a **loan** to buy the house.
14. dyed	*dyed*	The feather had been **dyed** yellow.
15. seller	*seller*	The buyer gave the **seller** money.
16. brake	*brake*	Step on the **brake** to stop.
17. soar	*soar*	Eagles **soar** across the sky.
18. steal	*steal*	Do not **steal** or damage goods.
19. stake	*stake*	A **stake** supports each plant.
20. waste	*waste*	Recycling does not **waste** material.

SORT THE SPELLING WORDS

1.–6. Write the pairs of spelling words that begin with a consonant cluster and that are pronounced the same but have different spellings and meanings.

7.–20. Write the pairs of spelling words that begin with a single consonant and that are pronounced the same but have different spellings and meanings.

REMEMBER THE SPELLING STRATEGY

Remember that **homophones** are words that sound the same but have different spellings and meanings: **roll** and **role**.

140

Pretest Sentences (See procedures on pages Z10–Z11.)

1. In our front yard stood a **lone** pine tree.
2. The glass jar will **break** if you drop it.
3. The man wore a belt around his **waist**.
4. After you have **passed** fourth grade, you will go into fifth grade.
5. After I ran, my muscles were **sore**.
6. Mother keeps potatoes in the **cellar** where it is cool.
7. A ball will **roll** down a hill.
8. The plant **died** from lack of water.
9. I drove **past** the zoo.
10. Aretha would rather eat chicken than **steak**.
11. Shanelle took the **role** of the big bad wolf in the school play.
12. The frame of that building is made of **steel**.
13. Will you please **loan** your pencil to me?
14. He **dyed** his white shirt blue.
15. That children's magazine is a good **seller**.
16. To stop the car, Dad put his foot on the **brake**.
17. The eagle was able to **soar** above the treetops.
18. A crow will **steal** shiny objects.
19. The surveyor will mark the property line with a **stake**.
20. We try not to **waste** water.

Spelling and Vocabulary

Word Meanings
Write the spelling word that goes with each meaning.
1. without company; by itself or oneself
2. a slice of beef
3. the middle part of the body
4. colored with dye
5. the part played by an actor
6. earlier than the present time
7. to come apart

Homophones
Write the spelling word that is a homophone for each word.
8. break
9. role
10. lone
11. past
12. dyed
13. stake
14. waist

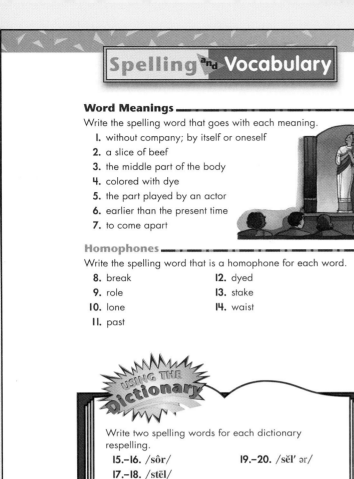

USING THE Dictionary

Write two spelling words for each dictionary respelling.
15.–16. /sôr/
17.–18. /stēl/
19.–20. /sěl' ər/

◆ ◆ ◆

Dictionary Check Be sure to check the respellings in your **Spelling Dictionary**.

Word Meanings
1. lone
2. steak
3. waist
4. dyed
5. role
6. past
7. break

Homophones
8. brake
9. roll
10. loan
11. passed
12. died
13. steak
14. waste

Using the Dictionary
15. sore
16. soar
17. steel
18. steal
19. cellar
20. seller

141

Developing Oral Language Skills

Have students work in pairs. The first student asks a question that includes one of the homophones from the spelling list. For example, the student might ask, "Does the **brake** work on your bicycle?" The second student responds with a sentence that uses the homophone for the spelling word in the question. For example, the second student might say, "No, and that caused me to **break** my arm." Have each pair of students see how many spelling words they can use this way.

MEETING INDIVIDUAL NEEDS
Providing More Help

On the chalkboard, present the homophone pairs in sentences. For example:

It is five minutes **past** the hour.
I don't think we **passed** that church before.

Underline each spelling word. Ask volunteers to read the sentences and explain what each homophone means. Then ask the students to make up sentences of their own using the spelling words.
★Students who need to study fewer words should use the **Alternate Word List**. This list is starred on page T140 in the Teacher Edition. The **Unit 23 Practice Masters** (*Teacher Resource Book*) provide additional practice with these words.

Unit 23 Practice Masters

Name _____

Practice Master Unit 23

| 1. roll | 3. break | 5. steal | 7. waist | 9. past |
| 2. role | 4. brake | 6. steel | 8. waste | 10. passed |

A. Write the word pairs that sound alike but have different spellings and meanings.
1. _____
2. _____
3. _____
4. _____
5. _____

B. Write the spelling word that goes with each meaning.
1. a strong metal
2. the middle part of the body
3. the part played by an actor
4. earlier than the present time
5. it slows down or stops a car
6. to take without permission
7. to move by turning over and over
8. to come apart
9. to use up carelessly

130

Practice Master Unit 23

| waist | past |
| waste | passed |

sentence. Write the words.

...e. Unscramble the circled ...inside the circles.

131

Objectives

Spelling and Reading

Students will
- **choose** and write the correct homophones.
- **write** pairs of homophones to complete sentences.

One-Minute Handwriting Hint

Keep the loop open in the lowercase **l**. Begin the letter with a wide undercurve, and then loop back and pull the slant stroke to the baseline.

WIDE UNDERCURVE — SLANT

Legible handwriting can boost spelling scores by as much as 20%.

Spelling and Reading

lone	break	waist	passed	sore
cellar	roll	died	past	steak
role	steel	loan	dyed	seller
brake	soar	steal	stake	waste

Choose the Homophones Choose the correct homophone for each sentence.

1. Please pass me a (roll, role) to eat.
2. Look at those seagulls (soar, sore) over the waves.
3. We try not to (waist, waste) the paper.
4. We need one more (steak, stake) to secure this tent.
5. She is playing the (roll, role) of the princess in the school play.
6. These paintings are on (lone, loan) from the museum.
7. Pele's knee was (sore, soar) after he fell.
8. He ate the soup before the (steak, stake).
9. A (lone, loan) horse stood in the field.
10. Please (brake, break) the seal to open the jar.
11. The dress with the black belt at the (waste, waist) looks nice.
12. When I go sledding, I use my foot as a (break, brake).

Complete the Sentences Write a homophone pair to complete each sentence.

13.–14. I remember that on our _____ trips we _____ that farmhouse.
15.–16. Why would anyone want to _____ a truckload of _____?
17.–18. The _____ showed us what was for sale in her _____.
19.–20. The flower _____ when the florist _____ it green.

Choose the Homophones
1. roll
2. soar
3. waste
4. stake
5. role
6. loan
7. sore
8. steak
9. lone
10. break
11. waist
12. brake

Complete the Sentences
13. past
14. passed
15. steal
16. steel
17. seller
18. cellar
19. died
20. dyed

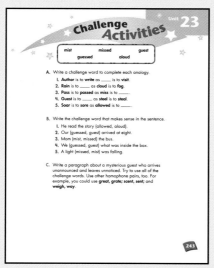

142

MEETING INDIVIDUAL NEEDS

Providing More Challenge

Challenge Words and **Challenge Activities** for Unit 23 appear on page 243. **Challenge Word Test Sentences** appear on page T243.

Unit 23 Challenge Activities

Weekly Test Options

Option 1:
One Spelling Word Per Sentence
(See procedures on pages Z10–Z11.)

1. Do not let the ball **roll** into the street.
2. I can take a ride while I have the **loan** of her bike.
3. The eagle can **soar** higher than most other birds.
4. The wild animal **died** from a lack of food.
5. You will have to pay for that if you **break** it.
6. That meat tastes like **steak**.
7. A **lone** animal walked through the forest that night.
8. I will play the main **role** in the school show.
9. His leg became **sore** after he fell on it.
10. Step on the **brake** if you want the car to stop.
11. This shirt is another color because I **dyed** it.
12. Push the **stake** into the ground so it holds down the tent.
13. Do not try to **steal** second base if there is not time.
14. That tiny woman has the smallest **waist**.
15. The **cellar** in our home is dug out of the dirt.

Proofread a Postcard

Six words are not spelled correctly on this postcard. Write those words correctly.

Hi Folks,
    Greetings from the *past* ~~passed~~. I'm in historic Williamstown, where a plate of *steak* ~~stake~~ and eggs once cost a few cents. We pay more than that today for a buttered *roll* ~~role~~. I may need a *loan* ~~lone~~ from you when I get back, since my waist is bigger than my wallet. But, seriously, I'm having fun, although my feet are *sore* ~~soar~~ from walking. This was a great *break* ~~brake~~ from my studies. See you soon.

Love,
Ted

Proofreading Marks

≡   Make a capital.
/   Make a small letter.
∧   Add something.
℘   Take out something.
⊙   Add a period.
⌗   New paragraph.
Ⓢ   Spelling error

Write a Postcard

Narrative Writing

Write a postcard about a place you have visited or can imagine. Be sure to mention
- where you are.
- what you have seen.
- what you have been doing.
- what you like or dislike about your trip.

Use as many spelling words as you can.

Writing Process

Prewriting
⇩
Drafting
⇩
Revising
⇩
Editing
⇩
Publishing

Proofread Your Writing During Editing

Proofread your writing for spelling errors as part of the editing stage in the writing process. Be sure to check each word carefully. Use a dictionary to check spelling if you are not sure.

143

Using the Writing Process

Before assigning **Write a Postcard** in this unit, see pages 258–259 in the Student Edition for a complete review of the writing process and additional writing assignments. You may also wish to refer to pages Z12–Z13 in the Teacher Edition.

Keeping a Spelling Journal

Encourage students to record the words they misspelled on the weekly test in a personal spelling journal. These words may be recycled for future study. Students may also wish to include words from their writing. See pages Z12–Z13 in the Teacher Edition for more information.

---

16. The teacher smiled at me as I walked **past** him.
17. The **steel** pipe is very heavy.
18. You will **waste** the food if you throw it away.
19. The **seller** wants Mother to buy a new ring.
20. Father **passed** me the ball.

Option 2:
Multiple Spelling Words Per Sentence
(See procedures on pages Z10–Z11.)

1. The **steel** pipe will **roll past** the car without hitting it.
2. Father **passed** me the piece of cloth he had **dyed**.
3. The **lone** bird will **soar** high into the sky.
4. The man showed how to **brake** as he played the **role** of a **seller** of used cars.
5. Father told us not to **waste** the good **steak**.
6. The bottle will **break** if you throw it down into the **cellar**.
7. Your **loan** of flowers for my table helps because mine have **died**.
8. My arms are **sore** from pounding the tent's **stake**.
9. Mother caught the young child around the **waist** as he began to **steal** the toast she was saving for the birds.

Option 3:
Standardized Test
(See *Teacher Resource Book,* Unit 23.)

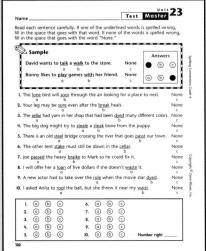

Unit 23 Test Master

Objectives

Strategy Words

Students will
- **review** words studied previously that are related to the spelling strategy.
- **preview** unknown words that are related to the spelling strategy.

Remind the students that the **Strategy Words** are related to the spelling strategy they have studied in this unit. The **Review Words** are below grade level, and the **Preview Words** are above grade level. You may wish to use the following sentences to introduce the words in context.

Review Words:
Words From Grade 3

1. The bird is cleaning **its** feathers.
2. I think **it's** going to be a sunny day.
3. Look over **there** on the table and see if you can find your book.
4. Joe and Sue will take a gift to **their** grandparents.
5. If **they're** late, they will miss the funny part of the show.

Preview Words:
Words From Grade 5

6. Use a **capital** letter to start each sentence.
7. The **capitol** building is in the next block.
8. He was so **vain** he combed his hair every few minutes.
9. There is a weather **vane** on our roof.
10. The nurse found a good **vein** in my arm for the medication.

Review Words
1. it's
2. their
3. they're
4. there
5. its

Preview Words
6. vein
7. capital
8. vane
9. vain
10. capitol

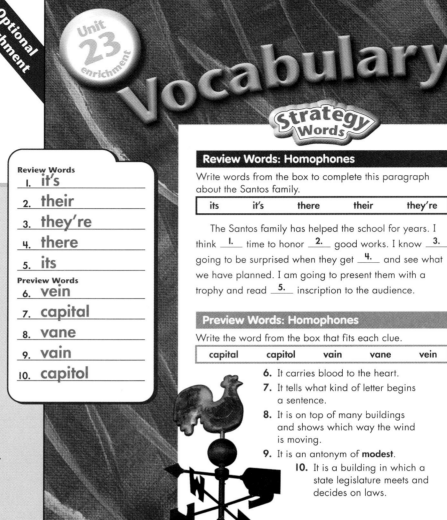

Vocabulary

Strategy Words

Review Words: Homophones

Write words from the box to complete this paragraph about the Santos family.

its	it's	there	their	they're

The Santos family has helped the school for years. I think __1.__ time to honor __2.__ good works. I know __3.__ going to be surprised when they get __4.__ and see what we have planned. I am going to present them with a trophy and read __5.__ inscription to the audience.

Preview Words: Homophones

Write the word from the box that fits each clue.

capital	capitol	vain	vane	vein

6. It carries blood to the heart.
7. It tells what kind of letter begins a sentence.
8. It is on top of many buildings and shows which way the wind is moving.
9. It is an antonym of **modest**.
10. It is a building in which a state legislature meets and decides on laws.

144

Unit 23 RECAP

You may wish to assign the **Unit 23 Homework Master** (*Teacher Resource Book*, Unit 23) as a fun way to recap the spelling words.

Unit 23 Homework Master

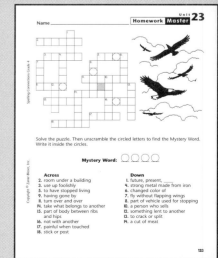

Name _____
Homework Master Unit 23

Solve the puzzle. Then unscramble the circled letters to find the Mystery Word. Write it inside the circles.

Mystery Word: ◯◯◯◯

Across
2. room under a building
3. use up foolishly
5. to have stopped living
9. having gone by
11. turn over and over
14. take what belongs to another
15. part of body between ribs and hips
16. not with another
17. painful when touched
18. stick or post

Down
1. future, present, ___
4. strong metal made from iron
6. changed color of
7. fly without flapping wings
8. part of vehicle used for stopping
10. a person who sells
12. something lent to another
13. to crack or split
14. a cut of meat

Spelling Connections Grade 4

Copyright © Zaner-Bloser, Inc.

133

Connections

Objectives

Content Words

Students will
- **expand** vocabulary with content-related words.
- **relate** the spelling strategy to words outside the basic spelling list.

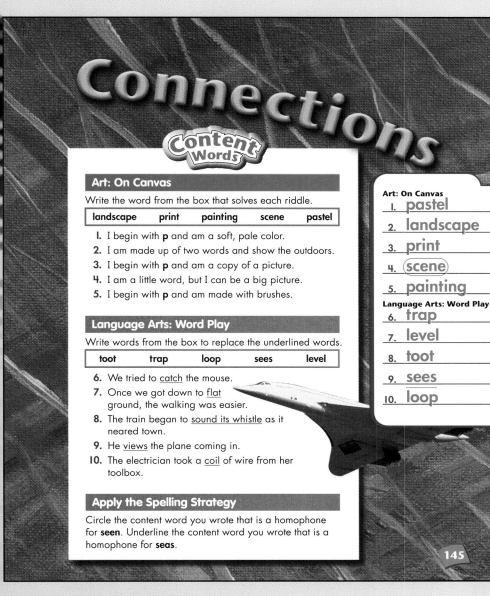

Content Words

Art: On Canvas

Write the word from the box that solves each riddle.

landscape	print	painting	scene	pastel

1. I begin with **p** and am a soft, pale color.
2. I am made up of two words and show the outdoors.
3. I begin with **p** and am a copy of a picture.
4. I am a little word, but I can be a big picture.
5. I begin with **p** and am made with brushes.

Language Arts: Word Play

Write words from the box to replace the underlined words.

toot	trap	loop	sees	level

6. We tried to <u>catch</u> the mouse.
7. Once we got down to <u>flat</u> ground, the walking was easier.
8. The train began to <u>sound its whistle</u> as it neared town.
9. He <u>views</u> the plane coming in.
10. The electrician took a <u>coil</u> of wire from her toolbox.

Apply the Spelling Strategy

Circle the content word you wrote that is a homophone for **seen**. Underline the content word you wrote that is a homophone for **seas**.

145

Art: On Canvas
1. pastel
2. landscape
3. print
4. (scene)
5. painting

Language Arts: Word Play
6. trap
7. level
8. toot
9. sees
10. loop

Content Words

Art: On Canvas

Review the meanings of these words with the students. You may wish to use these sentences to introduce the words in context.

1. We can paint a picture of the **landscape**.
2. When you finish typing that paper on the computer, you may **print** it.
3. Dad is **painting** the bedroom right now.
4. Take a picture of that street **scene** in Paris.
5. We like to use **pastel** colors when we paint.

Encourage the students to use these words to write an ad for a show at an art gallery.

Language Arts: Word Play

Review the meanings of these words with the students. You may wish to use these sentences to introduce the words in context.

6. The child wanted a horn on his little car that would really **toot**.
7. We built a playhouse with a **trap** door.
8. When we learn to write a small **l**, we must keep the **loop** open.
9. If the puppy **sees** us, he will follow us to school.
10. Mom measured out a **level** cup of flour for the cake.

Encourage the students to write a sentence in which each word is spelled both forward and backward.

Unit 24 Home Study Master

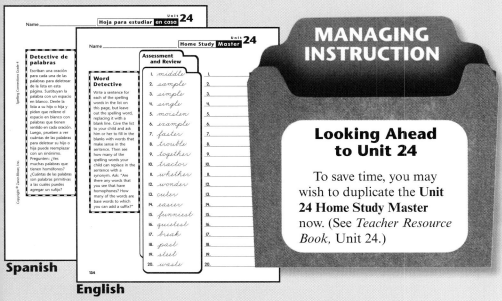

Spanish

English

MANAGING INSTRUCTION

Looking Ahead to Unit 24

To save time, you may wish to duplicate the **Unit 24 Home Study Master** now. (See *Teacher Resource Book,* Unit 24.)

Assessment Words

paddle	saddle
driven	dozen
heir	juggle
janitor	sunniest
driest	candle
trimmer	throne
clever	isle
handle	anger
forever	humble
aisle	smaller

Review Words

Unit 19
middle*	jungle
sample*	tickle
simple*	battle
single*	bottle
cattle	settle

Unit 20
moisten*	harden
example*	table
fasten*	lighten
trouble*	darken
brighten	double

Unit 21
together*	water
tractor*	rather
whether*	winter
wonder*	neither
either	silver

Unit 22
cuter*	safest
easier*	happier
funniest*	nearer
quietest*	kinder
kindest	nearest

Unit 23
break*	passed
past*	brake
steel*	waist
waste*	role
roll	steal

* Posttest sentences and the **Unit 24 Test Master** test these words. Students review all words listed.

MATERIALS

Student Edition
Pages 146–151

Teacher Edition
Pages T146A–T151

Other Resources
Spelling Connections Software
Spelling and Writing
  Transparencies (Writing Prompt
  and Writing Model) for Unit 24

Teacher Resource Book
Unit 24 Home Study Master
  (English or Spanish; students
  may use this sheet for review
  or home practice.)
Flip Folder Practice Master
Unit 24 Test Master

Visit our Web site, www.zaner-bloser.com

OBJECTIVES

Spelling and Assessment
Students will
- **assess** their progress in understanding the spelling strategies and patterns taught in Units 19–23.
- **connect** new words to the spelling strategies in Units 19–23.
- **write** new words that relate to the spelling strategies in Units 19–23.

Spelling and Review
Students will
- **review** the spelling strategies and words taught in Units 19–23.
- **learn** an alternative spelling study strategy.

Spelling and Writing
Students will
- **review** the concept of pronouns.
- **compose** a persuasive piece of writing about bicycle safety.
- **learn** a proofreading strategy.
- **proofread** for words that are often confused for each other.

MEETING INDIVIDUAL NEEDS
Learning Styles

 Visual

Have the students scramble the order of 15 spelling words on the five lists and then write them as continuous word chains. Have them exchange their word chains with each other and use crayons to separate the words with slashes.

 Auditory

Have the students work in pairs. Give each pair sufficient space at the chalkboard. One student of the pair says a spelling word and then writes the word on the chalkboard, leaving blanks for the letters that spell the vowel sounds. The other student of the pair supplies the missing letters and uses each word in a sentence. Then the students reverse roles and continue working together until they have used at least ten spelling words.

 Kinesthetic

Write several words on 3" × 5" cards and place them facedown on a table or desk. Have students choose a card and act out or illustrate the word. Have other students guess the word. The student acting out or illustrating the word may give a clue by writing the word in the air. Once the word is guessed, call on a student to write it correctly on the chalkboard. Possible words include **battle, tickle, moisten, tractor, winter,** and **water**.

Language and Cultural Differences

The final **le, er,** and **en** may be difficult for some students to hear and spell because of regional pronunciation differences or language backgrounds that do not include this sound. It is important for these students to hear and use each word in a meaningful context and associate the sound and the letters.

Ask the students to read along with you in their spelling books as you pronounce each spelling word. Have the students repeat each word after you. Then ask volunteers to use the words in sentences. Have other volunteers write the spelling words on the chalkboard.

MANAGING INSTRUCTION

3–5 Day Plan		Average	Below Average	Above Average
Day 1	**Day 1**	Assessment: Units 19–23, p. 146 (Option 1 or 2, p. T146)	Assessment: Units 19–23, p. 146 (Option 1 or 2, p. T146)	Assessment: Units 19–23, p. 146 (Option 1 or 2, p. T146)
	Day 2	Review: Units 19 and 20, p. 147	Review: Units 19 and 20, p. 147	Review: Units 19 and 20, p. 147 Review: Units 21 and 22, p. 148
Day 2	**Day 3**	Review: Units 21 and 22, p. 148	Review: Units 21 and 22, p. 148	Review: Unit 23, p. 149 Spelling Study Strategy, p. 149
	Day 4	Review: Unit 23, p. 149 Spelling Study Strategy, p. 149	Review: Unit 23, p. 149 Spelling Study Strategy, p. 149	Writer's Workshop, pages 150–151
Day 3	**Day 5**	Weekly Test, Option 1 or 2, p. T149	Weekly Test, Option 1 or 2, p. T149	Weekly Test, Option 1 or 2, p. T149
Writer's Workshop (pages 150 and 151) may be used anytime during this unit.				

Objectives

Spelling and Assessment

Students will
- **assess** their progress in understanding the spelling strategies and patterns taught in Units 19–23.
- **connect** new words to the spelling strategies in Units 19–23.
- **write** new words that relate to the spelling strategies taught in Units 19–23.

Unit **24**
Review Units 19–23

Assessment and Review

Unit 19
1. paddle ▲
2. handle ▲
3. saddle ▲
4. juggle ▲
5. candle ▲
6. humble ▲

Unit 20
7. driven
8. dozen

Unit 21
9. janitor
10. clever
11. forever
12. anger

Unit 22
13. driest
14. trimmer ▲
15. sunniest
16. smaller ▲

Unit 23
17. heir
18. aisle ▲
19. throne
20. isle ▲

Assessment Units 19–23

Each Assessment Word in the box fits one of the spelling strategies you have studied over the past five weeks. Read the spelling strategies. Then write each Assessment Word under the unit number it fits.

Unit 19 _____
1.–6. The second syllable in some words ends in **le**.

Unit 20 _____
7.–8. Words often end with **le** or **en**. Final **en** usually means "to make" or "to become."

Unit 21 _____
9.–12. The **schwa-r** sound is spelled in different ways: **er** in **water** and **or** in **major**.

Unit 22 _____
13.–16. Suffixes such as **-er** and **-est** are added to the ends of words to make new words: **kind, kinder, kindest**.

Unit 23 _____
17.–20. **Homophones** are words that sound the same but have different spellings and meanings.

paddle
driven
heir
janitor
driest
trimmer
clever
handle
forever
aisle
saddle
dozen
juggle
sunniest
candle
throne
isle
anger
humble
smaller

146

ASSESSMENT: UNITS 19–23

Option 1

Assessment Option 1 is the test that appears in the Student Edition on page 146. You may wish to have students take this test to determine their ability to recognize the spelling strategy in each unit and to match words not previously taught to that strategy. **Assessment Option 1** also serves as additional review and practice.

▲ Words designated with this symbol include more than one of the targeted spelling strategies. The answer key has placed them according to the most obvious spelling emphasis. However, if a student places a word in another category, and the word fits that generalization, accept that response. Remember, the objective is to place each word with any appropriate spelling generalization.

Option 2

Assessment Option 2 is a dictation test using the sentences on page T147. This test assesses students' ability to spell words not previously taught but that are exemplars of a spelling strategy. This test more specifically assesses students' ability to apply the spelling knowledge they have learned.

In either assessment test option, the words are identified by unit in the Teacher Edition. You may wish to index those misspelled words to the review exercises that follow in this unit. Determine which units students need to review and use the additional unit exercises found in this **Assessment and Review Unit** for reteaching the skill in a more focused way.

middle	sample	simple	single	cattle
jungle	tickle	battle	bottle	settle

These spelling words are missing letters. Write the spelling words.

1. j __ n __ le
2. cat __ __ e
3. s __ n __ le
4. bo __ __ le
5. ti __ __ le
6. mi __ dl __
7. __ et __ le
8. sam __ __ e
9. ba __ tl __
10. si __ p __ e

 Review   Unit 20: Final le, Final en

moisten	example	fasten	trouble	brighten
harden	table	lighten	darken	double

Write the spelling word that completes each sentence.

11. Drink some water to _____ your mouth.
12. Put four chairs around the _____.
13. Pull the shades down to _____ the room.
14. The sailor will _____ the boat to the dock with rope.
15. We will need to _____ the box of books before I can carry it.
16. The coach's hard work set a good _____ for his team.
17. Cold weather caused the water to _____ into ice.
18. We are having _____ with our television.
19. The morning sun began to _____ the room.
20. If you _____ five, you will get ten.

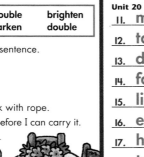

Unit 19
1. jungle
2. cattle
3. single
4. bottle
5. tickle
6. middle
7. settle
8. sample
9. battle
10. simple

Unit 20
11. moisten
12. table
13. darken
14. fasten
15. lighten
16. example
17. harden
18. trouble
19. brighten
20. double

147

Pretest Sentences: Assessment Words

(See procedures on pages Z10–Z11.)

1. We watched the boaters **paddle** across the lake.
2. The team will be **driven** to the game on buses.
3. The prince is **heir** to his father's crown.
4. A **janitor** sweeps the halls every night.
5. A desert is one of the **driest** places on earth.
6. Weeks of exercise gave me a **trimmer** body.
7. The magician knew several **clever** tricks.
8. Grab the pan by its **handle**.
9. That boring movie seemed to last **forever**.
10. Keep the **aisle** clear for others to pass through.
11. The rider tightened the **saddle** on her horse.
12. Eggs are usually sold by the **dozen**.
13. It can be hard trying to **juggle** several jobs at once.
14. Yesterday was the **sunniest** day of the week.
15. When the power went out, we had to light a **candle**.
16. The ambassadors bowed as they approached the **throne**.
17. We often vacation on a tropical **isle**.
18. Try to control your **anger** over the mistake.
19. The fairy tale is about a **humble** shoemaker.
20. Our kitchen is **smaller** than yours.

Objectives

Spelling and Review

Students will

- **review** the spelling strategy and words taught in Unit 21.
- **review** the spelling strategy and words taught in Unit 22.

Unit 21
1. together
2. either
3. neither
4. tractor
5. rather
6. winter
7. whether
8. water
9. wonder
10. silver

Unit 22
11. happier
12. nearest
13. safest
14. funniest
15. kinder
16. cuter
17. kindest
18. easier
19. quietest
20. nearer

Review Unit 21: Schwa-r er, or

| together | tractor | whether | wonder | either |
| water | rather | winter | neither | silver |

Write a spelling word for each clue.

1. It is an antonym for **apart**.
2. It begins with a **long e** sound spelled **ei**.
3. Add one letter to your answer for number 2.
4. You will find one of these on most farms.
5. Change one letter in **gather** to make this word.
6. It comes before spring.
7. A homophone for this word is **weather**.
8. Use this with soap.
9. The word **won** can be found in this word.
10. Some coins contain this.

Review Unit 22: Suffixes -er, -est

| cuter | easier | funniest | quietest | kindest |
| safest | happier | nearer | kinder | nearest |

Write the spelling word that completes each group of words.

11. happy, _____, happiest
12. near, nearer, _____
13. safe, safer, _____
14. funny, funnier, _____
15. kind, _____, kindest
16. cute, _____, cutest
17. kind, kinder, _____
18. easy, _____, easiest
19. quiet, quieter, _____
20. near, _____, nearest

148

Bulletin Board Idea

Books Worth Reading

On a bulletin board, list titles under "Fantasy and Science Fiction" and under "Mystery." List books under the categories as suggested reading.

Fantasy and Science Fiction: *James and the Giant Peach* by Roald Dahl. (Knopf, 1961); *The Lion, the Witch, and the Wardrobe* by C. S. Lewis. (HarperCollins, 1994); *A Wrinkle in Time* by Madeleine L'Engle. (Farrar, Straus, 1962).

Mystery: *Who Really Killed Cock Robin?* An Ecological Mystery by Jean George. (HarperCollins, 1991); *The House of Dies Drear* by Virginia Hamilton. (Macmillan, 1968); *Encyclopedia Brown Lends a Hand* by Donald J. Sobol. (Lodestar, 1974).

Have the students write brief summaries of these books or any other books they have read in these categories. Then display them on the bulletin board.

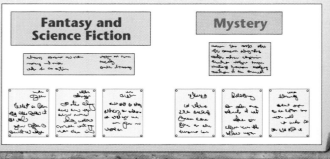

TI48

Review Unit 23: Homophones

break	past	steel	waist	roll
passed	brake	waist	role	steal

Write the homophone that completes each sentence.

1. We (passed, past) the school on our way to the game.
2. In the (passed, past), it took weeks to cross the ocean.
3. One should never (waist, waste) food.
4. The cook tied an apron around her (waist, waste).
5. If you drop the glass, it will surely (brake, break).
6. Use the (brake, break) to stop your bicycle.
7. Heavy trucks cross the river on a (steal, steel) bridge.
8. Put your money where no one can (steal, steel) it.
9. What is your (role, roll) in the play?
10. We watched the huge snowball (role, roll) down the hill.

Unit 23
1. passed
2. past
3. waste
4. waist
5. break
6. brake
7. steel
8. steal
9. role
10. roll

 Spelling Study Strategy

Sorting by Endings

One good way to practice spelling is to place words into groups according to some spelling pattern. Here is a way to practice some of the words you studied in the past few weeks.

1. Make five columns on a large piece of paper or on the chalkboard.

2. Write one of the following words at the top of each column: **apple, soften, sailor, power,** and **simplest.**

3. Have a partner choose a spelling word from Units 19 through 22 and say it aloud.

4. Write the spelling word under the word with the same ending.

149

Objectives

Spelling and Review

Students will
• **review** the spelling strategy and words taught in Unit 23.
• **learn** an alternative spelling study strategy.

Learning an Alternative Spelling Study Strategy

Students should always have a number of study strategies to draw from when it comes to learning their spelling words. **Sorting by Endings** is a fun way of differentiating sound and letter patterns. Encourage students to remember this spelling study strategy and to consider using it with any appropriate list they need to study and learn.

Weekly Test Options

Option 1:
One Spelling Word Per Sentence
(See procedures on pages Z10–Z11.)

1. I **wonder** what is for lunch today.
2. Give me an **example** of a preposition.
3. You must pay for that if you **break** it.
4. The boys gave the teacher a **simple** answer.
5. Father will go fishing **whether** it rains or not.
6. The rain will **moisten** the dry grass.
7. In the **past,** we have eaten lunch earlier.
8. Chad and I will go skating **together**.
9. I think math is **easier** than history.
10. Our teacher showed us a **sample** of the test questions.
11. The **steel** pipe is very heavy.
12. Kim didn't miss a **single** question on the test.
13. We must **fasten** the boat to the dock.
14. The library is the **quietest** room in school.
15. Don't stand in the **middle** of the road.
16. We try not to **waste** paper in our classroom.
17. I had no **trouble** finding your house.
18. This puppy is **cuter** than the white one.
19. The farmer drove the **tractor** to the barn.
20. That is the **funniest** joke I have ever heard.

Option 2:
Standardized Test

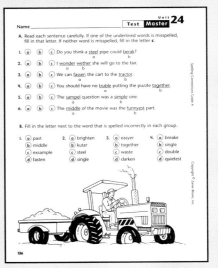

Unit 24 Test Master

(See *Teacher Resource Book,* Unit 24.)

Objectives

Spelling and Writing

Students will
- **review** the concept of pronouns.
- **compose** a persuasive piece of writing about bicycle safety. (See **Spelling and the Writing Process** below.)

Unit 24 enrichment

WRITER'S

Grammar, Usage, and Mechanics

Pronouns

Personal pronouns include the words **I, me, you, we, us, he, him, she, her, they, them,** and **it**. These words can be used in place of names for people and things.

Ida is here. **She** came early.

Possessive pronouns include the words **my, your, his, her, its, their,** and **our**. These pronouns show ownership.

Call **Guy**. **His** tickets are here.

Practice Activity

A. Write the boldfaced word in each sentence that is a pronoun.
1. The bird **is** carrying food to **its** babies.
2. **The** players are tired, so **they** want to stop.
3. Bart and **he** are co-captains **of** the men's team.
4. The lifeguard **put** sunscreen on **her** nose.
5. The vase of **colorful** flowers made **their** table look pretty.

B. Replace the underlined word or words with pronouns from the box.

them	he	we	its	their	she	our

6. All the cattle are waiting for <u>the cattle's</u> water.
7. Eric is late, so <u>Eric</u> may lose this seat.
8. Did you bring the lunches that <u>you and I</u> packed?
9. Mom is still at work, but <u>Mom</u> will be home soon.
10. The playful kitten tumbled around with <u>the kitten's</u> ball of yarn.

A
1. its
2. they
3. he
4. her
5. their

B
6. their
7. he
8. we
9. she
10. its

150

Persuasive Writing

Spelling and the Writing Process

You may wish to use this writing assignment to help students master the writing process. For other writing ideas, see pages 258–259 in the Student Edition.

Explain that students will write a composition in which they convince younger students to follow some bicycle safety rule, such as wearing a helmet or stopping at stop signs.

Prewriting Hint: You may wish to help students plan their writing by recommending the following graphic organizer. Have them replicate the graphic, filling in the blanks with details about the experience.

Safety Rule:	Always wear a bike helmet.
Reasons to follow it:	It protects your head if you fall.
Examples:	Allison fell and didn't get hurt.

Revising Hint: Remind students that when they revise what they have written, they should make sure that they have made their position clear and given reasons that are likely to appeal to their audience.

WORKSHOP

Proofreading Strategy

Circle and Check

Good writers always proofread their writing for spelling errors. Here's a strategy that you should try to proofread your papers.

Instead of reading your whole paper, look at just the first three or four words. Are they spelled correctly? If you are sure that they are correct, go on and check the next three or four words. If you are unsure of a word's spelling, circle the word and keep going. Look at your whole paper this way—one small group of words at a time.

When you are done looking, get a dictionary and check the spelling of all the circled words. Looking up the words later keeps you focused on the task of proofreading. It's also faster to look up several words at once. Try it!

Electronic Spelling

1. **angel**
2. **desert**
3. **choose**
4. **Which**
5. **wait**
6. **passed**

Electronic Spelling

Spell Checkers and Similar Words

A spell checker can help you with spelling, but it can't do the whole job. Many times writers confuse two words. They write one when they mean to write another. For example, don't **axis** and **axes** sound alike? Yet the earth does not revolve around an axes. Axes cut down trees.

Spell checkers are not as smart as you are. They can't tell which word belongs in a sentence. You need to know the spelling of words that are easy to confuse.

Practice on the sentences below. Find the misspelled word in each sentence. Write it correctly.

1. The artist drew a picture of an angle with wings.
2. Travelers in the dessert must carry plenty of water.
3. You may chose any seat on the bus.
4. Witch jacket did you bring?
5. Please weight until Leslie can join us.
6. Josh past right by us on the way to school.

151

Optional Enrichment

Objectives

Spelling and Writing

Students will
• **learn** a proofreading strategy.
• **proofread** for words that are often confused for each other.

Using Proofreading Strategies

Students are often unaware that there are a variety of techniques they can use to proofread their own writing. Building a repertory of strategies is important to improving students' writing and editing skills.

Spelling and Technology

The advent of word processing, computer protocols, and the Internet has actually increased, not lessened, the pressure on users to be better, more aware spellers. Spell checkers, for example, create circumstances in which the ability to discriminate between an acceptable and an unacceptable spelling is a critical skill. A homophone substitution, a correct spelling of the wrong word, an inadvertent word omission—these are examples of situations in computer usage that require a deeper understanding of spelling principles and a more adroit proofreading capability. It may be worthwhile to underscore this increased need as a whole-class discussion after students finish this unit's **Electronic Spelling** activity.

Unit 25 Home Study Master

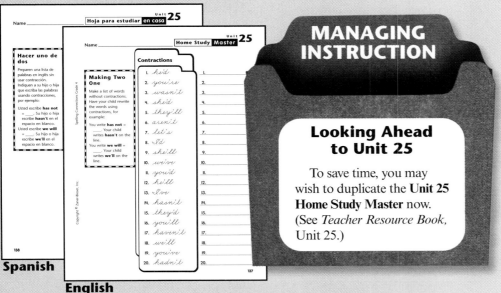

Spanish

English

MANAGING INSTRUCTION

Looking Ahead to Unit 25

To save time, you may wish to duplicate the **Unit 25 Home Study Master** now. (See *Teacher Resource Book*, Unit 25.)

Basic Spelling List

he'd	you'd
you're	he'll
wasn't	I've
she'd	hasn't
they'll	they'd
aren't	you'll
let's	haven't
I'd	we'll
she'll	you've
we've	hadn't

Strategy Words

Review

can't	I'll
didn't	I'm
doesn't	

Preview

couldn't	who's
weren't	who've
we'd	

Content Words

Language Arts: Parts of a Letter

closing	signature
heading	greeting
envelope	

Social Studies: Civics

election	vote
taxes	statehood
govern	

Individual Needs

Challenge Words

it'll	wouldn't
who'll	shouldn't
needn't	

Alternate Word List

he'd	I'd
you're	I've
wasn't	you'll
aren't	haven't
let's	we'll

MATERIALS

Student Edition
Pages 152–157
Challenge Activities, p. 244

Teacher Edition
Pages T152A–T157
Challenge Activities, p. T244

Other Resources
Spelling Connections Software
Unit 25 Word List Overhead
Transparency

Teacher Resource Book
Unit 25 Home Study Master
(English or Spanish; students
may pretest on this sheet or use
it for home practice.)
Unit 25 Homework Master
Unit 25 Practice Masters
Flip Folder Practice Master
Unit 25 Test Master

Visit our Web site, www.zaner-bloser.com

OBJECTIVES

Spelling and Thinking
Students will
- **read** the spelling words in list form and in context.
- **sort** the spelling words according to contractions for **will, not, us, have, had, would,** and **are.**
- **read** and remember this week's spelling strategy.

Spelling and Vocabulary
Students will
- **write** contractions from given words.
- **write** contractions that are opposites of given words in sentences.
- **use** the **Spelling Dictionary** to write spelling words from their dictionary respellings.

Spelling and Reading
Students will
- **complete** sentences using spelling words.
- **complete** a story using spelling words.

Spelling and Writing
Students will
- **proofread** a letter.
- **use** the writing process to write a letter of appeal.
- **proofread** their writing.

MEETING INDIVIDUAL NEEDS
Learning Styles

 Visual
Make two columns on the chalkboard. In one column, write the spelling words in random order. In the other, write the two words that make up each contraction. Call on students to take turns going to the chalkboard. Have each draw a line to match one contraction with the two words it represents. Then have each student circle the letter or letters in the two words that are replaced by the apostrophe in the contraction. Finally, have all the students write the contractions on paper.

 Auditory
Make up sentences like those below using the spelling words. Have the students chant each sentence, identify the spelling word, and write it three times.

He'd do it for you, **he would**.

We've always been friends, **we have**.

We **haven't** been gone long, **have not**.

 Kinesthetic
Have the students chant the sentences from the auditory activity. Then have them spell each contraction aloud. Ask them to sit and tap their feet for each letter in the word and stand to trace the apostrophe in the air.

Language and Cultural Differences

Although students are accustomed to using contractions in oral language, they may not always know what words the contractions replace. Mastering the spelling of a contraction lies in the students' understanding that two words have been compressed into one and that the missing letter or letters have been replaced by an apostrophe.

Explain that contractions are formed by putting two words together to make a single, shorter word that is faster and easier to say and write. Explain also that an apostrophe is used in place of the omitted letter(s). Go through the list of spelling words with the students and ask them to tell which two words make up each contraction and which letter or letters have been replaced by the apostrophe. Ask them to write a sentence for each contraction.

MANAGING INSTRUCTION

3–5 Day Plan		Average	Below Average	Above Average
Day 1	**Day 1**	Pretest Spelling Mini-Lesson, p. T152 Spelling and Thinking, p. 152	Pretest Spelling Mini-Lesson, p. T152 Spelling and Thinking, p. 152	Pretest Spelling and Thinking, p. 152
	Day 2	Spelling and Vocabulary, p. 153	Spelling and Vocabulary, p. 153 (or) Unit 25 Practice Master, A and B	Spelling and Vocabulary, p. 153 Spelling and Reading, p. 154
Day 2	**Day 3**	Spelling and Reading, p. 154	Spelling and Reading, p. 154 (or) Unit 25 Practice Master, C and D	Challenge Activities, p. 244
	Day 4	Spelling and Writing, p. 155 Unit 25 Homework Master	Spelling and Writing, p. 155	Spelling and Writing, p. 155 Unit 25 Homework Master
Day 3	**Day 5**	Weekly Test	Weekly Test	Weekly Test

Vocabulary Connections (pages 156 and 157) may be used anytime during this unit.

Objectives

Spelling and Thinking

Students will
- **read** the spelling words in list form and in context.
- **sort** the spelling words according to contractions for **will**, **not**, **us**, **have**, **had**, **would**, and **are**.
- **read** and remember this week's spelling strategy.

UNIT PRETEST

Use **Pretest Sentences** below. Refer to the self-checking procedures on student page 256. You may wish to use the **Unit 25 Word List Overhead Transparency** as part of the checking procedure.

TEACHING THE STRATEGY

Spelling Mini-Lesson

Ask volunteers to explain what contractions are. (**Contractions are shortened forms of words.**) Discuss the fact that we often use contractions when we speak. Contractions are written versions of the way some words sound when they are spoken together. Discuss the benefits— and possible shortcomings—of using contractions in writing and speech.

Write **you had** and **you would** on the chalkboard and explain that the contraction for both of these word pairs is the same: **you'd**. Write **you'd** on the board. Ask a volunteer to use the two different meanings of this contraction in a pair of sentences. Ask which letters are left out of **you had** to form **you'd** (**ha**) and which letters are left out of **you would** (**woul**). Point out that both vowels and consonants can be replaced by an apostrophe.

Read the list of spelling words and ask volunteers to identify the "long form" of each contraction.

Conclude by reading **Remember the Spelling Strategy** on page 152.

Order of answers may vary. will, not, or us

1. he'll
2. she'll
3. we'll ★
4. you'll ★
5. they'll
6. aren't ★
7. hadn't
8. hasn't
9. wasn't ★
10. haven't ★
11. let's ★

have, had, would, or are

12. I'd ★
13. he'd ★
14. she'd
15. you'd
16. they'd
17. I've ★
18. you've
19. we've
20. you're ★

152

READ THE SPELLING WORDS

1. he'd	*he'd*	We thought **he'd** been on vacation.
2. you're	*you're*	When **you're** ready, let us know.
3. wasn't	*wasn't*	I **wasn't** prepared for a storm.
4. she'd	*she'd*	She said **she'd** call her friend.
5. they'll	*they'll*	After dinner, **they'll** walk the dog.
6. aren't	*aren't*	Why **aren't** you shopping with Mom?
7. let's	*let's*	When we get tired, **let's** rest.
8. I'd	*I'd*	He thought **I'd** know his address.
9. she'll	*she'll*	If you play the piano, **she'll** sing.
10. we've	*we've*	Did you know **we've** been calling you?
11. you'd	*you'd*	If you had won, **you'd** know it.
12. he'll	*he'll*	He said **he'll** tell what happened.
13. I've	*I've*	I forgot to tell you that **I've** moved.
14. hasn't	*hasn't*	The cat **hasn't** eaten yet.
15. they'd	*they'd*	Each summer **they'd** visit each other.
16. you'll	*you'll*	After I bat, **you'll** be up.
17. haven't	*haven't*	Sorry, I **haven't** any change.
18. we'll	*we'll*	If you want to see us, **we'll** visit you.
19. you've	*you've*	Tell me when **you've** finished reading.
20. hadn't	*hadn't*	I **hadn't** yet thought of a good plan.

SORT THE SPELLING WORDS

1.–11. Write the spelling words in which **will**, **not**, or **us** has been shortened.

12.–20. Write the spelling words in which **have**, **had**, **would**, or **are** has been shortened.

REMEMBER THE SPELLING STRATEGY

Remember that a **contraction** is a shortened form of two words: **you're** means **you are**. An apostrophe (') shows where letters have been left out.

Pretest Sentences (See procedures on pages Z10–Z11.)

1. I asked Lavar if **he'd** go to the store with me.
2. Do you know that **you're** invited to the party?
3. Cathy said she **wasn't** going to the game.
4. Now **she'd** like to have some spinach.
5. My sisters said that **they'll** ride with us.
6. Pets **aren't** allowed on the beach.
7. This afternoon, **let's** go to town.
8. I said **I'd** rather walk than ride.
9. I know **she'll** trade books with me.
10. Every year **we've** visited our grandparents.
11. I invited you to the game because I thought **you'd** enjoy it.
12. If I ask Curtis to go by bus, I know **he'll** agree.
13. Did you know that **I've** already completed my project?
14. Beth **hasn't** had time to paint.
15. When I found my friends, **they'd** already eaten lunch.
16. If you study, **you'll** probably do well on the test.
17. I saw our neighbors move in, but I **haven't** met them.
18. My brother and I have decided that **we'll** play a word game.
19. We think **you've** a lot of talent!
20. Joe remembered that he **hadn't** done his homework.

Word Meanings

Write the spelling words that are contractions of these words.

1. I had or I would
2. let us
3. he will
4. he had or he would
5. we will
6. you are
7. I have
8. we have
9. they had or they would
10. she will

Opposites

Write the spelling word that means the opposite of the underlined word in each sentence.

11. Did you forget that we <u>had</u> bought our tickets?
12. I <u>have</u> ridden in a hot air balloon.
13. I could tell that this <u>was</u> your first ride.
14. We <u>are</u> afraid to ride in a helicopter.
15. This bus company <u>has</u> lost many suitcases.

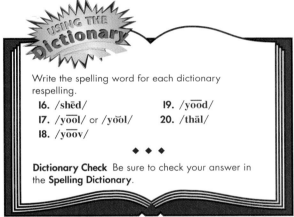

USING THE Dictionary

Write the spelling word for each dictionary respelling.

16. /shēd/
17. /yōol/ or /yŏŏl/
18. /yōov/
19. /yōod/
20. /thāl/

♦ ♦ ♦

Dictionary Check Be sure to check your answer in the **Spelling Dictionary**.

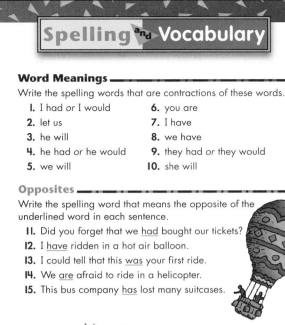

Word Meanings
1. I'd
2. let's
3. he'll
4. he'd
5. we'll
6. you're
7. I've
8. we've
9. they'd
10. she'll

Opposites
11. hadn't
12. haven't
13. wasn't
14. aren't
15. hasn't

Using the Dictionary
16. she'd
17. you'll
18. you've
19. you'd
20. they'll

153

Objectives

Spelling and Vocabulary

Students will
- **write** contractions from given words.
- **write** contractions that are opposites of given words in sentences.
- **use** the **Spelling Dictionary** to write spelling words from their dictionary respellings.

Developing Oral Language Skills

Have students work in pairs. The first student says a sentence using one of the contractions in the spelling word list. For example, the student might say, "We **haven't** seen Josh for days." The second student responds with a sentence that uses the uncontracted form of the contraction. For example, the second student might say, "I **have not** seen him either." Have students reverse roles and continue until all the spelling words have been used.

MEETING INDIVIDUAL NEEDS

Providing More Help

For each spelling word, write the two words from which each contraction is formed on a strip of construction paper. Cut out twenty paper apostrophes. Direct the students to use safety scissors to cut out the letters that are omitted when each contraction is formed. Then have them replace the letters by gluing or taping a paper apostrophe in their place. Tell them to tape the newly formed contractions to the chalkboard.
★Students who need to study fewer words should use the **Alternate Word List**. This list is starred on page T152 in the Teacher Edition. The **Unit 25 Practice Masters** (*Teacher Resource Book*) provide additional practice with these words.

Unit 25 Practice Masters

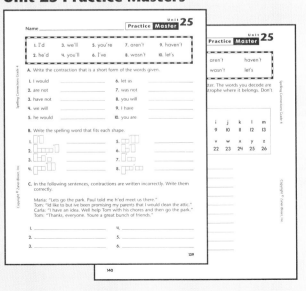

Spelling and Reading

Students will
- **complete** sentences using spelling words.
- **complete** a story using spelling words.

One-Minute Handwriting Hint

When joining the lowercase **v** to the letter **e,** swing right to form the loop of the letter **e.**

↓ SWING RIGHT

Legible handwriting can boost spelling scores by as much as 20%.

Complete the Sentences

1. haven't
2. you'll
3. she'll
4. aren't
5. hasn't
6. he'll
7. she'd
8. you're
9. we've
10. hadn't
11. they'll
12. you've
13. we'll
14. let's

Complete the Story

15. they'd
16. you'd
17. he'd
18. I'd
19. I've
20. wasn't

Spelling and Reading

he'd	you're	wasn't	she'd	they'll
aren't	let's	I'd	she'll	we've
you'd	he'll	I've	hasn't	they'd
you'll	haven't	we'll	you've	hadn't

Complete the Sentences Write the spelling words that best complete each sentence.

1.–2. Since you _____ been to the seashore, _____ have to ask directions.

3.–4. Sara says _____ find someone else to ride with if we _____ going.

5.–6. Jason's report card _____ arrived in the mail yet, so _____ have to go to the school to get it.

7.–8. Your grandmother would have written if _____ found the picture that _____ looking for.

9. In our class, _____ been studying early American explorers.

10. My parents were sure that they _____ forgotten their car keys.

11. Jesse and his sister say _____ be moving next week.

12.–13. We know _____ been waiting for us, but if you wait a little more, _____ both walk you home.

14. Our play is soon, so _____ practice our lines.

Complete the Story Write the spelling word that fits in each blank in the story.

Our school held a costume party. The guests dressed as something __15.__ like to be. I guess __16.__ be surprised at how many people dressed as cats! One boy said that __17.__ love to be a cat because they sleep so much.

I think __18.__ rather be a fish. I love to swim, and __19.__ spent hours watching the fish in my tank. So I dressed as a goldfish. There __20.__ another fish at the party!

I've
they'd
I'd
you'd
he'd
wasn't

154

MEETING INDIVIDUAL NEEDS

Providing More Challenge

Challenge Words and **Challenge Activities** for Unit 25 appear on page 244. **Challenge Word Test Sentences** appear on page T244.

Unit 25 Challenge Activities

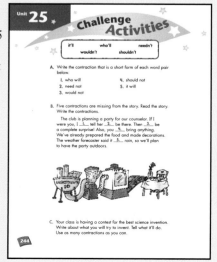

Weekly Test Options

Option 1:
One Spelling Word Per Sentence

(See procedures on pages Z10–Z11.)

1. She hopes **she'll** see an eagle.
2. I know **I've** seen the cave before.
3. Those children **haven't** had their lunch yet.
4. This afternoon **I'd** like to sleep on the cot.
5. We are sure that **we'll** be home before dark.
6. I know that **you're** my best friend.
7. He **hadn't** cleaned his bedroom until last week.
8. I thought you said **you'd** like to pet the geese.
9. Tomorrow, **let's** look at the birds in the cage.
10. They told me **they'll** do the dishes.
11. My uncle **hasn't** visited us for a year.
12. Father said **he'd** rather cook than clean.
13. I hope **you'll** be able to see the deer at dawn.
14. I **wasn't** able to ride the train.
15. Pat said that **she'd** like to rake the grass.

Spelling and Writing

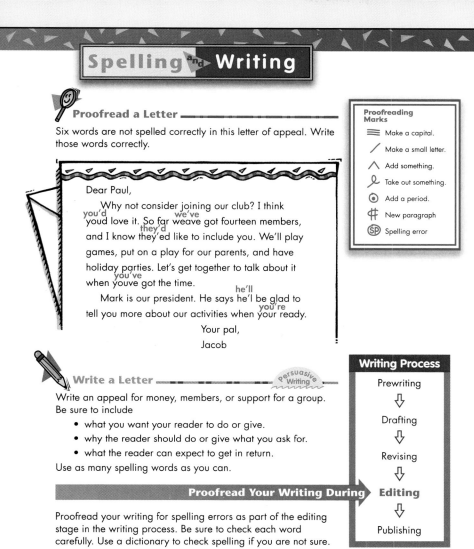

Proofread a Letter

Six words are not spelled correctly in this letter of appeal. Write those words correctly.

Dear Paul,

Why not consider joining our club? I think
you'd
youd love it. So far weave got fourteen members,
we've
and I know they'ed like to include you. We'll play
they'd
games, put on a play for our parents, and have
holiday parties. Let's get together to talk about it
you've
when youve got the time.
he'll
Mark is our president. He says he'l be glad to
you're
tell you more about our activities when your ready.

Your pal,

Jacob

Proofreading Marks

≡ Make a capital.
/ Make a small letter.
∧ Add something.
℘ Take out something.
⊙ Add a period.
⌗ New paragraph
ⓈⓅ Spelling error

Write a Letter

Persuasive Writing

Write an appeal for money, members, or support for a group. Be sure to include
• what you want your reader to do or give.
• why the reader should do or give what you ask for.
• what the reader can expect to get in return.
Use as many spelling words as you can.

Proofread Your Writing During → **Editing**

Proofread your writing for spelling errors as part of the editing stage in the writing process. Be sure to check each word carefully. Use a dictionary to check spelling if you are not sure.

Writing Process

Prewriting
⇩
Drafting
⇩
Revising
⇩
Editing
⇩
Publishing

155

Objectives

Spelling and Writing

Students will
• **proofread** a letter.
• **use** the writing process to write a letter of appeal.
• **proofread** their writing.

Using the Writing Process

Before assigning **Write a Letter,** see pages 258–259 in the Student Edition for a complete review of the writing process and additional writing assignments. You may also wish to refer to pages Z12–Z13 in the Teacher Edition.

Keeping a Spelling Journal

Encourage students to record the words they misspelled on the weekly test in a personal spelling journal. These words may be recycled for future study. Students may also wish to include words from their writing. See pages Z12–Z13 in the Teacher Edition for more information.

---

16. He thinks **he'll** have enough juice to drink.
17. The children **aren't** going to choose the colors.
18. I can see **you've** come a long way in your spelling.
19. They knew **they'd** stumble on the curb.
20. We feel as though **we've** seen enough of the circus.

Option 2:
Multiple Spelling Words Per Sentence
(See procedures on pages Z10–Z11.)

1. She knows **I'd** help her if **she'd** ask.
2. I think **he'd** come along if **you'd** invite him.
3. Tomorrow **she'll** ask you if **you're** able to go to the game.
4. If **you've** got tickets to the game, be sure you **aren't** late.
5. Since **I've** seen the show, **let's** leave early.
6. They said **they'd** help you pack if you **haven't** done it yet.
7. Mother **hadn't** seen her friend because she **wasn't** home.
8. He **hasn't** missed a day of school since **we've** lived here.
9. If **you'll** climb the tree, **we'll** climb it.
10. If **they'll** listen, **he'll** talk to them.

Option 3:
Standardized Test
(See *Teacher Resource Book,* Unit 25.)

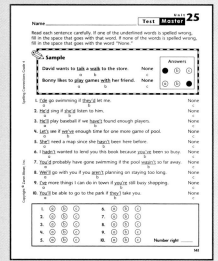

Unit 25 Test Master

Objectives

Strategy Words

Students will

- **review** words studied previously that are related to the spelling strategy.
- **preview** unknown words that are related to the spelling strategy.

Remind the students that the **Strategy Words** are related to the spelling patterns they have studied in this unit. The **Review Words** are below grade level, and the **Preview Words** are above grade level. You may wish to use the following sentences to introduce the words in context.

Review Words:
Words From Grade 3

1. I **can't** seem to get this paint off my hands.
2. We **didn't** get to go to the circus this year.
3. My sister **doesn't** like to leave her room messy.
4. **I'll** try to get my work finished before my friend comes.
5. I know that **I'm** going to spell all these words correctly.

Preview Words:
Words From Grade 5

6. The little boy **couldn't** reach the cookie jar.
7. Mark and Gloria **weren't** going to the park with us.
8. I thought **we'd** have a salad with dinner.
9. Do you know **who's** going to be at the party at Heather's house?
10. All **who've** met Kwan speak well of him.

Review Words

1. can't
2. I'll
3. didn't
4. I'm
5. doesn't

Preview Words

6. weren't
7. who've
8. couldn't
9. we'd
10. who's

Unit 25 enrichment

Vocabulary

Strategy Words

Review Words: Contractions

Write the word from the box that fits each definition or clue.

can't	didn't	doesn't	I'll	I'm

1. It means "not able to."
2. It combines a pronoun and the word **will**.
3. It combines a past tense verb with **not**.
4. It combines a pronoun and the word **am**.
5. It is the opposite of **does**.

Preview Words: Contractions

Write the word from the box that is the contraction for each pair of words.

couldn't	weren't	we'd	who's	who've

6. were not
7. who have
8. could not

9. we would *or* we had
10. who is

WHO'S

156

Unit 25 RECAP

You may wish to assign the **Unit 25 Homework Master** (*Teacher Resource Book,* Unit 25) as a fun way to recap the spelling words.

Unit 25 Homework Master

Name _____

Homework Master 25

Write a pronoun from the first column and a verb from the second column that go together to form a spelling word that is a contraction for the two words. Then write the spelling word. The first one is done as an example.

| I you he she we they | would will are have |

1. *I* + *would* = *I'd*
2. ___ + ___ = ___
3. ___ + ___ = ___
4. ___ + ___ = ___
5. ___ + ___ = ___
6. ___ + ___ = ___
7. ___ + ___ = ___
8. ___ + ___ = ___
9. ___ + ___ = ___
10. ___ + ___ = ___
11. ___ + ___ = ___
12. ___ + ___ = ___
13. ___ + ___ = ___
14. ___ + ___ = ___

Write the two words the contraction stands for.

15. aren't = ___ + ___
16. hadn't = ___ + ___
17. let's = ___ + ___
18. hasn't = ___ + ___
19. wasn't = ___ + ___
20. haven't = ___ + ___

142

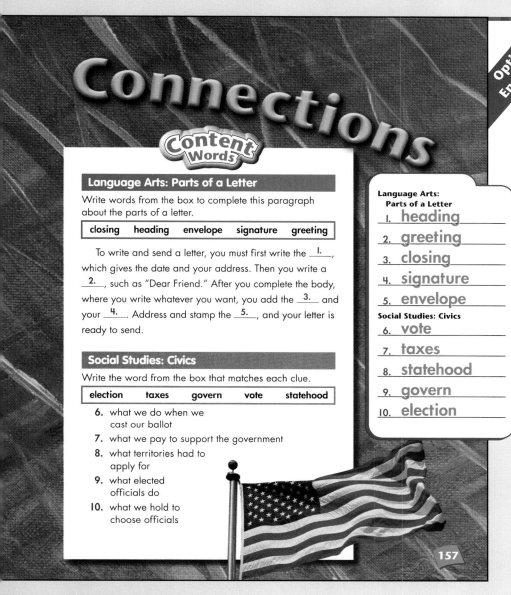

Connections

Content Words

Language Arts: Parts of a Letter

Write words from the box to complete this paragraph about the parts of a letter.

| closing | heading | envelope | signature | greeting |

To write and send a letter, you must first write the __1.__, which gives the date and your address. Then you write a __2.__, such as "Dear Friend." After you complete the body, where you write whatever you want, you add the __3.__ and your __4.__. Address and stamp the __5.__, and your letter is ready to send.

Social Studies: Civics

Write the word from the box that matches each clue.

| election | taxes | govern | vote | statehood |

6. what we do when we cast our ballot
7. what we pay to support the government
8. what territories had to apply for
9. what elected officials do
10. what we hold to choose officials

157

Language Arts: Parts of a Letter
1. heading
2. greeting
3. closing
4. signature
5. envelope

Social Studies: Civics
6. vote
7. taxes
8. statehood
9. govern
10. election

Objectives

Content Words

Students will
• **expand** vocabulary with content-related words.
• **relate** the spelling strategy to words outside the basic spelling list.

Content Words

Language Arts: Parts of a Letter

Review the meanings of these words with the students. You may wish to use these sentences to introduce the words in context.

1. The **closing** of a letter should be followed by a comma.
2. The **heading** goes at the top of the letter.
3. Remember to address the **envelope** correctly and neatly.
4. Your **signature** should be written by hand in cursive, not typewritten or hand-printed.
5. Each letter opens with a **greeting**.

Encourage the students to use these words to make a poster showing the main parts of a letter.

Social Studies: Civics

Review the meanings of these words with the students. You may wish to use these sentences to introduce the words in context.

6. The **election** of officers will be held next Tuesday during our home-room period.
7. Everyone must pay **taxes** promptly to avoid a penalty.
8. The President is the one who must **govern** our country.
9. It is a responsibility and an honor to **vote** for our leaders.
10. When did Texas gain **statehood**?

Encourage the students to use these words to make a campaign poster for a candidate in an election.

Unit 26 Home Study Master

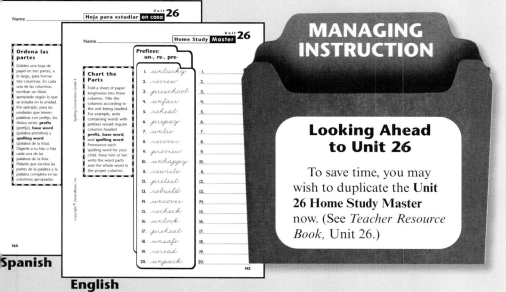

Spanish

English

MANAGING INSTRUCTION

Looking Ahead to Unit 26

To save time, you may wish to duplicate the **Unit 26 Home Study Master** now. (See *Teacher Resource Book*, Unit 26.)

Basic Spelling List

unlucky	rewrite
review	pretest
preschool	rebuild
unfair	uncover
reheat	recheck
prepay	unlock
untie	preheat
recover	unsafe
preview	reread
unhappy	unpack

Strategy Words

Review

preslice	rename
preplan	unkind
regroup	

Preview

prehistoric	refresh
prerecorded	unknown
reform	

Content Words

Language Arts: Handwriting

alphabet	strokes
letters	handwriting
cursive	

Math: Addition

addend	total
facts	arithmetic
addition	

Individual Needs

Challenge Words

uncertain	refill
unfriendly	presoak
reorder	

Alternate Word List

preschool	unhappy
unfair	rewrite
prepay	uncover
untie	unlock
recover	reread

MATERIALS

Student Edition

Pages 158–163
Challenge Activities, p. 245

Teacher Edition

Pages T158A–T163
Challenge Activities, p. T245

Other Resources

Spelling Connections Software
Unit 26 Word List Overhead
Transparency

Teacher Resource Book

Unit 26 Home Study Master
(English or Spanish; students
may pretest on this sheet or use
it for home practice.)
Unit 26 Homework Master
Unit 26 Practice Masters
Flip Folder Practice Master
Unit 26 Test Master

Visit our Web site, www.zaner-bloser.com

OBJECTIVES

Spelling and Thinking

Students will
• **read** spelling words in list form and in context.
• **sort** the words according to the prefixes **un-, re-,** and **pre-**.
• **read** and remember this week's spelling strategy.

Spelling and Vocabulary

Students will
• **write** spelling words for definitions.
• **write** spelling words that are synonyms for given words.
• **use** guide words in the **Spelling Dictionary** to locate spelling words.

Spelling and Reading

Students will
• **complete** sequences using spelling words.
• **replace** underlined words in sentences with spelling words.
• **complete** sentences using spelling words.

Spelling and Writing

Students will
• **proofread** a list.
• **use** the writing process to write a list of things to do.
• **proofread** their writing.

MEETING INDIVIDUAL NEEDS
Learning Styles

 Visual

Write the base word of each of the spelling words on 3" × 5" cards. Write the prefixes **un-, re-,** and **pre-** on separate cards. Place the prefix cards on the chalk tray or table. Divide the base word cards evenly among the students. Have the students take turns choosing prefix cards to go with their base word cards to form spelling words. Each time a word is formed, have every student write it on paper. When all of the words have been formed, have them check their lists with the spelling list.

 Auditory

Use the cards made in the visual activity. Have the students take turns placing each base word with each of the three prefixes. Ask them to pronounce the "words" that are formed and to tell which one is the spelling word. (For example, after pronouncing **unfair, prefair,** and **refair,** have the student point out that **unfair** is the spelling word.)

 Kinesthetic

Have the students use a felt-tip marker to write the spelling words on sheets of colored construction paper. Then have them draw a box around each prefix and circle each base word. Next, have them cut out the word from the sheet, cut the prefix away from the base word, and mix up the pieces. Finally, have them rearrange the pieces and write the spelling words on their papers.

Language and Cultural Differences

The **un-, re-,** and **pre-** prefixes may be difficult for some students to hear due to regional pronunciations or language background differences. It is important for students to hear and use these words in meaningful contexts so that they understand the meaning of the prefixes.

Write the spelling words on the chalkboard. Have the students pronounce each word aloud. Next, have them take turns circling the base words and boxing the prefixes. Then divide the words evenly among them and ask them to write sentences using their words. Have them read their sentences aloud.

MANAGING INSTRUCTION

3–5 Day Plan		Average	Below Average	Above Average
Day 1	**Day 1**	Pretest Spelling Mini-Lesson, p. T158 Spelling and Thinking, p. 158	Pretest Spelling Mini-Lesson, p. T158 Spelling and Thinking, p. 158	Pretest Spelling and Thinking, p. 158
	Day 2	Spelling and Vocabulary, p. 159	Spelling and Vocabulary, p. 159 (or) Unit 26 Practice Master, A and B	Spelling and Vocabulary, p. 159 Spelling and Reading, p. 160
Day 2	**Day 3**	Spelling and Reading, p. 160	Spelling and Reading, p. 160 (or) Unit 26 Practice Master, C and D	Challenge Activities, p. 245
	Day 4	Spelling and Writing, p. 161 Unit 26 Homework Master	Spelling and Writing, p. 161	Spelling and Writing, p. 161 Unit 26 Homework Master
Day 3	**Day 5**	Weekly Test	Weekly Test	Weekly Test
Vocabulary Connections (pages 162 and 163) may be used anytime during this unit.				

Objectives

Spelling and Thinking

Students will
- **read** spelling words in list form and in context.
- **sort** the words according to the prefixes **un-**, **re-**, and **pre-**.
- **read** and remember this week's spelling strategy.

UNIT PRETEST

Use **Pretest Sentences** below. Refer to the self-checking procedures on student page 256. You may wish to use the **Unit 26 Word List Overhead Transparency** as part of the checking procedure.

TEACHING THE STRATEGY

Spelling Mini-Lesson

Write **un-**, **re-**, and **pre-** on the chalkboard as headings. Tell the students that this lesson is about words with the prefixes **un-**, **re-**, and **pre-**.

Write these words on the chalkboard under the appropriate prefix: **untie, reread, preheat**. Ask the students to define each of these spelling words. Using these definitions, discuss ways in which the meaning of each base word changed when the prefix was added. For example, you may ask questions such as, "When do you preheat an oven?" (before you bake); "When do you reread a book?" (after you've already read it); "Is untying a knot the same as tying it?" (No; untying is the opposite of tying a knot.).

Tell the students that each prefix in this week's lesson has a specific meaning. Explain that **un-** means "not" or "the opposite of," **re-** means "again," and **pre-** means "ahead" or "before."

Read the spelling list aloud. Choose a variety of words and ask volunteers to discuss ways in which the prefixes change the meanings of the base words. (You may also wish to discuss that depending on how it is pronounced, **recover** can mean "to cover again," as in "to recover a chair," or "to get back," as in "to recover one's health.")

Conclude by reading **Remember the Spelling Strategy** on page 158.

TI58

Unit 26 — Prefixes: un-, re-, pre-

Order of answers may vary.

un-
1. unlucky
2. unfair ★
3. untie ★
4. unhappy ★
5. uncover ★
6. unlock ★
7. unsafe
8. unpack

re-
9. review
10. reheat
11. recover ★
12. rewrite ★
13. rebuild
14. recheck
15. reread ★

pre-
16. preschool ★
17. prepay ★
18. preview
19. pretest
20. preheat

Spelling and Thinking

READ THE SPELLING WORDS

1.	unlucky	*unlucky*	What an **unlucky** choice of seats!
2.	review	*review*	Let us **review** what we learned.
3.	preschool	*preschool*	The young child is in **preschool**.
4.	unfair	*unfair*	He took **unfair** advantage of us.
5.	reheat	*reheat*	They will **reheat** the vegetables.
6.	prepay	*prepay*	You must **prepay** your trip.
7.	untie	*untie*	I cannot **untie** the knot.
8.	recover	*recover*	We will **recover** the lost sock.
9.	preview	*preview*	They saw a **preview** of the movie.
10.	unhappy	*unhappy*	The lost child is **unhappy**.
11.	rewrite	*rewrite*	Please **rewrite** the letter in ink.
12.	pretest	*pretest*	A **pretest** prepares us for the test.
13.	rebuild	*rebuild*	Will you **rebuild** the damaged shed?
14.	uncover	*uncover*	We have to **uncover** the pan.
15.	recheck	*recheck*	Let me **recheck** that answer.
16.	unlock	*unlock*	Use this key to **unlock** the door.
17.	preheat	*preheat*	We **preheat** the oven before baking.
18.	unsafe	*unsafe*	Biking without a helmet is **unsafe**.
19.	reread	*reread*	I must **reread** the instructions.
20.	unpack	*unpack*	They will **unpack** after their trip.

SORT THE SPELLING WORDS

1.–8. Write the spelling words with the **un-** prefix.

9.–15. Write the spelling words with the **re-** prefix.

16.–20. Write the spelling words with the **pre-** prefix.

REMEMBER THE SPELLING STRATEGY

Remember that prefixes, like **un-**, **re-**, and **pre-**, are added to the beginnings of words to make new words: **pack, unpack; write, rewrite; pay, prepay.**

158

Pretest Sentences (See procedures on pages Z10–Z11.)

1. When she entered the contest and didn't win, Rhonda felt **unlucky**.
2. Today we will **review** our math lesson.
3. My little sister goes to **preschool**.
4. No one likes an **unfair** rule.
5. Mother decided to **reheat** the soup.
6. Dad wanted to **prepay** his taxes.
7. Demarcus will **untie** his shoelaces before taking off his shoes.
8. She will **recover** her strength quickly.
9. We saw a **preview** of the movie.
10. That puppy seems so **unhappy**.
11. Please proofread and **rewrite** your story.
12. We will take a math **pretest** today.
13. We had to **rebuild** the sand castle.
14. Each morning Joe will **uncover** his canary's cage.
15. Please **recheck** your addition.
16. She has a key to **unlock** the door.
17. The food will cook more quickly if you **preheat** the oven.
18. Crossing the street without looking both ways is very **unsafe**.
19. Shasta thinks that book is so good she plans to **reread** it.
20. It is time to **unpack** our suitcases.

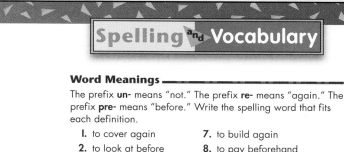

Spelling and Vocabulary

Word Meanings

The prefix **un-** means "not." The prefix **re-** means "again." The prefix **pre-** means "before." Write the spelling word that fits each definition.

1. to cover again
2. to look at before
3. to not be lucky
4. to read again
5. to heat beforehand
6. not fair
7. to build again
8. to pay beforehand
9. to write again
10. a place for children to go before they go to school
11. to check again

Synonyms

Write the spelling word that is a synonym for each word.

12. unlace
13. dangerous
14. reveal
15. sad
16. study
17. open

USING THE Dictionary

Guide words in a dictionary help you find a word easily. If the word you are looking for belongs alphabetically between a pair of guide words, then the word belongs on that page. Write the spelling word that would be found on the page in your **Spelling Dictionary** with these guide words.

18. player • print
19. record • ridge
20. Tues. • useless

Word Meanings
1. recover
2. preview
3. unlucky
4. reread
5. preheat
6. unfair
7. rebuild
8. prepay
9. rewrite
10. preschool
11. recheck

Synonyms
12. untie
13. unsafe
14. uncover
15. unhappy
16. review
17. unlock

Using the Dictionary
18. pretest
19. reheat
20. unpack

159

Developing Oral Language Skills

Review the meanings of the prefixes in this unit with the students. Then write the prefixes **un-, re-,** and **pre-** on the chalkboard. Ask a volunteer to use one of the spelling words in an oral sentence and then write the spelling word under the correct heading on the chalkboard. Have another volunteer go to the chalkboard, circle the prefix, and explain the meaning of the prefix. Repeat the process with the remaining spelling words.

MEETING INDIVIDUAL NEEDS

Providing More Help

Make a prefix wheel for each of the prefixes in this unit, as shown.

Have the students say the prefix and the base words on each wheel. Have each student spin the wheel and say the word formed by adding the prefix to the base word indicated by the spinner. Then have the student write the word on the chalkboard, underline the prefix, and use the word in a sentence.

★Students who need to study fewer words should use the **Alternate Word List**. This list is starred on page T158 in the Teacher Edition. The **Unit 26 Practice Masters** (*Teacher Resource Book*) provide additional practice with these words.

Unit 26 Practice Masters

Name _____

Practice **Master** Unit **26**

| 1. untie | 3. unlock | 5. unhappy | 7. rewrite | 9. prepay |
| 2. unfair | 4. uncover | 6. reread | 8. recover | 10. preschool |

A. Write the spelling words in alphabetical order.

1. _____
2. _____
3. _____
4. _____
5. _____
6. _____
7. _____
8. _____
9. _____
10. _____

B. Write the spelling word that is a synonym for each word.

1. unlace _____
2. reveal _____
3. sad _____
4. unfasten _____
5. nursery school _____
6. unjust _____
7. regain _____

145

Practice **Master** Unit **26**

rewrite   prepay
recover   preschool

...eries of events.

...hen circle the spelling word
Write the word.

146

Objectives

Spelling and Reading

Students will
- **complete** sequences using spelling words.
- **replace** underlined words in sentences with spelling words.
- **complete** sentences using spelling words.

One-Minute Handwriting Hint

Pause after the first under-curve in lowercase **p**. The over-curve ending crosses slightly above the baseline.

CROSS ABOVE BASELINE

Legible handwriting can boost spelling scores by as much as 20%.

Complete the Sequences

1. uncover
2. unpack
3. unlock
4. reheat
5. rebuild
6. untie
7. rewrite
8. recover

Replace the Words

9. reread
10. review
11. prepay
12. unlucky
13. recheck

Complete the Sentences

14. preheat
15. preview
16. preschool
17. pretest
18. unhappy
19. unsafe
20. unfair

Spelling and Reading

unlucky	review	preschool	unfair	reheat
prepay	untie	recover	preview	unhappy
rewrite	pretest	rebuild	uncover	recheck
unlock	preheat	unsafe	reread	unpack

Complete the Sequences A word in each series is missing a prefix. Write the spelling word to complete the sequence.

1. to wrap, to bake, to ____cover, to eat
2. to pack, to travel, to ____pack
3. to lock, to travel, to return, to ____lock
4. to cook, to cool, to ____heat, to eat
5. to build, to fall apart, to ____build
6. to put on, to tie, to ____tie, to take off
7. to write, to proofread, to ____write
8. to catch a cold, to be ill, to ____cover

Replace the Words Replace the underlined words with a spelling word with the same meaning.

9. I will <u>read</u> those directions <u>again</u>.
10. Please <u>look over and study</u> your notes again.
11. I will <u>pay ahead</u> for the book I ordered.
12. I have been <u>having bad luck</u> lately.
13. I am going to <u>check</u> my answers <u>again</u>.

Complete the Sentences Write the spelling word that best completes each sentence.

14. The cook will ____ the oven before he bakes the potatoes.
15. We are going to ____ our home movies before we show them to friends.
16. My four-year-old brother goes to ____.
17. What was your score on the spelling ____?
18. I will be ____ when my best friend moves.
19. Using a tool before you are taught how to use it is ____.
20. It is ____ to borrow a book and not return it.

160

MEETING INDIVIDUAL NEEDS

Providing More Challenge

Challenge Words and **Challenge Activities** for Unit 26 appear on page 245. **Challenge Word Test Sentences** appear on page T245.

Unit 26 Challenge Activities

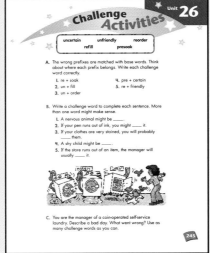

Weekly Test Options

Option 1:
One Spelling Word Per Sentence

(See procedures on pages Z10–Z11.)

1. Will you help me **untie** the string on the package?
2. The boys were **unhappy** because they lost the game.
3. Dad will **reheat** the stew for lunch.
4. We were able to **recover** our lost baggage.
5. Many young children go to **preschool**.
6. The door will not open until you **unlock** it.
7. You must **prepay** that amount before the book will be sent to you.
8. We can begin to eat as soon as you **uncover** the meat tray.
9. Always **rewrite** a letter neatly before you mail it.
10. She will **preheat** the oven before she bakes the bread.
11. Please **unpack** your clothes and stay a while.
12. I want to **rebuild** the old shed.
13. The **pretest** comes before the test on Friday.
14. The **unlucky** woman lost her baggage on the plane.

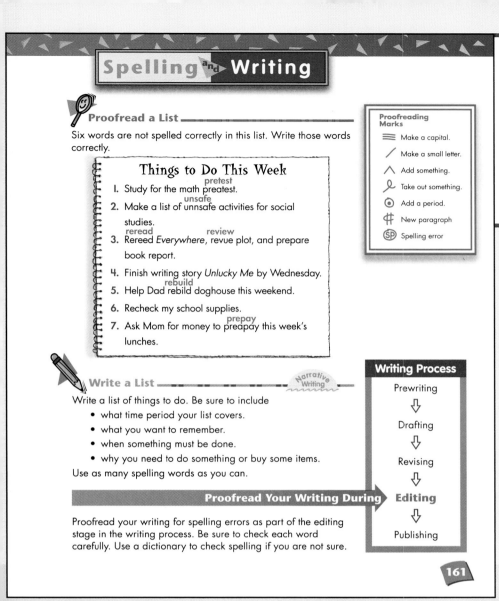

Spelling and Writing

Proofread a List

Six words are not spelled correctly in this list. Write those words correctly.

Things to Do This Week

1. Study for the math ~~preatest~~. *pretest*
2. Make a list of ~~unnsafe~~ activities for social studies. *unsafe*
3. ~~Rereed~~ *Everywhere*, ~~revue~~ plot, and prepare book report. *reread / review*
4. Finish writing story *Unlucky Me* by Wednesday.
5. Help Dad ~~rebild~~ doghouse this weekend. *rebuild*
6. Recheck my school supplies.
7. Ask Mom for money to ~~preapay~~ this week's lunches. *prepay*

Proofreading Marks

≡ Make a capital.
/ Make a small letter.
∧ Add something.
℘ Take out something.
⊙ Add a period.
New paragraph
SP Spelling error

Write a List

Narrative Writing

Write a list of things to do. Be sure to include
- what time period your list covers.
- what you want to remember.
- when something must be done.
- why you need to do something or buy some items.

Use as many spelling words as you can.

Writing Process

Prewriting
⇩
Drafting
⇩
Revising
⇩
Editing
⇩
Publishing

Proofread Your Writing During

Proofread your writing for spelling errors as part of the editing stage in the writing process. Be sure to check each word carefully. Use a dictionary to check spelling if you are not sure.

161

Objectives

Spelling and Writing

Students will
- **proofread** a list.
- **use** the writing process to write a list of things to do.
- **proofread** their writing.

Using the Writing Process

Before assigning **Write a List,** see pages 258–259 in the Student Edition for a complete review of the writing process and additional writing assignments. You may also wish to refer to pages Z12–Z13 in the Teacher Edition.

Keeping a Spelling Journal

Encourage students to record the words they misspelled on the weekly test in a personal spelling journal. These words may be recycled for future study. Students may also wish to include words from their writing. See pages Z12–Z13 in the Teacher Edition for more information.

---

15. I like the book so much that I **reread** it.
16. We saw a **preview** of the new movie.
17. It is **unsafe** to swim alone.
18. Try to **review** your notes before the test.
19. We wrote the rules so that none would be **unfair**.
20. You should **recheck** the price of that coat.

Option 2:
Multiple Spelling Words Per Sentence
(See procedures on pages Z10–Z11.)

1. The **pretest** was not an **unfair** test.
2. Carefully **unlock** the safe and **recover** the gems.
3. The **unlucky** and **unhappy** boy broke his watch at the **preview** of the show.
4. You must **prepay** before your child enters **preschool**.
5. I suggest you **rewrite** and **review** after you **reread** the book.
6. You have to **preheat** the stove to **reheat** the food.
7. Do not **rebuild** the house in the same **unsafe** spot.
8. First **untie** the string, then **uncover** the box.
9. Did you **unpack** the box and **recheck** for the lost part?

Option 3:
Standardized Test
(See *Teacher Resource Book,* Unit 26.)

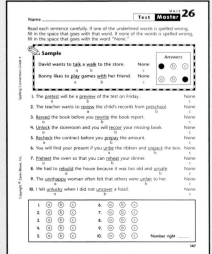

**Unit 26
Test Master**

T161

Objectives

Strategy Words

Students will
- **review** words studied previously that are related to the spelling strategy.
- **preview** unknown words that are related to the spelling strategy.

Remind the students that the **Strategy Words** are related to the spelling patterns they have studied in this unit. The **Review Words** are below grade level, and the **Preview Words** are above grade level. You may wish to use the following sentences to introduce the words in context.

Review Words:
Words From Grade 3

1. We will have the butcher **preslice** the ham.
2. The whole committee met to **preplan** the festival.
3. You need to **regroup** your troop and get ready to move on to the next objective.
4. I think we need to **rename** the puppy something that matches his personality.
5. That was certainly an **unkind** thing to say and calls for an apology.

Preview Words:
Words From Grade 5

6. It is exciting to study about **prehistoric** times.
7. The message on your answering machine is **prerecorded**.
8. We must **reform** this set of rules to something more appropriate to our class.
9. Please **refresh** my memory about the conversation we had last night.
10. The **unknown** factor in this problem is slowing down our progress on the project.

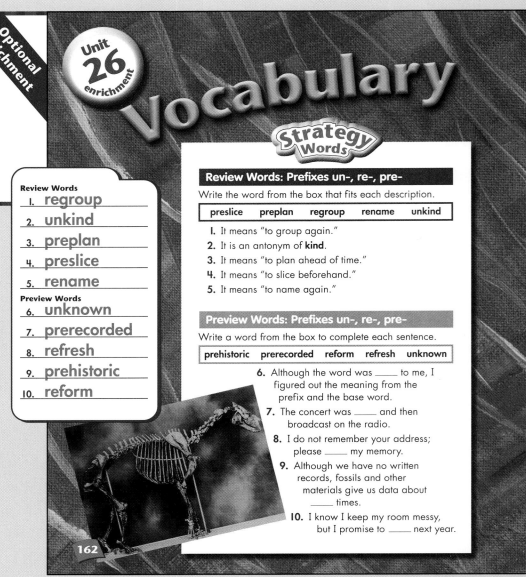

Unit 26 enrichment

Vocabulary

Strategy Words

Review Words
1. regroup
2. unkind
3. preplan
4. preslice
5. rename

Preview Words
6. unknown
7. prerecorded
8. refresh
9. prehistoric
10. reform

Review Words: Prefixes un-, re-, pre-

Write the word from the box that fits each description.

preslice	preplan	regroup	rename	unkind

1. It means "to group again."
2. It is an antonym of **kind**.
3. It means "to plan ahead of time."
4. It means "to slice beforehand."
5. It means "to name again."

Preview Words: Prefixes un-, re-, pre-

Write a word from the box to complete each sentence.

prehistoric	prerecorded	reform	refresh	unknown

6. Although the word was _____ to me, I figured out the meaning from the prefix and the base word.
7. The concert was _____ and then broadcast on the radio.
8. I do not remember your address; please _____ my memory.
9. Although we have no written records, fossils and other materials give us data about _____ times.
10. I know I keep my room messy, but I promise to _____ next year.

162

Unit 26 RECAP

You may wish to assign the **Unit 26 Homework Master** (*Teacher Resource Book*, Unit 26) as a fun way to recap the spelling words.

Unit 26 Homework Master

Name _____ Homework **Master** Unit **26**

Use the letter clues to write spelling words. Then circle the Mystery Word written from top to the bottom under the arrow. Write the word.

Mystery Word:

1. loosen or unfasten
2. remove contents of
3. dangerous or risky
4. to warm again
5. read printed material again
6. form letters or words again
7. to make over
8. to look over or study again
9. show to some before others

Unscramble the circled letters to find the missing spelling word. Write it inside the circles.

148

Connections

Content Words

Language Arts: Handwriting

Write words from the box to complete the paragraph.

| alphabet | letters | cursive | strokes | handwriting |

Our __1.__ is made up of twenty-six __2.__. Children usually learn __3.__ __4.__ after they have mastered printing. In this second kind of writing, the end __5.__ of letters are connected to the beginning of the next ones.

Math: Addition

Write the word from the box that completes each of these sentences.

| addend | facts | addition | total | arithmetic |

6. We use _____ to solve this problem: 5 + 4 = 9
7. The 5 in this problem is an _____.
8. The _____ of the two numbers is 9.
9. 2 × 3 = 6 and 2 × 4 = 8 are multiplication _____.
10. Questions 6 through 9 refer to _____ problems.

Apply the Spelling Strategy

Circle the one content word you wrote to which you could add the prefix **re-** or **pre-**.

j s z 2 a

163

Language Arts: Handwriting
1. alphabet
2. letters
3. cursive
4. handwriting
5. strokes

Math: Addition
6. addition
7. addend
8. (total)
9. facts
10. arithmetic

Objectives

Content Words

Students will
- **expand** vocabulary with content-related words.
- **relate** the spelling strategy to words outside the basic spelling list.

Content Words

Language Arts: Handwriting

Review the meanings of these words with the students. You may wish to use these sentences to introduce the words in context.

1. Most children are able to say the **alphabet** correctly before entering school.
2. Do you have trouble forming any of the **letters** when you write?
3. I was so happy to learn to write in **cursive**.
4. Practice the **strokes** needed to form your capital letters.
5. My teacher has such neat **handwriting**.

Encourage the students to write brief directions about learning to write, using these words in their directions.

Math: Addition

Review the meanings of these words with the students. You may wish to use these sentences to introduce the words in context.

6. When you write your math problem, label the **addend**.
7. You must commit your multiplication **facts** to memory in order to work the problems faster.
8. We will be doing the ten **addition** problems at the bottom of the page.
9. When you get the **total** to the problem, raise your hand.
10. Toby likes to do his **arithmetic** first.

Encourage the students to use these words to explain how to solve a math problem.

Unit 27 Home Study Master

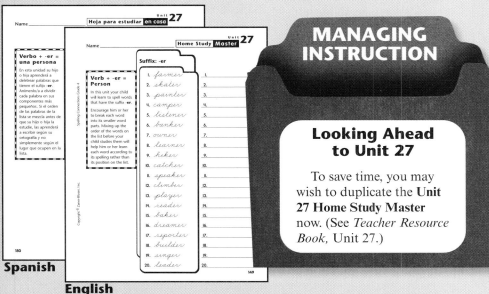

Spanish

English

MANAGING INSTRUCTION

Looking Ahead to Unit 27

To save time, you may wish to duplicate the **Unit 27 Home Study Master** now. (See *Teacher Resource Book,* Unit 27.)

Basic Spelling List

farmer	speaker
skater	climber
painter	player
camper	reader
listener	baker
banker	dreamer
owner	reporter
learner	builder
hiker	singer
catcher	leader

Strategy Words

Review

ladder	sadder
teacher	wider
redder	

Preview

commander	pitcher
gardener	publisher
homemaker	

Content Words

Social Studies: Pioneers

barter	pelt
hunter	feast
blanket	

Science: Joints

elbow	tendons
socket	pivot
hinge	

Individual Needs

Challenge Words

dancer	forester
jogger	letter carrier
jeweler	

Alternate Word List

farmer	player
painter	reader
listener	reporter
owner	builder
speaker	leader

MATERIALS

Student Edition
Pages 164–169
Challenge Activities, p. 246

Teacher Edition
Pages T164A–T169
Challenge Activities, p. T246

Other Resources
Spelling Connections Software
Unit 27 Word List Overhead
Transparency

Teacher Resource Book
Unit 27 Home Study Master
(English or Spanish; students
may pretest on this sheet or use
it for home practice.)
Unit 27 Homework Master
Unit 27 Practice Masters
Flip Folder Practice Master
Unit 27 Test Master

Visit our Web site, www.zaner-bloser.com

OBJECTIVES

Spelling and Thinking
Students will
- **read** the spelling words in list form and in context.
- **sort** the words according to whether the spelling of the base word changes before the suffix **-er** is added.
- **read** and remember this week's spelling strategy.

Spelling and Vocabulary
Students will
- **write** spelling words by adding the **-er** suffix to verbs to form nouns that complete sentences.
- **add** suffixes to base words to write spelling words.
- **use** the **Spelling Dictionary** respellings to write spelling words.

Spelling and Reading
Students will
- **solve** riddles using spelling words.
- **complete** sentences using spelling words.

Spelling and Writing
Students will
- **proofread** a description.
- **use** the writing process to write a description.
- **proofread** their writing.

MEETING INDIVIDUAL NEEDS
Learning Styles

 Visual
Since all the spelling words are nouns that name people, make word cards in the shape of human figures and write a spelling word on each card. Have each student choose a card and pronounce the word on it. Then have the student write the word and its definition on paper in his or her own words. Next, give each student five sheets of art paper. Have each student select five spelling words and write each word on a separate sheet of paper, illustrate it, and write its definition.

 Auditory
Use the word cards described in the visual activity. Have each student choose a card, pronounce the word on it, spell the word aloud, and state its definition. Next, have the students say each spelling word together. Call on individual students to tell how many syllables there are in each word. Then have each student make a list of the spelling words that have two syllables and a list of those that have three syllables. Ask them to underline the **-er** suffix in each word.

 Kinesthetic
Use the word cards described in the visual activity. Have the students take turns choosing a card and pantomiming the meaning of the word. Have the student who identifies the word stand and spell the word. Continue until each student has had at least one turn to act out a spelling word. Finally, ask the students to copy the spelling words on their papers and circle the **-er** suffix in each.

Language and Cultural Differences

The /er/ ending may be difficult for some students to pronounce because of language backgrounds that do not include this sound. For example, there is no sound similar to the /er/ sound in the Spanish language.

Using a tape recorder, pronounce each spelling word clearly and have a student echo the word. Next, have the student listen to the recording and then evaluate his or her pronunciation. Repeat the process with other students until all have said each word clearly. Have each student complete the activity for his or her dominant learning modality.

MANAGING INSTRUCTION

3–5 Day Plan		Average	Below Average	Above Average
Day 1	**Day 1**	Pretest Spelling Mini-Lesson, p. T164 Spelling and Thinking, p. 164	Pretest Spelling Mini-Lesson, p. T164 Spelling and Thinking, p. 164	Pretest Spelling and Thinking, p. 164
	Day 2	Spelling and Vocabulary, p. 165	Spelling and Vocabulary, p. 165 (or) Unit 27 Practice Master, A and B	Spelling and Vocabulary, p. 165 Spelling and Reading, p. 166
Day 2	**Day 3**	Spelling and Reading, p. 166	Spelling and Reading, p. 166 (or) Unit 27 Practice Master, C and D	Challenge Activities, p. 246
	Day 4	Spelling and Writing, p. 167 Unit 27 Homework Master	Spelling and Writing, p. 167	Spelling and Writing, p. 167 Unit 27 Homework Master
Day 3	**Day 5**	Weekly Test	Weekly Test	Weekly Test
Vocabulary Connections (pages 168 and 169) may be used anytime during this unit.				

Objectives

Spelling and Thinking

Students will
- **read** the spelling words in list form and in context.
- **sort** the words according to whether the spelling of the base word changes before the suffix **-er** is added.
- **read** and remember this week's spelling strategy.

UNIT PRETEST

Use **Pretest Sentences** below. Refer to the self-checking procedures on student page 256. You may wish to use the **Unit 27 Word List Overhead Transparency** as part of the checking procedure.

TEACHING THE STRATEGY

Spelling Mini-Lesson

Write **build** on the chalkboard. Ask the students to name a word that means "a person who builds." (builder) Write **builder** on the chalkboard. Repeat this procedure with **own, owner; farm, farmer**. Ask a volunteer to explain how **build, own,** and **farm** were changed into **builder, owner,** and **farmer**. (The suffix -er was added.) Ask what they can conclude about the meaning of the suffix **-er**. (It means "a person who does something.") Note that words ending in **-er** may also refer to animals or things, e.g., a cat is a **climber**.

Explain that all the words on this week's list were made by adding the suffix **-er** to a base word. Remind the students that a base word can stand alone without a suffix or prefix. Point out that **-er** is often added to verbs, such as **build,** to make nouns, such as **builder**.

Remind the students that when they add **-er** to a base word that ends in silent **e,** they must drop the **e** before adding the suffix. For example, when **er** is added to **hike,** the new word is **hiker,** not **hikeer**.

Encourage the students to talk about the kinds of jobs they would like to have. Write any spelling words they mention in the discussion on the chalkboard.

Conclude by reading **Remember the Spelling Strategy** on page 164.

Order of answers may vary.

just add -er
1. farmer ★
2. painter ★
3. camper
4. listener ★
5. banker
6. owner ★
7. learner
8. catcher
9. speaker ★
10. climber
11. player ★
12. reader ★
13. dreamer
14. reporter ★
15. builder ★
16. singer
17. leader ★

drop final e and add -er
18. skater
19. hiker
20. baker

READ THE SPELLING WORDS

1. farmer	*farmer*	The **farmer** milked his cows.
2. skater	*skater*	She was judged the best **skater**.
3. painter	*painter*	The **painter** stirred his paint.
4. camper	*camper*	We met a **camper** in the forest.
5. listener	*listener*	Drake is a good **listener**.
6. banker	*banker*	We got a loan from the **banker**.
7. owner	*owner*	Who is the **owner** of this farm?
8. learner	*learner*	A good **learner** pays attention.
9. hiker	*hiker*	Each **hiker** wore a backpack.
10. catcher	*catcher*	The **catcher** signaled to the pitcher.
11. speaker	*speaker*	That **speaker** was very entertaining.
12. climber	*climber*	A rock **climber** needs good equipment.
13. player	*player*	The team captain is a good **player**.
14. reader	*reader*	This book will please any **reader**.
15. baker	*baker*	Thanks to the **baker** for this bread.
16. dreamer	*dreamer*	He is a **dreamer** who has great ideas!
17. reporter	*reporter*	The **reporter** covered the fire.
18. builder	*builder*	The house was planned by the **builder**.
19. singer	*singer*	Each **singer** used the microphone.
20. leader	*leader*	He is the **leader** of the band.

SORT THE SPELLING WORDS

1.–17. Write the spelling words in which the **-er** suffix is added without changing the base word.

18.–20. Write the spelling words in which the final **e** is dropped from the base word before the **-er** suffix is added.

REMEMBER THE SPELLING STRATEGY

Remember that the suffix **-er** means "one who." A **player** is "one who plays." A **singer** is "one who sings."

164

Pretest Sentences (See procedures on pages Z10–Z11.)

1. Grandma has worked hard as a **farmer** for many years.
2. Fred enjoyed the performance of the ice **skater**.
3. My parents hired a **painter**.
4. The **camper** cooked a delicious meal over a campfire.
5. Lisa has learned to be a good **listener** by paying attention.
6. The **banker** explained how to open a savings account.
7. If something belongs to you, you are its **owner**.
8. A good **learner** listens in class.
9. We were surprised to see the **hiker** suddenly appear.
10. I am the **catcher** on our softball team.
11. Because Jack enjoys talking in front of crowds, he plans to be a **speaker**.
12. A mountain **climber** is very careful.
13. Salvador is the tallest **player** on the basketball team.
14. Linda is such a fast **reader** that she can read two books in one day.
15. Alan is an excellent **baker** and especially likes to bake bread.
16. Kim is a **dreamer** and is always making up stories.
17. The **reporter** works for the local newspaper.
18. Father enjoys his job as a **builder**.
19. Anaka was asked to be in the chorus because she is a good **singer**.
20. The president is the **leader** of the United States.

Spelling and Vocabulary

Word Meanings

The suffix **-er** can change a verb to a noun that means "someone who does something." Add the **-er** suffix to each underlined verb to write a noun that is a spelling word.

1. I often <u>hike</u> in the woods. I am a _____.
2. Missy will <u>play</u> goalie on a hockey team. She will be a _____.
3. I <u>listen</u> carefully. I am a good _____.
4. Walter likes to <u>speak</u> to large groups of people. He is a _____.
5. My cousin wants to <u>report</u> on sports for a newspaper. He wants to be a _____.
6. Mr. Brown can <u>farm</u> both his land and his father's. He is a successful _____.

Word Completion

Write a spelling word by adding the suffix that means "one who does something" to each of the following base words.

7. climb   9. own   11. dream
8. lead   10. paint   12. read

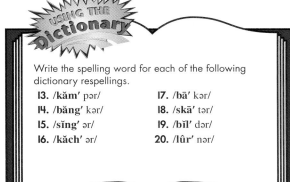

Write the spelling word for each of the following dictionary respellings.

13. /kăm′ pər/   17. /bā′ kər/
14. /băng′ kər/   18. /skā′ tər/
15. /sĭng′ ər/   19. /bĭl′ dər/
16. /kăch′ ər/   20. /lûr′ nər/

Word Meanings
1. hiker
2. player
3. listener
4. speaker
5. reporter
6. farmer

Word Completion
7. climber
8. leader
9. owner
10. painter
11. dreamer
12. reader

Using the Dictionary
13. camper
14. banker
15. singer
16. catcher
17. baker
18. skater
19. builder
20. learner

165

Developing Oral Language Skills

Remind the students that the **-er** suffix can change a verb into a noun. Have students work in pairs. One student writes one of the spelling words on a 3" × 5" card and says a sentence using that word. The partner then takes the card, covers the **-er** ending, and says a sentence using the verb form of the word. The students should continue the game, taking turns using the noun version or the verb version of the word.

MEETING INDIVIDUAL NEEDS

Providing More Help

Give each student twenty 3" × 5" cards. Read definitions for the spelling words aloud to the students and have them write those definitions on one side of the blank cards. Invent your own definitions, such as "one who plants seeds" (**farmer**) or "one who makes a house" (**builder**). Have the students write the spelling word that matches the definition on the reverse side of the card. You may have the students choose spelling partners and quiz each other on the definitions and spellings of the words.

★ Students who need to study fewer words should use the **Alternate Word List**. This list is starred on page T164 in the Teacher Edition. The **Unit 27 Practice Masters** (*Teacher Resource Book*) provide additional practice with these words.

Unit 27 Practice Masters

Objectives

Spelling and Reading

Students will
- **solve** riddles using spelling words.
- **complete** sentences using spelling words.

One-Minute Handwriting Hint

All of the letters of the same size should be even in height.

hiker

Legible handwriting can boost spelling scores by as much as 20%.

Solve the Riddles

1. baker
2. camper
3. learner
4. speaker
5. farmer
6. reader
7. owner
8. dreamer
9. banker
10. hiker

Complete the Sentences

11. climber
12. painter
13. player
14. leader
15. builder
16. skater
17. listener
18. reporter
19. singer
20. catcher

---

farmer	skater	painter	camper	listener
banker	owner	learner	hiker	catcher
speaker	climber	player	reader	baker
dreamer	reporter	builder	singer	leader

Solve the Riddles   Write the spelling word that solves each riddle.

1. I make fresh bread and rolls each day. Who am I?
2. I spend many nights in a tent. Who am I?
3. I study hard and learn my lessons. Who am I?
4. I am a box that sound comes from. What am I?
5. I take care of my animals and plow my fields. Who am I?
6. I spend all my spare time looking at words in books. Who am I?
7. I am looking for my lost dog. Who am I?
8. I see pictures in my sleep. Who am I?
9. I handle a lot of money every day. Who am I?
10. I go for long walks in the mountains. Who am I?

Complete the Sentences   Write a spelling word to complete each sentence.

11. A monkey is a natural tree _____.
12. The _____ captured the colors of the sunset.
13. She is a _____ on a baseball team.
14. Abraham Lincoln was a great _____.
15. That _____ is helping to put up the new shopping mall.
16. We went to the ice arena to watch the figure _____ perform.
17. A good _____ is as important as a good speaker.
18. The local television station sent its best news _____ to cover the mayor's speech.
19. She is a _____ with a beautiful soprano voice.
20. A pitcher and a _____ work together to strike out a batter.

166

MEETING INDIVIDUAL NEEDS

Providing More Challenge

Challenge Words and **Challenge Activities** for Unit 27 appear on page 246. **Challenge Word Test Sentences** appear on page T246.

Unit 27 Challenge Activities

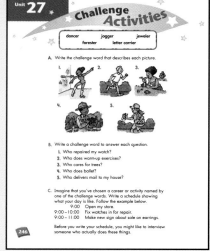

Weekly Test Options

Option 1:
One Spelling Word Per Sentence
(See procedures on pages Z10–Z11.)

1. We listened as the next **reader** took his turn.
2. The **camper** took enough supplies for two days.
3. My good friend is also a good **listener**.
4. The **painter** used those brushes.
5. The **skater** glided across the ice.
6. That short boy is the best **player** we have.
7. A **dreamer** wishes for things he may never have.
8. The bread was made by the **baker**.
9. Father will be the **catcher** for our baseball game.
10. This man is the **speaker** who will give the talk tonight.
11. The **leader** is at the front of the line.
12. Dad is a **singer** in the show.
13. The **hiker** climbed to the top before resting.
14. I returned the lost keys to the **owner**.
15. Whoever built this house is a good **builder**.

Spelling and Writing

 **Proofread a Description** _____

Six words are not spelled correctly in this description. Write those words correctly.

> ### A Lesson on Ice
>
> *painter*
> No paintir could have produced such a colorful picture. No reporter could have imagined a more *skater* exciting show. Each skatr, wearing a splendid costume, glided onto the ice. *speaker* The speeker roared the name of each star as he or she whipped around the arena, following the *leader* leeder of the group. The beautiful scene was the work of a *dreamer* dremer, and everyone in the audience became a *learner* leerner.

Proofreading Marks

- ☰ Make a capital.
- / Make a small letter.
- ∧ Add something.
- ℒ Take out something.
- ⊙ Add a period.
- ⌗ New paragraph
- ⑤Ⓟ Spelling error

✏ **Write a Description** _____ *Descriptive Writing*

Write a description of something you have seen. Be sure to include information such as

- where you were.
- what you saw.
- what you heard.
- how you felt.

Use as many spelling words as you can.

Proofread Your Writing During → Editing

Proofread your writing for spelling errors as part of the editing stage in the writing process. Be sure to check each word carefully. Use a dictionary to check spelling if you are not sure.

Writing Process

Prewriting
⇩
Drafting
⇩
Revising
⇩
Editing
⇩
Publishing

167

Objectives

Spelling and Writing

Students will
- **proofread** a description.
- **use** the writing process to write a description.
- **proofread** their writing.

Using the Writing Process

Before assigning **Write a Description,** see pages 258–259 in the Student Edition for a complete review of the writing process and additional writing assignments. You may also wish to refer to pages Z12–Z13 in the Teacher Edition.

Keeping a Spelling Journal

Encourage students to record the words they misspelled on the weekly test in a personal spelling journal. These words may be recycled for future study. Students may also wish to include words from their writing. See pages Z12–Z13 in the Teacher Edition for more information.

---

16. When I took music lessons, I was an eager **learner**.
17. He watched the **farmer** plow his fields.
18. A **climber** should wear strong boots.
19. The **reporter** tells us the news.
20. The **banker** will store the checks in the safe.

Option 2:
Multiple Spelling Words Per Sentence
(See procedures on pages Z10–Z11.)

1. A **dreamer** must try hard to become a good **listener**.
2. The baseball **catcher** hopes to be a good **player**.
3. The **farmer** will hire a **painter** to paint the house.
4. The **camper** is the **owner** of that tent.
5. That **hiker** is a good **climber**.
6. The **reporter** took notes as the **speaker** talked.
7. The **builder** hopes the **banker** will loan him some money.
8. The **skater** visited the **baker** on her way home from practice.
9. A good **reader** often seems to be a good **learner** as well.
10. That **singer** has been the group's **leader** for years.

Option 3:
Standardized Test
(See *Teacher Resource Book,* Unit 27.)

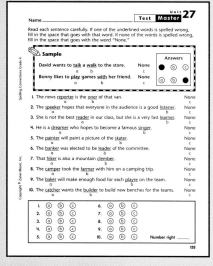

Unit 27 Test Master

T167

Objectives

Strategy Words

Students will

- **review** words studied previously that are related to the spelling strategy.
- **preview** unknown words that are related to the spelling strategy.

Remind the students that the **Strategy Words** relate to the spelling patterns they have studied in this unit. The **Review Words** are below grade level, and the **Preview Words** are above grade level. You may wish to use the following sentences to introduce the words in context.

Review Words:
Words From Grade 3

1. My dad will have to climb up the **ladder** to clean the leaves out of the gutters.
2. Our **teacher** told us about the Incas today.
3. When I am embarrassed, my face gets **redder** than an apple.
4. The movie got **sadder** by the minute.
5. One box is **wider** than the other.

Preview Words:
Words From Grade 5

6. The **commander** of the troop will speak to us now.
7. My sister is a **gardener,** and my brother likes to train horses.
8. A **homemaker** has a lot of responsibility and can stay busy every hour of the day.
9. Dakota is the **pitcher** for our team.
10. The **publisher** of the new book has many people working at the printing shop.

Review Words

1. teacher
2. sadder
3. redder
4. wider
5. ladder

Preview Words

6. pitcher
7. gardener
8. publisher
9. commander
10. homemaker

Vocabulary

Strategy Words

Review Words: Suffix -er

Write the word from the box that uses **-er** in each of the following ways.

ladder	teacher	redder	sadder	wider

1. The base word and the suffix **-er** mean "one who teaches."
2. The base word and the suffix **-er** mean "more sad."
3. The base word and the suffix **-er** mean "more red."
4. The base word and the suffix **-er** mean "more wide."
5. The **-er** is not a suffix. It is part of a word that means "a structure to climb on."

Preview Words: Suffix -er

Write the word from the box that fits each meaning.

commander	gardener	homemaker
pitcher	publisher	

6. one who pitches
7. one who gardens
8. one who publishes
9. one who commands
10. one who keeps or makes a home

168

Unit 27 RECAP

You may wish to assign the **Unit 27 Homework Master** (*Teacher Resource Book,* Unit 27) as a fun way to recap the spelling words.

Unit 27 Homework Master

Name

Homework Master 27

Circle the spelling words hidden in the puzzle.

```
r b a k e r b c a m p e r
e u p e a r b a c k e r s
p i a y b r a m o r a p k
r l i s t e n e r m s l a
e d n p r a k r e c i a t
i e t e o d e a p l n y r
d r e a m e r r o i g e e
e d r k o r f a r m e r s
l e a r n e r r e m a a
a r m l e a d e r r e r t
c a c h r t h s e w s c e
h c a t c h e r h i k e r
```

Use a spelling word to label each picture. Then draw two pictures of your own and label them with spelling words. Each one should show "one who" does something special.

1.
2.
3.
4.
5.
6.

154

Connections

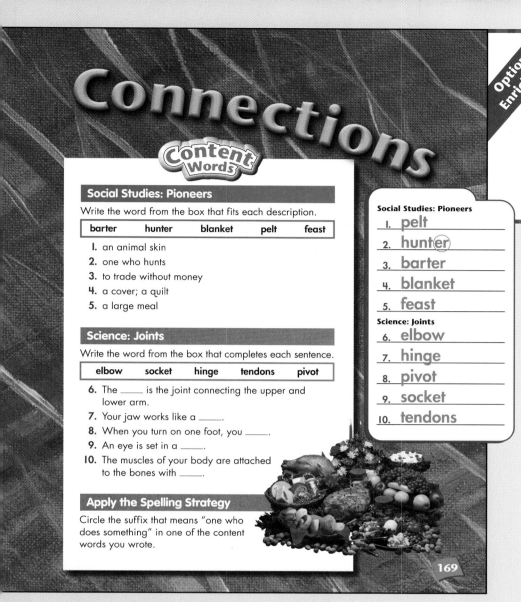

Content Words

Social Studies: Pioneers

Write the word from the box that fits each description.

barter	hunter	blanket	pelt	feast

1. an animal skin
2. one who hunts
3. to trade without money
4. a cover; a quilt
5. a large meal

Science: Joints

Write the word from the box that completes each sentence.

elbow	socket	hinge	tendons	pivot

6. The _____ is the joint connecting the upper and lower arm.
7. Your jaw works like a _____.
8. When you turn on one foot, you _____.
9. An eye is set in a _____.
10. The muscles of your body are attached to the bones with _____.

Apply the Spelling Strategy

Circle the suffix that means "one who does something" in one of the content words you wrote.

Social Studies: Pioneers
1. pelt
2. hunt(er)
3. barter
4. blanket
5. feast

Science: Joints
6. elbow
7. hinge
8. pivot
9. socket
10. tendons

169

Objectives

Content Words

Students will
- **expand** vocabulary with content-related words.
- **relate** the spelling strategy to words outside the basic spelling list.

Content Words

Social Studies: Pioneers

Review the meanings of these words with the students. You may wish to use these sentences to introduce the words in context.

1. At the open-air market we could **barter** with the merchants.
2. The deer disappeared when the **hunter** arrived.
3. We will need more than one **blanket** for the camping trip.
4. The animal **pelt** had been treated until it was very soft.
5. My parents planned a great **feast** for our family reunion.

Encourage the students to use these words in a paragraph about early settlers of America.

Science: Joints

Review the meanings of these words with the students. You may wish to use these sentences to introduce the words in context.

6. I hit my **elbow** on the corner of the door and made it sting.
7. The shoulder fits into a **socket** that allows it to move in a certain range.
8. A **hinge** allows a mollusk to open and close its shell.
9. There are many **tendons** in the arms and legs.
10. Can you **pivot** on your toes?

Encourage the students to make simple illustrations using these words as labels.

Unit 28 Home Study Master

Spanish

English

MANAGING INSTRUCTION

Looking Ahead to Unit 28

To save time, you may wish to duplicate the **Unit 28 Home Study Master** now. (See *Teacher Resource Book,* Unit 28.)

Basic Spelling List

joyful	powerful
helpless	helpful
restful	powerless
careless	careful
useful	restless
thankless	wasteful
peaceful	cheerful
hopeless	useless
thankful	playful
cloudless	thoughtful

Strategy Words

Review

airless	loveless
lawful	hurtful
landless	

Preview

awful	senseless
beautiful	weightless
homeless	

Content Words

Health: Injuries

ache	swollen
painful	clinic
aspirin	

Social Studies: Fishing

Canada	trawler
haddock	flounder
fishery	

Individual Needs

Challenge Words

boastful	sleepless
skillful	cordless
colorful	

Alternate Word List

helpless	helpful
careless	careful
useful	cheerful
peaceful	useless
powerful	thoughtful

MATERIALS

Student Edition

Pages 170–175
Challenge Activities, p. 247

Teacher Edition

Pages T170A–T175
Challenge Activities, p. T247

Other Resources

Spelling Connections Software
Unit 28 Word List Overhead
 Transparency

Teacher Resource Book

Unit 28 Home Study Master
 (English or Spanish; students
 may pretest on this sheet or use
 it for home practice.)
Unit 28 Homework Master
Unit 28 Practice Masters
Flip Folder Practice Master
Unit 28 Test Master

Visit our Web site, www.zaner-bloser.com

OBJECTIVES

Spelling and Thinking

Students will
- **read** the spelling words in list form and in context.
- **sort** the words according to the suffixes **-ful** and **-less**.
- **read** and remember this week's spelling strategy.

Spelling and Vocabulary

Students will
- **identify** and write spelling words that describe other words.
- **write** spelling words that are antonyms of given words.
- **find** spelling words in the **Writing Thesaurus** and list the number of synonyms given.

Spelling and Reading

Students will
- **replace** words in sentences with spelling words that are synonyms for the words.
- **complete** sentences using spelling words.
- **complete** comparisons using spelling words.

Spelling and Writing

Students will
- **proofread** a paragraph.
- **use** the writing process to write a narrative paragraph.
- **proofread** their writing.

MEETING INDIVIDUAL NEEDS
Learning Styles

Visual
Have the students discuss the types of pictures they might draw to illustrate some of the spelling words. Have them write and illustrate each word.

Auditory
Write each spelling word on separate 3" × 5" cards. On the back of each card, write a simple definition of the word, such as "full of help" for **helpful**. Have the students work in pairs, taking turns reading the definitions to each other. Have the listening student identify the word, spell it aloud, and then write the word. Have the student holding the card show the correct spelling.

Kinesthetic
Write the base word of each spelling word and the two suffixes on separate 3" × 5" cards. Place the base words in one container and the suffixes in another. Have the students take turns drawing a word from one container and a suffix from the other. If the cards form a spelling word, have the student hold up the base word and the suffix card, write the word on the chalkboard, and act it out. If the cards do not form a spelling word, have the student draw the other suffix card and complete the procedure.

Language and Cultural Differences

Some students may have difficulty with these suffixes. In many regions of the country, dialects and localisms in oral language often result in omissions, distortions, or other variations of final sounds. It is important for students to hear and use these words in meaningful contexts so that they understand the meaning of the suffixes that they are being asked to spell.

Pronounce each word and have the students repeat it as they read the word in their spelling books. Divide the spelling words among the students and have them define and illustrate their words. Combine their work to form an illustrated dictionary of the words in this unit.

MANAGING INSTRUCTION

3–5 Day Plan		Average	Below Average	Above Average
Day 1	Day 1	Pretest Spelling Mini-Lesson, p. T170 Spelling and Thinking, p. 170	Pretest Spelling Mini-Lesson, p. T170 Spelling and Thinking, p. 170	Pretest Spelling and Thinking, p. 170
	Day 2	Spelling and Vocabulary, p. 171	Spelling and Vocabulary, p. 171 (or) Unit 28 Practice Master, A and B	Spelling and Vocabulary, p. 171 Spelling and Reading, p. 172
Day 2	Day 3	Spelling and Reading, p. 172	Spelling and Reading, p. 172 (or) Unit 28 Practice Master, C and D	Challenge Activities, p. 247
	Day 4	Spelling and Writing, p. 173 Unit 28 Homework Master	Spelling and Writing, p. 173	Spelling and Writing, p. 173 Unit 28 Homework Master
Day 3	Day 5	Weekly Test	Weekly Test	Weekly Test
Vocabulary Connections (pages 174 and 175) may be used anytime during this unit.				

Objectives

Spelling and Thinking

Students will
- **read** the spelling words in list form and in context.
- **sort** the words according to the suffixes **-ful** and **-less**.
- **read** and remember this week's spelling strategy.

UNIT PRETEST

Use **Pretest Sentences** below. Refer to the self-checking procedures on student page 256. You may wish to use the **Unit 28 Word List Overhead Transparency** as part of the checking procedure.

TEACHING THE STRATEGY

Spelling Mini-Lesson

Write **help** on the chalkboard. Ask the students to name a word that means "full of help." (helpful) Write **helpful** beside **help**. Write **play** on the chalkboard. Ask the students to name a word that means "full of play." (playful) Write **playful** beside **play**. Ask a volunteer to explain how **help** and **play** were changed into **helpful** and **playful**. (The suffix -ful was added.) Ask what they can conclude about the meaning of the suffix **-ful**. (It means "full of something.")

Follow the same process with the suffix **-less**, using words such as **help, helpless,** and **power, powerless.** Guide the students to conclude that the suffix **-less** means "without."

Draw the students' attention to **helpful** and **helpless**. Ask them what they notice about the meanings of these words. (They are antonyms.) Explain that sometimes each of these suffixes can be added to the same base word to form antonyms. Invite the students to find other examples of antonyms on the spelling list. Write their responses on the chalkboard.

Conclude by reading **Remember the Spelling Strategy** on page 170.

Spelling and Thinking

Order of answers may vary.

-ful
1. joyful
2. restful
3. useful ★
4. peaceful ★
5. thankful
6. powerful ★
7. helpful ★
8. careful ★
9. wasteful
10. cheerful ★
11. playful
12. thoughtful ★

-less
13. helpless ★
14. careless ★
15. thankless
16. hopeless
17. cloudless
18. powerless
19. restless
20. useless ★

READ THE SPELLING WORDS

1.	joyful	*joyful*	She sang a **joyful,** happy song.
2.	helpless	*helpless*	We untangled the **helpless** butterfly.
3.	restful	*restful*	The quietness was **restful.**
4.	careless	*careless*	She tried not to be **careless.**
5.	useful	*useful*	A pen is a **useful** writing tool.
6.	thankless	*thankless*	Worry is a **thankless** activity.
7.	peaceful	*peaceful*	May your day be happy and **peaceful.**
8.	hopeless	*hopeless*	Finding the lost coin was **hopeless.**
9.	thankful	*thankful*	He is **thankful** for family and friends.
10.	cloudless	*cloudless*	The sky was **cloudless** and bright.
11.	powerful	*powerful*	Kindness is a **powerful** force.
12.	helpful	*helpful*	We try to be **helpful** at home.
13.	powerless	*powerless*	They felt **powerless** against the wind.
14.	careful	*careful*	Be **careful** not to slip on the tile.
15.	restless	*restless*	He was **restless** with nothing to do.
16.	wasteful	*wasteful*	Not recycling bottles is **wasteful.**
17.	cheerful	*cheerful*	We are **cheerful** most of the time.
18.	useless	*useless*	The toy is **useless** without a battery.
19.	playful	*playful*	Kittens are young, **playful** cats.
20.	thoughtful	*thoughtful*	The decision was a **thoughtful** one.

SORT THE SPELLING WORDS

1.–12. Write the spelling words with the suffix **-ful**.
13.–20. Write the spelling words with the suffix **-less**.

REMEMBER THE SPELLING STRATEGY

Remember that when you add **-ful** or **-less** to a word, you often do not need to change the spelling of the base word before adding the suffix: **help, helpful; rest, restless.**

170

Pretest Sentences (See procedures on pages Z10–Z11.)

1. The wedding celebration was a **joyful** one.
2. When Terry locked his keys in the car, he felt **helpless**.
3. Reading a good book can be **restful**.
4. Take your time and try not to be **careless**.
5. The wheel has been a very **useful** invention.
6. Doing the dishes can be a **thankless** task.
7. The river looked calm and **peaceful**.
8. It is **hopeless** to try to beat her at checkers.
9. I was **thankful** for the lovely gift.
10. The sky is blue and **cloudless**.
11. The train needs a **powerful** engine.
12. Lalisa was very **helpful** to her mother.
13. The old car engine was **powerless**.
14. Please be **careful** crossing the street.
15. She became **restless** during the movie.
16. Polluting water is thoughtless and **wasteful**.
17. I am **cheerful** most of the time.
18. A pencil without a point is **useless**.
19. The kittens were in a **playful** mood.
20. Lily is a most **thoughtful** friend.

Word Meanings

In each sentence, find and write a spelling word. It should describe the underlined word.

1. Tomorrow's party will be a joyful <u>celebration</u>.
2. JoAnn is a careful and hard-working <u>child</u>.
3. The <u>earthquake</u> was powerful enough to damage buildings.
4. Throwing away good food is a wasteful <u>act</u>.
5. The <u>people</u> were thankful for the rainfall.
6. <u>Humans</u> are powerless over the weather.
7. A <u>map</u> is useful when you take a long trip.
8. <u>People</u> who litter are careless.
9. She sent me a thoughtful <u>note</u> when I was sick.
10. My <u>teacher</u> is always helpful when I have a question.

Antonyms

Write the spelling word that is an antonym for each word below.

11. hopeful	13. cheerless	15. thankful
12. calm	14. cloudy	16. warlike
		17. useful

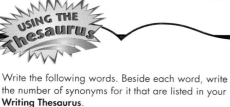

USING THE Thesaurus

Write the following words. Beside each word, write the number of synonyms for it that are listed in your **Writing Thesaurus**.

18. restful   19. helpless   20. playful

◆ ◆ ◆

Thesaurus Check Be sure to check for synonyms in your **Writing Thesaurus**.

Word Meanings
1. joyful
2. careful
3. powerful
4. wasteful
5. thankful
6. powerless
7. useful
8. careless
9. thoughtful
10. helpful

Antonyms
11. hopeless
12. restless
13. cheerful
14. cloudless
15. thankless
16. peaceful
17. useless

Using the Thesaurus
18. restful, 6
19. helpless, 4
20. playful, 3

171

MEETING INDIVIDUAL NEEDS

Providing More Help

Have the students play "Champ." Call on the students in turn to spell one of the spelling words. When the student spells the word correctly, he or she is said to have a **c** (the first letter of the word **champ**). The second time the student spells a word correctly, he or she gets an **h,** and so on. The first student to spell out **champ** by spelling five words correctly is the winner. If time permits, continue the rounds until all of the students become "champs."

★ Students who need to study fewer words should use the **Alternate Word List**. This list is starred on page T170 in the Teacher Edition. The **Unit 28 Practice Masters** (*Teacher Resource Book*) provide additional practice with these words.

Unit 28 Practice Masters

Name _____   Practice **Master** Unit **28**

1. helpful	3. useful	5. peaceful	7. thoughtful	9. useless
2. careful	4. cheerful	6. powerful	8. helpless	10. careless

A. Write the spelling word that describes the underlined noun in each sentence.

1. JoAnn is a careful and hard-working <u>child</u>. _____
2. The <u>earthquake</u> was powerful enough to damage buildings. _____
3. A <u>map</u> is useful when you take long trips. _____
4. <u>People</u> who litter are careless. _____
5. My <u>teacher</u> is always helpful when I have a question. _____

B. Write the spelling word that is an antonym for each word. Then write the base word of the spelling word.

1. capable _____
2. powerless _____
3. unhappy _____
4. careless _____
5. thoughtless _____

157

Practice **Master** Unit **28**

thoughtful	useless
helpless	careless

158

Objectives

Spelling and Reading

Students will
- **replace** words in sentences with spelling words that are synonyms for the words.
- **complete** sentences using spelling words.
- **complete** comparisons using spelling words.

One-Minute Handwriting Hint

The two loops in the lower-case **f** are equal in size. The lower loop ties at the baseline.

LOOPS ARE EQUAL

Legible handwriting can boost spelling scores by as much as 20%.

Replace the Words

1. thankful
2. careless
3. useless
4. careful
5. useful
6. thankless
7. restless
8. cheerful
9. powerless

Complete the Sentences

10. wasteful
11. peaceful
12. thoughtful
13. cloudless
14. hopeless

Complete the Comparisons

15. playful
16. helpless
17. helpful
18. joyful
19. powerful
20. restful

Spelling and Reading

joyful	helpless	restful	careless	useful
thankless	peaceful	hopeless	thankful	cloudless
powerful	helpful	powerless	careful	restless
wasteful	cheerful	useless	playful	thoughtful

Replace the Words Write the spelling word that is a synonym for each underlined word.

1. I am <u>grateful</u> that you offered to help.
2. I will never be a <u>reckless</u> driver.
3. A key without a lock is <u>worthless</u>.
4. Be <u>cautious</u> when crossing the street.
5. This flashlight may be <u>handy</u> tonight.
6. Although not <u>ungrateful</u>, she still refused my help.
7. He seemed to be <u>impatient</u> while he waited.
8. The shoppers were <u>good-humored</u> and friendly.
9. Without help the army was <u>lacking the strength</u> to attack.

Complete the Sentences Write the spelling word that best completes each sentence.

10. A thrifty person is not _____.
11. That nation will not wage war; it is a _____ country.
12. Sending a get-well card was very _____ of you.
13. The sky was clear and _____.
14. The lost climbers felt _____ until they saw the search plane.

Complete the Comparisons Choose a spelling word from the box that best completes each comparison.

15. A kitten with a ball is as _____ as a baby with a rattle.
16. The little lost puppy was as _____ as a newborn baby.
17. Your map was more _____ than mine.
18. The dinner was as _____ as a holiday celebration.
19. The engine in that machine is as _____ as the engine in a locomotive.
20. A ten-minute nap is not as _____ as a night's sleep.

helpless
restful
helpful
powerful
joyful
playful

172

MEETING INDIVIDUAL NEEDS

Providing More Challenge

Challenge Words and **Challenge Activities** for Unit 28 appear on page 247. **Challenge Word Test Sentences** appear on page T247.

Unit 28 Challenge Activities

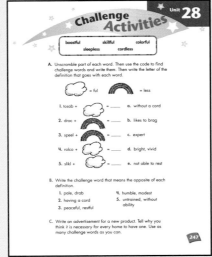

Weekly Test Options

Option 1:
One Spelling Word Per Sentence
(See procedures on pages Z10–Z11.)

1. Paper cups will be **useful** on our picnic.
2. I feel **helpless** when I cannot do something for myself.
3. Do not be **wasteful** with your food.
4. That rusted tool is **useless**.
5. We took a **restful** walk in the woods.
6. That **hopeless** feeling left when you decided to help.
7. The **powerful** engine pulled the train.
8. At first he was **thankless,** but later he thanked us.
9. The boy was **helpful** to his sister.
10. The sky was **cloudless**.
11. Be **careful** when you dive into the pool.
12. His bedroom was a **peaceful** place where he could think.
13. Mother was too **restless** to sleep.
14. I am always **cheerful** on my birthday.
15. We were glad to hear the **joyful** news.

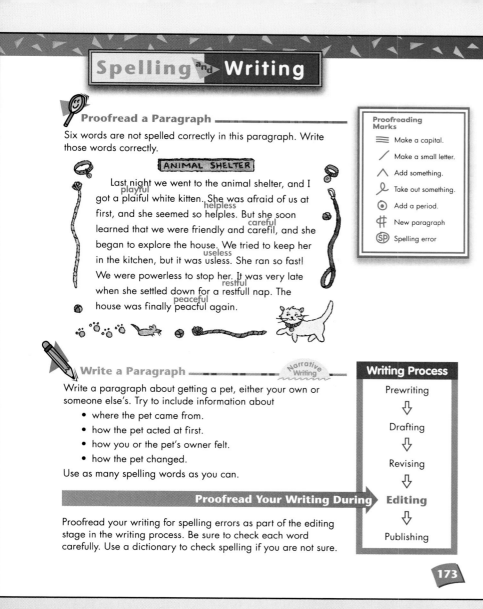

Spelling and Writing

Proofread a Paragraph

Six words are not spelled correctly in this paragraph. Write those words correctly.

ANIMAL SHELTER

Last night we went to the animal shelter, and I
got a plaiful white kitten. She was afraid of us at
playful
first, and she seemed so helpes. But she soon
helpless
learned that we were friendly and carefil, and she
careful
began to explore the house. We tried to keep her
in the kitchen, but it was usless. She ran so fast!
useless
We were powerless to stop her. It was very late
when she settled down for a restfull nap. The
restful
house was finally peacful again.
peaceful

Proofreading Marks

≡ Make a capital.
/ Make a small letter.
∧ Add something.
ℓ Take out something.
⊙ Add a period.
⌗ New paragraph.
SP Spelling error.

Write a Paragraph

Narrative Writing

Write a paragraph about getting a pet, either your own or someone else's. Try to include information about
- where the pet came from.
- how the pet acted at first.
- how you or the pet's owner felt.
- how the pet changed.

Use as many spelling words as you can.

Writing Process

Prewriting
⇩
Drafting
⇩
Revising
⇩
Editing
⇩
Publishing

Proofread Your Writing During

Proofread your writing for spelling errors as part of the editing stage in the writing process. Be sure to check each word carefully. Use a dictionary to check spelling if you are not sure.

173

16. I am **thankful** that you were so kind.
17. I am not **careless** with my homework.
18. The **playful** kitten jumped on the ball of string.
19. It was **thoughtful** of him to send a card.
20. The old battery was **powerless**.

Option 2:
Multiple Spelling Words Per Sentence
(See procedures on pages Z10–Z11.)

1. Do not be **wasteful** with these **useful** old books.
2. The **thoughtful** lady was **helpful** to her grandmother.
3. I am **careful** not to be **thankless**.
4. The temple seemed to be a **peaceful** and **joyful** place.
5. The **restless** child was becoming **careless** in his work.
6. I found a **restful** place to sit under the **cloudless** sky.
7. The **powerful** chief never felt **helpless**.
8. The **playful** child can find a use for even the most **useless** things.
9. I am **thankful** for my **cheerful** teacher.
10. I study hard so that I do not feel **hopeless** and **powerless** when I take tests.

Option 3:
Standardized Test
(See *Teacher Resource Book*, Unit 28.)

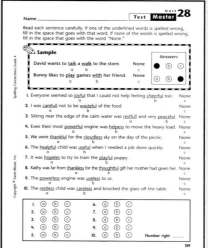

**Unit 28
Test Master**

Objectives

Strategy Words

Students will
- **review** words studied previously that are related to the spelling strategy.
- **preview** unknown words that are related to the spelling strategy.

Unit 28 enrichment

Vocabulary

Strategy Words

Remind the students that the **Strategy Words** relate to the spelling patterns they have studied in this unit. The **Review Words** are below grade level, and the **Preview Words** are above grade level. You may wish to use the following sentences to introduce the words in context.

Review Words:
Words From Grade 3

1. The room was so hot and stuffy, it felt **airless**.
2. Someone who obeys the law is being **lawful**.
3. Because of some poor business decisions, the man who had owned so much property suddenly found himself **landless**.
4. The group of strangers seemed **loveless** and lonely.
5. Be sure and add only one l to **hurtful**.

Preview Words:
Words From Grade 5

6. He had an **awful** feeling that he was going to do poorly on his cooking lesson.
7. That is a **beautiful** tree in your front yard.
8. The kitten we found had obviously been **homeless** for a long time.
9. That was such a **senseless** thing for me to do.
10. When the astronauts are in space, they are **weightless**.

Review Words
1. landless
2. lawful
3. hurtful
4. airless
5. loveless

Preview Words
6. homeless
7. beautiful
8. senseless
9. weightless
10. awful

Strategy Words

Review Words: Suffixes -ful, -less

Write the word from the box that fits each description.

airless	lawful	landless	loveless	hurtful

1. having no land
2. obeying the law
3. causing pain or injury
4. having no air
5. having no love

Preview Words: Suffixes -ful, -less

Write a word from the box to complete each sentence.

awful	beautiful	homeless	senseless	weightless

6. After the fire, the family was temporarily ____.
7. We saw a ____ sight as the sun disappeared over the ocean.
8. It is ____ to blame me for the windy and rainy weather.
9. The ____ astronauts floated around in their space capsule.
10. Because of delays and lost luggage, we had an ____ trip.

174

Unit 28 RECAP

You may wish to assign the **Unit 28 Homework Master** (*Teacher Resource Book*, Unit 28) as a fun way to recap the spelling words.

Unit 28 Homework Master

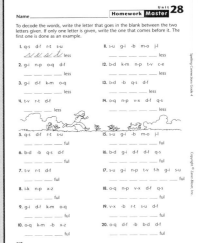

Connections

Objectives

Content Words

Students will
- **expand** vocabulary with content-related words.
- **relate** the spelling strategy to words outside the basic spelling list.

Content Words

Health: Injuries

Write words from the box to complete the paragraph.

| ache | painful | aspirin | swollen | clinic |

I always seem to have my shoelaces untied. Well, this morning, I tripped and hurt my ankle. It was __1.__ and __2.__ , so my father took me to the __3.__ to see my doctor. She said that nothing was broken, but that my ankle would __4.__ for a while. My father asked if he could give me __5.__ for the pain. Then the doctor told me to keep my shoes tied!

Social Studies: Fishing

Write the word from the box that matches each clue.

| Canada | haddock | fishery | trawler | flounder |

6. It is a fishing boat.
7. It is a country.
8. This is a fish with a **dock** in its name.
9. It is a place where fish are caught.
10. This is a flat fish with both eyes on top of its head.

Apply the Spelling Strategy

Circle the suffix that means "full of" in one of the content words you wrote.

Health: Injuries
Order of answers 1 and 2 may vary.

1. pain(ful) or
2. swollen
3. clinic
4. ache
5. aspirin

Social Studies: Fishing

6. trawler
7. Canada
8. haddock
9. fishery
10. flounder

175

Content Words

Health: Injuries

Review the meanings of these words with the students. You may wish to use these sentences to introduce the words in context.

1. I have an **ache** in my side from when I fell the other day.
2. A broken leg can be very **painful** until it has been set and put into a cast.
3. My doctor told me to take some **aspirin**.
4. We need to put some ice on your **swollen** jaw.
5. The **clinic** is open all night in case of emergency.

Encourage the students to use these words to write a television commercial for a miracle medicine.

Social Studies: Fishing

Review the meanings of these words with the students. You may wish to use these sentences to introduce the words in context.

6. My brother likes to go fishing in **Canada**.
7. He especially wants to catch **haddock**.
8. Not too far from here is a **fishery** where trout are raised.
9. The motor on the **trawler** was very quiet.
10. A **flounder** is a flatfish that is very tasty.

Encourage the students to use these words as labels on a bulletin board display about fishing.

Unit 29 Home Study Master

Spanish

English

MANAGING INSTRUCTION

Looking Ahead to Unit 29

To save time, you may wish to duplicate the **Unit 29 Home Study Master** now. (See *Teacher Resource Book,* Unit 29.)

Basic Spelling List

January	November
February	December
March	calendar
April	Sunday
May	Monday
June	Tuesday
July	Wednesday
August	Thursday
September	Friday
October	Saturday

Strategy Words

Review
month	summer
monthly	sunshine
spring	

Preview
bimonthly	twenty-seven
biweekly	up-to-date
daily	

Content Words

Language Arts: Research
define	paperback
library	entry
dictionary	

Social Studies: Pioneers
colony	pumpkin
provide	pilgrim
cranberry	

Individual Needs

Challenge Words
Chanukah	Passover
Christmas	Thanksgiving
Easter	

Alternate Word List
February	Sunday
March	Monday
April	Wednesday
June	Friday
July	Saturday

MATERIALS

Student Edition
Pages 176–181
Challenge Activities, p. 248

Teacher Edition
Pages T176A–T181
Challenge Activities, p. T248

Other Resources
Spelling Connections Software
Unit 29 Word List Overhead
Transparency

Teacher Resource Book
Unit 29 Home Study Master
(English or Spanish; students
may pretest on this sheet or use
it for home practice.)
Unit 29 Homework Master
Unit 29 Practice Masters
Flip Folder Practice Master
Unit 29 Test Master

Visit our Web site, www.zaner-bloser.com

OBJECTIVES

Spelling and Thinking
Students will
- **read** the spelling words in list form and in context.
- **sort** the spelling words by number of syllables.
- **read** and remember this week's spelling strategy.

Spelling and Vocabulary
Students will
- **complete** sentences using spelling words that name months.
- **unscramble** letters to write spelling words.
- **use** the **Spelling Dictionary** to write spelling words for word histories.

Spelling and Reading
Students will
- **complete** sentences using spelling words.
- **write** the names of the months to complete a poem.

Spelling and Writing
Students will
- **proofread** a paragraph.
- **use** the writing process to write a paragraph of useful hints.
- **proofread** their writing.

MEETING INDIVIDUAL NEEDS
Learning Styles

Visual

Write each spelling word on a 3" × 5" card. Then cut the word in half. Shuffle the word pieces and distribute several to each student. Have students study the pieces and identify the spelling words from seeing just half of each word. Then have them write the words on their papers. Have the students exchange pieces with their classmates until everyone has identified and written all the spelling words.

Auditory

Write each spelling word on a separate piece of paper and divide the words among the students. Call on each student to use her or his words in sentences, spelling out the spelling words. For example, a student might say, "In J-U-L-Y I like to go swimming and read books in the shade." Have the other students repeat aloud the spelling of the word. Then have all the students write the word on their papers.

Kinesthetic

Use the cut-apart words from the visual activity. Distribute the word pieces to the students, and have them trace over the segments of each letter with their fingers. Then have them compare their word parts with their classmates' and match the halves of the words. Finally, have the students write the words.

Language and Cultural Differences

The pronunciation of the words in this unit may vary among your students due to regional pronunciation differences or language backgrounds that do not include these sound-symbol relationships. Nevertheless, correct spelling can be achieved without exact pronunciation, provided that the student has the opportunity to associate the meaning of a word with the visual sequence of letters required to spell it.

Post a large calendar in the classroom to demonstrate the meaning of the days of the week and the months of the year. Write the spelling words on 3" × 5" cards. Then have a volunteer shuffle the cards, choose a card at random, and match it to the name of the day or month on the calendar. Continue until all the spelling words have been used. Then have the students write **calendar** and the names of the days and the months in order on their papers.

MANAGING INSTRUCTION

3–5 Day Plan		Average	Below Average	Above Average
Day 1	**Day 1**	Pretest Spelling Mini-Lesson, p. T176 Spelling and Thinking, p. 176	Pretest Spelling Mini-Lesson, p. T176 Spelling and Thinking, p. 176	Pretest Spelling and Thinking, p. 176
	Day 2	Spelling and Vocabulary, p. 177	Spelling and Vocabulary, p. 177 (or) Unit 29 Practice Master, A and B	Spelling and Vocabulary, p. 177 Spelling and Reading, p. 178
Day 2	**Day 3**	Spelling and Reading, p. 178	Spelling and Reading, p. 178 (or) Unit 29 Practice Master, C and D	Challenge Activities, p. 248
	Day 4	Spelling and Writing, p. 179 Unit 29 Homework Master	Spelling and Writing, p. 179	Spelling and Writing, p. 179 Unit 29 Homework Master
Day 3	**Day 5**	Weekly Test	Weekly Test	Weekly Test

Vocabulary Connections (pages 180 and 181) may be used anytime during this unit.

Objectives

Spelling and Thinking

Students will
- **read** the spelling words in list form and in context.
- **sort** the spelling words by number of syllables.
- **read** and remember this week's spelling strategy.

UNIT PRETEST

Use **Pretest Sentences** below. Refer to the self-checking procedures on student page 256. You may wish to use the **Unit 29 Word List Overhead Transparency** as part of the checking procedure.

TEACHING THE STRATEGY

Spelling Mini-Lesson

Write the word **calendar** on the chalkboard and ask the students to name all the words they would expect to find on a calendar page. When all the days of the week are mentioned, ask these questions:

"What do all the words have in common?" (All begin with a capital letter; all end in day.); "Which word has a silent consonant?" (Wednesday); "Which word looks like a compound word?" (Sunday)

Tell students that the name for each day has an interesting history. Ask volunteers to find each day in the **Spelling Dictionary** and describe its word history.

Tell students to stand if their birthday is in **January**. Invite a standing student to write **January** on the board. Follow this process for each month. (If no one has a birthday in a particular month, write the month yourself.) When all months are written, ask the students these questions:

"Which month has a silent consonant?" (February) "Which months have only one syllable?" (March, May, June) "Which months have similar spellings?" (January, February; June, July; September, November, December)

Conclude by reading **Remember the Spelling Strategy** on page 176.

Order of answers may vary.

one syllable
1. March ★
2. May
3. June ★

two syllables
4. April ★
5. July ★
6. August
7. Sunday ★
8. Monday ★
9. Tuesday
10. Wednesday ★
11. Thursday
12. Friday ★

three or more syllables
13. January
14. February ★
15. September
16. October
17. November
18. December
19. calendar
20. Saturday ★

READ THE SPELLING WORDS

1.	January	*January*	The new year begins on **January** 1.
2.	February	*February*	Valentine's Day is **February** 14.
3.	March	*March*	**March** is named for the god Mars.
4.	April	*April*	**April** is a month with thirty days.
5.	May	*May*	Mother's Day is celebrated in **May**.
6.	June	*June*	School vacation begins in **June**.
7.	July	*July*	**July** Fourth is Independence Day.
8.	August	*August*	Many people vacation in **August**.
9.	September	*September*	Thirty days has **September**.
10.	October	*October*	**October** ends with Halloween.
11.	November	*November*	Elections are held in **November**.
12.	December	*December*	**December** ends the year.
13.	calendar	*calendar*	Mark today's date on the **calendar**.
14.	Sunday	*Sunday*	**Sunday** begins a new week.
15.	Monday	*Monday*	On **Monday** we go back to school.
16.	Tuesday	*Tuesday*	**Tuesday** comes early in the week.
17.	Wednesday	*Wednesday*	**Wednesday** falls in midweek.
18.	Thursday	*Thursday*	Thanksgiving falls on **Thursday**.
19.	Friday	*Friday*	**Friday** ends the work week.
20.	Saturday	*Saturday*	School is not held on **Saturday**.

SORT THE SPELLING WORDS

1.–3. Write the spelling words with one syllable.

4.–12. Write the spelling words with two syllables.

13.–20. Write the spelling words with three or more syllables.

REMEMBER THE SPELLING STRATEGY

Remember that it is important to learn to spell the names of the months of the year and the days of the week. These words always begin with a capital letter.

176

Pretest Sentences (See procedures on pages Z10–Z11.)

1. The first month of the year is **January**.
2. Abraham Lincoln's birthday is in **February**.
3. **March** is sometimes a windy month here.
4. The fourth month of the year is **April**.
5. Memorial Day is celebrated in **May**.
6. Our garden has many flowers in **June**.
7. Independence Day is celebrated in the month of **July**.
8. **August** is often a very hot month.
9. In some states, students begin the school year in **September**.
10. Hiking can be very pleasant during the month of **October**.
11. Thanksgiving is in the month of **November**.
12. The last month of the year is **December**.
13. I write important notes on the **calendar**.
14. The first day of the week is **Sunday**.
15. Most people go to school or work on **Monday**.
16. The third day of the week is **Tuesday**.
17. **Wednesday** is named for the Viking god, Woden.
18. **Thursday** is named after Thor, the Viking god of thunder.
19. We will take a spelling test on **Friday**.
20. **Saturday** is named after Saturn, a Roman god.

Word Meanings

Write the name of the month that completes each sentence.

1. In _____ we celebrate Independence Day.
2. I will wear a costume on the thirty-first day of _____.
3. Mom will try to fool me on the first day of _____.
4. I will send you a valentine in _____.
5. In _____ we will have a Memorial Day picnic.
6. When spring begins, in _____, I will fly my kite.
7. In the Northern Hemisphere, summer begins late in the month of _____.
8. The month before the last month of the year is _____.
9. Labor Day always falls on the first Monday of _____.

Word Structure

Unscramble the letters to write spelling words. Begin the names of the months with a capital letter.

10. auyjnar
11. utgsua
12. eembrcde
13. alncedra

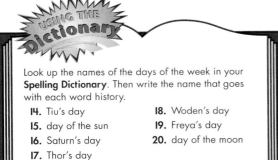

USING THE Dictionary

Look up the names of the days of the week in your **Spelling Dictionary**. Then write the name that goes with each word history.

14. Tiu's day
15. day of the sun
16. Saturn's day
17. Thor's day
18. Woden's day
19. Freya's day
20. day of the moon

Word Meanings

1. July
2. October
3. April
4. February
5. May
6. March
7. June
8. November
9. September

Word Structure

10. January
11. August
12. December
13. calendar

Using the Dictionary

14. Tuesday
15. Sunday
16. Saturday
17. Thursday
18. Wednesday
19. Friday
20. Monday

177

Objectives

Spelling and Vocabulary

Students will
- **complete** sentences using spelling words that name months.
- **unscramble** letters to write spelling words.
- **use** the **Spelling Dictionary** to write spelling words for word histories.

Developing Oral Language Skills

Write **February** on the chalkboard. Have several students pronounce the word and note whether the first **r** is pronounced. Remind students that many words in the English language are misspelled because they are commonly pronounced much differently than the spelling would indicate.

Write **colonel, crochet, diaper, mischievous, sherbet** and **veterinary** on the chalkboard. Encourage several students to say each word as the other students listen carefully to their pronunciations. Then write the dictionary respelling beside each word: /kûr′ nəl/, /krō shā′/, /dī′ pər/, /mĭs′ chə vəs/, /shûr′ bûrt′/, /vĕt′ rə nĕr′ ē/.

Have students pronounce the words again, this time according to their dictionary respellings. Ask them to compare their pronunciation with how the word is spelled.

MEETING INDIVIDUAL NEEDS

Providing More Help

Have the students say each word in unison, clapping softly for each syllable they pronounce. Ask volunteers to write the spelling words on the chalkboard with spaces between the syllables. Next, have the students copy the words in syllable form from the chalkboard, and then have them write each word beside its syllable form.

★Students who need to study fewer words should use the **Alternate Word List**. This list is starred on page T176 in the Teacher Edition. The **Unit 29 Practice Masters** (*Teacher Resource Book*) provide additional practice with these words.

Unit 29 Practice Masters

Objectives

Spelling and Reading

Students will
• **complete** sentences using spelling words.
• **write** the names of the months to complete a poem.

One-Minute Handwriting Hint

A smooth and even line is maintained by relaxing the hand and using the proper writing instrument. Do not press too hard on the pen or pencil or you will get a heavy or uneven line.

July

Legible handwriting can boost spelling scores by as much as 20%.

Complete the Sentences
1. Monday
2. Wednesday
3. Thursday
4. Saturday
5. Friday
6. Sunday
7. Tuesday
8. calendar

Complete the Poem
9. January
10. February
11. March
12. April
13. May
14. June
15. July
16. August
17. September
18. October
19. November
20. December

Spelling ^{and} Reading

January	February	March	April	May
June	July	August	September	October
November	December	calendar	Sunday	Monday
Tuesday	Wednesday	Thursday	Friday	Saturday

Complete the Sentences   Write a spelling word to complete each sentence.

1. After all the yard work I did last weekend, I was glad to go back to school on _____.
2. With three days on either side of it, _____ is the middle of the week.
3. Thanksgiving falls on the fourth _____ of November.
4. _____ is the last weekday but the first day of the weekend.
5. The last day of school each week is _____.
6. The first day of the week on many calendars is _____.
7. _____ is the day that follows Monday.
8. Jim writes the date of every away game in his _____.

Complete the Poem   Write the names of the months to complete this poem.

In __9.__ the new year starts.
__10.__ brings Valentine hearts.
In __11.__ the winds will come and go.
In __12.__ we usually don't see snow.
In __13.__ the green grass grows, and soon
School will end in the month of __14.__.
And maybe we'll watch a parade go by
On our own most special Fourth of __15.__.
__16.__ is usually hot, not cool.
__17.__ sees us back in school.
In __18.__ the leaves turn gold,
And in __19.__ the weather turns cold.
So now let's give a little cheer
For __20.__, which ends the year.

178

MEETING INDIVIDUAL NEEDS

Providing More Challenge

Challenge Words and **Challenge Activities** for Unit 29 appear on page 248. **Challenge Word Test Sentences** appear on page T248.

Unit 29 Challenge Activities

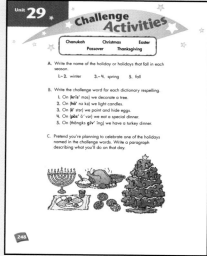

Unit 29

Challenge Activities

Chanukah   Christmas   Easter
Passover   Thanksgiving

A. Write the name of the holiday or holidays that fall in each season.
1.–2. winter   3.–4. spring   5. fall

B. Write the challenge word for each dictionary respelling.
1. On (kris' mas) we decorate a tree.
2. On (hä' nə kə) we light candles.
3. On (ē' stər) we paint and hide eggs.
4. On (pás' ō vər) we eat a special dinner.
5. On (thăngks giv' ing) we have a turkey dinner.

C. Pretend you're planning to celebrate one of the holidays named in the challenge words. Write a paragraph describing what you'll do on that day.

248

Weekly Test Options

Option 1:
One Spelling Word Per Sentence
(See procedures on pages Z10–Z11.)

1. I have to return the sweater on **Thursday**.
2. We enjoyed going to the beach in **August**.
3. I will mark your birthday on my **calendar**.
4. **February** has the fewest days.
5. Mother went shopping on **Tuesday**.
6. Grandmother visits us every **January**.
7. He will play football in **September**.
8. Many people do not work on **Sunday**.
9. We bought a new car last **March**.
10. The builder will fix the roof on **Friday**.
11. I wrote to my uncle in **December**.
12. We went to the dentist on **Wednesday**.
13. Father has to give a speech in **July**.
14. We go back to school on **Monday**.
15. In **May** the bus station is always busy.

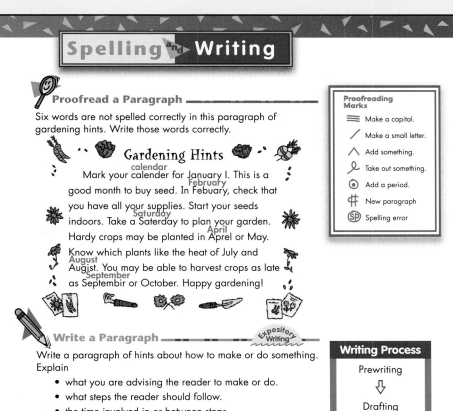

Spelling and Writing

Proofread a Paragraph

Six words are not spelled correctly in this paragraph of gardening hints. Write those words correctly.

Gardening Hints

calendar
Mark your calender for January 1. This is a good month to buy seed. In **Febuary**, check that (February)
you have all your supplies. Start your seeds indoors. Take a **Saterday** to plan your garden. (Saturday)
Hardy crops may be planted in **Aprel** or May. (April)
Know which plants like the heat of July and **Augest**. You may be able to harvest crops as late (August)
as **Septembir** or October. Happy gardening! (September)

Proofreading Marks

≡ Make a capital.
/ Make a small letter.
∧ Add something.
℘ Take out something.
⊙ Add a period.
⌗ New paragraph
🆂🅿 Spelling error

Write a Paragraph

Expository Writing

Write a paragraph of hints about how to make or do something. Explain

- what you are advising the reader to make or do.
- what steps the reader should follow.
- the time involved in or between steps.
- the things to be aware of.
- the advantages of following your advice.

Use as many spelling words as you can.

Proofread Your Writing During

Proofread your writing for spelling errors as part of the editing stage in the writing process. Be sure to check each word carefully. Use a dictionary to check spelling if you are not sure.

Writing Process

Prewriting
⇩
Drafting
⇩
Revising
⇩
Editing
⇩
Publishing

179

Using the Writing Process

Before assigning **Write a Paragraph,** see pages 258–259 in the Student Edition for a complete review of the writing process and additional writing assignments. You may also wish to refer to pages Z12–Z13 in the Teacher Edition.

Keeping a Spelling Journal

Encourage students to record the words they misspelled on the weekly test in a personal spelling journal. These words may be recycled for future study. Students may also wish to include words from their writing. See pages Z12–Z13 in the Teacher Edition for more information.

---

16. We are going to rebuild the birdhouse in **April**.
17. Mother bought a new dress on **Saturday**.
18. Many schools close for the summer in **June**.
19. We invited the fire chief to be our speaker in **November**.
20. We will pick the apples in **October**.

Option 2:
Multiple Spelling Words Per Sentence
(See procedures on pages Z10–Z11.)

1. The **calendar** shows **Saturday** as the last day of the week.
2. I am going to stay with my friend on **Sunday** and **Monday**.
3. We go swimming in **July** and **August**.
4. Father has to work on **Thursday** and **Friday**.
5. Mother rode the train to work in **January** and **February**.
6. Grandmother will stay with us from **October** until **December**.
7. The months I like best are **September** and **November**.
8. We will go to the show in **May** or **June**.
9. We are going to the circus on **Tuesday** or **Wednesday**.
10. I was born in **March,** and my mother was born in **April**.

Option 3:
Standardized Test
(See *Teacher Resource Book,* Unit 29.)

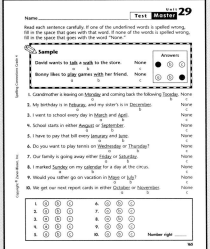

Unit 29 Test Master

TI79

Objectives

Strategy Words

Students will
- **review** words studied previously that are related to the spelling strategy.
- **preview** unknown words that are related to the spelling strategy.

Remind the students that the **Strategy Words** relate to the spelling words they have studied in this unit. The **Review Words** are below grade level, and the **Preview Words** are above grade level. You may wish to use the following sentences to introduce the words in context.

Review Words:
Words From Grade 3

1. Each **month** we have a special project that our class enjoys.
2. Our Girl Scout Troop meets **monthly**.
3. In the **spring** all our tulips will be in bloom.
4. This **summer** we plan to visit my grandparents.
5. The **sunshine** came as a relief after the storm.

Preview Words:
Words From Grade 5

6. Our art class is held **bimonthly**.
7. Our gym class meets **biweekly**.
8. Reading is a **daily** subject.
9. My big sister will be **twenty-seven** on Friday.
10. I will keep you **up-to-date** on our plans for the class trip to the art museum.

Review Words
1. monthly
2. summer
3. sunshine
4. month
5. spring

Preview Words
6. daily
7. biweekly
8. up-to-date
9. bimonthly
10. twenty-seven

Review Words: Calendar Words

Write the word from the box that matches each description.

month	monthly	spring	summer	sunshine

1. happening on a regular schedule, about thirty days apart
2. the season that comes between spring and fall
3. light from the sun
4. a period of time, usually a little more than 4 weeks
5. the season noted for showers, flowers, and warming weather

Preview Words: Calendar Words

Write the word from the box that completes each sentence.

bimonthly		biweekly		daily
	twenty-seven		up-to-date	

6. Since I happen every day, you can say I am a _____ event.
7. I am a magazine that is published once every two weeks, so you can call me a _____ magazine.
8. I am a hyphenated word that means "modern; timely." You could say I am _____.
9. I am a meeting that is held once every two months. Everyone calls me the _____ meeting.
10. My nearest whole-number neighbors are twenty-six and twenty-eight. You know my name as _____.

180

Unit 29 RECAP

You may wish to assign the **Unit 29 Homework Master** (*Teacher Resource Book*, Unit 29) as a fun way to recap the spelling words.

Unit 29 Homework Master

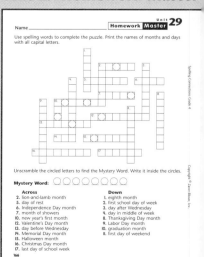

Connections

Objectives

Content Words

Students will
- **expand** vocabulary with content-related words.
- **relate** the spelling strategy to words outside the basic spelling list.

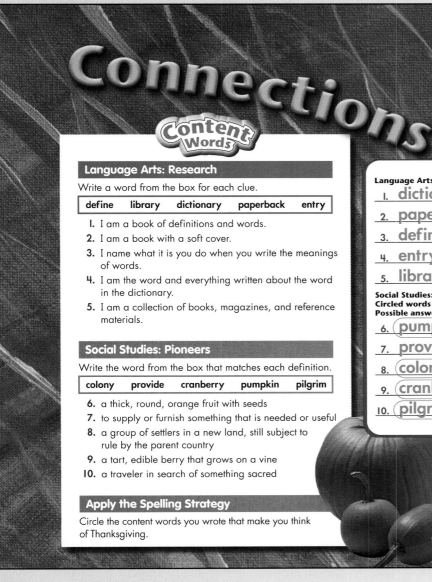

Content Words

Language Arts: Research

Write a word from the box for each clue.

| define | library | dictionary | paperback | entry |

1. I am a book of definitions and words.
2. I am a book with a soft cover.
3. I name what it is you do when you write the meanings of words.
4. I am the word and everything written about the word in the dictionary.
5. I am a collection of books, magazines, and reference materials.

Social Studies: Pioneers

Write the word from the box that matches each definition.

| colony | provide | cranberry | pumpkin | pilgrim |

6. a thick, round, orange fruit with seeds
7. to supply or furnish something that is needed or useful
8. a group of settlers in a new land, still subject to rule by the parent country
9. a tart, edible berry that grows on a vine
10. a traveler in search of something sacred

Apply the Spelling Strategy

Circle the content words you wrote that make you think of Thanksgiving.

181

Language Arts: Research
1. dictionary
2. paperback
3. define
4. entry
5. library

Social Studies: Pioneers
Circled words will vary.
Possible answers are shown.
6. (pumpkin)
7. provide
8. (colony)
9. (cranberry)
10. (pilgrim)

Content Words

Language Arts: Research

Review the meanings of these words with the students. You may wish to use these sentences to introduce the words in context.

1. You need to **define** each spelling word and use it in a sentence.
2. We will go to the **library** so you can research your topic.
3. Keep your **dictionary** handy while you are studying.
4. The new stories we will be reading are in **paperback** books.
5. Look for the **entry** word in the reference book to help you find the information more quickly.

Encourage the students to use these words in a paragraph about a trip to the library.

Social Studies: Pioneers

Review the meanings of these words with the students. You may wish to use these sentences to introduce the words in context.

6. Can you find information about the first **colony** in the new land?
7. There are many reference books to **provide** you with the facts you need.
8. Mother will make a **cranberry** salad for the special feast we are having at our school.
9. That is the largest **pumpkin** I have ever seen.
10. Will you be dressing as a **pilgrim** in the play?

Encourage the students to use these words to write about the first Thanksgiving.

Unit 30 Home Study Master

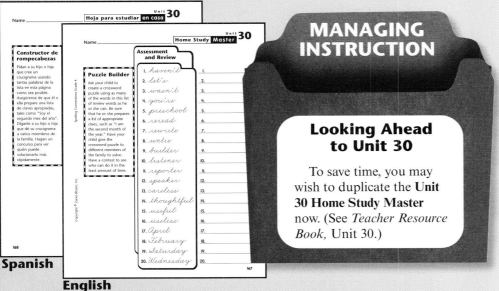

Spanish

English

MANAGING INSTRUCTION

Looking Ahead to Unit 30

To save time, you may wish to duplicate the **Unit 30 Home Study Master** now. (See *Teacher Resource Book,* Unit 30.)

Assessment Words

preset	keeper
would've	harmful
biker	mightn't
painless	unemployed
could've	weekly
endless	should've
yearly	adventurer
kicker	glassful
unload	preflight
retell	blissful

Review Words

Unit 25
haven't*	he'd
let's*	I'd
wasn't*	we'll
you're*	you'll
aren't	I've

Unit 26
preschool*	unlock
reread*	recover
rewrite*	unfair
untie*	unhappy
prepay	uncover

Unit 27
builder*	painter
listener*	player
reporter*	owner
speaker*	leader
reader	farmer

Unit 28
careless*	cheerful
thoughtful*	peaceful
useless*	careful
useful*	helpless
helpful	powerful

Unit 29
April*	Friday
February*	July
Saturday*	Monday
Wednesday*	March
Sunday	June

* Posttest sentences and the **Unit 30 Test Master** test these words. Students review all words listed.

MATERIALS

Student Edition
Pages 182–187

Teacher Edition
Pages T182A–T187

Other Resources
Spelling Connections Software
Spelling and Writing
   Transparencies (Writing Prompt
   and Writing Model) for Unit 30

Teacher Resource Book
Unit 30 Home Study Master
   (English or Spanish; students
   may use this sheet for review or
   home practice.)
Flip Folder Practice Master
Unit 30 Test Master

Visit our Web site, www.zaner-bloser.com

OBJECTIVES

Spelling and Assessment
Students will
- **assess** their spelling success by matching new words to the spelling strategies presented in Units 25–29.
- **connect** new words to the spelling strategies in Units 25–29.
- **write** new words that relate to the spelling strategies taught in Units 25–29.

Spelling and Review
Students will
- **review** and practice the spelling strategies and words in Units 25–29.
- **learn** an alternative spelling study strategy.

Spelling and Writing
Students will
- **review** the concept of adjectives.
- **compose** a narrative piece of writing that tells a biographical incident about a famous person.
- **learn** a proofreading strategy.
- **proofread** for correct spelling of chart heads.

MEETING INDIVIDUAL NEEDS
Learning Styles

Visual
Have the students discuss the types of pictures they might draw to illustrate some of the spelling words. Have them write and illustrate each word.

Auditory
Write each spelling word on a separate piece of paper and divide the words among the students. Call on each student to use her or his word in a sentence, spelling out the word. For example, a student might say, "In J-U-L-Y I like to go swimming and read books in the shade." Have the other students repeat aloud the spelling of the word. Then have all the students write the word on their papers.

Kinesthetic
Have the students write the spelling words with a felt-tip marker on sheets of colored construction paper. Then have them draw a box around each prefix or suffix and circle each base word. Next have them cut out the word from the sheet, cut the prefix or suffix away from the base word, and mix up the pieces. Finally, have them rearrange the pieces and write the spelling words on their papers.

Language and Cultural Differences

The **un-, re-,** and **pre-** prefixes may be difficult for some students to hear because of regional pronunciation differences or first-language backgrounds. Students may not hear or pronounce a particular sound in the standard way. Also, the **schwa-r** ending may be difficult for some students to pronounce. For example, there is no sound similar to the **schwa** sound in the Spanish language. Be aware of the individual problems. Begin by stressing the word meanings. Use pictures if necessary.

Use a tape recorder to record this activity. Pronounce each spelling word clearly and have a student repeat the word. Next, have the student listen to the recording and then evaluate his or her pronunciation. Repeat the process with other students until all have said each word clearly. Have each student complete the activity for the dominant learning modality.

MANAGING INSTRUCTION

3–5 Day Plan		Average	Below Average	Above Average
Day 1	**Day 1**	Assessment: Units 25–29, p. 182 (Option 1 or 2, p. T182)	Assessment: Units 25–29, p. 182 (Option 1 or 2, p. T182)	Assessment: Units 25–29, p. 182 (Option 1 or 2, p. T182)
	Day 2	Review: Units 25 and 26, p. 183	Review: Units 25 and 26, p. 183	Review: Units 25 and 26, p. 183 Review: Units 27 and 28, p. 184
Day 2	**Day 3**	Review: Units 27 and 28, p. 184	Review: Units 27 and 28, p. 184	Review: Unit 29, p. 185 Spelling Study Strategy, p. 185
	Day 4	Review: Unit 29, p. 185 Spelling Study Strategy, p. 185	Review: Unit 29, p. 185 Spelling Study Strategy, p. 185	Writer's Workshop, pages 186–187
Day 3	**Day 5**	Weekly Test, Option 1 or 2, p. T185	Weekly Test, Option 1 or 2, p. T185	Weekly Test, Option 1 or 2, p. T185

Writer's Workshop (pages 186 and 187) may be used anytime during this unit.

Objectives

Spelling and Assessment

Students will
- **assess** their spelling success by matching new words to the spelling strategies presented in Units 25–29.
- **connect** new words to the spelling strategies in Units 25–29.
- **write** new words that relate to the spelling strategies taught in Units 25–29.

Assessment and Review

Unit 25
1. would've
2. could've
3. mightn't
4. should've

Unit 26
5. preset
6. unload
7. retell
8. unemployed
9. preflight

Unit 27
10. biker
11. kicker
12. keeper
13. adventurer

Unit 28
14. painless
15. endless
16. harmful
17. glassful
18. blissful

Unit 29
19. yearly
20. weekly

182

Assessment / Units 25–29

Each Assessment Word in the box fits one of the spelling strategies you have studied over the past five weeks. Read the spelling strategies. Then write each Assessment Word under the unit number it fits.

Unit 25 _____

1.–4. A contraction is a shortened form of two words: **you're** means **you are.** An apostrophe (') shows where letters have been left out.

Unit 26 _____

5.–9. Prefixes, like **un-, re-,** and **pre-,** are added to the beginnings of words to make new words: **pack, unpack; write, rewrite; pay, prepay.**

Unit 27 _____

10.–13. The suffix **-er** means "one who." A **player** is "one who plays." A **singer** is "one who sings."

Unit 28 _____

14.–18. When you add **-ful** or **-less** to a word, you often do not need to change the spelling of the base word before adding the suffix: **help, helpful; rest, restless.**

Unit 29 _____

19.–20. It is important to learn to spell the names of the months of the year and the days of the week.

preset
would've
biker
painless
could've
endless
yearly
kicker
unload
retell
keeper
harmful
mightn't
unemployed
weekly
should've
adventurer
glassful
preflight
blissful

ASSESSMENT: UNITS 25–29

Option 1

Assessment Option 1 is the test that appears in the Student Edition on page 182. You may wish to have students take this test to determine their ability to recognize the spelling strategy in each unit and to match words not previously taught to that strategy. **Assessment Option 1** also serves as additional review and practice.

Option 2

Assessment Option 2 is a dictation test using the sentences on page T183. This test assesses students' ability to spell words not previously taught but that are exemplars of a spelling strategy. This test more specifically assesses students' ability to apply the spelling knowledge they have learned.

In either assessment test option, the words are identified by unit in the Teacher Edition. You may wish to index those misspelled words to review exercises that follow in this unit. Determine which units students need to review and use additional unit exercises found in this **Assessment and Review Unit** for reteaching the skill in a more focused way.

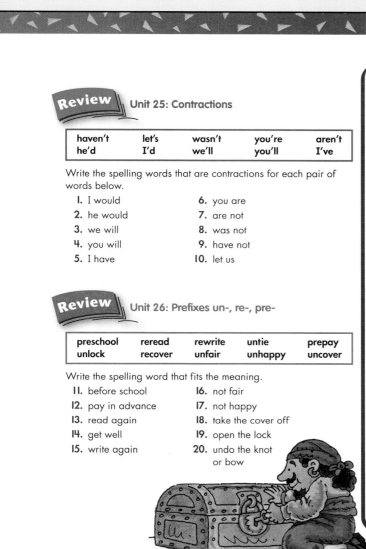

Review — Unit 25: Contractions

haven't	let's	wasn't	you're	aren't
he'd	I'd	we'll	you'll	I've

Write the spelling words that are contractions for each pair of words below.

1. I would
2. he would
3. we will
4. you will
5. I have

6. you are
7. are not
8. was not
9. have not
10. let us

Review — Unit 26: Prefixes un-, re-, pre-

preschool	reread	rewrite	untie	prepay
unlock	recover	unfair	unhappy	uncover

Write the spelling word that fits the meaning.

11. before school
12. pay in advance
13. read again
14. get well
15. write again

16. not fair
17. not happy
18. take the cover off
19. open the lock
20. undo the knot or bow

Unit 25
1. I'd
2. he'd
3. we'll
4. you'll
5. I've
6. you're
7. aren't
8. wasn't
9. haven't
10. let's

Unit 26
11. preschool
12. prepay
13. reread
14. recover
15. rewrite
16. unfair
17. unhappy
18. uncover
19. unlock
20. untie

183

Objectives

Spelling and Review

Students will
• **review** and practice the spelling strategy and words in Unit 25.
• **review** and practice the spelling strategy and words in Unit 26.

Assessing Progress: The Spelling Journal

If your students have been keeping a personal spelling journal, a periodical review of these journals can be a rich assessment tool. Students should include the words they have misspelled from each unit spelling test. They should also be encouraged to write the words they consistently misspell in their own writing and content-area words that present a challenge. Being able to discriminate the words in their everyday writing whose spelling they need to master is a powerful spelling skill.

Pretest Sentences: Assessment Words
(See procedures on pages Z10–Z11.)

1. Always **preset** your alarm when you want to get up early.
2. If you had been there, I **would've** seen you.
3. He was the only **biker** on the trail.
4. The doctor promised a **painless** shot.
5. This fire **could've** been prevented.
6. Sometimes the day seems **endless**.
7. It is time for my **yearly** checkup.
8. Jake is becoming a very good **kicker**.
9. You should **unload** your suitcase as soon as you can.
10. They asked her to **retell** the story.
11. She wanted to become a **keeper** at the zoo.
12. Poison ivy can be **harmful**.
13. The package **mightn't** arrive on time.
14. This program will help the **unemployed** get jobs.
15. We are given a **weekly** spelling test.

16. Hal **should've** studied for the math test.
17. We read a book about an early **adventurer**.
18. I offered the worker a **glassful** of lemonade.
19. The pilot performed a **preflight** check of the plane.
20. Our vacation gave us a **blissful** change from work.

Objectives

Spelling and Review

Students will
- **review** and practice the spelling strategy and words in Unit 27.
- **review** and practice the spelling strategy and words in Unit 28.

Unit 27
1. farmer
2. builder
3. player
4. owner
5. reader
6. leader
7. listener
8. reporter
9. painter
10. speaker

Unit 28
11. careless
12. powerful
13. useless
14. useful
15. helpless
16. helpful
17. cheerful
18. thoughtful
19. careful
20. peaceful

Review Unit 27: Suffix -er

builder	listener	reporter	speaker	reader
painter	player	owner	leader	farmer

Write the spelling word that completes each sentence.

1. If you farm, you are a _____.
2. If you build things, you are a _____.
3. If you have a role in a game, you are a _____.
4. If you own a bike, you are its _____.
5. If you can read, you are a _____.
6. If you direct a band, you are its _____.
7. If you listen to a speaker, you are a _____.
8. If you report stories for a newspaper, you are a _____.
9. If you paint pictures or houses, you are a _____.
10. If you give a speech, you are a _____.

Review Unit 28: Suffixes -ful, -less

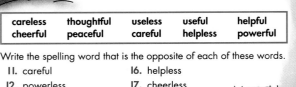

careless	thoughtful	useless	useful	helpful
cheerful	peaceful	careful	helpless	powerful

Write the spelling word that is the opposite of each of these words.

11. careful
12. powerless
13. useful
14. useless
15. helpful
16. helpless
17. cheerless
18. thoughtless
19. careless
20. warlike

184

Bulletin Board Idea

The History of Writing

Display photographs of cuneiform tablets, papyrus scrolls, and illuminated texts. You may want to include the following information under the displays:

Wedge-shaped writing, called **cuneiform,** was invented around 5,000 years ago. The papyrus scrolls used in the ancient world were made from the stems of papyrus reeds. Handmade books were written on parchment, a heavy paper made of animal skin. The printing press made books much less expensive. Before that, most people could not read. Computers make it possible to store entire books on computer disks.

The History of Writing

Cuneiform **Papyrus Scrolls** **Books** **Computers**

Unit 29: Calendar Words

April	February	Saturday	Wednesday	Sunday
Friday	July	Monday	March	June

Write the spelling word for each clue.

1. This word ends with a **long e** sound.
2. This word has an **r-controlled** vowel.
3. This word begins with a **long a** sound.
4. This word has a **vowel-consonant-e** spelling pattern.
5. This word ends with a **long i** sound.
6.–10. List the five spelling words that name days according to their order in the week.

GAME Spelling Study Strategy

Word Swap

Practicing spelling words can be fun if you make it into a game. Here's an idea you can try with a friend.

1. Swap spelling lists with a partner. Ask your partner to read your list and tell you if there are any words she or he doesn't know how to say. Say those words for your partner.

2. Ask your partner to read the first word on your list. Write the word on a piece of scrap paper.

3. Ask your partner to check your spelling. If you spelled the word correctly, your partner should say the next word on your list. If you did not spell the word correctly, ask your partner to spell the word out loud for you. Write the correct spelling.

4. Keep going until you have practiced five words. Then trade roles. You will say the first word on your partner's list, and your partner will try to write the word correctly.

5. Keep taking turns until you and your partner have practiced all the words on your lists.

185

Unit 29

1. February
2. March
3. April
4. June
5. July
6. Sunday
7. Monday
8. Wednesday
9. Friday
10. Saturday

Objectives

Spelling and Review

Students will
- **review** and practice the spelling strategy and words in Unit 29.
- **learn** an alternative spelling study strategy.

Learning an Alternative Spelling Study Strategy

Students should always have a number of study strategies to draw from when it comes to learning their spelling words. **Word Swap** is a fun way of differentiating sound and letter patterns. Encourage students to remember this spelling study strategy and to consider using it with any appropriate list they need to study and learn.

Weekly Test Options

Option 1:
One Spelling Word Per Sentence
(See procedures on pages Z10–Z11.)

1. Please help me **untie** the package.
2. Avoid making **careless** mistakes on the test.
3. I am glad that you are a good **listener**.
4. Many young children go to **preschool**.
5. Those children **haven't** walked to school yet.
6. My uncle is a **builder** of homes.
7. It was **thoughtful** of him to send me a letter on my birthday.
8. If you want to, **let's** look at the birds in the nest.
9. We are going to rebuild the birdhouse in **April**.
10. The tractor was **useful** for plowing the field.
11. I **wasn't** able to ride the train.
12. It is **useless** to think the sun will shine when it is raining.
13. My birthday is in **February**.
14. Mother bought a new dress on **Saturday**.
15. I feel **you're** my best friend.
16. I will **rewrite** the letter before I mail it.
17. The **reporter** tells us the news.
18. This man is the **speaker** I asked about
19. I liked the book so much that I **reread** it.
20. We went to the cottage on **Wednesday**.

Option 2:
Standardized Test

Unit 30
Test Master

(See *Teacher Resource Book,* Unit 30.)

Objectives

Spelling and Writing

Students will
- **review** the concept of adjectives.
- **compose** a narrative piece of writing that tells a biographical incident about a famous person. (See **Spelling and the Writing Process** below.)

WRITER'S

Unit **30** enrichment

Adjectives

An adjective usually describes a noun or a pronoun. It tells what the noun or pronoun is like. Adjectives can tell what kind, how many, or which one.

- what kind:
    The **friendly** dog wagged its **bushy** tail.
- how many:
    We ate **three** pizzas in **one** hour!
- which one:
    This computer cannot solve **that** problem.

A
1. correct
2. dull
3. chilly
4. delicious
5. soft

Answers may differ. Likely answers are given.

B
6. cheerful
7. careless
8. powerful
9. useless
10. thoughtful

Practice Activity

A. Write the adjective in each sentence.
1. Tara looked for the correct key.
2. Don't use a dull pencil.
3. Yesterday was a chilly day for a picnic.
4. What a delicious drink you made!
5. I snuggled in the soft blanket.

B. Fill in the blank with other adjectives from the spelling lists in Units 25–29.
6. Jon wore a _____ smile.
7. One _____ act could ruin the project.
8. A _____ storm damaged trees and buildings.
9. Throw out that _____ lamp.
10. I appreciate your _____ act of kindness.

186

 Narrative Writing

Spelling and the Writing Process

You may wish to use this writing assignment to help students master the writing process. For other writing ideas, see pages 258–259 in the Student Edition.

Explain that students will write a composition in which they relate some well-known true incident that happened to a famous person.

Prewriting Hint: You may wish to help students plan their writing by recommending the chart on this page. Have them replicate the chart, filling in the blanks with details and steps.

The name of the person:	George Crum, a Native American chef
The setting (when and where):	Saratoga Springs, NY, 1853
The beginning:	Guest kept complaining about the potatoes
The middle:	Crum sliced them thinner
The end:	The potato chip was invented

Revising Hint: Remind students that when they revise what they have written, they should add details that help readers understand when things happened and why they happened.

Objectives

Spelling and Writing

Students will
- **learn** a proofreading strategy.
- **proofread** for correct spelling of chart heads.

Proofreading Strategy

One at a Time!

Good writers always proofread their writing for spelling mistakes. Here's a strategy that you can use to proofread your papers.

Focus on one kind of mistake at a time. First, skim your paper and look for only one kind of problem, such as word endings. Then, look for another kind of problem, such as words that sound alike or contractions.

It will take only a few minutes to check for each problem, so this method does not take long. And you'll be surprised by how easy it is to find problems when you look for only one kind. Try it!

Electronic Spelling

Graphics

Computers allow you to make graphics quickly and easily. You can make a chart or a timetable in just a few seconds, and it will look good and help your readers understand certain kinds of information.

Your readers will not understand your charts, though, if the heads are misspelled. The heads are the words that explain what each row or column contains. Make sure you double-check the spelling of these.

Look at the chart heads below. Which have misspelled words? Write the words correctly. Write **OK** if a head is correct.

1. Name of Playor
2. Wednsday Classes
3. Morning Speaker
4. Pet's Owner
5. Games in Febuary
6. Weakly Jobs

Electronic Spelling
1. Player
2. Wednesday
3. OK
4. OK
5. February
6. Weekly

187

Using Proofreading Strategies

Students are often unaware that there are a variety of approaches to proofreading their own writing. Building a repertory of strategies is important to improving students' writing and editing skills.

Spelling and Technology

The advent of word processing, computer protocols, and the Internet has actually increased, not lessened, the pressure on users to be better, more aware spellers. Spell checkers, for example, create circumstances in which the ability to discriminate between an acceptable and an unacceptable spelling is a critical skill. A homophone substitution, a correct spelling of the wrong word, an inadvertent word omission— these are examples of situations in computer usage that require a deeper understanding of spelling principles and a more adroit proofreading capability. It may be worthwhile to underscore this increased need as a whole-class discussion after students finish this unit's **Electronic Spelling** activity.

Unit 31 Home Study Master

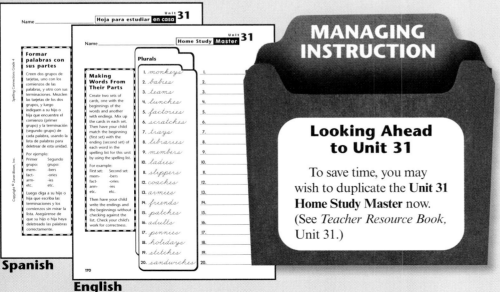

MANAGING INSTRUCTION

Looking Ahead to Unit 31

To save time, you may wish to duplicate the **Unit 31 Home Study Master** now. (See *Teacher Resource Book*, Unit 31.)

Spanish

English

Basic Spelling List

monkeys	slippers
babies	coaches
teams	armies
lunches	friends
factories	patches
scratches	adults
trays	pennies
libraries	holidays
members	stitches
ladies	sandwiches

Strategy Words

Review

apples	flags
branches	inches
drums	

Preview

envelopes	pianos
essays	valleys
heroes	

Content Words

Science: Volcanoes

ashes	volcano
magma	lava
cinders	

Math: Multiplication

factor	times
product	multiplication
groups	

Individual Needs

Challenge Words

menus	hobbies
sponges	strawberries
arches	

Alternate Word List

babies	ladies
teams	armies
lunches	friends
libraries	patches
members	holidays

MATERIALS

Student Edition
Pages 188–193
Challenge Activities, p. 249

Teacher Edition
Pages T188A–T193
Challenge Activities, p. T249

Other Resources
Spelling Connections Software
Unit 31 Word List Overhead
Transparency

Teacher Resource Book
Unit 31 Home Study Master
(English or Spanish; students
may pretest on this sheet or use
it for home practice.)
Unit 31 Homework Master
Unit 31 Practice Masters
Flip Folder Practice Master
Unit 31 Test Master

Visit our Web site, www.zaner-bloser.com

OBJECTIVES

Spelling and Thinking
Students will
- **read** the spelling words in list form and in context.
- **sort** the spelling words according to whether they form their plurals by adding **-s** to the base word, **-es** to the base word, or changing the **y** to **i** before adding **-es**.
- **read** and remember this week's spelling strategy.

Spelling and Vocabulary
Students will
- **write** spelling words that match definitions.
- **write** spelling words by adding **-es** to base words.
- **match** words, their meanings, and their plural forms.

Spelling and Reading
Students will
- **add** the **-es** ending to given words to write spelling words in sentences.
- **write** spelling words to complete a series of meaning-related words.
- **complete** a paragraph using spelling words.

Spelling and Writing
Students will
- **proofread** a story.
- **use** the writing process to write a story about something they did.
- **proofread** their writing.

MEETING INDIVIDUAL NEEDS
Learning Styles

Visual

Have each student illustrate at least five of the spelling words by drawing pictures of the objects they represent. Have the students hide each spelling word in three places within the drawing. Then have the students exchange drawings and find each other's hidden words.

Auditory

Have the students work in pairs. Have one student say the base word of a spelling word. Have the other student spell the correct plural ending. Then have both students pronounce the spelling word together. Finally, have them write the word three times. Each pair should continue in this way until the students have pronounced and spelled all the spelling words.

Kinesthetic

Pass out three 3" × 3" squares of construction paper to each student. Have each student write **e** on one square, **ie** on another square, and **s** on the third square. Write the base words of the spelling words on the chalkboard. As you point to each base word and say it, have the students hold up the correct card or cards that form the plural. Then call on a student to stand and spell the word aloud, showing the appropriate card or cards as she or he spells the plural ending.

Language and Cultural Differences

The plural forms in this unit may cause difficulty due to their irregular spelling patterns. Write the words **monkey** and **library** on the chalkboard. Tell the students that when a singular noun ends with a vowel + **y**, the word is made plural by adding **-s**. Ask a volunteer to circle the final vowel + **y** in **monkey** with colored chalk. Explain again that words ending with a vowel + **y** need only the letter **s** to form the plural. Write **monkey** again on the chalkboard, and add the **-s** to make it plural. Next, demonstrate that a word ending with the consonant + **y** pattern is made plural by changing the **y** to **i** and adding **-es**. Ask a volunteer to circle the final two letters in **library** with different-colored chalk to show that it ends with a consonant + **y**. In this case, the **y** is changed to **i** and **-es** is added to form the plural. As you explain this, write **library** again on the chalkboard. Then erase the **y**, add **i**, and then add **-es**. Have the students spell the two plural nouns in unison. Write the base words of the remaining spelling words on the chalkboard, and have the students take turns going to the board to change these singular nouns to their plural forms.

MANAGING INSTRUCTION

3–5 Day Plan		Average	Below Average	Above Average
Day 1	**Day 1**	Pretest Spelling Mini-Lesson, p. T188 Spelling and Thinking, p. 188	Pretest Spelling Mini-Lesson, p. T188 Spelling and Thinking, p. 188	Pretest Spelling and Thinking, p. 188
	Day 2	Spelling and Vocabulary, p. 189	Spelling and Vocabulary, p. 189 (or) Unit 31 Practice Master, A and B	Spelling and Vocabulary, p. 189 Spelling and Reading, p. 190
Day 2	**Day 3**	Spelling and Reading, p. 190	Spelling and Reading, p. 190 (or) Unit 31 Practice Master, C and D	Challenge Activities, p. 249
	Day 4	Spelling and Writing, p. 191 Unit 31 Homework Master	Spelling and Writing, p. 191	Spelling and Writing, p. 191 Unit 31 Homework Master
Day 3	**Day 5**	Weekly Test	Weekly Test	Weekly Test

Vocabulary Connections (pages 192 and 193) may be used anytime during this unit.

Objectives

Spelling and Thinking

Students will
- **read** the spelling words in list form and in context.
- **sort** the spelling words according to whether they form their plurals by adding **-s** to the base word, **-es** to the base word, or changing the **y** to **i** before adding **-es**.
- **read** and remember this week's spelling strategy.

UNIT PRETEST

Use **Pretest Sentences** below. Refer to the self-checking procedures on student page 256. You may wish to use the **Unit 31 Word List Overhead Transparency** as part of the checking procedure.

TEACHING THE STRATEGY

Spelling Mini-Lesson

Explain that all the words on this week's list are plurals; they name "more than one."

Write three headings on the board: **Add -s, Add -es, Change final y to i and add -es.** Ask students to identify words that fit each spelling pattern. Ask volunteers to come to the board and write each word in the proper column.

Direct students' attention to the column headed **Add -es.** Ask, "What do you notice about the spelling of the base word of these plurals?" (They end in ch or tch.) Ask, "What does that tell you about spelling plurals?" (If the base word ends in ch or tch, form the plural by adding -es.)

Direct students' attention to **monkeys** and **holidays** on the board. Ask them to compare these spellings to those of the words in the column headed **Change final y to i and add -es.** Ask, "Why didn't the final **y** in **monkeys** and **holidays** change to **i**? Why wasn't **-es** added to these words?" Guide them to conclude that because the final **y** in **monkeys** and **holidays** is preceded by a vowel, **y** remains **y**. Tell them that when a word ends in a consonant followed by a **y** that has the **long e** sound, the plural is formed by changing the **y** to **i** and then adding **-es.**

Read **Remember the Spelling Strategy** on page 188.

TI88

Order of answers may vary.

-s to base word
1. monkeys
2. teams ★
3. trays
4. members ★
5. slippers
6. friends ★
7. adults
8. holidays ★

-es to base word
9. lunches ★
10. scratches
11. coaches
12. patches ★
13. stitches
14. sandwiches

y to i before -es added
15. babies ★
16. factories
17. libraries ★
18. ladies ★
19. armies ★
20. pennies

READ THE SPELLING WORDS

1.	monkeys	*monkeys*	I like to watch **monkeys** at the zoo.
2.	babies	*babies*	We have to feed **babies** often.
3.	teams	*teams*	Both **teams** ran onto the field.
4.	lunches	*lunches*	Does the school serve hot **lunches**?
5.	factories	*factories*	Some items are made in **factories**.
6.	scratches	*scratches*	Our cat **scratches** on a padded post.
7.	trays	*trays*	They served **trays** of cookies.
8.	libraries	*libraries*	Most **libraries** lend books.
9.	members	*members*	There are thirty **members** in the club.
10.	ladies	*ladies*	Three **ladies** hosted the luncheon.
11.	slippers	*slippers*	My bathrobe and **slippers** are warm.
12.	coaches	*coaches*	The soccer team has two **coaches**.
13.	armies	*armies*	Both **armies** sent in troops.
14.	friends	*friends*	Amy, Paul, and I are good **friends**.
15.	patches	*patches*	We sewed **patches** on the worn spots.
16.	adults	*adults*	Children and **adults** like to read.
17.	pennies	*pennies*	I have more **pennies** than dimes.
18.	holidays	*holidays*	My sister is home for the **holidays**.
19.	stitches	*stitches*	That cut required fourteen **stitches**.
20.	sandwiches	*sandwiches*	We ate **sandwiches** at the picnic.

SORT THE SPELLING WORDS

Write the spelling words that form their plural by
- 1.–8. adding **-s** to the base word.
- 9.–14. adding **-es** to the base word.
- 15.–20. changing the final **y** to **i** before adding **-es**.

REMEMBER THE SPELLING STRATEGY

Remember that plural nouns name more than one person, place, or thing. Plurals are formed in different ways: add **-s** (**trays**), add **-es** (**lunches**), or change final **y** to **i** and add **-es** (**pennies**).

188

Pretest Sentences (See procedures on pages Z10–Z11.)

1. We watched the playful **monkeys** at the zoo.
2. The twins were beautiful **babies**.
3. Jeff and Vincent are on opposing **teams**.
4. Many students bring their **lunches** to school.
5. We saw several **factories** as we drove through the town.
6. The kitten **scratches** the rug with its claws.
7. The waiters carried the food on **trays**.
8. People talk quietly in **libraries**.
9. Gail and Tommy are **members** of the band.
10. My mother was one of the **ladies** who was given an award.
11. Juana has fluffy white **slippers**.
12. After the football game, the **coaches** congratulated the team.
13. Countries are protected by **armies**.
14. Terry and Diana are sisters and best **friends**.
15. The jacket was so worn that I had to sew **patches** on the elbows.
16. People who are twenty-one years old are considered **adults**.
17. There are many **pennies** in the wishing well.
18. Can you name three school **holidays**?
19. Carmen can knit many fancy **stitches**.
20. I made two **sandwiches** for my lunch.

Spelling and Vocabulary

Word Meanings

Write the spelling word that goes with each meaning.

1. very young children; infants
2. grown-ups
3. animals that have long tails
4. women
5. people one knows and likes
6. places where books and reference materials are kept
7. days on which people celebrate an event or honor a person
8. players on the same side in a game

Word Structure

The **-es** ending added to singular nouns forms a plural noun and also creates a new syllable. Write the spelling words by adding the syllables.

9. scratch + es = _____
10. sand + wich + es = _____
11. stitch + es = _____
12. coach + es = _____
13. lunch + es = _____
14. patch + es = _____

Write the plural form of the words with the following meanings:

15. a large group of soldiers
16. a person belonging to a group
17. a low, comfortable shoe
18. a place where goods are manufactured
19. one cent
20. a flat, shallow holder with a low rim

189

Word Meanings
1. babies
2. adults
3. monkeys
4. ladies
5. friends
6. libraries
7. holidays
8. teams

Word Structure
9. scratches
10. sandwiches
11. stitches
12. coaches
13. lunches
14. patches

Using the Dictionary
15. armies
16. members
17. slippers
18. factories
19. pennies
20. trays

Objectives

Spelling and Vocabulary

Students will
- **write** spelling words that match definitions.
- **write** spelling words by adding **-es** to base words.
- **match** words, their meanings, and their plural forms.

Developing Oral Language Skills

The word **libraries** (/lī′ brĕr′ ēz/) is sometimes misspelled because it is mispronounced. Write **libraries** on the chalkboard. Have students pronounce **libraries** and note whether they pronounce the first **r**. If they do not pronounce the first **r**, remind them of the correct pronunciation and have them practice pronouncing **libraries** correctly several times.

MEETING INDIVIDUAL NEEDS

Providing More Help

Have the students illustrate on word cards the singular nouns that are the base words of the spelling words. Then have the students exchange their card sets with classmates. Tell them to decide what each picture illustrates and to write the plural form of that noun on the back of the card.

★ Students who need to study fewer words should use the **Alternate Word List**. This list is starred on page T188 in the Teacher Edition. The **Unit 31 Practice Masters** (*Teacher Resource Book*) provide additional practice with these words.

Unit 31 Practice Masters

Name_____

Practice Master Unit **31**

| 1. teams | 3. holidays | 5. lunches | 7. babies | 9. armies |
| 2. members | 4. friends | 6. patches | 8. ladies | 10. libraries |

A. Write the plural for each word below.

1. patch _____   6. member _____
2. library _____   7. army _____
3. team _____   8. friend _____
4. holiday _____   9. lady _____
5. baby _____   10. lunch _____

B. Write the spelling word that goes with each meaning.

1. very young children; infants _____
2. women; well-behaved young girls _____
3. people one knows and likes _____
4. pieces of cloth sewn over holes or tears _____
5. meals usually in the middle of the day _____
6. days when most people do not work _____
7. places where books and reference materials are kept _____

C. Write the six spelling words that name groups of people.

1. _____   4. _____
2. _____   5. _____
3. _____   6. _____

172

Practice Master Unit **31**

| babies | armies |
| ladies | libraries |

Down
large groups of soldiers
special days of celebration
people one knows and likes
people belonging to a group
meals eaten at midday

173

Spelling Connections Grade 4   Copyright © Zaner-Bloser, Inc.

Objectives

Spelling and Reading

Students will

- **add** the **-es** ending to given words to write spelling words in sentences.
- **write** spelling words to complete a series of meaning-related words.
- **complete** a paragraph using spelling words.

One-Minute Handwriting Hint

The lowercase **s** contains two pauses. The first pause occurs at the end of the undercurve beginning. The second pause occurs before the undercurve ending. Do not loop the letter.

PAUSE

PAUSE

Legible handwriting can boost spelling scores by as much as 20%.

Complete the Sentences

1. patches
2. stitches
3. scratches
4. coaches
5. lunches

Complete the Groups

6. babies
7. sandwiches
8. teams
9. monkeys
10. slippers
11. pennies
12. holidays
13. trays
14. ladies
15. armies
16. factories

Complete the Paragraph

17. libraries
18. adults
19. friends
20. members

190

Spelling and Reading

monkeys	babies	teams	lunches	factories
scratches	trays	libraries	members	ladies
slippers	coaches	armies	friends	patches
adults	pennies	holidays	stitches	sandwiches

Complete the Sentences The endings **-s** and **-es** can also be added to verbs. Add **-s** or **-es** to each word in parentheses to make the verb that completes the sentence.

1. Grandmother often _____ my torn clothes. (patch)
2. This old sewing machine still _____ well. (stitch)
3. My pet rooster always _____ in the dirt. (scratch)
4. Mr. Harris _____ a very successful team. (coach)
5. Aunt Ruth often _____ with her friends. (lunch)

Complete the Groups Write the spelling word that belongs in each of the following groups.

6. infants, tots, _____
7. soups, salads, _____
8. squads, crews, _____
9. camels, zebras, _____
10. boots, shoes, _____
11. dimes, nickels, _____
12. Sundays, weekends, _____
13. plates, platters, _____
14. gentlemen, women, _____
15. air forces, navies, _____
16. mills, plants, _____

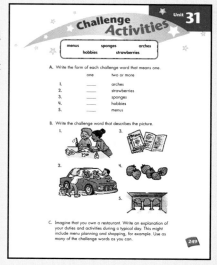

Complete the Paragraph Write the spelling words that best complete the paragraph.

Besides providing books to borrow, many __17.__ offer interesting activities and convenient meeting places for both children and __18.__. Preschoolers can enjoy story hours, and students can meet their __19.__ to work on projects together. People can become __20.__ of book clubs, computer societies, and drama groups. Do you know what activities your library offers?

MEETING INDIVIDUAL NEEDS

Providing More Challenge

Challenge Words and **Challenge Activities** for Unit 31 appear on page 249. **Challenge Word Test Sentences** appear on page T249.

Unit 31 Challenge Activities

Challenge Activities Unit 31

menus	sponges	arches
hobbies	strawberries	

A. Write the form of each challenge word that means one.

	one	two or more
1.	_____	arches
2.	_____	strawberries
3.	_____	sponges
4.	_____	hobbies
5.	_____	menus

B. Write the challenge word that describes the picture.

C. Imagine that you own a restaurant. Write an explanation of your duties and activities during a typical day. This might include menu planning and shopping, for example. Use as many of the challenge words as you can.

249

Weekly Test Options

Option 1:
One Spelling Word Per Sentence

(See procedures on pages Z10–Z11.)

1. We had to put two **patches** on the bike tire.
2. The **teams** will play football on Saturday.
3. Father had **scratches** on his leg from falling on the stones.
4. Put the **pennies** in your bank.
5. Many people work in large **factories**.
6. The **adults** took the children to the zoo.
7. The doctor put **stitches** in my knee because the cut was so deep.
8. The **monkeys** jumped from tree to tree.
9. You can find books in **libraries**.
10. Take the hot food off the **trays**.
11. The **armies** of the two nations fought bravely.
12. The **coaches** taught us to play football.
13. Mother put **slippers** on her feet.

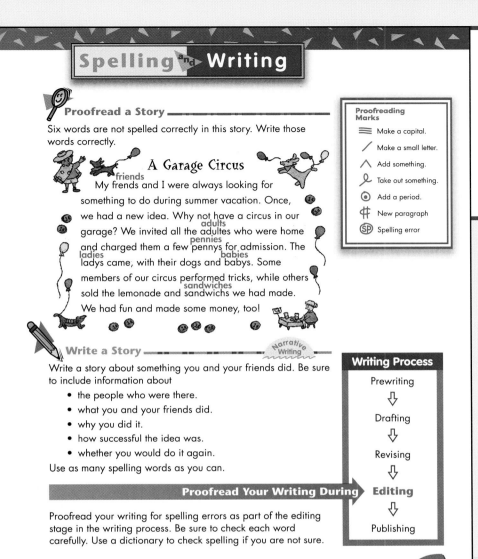

Spelling and Writing

Proofread a Story

Six words are not spelled correctly in this story. Write those words correctly.

A Garage Circus

friends
My friends and I were always looking for
something to do during summer vacation. Once,
we had a new idea. Why not have a circus in our
adults
garage? We invited all the adultes who were home
pennies
and charged them a few pennys for admission. The
ladies   *babies*
ladys came, with their dogs and babys. Some
members of our circus performed tricks, while others
sandwiches
sold the lemonade and sandwichs we had made.
We had fun and made some money, too!

Proofreading Marks

≡ Make a capital.
/ Make a small letter.
∧ Add something.
ℒ Take out something.
⊙ Add a period.
⌗ New paragraph.
SP Spelling error

Write a Story

Narrative Writing

Write a story about something you and your friends did. Be sure to include information about

- the people who were there.
- what you and your friends did.
- why you did it.
- how successful the idea was.
- whether you would do it again.

Use as many spelling words as you can.

Proofread Your Writing During

Writing Process

Prewriting
⇩
Drafting
⇩
Revising
⇩
Editing
⇩
Publishing

Proofread your writing for spelling errors as part of the editing stage in the writing process. Be sure to check each word carefully. Use a dictionary to check spelling if you are not sure.

191

---

14. Most **holidays** are marked on the calendar.
15. My **friends** are not all the same age.
16. The **ladies** will wear long dresses to the affair.
17. The **babies** are happy most of the day.
18. The man and his wife are both **members** of the club.
19. We had **sandwiches** and milk for lunch.
20. Do not forget to pack **lunches** for the field trip.

Option 2:
Multiple Spelling Words Per Sentence
(See procedures on pages Z10–Z11.)

1. We were asked to serve **lunches** on **trays** to the **adults**.
2. The **sandwiches** were served to **members** of both **teams**.
3. His pet **monkeys** made **scratches** on the tables and chairs.
4. We had only **pennies** to spend over the **holidays**.
5. The **armies** protected the land around the **factories**.
6. We used small **stitches** to put **patches** on the **slippers**.
7. The **coaches** found books on sports in the **libraries**.
8. My **friends** and I saw many **ladies** with their **babies** at the park.

Option 3:
Standardized Test
(See *Teacher Resource Book,* Unit 31.)

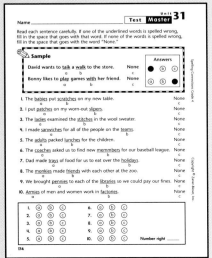

Unit 31
Test Master

Objectives

Strategy Words

Students will
- **review** words studied previously that are related to the spelling strategy.
- **preview** unknown words that are related to the spelling strategy.

Remind the students that the **Strategy Words** relate to the spelling patterns they have studied in this unit. The **Review Words** are below grade level, and the **Preview Words** are above grade level. You may wish to use the following sentences to introduce the words in context.

Review Words:
Words From Grade 3
1. We will bob for **apples** at the party.
2. The kite got caught in the **branches** of the tree.
3. My friend will play the **drums** in our school band.
4. The **flags** really fly in this windy weather.
5. One foot is the same as twelve **inches**.

Preview Words:
Words From Grade 5
6. Close the **envelopes** before you drop them in the mailbox.
7. We will need to write at least three **essays** in history this year.
8. Can you name some **heroes** from our nation's history?
9. I will look at some **pianos** while they are on sale.
10. Wild animals live all through the hills and **valleys** of this part of the country.

Unit 31 enrichment

Vocabulary

Strategy Words

Review Words: Plurals

Write the word from the box that matches each description.

apples	branches	drums	flags	inches

1. They are musical instruments played by striking them with sticks.
2. They are small units of measure.
3. We fly them on holidays, such as the Fourth of July.
4. We eat these raw or cooked.
5. Found on trees; leaves and flowers grow on them.

Preview Words: Plurals

Write the word from the box that matches each definition.

envelopes	essays	heroes	pianos	valleys

6. brave people
7. paper wrappers you put letters into
8. a plural word for one kind of musical instrument
9. short written compositions
10. a plural word naming the kind of land you might find between mountains

Review Words
1. drums
2. inches
3. flags
4. apples
5. branches

Preview Words
6. heroes
7. envelopes
8. pianos
9. essays
10. valleys

192

Unit 31 Homework Master

Unit 31 RECAP

You may wish to assign the **Unit 31 Homework Master** (*Teacher Resource Book,* Unit 31) as a fun way to recap the spelling words.

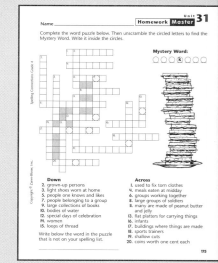

Connections

Objectives

Content Words

Students will
- **expand** vocabulary with content-related words.
- **relate** the spelling strategy to words outside the basic spelling list.

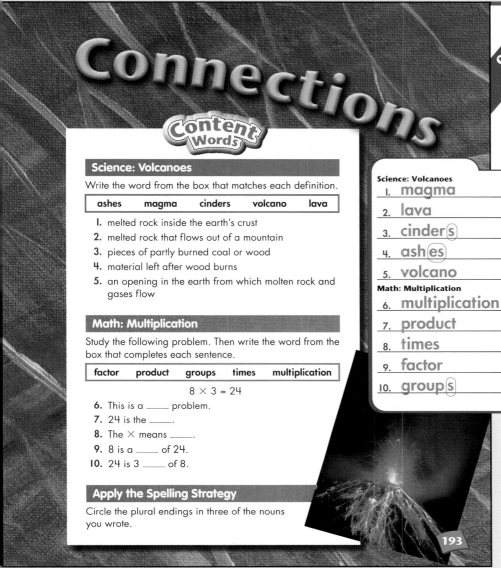

Content Words

Science: Volcanoes

Write the word from the box that matches each definition.

ashes	magma	cinders	volcano	lava

1. melted rock inside the earth's crust
2. melted rock that flows out of a mountain
3. pieces of partly burned coal or wood
4. material left after wood burns
5. an opening in the earth from which molten rock and gases flow

Math: Multiplication

Study the following problem. Then write the word from the box that completes each sentence.

factor	product	groups	times	multiplication

$$8 \times 3 = 24$$

6. This is a _____ problem.
7. 24 is the _____.
8. The $\times$ means _____.
9. 8 is a _____ of 24.
10. 24 is 3 _____ of 8.

Apply the Spelling Strategy

Circle the plural endings in three of the nouns you wrote.

193

Science: Volcanoes
1. magma
2. lava
3. cinder(s)
4. ash(es)
5. volcano

Math: Multiplication
6. multiplication
7. product
8. times
9. factor
10. group(s)

Content Words

Science: Volcanoes

Review the meanings of these words with the students. You may wish to use these sentences to introduce the words in context.

1. We had a lot of **ashes** left at the campfire after our roaring bonfire last night.
2. The **magma** lay steaming just below the earth's crust.
3. The highway department put **cinders** on the icy roads.
4. We visited the site of a **volcano** that is no longer active.
5. The **lava** from the volcanic eruption covered the little village.

Encourage the students to use these words in a paragraph explaining how a volcano is formed.

Math: Multiplication

Review the meanings of these words with the students. You may wish to use these sentences to introduce the words in context.

6. What **factor** is multiplied by three to make six?
7. The answer to a multiplication problem is called a **product**.
8. How many **groups** of ten make fifty?
9. Four **times** three equals twelve.
10. We will do each **multiplication** problem on the page.

Encourage the students to use these words to start a dictionary of math terms.

Unit 32 Home Study Master

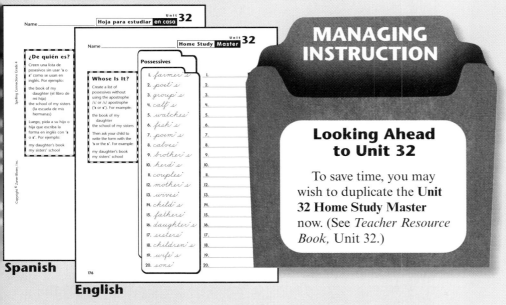

Spanish

English

MANAGING INSTRUCTION

Looking Ahead to Unit 32

To save time, you may wish to duplicate the **Unit 32 Home Study Master** now. (See *Teacher Resource Book,* Unit 32.)

Basic Spelling List

farmer's	couples'
poets'	mother's
group's	wives'
calf's	child's
watches'	fathers'
fish's	daughter's
poem's	sisters'
calves'	children's
brother's	wife's
herd's	sons'

Strategy Words

Review
city('s)	grandfather('s)
geese('s)	pies(')
grandmother('s)	

Preview
actor(s')	youth('s)
artist('s)	tourist(s')
company('s)	

Content Words

Health: Illnesses
disease	virus
infect	immune
hospital	

Science: Conductivity
acid	metal
crystal	battery
antenna	

Individual Needs

Challenge Words
infant's	umpires'
nephew's	runners'
crowd's	

Alternate Word List
watches'	fathers'
fish's	sisters'
brother's	children's
mother's	wife's
child's	sons'

MATERIALS

Student Edition
Pages 194–199
Challenge Activities, p. 250

Teacher Edition
Pages T194A–T199
Challenge Activities, p. T250

Other Resources
Spelling Connections Software
Unit 32 Word List Overhead
  Transparency

Teacher Resource Book
Unit 32 Home Study Master
  (English or Spanish; students
  may pretest on this sheet or use
  it for home practice.)
Unit 32 Homework Master
Unit 32 Practice Masters
Flip Folder Practice Master
Unit 32 Test Master

Visit our Web site, www.zaner-bloser.com

OBJECTIVES

Spelling and Thinking
Students will
- **read** the spelling words in list form and in context.
- **sort** the spelling words according to final **-'s** and **-s'** spellings of possessive nouns.
- **read** and remember this week's spelling strategy.

Spelling and Vocabulary
Students will
- **write** spelling words for meaning clues.
- **change** singular possessive forms to plural possessive forms to write spelling words.
- **write** spelling words by changing plural possessive forms to singular possessive forms.

- **use** the **Spelling Dictionary** to verify the possessive form of a spelling word.

Spelling and Reading
Students will
- **complete** sentences with the correct possessive forms of given spelling words.
- **write** the correct possessive forms to complete phrases.

Spelling and Writing
Students will
- **proofread** an ad.
- **use** the writing process to write an ad.
- **proofread** their writing.

MEETING INDIVIDUAL NEEDS
Learning Styles

Visual

Have the students draw pictures to illustrate each possessive noun. Then write each spelling word on the chalkboard, double-spacing between the letters of each word and leaving out the apostrophe. Call on several students to place an apostrophe in the correct place to form the possessive. Have the students write the words on their papers as captions for the pictures they have drawn.

Auditory

Most of the spelling words are homophones of plural words. Have the students write a sentence for each spelling word. Have them write another sentence for the plural homophone of each spelling word. Say a spelling word and call on a student to say her or his sentences aloud, spelling out the spelling word and clapping when she or he says "apostrophe."

Kinesthetic

Write each spelling word on a card and attach it to an object. Then write the singular nouns once and the plural nouns two or three times, all on separate slips of paper. Give a slip to each student, with instructions to find the object that "belongs" to his or her slip. For example, the student who holds **brother** would look for the object, perhaps a book, labeled **brother's**. Have each student say a sentence showing the relationship between the spelling word and the object.

Language and Cultural Differences

The pronunciation and spelling of possessive word forms may be difficult for Spanish-speaking students because the concept of one word showing possession does not exist in the Spanish language. Explain that possessives are words showing ownership. Explain that they are formed in these ways: (1) by adding an apostrophe followed by an **s** (**'s**) to singular nouns (**boy's, girl's**) and some plurals (**children's**) and (2) by adding an apostrophe (**'**) to plural nouns ending in **s** (**sons', wives'**).

Write the base word of each singular possessive noun on the chalkboard. Have the students go to the chalkboard and write the singular possessive form of the word. Ask each student to use the base word in one sentence and the singular possessive form in another sentence.

Follow the same procedure with the plural possessive nouns, but have each student who goes to the chalkboard write the plural form before writing the plural possessive.

Then ask the student to say one sentence using the base word, another using its plural, and a third sentence using the plural possessive.

MANAGING INSTRUCTION

3–5 Day Plan		Average	Below Average	Above Average
Day 1	**Day 1**	Pretest Spelling Mini-Lesson, p. T194 Spelling and Thinking, p. 194	Pretest Spelling Mini-Lesson, p. T194 Spelling and Thinking, p. 194	Pretest Spelling and Thinking, p. 194
	Day 2	Spelling and Vocabulary, p. 195	Spelling and Vocabulary, p. 195 (or) Unit 32 Practice Master, A and B	Spelling and Vocabulary, p. 195 Spelling and Reading, p. 196
Day 2	**Day 3**	Spelling and Reading, p. 196	Spelling and Reading, p. 196 (or) Unit 32 Practice Master, C and D	Challenge Activities, p. 250
	Day 4	Spelling and Writing, p. 197 Unit 32 Homework Master	Spelling and Writing, p. 197	Spelling and Writing, p. 197 Unit 32 Homework Master
Day 3	**Day 5**	Weekly Test	Weekly Test	Weekly Test
Vocabulary Connections (pages 198 and 199) may be used anytime during this unit.				

Objectives

Spelling and Thinking

Students will
- **read** the spelling words in list form and in context.
- **sort** the spelling words according to final **-'s** and **-s'** spellings of possessive nouns.
- **read** and remember this week's spelling strategy.

UNIT PRETEST

Use **Pretest Sentences** below. Refer to the self-checking procedures on student page 256. You may wish to use the **Unit 32 Word List Overhead Transparency** as part of the checking procedure.

TEACHING THE STRATEGY

Spelling Mini-Lesson

On the chalkboard, write **The calf's mother is that large brown cow**. Ask, "Whose mother are we talking about?" (the calf); "How do we know?" (because **'s** was added to calf)

Explain that **'s** can be added to a singular noun to show possession or ownership. Tell them **calf's** is a possessive noun.

On the chalkboard, write **Where are the calves' mothers**? Discuss how the spellings of **calf's** and **calves'** differ. Point out that when a plural noun ends in **s**, an apostrophe shows possession. Ask students to find other plural possessives on the spelling list that were formed in this way. (couples', poets', sons', wives', sisters', watches', fathers')

Write **herd, group,** and **children**. Ask the students if these words are singular or plural. Ask them how they think the possessive of each word is formed. Explain that when a plural word does not end in **s,** the plural is formed by adding **'s**.

Challenge students to find the spelling word that is spelled the same whether it's singular possessive or plural possessive. (fish's) You may wish to note that the plural form can also be written **fishes**.

Conclude by reading **Remember the Spelling Strategy** on page 194.

Order of answers may vary.

-'s
1. farmer's
2. group's
3. calf's
4. fish's ★
5. poem's
6. brother's ★
7. herd's
8. mother's ★
9. child's ★
10. daughter's
11. children's ★
12. wife's ★

-s'
13. poets'
14. watches' ★
15. calves'
16. couples'
17. wives'
18. fathers' ★
19. sisters' ★
20. sons' ★

READ THE SPELLING WORDS

1.	farmer's	*farmer's*	We brought in the **farmer's** crops.
2.	poets'	*poets'*	The **poets'** haikus were read.
3.	group's	*group's*	They finished the **group's** work.
4.	calf's	*calf's*	A **calf's** legs are long and weak.
5.	watches'	*watches'*	The **watches'** faces were identical.
6.	fish's	*fish's*	That **fish's** tail is forked.
7.	poem's	*poem's*	The **poem's** last line was a surprise.
8.	calves'	*calves'*	The **calves'** mothers watch over them.
9.	brother's	*brother's*	This is my **brother's** book.
10.	herd's	*herd's*	The **herd's** pasture is on the hill.
11.	couples'	*couples'*	We accepted the **couples'** ideas.
12.	mother's	*mother's*	Anna is my **mother's** best friend.
13.	wives'	*wives'*	They listened to their **wives'** ideas.
14.	child's	*child's*	Read a **child's** book to youngsters.
15.	fathers'	*fathers'*	The coach liked the **fathers'** plans.
16.	daughter's	*daughter's*	Her **daughter's** name is Pamela.
17.	sisters'	*sisters'*	The **sisters'** reunion was a success.
18.	children's	*children's*	We heard the **children's** laughter.
19.	wife's	*wife's*	He appreciated his **wife's** gift.
20.	sons'	*sons'*	All his **sons'** names begin with **J**.

SORT THE SPELLING WORDS

1.–12. Write the spelling words that end with an apostrophe **s** (**-'s**).

13.–20. Write the spelling words that end with an **s** apostrophe (**-s'**).

REMEMBER THE SPELLING STRATEGY

Remember that possessive nouns show ownership. Add an apostrophe and **s** (**'s**) to show possession when a noun is singular: **calf's**. Add an apostrophe (**'**) to show ownership when a plural noun ends in **-s: calves'**. When a noun is plural and does **not** end in **-s,** add an apostrophe and **s** (**'s**) to show ownership: **children's**.

194

Pretest Sentences (See procedures on pages Z10–Z11.)

1. Mrs. Lee bought the **farmer's** apples.
2. Local **poets'** poems were often read.
3. Jill took the **group's** phone number.
4. The **calf's** fur was soft.
5. The **watches'** bands are different colors.
6. That **fish's** tail is pretty.
7. Please put quotation marks around the **poem's** title.
8. The **calves'** owners were all farmers.
9. Juan borrowed his **brother's** bike.
10. We rode out to the **herd's** pasture.
11. The **couples'** tables were filled at the restaurant.
12. I think your **mother's** job is interesting.
13. They talked about their **wives'** careers.
14. He was proud of his **child's** honesty.
15. Their **fathers'** crafts were shown.
16. She will go to her **daughter's** recital.
17. We liked our **sisters'** bowling scores.
18. Dad washed the **children's** clothes.
19. Mr. Smith is a friend of his **wife's** brother.
20. Their **sons'** team won the game.

Spelling and Vocabulary

Word Meanings

Write a possessive noun to complete the equation.

1. The tail of one calf = one _____ tail.
2. A playground for more than one child = a _____ playground.
3. The fields of one farmer = one _____ fields.
4. The bands of three watches = the _____ bands.

Plural Possessives

Each word below is the singular possessive form of a noun. Write the spelling word that is the plural possessive form of the same noun.

5. calf's	7. poet's	9. son's	11. sister's
6. wife's	8. couple's	10. father's	

Singular Possessives

Each word below is the plural possessive form of a noun. Write the word that is the singular possessive form of the same noun.

12. herds'	14. groups'	16. children's	18. brothers'
13. wives'	15. poems'	17. mothers'	19. daughters'

USING THE Dictionary

20. Which spelling word can be used as a singular possessive and a plural possessive? Check your answer by finding the base word and a plural form of the word in your **Spelling Dictionary**.

◆ ◆ ◆

Dictionary Check Be sure to check the plural form of the word in your **Spelling Dictionary**.

Word Meanings
1. calf's
2. children's
3. farmer's
4. watches'

Plural Possessives
5. calves'
6. wives'
7. poets'
8. couples'
9. sons'
10. fathers'
11. sisters'

Singular Possessives
12. herd's
13. wife's
14. group's
15. poem's
16. child's
17. mother's
18. brother's
19. daughter's

Using the Dictionary
20. fish's

195

Objectives

Spelling and Vocabulary

Students will

- **write** spelling words for meaning clues.
- **change** singular possessive forms to plural possessive forms to write spelling words.
- **write** spelling words by changing plural possessive forms to singular possessive forms.
- **use** the **Spelling Dictionary** to verify the possessive form of a spelling word.

Developing Oral Language Skills

Have students work in pairs. The first student recites a phrase using one of the spelling words. For example, the student might say, "one **child's** toy" or "those **calves'** pasture." The second student must respond with a phrase using another spelling word. However, if the first student's phrase uses a singular possessive, the second student must use a plural possessive in his or her phrase, and vice versa.

MEETING INDIVIDUAL NEEDS

Providing More Help

Use each spelling word in a sentence and have volunteers identify whether it is singular or plural. Then have each student use the word in a phrase that shows clearly the meaning of the word. Finally, have the students choose spelling partners and write their own sentences using the spelling words. Have the partners check each other's work.

★Students who need to study fewer words should use the **Alternate Word List**. This list is starred on page T194 in the Teacher Edition. The **Unit 32 Practice Masters** (*Teacher Resource Book*) provide additional practice with these words.

Unit 32 Practice Masters

Name_____ **Practice Master** Unit 32

| 1. wife's | 3. mother's | 5. sons' | 7. watches' | 9. children's |
| 2. child's | 4. brother's | 6. sisters' | 8. fathers' | 10. fish's |

A. The incorrect possessive form is used in each sentence below. Write the correct form.

1. I laughed at my brothers' joke when he told it. _____
2. My mothers' car is in the driveway. _____
3. Her two son's toys were neatly put away. _____
4. My dad and I went to the father's picnic. _____
5. We played with the childs' toy. _____
6. His wifes' friend is going, too. _____

B. Write the spelling word that is the possessive form of each word. Then write the name of something that each might own or have. The first one is done for you.

1. brother _brother's bike_
2. wife _____
3. mother _____
4. sons _____
5. children _____
6. fish _____
7. sisters _____
8. child _____
9. fathers _____
10. watches _____

178

Practice Master Unit 32

| watches' | children's |
| fathers' | fish's |

...ssive form of a noun. Write the ...ssive form of the same noun.

...le **S** if the possessive is singular.
...rd is either singular or plural.

	S	P
	S	P
	S	P
	S	P
	S	P
	S	P
	S	P
	S	P
	S	P
	S	P

179

Objectives

Spelling and Reading

Students will
• **complete** sentences with the correct possessive forms of given spelling words.
• **write** the correct possessive forms to complete phrases.

One-Minute Handwriting Hint

The spacing between letters should look even. The joining stroke controls the spacing between letters. Swing wide as you join letters. There should be enough space between letters to insert a small oval.

poets'

Legible handwriting can boost spelling scores by as much as 20%.

Complete the Sentences

1. calf's
2. fathers'
3. herd's
4. child's
5. poets'
6. watches'
7. sisters'
8. daughter's
9. brother's
10. mother's
11. sons'
12. couples'

Form the Possessives

13. poem's
14. group's
15. wife's
16. farmer's
17. calves'
18. children's
19. fish's
20. wives'

Spelling and Reading

farmer's	poets'	group's	calf's	watches'
fish's	poem's	calves'	brother's	herd's
couples'	mother's	wives'	child's	fathers'
daughter's	sisters'	children's	wife's	sons'

Complete the Sentences Complete each sentence by writing the correct possessive form of each of the words in parentheses.

1. This is the spotted _____ collar. (calf)
2. All the _____ names are on this list. (father)
3. The farmer painted the _____ barn. (herd)
4. Thursday was the sick _____ last day of school. (child)
5. Three _____ works were read at the library program. (poet)
6. All the _____ bands are made of the same material. (watch)
7. Both of my _____ rooms are decorated differently. (sister)
8. His only _____ birthday is in June. (daughter)
9. I laughed at my _____ joke when he told it. (brother)
10. My _____ car is in the driveway. (mother)
11. Her two _____ toys were neatly put away. (son)
12. My mom and dad went to the _____ picnic. (couple)

Form the Possessives Write the spelling word that is the possessive form of each word.

13. the lines of the poem; the _____ lines
14. the project of the group; the _____ project
15. the idea of the wife; the _____ idea
16. the crop of the farmer; the _____ crop
17. the feed for the calves; the _____ feed
18. the faces of the children; the _____ faces
19. the fins of the fish; the _____ fins
20. the meeting of the wives; the _____ meeting

196

MEETING INDIVIDUAL NEEDS

Providing More Challenge

Challenge Words and **Challenge Activities** for Unit 32 appear on page 250. **Challenge Word Test Sentences** appear on page T250.

Unit 32 Challenge Activities

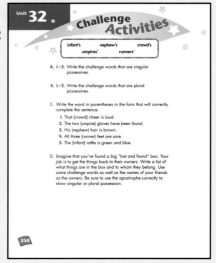

Unit 32

Challenge Activities

infant's   nephew's   crowd's
umpires'   runners'

A. 1.–3. Write the challenge words that are singular possessives.

B. 1.–2. Write the challenge words that are plural possessives.

C. Write the word in parentheses in the form that will correctly complete the sentence.
1. That (crowd) cheer is loud.
2. The two (umpire) gloves have been found.
3. His (nephew) hair is brown.
4. All three (runner) feet are sore.
5. The (infant) rattle is green and blue.

D. Imagine that you've found a big "lost and found" box. Your job is to get the things back to their owners. Write a list of what things are in the box and to whom they belong. Use some challenge words as well as the names of your friends as the owners. Be sure to use the apostrophe correctly to show singular or plural possession.

250

Weekly Test Options

Option 1:
One Spelling Word Per Sentence
(See procedures on pages Z10–Z11.)

1. My **mother's** slippers are under her bed.
2. The **watches'** prices have a wide range.
3. My **brother's** car is red.
4. The **calf's** mother is in the barn.
5. Most of their **wives'** friends will be here soon.
6. Her **daughter's** balloon is yellow.
7. Our **fathers'** jobs are close to our homes.
8. The **poem's** words made me happy.
9. My mother and father joined in the **couples'** dance.
10. The **herd's** range covers many miles.
11. All of those **poets'** poems are very short.
12. My **wife's** watch is made of silver.
13. The **children's** goats won first prize at the fair.
14. Our **sons'** houses are on the same street.
15. All of the **group's** baggage was found.
16. The **child's** pillow is on her bed.

T196

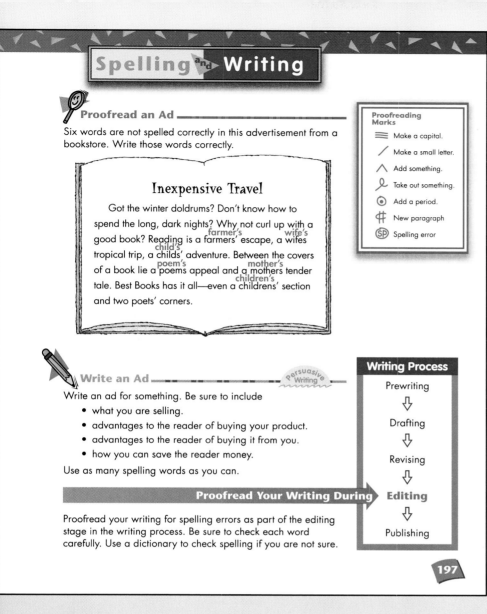

Spelling *and* Writing

🔍 Proofread an Ad

Six words are not spelled correctly in this advertisement from a bookstore. Write those words correctly.

Inexpensive Travel

Got the winter doldrums? Don't know how to spend the long, dark nights? Why not curl up with a good book? Reading is a farmers' escape, a wifes
farmer's   wife's
child's
tropical trip, a childs' adventure. Between the covers
poem's   mother's
of a book lie a poems appeal and a mothers tender
children's
tale. Best Books has it all—even a childrens' section and two poets' corners.

Proofreading Marks

≡ Make a capital.

/ Make a small letter.

∧ Add something.

℘ Take out something.

⊙ Add a period.

⌗ New paragraph

Ⓢ Spelling error

✏️ Write an Ad
Persuasive Writing

Write an ad for something. Be sure to include
- what you are selling.
- advantages to the reader of buying your product.
- advantages to the reader of buying it from you.
- how you can save the reader money.

Use as many spelling words as you can.

Proofread Your Writing During ➡ Editing

Proofread your writing for spelling errors as part of the editing stage in the writing process. Be sure to check each word carefully. Use a dictionary to check spelling if you are not sure.

Writing Process

Prewriting
⇩
Drafting
⇩
Revising
⇩
Editing
⇩
Publishing

197

Objectives

Spelling and Writing

Students will
- **proofread** an ad.
- **use** the writing process to write an ad.
- **proofread** their writing.

Using the Writing Process

Before assigning **Write an Ad,** see pages 258–259 in the Student Edition for a complete review of the writing process and additional writing assignments. You may also wish to refer to pages Z12–Z13 in the Teacher Edition.

Keeping a Spelling Journal

Encourage students to record the words they misspelled on the weekly test in a personal spelling journal. These words may be recycled for future study. Students may also wish to include words from their writing. See pages Z12–Z13 in the Teacher Edition for more information.

---

17. The **calves'** feed was brought to the barn.
18. The **farmer's** crops are planted in the field.
19. Our **sisters'** birthdays are on the same day.
20. The **fish's** eyes are always open.

Option 2:
Multiple Spelling Words Per Sentence
(See procedures on pages Z10–Z11.)

1. Most of the **watches'** parts were made at her **daughter's** shop.
2. Many of the young **poets'** works were printed in the **children's** book.
3. The **calves'** mothers were out in the **farmer's** field.
4. Their **wives'** friends live near our **fathers'** homes.
5. That **calf's** mother is the **herd's** oldest cow.
6. His **wife's** friend read the **poem's** few lines.
7. My **brother's** friend took care of both **couples'** dogs.
8. The **sons'** wives stayed at their **sisters'** homes.
9. The **child's** job was to measure the **fish's** food.
10. Will the **group's** members meet at your **mother's** house?

Option 3:
Standardized Test
(See *Teacher Resource Book,* Unit 32.)

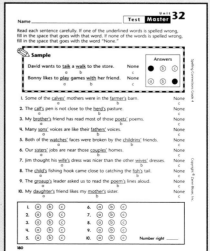

**Unit 32
Test Master**

Objectives

Strategy Words

Students will
- **review** words studied previously that are related to the spelling strategy.
- **preview** unknown words that are related to the spelling strategy.

Remind the students that the **Strategy Words** relate to the spelling patterns they have studied in this unit. The **Review Words** are below grade level, and the **Preview Words** are above grade level. You may wish to use the following sentences to introduce the words in context.

Review Words:
Words From Grade 3

1. Our **city's** government seems to run pretty smoothly.
2. I think the **geese's** nests are all located around the lake.
3. My **grandmother's** house holds lots of special memories for me.
4. Our **grandfather's** barn was always kept very clean.
5. The **pies'** crusts are especially flaky.

Preview Words:
Words From Grade 5

6. The **actors'** roles were very difficult to learn in the short period of time they were given.
7. At the bottom of the picture was the **artist's** signature.
8. We have our **company's** logo on all our letterhead.
9. Did you notice the **youth's** even teeth?
10. Halfway up the mountain was a **tourists'** stop for food and beverages.

Review Words
1. city's
2. pies'
3. grandmother's
4. grandfather's
5. geese's

Preview Words
6. youth's
7. actors'
8. tourists'
9. artist's
10. company's

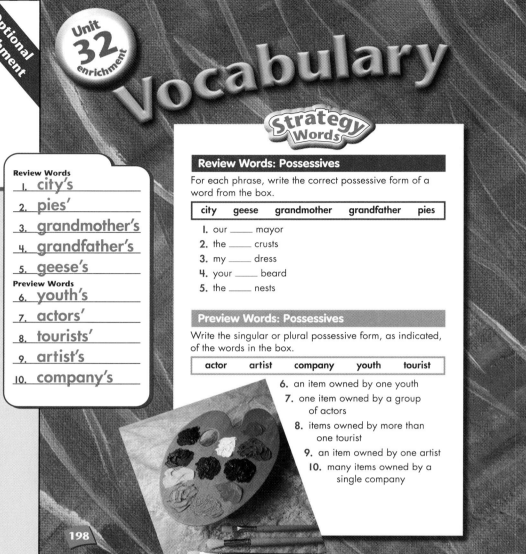

Strategy Words

Review Words: Possessives

For each phrase, write the correct possessive form of a word from the box.

city	geese	grandmother	grandfather	pies

1. our _____ mayor
2. the _____ crusts
3. my _____ dress
4. your _____ beard
5. the _____ nests

Preview Words: Possessives

Write the singular or plural possessive form, as indicated, of the words in the box.

actor	artist	company	youth	tourist

6. an item owned by one youth
7. one item owned by a group of actors
8. items owned by more than one tourist
9. an item owned by one artist
10. many items owned by a single company

198

Unit 32 RECAP

You may wish to assign the **Unit 32 Homework Master** (*Teacher Resource Book*, Unit 32) as a fun way to recap the spelling words.

Unit 32 Homework Master

Name _____ Homework Master Unit 32

Alphabetize the following words. Then circle **S** if the possessive is singular. Circle **P** if the possessive is plural. One word is either singular or plural. Circle **S** and **P**.

1. calf's _____ S P
2. fathers' _____ S P
3. wife's _____ S P
4. watches' _____ S P
5. poem's _____ S P
6. sisters' _____ S P
7. child's _____ S P
8. wives' _____ S P
9. farmer's _____ S P
10. sons' _____ S P
11. mother's _____ S P
12. poets' _____ S P
13. brother's _____ S P
14. calves' _____ S P
15. daughter's _____ S P
16. couples' _____ S P
17. herd's _____ S P
18. fish's _____ S P
19. group's _____ S P
20. children's _____ S P

Connections

Objectives

Content Words

Students will
- **expand** vocabulary with content-related words.
- **relate** the spelling strategy to words outside the basic spelling list.

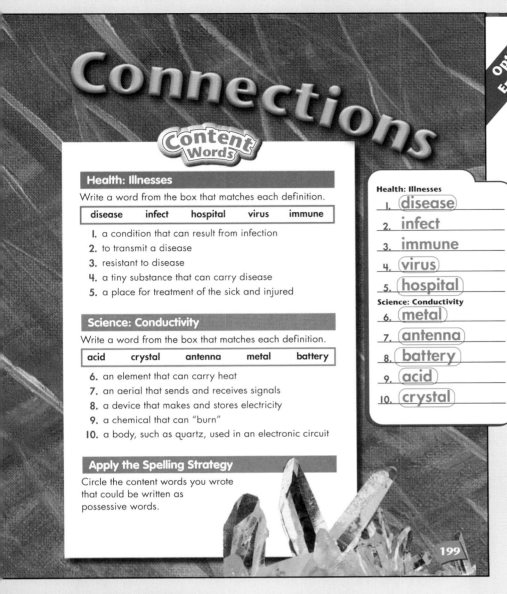

Content Words

Health: Illnesses

Write a word from the box that matches each definition.

disease	infect	hospital	virus	immune

1. a condition that can result from infection
2. to transmit a disease
3. resistant to disease
4. a tiny substance that can carry disease
5. a place for treatment of the sick and injured

Science: Conductivity

Write a word from the box that matches each definition.

acid	crystal	antenna	metal	battery

6. an element that can carry heat
7. an aerial that sends and receives signals
8. a device that makes and stores electricity
9. a chemical that can "burn"
10. a body, such as quartz, used in an electronic circuit

Apply the Spelling Strategy

Circle the content words you wrote that could be written as possessive words.

Health: Illnesses
1. disease
2. infect
3. immune
4. virus
5. hospital

Science: Conductivity
6. metal
7. antenna
8. battery
9. acid
10. crystal

199

Health: Illnesses

Review the meanings of these words with the students. You may wish to use these sentences to introduce the words in context.

1. The animals seemed to get the same **disease** each spring.
2. One sick child can **infect** several others.
3. If someone is seriously hurt, we should take that person to the **hospital**.
4. A **virus** of some kind had infected all the chickens.
5. We get shots to make us **immune** to certain kinds of flu.

Encourage the students to use these words to create a poster promoting a good health habit.

Science: Conductivity

Review the meanings of these words with the students. You may wish to use these sentences to introduce the words in context.

6. An **acid** can eat away at whatever it touches.
7. Early radios needed **crystal** to work.
8. Dad put an **antenna** on the roof so we could get better reception on our TV.
9. Most types of **metal** are good conductors of electricity.
10. We had to jump-start the car this morning because the **battery** was dead.

Encourage the students to use an encyclopedia or similar reference book to find out how a radio works. Then have them use these words to write an explanation.

Unit 33 Home Study Master

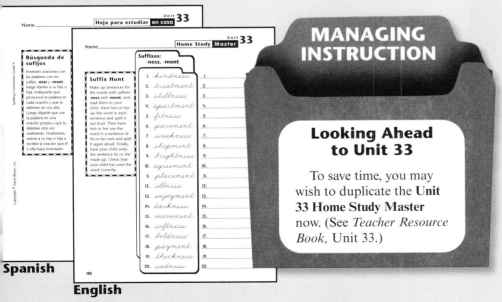

Spanish

English

MANAGING INSTRUCTION

Looking Ahead to Unit 33

To save time, you may wish to duplicate the **Unit 33 Home Study Master** now. (See *Teacher Resource Book,* Unit 33.)

Basic Spelling List

kindness	placement
treatment	illness
stillness	enjoyment
apartment	darkness
fitness	movement
pavement	softness
weakness	boldness
shipment	payment
brightness	thickness
agreement	sadness

Strategy Words

Review

high(ness)	round(ness)
pave(ment)	mild(ness)
right(ness)	

Preview

argument	sickness
employment	tardiness
government	

Content Words

Language Arts: Punctuation

colon	statement
sentence	period
comma	

Social Studies: Deserts

arid	nomad
dune	travel
migrate	

Individual Needs

Challenge Words

smoothness	emptiness
restfulness	wonderment
happiness	

Alternate Word List

kindness	enjoyment
stillness	darkness
apartment	movement
agreement	thickness
illness	sadness

MATERIALS

Student Edition

Pages 200–205
Challenge Activities, p. 251

Teacher Edition

Pages T200A–T205
Challenge Activities, p. T251

Other Resources

Spelling Connections Software
Unit 33 Word List Overhead
Transparency

Teacher Resource Book

Unit 33 Home Study Master
(English or Spanish; students
may pretest on this sheet or use
it for home practice.)
Unit 33 Homework Master
Unit 33 Practice Masters
Flip Folder Practice Master
Unit 33 Test Master

Visit our Web site, www.zaner-bloser.com

OBJECTIVES

Spelling and Thinking

Students will
- **read** the spelling words in list form and in context.
- **sort** the spelling words according to the **-ness** or **-ment** suffix.
- **read** and remember this week's spelling strategy.

Spelling and Vocabulary

Students will
- **write** spelling words for definitions.
- **add** suffixes to base words to write spelling words.
- **use** the **Writing Thesaurus** to write spelling words that are synonyms for given words.

Spelling and Reading

Students will
- **complete** sentences using spelling words.
- **complete** a paragraph using spelling words.
- **write** spelling words that are antonyms of given words.

Spelling and Writing

Students will
- **proofread** a note.
- **use** the writing process to write a note.
- **proofread** their writing.

MEETING INDIVIDUAL NEEDS
Learning Styles

Visual

Make a word wheel. Arrange and label it as shown.

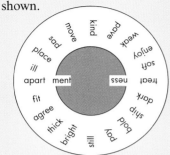

Have a student turn the wheel to form a spelling word while others watch. Have the student pronounce the word while the other students write it on their papers. Then have other students take turns with the wheel until all of the spelling words have been formed and written.

Auditory

Follow the procedure described in the visual activity. Have the students say each word they form, spell it aloud, and use it in a sentence. Tape record the students. When playing back the tape, have the students clap out the syllables of each word.

Kinesthetic

Assign each of the students a base word from the spelling list to write on an index card. Next, give each student two small pieces of construction paper and have them write the **-ness** suffix on one and the **-ment** suffix on the other. Have the students help each other tape the **-ness** to the backs of their left hands and the **-ment** to the backs of their right hands. Have a student hold up a base word card. Ask the other students to spell the base word aloud, clapping for each letter in the base word and then raising the appropriate hand for the suffix that forms the spelling word. Then have the students write each spelling word.

Language and Cultural Differences

Some Spanish-speaking students may confuse the suffix **-ment** with the Spanish suffix **-mente,** which indicates an adverb. Have the students pronounce each spelling word. Listen to be sure they do not add the **long a** sound to the end of the words having the **-ment** suffix.

Next, have the students write each word and circle the suffix. Discuss the meaning of each base word and its affixed form, comparing their meanings.

Have each student complete the activity for his or her dominant learning modality.

MANAGING INSTRUCTION

3–5 Day Plan		Average	Below Average	Above Average
Day 1	**Day 1**	Pretest Spelling Mini-Lesson, p. T200 Spelling and Thinking, p. 200	Pretest Spelling Mini-Lesson, p. T200 Spelling and Thinking, p. 200	Pretest Spelling and Thinking, p. 200
	Day 2	Spelling and Vocabulary, p. 201	Spelling and Vocabulary, p. 201 (or) Unit 33 Practice Master, A and B	Spelling and Vocabulary, p. 201 Spelling and Reading, p. 202
Day 2	**Day 3**	Spelling and Reading, p. 202	Spelling and Reading, p. 202 (or) Unit 33 Practice Master, C and D	Challenge Activities, p. 251
	Day 4	Spelling and Writing, p. 203 Unit 33 Homework Master	Spelling and Writing, p. 203	Spelling and Writing, p. 203 Unit 33 Homework Master
Day 3	**Day 5**	Weekly Test	Weekly Test	Weekly Test
Vocabulary Connections (pages 204 and 205) may be used anytime during this unit.				

Objectives

Spelling and Thinking

Students will
- **read** the spelling words in list form and in context.
- **sort** the spelling words according to the **-ness** or **-ment** suffix.
- **read** and remember this week's spelling strategy.

UNIT PRETEST

Use **Pretest Sentences** below. Refer to the self-checking procedures on student page 256. You may wish to use the **Unit 33 Word List Overhead Transparency** as part of the checking procedure.

TEACHING THE STRATEGY

Spelling Mini-Lesson

Tell the students that in this lesson the spelling words have either the suffix **-ness** or the suffix **-ment**. Ask the students to give examples of any words they know that have these suffixes. Write their responses on the chalkboard.

Ask the students to look up the two suffixes in the **Spelling Dictionary**. Read the definitions with the students. Ask the students to look at the words on the spelling list. Ask, "How does the definition of **-ness** relate to the meanings of the spelling words with that suffix? How does the definition of **-ment** relate to the meanings of the spelling words with that suffix?" Discuss these relationships until the students gain a greater understanding of the way these suffixes change the meanings of base words. Encourage the students to think creatively to explain words like **apartment** and **shipment**.

Read **Remember the Spelling Strategy** on page 200.

Spelling and Thinking

Order of answers may vary.

-ness
1. kindness ★
2. stillness ★
3. fitness
4. weakness
5. brightness
6. illness ★
7. darkness ★
8. softness
9. boldness
10. thickness ★
11. sadness ★

-ment
12. treatment
13. apartment ★
14. pavement
15. shipment
16. agreement ★
17. placement
18. enjoyment ★
19. movement ★
20. payment

READ THE SPELLING WORDS

1.	kindness	*kindness*	He always treats people with **kindness**.
2.	treatment	*treatment*	When you are ill, you need **treatment**.
3.	stillness	*stillness*	I left in the **stillness** of the night.
4.	apartment	*apartment*	She lives in a large **apartment**.
5.	fitness	*fitness*	They use **fitness** equipment at home.
6.	pavement	*pavement*	The **pavement** was wet with rain.
7.	weakness	*weakness*	Arriving late is his **weakness**.
8.	shipment	*shipment*	A **shipment** of goods arrived today.
9.	brightness	*brightness*	The sun's **brightness** made me squint.
10.	agreement	*agreement*	We will try to reach an **agreement**.
11.	placement	*placement*	Father works at a **placement** bureau.
12.	illness	*illness*	He is at home because of **illness**.
13.	enjoyment	*enjoyment*	Her **enjoyment** of the movie was clear.
14.	darkness	*darkness*	I stumbled in the **darkness**.
15.	movement	*movement*	We studied the **movement** of the stars.
16.	softness	*softness*	The blanket's **softness** was comforting.
17.	boldness	*boldness*	The **boldness** of his plan surprised us.
18.	payment	*payment*	Expect the first **payment** next week.
19.	thickness	*thickness*	She measured the **thickness** of the wall.
20.	sadness	*sadness*	He has known great **sadness** and joy.

SORT THE SPELLING WORDS

1.–11. Write the spelling words that have the **-ness** suffix.
12.–20. Write the spelling words that have the **-ment** suffix.

REMEMBER THE SPELLING STRATEGY

Remember that the suffix **-ness** means "a condition or quality": **kindness**. The suffix **-ment** means "the result of an action": **enjoyment**.

200

Pretest Sentences (See procedures on pages Z10–Z11.)

1. Jamal was thankful for Yoko's **kindness**.
2. The boards for our deck received a special weatherproofing **treatment**.
3. The weather was calm, and there was a **stillness** in the night.
4. Mary Beth lives in an **apartment**.
5. The **fitness** program helped Sarah to stay healthy and strong.
6. We play basketball on the smooth **pavement**.
7. The X-ray showed no **weakness** in the steel beam.
8. Will the next **shipment** of tires be sent by truck?
9. The **brightness** of the material's colors makes it beautiful.
10. We made an **agreement** to work together on the project.
11. Dad hopes to find a job through a **placement** agency.
12. Lacole has not had even a slight **illness** in years.
13. Her smiling face showed her **enjoyment**.
14. We waited for **darkness** so we could gaze at the stars.
15. The instructor explained each **movement** of the dance.
16. You could feel the **softness** of the cotton.
17. We could see **boldness** in the way she played tennis.
18. We made a **payment** of ten dollars.
19. The price of the plywood depends on the wood's **thickness**.
20. When her best friend moved away, Shada felt **sadness**.

Spelling and Vocabulary

Word Meanings

Write the spelling word that goes with each definition.

1. the condition of being physically healthy
2. the result of an understanding between people
3. the condition of being sad or gloomy
4. the quality of being kind and generous
5. the act of placing something
6. the condition or feeling of being weak
7. the condition of being heavy or thick
8. the result of paying something
9. the result of covering a road with a hard, smooth surface
10. the result of changing position or location

Word Structure

Add a suffix to each of the following base words to write a spelling word.

11. treat
12. bold
13. still
14. bright
15. enjoy
16. soft

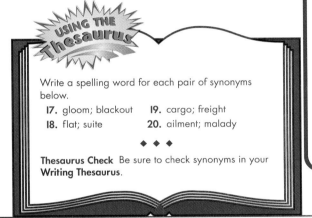

USING THE Thesaurus

Write a spelling word for each pair of synonyms below.

17. gloom; blackout
18. flat; suite
19. cargo; freight
20. ailment; malady

◆ ◆ ◆

Thesaurus Check Be sure to check synonyms in your **Writing Thesaurus**.

Word Meanings
1. fitness
2. agreement
3. sadness
4. kindness
5. placement
6. weakness
7. thickness
8. payment
9. pavement
10. movement

Word Structure
11. treatment
12. boldness
13. stillness
14. brightness
15. enjoyment
16. softness

Using the Thesaurus
17. darkness
18. apartment
19. shipment
20. illness

201

Objectives

Spelling and Vocabulary

Students will
- **write** spelling words for definitions.
- **add** suffixes to base words to write spelling words.
- **use** the **Writing Thesaurus** to write spelling words that are synonyms for given words.

Developing Oral Language Skills

Have students work in pairs. The first student asks a question that includes the base word of one of the words in the spelling list. For example, the first student might ask, "Did you **enjoy** the movie?" The second student answers the question. The answer must include the spelling word formed from that base word. For example, the second student might answer, "My **enjoyment** could not have been greater."

MEETING INDIVIDUAL NEEDS

Providing More Help

Have the students work in pairs. Assign the **-ness** suffix to one student in each pair and the **-ment** suffix to the other. Have each partner create word problems with the spelling words that contain her or his suffix. For example: **enjoy + ment = ?** Then have the partners exchange papers and write the spelling words that solve the problems. Have them check each other's papers.
★ Students who need to study fewer words should use the **Alternate Word List**. This list is starred on page T200 in the Teacher Edition. The **Unit 33 Practice Masters** (*Teacher Resource Book*) provide additional practice with these words.

Unit 33 Practice Masters

Name_____

Practice **Master** Unit **33**

1. illness 3. kindness 5. stillness 7. enjoyment 9. apartment
2. sadness 4. darkness 6. thickness 8. movement 10. agreement

A. Add the suffix **-ness** or **-ment** to each base word to make spelling words.

1. agree _____
2. thick _____
3. dark _____
4. ill _____
5. apart _____
6. sad _____
7. enjoy _____
8. move _____
9. still _____
10. kind _____

B. Write the spelling word that goes with each meaning.

1. an understanding between two parties _____
2. the quality of being kind and generous _____
3. the condition of being sad or gloomy _____
4. a building housing more than one family _____
5. change in position or location _____

184

Practice **Master** Unit **33**

enjoyment apartment
movement agreement

... for each word.

... words. Write the words.

185

Objectives

Spelling and Reading

Students will
- **complete** sentences using spelling words.
- **complete** a paragraph using spelling words.
- **write** spelling words that are antonyms of given words.

One-Minute Handwriting Hint

PENCIL POSITION

LEFT-HANDED

RIGHT-HANDED

Legible handwriting can boost spelling scores by as much as 20%.

Complete the Sentences
1. shipment
2. pavement
3. kindness
4. thickness
5. movement
6. payment
7. agreement
8. boldness
9. placement
10. treatment

Complete the Paragraph
11. stillness
12. apartment
13. fitness
14. weakness
15. enjoyment

Write the Antonyms
16. softness
17. illness
18. brightness
19. sadness
20. darkness

202

Spelling and Reading

kindness	treatment	stillness	apartment
fitness	pavement	weakness	shipment
brightness	agreement	placement	illness
enjoyment	darkness	movement	softness
boldness	payment	thickness	sadness

Complete the Sentences Write a spelling word by adding **-ness** or **-ment** to each underlined word.

1. The <u>ship</u> is carrying a large ____.
2. When they <u>pave</u> this road, the ____ will be easier to ride on.
3. <u>Kind</u> people bring out ____ in others.
4. This <u>thick</u> board is the same ____ as those other boards.
5. As you <u>move</u> your arms, follow the ____ of the dance director.
6. Please <u>pay</u> your bill by sending your ____ by mail.
7. We <u>agree</u> that he should sign the ____ today.
8. His <u>bold</u> words match the ____ of his personality.
9. As you <u>place</u> the pieces in the jigsaw puzzle, their ____ will help create a picture.
10. The doctors will <u>treat</u> certain injuries at a special ____ center.

Complete the Paragraph Write words from the box to complete the paragraph.

The accident left Martha weak. Each day, in the __11.__ of her small __12.__, she worked with physical __13.__ equipment to overcome her __14.__. Although it was hard work, she felt much __15.__ because she knew that one day she would be strong again.

> fitness
> weakness
> stillness
> enjoyment
> apartment

Write the Antonyms Write the spelling word that is an antonym of each of the following words.

16. hardness
17. health
18. dimness
19. happiness
20. brightness

MEETING INDIVIDUAL NEEDS

Providing More Challenge

Challenge Words and **Challenge Activities** for Unit 33 appear on page 251. **Challenge Word Test Sentences** appear on page T251.

Unit 33 Challenge Activities

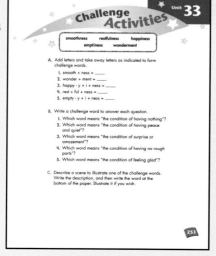

Weekly Test Options

Option 1:
One Spelling Word Per Sentence
(See procedures on pages Z10–Z11.)

1. The sky at night is filled with **darkness**.
2. We agreed on the **placement** of the painting.
3. The **thickness** of the book made it heavy to carry.
4. He recovered quickly from his **illness**.
5. Many people live in that **apartment** building.
6. There is often a sudden **stillness** before a storm.
7. The two friends made an **agreement**.
8. Feel the **softness** of the baby's skin.
9. The nurse's **treatment** of people showed her concern.
10. The **fitness** teacher was in good shape.
11. We walked along the path in the **brightness** of the moon.
12. A child gets a lot of **enjoyment** from going to the circus.
13. The coach was known for his **boldness**.
14. We will pay the last **payment** on our bill.
15. After he talked to his parents, his **sadness** ended.

T202

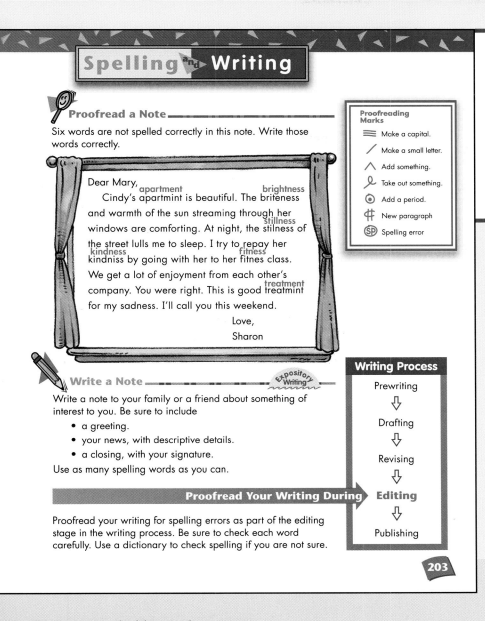

Spelling and Writing

Proofread a Note

Six words are not spelled correctly in this note. Write those words correctly.

Dear Mary,
    Cindy's apartmint is beautiful. The briteness and warmth of the sun streaming through her windows are comforting. At night, the stilness of the street lulls me to sleep. I try to repay her kindniss by going with her to her fitnes class. We get a lot of enjoyment from each other's company. You were right. This is good treatmint for my sadness. I'll call you this weekend.

              Love,

              Sharon

(corrections: apartment, brightness, stillness, kindness, fitness, treatment)

Proofreading Marks

≡	Make a capital.
/	Make a small letter.
∧	Add something.
℮	Take out something.
⊙	Add a period.
¶	New paragraph
SP	Spelling error

Write a Note

Expository Writing

Write a note to your family or a friend about something of interest to you. Be sure to include
- a greeting.
- your news, with descriptive details.
- a closing, with your signature.

Use as many spelling words as you can.

Writing Process

Prewriting
⇩
Drafting
⇩
Revising
⇩
Editing
⇩
Publishing

Proofread Your Writing During

Proofread your writing for spelling errors as part of the editing stage in the writing process. Be sure to check each word carefully. Use a dictionary to check spelling if you are not sure.

203

Objectives

Spelling and Writing

Students will
- **proofread** a note.
- **use** the writing process to write a note.
- **proofread** their writing.

Using the Writing Process

Before assigning **Write a Note,** see pages 258–259 in the Student Edition for a complete review of the writing process and additional writing assignments. You may also wish to refer to pages Z12–Z13 in the Teacher Edition.

Keeping a Spelling Journal

Encourage students to record the words they misspelled on the weekly test in a personal spelling journal. These words may be recycled for future study. Students may also wish to include words from their writing. See pages Z12–Z13 in the Teacher Edition for more information.

---

16. The trees swayed with a gentle **movement**.
17. She showed **kindness** by being nice to others.
18. A **shipment** of goods will be sent to the market.
19. A **weakness** in your ankle is what made you fall down.
20. The black **pavement** gets hot in the sun.

Option 2:
Multiple Spelling Words Per Sentence
(See procedures on pages Z10–Z11.)

1. Check the towels for **thickness** and **softness**.
2. The icy **pavement** needs a **treatment** of salt.
3. We had an **agreement** to make the **payment** on time.
4. The **shipment** of goods was left at our new **apartment**.
5. There was no **movement** in the **stillness** of the night.
6. The **brightness** of the fire was welcome in the **darkness**.
7. His **illness** caused **sadness** in his family.
8. It took **boldness** to make sure that the **placement** of the football was just right for the kick.
9. We go to the **fitness** club for **enjoyment** and good health.
10. Showing **kindness** to others is not a **weakness**.

Option 3:
Standardized Test
(See *Teacher Resource Book,* Unit 33.)

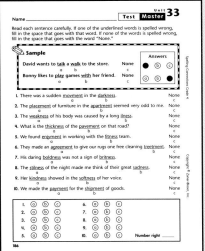

Unit 33 Test Master

T203

Objectives

Strategy Words

Students will
- **review** words studied previously that are related to the spelling strategy.
- **preview** unknown words that are related to the spelling strategy.

Vocabulary

Remind the students that the **Strategy Words** relate to the spelling patterns they have studied in this unit. The **Review Words** are below grade level, and the **Preview Words** are above grade level. You may wish to use the following sentences to introduce the words in context.

Review Words:
Words From Grade 3

1. The mountains were so **high** that their **highness** was awesome.
2. They were going to **pave** the road so it would have smooth **pavement**.
3. Your **right** behavior is a **rightness** that others can admire.
4. The puppy's **round** tummy had a **roundness** that made me laugh.
5. Her **mild** manner is a **mildness** that I respect.

Preview Words:
Words From Grade 5

6. It is not worth it to have an **argument** with your best friend.
7. My parents are pleased with their new **employment** opportunities.
8. Our **government** tries to be helpful to the people of the world as well as to our own nation.
9. His mysterious **sickness** lasted for about a week, then suddenly disappeared.
10. Your frequent **tardiness** at school will cause you to get far behind in your studies.

Review Words
1. **roundness**
2. **highness**
3. **pavement**
4. **rightness**
5. **mildness**

Preview Words
6. **sickness**
7. **argument**
8. **tardiness**
9. **employment**
10. **government**

Review Words: Suffixes –ness, –ment

Write a word for each clue by adding the suffix **-ness** or **-ment** to a word in the box.

high	pave	right	round	mild

1. describes one quality of a ball
2. refers to height
3. refers to the surface of a road
4. is an antonym of **wrongness**
5. might be used to describe the weather or a spice

Preview Words: Suffixes –ness, –ment

Write the word from the box that is the correct synonym or antonym.

argument	employment	government
	sickness	tardiness

6. a synonym of **illness**
7. an antonym of **agreement**
8. a synonym of **lateness**
9. an antonym of **unemployment**
10. a synonym of **administration**

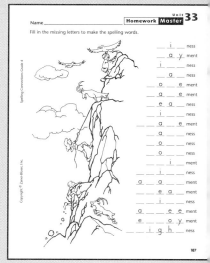

204

Unit
33
RECAP

You may wish to assign the **Unit 33 Homework Master** (*Teacher Resource Book*, Unit 33) as a fun way to recap the spelling words.

Unit 33 Homework Master

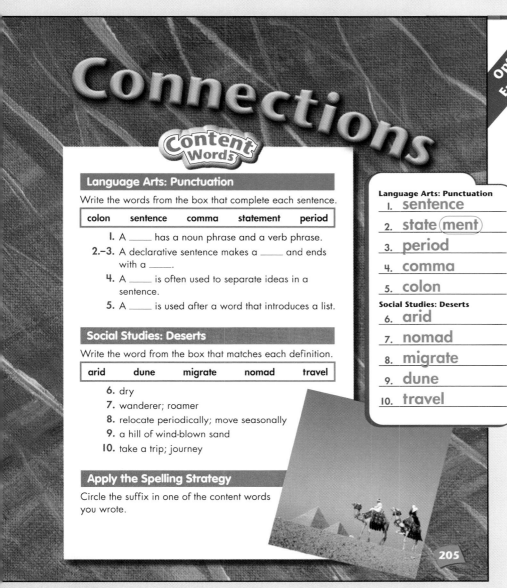

Connections

Content Words

Language Arts: Punctuation

Write the words from the box that complete each sentence.

colon	sentence	comma	statement	period

1. A _____ has a noun phrase and a verb phrase.
2.–3. A declarative sentence makes a _____ and ends with a _____.
4. A _____ is often used to separate ideas in a sentence.
5. A _____ is used after a word that introduces a list.

Social Studies: Deserts

Write the word from the box that matches each definition.

arid	dune	migrate	nomad	travel

6. dry
7. wanderer; roamer
8. relocate periodically; move seasonally
9. a hill of wind-blown sand
10. take a trip; journey

Apply the Spelling Strategy

Circle the suffix in one of the content words you wrote.

Language Arts: Punctuation
1. sentence
2. state(ment)
3. period
4. comma
5. colon

Social Studies: Deserts
6. arid
7. nomad
8. migrate
9. dune
10. travel

205

Objectives

Content Words

Students will
- **expand** vocabulary with content-related words.
- **relate** the spelling strategy to words outside the basic spelling list.

Content Words

Language Arts: Punctuation

Review the meanings of these words with the students. You may wish to use these sentences to introduce the words in context.

1. The **colon** is used just before naming a list of things.
2. Be sure each **sentence** has a subject and a verb.
3. Use a **comma** between the day and the year when you are writing the date.
4. He will make a **statement** about the front-page news story.
5. Always put a **period** after the abbreviation for Mister.

Encourage the students to use these words to write rules for punctuation.

Social Studies: Deserts

Review the meanings of these words with the students. You may wish to use these sentences to introduce the words in context.

6. When we speak about a desert being **arid,** we are saying that it is a hot and dry area.
7. As the wind blows the sand against that fence, it will create a large **dune**.
8. Many birds **migrate** to the south in cold weather.
9. A **nomad** is a wanderer.
10. We like to **travel** to warm places during the cooler months of the year.

Encourage the students to use these words to write a story set in the desert.

Unit 34 Home Study Master

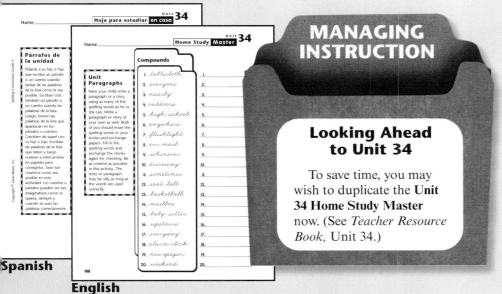

Spanish

English

MANAGING INSTRUCTION

Looking Ahead to Unit 34

To save time, you may wish to duplicate the **Unit 34 Home Study Master** now. (See *Teacher Resource Book,* Unit 34.)

Basic Spelling List

tablecloth	sometimes
everyone	seat belt
nearby	basketball
outdoors	mailbox
high school	baby sitter
anywhere	upstairs
flashlight	everyday
air mail	alarm clock
whenever	newspaper
driveway	weekend

Strategy Words

Review

anybody	someone
anything	something
everything	

Preview

downstairs	itself
good-bye	peanut butter
homework	

Content Words

Science: The Sun

core	sunspot
solar	halo
eclipse	

Science: Earthquakes

aftershock	totter
terror	fault
earthquake	

Individual Needs

Challenge Words

yearbook	third base
floodlight	zip code
field trip	

Alternate Word List

everyone	sometimes
nearby	basketball
outdoors	upstairs
anywhere	everyday
whenever	newspaper

MATERIALS

Student Edition

Pages 206–211
Challenge Activities, p. 252

Teacher Edition

Pages T206A–T211
Challenge Activities, p. T252

Other Resources

Spelling Connections Software
Unit 34 Word List Overhead
Transparency

Teacher Resource Book

Unit 34 Home Study Master
(English or Spanish; students
may pretest on this sheet or use
it for home practice.)
Unit 34 Homework Master
Unit 34 Practice Masters
Flip Folder Practice Master
Unit 34 Test Master

Visit our Web site, www.zaner-bloser.com

OBJECTIVES

Spelling and Thinking

Students will
- **read** the spelling words in list form and in context.
- **sort** the spelling words according to whether they are joined or two-word compounds.
- **read** and remember this week's spelling strategy.

Spelling and Vocabulary

Students will
- **write** spelling words for definitions.
- **write** spelling words that are antonyms of given words.
- **find** spelling words in the **Spelling Dictionary** and identify their parts of speech.

Spelling and Reading

Students will
- **replace** underlined phrases in sentences with spelling words.
- **complete** sentences using spelling words.
- **solve** analogies using spelling words.

Spelling and Writing

Students will
- **proofread** a notice.
- **use** the writing process to write a notice.
- **proofread** their writing.

MEETING INDIVIDUAL NEEDS
Learning Styles

Visual

Construct two spinners like the ones shown.

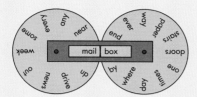

Write the first word of some of the closed compound words around the circle on the left. Write the second word around the circle on the right. Cut out a window in the tagboard and fasten the circles. Have the students form compound words, write the words, and use them in sentences.

Auditory

Make lists of five words each. Use the words that make up the compound words in the spelling list. In each list, include only one pair of words that can combine to form a compound word. For example, from the list **firm, doors, cube, bold,** and **out,** the word **outdoors** can be formed. Read the lists to the students. Have them take turns identifying the two words that make each spelling word and spell it into a tape recorder. Then have the students listen to themselves on tape and write the words.

Kinesthetic

Make forty tagboard strips and label them with the base words of the spelling words. Play a game called "Musical Compound Words" by giving each student a word strip and then playing some music. While the music is playing, each student must find another student who has a word that will form a compound with his or her word. Stop the music and have the students who have found their word partners say and spell the words they have formed. Have the students exchange word strips and play as many rounds of the game as time permits.

Language and Cultural Differences

Compound words may be difficult to spell, depending on the spelling of the words that form the compound. Once students see that compound words are simply two or more words written together, their spelling task will be facilitated.

Write the word **basketball** on the chalkboard. Pronounce the word and ask the students to listen for the two words that make the compound word. Explain that a **basketball** is a ball that is thrown into a basket. Have the students give the meanings of the other spelling words using the definitions of the words within the compounds.

MANAGING INSTRUCTION

3–5 Day Plan		Average	Below Average	Above Average
Day 1	Day 1	Pretest Spelling Mini-Lesson, p. T206 Spelling and Thinking, p. 206	Pretest Spelling Mini-Lesson, p. T206 Spelling and Thinking, p. 206	Pretest Spelling and Thinking, p. 206
	Day 2	Spelling and Vocabulary, p. 207	Spelling and Vocabulary, p. 207 (or) Unit 34 Practice Master, A and B	Spelling and Vocabulary, p. 207 Spelling and Reading, p. 208
Day 2	Day 3	Spelling and Reading, p. 208	Spelling and Reading, p. 208 (or) Unit 34 Practice Master, C and D	Challenge Activities, p. 252
	Day 4	Spelling and Writing, p. 209 Unit 34 Homework Master	Spelling and Writing, p. 209	Spelling and Writing, p. 209 Unit 34 Homework Master
Day 3	Day 5	Weekly Test	Weekly Test	Weekly Test
Vocabulary Connections (pages 210 and 211) may be used anytime during this unit.				

Objectives

Spelling and Thinking

Students will
- **read** the spelling words in list form and in context.
- **sort** the spelling words according to whether they are joined or two-word compounds.
- **read** and remember this week's spelling strategy.

UNIT PRETEST

Use **Pretest Sentences** below. Refer to the self-checking procedures on student page 256. You may wish to use the **Unit 34 Word List Overhead Transparency** as part of the checking procedure.

TEACHING THE STRATEGY

Spelling Mini-Lesson

Explain that compound words are formed by combining two or more words and that the meaning of the compound is usually related to the meaning of the words within it. Explain that new compound words are always being formed. For example, **air mail** has only been in use since the invention of the airplane. Encourage the students to look at the words on the spelling list and to try to identify compound words that probably were not used 200 years ago (e.g., **driveway, seat belt, basketball, flashlight**). Pursue this activity as much as possible to point out how language is always changing. Explain that speakers bring new compounds into the language, and writers change the way compounds are written. Some words, such as **smallpox, paperback,** and **toothache,** were originally open compounds but are now closed compounds.

Read the spelling words aloud. Discuss how the meanings of the individual words that make up a compound affect the meaning of the compound. For example, the **weekend** comes at the "end of the week." You may wish to note that **basketball** is so named because the ball was originally thrown into a bottomless peach basket!

Conclude by reading **Remember the Spelling Strategy** on page 206.

T206

Order of answers may vary.
one-word compounds
1. tablecloth
2. everyone ★
3. nearby ★
4. outdoors ★
5. anywhere ★
6. flashlight
7. whenever ★
8. driveway
9. sometimes ★
10. basketball ★
11. mailbox
12. upstairs ★
13. everyday ★
14. newspaper ★
15. weekend

two-word compounds
16. high school
17. air mail
18. seat belt
19. baby sitter
20. alarm clock

Unit **34**
Compounds

 Spelling **and** Thinking

READ THE SPELLING WORDS

1. tablecloth	tablecloth	We use a red and white **tablecloth**.
2. everyone	everyone	Was **everyone** at the soccer game?
3. nearby	nearby	We walk to school, which is **nearby**.
4. outdoors	outdoors	We play **outdoors** when it is warm.
5. high school	high school	My older brother is in **high school**.
6. anywhere	anywhere	You may sit **anywhere** you wish.
7. flashlight	flashlight	I need a **flashlight** to find my way.
8. air mail	air mail	A plane carrying **air mail** landed.
9. whenever	whenever	We can go **whenever** he is ready.
10. driveway	driveway	The car is parked in the **driveway**.
11. sometimes	sometimes	I walk to school **sometimes**.
12. seat belt	seat belt	Use your **seat belt** when in a car.
13. basketball	basketball	She is our new **basketball** coach.
14. mailbox	mailbox	I dropped the letter in the **mailbox**.
15. baby sitter	baby sitter	She is a **baby sitter** for the twins.
16. upstairs	upstairs	My bedroom is **upstairs**.
17. everyday	everyday	That is one of my **everyday** chores.
18. alarm clock	alarm clock	I set the **alarm clock** for 7:30.
19. newspaper	newspaper	We read a **newspaper** every day.
20. weekend	weekend	The **weekend** at the lake will be fun.

SORT THE SPELLING WORDS

1.–15. Write the compound words on the spelling list that are written as one word.

16.–20. Write the spelling words that are two-word compounds.

REMEMBER THE SPELLING STRATEGY

Remember that a compound word is formed from two or more smaller words. Closed compounds are written as one word: **newspaper**. Open compounds are written as two or more words: **air mail**.

206

Pretest Sentences (See procedures on pages Z10–Z11.)

1. Let us put a **tablecloth** on the table.
2. We will begin when **everyone** is here.
3. Lamar walks to school because he lives **nearby**.
4. Farmers often work **outdoors**.
5. She will graduate from **high school** soon.
6. We could not find Dan **anywhere**.
7. We keep a **flashlight** in our car.
8. A letter usually arrives sooner if you send it by **air mail**.
9. Please visit us **whenever** you can.
10. Mom parked the car in the **driveway**.
11. Lacara and I **sometimes** play tennis.
12. Terry wears a **seat belt** in the car.
13. The player bounced the **basketball**.
14. She put the letters in the **mailbox**.
15. Our **baby sitter** is a good storyteller.
16. I walked **upstairs** to the third floor.
17. I do my **everyday** chores after school.
18. Please set the **alarm clock**.
19. Father likes to read the **newspaper**.
20. We will go skiing this **weekend**.

Spelling and Vocabulary

Word Meanings

Write the spelling word that has the same or almost the same meaning as each of the following phrases.

1. a person who takes care of a baby
2. a paper that has news in it
3. a game in which a ball is thrown through a basket
4. a school that usually includes grades nine through twelve
5. the two days at the end of the week

Antonyms

Write a spelling word that is an antonym for each of the following words.

6. faraway
7. downstairs
8. indoors
9. no one
10. nowhere

USING THE Dictionary

Find the following words in your **Spelling Dictionary**. Write each word. Then write **n.**, **adj.**, **adv.**, or **conj.** after it to name the part of speech it usually has.

11. whenever	16. flashlight
12. seat belt	17. sometimes
13. tablecloth	18. driveway
14. everyday	19. air mail
15. mailbox	20. alarm clock

Word Meanings
1. baby sitter
2. newspaper
3. basketball
4. high school
5. weekend

Antonyms
6. nearby
7. upstairs
8. outdoors
9. everyone
10. anywhere

Using the Dictionary
11. whenever, conj.
12. seat belt, n.
13. tablecloth, n.
14. everyday, adj.
15. mailbox, n.
16. flashlight, n.
17. sometimes, adv.
18. driveway, n.
19. air mail, n.
20. alarm clock, n.

207

Developing Oral Language Skills

Divide the class into pairs of students. Give each pair twenty 3" × 5" cards, and have the students write one spelling word on each card. The first partner shuffles the cards, places them facedown on the table or desk, draws the top card, and says the first word of the compound word on that card. Without looking at the card, the partner says the second word of the compound as quickly as possible. Have the partners take turns calling out the first word and responding with the second word as quickly as they can until all the spelling words have been used.

MEETING INDIVIDUAL NEEDS

Providing More Help

Write the compound words on the chalkboard with the two base words in reverse order. For example, write **nearby** as **bynear**. Have the students write the words correctly on their papers.

★ Students who need to study fewer words should use the **Alternate Word List**. This list is starred on page T206 in the Teacher Edition. The **Unit 34 Practice Masters** (*Teacher Resource Book*) provide additional practice with these words.

Unit 34 Practice Masters

Name_____

Practice Master 34

1. nearby	3. everyday	5. everyone	7. outdoors	9. upstairs
2. anywhere	4. sometimes	6. whenever	8. newspaper	10. basketball

A. Write the spelling word that is an antonym for each word.

1. faraway _____
2. downstairs _____
3. inside _____
4. no one _____
5. nowhere _____

B. Find each of the spelling words in your **Spelling Dictionary**. Write the word. Then write **n.**, **adj.**, **adv.**, **pron.**, or **conj.** to name the part of speech of the word.

1. nearby _____
2. anywhere _____
3. everyday _____
4. sometimes _____
5. everyone _____
6. whenever _____
7. outdoors _____
8. newspaper _____
9. upstairs _____
10. basketball _____

190

Practice Master 34

outdoors   upstairs
newspaper   basketball

a compound word. Write the

me	out	doors
ws	basket	stairs

ue to a spelling word. Write the
example.

191

Objectives

Spelling and Reading

Students will
- **replace** underlined phrases in sentences with spelling words.
- **complete** sentences using spelling words.
- **solve** analogies using spelling words.

One-Minute Handwriting Hint

The undercurve ending of the lowercase **e** curves up and right to form the top of the letter **a**. The downstroke of the letter **a** retraces the joining slightly and then curves down. Be sure to close the oval in the letter **a**.

FORMS TOP OF LETTER

Legible handwriting can boost spelling scores by as much as 20%.

Replace the Words
1. Everyone
2. baby sitter
3. air mail
4. newspaper
5. sometimes

Complete the Sentences
6. seat belt
7. everyday
8. alarm clock
9. outdoors
10. driveway
11. mailbox
12. flashlight
13. tablecloth
14. basketball
15. whenever

Solve the Analogies
16. weekend
17. high school
18. nearby
19. upstairs
20. anywhere

Spelling and Reading

tablecloth	everyone	nearby	outdoors
high school	anywhere	flashlight	air mail
whenever	driveway	sometimes	seat belt
basketball	mailbox	baby sitter	upstairs
everyday	alarm clock	newspaper	weekend

Replace the Words   Replace the underlined part of each sentence with a spelling word.
1. Every person can be seated now.
2. The person who takes care of children arrived.
3. Our post office has a special slot for mail that is sent by air.
4. We subscribe to a daily news printed on sheets of paper.
5. I now and then listen to the radio.

Complete the Sentences   Write the spelling word that completes each sentence.
6. I always wear a _____ when riding in a car.
7. We have old dishes that Mom calls her _____ tableware.
8. I was late yesterday because my _____ did not ring.
9. I would rather be _____ than indoors.
10. My father parks his car in our _____.
11. Was there a letter in the _____?
12. I need a bright _____ for my camping trips.
13. Please put the lace _____ on the table.
14. Our school will have a _____ game tonight.
15. I squint _____ the sun is in my eyes.

Solve the Analogies   Write a spelling word to solve each analogy.
16. **Wednesday** is to **weekday** as **Saturday** is to _____.
17. **Fourth grade** is to **elementary school** as **tenth grade** is to _____.
18. **Distant** is to **faraway** as **close** is to _____.
19. **First floor** is to **downstairs** as **second floor** is to _____.
20. **No one** is to **anyone** as **nowhere** is to _____.

208

MEETING INDIVIDUAL NEEDS

Providing More Challenge

Challenge Words and **Challenge Activities** for Unit 34 appear on page 252. **Challenge Word Test Sentences** appear on page T252.

Unit 34 Challenge Activities

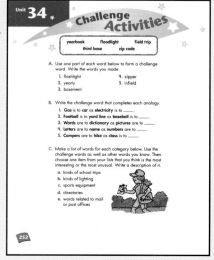

Weekly Test Options

Option 1:
One Spelling Word Per Sentence
(See procedures on pages Z10–Z11.)

1. I go swimming **whenever** it is hot.
2. Some states have a law that says you must wear your **seat belt** in the car.
3. A car drove up the **driveway**.
4. I will change out of my **everyday** clothes and wear something new to the party.
5. There are many classrooms in the **high school**.
6. Baseball is usually played **outdoors**.
7. Put the letters into the **mailbox**.
8. The package was sent by **air mail**.
9. I read the **newspaper** before breakfast.
10. Our **baby sitter** has some fun ideas.
11. We sat **nearby** and watched the show.
12. Turn the **flashlight** on so you can see.
13. We **sometimes** eat outside.
14. The **tablecloth** looks pretty on the table.

T208

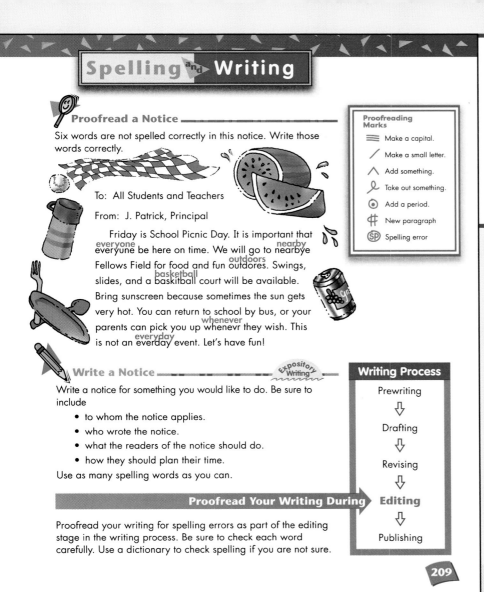

Spelling and Writing

Proofread a Notice

Six words are not spelled correctly in this notice. Write those words correctly.

To: All Students and Teachers

From: J. Patrick, Principal

Friday is School Picnic Day. It is important that *everyone* everyune be here on time. We will go to *nearby* nearbye Fellows Field for food and fun *outdoors* outdores. Swings, slides, and a *basketball* baskitball court will be available. Bring sunscreen because sometimes the sun gets very hot. You can return to school by bus, or your parents can pick you up *whenever* whenevr they wish. This is not an *everyday* everday event. Let's have fun!

Proofreading Marks

≡ Make a capital.

/ Make a small letter.

∧ Add something.

⌇ Take out something.

⊙ Add a period.

⌗ New paragraph.

(SP) Spelling error

Write a Notice

Expository Writing

Write a notice for something you would like to do. Be sure to include
- to whom the notice applies.
- who wrote the notice.
- what the readers of the notice should do.
- how they should plan their time.

Use as many spelling words as you can.

Proofread Your Writing During

Writing Process

Prewriting
⇩
Drafting
⇩
Revising
⇩
Editing
⇩
Publishing

Proofread your writing for spelling errors as part of the editing stage in the writing process. Be sure to check each word carefully. Use a dictionary to check spelling if you are not sure.

209

Using the Writing Process

Before assigning **Write a Notice,** see pages 258–259 in the Student Edition for a complete review of the writing process and additional writing assignments. You may also wish to refer to pages Z12–Z13 in the Teacher Edition.

Keeping a Spelling Journal

Encourage students to record the words they misspelled on the weekly test in a personal spelling journal. These words may be recycled for future study. Students may also wish to include words from their writing. See pages Z12–Z13 in the Teacher Edition for more information.

---

15. My bedroom is **upstairs**.
16. The **alarm clock** will ring early in the morning.
17. Father will take us **anywhere** we want to go today.
18. Let us go camping this **weekend**.
19. We will play **basketball**.
20. We want **everyone** to come to the party.

Option 2:
Multiple Spelling Words Per Sentence
(See procedures on pages Z10–Z11.)

1. We kept the **flashlight outdoors** in the tent.
2. My sister in **high school** has several **everyday** chores.
3. You will find the **newspaper** in the **mailbox** at the end of the **driveway**.
4. A **tablecloth** is **sometimes** placed on the picnic table.
5. I wear a **seat belt whenever** I ride in a car.
6. I do not set the **alarm clock** on the **weekend**.
7. We include **everyone** in our **basketball** games.
8. The **baby sitter** went **upstairs** to put the baby to bed.
9. We can get **air mail** from **anywhere** in the nation, as well as letters from **nearby** towns.

Option 3:
Standardized Test
(See *Teacher Resource Book,* Unit 34.)

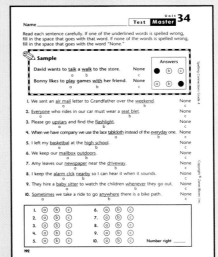

Unit 34 Test Master

T209

Vocabulary

Objectives

Strategy Words

Students will
- **review** words studied previously that are related to the spelling strategy.
- **preview** unknown words that are related to the spelling strategy.

Remind the students that the **Strategy Words** relate to the spelling patterns they have studied in this unit. The **Review Words** are below grade level, and the **Preview Words** are above grade level. You may wish to use the following sentences to introduce the words in context.

Review Words:
Words From Grade 3

1. Is there **anybody** at the front door to greet visitors?
2. I do not see **anything** in this drawer that will work to open that can.
3. Make sure **everything** is ready for the family reunion.
4. Will **someone** please put those books back on the shelf?
5. Put **something** to eat in your backpack, as it will be a long hike.

Preview Words:
Words From Grade 5

6. Take your toys and books **downstairs** and play in the playroom.
7. Tell your mom and dad **good-bye** when you leave for the store.
8. How much **homework** do you have tonight?
9. The puppy scratched **itself** behind the ears.
10. He wanted some **peanut butter** sandwiches and an apple for his lunch.

Review Words
1. someone
2. something
3. everything
4. anything
5. anybody

Preview Words
6. good-bye
7. itself
8. peanut butter
9. homework
10. downstairs

Review Words: Compounds

Write the word from the box that matches each of the following descriptions.

anybody	anything	everything	someone	something

1. I am a two-syllable word ending in **one**.
2. I am a two-syllable word ending in **thing**.
3. I am a three-syllable word meaning "all things."
4. I am a three-syllable word beginning with **any**.
5. I am a four-syllable word meaning "any person."

Preview Words: Compounds

Write the word from the box that matches each clue.

downstairs	good-bye	homework
	itself	peanut butter

6. an antonym of **hello**
7. himself, herself, _____
8. an open compound naming something good to eat
9. a closed compound meaning "work that is done at home"
10. a location in a building

210

Unit 34 RECAP

You may wish to assign the **Unit 34 Homework Master** (*Teacher Resource Book*, Unit 34) as a fun way to recap the spelling words.

Unit 34 Homework Master

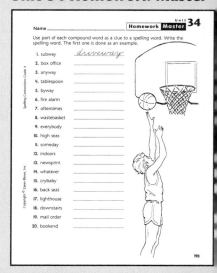

Name _____

Homework Master Unit 34

Use part of each compound word as a clue to a spelling word. Write the spelling word. The first one is done as an example.

1. subway _driveway_
2. box office
3. anyway
4. tablespoon
5. byway
6. fire alarm
7. oftentimes
8. wastebasket
9. everybody
10. high seas
11. someday
12. indoors
13. newsprint
14. whatever
15. crybaby
16. back seat
17. lighthouse
18. downstairs
19. mail order
20. bookend

Spelling Connections Grade 4
Copyright © Zaner-Bloser, Inc.

193

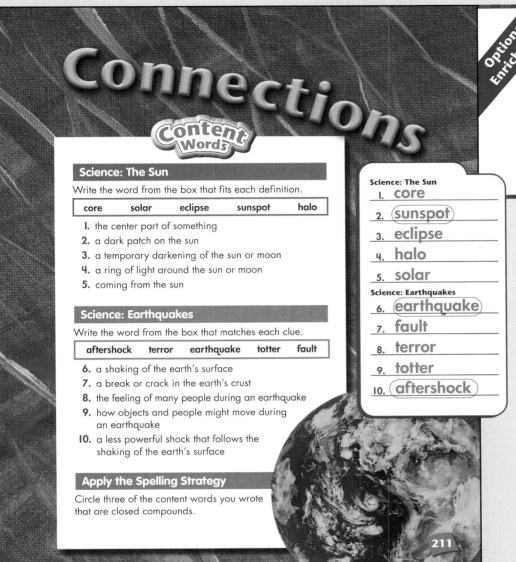

Connections

Content Words

Science: The Sun

Write the word from the box that fits each definition.

core	solar	eclipse	sunspot	halo

1. the center part of something
2. a dark patch on the sun
3. a temporary darkening of the sun or moon
4. a ring of light around the sun or moon
5. coming from the sun

Science: Earthquakes

Write the word from the box that matches each clue.

aftershock	terror	earthquake	totter	fault

6. a shaking of the earth's surface
7. a break or crack in the earth's crust
8. the feeling of many people during an earthquake
9. how objects and people might move during an earthquake
10. a less powerful shock that follows the shaking of the earth's surface

Apply the Spelling Strategy

Circle three of the content words you wrote that are closed compounds.

211

Science: The Sun
1. core
2. sunspot
3. eclipse
4. halo
5. solar

Science: Earthquakes
6. earthquake
7. fault
8. terror
9. totter
10. aftershock

Objectives

Content Words

Students will
- **expand** vocabulary with content-related words.
- **relate** the spelling strategy to words outside the basic spelling list.

Content Words

Science: The Sun

Review the meanings of these words with the students. You may wish to use these sentences to introduce the words in context.

1. What makes up the **core** of the earth?
2. Many people heat their homes with **solar** energy.
3. The class wanted to talk about the lunar **eclipse** that took place last night.
4. A **sunspot** is a dark place that appears on the surface of the sun.
5. The ring of light that surrounds the moon is called a **halo**.

Encourage the students to use these words to start a glossary of scientific terms.

Science: Earthquakes

Review the meanings of these words with the students. You may wish to use these sentences to introduce the words in context.

6. An **aftershock** took place following the terrible quake.
7. Many people experienced **terror** as the movement of the earth grew more intense.
8. The **earthquake** was particularly frightening for those who experienced it.
9. We were so unsteady on our feet that we began to **totter**.
10. A crack in the earth's crust is called a **fault**.

Encourage the students to use these words to write a brief newspaper article about a real or imaginary earthquake.

Unit 35 Home Study Master

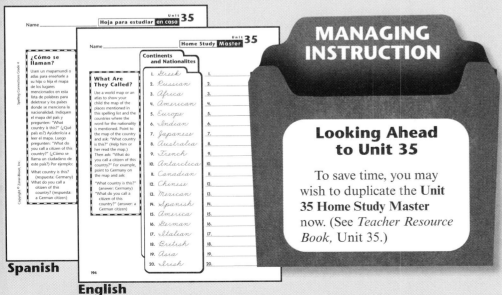

Spanish

English

MANAGING INSTRUCTION

Looking Ahead to Unit 35

To save time, you may wish to duplicate the **Unit 35 Home Study Master** now. (See *Teacher Resource Book,* Unit 35.)

Basic Spelling List

Greek	Canadian
Russian	Chinese
Africa	Mexican
American	Spanish
Europe	America
Indian	German
Japanese	Italian
Australia	British
French	Asia
Antarctica	Irish

Strategy Words

Review

street	west
east	south
earth	

Preview

California	Texas
Colorado	Washington
New York	

Content Words

Social Studies: Geography

arctic	strait
polar	iceberg
continent	

Math: Ordinal Numbers

ninth	fourteenth
thirteenth	twelfth
eleventh	

Individual Needs

Challenge Words

yen	franc
lira	shilling
peso	

Alternate Word List

Africa	Mexican
American	Spanish
Indian	America
French	Asia
Chinese	Irish

MATERIALS

Student Edition
Pages 212–217
Challenge Activities, p. 253

Teacher Edition
Pages T212A–T217
Challenge Activities, p. T253

Other Resources
Spelling Connections Software
Unit 35 Word List Overhead
Transparency

Teacher Resource Book
Unit 35 Home Study Master
(English or Spanish; students
may pretest on this sheet or use
it for home practice.)
Unit 35 Homework Master
Unit 35 Practice Masters
Flip Folder Practice Master
Unit 35 Test Master

Visit our Web site, www.zaner-bloser.com

OBJECTIVES

Spelling and Thinking
Students will
- **read** the spelling words in list form and in context.
- **sort** the spelling words according to whether they name continents or nationalities.
- **read** and remember this week's spelling strategy.

Spelling and Vocabulary
Students will
- **write** spelling words by matching nationalities to country names.
- **write** spelling words that are names of continents beginning and ending with **a**.
- **write** spelling words that contain given smaller words.
- **use** the **Spelling Dictionary** to alphabetize spelling words.

Spelling and Reading
Students will
- **write** spelling words that name categories for a group of meaning-related words.
- **complete** sentences using spelling words.

Spelling and Writing
Students will
- **proofread** an ad.
- **use** the writing process to write an ad.
- **proofread** their writing.

MEETING INDIVIDUAL NEEDS
Learning Styles

Visual

On a large map of the world, have volunteers point out each continent and the country of each nationality as you pronounce each spelling word. Then have the students write the words.

Divide the spelling words among the students and have them trace and cut out the shapes of the continents and the nations that are represented. Have the students use these patterns to draw the shapes on colored pieces of construction paper. Then have them write the appropriate spelling word in large letters on each shape. Display their work.

Auditory

Have the students sit in a circle. Pronounce a spelling word and ask a student to say the first letter. (Remind the students that the first letter of each spelling word will be an uppercase letter.) Have the next student in clockwise order say the second letter of the word. Have the students continue to spell the letters of the word until the last letter is named. Then have the next student in line pronounce the word. If a student makes a mistake, start over again from the first student. Continue this activity until all the spelling words have been pronounced and spelled.

Kinesthetic

Write each spelling word on a small strip of paper. Using a large relief globe, if available, have the students attach each spelling word to the appropriate nation or continent. Then pronounce one word at a time, and have a volunteer find the nation or continent it represents and run her or his fingers over its contours and borders. Then have all of the students write the spelling words on their papers.

Language and Cultural Differences

Because of regional dialects or different language backgrounds, the students' pronunciation of the words in this unit may vary. Correct spelling can be achieved without exact pronunciation, however, provided that the student has the opportunity to associate the meaning of the word with the visual sequence of letters that spell it. Through the use of a world map or globe, demonstrate the meanings of the spelling words several times.

Ask the students to read along with you in their spelling books as you pronounce each spelling word. Have them repeat each word in unison. Then ask the students to tell you something about the meaning of each word. Clarify and expand on the students' definitions if necessary.

MANAGING INSTRUCTION

3–5 Day Plan		Average	Below Average	Above Average
Day 1	**Day 1**	Pretest Spelling Mini-Lesson, p. T212 Spelling and Thinking, p. 212	Pretest Spelling Mini-Lesson, p. T212 Spelling and Thinking, p. 212	Pretest Spelling and Thinking, p. 212
	Day 2	Spelling and Vocabulary, p. 213	Spelling and Vocabulary, p. 213 (or) Unit 35 Practice Master, A and B	Spelling and Vocabulary, p. 213 Spelling and Reading, p. 214
Day 2	**Day 3**	Spelling and Reading, p. 214	Spelling and Reading, p. 214 (or) Unit 35 Practice Master, C and D	Challenge Activities, p. 253
	Day 4	Spelling and Writing, p. 215 Unit 35 Homework Master	Spelling and Writing, p. 215	Spelling and Writing, p. 215 Unit 35 Homework Master
Day 3	**Day 5**	Weekly Test	Weekly Test	Weekly Test

Vocabulary Connections (pages 216 and 217) may be used anytime during this unit.

Objectives

Spelling and Thinking

Students will
- **read** the spelling words in list form and in context.
- **sort** the spelling words according to whether they name continents or nationalities.
- **read** and remember this week's spelling strategy.

UNIT PRETEST

Use **Pretest Sentences** below. Refer to the self-checking procedures on student page 256. You may wish to use the **Unit 35 Word List Overhead Transparency** as part of the checking procedure.

TEACHING THE STRATEGY

Spelling Mini-Lesson

Ask the students to tell about countries outside the United States that they have lived in, visited, or know about. Write these countries' names on the chalkboard. (You may wish to use a world map or a globe and ask students to locate these countries.)

Remind the students that a continent is a huge land mass that contains one or more countries. Ask the students to identify the continent on which each of the countries they have named is located.

Ask, "Which continents are on the spelling list?" (Antarctica, Asia, Europe, Africa, Australia) (**Note: Australia** is both a country and a continent. You may wish to point out that **America** can refer to either North America, South America, or the United States.)

Ask the students what the rest of the spelling words name. (the people or language of a specific country) Ask volunteers to identify the country related to selected peoples or languages.

If any students speak one of the languages on the list, encourage them to share words in that language.

Read the spelling list with the students. Clarify that **Indian** usually refers to people from India.

Conclude by reading **Remember the Spelling Strategy** on page 212.

T212

Unit 35
Continents and Nationalities

Order of answers may vary.

continents
1. Africa ★
2. Europe
3. Australia
4. Antarctica
5. America ★
6. Asia ★

nationalities
7. Greek
8. Russian
9. American ★
10. Indian ★
11. Japanese
12. French ★
13. Canadian
14. Chinese ★
15. Mexican ★
16. Spanish ★
17. German
18. Italian
19. British
20. Irish ★

Spelling and Thinking

READ THE SPELLING WORDS

1.	Greek	*Greek*	He is of **Greek** ancestry.
2.	Russian	*Russian*	Our dog is a **Russian** wolfhound.
3.	Africa	*Africa*	They went on a safari in **Africa**.
4.	American	*American*	That is an **American** automobile.
5.	Europe	*Europe*	She traveled in **Europe** all summer.
6.	Indian	*Indian*	The **Indian** capital is New Delhi.
7.	Japanese	*Japanese*	We saw a **Japanese** temple.
8.	Australia	*Australia*	**Australia** is a small continent.
9.	French	*French*	I studied the **French** language.
10.	Antarctica	*Antarctica*	**Antarctica** is a cold, icy continent.
11.	Canadian	*Canadian*	Ontario is a **Canadian** province.
12.	Chinese	*Chinese*	The **Chinese** have an ancient culture.
13.	Mexican	*Mexican*	Do you cook **Mexican** dishes?
14.	Spanish	*Spanish*	Are your relatives of **Spanish** descent?
15.	America	*America*	**America** consists of two continents.
16.	German	*German*	We watched the **German** folk dancers.
17.	Italian	*Italian*	I love **Italian** food.
18.	British	*British*	Which countries are **British**?
19.	Asia	*Asia*	Laos is a country in **Asia**.
20.	Irish	*Irish*	We enjoy singing **Irish** songs.

SORT THE SPELLING WORDS

1.–6. Write the spelling words that name continents.

7.–20. Write the spelling words that name nationalities.

REMEMBER THE SPELLING STRATEGY

Remember that it is important to be able to spell the names of the continents and nationalities correctly.

212

Pretest Sentences (See procedures on pages Z10–Z11.)

1. At **Greek** festivals the men perform entertaining dances.
2. My cousin is learning to speak the **Russian** language.
3. Egypt is a country in **Africa**.
4. George Washington was the first **American** president.
5. **Europe** is the sixth largest continent.
6. **Indian** food usually contains spices.
7. **Japanese** people make many products to export.
8. A continent located south of the equator is **Australia**.
9. Some restaurants serve various kinds of **French** food.
10. The coldest continent is **Antarctica**.
11. The **Canadian** provinces are located north of the continental United States.
12. Many people enjoy **Chinese** food.
13. Mexico is the native land of **Mexican** people.
14. Is the **Spanish** language taught in our high school?
15. The United States of America is often called "**America**."
16. Many **German** people speak other languages.
17. People all over the world enjoy **Italian** foods.
18. Most **British** people come from Great Britain.
19. **Asia** is a very large continent.
20. Many **Irish** people live in the United States.

Spelling and Vocabulary

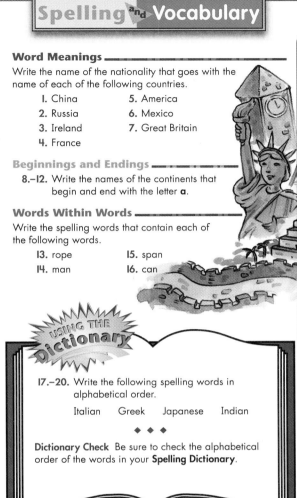

Word Meanings

Write the name of the nationality that goes with the name of each of the following countries.

1. China
2. Russia
3. Ireland
4. France
5. America
6. Mexico
7. Great Britain

Beginnings and Endings

8.–12. Write the names of the continents that begin and end with the letter **a**.

Words Within Words

Write the spelling words that contain each of the following words.

13. rope
14. man
15. span
16. can

USING THE Dictionary

17.–20. Write the following spelling words in alphabetical order.

Italian   Greek   Japanese   Indian

◆ ◆ ◆

Dictionary Check Be sure to check the alphabetical order of the words in your **Spelling Dictionary**.

Word Meanings
1. Chinese
2. Russian
3. Irish
4. French
5. American
6. Mexican
7. British

Beginnings and Endings
Order of answers may vary.
8. Africa
9. Australia
10. Antarctica
11. America
12. Asia

Words Within Words
13. Europe
14. German
15. Spanish
16. Canadian

Using the Dictionary
17. Greek
18. Indian
19. Italian
20. Japanese

213

Objectives

Spelling and Vocabulary

Students will
- **write** spelling words by matching nationalities to country names.
- **write** spelling words that are names of continents beginning and ending with **a**.
- **write** spelling words that contain given smaller words.
- **use** the **Spelling Dictionary** to alphabetize spelling words.

Developing Oral Language Skills

Write **Antarctica** on the chalkboard. Have students pronounce **Antarctica** (/ănt **ärk′** tĭ kə/) and note whether the first **t** and the first **c** are pronounced. Explain to students that the word **Antarctica** is often misspelled because the first **t** and first **c** are omitted from the pronunciation. If necessary, remind students to pronounce these letters and have them practice saying the word several times.

MEETING INDIVIDUAL NEEDS

Providing More Help

Assign a spelling word to each student. Call on each student to stand and give a clue about her or his spelling word. Have each say, "I am thinking of a place that . . . " or "I am thinking of some people who . . ." and then give a clue about the continent or nationality named by their spelling word. Have the other students try to guess the word and write it on their papers. Continue this activity until all the spelling words have been used.

★ Students who need to study fewer words should use the **Alternate Word List**. This list is starred on page T212 in the Teacher Edition. The **Unit 35 Practice Masters** (*Teacher Resource Book*) provide additional practice with these words.

Unit 35 Practice Masters

Name _____   Practice **Master** Unit **35**

| 1. Asia | 3. America | 5. French | 7. Mexican | 9. Chinese |
| 2. Africa | 4. Irish | 6. Indian | 8. Spanish | 10. American |

A. The groups of people listed below come from the continents in the spelling list. Write the name of the continent that each group comes from.

1. African _____
2. Asian _____
3. American _____

B. Read each sentence carefully and find the misspelled word(s) or the capitalization error(s). Write the spelling word correctly.

1. An Amerecin citizen can vote at the age of eighteen. _____
2. James Joyce was a famous irish writer. _____
3. The Indean government meets in New Delhi, India's capital. _____
4. The mexican people speak Spanesh. _____
5. Renoir was a famous Fench artist. _____
6. The Chinees people live in one of the largest countries in the world. _____

196

Practice **Master** Unit **35**

| Mexican | Chinese |
| Spanish | American |

197

T213

Objectives

Spelling and Reading

Students will
- **write** spelling words that name categories for a group of meaning-related words.
- **complete** sentences using spelling words.

Name the Categories
1. Chinese
2. Canadian
3. Irish
4. Antarctica
5. Australia
6. French
7. British
8. Greek

Complete the Sentences
9. Asia
10. America
11. Indian
12. Italian
13. Mexican
14. Spanish
15. Russian
16. Europe
17. Japanese
18. American
19. German
20. Africa

Spelling and Reading

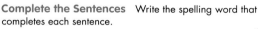

Greek	Russian	Africa	American
Europe	Indian	Japanese	Australia
French	Antarctica	Canadian	Chinese
Mexican	Spanish	America	German
Italian	British	Asia	Irish

Name the Categories Write the spelling word that is suggested by each of the following groups of words.

1. panda bears, chopsticks, Great Wall
2. maple leaf, hockey, provinces
3. shamrocks, Blarney Stone, green fields
4. snow, ice, whales, penguins
5. kangaroos, koala bears, boomerangs
6. Paris, berets, Eiffel Tower
7. Big Ben, London, Buckingham Palace
8. Olympics, mythology, Athens

Complete the Sentences Write the spelling word that completes each sentence.

9. The largest continent in the world is _____.
10. The United States is in North _____.
11. A sari is a dress worn by many _____ women.
12. Rome is an _____ city.
13. _____ festivals are called **fiestas**.
14. Madrid is a _____ city.
15. *Sputnik I* was a _____ spacecraft, the first to orbit the earth.
16. France and Spain are countries in _____.
17. **Origami** is the _____ art of folding paper.
18. The two _____ continents are South America and North America.
19. Berlin is a large _____ city.
20. You can go on a jungle safari in _____.

MEETING INDIVIDUAL NEEDS

Providing More Challenge

Challenge Words and **Challenge Activities** for Unit 35 appear on page 253. **Challenge Word Test Sentences** appear on page T253.

Unit 35 Challenge Activities

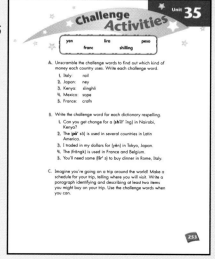

Weekly Test Options

Option 1:
One Spelling Word Per Sentence
(See procedures on pages Z10–Z11.)

1. My grandfather can speak **German**.
2. There are jungles and deserts in **Africa**.
3. We used **Italian** bread to make our sandwiches.
4. His **British** friend came for a visit last February.
5. My uncle drives a **Japanese** car.
6. There are many states in **America**.
7. The **Canadian** flag is red and white.
8. The **Irish** singer wore a green cap.
9. My brother wants to sail to **Europe**.
10. The **Russian** dancer has very quick movements.
11. We study about **Asia** in school.
12. Some **Mexican** food tastes very spicy.
13. Mother saw wild animals in **Australia**.
14. I enjoy **Chinese** food.
15. **Antarctica** is empty and cold.

Proofread an Ad

Six words are not spelled correctly in this travel ad. Write those words correctly.

Omniworld
Offers It All

Do you want to sweat in a jungle in Africa,
                        Antarctica   *Europe*
shiver in Antartica, visit Europ, photograph
kangaroos in Australia, or explore South
    America   *Greek*
Americka? We have it all: Greak food, Irish
                Chinese
hospitality, the Chineese Great Wall! Visit or call
        Canadian
our Canadien or American offices today.

Proofreading Marks

≡ Make a capital.
/ Make a small letter.
∧ Add something.
℘ Take out something.
⊙ Add a period.
⌗ New paragraph
ⓢⓟ Spelling error

Write an Ad

Persuasive Writing

Write a travel ad about a place you have visited or would like to visit. Be sure to include

• the name of the company placing the ad.
• what the company has to offer.
• suggested prices.
• why the reader should choose to go.
• how the reader can get more information.

Use as many spelling words as you can.

Proofread Your Writing During ➤

Proofread your writing for spelling errors as part of the editing stage in the writing process. Be sure to check each word carefully. Use a dictionary to check spelling if you are not sure.

Writing Process

Prewriting
⇩
Drafting
⇩
Revising
⇩
Editing
⇩
Publishing

215

Objectives

Spelling and Writing

Students will
• **proofread** an ad.
• **use** the writing process to write an ad.
• **proofread** their writing.

Using the Writing Process

Before assigning **Write an Ad,** see pages 258–259 in the Student Edition for a complete review of the writing process and additional writing assignments. You may also wish to refer to pages Z12–Z13 in the Teacher Edition.

Keeping a Spelling Journal

Encourage students to record the words they misspelled on the weekly test in a personal spelling journal. These words may be recycled for future study. Students may also wish to include words from their writing. See pages Z12–Z13 in the Teacher Edition for more information.

---

16. That **Indian** student is a visitor to the United States.
17. Would you like to meet the **Greek** skater?
18. The **American** flag has three colors.
19. The **French** cook prepares delicious meals.
20. Listen to the **Spanish** lady sing.

Option 2:
Multiple Spelling Words Per Sentence
(See procedures on pages Z10–Z11.)

1. We went to **Africa** and **Asia**.
2. The **American** ship will sail from **America** to **Europe**.
3. I will visit **Australia** before going to **Antarctica**.
4. The **Greek** woman and the **Irish** girl are friends.
5. I used **French** cheese in that **German** dish.
6. The **Italian** lady enjoys **Chinese** and **Mexican** food.
7. The shop sold **Canadian** wool suits and **Indian** cotton dresses.
8. The **British** ship sailed from a **Russian** port.
9. Since the **Japanese** woman did not speak **Spanish,** she could not understand the visitor.

Option 3:
Standardized Test
(See *Teacher Resource Book,* Unit 35.)

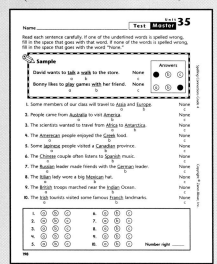

Unit 35 Test Master

Objectives

Strategy Words

Students will
- **review** words studied previously that are related to the spelling strategy.
- **preview** unknown words that are related to the spelling strategy.

Remind the students that the **Strategy Words** relate to the content they have studied in this unit. The **Review Words** are below grade level, and the **Preview Words** are above grade level. You may wish to use the following sentences to introduce the words in context.

Review Words:
Words From Grade 3
1. Look both ways before crossing the **street**.
2. The sun rises in the **east** and goes down in the western skies.
3. Our **earth** rotates on its axis as it follows its path around the sun.
4. As we travel **west,** we see lots of beautiful mountains and canyons.
5. Is your house north or **south** of the park?

Preview Words:
Words From Grade 5
6. We drove along the coast of **California,** seeing the ocean on one side and the beautiful redwood trees on the other.
7. In **Colorado** we visited dwellings of American Indians.
8. **New York** is a very large and busy city.
9. **Texas** is a state that has many cattle ranches.
10. The apples from **Washington** are the prettiest and juiciest I have ever eaten.

T216

Review Words
1. west
2. street
3. south
4. east
5. earth

Preview Words
6. California
7. Washington
8. New York
9. Colorado
10. Texas

Vocabulary

Review Words: Continents and Nationalities

Write the word from the box that answers each word problem.

street	east	earth	west	south

1. best – b + w = _____
2. strong – ong + feet – f = _____
3. mouths – s – m + s = _____
4. feasting – f – ing = _____
5. dreary – dr – y + th = _____

Preview Words: Continents and Nationalities

Write the word from the box that matches each state description.

California	Colorado	New York	Texas	Washington

6. a state bordered on the north by Oregon and on the west by the Pacific Ocean
7. a state bordered by Oregon, Idaho, and Canada
8. a state and a city in the Northeast
9. the Rocky Mountain state whose capital is Denver
10. the largest of the south-central states

216

Unit 35 RECAP

You may wish to assign the **Unit 35 Homework Master** (*Teacher Resource Book,* Unit 35) as a fun way to recap the spelling words.

Unit 35 Homework Master

Name _____   Homework **Master** Unit 35

Each group of letters can be used to make a spelling word. Unscramble the letters and write the words.

1. pe Erou
2. cAr amie
3. tAr act cain
4. his lr
5. name rG
6. his triB
7. cane Mix
8. his panS
9. and Can ia
10. see pan Ja

11. i Asa
12. afrAic
13. trail us Aa
14. kreeG
15. her Fnc
16. Inn adi
17. tail an I
18. Rain us s
19. he is enC
20. name cAr i

Make as many words as possible from the word **American**.

199

Connections

Content Words

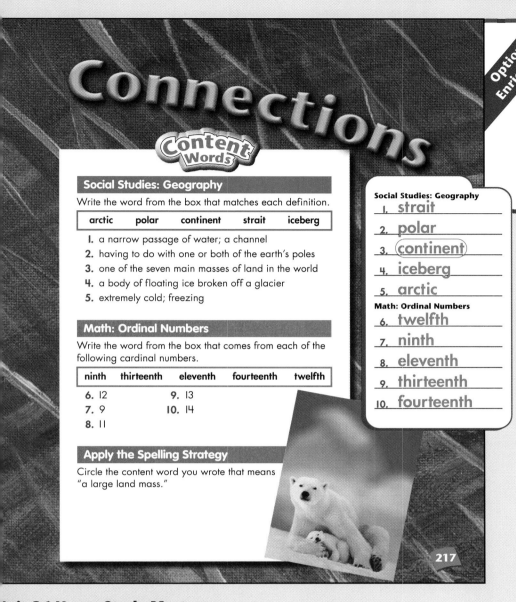

Social Studies: Geography

Write the word from the box that matches each definition.

arctic	polar	continent	strait	iceberg

1. a narrow passage of water; a channel
2. having to do with one or both of the earth's poles
3. one of the seven main masses of land in the world
4. a body of floating ice broken off a glacier
5. extremely cold; freezing

Math: Ordinal Numbers

Write the word from the box that comes from each of the following cardinal numbers.

ninth	thirteenth	eleventh	fourteenth	twelfth

6. 12   9. 13
7. 9   10. 14
8. 11

Apply the Spelling Strategy

Circle the content word you wrote that means "a large land mass."

Social Studies: Geography
1. strait
2. polar
3. continent
4. iceberg
5. arctic

Math: Ordinal Numbers
6. twelfth
7. ninth
8. eleventh
9. thirteenth
10. fourteenth

217

Objectives

Content Words

Students will
- **expand** vocabulary with content-related words.
- **relate** the spelling strategy to words outside the basic spelling list.

Content Words

Social Studies: Geography

Review the meanings of these words with the students. You may wish to use these sentences to introduce the words in context.

1. The **arctic** areas are very cold.
2. We might even see a **polar** bear, if we keep a sharp lookout.
3. Which is the largest **continent**?
4. The large cruise ship sailed carefully through the **strait**.
5. The *Titanic* hit an **iceberg,** which caused it to sink.

Encourage the students to use these words to write a description of a cold part of the earth.

Math: Ordinal Numbers

Review the meanings of these words with the students. You may wish to use these sentences to introduce the words in context.

6. We will be making our **ninth** trip to the western part of the country.
7. The **thirteenth** day of the month is on a Monday.
8. Please have the elevator stop on the **eleventh** floor.
9. The **fourteenth** caller to the radio program won a prize.
10. This will be the **twelfth** night of the festivities.

Encourage the students to use these words to write a series of sentences about things such as birthdays or historic events that happened on certain dates.

Unit 36 Home Study Master

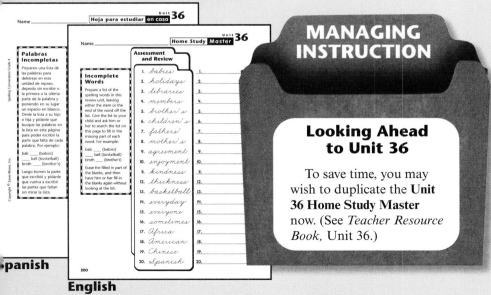

Spanish

English

MANAGING INSTRUCTION

Looking Ahead to Unit 36

To save time, you may wish to duplicate the **Unit 36 Home Study Master** now. (See *Teacher Resource Book,* Unit 36.)

Assessment Words

families	questions
parents'	teacher's
Dutch	Portuguese
prepayment	peacefulness
home run	meantime
turtleneck	Cuban
cheerfulness	treaties
Korean	aunt's
friend's	swiftness
matches	applesauce

Review Words

Unit 31

babies*	lunches
holidays*	teams
libraries*	armies
members*	patches
friends	ladies

Unit 32

brother's*	fish's
children's*	sisters'
fathers'*	wife's
mother's*	child's
watches'	sons'

Unit 33

agreement*	movement
enjoyment*	apartment
kindness*	illness
thickness*	sadness
stillness	darkness

Unit 34

basketball*	outdoors
everyday*	nearby
everyone*	anywhere
sometimes*	whenever
newspaper	upstairs

Unit 35

Africa*	Mexican
American*	Indian
Chinese*	America
Spanish*	Irish
Asia	French

* Posttest sentences and the **Unit 36 Test Master** test these words. Students review all words listed.

MATERIALS

Student Edition

Pages 218–223

Teacher Edition

Pages T218A–T223

Other Resources

Spelling Connections Software
Spelling and Writing
  Transparencies (Writing Prompt
  and Writing Model) for Unit 36

Teacher Resource Book

Unit 36 Home Study Master
  (English or Spanish; students
  may use this sheet for review
  or home practice.)
Flip Folder Practice Master
Unit 36 Test Master

Visit our Web site, www.zaner-bloser.com

OBJECTIVES

Spelling and Assessment

Students will
- **assess** their progress in understanding the spelling strategies and patterns taught in Units 31–35.
- **connect** new words to the spelling strategies in Units 31–35.
- **write** new words that relate to the spelling strategies taught in Units 31–35.

Spelling and Review

Students will
- **review** the spelling strategies and words taught in Units 31–35.
- **learn** an alternative spelling study strategy.

Spelling and Writing

Students will
- **review** the concept of adverbs.
- **compose** an expository piece of writing that gives information about weather.
- **learn** a proofreading strategy.
- **proofread** for correct spelling of state abbreviations.

MEETING INDIVIDUAL NEEDS
Learning Styles

 Visual

Have each student illustrate at least three of the spelling words reviewed in this unit by drawing pictures of the objects or ideas they represent. Possible words include **kindness, sadness, basketball,** and **friends**. Have the students hide each spelling word itself in three places within the drawing. Then have the students exchange drawings and find each other's hidden words.

 Auditory

Have students work in pairs. Have one student say and spell the base word or one part of a compound, depending on the unit spelling strategy being emphasized. Have the other student say and spell the word with its ending—a plural form, a possessive form, a form with a suffix, or a compound word. Then have both students pronounce the spelling word together. Finally, have students write the word three times. Each pair should continue in this way until the students have pronounced and spelled all the words being studied.

 Kinesthetic

To reinforce spelling of plurals, possessives, and suffixes, use small squares of construction paper that have plural endings (**-s, -es, -ies**), possessive endings (**-'s, -s'**), or suffixes (**-ness, -ment**). Give each child enough squares to write one ending on each square. Write the base words on the chalkboard. Point to each word and say it. Then say the form you are emphasizing. (If it is a possessive, use the word in a sentence.) Have students hold up the correct card that shows the ending. Call on a student to stand and spell the word aloud, raising the appropriate card high while spelling the word.

Language and Cultural Differences

Some words may present difficulties because of differences in language background or regional pronunciation. For example, the pronunciation and spelling of possessive word forms may be difficult for Spanish-speaking students because the concept of one word showing possession does not exist in the Spanish language. Also, some Spanish-speaking students may confuse the suffix **-ment** with the Spanish suffix **-mente,** which indicates an adverb. Have students pronounce each spelling word. Work with students as they write the words. Have them circle the part of each word that shows it is plural, that it is a possessive, or that it has a suffix. Discuss the meaning of each base word and its affixed form.

MANAGING INSTRUCTION

3–5 Day Plan		Average	Below Average	Above Average
Day 1	Day 1	Assessment: Units 31–35, p. 218 (Option 1 or 2, p. T218)	Assessment: Units 31–35, p. 218 (Option 1 or 2, p. T218)	Assessment: Units 31–35, p. 218 (Option 1 or 2, p. T218)
	Day 2	Review: Units 31 and 32, p. 219	Review: Units 31 and 32, p. 219	Review: Units 31 and 32, p. 219 Review: Units 33 and 34, p. 220
Day 2	Day 3	Review: Units 33 and 34, p. 220	Review: Units 33 and 34, p. 220	Review: Unit 35, p. 221 Spelling Study Strategy, p. 221
	Day 4	Review: Unit 35, p. 221 Spelling Study Strategy, p. 221	Review: Unit 35, p. 221 Spelling Study Strategy, p. 221	Writer's Workshop, pages 222–223
Day 3	Day 5	Weekly Test, Option 1 or 2, p. T221	Weekly Test, Option 1 or 2, p. T221	Weekly Test, Option 1 or 2, p. T221
Writer's Workshop (pages 222 and 223) may be used anytime during this unit.				

Objectives

Spelling and Assessment

Students will
- **assess** their progress in understanding the spelling strategies and patterns taught in Units 31–35.
- **connect** new words to the spelling strategies in Units 31–35.
- **write** new words that relate to the spelling strategies taught in Units 31–35.

Assessment and Review

Assessment Units 31–35

Each Assessment Word in the box fits one of the spelling strategies you have studied over the past five weeks. Read the spelling strategies. Then write each Assessment Word under the unit number it fits.

Unit 31 _____

1.–4. Plural nouns name more than one person, place, or thing. Plurals are formed in different ways: add **-s** (trays), add **-es** (lunches), or change final **y** to **i** and add **-es** (pennies).

Unit 32 _____

5.–8. Possessive nouns show ownership. Add an apostrophe and **s** (**'s**) to show possession when a noun is singular: **calf's**. Add an apostrophe (**'**) to show ownership when a plural noun ends in **-s: calves'**. When a noun is plural and does **not** end in **-s,** add an apostrophe and **s** (**'s**) to show ownership: **children's**.

Unit 33 _____

9.–12. The suffix **-ness** means "a condition or quality": **kindness**. The suffix **-ment** means "the result of an action": **enjoyment**.

Unit 34 _____

13.–16. A compound word is formed from two or more smaller words. Closed compounds are written as one word: **newspaper**. Open compounds are written as two or more words: **air mail**.

Unit 35 _____

17.–20. It is important to be able to spell the names of the continents and nationalities correctly.

Unit 31
1. families
2. matches
3. questions
4. treaties

Unit 32
5. parents'
6. friend's
7. teacher's
8. aunt's

Unit 33
9. prepayment
10. cheerfulness
11. peacefulness
12. swiftness

Unit 34
13. home run
14. turtleneck
15. meantime
16. applesauce

Unit 35
17. Dutch
18. Korean
19. Portuguese
20. Cuban

families
parents'
Dutch
prepayment
home run
turtleneck
cheerfulness
Korean
friend's
matches
questions
teacher's
Portuguese
peacefulness
meantime
Cuban
treaties
aunt's
swiftness
applesauce

218

ASSESSMENT: UNITS 31–35

Option 1

Assessment Option 1 is the test that appears in the Student Edition on page 218. You may wish to have students take this test to determine their ability to recognize the spelling strategy in each unit and to match words not previously taught to that strategy. **Assessment Option 1** also serves as additional review and practice.

▲ Words designated with this symbol include more than one of the targeted spelling strategies. The answer key has placed them according to the most obvious spelling emphasis. However, if a student places a word in another category, and the word fits that generalization, accept that response. Remember, the objective is to place each word with any appropriate spelling generalization.

Option 2

Assessment Option 2 is a dictation test using the sentences on page T219. This test assesses students' ability to spell words not previously taught but that are exemplars of a spelling strategy. This test more specifically assesses students' ability to apply the spelling knowledge they have learned.

In either assessment test option, the words are identified by unit in the Teacher Edition. You may wish to index those misspelled words to the review exercises that follow in this unit. Determine which units students need to review and use the additional unit exercises found in this **Assessment and Review Unit** for reteaching the skill in a more focused way.

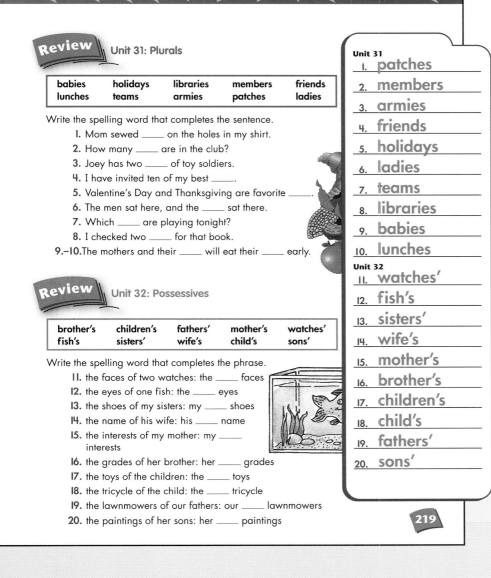

Review — Unit 31: Plurals

babies	holidays	libraries	members	friends
lunches	teams	armies	patches	ladies

Write the spelling word that completes the sentence.

1. Mom sewed _____ on the holes in my shirt.
2. How many _____ are in the club?
3. Joey has two _____ of toy soldiers.
4. I have invited ten of my best _____.
5. Valentine's Day and Thanksgiving are favorite _____.
6. The men sat here, and the _____ sat there.
7. Which _____ are playing tonight?
8. I checked two _____ for that book.
9.–10. The mothers and their _____ will eat their _____ early.

Review — Unit 32: Possessives

brother's	children's	fathers'	mother's	watches'
fish's	sisters'	wife's	child's	sons'

Write the spelling word that completes the phrase.

11. the faces of two watches: the _____ faces
12. the eyes of one fish: the _____ eyes
13. the shoes of my sisters: my _____ shoes
14. the name of his wife: his _____ name
15. the interests of my mother: my _____ interests
16. the grades of her brother: her _____ grades
17. the toys of the children: the _____ toys
18. the tricycle of the child: the _____ tricycle
19. the lawnmowers of our fathers: our _____ lawnmowers
20. the paintings of her sons: her _____ paintings

Unit 31

1. patches
2. members
3. armies
4. friends
5. holidays
6. ladies
7. teams
8. libraries
9. babies
10. lunches

Unit 32

11. watches'
12. fish's
13. sisters'
14. wife's
15. mother's
16. brother's
17. children's
18. child's
19. fathers'
20. sons'

219

Objectives

Spelling and Review

Students will
- **review** the spelling strategy and words taught in Unit 31.
- **review** the spelling strategy and words taught in Unit 32.

Assessing Progress: The Spelling Journal

If your students have been keeping a personal spelling journal, a periodical review of these journals can be a rich assessment tool. Students should include the words they have misspelled from each unit spelling test. They also should be encouraged to write the words they consistently misspell in their own writing and content-area words that present a challenge. Being able to discriminate the words in their everyday writing whose spelling they need to master is a powerful spelling skill.

Pretest Sentences: Assessment Words
(See procedures on pages Z10–Z11.)

1. The picnic tables are reserved for large **families**.
2. We've hidden our **parents'** anniversary presents.
3. These **Dutch** tulips are very colorful.
4. Because we were going to be out of town, we arranged for a **prepayment** for our rent.
5. The record-breaking **home run** brought a great cheer.
6. I got a new **turtleneck** sweater for my birthday.
7. You can count on her **cheerfulness**.
8. We plan to buy a **Korean** automobile.
9. I am going to my **friend's** house.
10. This shirt **matches** these socks.
11. Do you have any **questions** about the assignment?
12. We waited for the **teacher's** signal to begin.
13. The ship sailed past the **Portuguese** coastline.
14. I enjoy the **peacefulness** of the quiet garden.
15. Lunch will be served, but in the **meantime,** here are some crackers.
16. That restaurant serves **Cuban** food.
17. Many **treaties** have been signed in this palace.
18. I used my **aunt's** recipe to make this soup.
19. The jaguar is known for its **swiftness**.
20. Serve the **applesauce** for dessert.

Objectives

Spelling and Review

Students will
- **review** the spelling strategy and words taught in Unit 33.
- **review** the spelling strategy and words taught in Unit 34.

Unit 33
1. kindness
2. thickness
3. apartment
4. darkness
5. agreement
6. sadness
7. movement
8. enjoyment
9. illness
10. stillness

Unit 34
11. anywhere
12. everyone
13. basketball
14. outdoors
15. newspaper
16. whenever
17. everyday
18. upstairs
19. sometimes
20. nearby

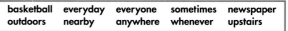

Review Unit 33: Suffixes -ness, -ment

| agreement | enjoyment | kindness | thickness | stillness |
| movement | apartment | illness | sadness | darkness |

Write the spelling word whose base word rhymes with the word below.

1. mind   5. free
2. sick   6. mad
3. smart   7. prove
4. spark   8. employ

Write the spelling word that goes with each base word.

9. ill   10. still

Review Unit 34: Compounds

| basketball | everyday | everyone | sometimes | newspaper |
| outdoors | nearby | anywhere | whenever | upstairs |

Write the word that completes each sentence.

11. I looked all over but couldn't find my watch _____.
12. Nearly _____ agreed that this is best.
13. What time should we be at the gym for the _____ game?
14. Instead of staying indoors, we're going to go _____.
15. I read the article in the _____.
16. I'll be ready _____ you are.
17. These are our special dishes, and those are our _____ ones.
18. Stay here and look downstairs while I look _____.
19. Usually I eat cereal for breakfast, but _____ I have muffins.
20. Is the school far away, or is it _____?

220

Bulletin Board Idea

The Travel Agency

1. Explain that travel agents plan trips for people who want to travel to any place in the world.
2. Make a collection of brochures, guidebooks, schedules of transportation, and maps. Display them on a large table.
3. Have students work in pairs or in small groups to learn how to read timetables, maps, and brochures.
4. Have the groups write a plan for a trip to a place of their choice. Have them tell what the visitor can expect to see and do on the trip.
5. Students might use pieces of yarn to show their travel routes.

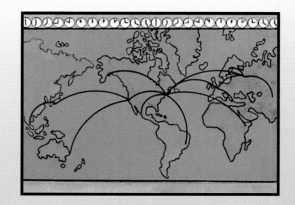

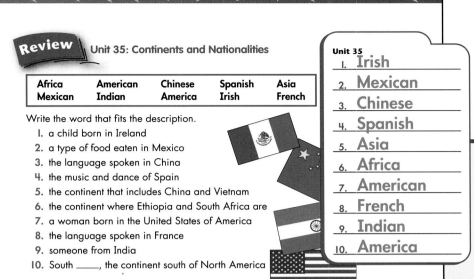

Review — Unit 35: Continents and Nationalities

Africa	American	Chinese	Spanish	Asia
Mexican	Indian	America	Irish	French

Write the word that fits the description.

1. a child born in Ireland
2. a type of food eaten in Mexico
3. the language spoken in China
4. the music and dance of Spain
5. the continent that includes China and Vietnam
6. the continent where Ethiopia and South Africa are
7. a woman born in the United States of America
8. the language spoken in France
9. someone from India
10. South _____, the continent south of North America

Unit 35

1. Irish
2. Mexican
3. Chinese
4. Spanish
5. Asia
6. Africa
7. American
8. French
9. Indian
10. America

Spelling Study Strategy

Sorting by Endings

One good way to practice spelling words is to place words into groups according to some spelling pattern. Here is a way to practice some of the spelling words you have been studying in the past few weeks.

1. Make six columns across a large piece of paper.
2. Write one of these words, including the underlined parts, at the top of each column: **lunches, friends, brother's, fathers', darkness, enjoyment**.
3. Have a partner choose a spelling word from Units 31, 32, and 33 and say it aloud.
4. Write the spelling word in the column under the word with the same ending.

221

Objectives

Spelling and Review

Students will
- **review** the spelling strategy and words taught in Unit 35.
- **learn** an alternative spelling study strategy.

Learning an Alternative Spelling Study Strategy

Students should always have a number of study strategies to draw from when it comes to learning their spelling words. **Sorting by Endings** is a fun way of differentiating sound and letter patterns. Encourage students to remember this spelling study strategy and to consider using it with any appropriate list they need to study and learn.

Weekly Test Options

Option 1:
One Spelling Word Per Sentence
(See procedures on pages Z10–Z11.)

1. An **agreement** was made between them.
2. The **babies** were quiet.
3. We will play **basketball** in the gym.
4. My **brother's** car is red.
5. That folk tale is from **Africa**.
6. A child gets a lot of **enjoyment** from going to the circus.
7. I'll change from my **everyday** clothes and put on something new for the party.
8. Most **holidays** are listed on the calendar.
9. Most of our **fathers'** jobs are close to home.
10. There are more than books in **libraries**.
11. The **American** flag has three colors.
12. His **kindness** was rewarded at last.
13. The **children's** goats are at the fair.
14. We want **everyone** to come to the party.
15. These people are **members** of the club.
16. The **Chinese** New Year's celebration lasts days.
17. We learned to count in **Spanish**.
18. The **thickness** of the book made it hard to hold in my hands.
19. My **mother's** slippers are under her bed.
20. We **sometimes** eat outside.

Unit 36 Test Master

(See *Teacher Resource Book*, Unit 36.)

Option 2:
Standardized Test

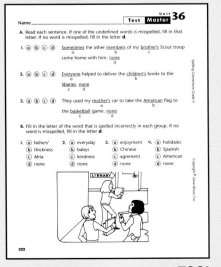

T221

Objectives

Spelling and Writing

Students will
• **review** the concept of adverbs.
• **compose** an expository piece of writing that gives information about weather. (See **Spelling and the Writing Process** below.)

Optional Enrichment

A
1. carelessly
2. cheerfully
3. softly
4. carefully
5. excitedly

B
6. loudly
7. no
8. noisily
9. suddenly
10. completely

Grammar, Usage, and Mechanics

Adverbs

An adverb that ends in **-ly** usually tells about a verb. It tells how something is done, or how often it is done.

The actor walked **quietly** across the stage.

The hare ran **quickly**.

Slowly but **surely,** the tortoise won the race.

Practice Activity

A. Write the adverb in each sentence below.
1. Someone carelessly left a shoe on the floor.
2. Tawana smiled cheerfully at the audience.
3. People are sleeping, so talk softly.
4. George packed his suitcase carefully.
5. With trembling hands, I excitedly opened the huge envelope.

B. Which sentences contain adverbs? Write the adverbs you see in each sentence. Write **no** if a sentence has no adverb.
6. The audience cheered loudly for both teams.
7. I love staying in this quiet library.
8. Your brother's watch ticks noisily.
9. The door slammed suddenly and startled me.
10. The delicious aroma filled the room completely.

222

Spelling and the Writing Process

Expository Writing

You may wish to use this writing assignment to help students master the writing process. For other writing ideas, see pages 258–259 in the Student Edition.

Explain that students will write a composition in which they report on a weather phenomenon, such as a tornado.

Prewriting Hint: You may wish to help students plan their writing by recommending the questions in the graphic organizer on this page. Have them copy the questions and find answers.

What?	tornadoes; wildly spinning storm that creates funnel shaped clouds
When?	mostly spring, summer
Where?	tornado alley in the US
Why?	

Revising Hint: Remind students that when they revise what they have written they should check any facts or statistics carefully for accuracy. Encourage them to include illustrations or other graphics.

Proofreading Strategy

Box It Up!

Good writers always proofread their writing for spelling errors. Here's a strategy that you can use to proofread your work.

Cut a small hole or box in a piece of paper. Slide it over your writing so that just one or two words appear inside the box. You won't be able to see a whole sentence. Instead of reading **The rocket blasted off into space,** you might see **rocket blasted** or **off into**.

This may sound like a strange way to proofread, but boxing in a few words at a time helps you focus on the spelling of words. You pay no attention to their meanings this way. Try it!

Electronic Spelling

1. Arkansas
2. Colorado
3. Iowa
4. Mississippi
5. Nebraska
6. Massachusetts

Searching for Information

Computers and the Internet allow you to find information quickly and easily. However, you must know how to look. You can tell your search engine to look for a key word in a source. Suppose you wanted information on a state. In this case, you could type in the two-letter postal abbreviation, such as **NY** for **New York**.

Many of these abbreviations look alike. Can you tell which are which? Write the name of the state that matches each abbreviation.

1. Does AR stand for Arkansas or Arizona?
2. Does CO stand for Connecticut or Colorado?
3. Does IA stand for Indiana or Iowa?
4. Does MS stand for Missouri or Mississippi?
5. Does NE stand for Nebraska or Nevada?
6. Does MA stand for Massachusettes or Maine?

223

Objectives

Spelling and Writing

Students will
- **learn** a proofreading strategy.
- **proofread** for correct spelling of state abbreviations.

Using Proofreading Strategies

Students are often unaware that there are a variety of approaches to proofreading their own writing. Building a repertory of strategies is important to improving students' writing and editing skills.

Spelling and Technology

The advent of word processing, computer protocols, and the Internet has actually increased, not lessened, the pressure on users to be better, more aware spellers. Spell checkers, for example, create circumstances in which the ability to discriminate between an acceptable and an unacceptable spelling is a critical skill. A homophone substitution, a correct spelling of the wrong word, an inadvertent word omission—these are examples of situations in computer usage that require a deeper understanding of spelling principles and a more adroit proofreading capability. It may be worthwhile to underscore this increased need as a whole-class discussion after students finish this unit's **Electronic Spelling** activity.

Challenge Activities

perhaps	catfish	ticket
	begun	vinegar

The **Challenge Words, Challenge Activities,** and **Challenge Word Test Sentences** (provided in the Teacher Edition) were developed for students who have mastered the spelling list in the Student Edition. The **Challenge Words** are high-frequency words one to two grade levels above the level of the basic spelling list.

Challenge Words do not appear in the **Spelling Dictionary** so students will have the additional challenge of researching word meanings, as needed, in other reference materials.

A
1. perhaps
2. catfish
3. begun
4. ticket
5. vinegar

B
1. begun
2. ticket
3. catfish
4. Perhaps
5. vinegar

C
Answers will vary.

A. Write the challenge word that fits each group.

1. maybe, possibly, _____
2. trout, perch, _____
3. started, gone, _____
4. check, bill, _____
5. salad, oil, _____

B. Correct the misspelling in each challenge word. Write the word.

1. The performance has already beggun.
2. Do you have the tiket for the show?
3. Can you believe that there is an act with a catfesh as a magician!
4. Purhaps we can learn some tricks!
5. This viniger is very sour!

C. Write a paragraph to describe this make-believe catfish performer in the picture. Tell a little about how it is dressed, and describe one of the tricks. Use the challenge words, when you can, as well as other words of your choice.

Challenge Word Test Sentences

1. **Perhaps** we will go to the fair.
2. Do **catfish** live in this muddy brook?
3. He spent all of his money for a train **ticket**.
4. Snow has **begun** to fall on the ground.
5. She put **vinegar** and oil on her lettuce salad.

fuse	female	trapeze
antelope	otherwise	

A. Write the challenge word that rhymes with each word below. After each challenge word, write **a, e, i, o,** or **u** to tell which long vowel sound you hear in the word. One word has two different long vowel sounds in it.

1. detail
2. cantaloupe
3. green peas
4. pews
5. surprise

B. Use the letter that comes before each letter of the alphabet in the underlined words to write the challenge words.

Example: dbqf = cape

1. Can an boufmpqf run swiftly?
2. Does a gvtf have to do with electricity?
3. Is your mom a gfnbmf?
4. Can you find a usbqaf in an oven?
5. If I think puifsxjtf, am I right?

Now go back and answer **Yes** or **No** to each question.

C. Make up at least ten sentences with the words "If I were . . . I might be. . . ." Use challenge words and other words you know to complete the sentences. For example, "If I were on a car, I might be a tire" or "If I were made of ice, I might be a cube." Choose one of your sentences to illustrate.

A
1. female; e, a
2. antelope; o
3. trapeze; e
4. fuse; u
5. otherwise; i

B
1. antelope; Yes
2. fuse; Yes
3. female; Yes
4. trapeze; No
5. otherwise; No or Yes

C
Answers will vary.

225

Challenge Word Test Sentences

1. The man will carefully light the end of the **fuse.**
2. Our **female** cat gave birth to four cute kittens.
3. We saw two men swing on a **trapeze** at the circus.
4. The **antelope** is an animal that can run very fast.
5. You should leave now; **otherwise,** you will be late.

Challenge Activities

nickname	stadium	replay
regain	trainer	

A
1. regain
2. stadium
3. nickname
4. replay
5. trainer

B
1. nickname
2. stadium
3. trainer
4. replay
5. regain

C
Answers will vary.

A. Look at the vowel spellings for **long a** in the words below. Write the word that does not belong in each group.

1. flavor, stadium, regain, able
2. stadium, aim, rail, trainer
3. anyway, relay, nickname, holiday
4. trailer, rail, replay, brain
5. lazy, lady, paper, trainer

B. Write the challenge word that fits each "What Am I?" statement.

1. Sometimes I am Patty, and other times I am Tricia, Patsy, or "Smartie."
2. I am huge. I have a playing field, bleachers, reserved seats, and a scoreboard.
3. I am someone who teaches and helps athletes prepare for sports competitions.
4. You see me on television. Sometimes I'm in slow motion. I'm often seen as an exciting part of a game, such as a football touchdown.
5. I have a prefix that means "do again."

C. Imagine that you are a radio sports announcer. You have just witnessed a football game or some other sports event. First tell who you are and where you are broadcasting from. Write what you would say about the highlights in the exciting game. Try to use all the challenge words. You might wish to make your classmates players on the teams.

226

Challenge Word Test Sentences

1. The girl told us her **nickname** instead of her given name.
2. Will the next football game be played in the new **stadium**?
3. The team will look at a **replay** of the game.
4. We will **regain** the lead in the game if we score two points.
5. The animal **trainer** taught the dog a trick.

Challenge Activities

wreath	treason	keenly
breed	belief	

A. Write the challenge words that rhyme with the words below.

1. relief
2. creed
3. queenly
4. reason
5. beneath

B. Write a challenge word to complete each sentence.

1. If you betray your country by aiding the enemy, you are guilty of _____.
2. If you have faith in something, you have a _____.
3. If your eyes are sharp, you see _____.
4. A ring made of flowers, leaves, or small branches is a _____.
5. A group of animals, such as beagles, can be called a _____.

C. List several answers to each question below. Look over your lists to see whether one of your answers suggests something you could write about. Then write a short paragraph using the word or words you selected.

1. What are some names for different breeds of dogs?
2. Where might a person put a wreath?
3. What do you feel keenly, or very strongly, about?

A
1. belief
2. breed
3. keenly
4. treason
5. wreath

B
1. treason
2. belief
3. keenly
4. wreath
5. breed

C
Answers will vary.

227

Challenge Word Test Sentences
1. Father hung a **wreath** of evergreens on the door.
2. What she said amounts to **treason**.
3. When I cut my finger, I felt the pain **keenly**.
4. The rancher will **breed** calves for beef.
5. It is our **belief** that the team will win.

Challenge Activities

dial	rely	hydrant
lightly	blight	

A. Write the challenge word that matches each vowel pattern and goes with each definition. Circle the letter or letters that spell the **long i** sound.

1. control knob   __ i __ __
2. disease   __ __ i g h __
3. fireplug   __ y __ __ __ __ __
4. without force   __ i g h __ __ __
5. depend   __ __ __ y

B. Write the letter that tells which meaning of **lightly** is used in the sentence.

    a. with little weight or pressure
    b. a little amount of something
    c. not seriously
    d. without serious penalty

1. My uncle says that he'll buy me a pony, but I take it lightly.
2. I wasn't hungry, so I ate lightly at lunch.
3. The principal let the tardy student off lightly.
4. Please press down lightly to glue each corner.

C. Answer each question with several examples. If you wish, add details to explain your answers.

1. What things have a dial?
2. When should you rely on others?
3. Why do we have fire hydrants?
4. What might you hear that you would take lightly?

A
1. d i al
2. bl igh t
3. h y drant
4. l igh tly
5. rel y

B
1. c.
2. b.
3. d.
4. a.

C
Answers will vary.

228

Challenge Word Test Sentences

1. I had to **dial** the number a second time.
2. You can usually **rely** on a friend for help.
3. Every corner in the town has a fire **hydrant**.
4. A soft breeze blew **lightly** in the night air.
5. Last year a **blight** hurt our apple trees.

Challenge Activities

bonus	banjo	poach
decode	following	

A. Write the challenge word that fits with each group.

1. gift, reward, _____
2. unscramble, solve, _____
3. guitar, ukulele, _____
4. fry, boil, _____
5. leading, passing, _____

B. Write the challenge word that completes each analogy.

1. **Tuba** is to **trumpet** as **ukulele** is to _____.
2. **Extra** is to **more** as _____ is to **reward**.
3. **Read** is to **greeting card** as _____ is to **secret message**.
4. **Fish** is to **broil** as **eggs** are to _____.
5. **Pass** is to **passing** as **follow** is to _____.

A
1. bonus
2. decode
3. banjo
4. poach
5. following

B
1. banjo
2. bonus
3. decode
4. poach
5. following

C
Answers will vary.

C. Choose a challenge word. Write it at the top of your paper. Then write **Who? What? Where? Why?** and **When?** along the left-hand edge of the paper. Write questions using the **W**-words and the challenge word. Then think about how you could answer each question. Use your questions and answers to write a paragraph.

229

Challenge Word Test Sentences

1. We were paid a **bonus** for a job well done.
2. Does she have a **banjo** lesson after school?
3. Mom will **poach** the eggs in the morning.
4. Some children think it is fun to **decode** a message.
5. Is that dog **following** the scent of a deer?

menu	fuel	nephew
duties	blueberry	

A
1. nephew
2. menu
3. duties
4. blueberry
5. fuel

B
1. duties
2. menu
3. nephew
4. fuel
5. blueberry

C
Answers will vary.

A. Write the challenge word that completes each analogy.

1. **Sister** is to **brother** as **niece** is to _____.
2. **Telephone numbers** are to **directory** as **dinners** are to _____.
3. **Berry** is to **berries** as **duty** is to _____.
4. **Vegetable** is to **carrot** as **fruit** is to _____.
5. **Portable radio** is to **batteries** as **car** is to _____.

B. Write a challenge word to answer each question.

1. I am things you ought to do. What am I?
2. I am something you read and order from in a restaurant. What am I?
3. I am a boy who is the son of your sister or brother. What is my relationship to you?
4. I am used to produce heat in homes or power in automobiles. What am I?
5. You can pick me and put me in a dish with other fruit or into a pie. What am I?

C. Imagine that you have each job mentioned below. You think your job is very interesting and special. Write what some of your duties are. Use some of the challenge words.

1. You work at a gasoline station.
2. You are in charge of preparing menus in a famous restaurant.
3. You grow fruit and sell it.

230

Challenge Word Test Sentences

1. I will place my order after I read the **menu**.
2. A car runs on **fuel**.
3. Her **nephew** is in first grade.
4. One of my **duties** is to feed the dog.
5. Would you like a piece of **blueberry** pie?

Challenge Activities

| spout | bountiful | scowl |
| hoist | buoyant | |

A. Write the challenge word that best replaces each underlined phrase.

1. She likes to swim with an inner tube because it is <u>able to float</u>.
2. The <u>angry frown</u> showed how he felt when the team lost the game.
3. The hot water came from the kettle's <u>narrow opening</u>.
4. The heavy ropes helped them <u>lift up</u> the box off the ship and onto the dock.
5. The pirate's chest overflowed with <u>more than enough</u> treasure.

B. Write the challenge word for each number to complete the story.

What was that in the water? It looked heavy but it floated on the surface, so it was __1.__. I eased our boat over to it and tried to __2.__ it in, but it weighed a ton. A __3.__ on each of our faces showed how unhappy we were. We hoped it would overflow with a __4.__ treasure! Finally, we got it out of the water and opened it. What do you think it was? A trunkful of toy, wind-up whales! We couldn't resist trying them, so we put them in the water. They began to __5.__!

C. Write a tall tale about your own treasure hunt. Exaggerate as much as you can. Use some of the challenge words.

A
1. buoyant
2. scowl
3. spout
4. hoist
5. bountiful

B
1. buoyant
2. hoist
3. scowl
4. bountiful
5. spout

C
Answers will vary.

231

Challenge Word Test Sentences
1. Some milk might spill from that **spout**.
2. The weeds are **bountiful** in our garden.
3. Why does that man have a **scowl** on his face?
4. The little girl needed a **hoist** over the high fence.
5. Because a ship is **buoyant**, it stays on top of the water.

audio	naughty	oriole
toward	dinosaur	

A
1. dinosaur
2. oriole; No
3. audio; Yes
4. naughty; No
5. oriole
6. toward; No

B
1. dinosaur
2. naughty
3. oriole
4. audio
5. toward

C
Answers will vary.

A. Replace the definition in ( ) with a challenge word. Write the word. Then answer the question with **Yes** or **No**.

 1.–2. Could a (prehistoric reptile) perch daintily on the head of an (orange songbird)?

 3. Can (relating to sound) refer to a television set?

 4. Can shoes be (behaving badly)?

 5.–6. Can an (orange songbird) swim (in the direction of) land?

B. Read each group of words. Write the challenge word you associate with each group.

 1. brontosaurus, stegosaurus, styracosaurus

 2. overturned water dish, chewed book, muddy paws

 3. Baltimore, songbird, orange and black feathers

 4. AM/FM, stereo, radio

 5. forward, near

C. Pretend that a dinosaur was playing a loud radio while you were trying to read. Write a paragraph describing what you would do. Use as many challenge words as possible.

232

Challenge Word Test Sentences
1. Dad fixed the **audio** part of the tape.
2. The **naughty** boy ate a piece of cake before supper.
3. An **oriole** is a bird with black and orange feathers.
4. The class walked slowly **toward** the door.
5. A **dinosaur** was a huge animal with a tiny brain.

Challenge Activities

terse	burden	skirted
reindeer	earrings	

A. Use the clues in each equation to make a challenge word. Write the word.

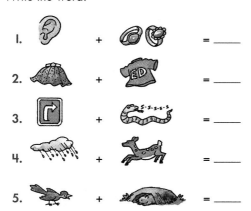

1. [ear] + [earrings] = ____

2. [hat] + [ED shirt] = ____

3. [right turn] + [snake s-s-s-s-s] = ____

4. [rain] + [deer] = ____

5. [bird] + [den nest] = ____

A
1. earrings
2. skirted
3. terse
4. reindeer
5. burden

B
1. terse
2. skirted
3. earrings
4. burden
5. reindeer

C
Answers will vary.

B. Write the challenge words for the **R** puzzle. Use the definitions as clues.

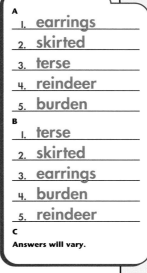

1. __ __ R __ __ — brief
2. __ __ __ R __ __ — passed around or avoided
3. __ __ __ R __ __ __ — jewelry worn on the ears
4. __ __ R __ __ — a load
5. R __ __ __ __ __ __ __ — animal with antlers

C. Imagine that a reindeer is a rock star. Write a story about his or her adventures. Use as many challenge words as possible.

233

Challenge Word Test Sentences

1. The grumpy man gave a **terse** reply.
2. A strong donkey could carry that **burden**.
3. The children **skirted** the muddy part of the playground.
4. Some people eat **reindeer** meat.
5. Are those **earrings** really made out of gold?

Challenge Activities

arch   harness   tardy
glare   snare

A

1. glare
2. tardy
3. harness
4. snare
5. arch

B

1. harness
2. glared
3. tardy
4. snare
5. arch

C
Answers will vary.

A. Write the challenge words that match the definitions below.

1. an angry look; a bright light
2. late or delayed
3. leather straps and bands
4. trap or catch
5. a curved structure that carries weight over an opening; to form a curve

B. 1.–5. Find the misspelled challenge words or forms of them in the story. Write each one correctly.

My horse and I were walking along a road. It was hot, so I took off his harnes. Instead of walking slowly with me, he galloped off. I glaired at him, but he would not come back. I was afraid I'd be tardie for dinner, so I ran after him. I was finally able to snair him and bring him through the gate with the arrch and into the corral. I quickly washed my hands and face and went into the kitchen.

"I was just about to call you to dinner," Dad said.

C. Write a mystery story about something missing or unusual. Use some of the challenge words to tell about the mystery and to describe clues. Perhaps you can tell about a ranch and a missing saddle from the tack room where all the horses' equipment is stored.

234

Challenge Word Test Sentences

1. Is that **arch** made of stone, brick, or marble?
2. Please help **harness** the horse to the plow.
3. Some children were **tardy** for school because of the storm.
4. Bright lights give off a **glare**.
5. A small animal has been caught in the **snare**.

Challenge Activities

wealth	threat	pheasant
biscuit	tortoise	

A. "Pick" or take out the flowers in these sentences. Write a challenge word to replace each one.

1. The rose would taste delicious with jam.

2. Was that a daisy I saw fly by?

3. The tulip pulled its head back into its shell.

4. The gray cloud was a dandelion to the picnic.

5. The millionaire offered to donate some of his great sunflower to build a new hospital.

B. Write a challenge word to complete each sentence.

1. A _____ is a kind of bread.

2. A _____ may be a sign of trouble.

3. A _____ is a kind of bird.

4. A _____ is a kind of turtle.

5. _____ is a large amount of riches.

C. Write a fable about a tortoise and a pheasant. Use some of the challenge words to tell what happens. Many fables end with a wise saying that sums up the fable. Use one of the sayings below or another one that you know. You may want to make up your own wise saying!

1. Nothing ventured, nothing gained.

2. He who laughs last, laughs best.

3. Don't count your chickens before they're hatched.

A
1. biscuit
2. pheasant
3. tortoise
4. threat
5. wealth

B
1. biscuit
2. threat
3. pheasant
4. tortoise
5. Wealth

C
Answers will vary.

235

Challenge Word Test Sentences

1. He is a man of great **wealth**.

2. Litter on the sidewalk can be a **threat** to safety.

3. Do you like the taste of **pheasant**?

4. A **biscuit** is made with flour and baking powder.

5. Does a **tortoise** live on land?

Challenge Activities

gnaw	gnat	cough
prompt	knuckle	

A. Write a challenge word to go with each clue.

1. a joint in your finger
2. quick
3. to bite on something, such as a bone
4. a small flying insect
5. a sound you often make when you have a cold

B. Look at the dictionary respelling in parentheses. Then write the challenge word it stands for.

1. The restaurant gave us (prŏmpt) service.
2. I scratched my (**nuk'** əl) on the bricks.
3. We gave the dog a bone to (nô).
4. The (năt) tried to bite me.
5. Does your cold make you (kôf)?

C. A gnat who wants to go into business has asked you to write an ad for the local newspaper. Since a gnat can fly, what business might the gnat select? How could the gnat's small size help it get in and out of certain places? Use some challenge words in the ad.

A
1. knuckle
2. prompt
3. gnaw
4. gnat
5. cough

B
1. prompt
2. knuckle
3. gnaw
4. gnat
5. cough

C
Answers will vary.

236

Challenge Word Test Sentences

1. A mouse can **gnaw** a piece of rope.
2. A **gnat** looks like a small fly.
3. Always cover your mouth when you **cough**.
4. The teacher asked us to be **prompt**.
5. A **knuckle** is a part of the human hand.

Challenge Activities

quartz	quaint	quiver
squid	squirt	

A. Add a challenge word with the same beginning sound to each group. Be sure not to add the challenge word that is already in the list. The words are in alphabetical order.

1. _____, quartz, quiet, quiver
2. squad, squeal, squid, _____
3. quaint, _____, quill, quiver
4. squeeze, _____, squirm, squirt
5. quaint, quartz, quiet, _____

B. What am I? Write the challenge word that answers each description.

1. I'm an animal that looks like an octopus.
2. I'm a hard rock.
3. I'm what you can do with a hose.
4. I'm what you do when you shake just a little.
5. I'm attractive in an old-fashioned way.

C. Write two tongue twisters. Use two challenge words in each sentence and underline them. Try to make most of the words in your sentences start with the same sound.

Example: Can quartz quiver quite quickly?

Answer key

A
1. quaint
2. squirt
3. quartz
4. squid
5. quiver

B
1. squid
2. quartz
3. squirt
4. quiver
5. quaint

C
Answers will vary.

Challenge Word Test Sentences

1. Is **quartz** a hard rock?
2. Grandmother and Grandfather live in a **quaint** house.
3. My body began to **quiver** when I saw the flames.
4. A **squid** is a sea animal with ten arms.
5. Did you ever **squirt** a friend with a water hose?

Challenge Activities

gadget	gelatin	engage
beverage	rummage	

A
1. bevera(g)e
2. enga(g)e
3. gad(g)et
4. rumma(g)e
5. (g)elatin

B
1. beverage
2. gadget
3. rummage
4. engage
5. gelatin

C
Answers will vary.

A. Write the challenge word by adding the missing consonants. Circle the **g** that stands for the **/j/** sound in each word you write.

1. __ e __ e __ a __ e
2. e __ __ a __ e
3. __ a __ __ e __
4. __ u __ __ a __ e
5. __ e __ a __ i __

B. Write the challenge word for each definition.

1. something to drink
2. a small mechanical object
3. to search for something by moving things around
4. to keep busy or to hire
5. a jellylike substance

C. You have found a mysterious-looking gadget. Write a detailed description of it, and tell what you think it is used for. If you wish, draw a picture of the strange gadget.

Challenge Word Test Sentences

1. What does the funny **gadget** do?
2. Mother will use a package of fruit **gelatin** to make the salad.
3. Father likes to **engage** in conversation with his friends.
4. I chose milk as a **beverage** to drink with dinner.
5. Some animals will **rummage** in trash for food.

Challenge Activities

meddle	wriggle	sparkle
	brittle	tangle

A. Write the challenge word that best completes each sentence.

1. Dried leaves and eggshells are _____.
2. To "butt in" or "intrude" is to _____.
3. A diamond or crystal will _____.
4. Hair, yarn, or string can _____.
5. A worm or a snake can _____.

s-s-s-s-s

B. Add and subtract letters to find challenge words. Write the challenge word that solves each problem.

1. wrbr – wr + i + tet – e + le = _____
2. spdl – dl + dark – d + le = _____
3. pdm – pd + edd + le = _____
4. stan – s + bgle – b = _____
5. w + rig + bg – b + le = _____

C. Imagine that your spacecraft has just landed on a planet with very strange but friendly surroundings. Write an entry for your captain's journal describing what you see. Use as many challenge words as you can.

A
1. brittle
2. meddle
3. sparkle
4. tangle
5. wriggle

B
1. brittle
2. sparkle
3. meddle
4. tangle
5. wriggle

C
Answers will vary.

239

Challenge Word Test Sentences

1. Please do not **meddle** unless I ask you for help.
2. The teacher told us not to **wriggle** in our seats.
3. His eyes suddenly **sparkle** with joy when he hears good news.
4. Drink milk so your bones will not become **brittle**.
5. It is very easy to **tangle** a ball of yarn.

Unit 20

Challenge Activities

unable	whistle	beaten
wooden	woolen	

A
1. beaten
2. wooden
3. unable
4. whistle
5. woolen

B
1. beaten
2. unable
3. whistle
4. woolen
5. wooden

C
Answers will vary.

A. Write the challenge word that answers the question.

1. What do you call an egg if the white and yolk are mixed together?
2. If a table isn't made of plastic, what kind of table might it be?
3. What means the same as **cannot**?
4. What can you do with a tune rather than sing it?
5. What type of blanket feels good on a chilly night?

B. Change one, two, or three letters in the underlined word in each sentence and write the challenge word that makes the most sense.

1. I have <u>beetle</u> the eggs.
2. I am <u>stable</u> to lift the heavy box.
3. The counselor blew a <u>whisper</u>.
4. Is this a <u>wooden</u> blanket?
5. Dad made a <u>woolen</u> train.

C. Pretend you are a carpenter. Write directions for making something out of wood. Use some of the challenge words.

240

Challenge Word Test Sentences
1. Most of the students were **unable** to finish the test.
2. Dad likes to **whistle** when he takes a bath.
3. Our team was badly **beaten** at the last baseball game.
4. That lamp has a **wooden** base.
5. I wore a warm **woolen** shirt when I went out.

halter	barber	rubber
razor	anchor	

A. Write the challenge word that goes with each spelling clue below.

   1. Which word has the **k** sound spelled **ch**?
   2. Which word rhymes with **harbor**?
   3. Which word has **long a** spelled **a**?
   4. Which word has double **b**'s?
   5. Which word begins with **h** and ends with **er**?

B. Unscramble each underlined word to find the challenge word that goes with each definition. Write the word.

   1. relhat A leather headgear for leading a horse is a _____.
   2. brerbu An article of footwear worn in the rain is a _____.
   3. brebra A person who cuts hair and trims beards is a _____.
   4. chonra A heavy object that keeps boats from drifting is an _____.
   5. zorar A tool for cutting is a _____.

C. Write about a real or an imaginary time when you had your hair cut. Did anything unusual happen? Use some challenge words if you can.

A
   1. anchor
   2. barber
   3. razor
   4. rubber
   5. halter

B
   1. halter
   2. rubber
   3. barber
   4. anchor
   5. razor

C
Answers will vary.

241

Challenge Word Test Sentences
   1. A **halter** fits around the head of a horse.
   2. The **barber** must cut my hair every four weeks.
   3. Car tires are made of **rubber**.
   4. That knife is as sharp as a **razor**.
   5. The **anchor** dropped deep into the sea.

Challenge Activities

bluest	healthier	healthiest
	heavier	heaviest

A. Unscramble the challenge words and write them correctly.

1. t e s b u l

2. h e a l i t e r h

3. s e l t h a t i e h

4. v e i r e a h

5. s t e a v i e h

B. Write the missing challenge words to describe the pictures.

1. blue   bluer _____

2.–3. healthy _____ _____

4.–5. heavy _____ _____

C. Describe five imaginary people. Give them names. Write a sentence about each one. Try to use challenge words in each sentence.

242

A

1. bluest
2. healthier
3. healthiest
4. heavier
5. heaviest

B

1. bluest
2. healthier
3. healthiest
4. heavier
5. heaviest

C
Answers will vary.

Challenge Word Test Sentences

1. The sky is the **bluest** I have ever seen it.
2. This plant looks **healthier** than that one.
3. This is the **healthiest** crop of wheat he has ever grown.
4. Cats are **heavier** than mice.
5. Is a lion one of the **heaviest** animals on earth?

Challenge Activities

> mist   missed   guest
>
> guessed   aloud

A. Write a challenge word to complete each analogy.

    I. Author is to **write** as _____ is to **visit**.

    2. Rain is to _____ as **cloud** is to **fog**.

    3. Pass is to **passed** as **miss** is to _____.

    4. Guest is to _____ as **steel** is to **steal**.

    5. Soar is to **sore** as **allowed** is to _____.

B. Write the challenge word that makes sense in the sentence.

    I. He read the story (allowed, aloud).

    2. Our (guessed, guest) arrived at eight.

    3. Mom (mist, missed) the bus.

    4. We (guessed, guest) what was inside the box.

    5. A light (missed, mist) was falling.

C. Write a paragraph about a mysterious guest who arrives unannounced and leaves unnoticed. Try to use all of the challenge words. Use other homophone pairs, too. For example, you could use **great, grate; scent, sent;** and **weigh, way**.

A
1. guest
2. mist
3. missed
4. guessed
5. aloud

B
1. aloud
2. guest
3. missed
4. guessed
5. mist

C
Answers will vary.

243

Challenge Word Test Sentences

1. A fine **mist** fell softly on the still lake.
2. She **missed** the train for the third time this month.
3. Mother will invite a **guest** to dinner.
4. He **guessed** the right answer on the first try.
5. Most children like to read **aloud**.

it'll	who'll	needn't
	wouldn't	shouldn't

A. Write the contraction that is a short form of each word pair below.

1. who will
2. need not
3. would not

4. should not
5. it will

B. Five contractions are missing from the story. Read the story. Write the contractions.

The club is planning a party for our counselor. If I were you, I __1.__ tell her __2.__ be there. Then __3.__ be a complete surprise! Also, you __4.__ bring anything. We've already prepared the food and made decorations. The weather forecaster said it __5.__ rain, so we'll plan to have the party outdoors.

C. Your class is having a contest for the best science invention. Write about what you will try to invent. Tell what it'll do. Use as many contractions as you can.

A
1. who'll
2. needn't
3. wouldn't
4. shouldn't
5. it'll

B
Order of answers 4 and 5 may vary.
1. wouldn't
2. who'll
3. it'll
4. needn't
5. shouldn't

C
Answers will vary.

Challenge Word Test Sentences

1. **It'll** take the crew three days to pave this highway.
2. **Who'll** care for her bird while she's away?
3. You **needn't** speak so loudly.
4. **Wouldn't** it be fun to dig in the sand?
5. Girls and boys **shouldn't** throw stones.

Challenge Activities

uncertain	unfriendly	reorder
refill	presoak	

A. The wrong prefixes are matched with base words. Think about where each prefix belongs. Write each challenge word correctly.

1. re + soak
2. un + fill
3. un + order
4. pre + certain
5. re + friendly

B. Write a challenge word to complete each sentence. More than one word might make sense.

1. A nervous animal might be ____.
2. If your pen runs out of ink, you might ____ it.
3. If your clothes are very stained, you will probably ____ them.
4. A shy child might be ____.
5. If the store runs out of an item, the manager will usually ____ it.

C. You are the manager of a coin-operated self-service laundry. Describe a bad day. What went wrong? Use as many challenge words as you can.

245

A
1. presoak
2. refill
3. reorder
4. uncertain
5. unfriendly

B
1. uncertain
2. refill
3. presoak
4. unfriendly
5. reorder

C
Answers will vary.

Challenge Word Test Sentences

1. The student was **uncertain** of the answer.
2. The shy person only appeared to be **unfriendly**.
3. Father forgot to **reorder** new checks.
4. Please **refill** the tray for ice cubes.
5. Mother had to **presoak** the collar of this white shirt.

Challenge Activities

dancer	jogger	jeweler
forester	letter carrier	

A. Write the challenge word that describes each picture.

1.
2.
3.

4.
5.

B. Write a challenge word to answer each question.

1. Who repaired my watch?
2. Who does warm-up exercises?
3. Who cares for trees?
4. Who does ballet?
5. Who delivers mail to my house?

C. Imagine that you've chosen a career or activity named by one of the challenge words. Write a schedule showing what your day is like. Follow the example below.

9:00	Open my store.
9:00 – 10:00	Fix watches in for repair.
10:00 – 11:00	Make new sign about sale on earrings.

Before you write your schedule, you might like to interview someone who actually does these things.

246

A
1. dancer
2. jogger
3. jeweler
4. forester
5. letter carrier

B
1. jeweler
2. dancer, jogger
3. forester
4. dancer
5. letter carrier

C
Answers will vary.

Challenge Word Test Sentences

1. A **dancer** should practice every day.
2. A **jogger** often jogs four or more times each week.
3. Her daughter bought these earrings from a **jeweler**.
4. A **forester** showed us how to plant the trees.
5. Does a **letter carrier** walk more than a mile a day?

Challenge Activities

boastful	skillful	colorful
sleepless	cordless	

A. Unscramble part of each word. Then use the code to find challenge words and write them. Then write the letter of the definition that goes with each word.

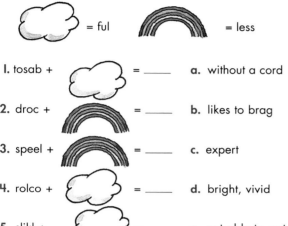

= ful   = less

1. tosab + = ____   **a.** without a cord

2. droc + = ____   **b.** likes to brag

3. speel + = ____   **c.** expert

4. rolco + = ____   **d.** bright, vivid

5. slikl + = ____   **e.** not able to rest

A
1. boastful; b
2. cordless; a
3. sleepless; e
4. colorful; d
5. skillful; c

B
1. colorful
2. cordless
3. sleepless
4. boastful
5. skillful

C
Answers will vary.

B. Write the challenge word that means the opposite of each definition.

1. pale, drab
2. having a cord
3. peaceful, restful
4. humble, modest
5. untrained, without ability

C. Write an advertisement for a new product. Tell why you think it is necessary for every home to have one. Use as many challenge words as you can.

247

Challenge Word Test Sentences

1. His uncle is a very **boastful** person.
2. A **skillful** reporter must write well.
3. This tulip has very **colorful** petals.
4. The doctor spent another **sleepless** night.
5. The **cordless** telephone is very useful outside the house.

Challenge Activities

Chanukah	Christmas	Easter
	Passover	Thanksgiving

A. Order of answers may vary.

1. Chanukah
2. Christmas
3. Passover
4. Easter
5. Thanksgiving

B
1. Christmas
2. Chanukah
3. Easter
4. Passover
5. Thanksgiving

C
Answers will vary.

A. Write the name of the holiday or holidays that fall in each season.

   1.–2. winter   **3.–4.** spring   **5.** fall

B. Write the challenge word for each dictionary respelling.

   1. On (**krĭs′** məs) we decorate a tree.
   2. On (**hä′** nə kə) we light candles.
   3. On (**ē′** stər) we paint and hide eggs.
   4. On (**păs′** ō′ vər) we eat a special dinner.
   5. On (thăngks **gĭv′** ĭng) we have a turkey dinner.

C. Pretend you're planning to celebrate one of the holidays named in the challenge words. Write a paragraph describing what you'll do on that day.

Challenge Word Test Sentences

   1. The season of **Chanukah** is a joyful one.
   2. We sing happy songs at **Christmas**.
   3. They always have an egg hunt at **Easter**.
   4. **Passover** is a thankful time of the year.
   5. Grandmother and Grandfather always eat **Thanksgiving** dinner with us.

Challenge Activities

menus	sponges	arches
hobbies		strawberries

A. Write the form of each challenge word that means one.

	one	two or more
1.	_____	arches
2.	_____	strawberries
3.	_____	sponges
4.	_____	hobbies
5.	_____	menus

B. Write the challenge word that describes the picture.

1.

2.

3.

4.

5.

A
1. arch
2. strawberry
3. sponge
4. hobby
5. menu

B
1. hobbies
2. sponges
3. menus
4. strawberries
5. arches

C
Answers will vary.

C. Imagine that you own a restaurant. Write an explanation of your duties and activities during a typical day. This might include menu planning and shopping, for example. Use as many of the challenge words as you can.

249

Challenge Word Test Sentences

1. Please place the **menus** beside the glasses.
2. We used four **sponges** to soak up the water.
3. The **arches** of this bridge are gigantic.
4. Two of her **hobbies** are baking cakes and playing baseball.
5. Mother will cook the **strawberries** to make jelly.

Challenge Activities

infant's	nephew's	crowd's
umpires'		runners'

A. **1.–3.** Write the challenge words that are singular possessives.

B. **1.–2.** Write the challenge words that are plural possessives.

C. Write the word in parentheses in the form that will correctly complete the sentence.

1. That (crowd) cheer is loud.
2. The two (umpire) gloves have been found.
3. His (nephew) hair is brown.
4. All three (runner) feet are sore.
5. The (infant) rattle is green and blue.

D. Imagine that you've found a big "lost and found" box. Your job is to get the things back to their owners. Write a list of what things are in the box and to whom they belong. Use some challenge words as well as the names of your friends as the owners. Be sure to use the apostrophe correctly to show singular or plural possession.

A
Order of answers may vary.
1. infant's
2. nephew's
3. crowd's

B
Order of answers may vary.
1. runners'
2. umpires'

C
1. crowd's
2. umpires'
3. nephew's
4. runners'
5. infant's

D
Answers will vary.

250

Challenge Word Test Sentences

1. The **infant's** cry woke the other children.
2. Is this your **nephew's** baseball glove?
3. A **crowd's** loud cheer might help a team win.
4. The **umpires'** calls were not the same, so they met to talk.
5. The **runners'** shirts were very wet after the race.

Challenge Activities

smoothness	restfulness	happiness
emptiness	wonderment	

A. Add letters and take away letters as indicated to form challenge words.

1. smooth + ness = _____
2. wonder + ment = _____
3. happy - y + i + ness = _____
4. rest + ful + ness = _____
5. empty - y + i + ness = _____

B. Write a challenge word to answer each question.

1. Which word means "the condition of having nothing"?
2. Which word means "the condition of having peace and quiet"?
3. Which word means "the condition of surprise or amazement"?
4. Which word means "the condition of having no rough parts"?
5. Which word means "the condition of feeling glad"?

C. Describe a scene to illustrate one of the challenge words. Write the description, and then write the word at the bottom of the paper. Illustrate it if you wish.

A
1. smoothness
2. wonderment
3. happiness
4. restfulness
5. emptiness

B
1. emptiness
2. restfulness
3. wonderment
4. smoothness
5. happiness

C
Answers will vary.

251

Challenge Word Test Sentences

1. The **smoothness** of the baby's skin made it soft to touch.
2. The **restfulness** of the music put the baby to sleep.
3. Your kindness has brought me much **happiness**.
4. The **emptiness** in his life made him sad.
5. The child's eyes were full of **wonderment**.

Challenge Activities

yearbook	floodlight	field trip
third base	zip code	

A. Use one part of each word below to form a challenge word. Write the words you made.

1. flashlight
2. yearly
3. basement
4. zipper
5. infield

B. Write the challenge word that completes each analogy.

1. **Gas** is to **car** as **electricity** is to _____.
2. **Football** is to **yard line** as **baseball** is to _____.
3. **Words** are to **dictionary** as **pictures** are to _____.
4. **Letters** are to **name** as **numbers** are to _____.
5. **Campers** are to **hike** as **class** is to _____.

C. Make a list of words for each category below. Use the challenge words as well as other words you know. Then choose one item from your lists that you think is the most interesting or the most unusual. Write a description of it.

a. kinds of school trips
b. kinds of lighting
c. sports equipment
d. directories
e. words related to mail or post offices

252

A
1. floodlight
2. yearbook
3. third base
4. zip code
5. field trip

B
1. floodlight
2. third base
3. yearbook
4. zip code
5. field trip

C
Answers will vary.

Challenge Word Test Sentences

1. The students in the eighth grade have a **yearbook**.
2. Only a **floodlight** could be seen in the fog.
3. Our class will take a **field trip** in the spring.
4. The umpire on **third base** is my brother's friend.
5. I forgot to write the **zip code** on the letter.

Challenge Activities

yen	lira	peso
franc	shilling	

A. Unscramble the challenge words to find out which kind of money each country uses. Write each challenge word.

1. Italy: rail
2. Japan: ney
3. Kenya: slinghli
4. Mexico: sope
5. France: crafn

B. Write the challenge word for each dictionary respelling.

1. Can you get change for a (**shĭl′** ĭng) in Nairobi, Kenya?
2. The (**pā′** sō) is used in several countries in Latin America.
3. I traded in my dollars for (yĕn) in Tokyo, Japan.
4. The (frăngk) is used in France and Belgium.
5. You'll need some (**lîr′** ə) to buy dinner in Rome, Italy.

C. Imagine you're going on a trip around the world! Make a schedule for your trip, telling where you will visit. Write a paragraph identifying and describing at least two items you might buy on your trip. Use the challenge words when you can.

A
1. lira
2. yen
3. shilling
4. peso
5. franc

B
1. shilling
2. peso
3. yen
4. franc
5. lira

C
Answers will vary.

253

Challenge Word Test Sentences

1. A **yen** once meant only a round object.
2. A **lira** can be a coin or paper money.
3. There are many places where a **peso** is used as money.
4. The French coin for one **franc** is about the same size as an American quarter.
5. A **shilling** is a coin once used in England.

WRITER'S HANDBOOK
Contents

The list of high frequency writing words on pages 262–266 was taken from *Teaching Kids to Spell* by J. Richard Gentry and Jean Gillet (Heinemann, 1993).

255

Spelling Strategy
When You Take a Test

1 **Get** ready for the test. Make sure your paper and pencil are ready.

2 **Listen** carefully as your teacher says each word and uses it in a sentence. Don't write before you hear the word **and** the sentence.

3 **Write** the word carefully. Make sure your handwriting is easy to read. If you want to print your words, ask your teacher.

4 **Use** a pen to correct your test. Look at the word as your teacher says it.

5 **Say** the word aloud. Listen carefully as your teacher spells the word. Say each letter aloud. Check the word one letter at a time.

6 **Circle** any misspelled parts of the word.

7 **Look** at the correctly written word. Spell the word again. Say each letter out loud.

8 **Write** any misspelled word correctly.

Spelling Strategy
When You Write a Paper

1 **Think** of the exact word you want to use.

2 **Write** the word, if you know how to spell it.

3 **Say** the word to yourself, if you are not sure how to spell it.

4 **Picture** what the word looks like when you see it written.

5 **Write** the word.

6 **Ask** yourself whether the word looks right.

7 **Check** the word in a dictionary if you are not sure.

257

SPELLING AND THE Writing Process

Writing anything—a friendly letter, a paper for school—usually follows a process. The writing process has five steps. It might look like this if you tried to draw a picture of it:

Prewriting · Drafting · Revising · Editing · Publishing

Part of that writing process forms a loop. That is because not every writing task is the same. It is also because writers often jump back and forth between the steps as they change their minds and think of new ideas.

Here is a description of each step:

Prewriting This is thinking and planning ahead to help you write.

Drafting This means writing your paper for the first time. You usually just try to get your ideas down on paper. You can fix them later.

Revising This means fixing your final draft. Here is where you rewrite, change, and add words.

Editing This is where you feel you have said all you want to say. Now you proofread your paper for spelling errors and errors in grammar and punctuation.

Publishing This is making a copy of your writing and sharing it with your readers. Put your writing in a form that your readers will enjoy.

Confident spellers are better writers. Confident writers understand better their own writing process. Know the five steps. Know how they best fit the way you write.

258

SPELLING AND
Writing Ideas

Being a good speller can help make you a more confident writer. Writing more can make you a better writer. Here are some ideas to get you started.

 Ideas for Descriptive Writing

You might…
- describe something very, very small and something very, very big.
- describe something from the point of view of an insect.
- describe your most prized possession.

 Ideas for Narrative Writing

You might…
- write a story about your first visit to someplace new.
- write a story about an event that helped you "grow up."
- write a story about a bad day or a best day playing your favorite sport.

 Ideas for Persuasive Writing

You might…
- try to persuade your classmates to read a book you like.
- try to persuade your parents to let you have a pet.
- try to persuade your teacher to change a class rule.

 Ideas for Expository Writing

You might…
- write how to prepare your favorite dish.
- inform your classmates how to create a craft object.
- write instructions on how to care for a lawn mower or carpentry tool.

 More Ideas for Expository Writing

You might…
- find out how your local government works and write a report.
- interview an animal caregiver and write a report about the job.
- choose a career you might like and write a report about it.

259

Manuscript Handwriting Models

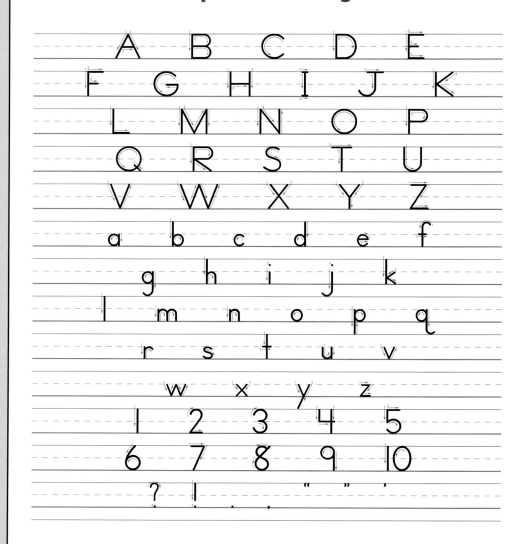

Cursive Handwriting Models

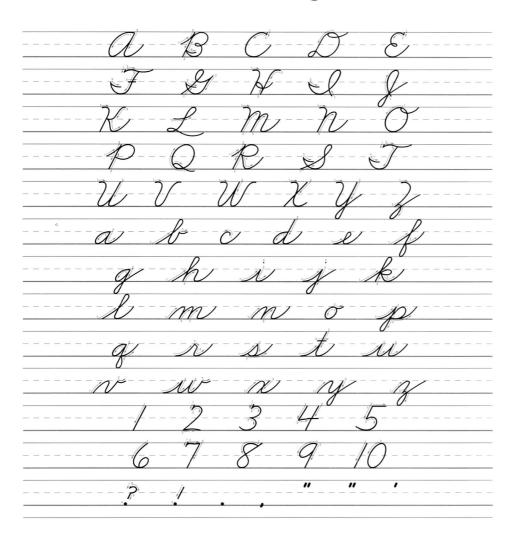

High Frequency Writing Words

A

a
about
afraid
after
again
air
all
almost
also
always
am
America
an
and
animal
animals
another
any
anything
are
around
as
ask
asked
at
ate
away

B

baby
back
bad
ball
balloons
baseball
basketball
be
bear
beautiful
because
become
bed
been
before
being
believe
best
better
big
bike
black
boat
book

books
both
boy
boys
bring
broke
brother
build
bus
but
buy
by

C

call
called
came
can
candy
can't
car
care
cars
cat
catch
caught
change

charge
children
Christmas
circus
city
class
clean
clothes
come
comes
coming
could
couldn't
country
cut

D

Dad
day
days
decided
did
didn't
died
different
dinner
do

does
doesn't
dog
dogs
doing
done
don't
door
down
dream

E

each
earth
eat
eighth
else
end
enough
even
every
everybody
everyone
everything
except
eyes

F

family
fast
father
favorite
feel
feet
fell
few
field
fight
finally
find
fire
first
fish
five
fix
food
football
for
found
four
free
Friday
friend
friends
from

front
fun
funny
future

G

game
games
gas
gave
get
gets
getting
girl
girls
give
go
God
goes
going
good
got
grade
grader
great
ground
grow

H

had
hair
half
happened
happy
hard
has
have
having
he
head
heard
help
her
here
he's
high
hill
him
his
hit
home
homework
hope
horse
horses
hot

263

hour
house
how
hurt

I

I
I'd
if
I'm
important
in
into
is
it
its
it's

J

job
jump
just

K

keep
kept
kids

killed
kind
knew
know

L

lady
land
last
later
learn
leave
left
let
let's
life
like
liked
likes
little
live
lived
lives
long
look
looked
looking
lost

lot
lots
love
lunch

M

mad
made
make
making
man
many
math
may
maybe
me
mean
men
might
miss
Mom
money
more
morning
most
mother
mouse
move

Mr.
Mrs.
much
music
must
my
myself

N

name
named
need
never
new
next
nice
night
no
not
nothing
now

O

of
off
oh
OK
old

264

on
once
one
only
or
other
our
out
outside
over
own

P

parents
park
party
people
person
pick
place
planet
play
played
playing
police
president
pretty
probably

problem
put

R

ran
read
ready
real
really
reason
red
responsibilities
rest
ride
riding
right
room
rules
run
running

S

said
same
saw
say
scared
school

schools
sea
second
see
seen
set
seventh
she
ship
shot
should
show
sick
since
sister
sit
sleep
small
snow
so
some
someone
something
sometimes
soon
space
sport
sports

start
started
states
stay
still
stop
stopped
store
story
street
stuff
such
sudden
suddenly
summer
sure
swimming

T

take
talk
talking
teach
teacher
teachers
team
tell
than

265

High Frequency Writing Words (continued)

Thanksgiving
that
that's
the
their
them
then
there
these
they
they're
thing
things
think
this
thought
three
through
throw
time
times
to
today
together
told
too
took

top
tree
trees
tried
trip
trouble
try
trying
turn
turned
TV
two

U

united
until
up
upon
us
use
used

V

very

W

walk
walked
walking
want
wanted
war
was
wasn't
watch
water
way
we
week
weeks
well
went
were
what
when
where
which
while
white
who
whole
why
will
win
winter
wish
with
without
woke
won
won't
work
world
would
wouldn't

Y

yard
year
years
yes
you
your
you're

Guide Words

The **guide words** at the top of each dictionary page can help you find the word you want quickly. The first guide word tells you the first word on that page. The second guide word tells you the last word on that page. The entries on the page fall in alphabetical order between these two guide words.

Entries

Words you want to check in the dictionary are called **entries**. Entries provide a lot of information besides the correct spelling. Look at the sample entry below.

Tips for Finding a Word in a Dictionary

- Practice using guide words in a dictionary. Think of words to spell. Then use the guide words to find each word's entry. Do this again and again until you can use guide words easily.

- Some spellings are listed with the base word. To find **easiest,** you would look up **easy**. To find **remaining,** you would look up **remain**. To find **histories,** you would look up **history**.

- If you do not know how to spell a word, guess the spelling before looking it up. Try to find the first three letters of the word. (If you just use the first letter, you will probably take too long.)

- If you can't find a word, think of how else it might be spelled. For example, if a word starts with the **/k/ sound,** the spelling might begin with **k, c,** or even **ch**.

Mini-Lessons on Dictionary Usage

Pronunciation
Key T268

Dictionary
Features.............T270

---

entry the correct spelling, sometimes broken into syllables

pronunciation

definition to be sure you have the correct entry word

po•ny /pō′ nē/ *n.* (**po•nies** *pl.*) a kind of horse that is small in size when fully grown. *Children ride a pony at an amusement park.*

sample sentence to make the definition clearer

other spellings other word forms, including plurals that change the spelling of the base word

267

You may wish to use these mini-lessons to help your students better utilize the **Spelling Dictionary**.

Objective

Students will
• **become** familiar with and use the **Pronunciation Key**.

Dictionary Mini-Lesson: Pronunciation Key

Tell the students that a **Pronunciation Key** appears on every second page in the **Spelling Dictionary**. Ask the students to find a **Pronunciation Key**. (It first appears on page 269.)

Explain that each symbol in the **Pronunciation Key** represents a sound in the English language. The word(s) that follow each symbol include that sound. The letters that spell the sound in each word are printed in bold type. Tell the students that these symbols are used in the dictionary respellings that appear in the **Spelling Dictionary**.

Remind the students that, in a dictionary respelling, a syllable that receives primary stress, or accent, is printed in bold type and is followed by an accent mark. A syllable that receives secondary stress is printed in regular type and is followed by an accent mark.

---

a•ble /ā′ bəl/ *adj.* having power, skill, or talent. *With practice you will be able to play the piano.*

ache /āk/ *n.* a pain that continues. *The ache in the boy's tooth stopped after he saw the dentist.*

ac•id /ăs′ ĭd/ *n.* a chemical compound that can "burn" or "eat" other materials. *You learn to handle acid safely in science class.*

ad•dend /ăd′ ĕnd/ or /ə dĕnd′/ *n.* a number to be added to another number. *In the example 50 + 25 = 75, the numbers 25 and 50 are addends.*

ad•di•tion¹ /ə dĭsh′ ən/ *n.* the adding of one number to another to get a total. *2 + 2 = 4 is an example of addition.*

ad•di•tion² /ə dĭsh′ ən/ *adj.* having to do with adding numbers: *an addition problem.*

ad•jec•tive /ăj′ ĭk′ tĭv/ *n.* a word used to describe or modify a noun. *"Sunny" is an adjective that could describe the noun "day."*

a•dult /ə dŭlt′/ or /ăd′ ŭlt/ *n.* a grown person. *You may vote when you are an adult.*

ad•verb /ăd′ vûrb/ *n.* a word used to describe or modify a verb. *The students were asked to use the adverb "joyfully" in a sentence.*

Af•ri•ca /ăf′ rĭ kə/ *n.* a large continent that lies south of Europe. *The explorer visited jungles and deserts in Africa.*

af•ter•shock /ăf′ tər shŏk/ *n.* a minor shock that follows an earthquake. *Because the earthquake was so slight, the aftershock was not even felt.*

a•gree /ə grē′/ *v.* to have the same opinion. *We all agree that Mr. Jansen would make a good mayor.*

a•gree•ment /ə grē′ mənt/ *n.* an arrangement or understanding between two persons or groups. *The students came to an agreement about the best day for the litter cleanup.*

a•head /ə hĕd′/ *adv.* in advance; in front. *Dad walked ahead to look for a campsite.*

---

aim /ām/ *v.* to point at; to direct toward. *Aim the arrow at the center of the target.*

air mail /âr′ māl/ *n.* mail carried by airplanes. *The air mail is placed in special bags.*

air•port /âr′ pôrt/ or /-pōrt/ *n.* a place where airplanes take off and land. *John picked up Betty at the airport.*

air•y /âr′ ē/ *adj.* light; breezy. *The balcony of our apartment is a cool and airy place to sit.*

a•larm /ə lärm′/ *n.* a warning signal that danger is near. *The alarm went off moments after the fire started.*

a•larm clock /ə lärm′ klŏk/ *n.* a clock that can be set to ring or buzz at a certain time. *My alarm clock wakes me up at seven every morning.*

alarm clock

a•live /ə lĭv′/ *adj.* living; not dead. *People sometimes forget that trees are alive.*

a•lone /ə lōn′/ *adv.* without anyone else. *The box was too heavy for one person to lift alone.*

al•pha•bet /ăl′ fə bĕt/ *n.* the letters of a language arranged in order. *The first three letters of the English alphabet are a, b, and c.*

al•read•y /ôl rĕd′ ē/ *adv.* by this time; before. *We stopped to visit, but they had already left.*

al•so /ôl′ sō/ *adv.* too; in addition; likewise. *Geraniums grow well not only in flowerpots, but also in gardens.*

al•ti•tude /ăl′ tĭ tōōd/ or /-tyōōd/ *n.* height above sea level. *The altitude of the mountain pass was 9,500 feet.*

A•mer•i•ca /ə mĕr′ ĭ kə/ *n.* the continents of the western hemisphere; North and South America. *The United States of America is often called America.*

A•mer•i•can¹ /ə mĕr′ ĭ kən/ *n.* one born or living in America. *A citizen of the United States is an American.*

A•mer•i•can² /ə mĕr′ ĭ kən/ *adj.* of or from the United States. *The American flag is red, white, and blue.*

a•mount /ə mount′/ *n.* the total or sum. *We raised the amount of money needed for the books.*

Ask volunteers to read the sample words in the **Pronunciation Key** and to name the letters in dark type that spell the sounds. Encourage the class to name other words that have these sounds. Remind the students that two or more letters may spell a single sound. (For example, **ai** spells /ā/ and **dge** spells /j/.)

Pronounce several spelling words and write them on the chalkboard. Ask the students to use the **Pronunciation Key** to write a dictionary respelling for each word. Then ask them to check their answers in the **Spelling Dictionary**.

an•kle /ăng′ kəl/ *n.* the joint connecting the foot with the leg. *My new sneakers are high enough to cover my ankles.*

an•swer /ăn′ sər/ *n.* **a.** a reply. *I must send my answer to her letter quickly.* **b.** a solution. *I know the answer to that math problem.*

Ant•arc•ti•ca /ănt ärk′ tĭ kə/ *n.* the continent at the South Pole. *The coldest continent on the earth is Antarctica.*

an•ten•na /ăn těn′ ə/ *n.* equipment for sending or receiving radio or television broadcasts. *Adjusting the TV antenna may improve the picture.*

an•y•way /ěn′ ē wā′/ *adv.* no matter what may happen; anyhow. *It may rain tomorrow, but we are going to have the picnic anyway.*

an•y•where /ěn′ ē hwâr′/ *adv.* at or to any place. *If you're going anywhere near a hardware store, bring me some nails.*

a•part /ə pärt′/ *adv.* to pieces; in separate pieces. *The puzzle fell apart when it slipped off the table.*

a•part•ment /ə pärt′ mənt/ *n.* a group of rooms to live in, generally in a building housing more than one family. *They live in an apartment on the second floor.*

Apr. April.

A•pril /ā′ prəl/ *n.* the fourth month of the year. *We should have some warmer weather in April.*

arc•tic[1] /ärk′ tĭk/ *n.* the region around or near the North Pole. *Scientists have been able to study the arctic in submarines.*

arc•tic[2] /ärk′ tĭk/ *adj.* extremely cold; freezing. *The winter months brought arctic temperatures.*

aren′t /ärnt/ are not.

ar•id /ăr′ ĭd/ *adj.* dry. *The desert has an arid climate.*

a•rith•me•tic /ə rĭth′ mə tĭk/ *n.* the study and use of numbers. *Arithmetic includes addition, subtraction, multiplication, and division.*

ar•my /är′ mē/ *n.* (**ar•mies** *pl.*) a large group of people who are organized and trained to serve as soldiers. *The United States Army fought in Europe during World War II.*

Pronunciation Key

ă	pat	ŏ	pot	th	thin
ā	pay	ō	toe	*th*	this
âr	care	ô	paw, for	hw	which
ä	father	oi	noise	zh	vision
ě	pet	ou	out	ə	about,
ē	be	ŏŏ	took		item,
ĭ	pit	ōō	boot		pencil,
ī	pie	ŭ	cut		gallop,
îr	pier	ûr	urge		circus

ash /ăsh/ *n.* (**ash•es** *pl.*) the remains of a thing that has been burned. *We can use this pail to empty the ashes from the fireplace.*

A•sia /ā′ zhə/ *n.* the large continent that lies east of Europe. *The largest continent on the earth is Asia.*

as•pi•rin /ăs′ pə rĭn/ or /-prĭn/ *n.* a mild medicine in the form of a tablet or liquid used to relieve fever or minor pain. *The doctor told Lani to take aspirin for her cold.*

auc•tion /ôk′ shən/ *n.* a public sale at which property is sold to the highest bidder. *Mrs. Evans bought an antique vase at the auction.*

Aug. August.

Au•gust /ô′ gəst/ *n.* the eighth month of the year. *August has thirty-one days.*

Aus•tra•lia /ô strāl′ yə/ *n.* the island continent between the Pacific and Indian oceans. *At the zoo we saw a kangaroo from Australia.*

a•while /ə hwīl′/ *adv.* for a short time. *Let's rest awhile before we continue driving.*

ba•by /bā′ bē/ *n.* (**ba•bies** *pl.*) a very young child; an infant. *The baby had not learned to stand up yet.*

ba•by sit•ter /bā′ bē sĭt′ ər/ *n.* one who takes care of young children. *John's mother called a baby sitter to stay with him while she was out.*

baby

Spelling Dictionary

Using the Spelling Dictionary

You may wish to use these mini-lessons to help your students better utilize the **Spelling Dictionary**.

Objective

Students will
• **become** familiar with and use the **Spelling Dictionary**.

Dictionary Mini-Lesson: Dictionary Features

Ask the students to name some of the uses of a dictionary. (Dictionaries are used to look up the meanings, spellings, and pronunciations of words. Many dictionaries also give the histories, or etymologies, of words.)

Tell the students that their **Spelling Dictionaries** give them information about their spelling words. As the students look through the **Spelling Dictionary**, point out the following:

• Entry words are listed in alphabetical order, and each word is followed by its respelling, its part of speech, and its definition.

• Each definition is followed by a sentence or phrase that shows how the word is used.

Read the information on the **Using the Dictionary** page in the Student Edition with the students. Use the sample entry and the following additional information to discuss the **Spelling Dictionary:**

---

badge /băj/ *n.* something worn to show that a person is a member of a group or organization. *Each firefighter wore a badge.*

bag • gage /băg′ ĭj/ *n.* suitcases; luggage. *Airline passengers may pick up their baggage inside the terminal.*

bak • er /bā′ kər/ *n.* a person who makes and sells breads and pastries. *We ordered a special birthday cake from the baker.*

bank • er /băng′ kər/ *n.* a person who owns or runs a bank. *We talked to the banker about opening a savings account.*

barge /bärj/ *n.* a long, flat, unpowered boat used for transporting freight. *The tugboat pulled a barge that carried lumber.*

barn /bärn/ *n.* a farm building in which to house animals and store grain and hay. *The largest barn on the farm was filled with animals.*

barn

bar • ri • er /băr′ ē ər/ *n.* a boundary or limit. *The fence forms a barrier against intruders.*

bar • ter /bär′ tər/ *v.* to trade without the exchange of money. *She used her handmade ornaments to barter for the oriental rug.*

bas • ket • ball /băs′ kĭt bôl′/ *n.* **a.** a game in which points are scored by throwing a ball through a basket. *Basketball is usually played indoors.* **b.** the ball used in this game. *Our basketball had lost all its air.*

bass /bās/ *n.* **a.** in music, the range of notes that are lower in tone than the other notes. *A piano player plays the bass with the left hand.* **b.** a person who sings the lowest part. *A man with a deep voice is a bass.*

bas • soon /bə sōōn′/ *n.* a large woodwind instrument with a low tone. *The bassoon can have a mournful sound.*

bat • ter • y /băt′ ə rē/ *n.* (**bat•ter•ies** *pl.*) an electric cell used to produce a current. *My radio operates on a battery.*

bat • tle /băt′ l/ *n.* a fight between armies, navies, etc., during a war. *That battle was the turning point of the war.*

be • came /bĭ kām′/ *v.* past tense of **become**.

be • cause /bĭ kôz′/ *conj.* for the reason that. *I study because I want to learn.*

be • come /bĭ kŭm′/ *v.* (**be•comes, be•came, be•come, be•com•ing**) to come to be. *The weather will become warmer in spring.*

bee • tle /bēt′ l/ *n.* an insect that has four wings, two of which form a hard, shiny covering. *A ladybug is a small beetle that eats insects that harm garden plants.*

be • gan /bĭ găn′/ *v.* past tense of **begin**.

be • gin /bĭ gĭn′/ *v.* (**be•gins, be•gan, be•gun, be•gin•ning**) to start. *We will begin our school day with a math lesson.*

be • lieve /bĭ lēv′/ *v.* (**be•lieves, be•lieved, be•liev•ing**) to accept something as true or real. *Do you believe that cats have nine lives?*

be • side /bĭ sīd′/ *prep.* at the side of; near to. *The carton was left beside the trash can.*

be • tween /bĭ twēn′/ *prep.* in the space that separates two things. *There were four people between me and the door.*

be • ware /bĭ wâr′/ *v.* to be cautious of. *Beware of the undertow when you swim in the ocean.*

bit • ter /bĭt′ ər/ *adj.* tasting sharp and unpleasant. *Do you think black walnuts have a bitter taste?*

black • en /blăk′ ən/ *v.* to make black or dark. *Use a pencil to blacken the circle that matches the correct answer.*

blame¹ /blām/ *v.* (**blames, blamed, blam•ing**) to put the responsibility for something bad on a person or thing. *Don't blame yourself; it wasn't your fault.*

blame² /blām/ *n.* responsibility for a fault. *The pilot put the blame for the delay on the fog.*

blan • ket /blăng′ kĭt/ *n.* a heavy woven piece of cloth used to keep one warm. *I sleep under a wool blanket in the winter.*

blos • som¹ /blŏs′ əm/ *n.* the flower of a plant or tree. *The orange blossom smells sweet.*

blos • som² /blŏs′ əm/ *v.* to bloom; to produce flowers. *The trees blossom early in warm weather.*

• **Guide Words:** The guide words at the top of each dictionary page show the first and last entries on that page. A word that comes between the guide words alphabetically will appear on that page.

• **Entry:** The entry is made up of the entry word and the information about it (i.e., the phonetic spelling, part(s) of speech, definition(s), sample sentence(s), inflected forms, and homophones and etymology, if any).

blue jeans /bloo' jēnz'/ *n.* pants made out of denim. *He likes to wear blue jeans when he goes skiing.*

boast /bōst/ *v.* to brag; to talk too much about yourself and about what you can do. *Judy likes to boast about how fast she can run.*

bold /bōld/ *adj.* not afraid to face danger; brave and daring. *The bold gymnast attempted a difficult vault.*

bold • ness /bōld' nĭs/ *n.* the state of being bold; bravery; daring. *We were surprised by the boldness of the fawn in leaving its safe hiding place.*

bot • tle¹ /bŏt' l/ *n.* a holder for liquids. *I think juice tastes better from a glass bottle than from a can.*

bot • tle² /bŏt' l/ *v.* (**bot•tles, bot•tled, bot•tling**) to put into bottles. *Milk must be bottled under very clean conditions.*

bought /bôt/ *v.* past tense of **buy**.

brag /brăg/ *v.* (**brags, bragged, brag•ging**) to boast; to talk too much about how good you are or how much you have. *Charles often brags about his new radio.*

brain /brān/ *n.* the mass of nerve tissue in the skull that controls the body and stores knowledge. *Your brain constantly tells your heart to beat.*

brake /brāk/ *n.* a thing that slows down or stops a car, a machine, a bicycle, etc. *The driver pressed on the brake when the traffic light turned red.*

▶ **Brake** sounds like **break**.

bread /brĕd/ *n.* a food baked from dough made with flour or meal. *Sandwiches are made with bread.*

break /brāk/ *v.* (**breaks, broke, bro•ken, break•ing**) to come apart; to separate into pieces. *The dish will break if it falls on the floor.*

▶ **Break** sounds like **brake**.

break • fast /brĕk' fəst/ *n.* the first meal of the day. *Jim ate a good breakfast of orange juice, cereal, toast, and milk.*

breeze /brēz/ *n.* a light, gentle wind. *The flag barely moved in the breeze.*

brick /brĭk/ *n.* a block of baked clay used for building or paving. *Many houses and apartment buildings are built with bricks.*

Pronunciation Key

ă	pat	ŏ	pot	th	thin
ā	pay	ō	toe	th	this
âr	care	ô	paw, for	hw	which
ä	father	oi	noise	zh	vision
ĕ	pet	ou	out	ə	about,
ē	be	ŏŏ	took		item,
ĭ	pit	ōō	boot		pencil,
ī	pie	ŭ	cut		gallop,
îr	pier	ûr	urge		circus

---

bridge /brĭj/ *n.* a structure built over a river or a valley for people or vehicles to cross. *Thousands of cars a day cross the Mississippi River on bridges.*

bridge

brief /brēf/ *adj.* short; quick; direct. *Our meeting was brief.*

bright • en /brīt' ən/ *v.* to lighten; to make or become bright. *The lamp will brighten the living room.*

bright • ness /brīt' nĭs/ *n.* the state or quality of shining or giving light. *The moon's brightness made it easy to see at night.*

bring /brĭng/ *v.* (**brings, brought, bring•ing**) to take along. *Be sure to bring a gift to our party.*

Brit • ain /brĭt' ən/ *n.* the country that includes England, Scotland, and Wales. *Britain is separated from the rest of Europe by the English Channel.*

Brit • ish¹ /brĭt' ĭsh/ *adj.* of or from Britain. *British woolens are famous for their fine quality.*

Brit • ish² /brĭt' ĭsh/ *n.* the people of Britain. *The British drive on the left side of the road.*

broth • er /brŭth' ər/ *n.* a boy or man having the same parents as another person. *The girl had three older brothers and one younger sister.*

brought /brôt/ *v.* past tense of **bring**.

bub • ble¹ /bŭb' əl/ *n.* a thin, round film of liquid that forms a ball around a pocket of gas or air. *The slightest touch can pop a bubble.*

Spelling Dictionary

- **Part of Speech:** The **Spelling Dictionary** gives the entry word's most frequently used part of speech. If a word is commonly used as more than one part of speech, a separate entry is provided for each usage.

- **Definitions/Sample Sentences:** Each definition is followed by a sentence that shows how the word is used. The form of the word in the sentence may vary from the entry word to provide additional information about the word's usage.

- **Homophones:** Common homophones are identified.

- **Inflected Forms:** The students should look for inflected forms of the spelling words under the base words. Inflected forms are shown only if the spelling of the base word changes when the ending is added.

- **Etymologies:** Etymologies, or word histories, are sometimes included. The etymology shows the words from which the entry word was derived. The earliest source is shown last. For more information on the histories of the spelling words, the students should refer to a standard dictionary.

- **Entry Word:** The entry word is usually a base word—that is, a word to which an inflected ending has not been added. The entry word is divided into syllables to show how it should be hyphenated.

- **Phonetic Spelling:** The phonetic spelling uses the symbols shown in the **Pronunciation Key** to show how the word is pronounced. Sometimes phonetic spellings showing alternative pronunciations of a word are also provided.

bub • ble² /bŭb′ əl/ *v.* (**bub•bles, bub•bled, bub•bling**) to form bubbles. *The soup will bubble when it is hot.*

build /bĭld/ *v.* (**builds, built, build•ing**) to make; to put together. *Doug wants to build a model house out of toothpicks.*

build • er /bĭl′ dər/ *n.* a person whose business is putting up buildings. *My uncle is a builder working on the new school buildings.*

built /bĭlt/ *v.* past tense of **build.**

burst /bûrst/ *v.* (**bursts, burst, burst•ing**) to break open suddenly. *The balloon will burst if it touches the hot light.*

but • ton¹ /bŭt′ n/ *n.* a small, flat, hard, round piece used to fasten two parts of a garment by fitting through a slit. *The top button on my coat is loose.*

but • ton² /bŭt′ n/ *v.* to fasten with buttons. *I buttoned my shirt.*

buy /bī/ *v.* (**buys, bought, buy•ing**) to purchase. *Sally needs to buy a new pair of shoes before winter.*

cab • bage /kăb′ ĭj/ *n.* a vegetable with thick leaves growing tightly together in a solid ball. *Cabbage can be eaten raw or cooked.*

cal • en • dar /kăl′ ən dər/ *n.* a table or chart used to keep track of days, weeks, and months. *We must remember to change our classroom calendar on the first day of the month.*

calf /kăf/ *n.* (**calves** *pl.*) a young cow or bull. *A calf can walk soon after it is born.*

calm /käm/ *adj.* quiet; peaceful; motionless. *There wasn't even a breeze on that calm evening.*

calves /kăvz/ *n.* plural of **calf.**

camp • er /kăm′ pər/ *n.* **a.** a person who lives outdoors for a period of time, usually in a tent. *The campers pitched their tent next to a stream.* **b.** a van or trailer equipped for camping. *The family moved into the camper as the storm approached.*

Can • a • da /kăn′ ə də/ *n.* the country north of the United States. *Canada is larger than the United States, but it has fewer people.*

Ca • na • di • an¹ /kə nā′ dē ən/ *adj.* of or from Canada. *Many U.S. hockey teams have Canadian players.*

Ca • na • di • an² /kə nā′ dē ən/ *n.* one born or living in Canada. *Many Canadians speak French.*

ca • nal /kə năl′/ *n.* a waterway dug across land to connect two bodies of water. *The Panama Canal connects the Pacific Ocean and the Atlantic Ocean.*

ca • nar • y /kə nâr′ ē/ *n.* (**ca•nar•ies** *pl.*) a songbird with bright greenish and yellow feathers. *The canary got its name from the Canary Islands.*

card • board /kärd′ bôrd/ or /-bōrd/ *n.* a kind of stiff, heavy paper used in making boxes, posters, etc. *We drew posters for our school play on large pieces of cardboard.*

care • ful /kâr′ fəl/ *adj.* cautious; full of care. *Be careful when you cross the busy street.*

care • less /kâr′ lĭs/ *adj.* reckless; not cautious. *You can't afford to be careless with matches.*

car • go /kär′ gō/ *n.* the freight carried on a ship or other vehicle. *The barge carried a cargo of lumber to the mill.*

car • ry /kăr′ rē/ *v.* (**car•ries, car•ried, car•ry•ing**) to transport from one place to another. *She will carry the young lamb into the barn.*

cart /kärt/ *n.* **a.** a two-wheeled vehicle pulled by a horse or other animal. *The pony pulled a cart in the parade.* **b.** a small vehicle moved by hand. *I will push the grocery cart.*

case /kās/ *n.* a large box; a container. *The music teacher carries her violin in a case.*

catch /kăch/ *v.* (**catch•es, caught, catch•ing**) to seize or retrieve; to capture. *Tonight would be a good night to catch fireflies.*

catch • er /kăch′ ər/ *n.* one who catches, especially the player behind home plate in a baseball game. *The catcher can tell the pitcher which pitch to throw.*

cat • tle /kăt′ l/ *n.* cows, bulls, or oxen. *The cattle eat grass in the pasture.*

cattle

caught /kôt/ *v.* past tense of **catch**.

cause[1] /kôz/ *n.* a person or thing that makes something happen. *A snowstorm was the cause of the slow traffic.*

cause[2] /kôz/ *v.* (**caus•es, caused, caus•ing**) to make happen. *The rain caused a leak in the roof.*

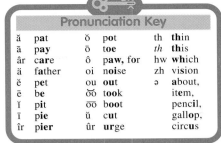

caught

cel•lar /sĕl′ ər/ *n.* an underground room, used for storage. *The family next door fixed up the cellar as a playroom for their children.*

▶ **Cellar** sounds like **seller**.

cel•lo /chĕl′ ō/ *n.* a large stringed instrument in the violin family. *The cello has a deep, rich tone.*

cen•ti•me•ter /sĕn′ tə mē′ tər/ *n.* a measure of length equal to one one-hundredth of a meter. *It takes about two centimeters to make one inch.*

cen•tu•ry /sĕn′ chə rē/ *n.* (**cen•tu•ries** *pl.*) a period of one hundred years. *The Statue of Liberty was built over a century ago.*

cer•tain /sûr′ tn/ *adj.* confident; sure; convinced. *She was certain you would win.*

charge[1] /chärj/ *v.* **a.** to ask for as payment. *That store will charge two dollars for that notebook.* **b.** to postpone payment on by recording the amount owed. *Charge the groceries to my account.*

charge[2] /chärj/ *n.* **a.** an amount asked or made as payment. *There is no charge for this service.* **b.** care; supervision: *the scientist in charge of the project.*

charm /chärm/ *v.* to delight; to please. *The child's smile charmed the audience.*

chart[1] /chärt/ *n.* information given in the form of graphs, maps, and tables. *Newspapers often print weather charts.*

chart[2] /chärt/ *v.* to make a map or diagram of. *My job is to chart our class's spelling progress.*

chase /chās/ *v.* (**chas•es, chased, chas•ing**) to run after; to try to catch. *In this game the players must chase the one with the ball.*

cheer[1] /chîr/ *n.* happiness; comfort. *A fire in the fireplace brings warmth and cheer to the room.*

Pronunciation Key

ă	pat	ŏ	pot	th	thin
ā	pay	ō	toe	th	this
âr	care	ô	paw, for	hw	which
ä	father	oi	noise	zh	vision
ĕ	pet	ou	out	ə	about,
ē	be	ŏŏ	took		item,
ĭ	pit	ōō	boot		pencil,
ī	pie	ŭ	cut		gallop,
îr	pier	ûr	urge		circus

cheer[2] /chîr/ *v.* to shout words of approval; to encourage by yelling. *We all cheered for our star player as he came on the field.*

cheer•ful /chîr′ fəl/ *adj.* happy; joyful. *Kari gave a cheerful smile.*

chick•en /chĭk′ ən/ *n.* a bird raised for its meat and its eggs; a hen or rooster. *Some chickens lay brown eggs.*

chick•en pox /chĭk′ ən pŏks/ *n.* a disease that causes a slight fever and a rash. *When Carl had chicken pox, it was hard for him to keep from scratching.*

chief /chēf/ *n.* a leader; a head of a tribe or group. *The chief leads the tribal council.*

child /chīld/ *n.* (**chil•dren** *pl.*) a young boy or girl. *Corey is the only child absent today.*

chil•dren /chĭl′ drən/ *n.* plural of **child**.

Chi•na /chī′ nə/ *n.* a country in eastern Asia. *China has more people than any other country.*

Chi•nese[1] /chī nēz′/ *adj.* of or from China. *Our city's zoo has a Chinese panda.*

Chi•nese[2] /chī nēz′/ *n.* **a.** the people of China. *Many Chinese live in rural areas.* **b.** the language of China. *Mr. Chang can speak Chinese.*

choice /chois/ *n.* a decision; a selection. *For dinner we will go to a restaurant of your choice.*

choose /chōōz/ *v.* (**choos•es, chose, cho•sen, choos•ing**) to select; to decide upon; to pick. *I will let you choose which color you would like.*

chose /chōz/ *v.* past tense of **choose**.

chuck•le /chŭk′ əl/ *n.* a small, quiet laugh. *His funny speech caused chuckles in the audience.*

273

cin • der /sĭn′ dər/ *n.* a piece of coal or wood that is only partly burned. *We spread cinders on the sidewalk on icy days.*

clar • i • net /klăr′ ə nĕt′/ *n.* a woodwind instrument with a bell-shaped end. *A clarinet has finger holes and keys for different notes.*

clay /klā/ *n.* soft, sticky earth that can be molded into different forms and then hardened in ovens. *Bricks, pottery, and tiles may be made of clay.*

clear /klîr/ *adj.* **a.** having no clouds; bright. *The sun shone in the clear sky.* **b.** distinct; not fuzzy. *I cannot get a clear picture on this TV station.*

climb /klīm/ *v.* to go up, often using both hands and feet; to move on a steep slope. *The club members climb mountains all over the state.*

climb • er /klī′ mər/ *n.* one who climbs. *Her goal was to become a mountain climber.*

clin • ic /klĭn′ ĭk/ *n.* a center like a hospital that provides care for outpatients. *Since his injuries were minor, he could be treated at the clinic.*

clos • ing /klō′ zĭng/ *n.* a phrase used to end a letter. *"Sincerely yours" is a common closing.*

clothes /klōz/ or /klō*thz*/ *n. pl.* garments; articles of dress; clothing. *Some people order all their clothes through a catalog.*

cloud • less /kloud′ lĭs/ *adj.* free of clouds; without clouds. *The cloudless sky was a brilliant blue.*

clue /kloō/ *n.* a piece of information that helps solve a problem or mystery. *In this game we use word clues to solve the puzzle.*

coach /kōch/ *n.* (**coach•es** *pl.*) a person who trains athletes; a person who teaches. *The basketball coach is happy when the team plays well.*

coast /kōst/ *n.* the seashore; land along the sea or ocean. *There are many beaches along the coast of the Pacific Ocean.*

coast • al /kōs′ təl/ *adj.* of or having to do with the coast or seashore. *Coastal waters are shallow.*

coil /koil/ *v.* to wind in spirals or rings; to wind around and around. *The snake coiled around the log.*

col • lar /kŏl′ ər/ *n.* the part of a shirt or coat that circles the neck. *He loosened his tie and his collar.*

co • lon /kō′ lən/ *n.* a punctuation mark (:) that introduces a list or phrase. *Use a colon before listing the names.*

col • o • ny /kŏl′ ə nē/ *n.* (**col•o•nies** *pl.*) a group of people with similar interests who live in a particular area. *The Pilgrims' colony grew as more people arrived.*

comb

comb¹ /kōm/ *n.* a tool with teeth, used to smooth or arrange the hair. *Most people carry a brush or comb.*

comb² /kōm/ *v.* to search carefully. *We will comb the room to find the contact lens.*

com • et /kŏm′ ĭt/ *n.* a heavenly body that looks like a star but has a tail of vapor. *A comet moves in orbit around the sun.*

com • ma /kŏm′ ə/ *n.* a punctuation mark (,) used to show a separation of words or ideas. *Commas separate items in a list.*

com • pare /kəm pâr′/ *v.* (**com•pares, com•pared, com•par•ing**) to examine things for similarities or differences. *If you compare prices, you can save money when you shop.*

con • ti • nent /kŏn′ tə nənt/ *n.* one of the seven main masses of land in the world. *We live on the continent of North America.*

core /kôr/ or /kōr/ *n.* the innermost part of something; the center; the middle. *The core of the earth contains solid metals.*

cor • ral /kə răl′/ *n.* a fenced-in place for horses, cattle, or other livestock. *Horseback riding lessons are given in the smaller corral.*

cot • tage /kŏt′ ĭj/ *n.* a small house. *We spent our vacation in a cottage on the beach.*

cou • ple /kŭp′ əl/ *n.* **a.** two of anything. *They will have to wait a couple of hours for the train.* **b.** a man and woman together. *That couple dances well together.*

Spelling Dictionary

craft /krăft/ *n.* **a.** skill in doing or making something. *Maria has taken up the craft of basketmaking.* **b.** a handmade item. *The crafts displayed at the fair included quilts and pottery.*

crag /krăg/ *n.* a steep mass of rock forming a cliff. *The climber reached a crag near the top of the mountain.*

cran•ber•ry /krăn′ bĕr′ ē/ *n.* (**cran•ber•ries** *pl.*) a red berry that grows on low shrubs in wet ground. *Cranberries are used in sauce and juice.*

cray•on /krā′ ŏn′/ *n.* a stick of colored wax or chalk used for drawing. *The children used crayons to add details to their paintings.*

crowd¹ /kroud/ *n.* many people gathered together. *I lost my brother in the crowd.*

crowd² /kroud/ *v.* to push or squeeze together in a small space. *The people crowded into the small room.*

crust /krŭst/ *n.* the outer surface of a loaf of bread. *Rye bread often has a dark crust.*

crys•tal /krĭs′ təl/ *n.* a clear, hard mineral with flat, regularly arranged surfaces. *Quartz is a common crystal.*

cube /kyoōb/ *n.* a solid figure with six square sides. *Not all ice cubes are actually in the shape of a cube.*

cure /kyoŏr/ *n.* a remedy. *Scientists have not yet found a cure for the common cold.*

cur•sive /kûr′ sĭv/ *adj.* written with the letters joined together. *Children begin to learn cursive writing when they have mastered printing.*

curve /kûrv/ *n.* a smooth bend in a line or road. *The sign warned us of a sharp curve just ahead.*

cute /kyoōt/ *adj.* delightfully attractive or appealing. *The child looked cute in her rabbit costume.*

cy•cle /sī′ kəl/ *n.* a series of events that occur over and over in the same order. *The seasons of the year form a cycle.*

Pronunciation Key

ă	pat	ŏ	pot	th	thin
ā	pay	ō	toe	th	this
âr	care	ô	paw, for	hw	which
ä	father	oi	noise	zh	vision
ĕ	pet	ou	out	ə	about,
ē	be	ŏŏ	took		item,
ĭ	pit	ōō	boot		pencil,
ī	pie	ŭ	cut		gallop,
îr	pier	ûr	urge		circus

damp•en /dăm′ pən/ *v.* to make moist or wet. *Dampen the cloth before you begin cleaning.*

dan•ger /dān′ jər/ *n.* peril; chance of injury or harm. *Learning safety rules can help you avoid danger.*

dark•en /där′ kən/ *v.* to make dark. *He darkened the room by pulling down the shades.*

dark•ness /därk′ nĭs/ *n.* the state or quality of being without light or brightness. *The darkness of the sky told us a storm was coming.*

daugh•ter /dô′ tər/ *n.* a female child. *A princess is the daughter of a king or a queen.*

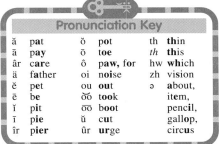

daughter

deal /dēl/ *v.* (**deals, dealt, deal•ing**) to handle in a certain way; to cope. *It is important to know how to deal with emergencies.*

death /dĕth/ *n.* a dying; the ending of life or existence. *The movie ended with the death of the villain.*

dec•ade /dĕk′ ād/ *n.* a period of ten years. *The royal family ruled the country for a decade.*

Dec. December.

De•cem•ber /dĭ sĕm′ bər/ *n.* the twelfth and final month of the year. *The shortest day of the year comes in December.*

dec•i•me•ter /dĕs′ ə mē′ tər/ *n.* a measure of length equal to one-tenth of a meter. *There are ten decimeters in one meter.*

de•fine /dĭ fīn′/ *v.* (**de•fines, de•fined, de•fin•ing**) to describe the meaning of; to explain. *The dictionary defines words.*

de•gree /dĭ grē′/ *n.* a unit used to measure temperature. *Water freezes at thirty-two degrees Fahrenheit.*

de•nom•i•na•tor /dĭ nŏm′ ə nā′ tər/ *n.* the bottom number in a fraction. *In the fraction $\frac{5}{8}$, 8 is the denominator.*

dense /dĕns/ *adj.* crowded together; thickly settled. *Cities are areas of dense population.*

de•pot /dē′ pō/ *n.* a station for trains or buses. *We went to the depot to meet his train.*

des•sert /dĭ zûrt′/ *n.* a food, usually sweet, served at the end of a meal. *I had an apple for dessert.*

dew /dōō/ or /dyōō/ *n.* water droplets that form at night on cool surfaces. *In the morning you may see dew on the leaves.*
▶ **Dew** sounds like **due.**

dic•tion•ar•y /dĭk′ shə nĕr′ ē/ *n.* (**dic•tion•ar•ies** *pl.*) a book that explains the words used in a language. *A dictionary gives definitions, pronunciations, and word histories.*

die /dī/ *v.* (**dies, died, dy•ing**) to stop living or existing. *The tree will die if it is not watered.*
▶ **Die** sounds like **dye.**

di•et /dī′ ĭt/ *n.* a special choice of foods for improving or maintaining health. *Mr. Collins is on a special diet to control his weight.*

di•gest /dī jĕst′/ or /dĭ-/ *v.* to turn food into a form the body can use. *Special juices in your stomach help your body digest food.*

dine /dīn/ *v.* (**dines, dined, din•ing**) to eat dinner. *We dine at seven o'clock.*

dis•cov•er /dĭ skŭv′ ər/ *v.* to find out. *If you read further you may discover the meaning of the word.*

dis•ease /dĭ zēz′/ *n.* a sickness; an illness. *Most common diseases, such as colds, are caused by germs.*

div•i•dend /dĭv′ ĭ dĕnd′/ *n.* the number to be divided. *In 60 ÷ 2 = 30, 60 is the dividend.*

di•vi•sion /dĭ vĭzh′ ən/ *n.* the act or process of dividing. *Division is the opposite of multiplication.*

di•vi•sor /dĭ vī′ zər/ *n.* a number by which another number is divided. *In 60 ÷ 2 = 30, 2 is the divisor.*

dodge /dŏj/ *v.* (**dodg•es, dodged, dodg•ing**) to try to avoid; to stay away from. *The batter stepped back from the plate to dodge the bad pitch.*

dou•ble /dŭb′ əl/ *v.* (**dou•bles, dou•bled, dou•bling**) to make or become twice as great. *The bread dough will double in size as it rises.*

doubt /dout/ *v.* to be unsure or uncertain. *I doubt that the Cortez family is home from vacation.*

drag /drăg/ *v.* (**drags, dragged, drag•ging**) to pull slowly along the ground; to haul. *They drag the sled to the top of the hill and then slide down.*

dream•er /drē′ mər/ *n.* one who dreams; one who has visions of the future. *Dreamers often have the ideas that make inventions possible.*

drive /drīv/ *v.* (**drives, drove, driv•en, driv•ing**) to operate a vehicle. *Marsha's uncle drives a school bus.*

drive•way /drīv′ wā/ *n.* a road connecting a building to the street. *We park our car in our driveway.*

driveway

drove /drōv/ *v.* past tense of **drive.**

due /dōō/ or /dyōō/ *adj.* expected; scheduled to arrive. *The bus is not due for two hours.*
▶ **Due** sounds like **dew.**

du•et /dōō ĕt′/ or /dyōō-/ *n.* a musical composition for two voices or instruments. *The brother and sister performed a duet in the talent show.*

dune /dōōn/ or /dyōōn/ *n.* a rounded hill of sand piled up by the wind. *Sand dunes are often formed in deserts.*

dye /dī/ *v.* (**dyes, dyed, dye•ing**) to give color to something or change its color. *Today we learned to dye fabric in art class.*
▶ **Dye** sounds like **die.**

Spelling Dictionary

ea•ger /ē′ gər/ *adj.* excitedly or impatiently wanting or expecting something. *We were eager for school to begin that day.*

ea•gle /ē′ gəl/ *n.* a large bird of prey with a hooked beak. *The bald eagle is the symbol of the United States.*

eagle

ear /îr/ *n.* the organ by which animals and humans hear. *Parts of the ear are located both inside and outside the head.*

earth•quake /ûrth′ kwāk′/ *n.* a movement of the earth's surface, sometimes caused by volcanic activity. *Earthquakes are often followed by mild aftershocks.*

ea•sy /ē′ zē/ *adj.* (**eas•i•er, eas•i•est;** **eas•i•ly** *adv.*) not hard or difficult. *The quiz was easy for me because I had studied hard.*

ech•o¹ /ĕk′ ō/ *n.* (**ech•oes** *pl.*) a repeated sound caused by sound waves bouncing off a surface. *We heard an echo when we shouted into the cave.*

ech•o² /ĕk′ ō/ *v.* to send back a sound. *Tunnels often echo.*

e•clipse /ĭ klĭps′/ *n.* the apparent covering of the sun or the moon by the other when their paths cross. *During a solar eclipse the sun is blocked from view by the moon.*

edge /ĕj/ *n.* border; side. *The cup fell from the edge of the table.*

ei•ther /ē′ thər/ or /ī′-/ *adj.* one or the other of two. *I couldn't run faster than either one of my friends.*

el•bow /ĕl′ bō/ *n.* the joint that allows the arm to bend. *I rolled my sleeves up above my elbows.*

e•lec•tion /ĭ lĕk′ shən/ *n.* a choosing or selecting by voting. *We held an election to choose a class president.*

e•lev•enth¹ /ĭ lĕv′ ənth/ *adj.* next after the tenth. *The eleventh shopper in the new store won a prize.*

e•lev•enth² /ĭ lĕv′ ənth/ *n.* one of eleven equal parts. *It's hard to divide something into elevenths.*

else /ĕls/ *adj.* other; different. *Would you rather ride with someone else?*

-en a suffix that means "to cause to be," used to form verbs: *tighten.*

en•gine /ĕn′ jĭn/ *n.* a machine that changes fuel and energy into motion. *Most automobile engines use gasoline.*

Eng•land /ĭng′ glənd/ *n.* the southern part of the island of Great Britain. *London is the capital city of England.*

en•joy /ĕn joi′/ *v.* to get pleasure from. *Did you enjoy the movie last night?*

en•joy•ment /ĕn joi′ mənt/ *n.* the state of enjoying. *Her enjoyment of the play was evident from her delighted smile.*

e•nough /ĭ nŭf′/ *adj.* as much or as many as needed. *The campers had enough food and water for three days.*

en•ter /ĕn′ tər/ *v.* to come or go into. *The students enter the school through the doorway closest to their classrooms.*

en•try /ĕn′ trē/ *n.* (**en•tries** *pl.*) a word listed in a dictionary, along with all related information given about it. *A dictionary entry usually includes a pronunciation and one or more definitions.*

en•ve•lope /ĕn′ və lōp′/ or /ŏn′-/ *n.* a paper cover used to hold letters and other materials. *Always include the ZIP code when you address an envelope.*

Spelling Dictionary

277

e • qual • ly /ē′ kwə lē/ *adv.* in the same way or amount. *The two students were equally responsible for delivering the message.*

-er a suffix, used to form nouns, that means: **a.** one who: *swimmer.* **b.** thing that: *toaster.*

Eu • rope /yŏor′ əp/ *n.* the continent east of the Atlantic Ocean and west of Asia. *Our teacher visited France and Spain on her trip to Europe.*

ev • er • green /ĕv′ ər grēn′/ *n.* a shrub, bush, or tree that stays green all year. *The branches of evergreens are sometimes used as decorations in the winter.*

eve • ry • day /ĕv′ rē dā′/ *adj.* ordinary; all right for the usual day or event. *You should wear your everyday clothes to play outside.*

eve • ry • one /ĕv′ rē wŭn′/ *pron.* each person; everybody. *Everyone in the class received a permission slip for the field trip.*

ex • am • ple /ĭg zăm′ pəl/ *n.* a sample; a model; something that may be imitated. *If you don't understand how to do the problems, look at the example.*

ex • ert /ĭg zûrt′/ *v.* to put forth; to put into use. *If you exert pressure on the window, it will open.*

ex • plode /ĭk splōd′/ *v.* (**ex•plodes, ex•plod•ed, ex•plod•ing**) to burst violently. *Fireworks explode with a flash of color.*

eye /ī/ *n.* the part of the body with which humans and animals see. *Tears keep your eyes moist.*

fact /făkt/ *n.* something known and proved to be true. *It is a fact that gravity causes objects to fall to the earth.*

fac • tor /făk′ tər/ *n.* any of the numbers that can be multiplied together to form a given product. *The factors of 6 are 1, 2, 3, and 6.*

fac • to • ry /făk′ tə rē/ *n.* (**fac•to•ries** *pl.*) a plant where goods are manufactured. *Much of the work in a factory is done by machines.*

fail /fāl/ *v.* to be unsuccessful. *The pirates failed to find the treasure they had hidden.*

fame /fām/ *n.* the state of being well-known; respect; recognition. *George Washington was a man of great fame.*

farm /färm/ *v.* to raise crops or animals as a profession; to cultivate land. *The Ellisons farm their own land.*

farm • er /fär′ mər/ *n.* a person who owns or operates a farm. *Farmers often store chopped corn in tall towers called silos.*

fas • ten /făs′ ən/ *v.* to join; to attach. *We can fasten this lamp to the wall over my desk.*

fa • ther /fä′ thər/ *n.* the male parent. *My father helped me study my spelling.*

fault /fôlt/ *n.* **a.** a mistake; an error. *I'm sorry; it was my fault.* **b.** a break or crack in the earth's crust. *The earthquake revealed a fault that runs through the valley.*

fa • vor /fā′ vər/ *n.* **a.** a kind or thoughtful act. *We did him a favor by mowing his lawn.* **b.** a small gift. *Each child received a balloon as a party favor.*

fear¹ /fîr/ *n.* a feeling of fright or alarm. *Dogs show fear by putting their tails between their legs.*

fear² /fîr/ *v.* to be afraid of. *My little sister fears thunder and lightning.*

feast /fēst/ *n.* a large meal, often with entertainment; a banquet. *We ate so much at the feast that we all felt stuffed.*

feath • er /fĕth′ ər/ *n.* one of the light, flat parts that form the outer covering of birds. *Feathers protect birds from cold and injury.*

Feb. February.

Feb • ru • ar • y /fĕb′ rōō ĕr′ ē/ *n.* the second month of the year. *February is the shortest month.*

feel /fēl/ *v.* (**feels, felt, feel•ing**) **a.** to sense by touch. *Feel how soft this cloth is!* **b.** to have a feeling or emotion. *I feel happy.*

felt /fĕlt/ *v.* past tense of **feel.**

fer • ry /fĕr′ ē/ *n.* (**fer•ries** *pl.*) a boat used to transport people or goods across a narrow body of water. *The ferry takes cars across the channel every day.*

ferry

fe•ver /fē′ vər/ *n.* a body temperature that is higher than normal. *Juanita had a cold and a slight fever.*

few /fyōō/ *adj.* not many. *Few copies of this rare book are available.*

field /fēld/ *n.* a piece of open land, usually part of a farm, often used for planting crops. *Some wheat fields are several miles wide.*

fif•ti•eth¹ /fĭf′ tē ĭth/ *adj.* next after the forty-ninth. *The couple celebrated their fiftieth year of marriage.*

fif•ti•eth² /fĭf′ tē ĭth/ *n.* one of fifty equal parts. *A coin worth two cents would be a fiftieth of a dollar.*

fight /fīt/ *v.* (**fights, fought, fight•ing**) to oppose strongly, especially in battle. *Our team tried to fight well, but the other team won.*

firm /fûrm/ *adj.* hard; solid. *They left the muddy road and walked on firm ground.*

fish /fĭsh/ *n.* (**fish** or **fish•es** *pl.*) an animal that lives in water, has fins, and breathes through gills. *Most fish have scales covering their bodies.*

fish

fish•er•y /fĭsh′ ə rē/ *n.* (**fish•er•ies** *pl.*) a place where fish can be caught; fishing ground. *Tuna are caught in Pacific fisheries.*

fit•ness /fĭt′ nĭs/ *n.* the state of being in good physical condition. *Many people exercise for greater fitness.*

flash•light /flăsh′ līt′/ *n.* a small light powered by batteries. *Campers carry flashlights to find their way in the dark.*

fla•vor /flā′ vər/ *n.* a particular taste. *Lemonade can have a sweet or tart flavor.*

flight /flīt/ *n.* a scheduled trip on an airplane. *The next flight to Chicago departs at 3:05.*

flood /flŭd/ *n.* water that flows over normally dry land. *The low bridge was under water for an hour after the flash flood.*

floun•der /floun′ dər/ *n.* a flat fish. *Baked flounder is a popular item on the menu.*

Pronunciation Key

ă	pat	ŏ	pot	th	thin
ā	pay	ō	toe	*th*	this
âr	care	ô	paw, for	hw	which
ä	father	oi	noise	zh	vision
ĕ	pet	ou	out	ə	about,
ē	be	ŏŏ	took		item,
ĭ	pit	ōō	boot		pencil,
ī	pie	ŭ	cut		gallop,
îr	pier	ûr	urge		circus

flour /flour/ *n.* a fine powder of ground grain, usually wheat. *Flour is used in making breads.*

► **Flour** sounds like **flower**.

flow•er /flou′ ər/ *n.* the blossom of a plant. *Many flowers bloom in the spring.*

► **Flower** sounds like **flour**.

flu /flōō/ *n.* a very contagious disease that causes fever, aches, and tiredness; influenza. *Ann stayed in bed for a week with the flu.*

flute /flōōt/ *n.* a woodwind instrument with a side opening across which a player blows. *The flute makes a high, soft sound.*

foil /foil/ *n.* a sheet of metal so thin it seems like paper. *The sandwiches are wrapped in aluminum foil.*

fold /fōld/ *v.* to close or bend parts of something together in order to fit it into a smaller space. *When we take down the flag, we fold it into the shape of a triangle.*

for•est /fôr′ ĭst/ *n.* an area covered with trees; a woods. *We found pine cones in the forest.*

for•get /fôr gĕt′/ or /fər-/ *v.* (**for•gets, for•got, for•got•ten, for•get•ting**) to fail to remember. *He sometimes forgets his umbrella on rainy days.*

for•got /fôr gŏt′/ or /fər-/ *v.* past tense of **forget**.

forth /fôrth/ or /fōrth/ *adv.* forward; onward. *From that day forth the princess lived happily.*

for•ty /fôr′ tē/ *n.* one more than thirty-nine; four times ten; 40. *Her father's age is forty.*

fought /fôt/ past tense of **fight**.

four•teenth¹ /fôr tēnth'/ or /fōr-/ *adj.* next after the thirteenth. *This is the store's fourteenth year in business.*

four•teenth² /fôr tēnth'/ or /fōr-/ *n.* one of fourteen equal parts. *Two is one four-teenth of twenty-eight.*

frac•tion /frăk' shən/ *n.* one or more of the equal parts into which a thing is divided. *The fraction ¾ represents three of four equal parts.*

France /frăns/ *n.* a country in western Europe. *The Eiffel Tower is in Paris, France.*

French¹ /frĕnch/ *adj.* of or from France. *A beret is a soft French cap.*

French² /frĕnch/ *n.* **a.** the national language of France, also spoken in other parts of the world. *Can you speak French?* **b.** the people of France. *The French consider cooking an art.*

Fri. Friday.

Fri•day /frī' dē/ or /-dā/ *n.* the sixth day of the week. *Friday is the end of the school week.* [Old English *Frigedæg,* Freya's day.]

friend /frĕnd/ *n.* a person one knows and likes. *Erin and I are good friends.*

fright /frīt/ *n.* a sudden fear. *The village was filled with fright when the forest fire started.*

fruit /frōōt/ *n.* (**fruit** or **fruits** *pl.*) the part of certain plants that contains seeds and is good to eat. *Oranges, grapes, and pears are types of fruit.*

fruit

-ful a suffix that means: **a.** full of or having, used to form adjectives: *meaningful.* **b.** the amount that fills, used to form nouns: *cupful.*

fun•ny /fŭn' ē/ *adj.* (**fun•ni•er, fun•ni•est**) causing laughter or amusement. *The joke was funny.*

gas /găs/ *n.* (**gas•es** *pl.*) **a.** a light substance that is neither a solid nor a liquid. *Oxygen is a gas.* **b.** a short word for gasoline. *Fill the tank with unleaded gas.*

gath•er /găth' ər/ *v.* to bring or come together. *When clouds gather it often means rain.*

gem /jĕm/ *n.* a precious stone. *Diamonds and emeralds are gems.*

gen•tle /jĕn' tl/ *adj.* light; soft. *The gentle breeze rustled through the leaves.*

Ger•man¹ /jûr' mən/ *adj.* of or from Germany. *Oktoberfest is a German festival.*

Ger•man² /jûr' mən/ *n.* **a.** one born or living in Germany. *The composer Bach was a famous German.* **b.** the language spoken in Germany, Austria, and parts of Switzerland. *Many English words come from German.*

Ger•ma•ny /jûr' mə nē/ *n.* a country in north-central Europe. *Between 1949 and 1989, Germany was divided into East Germany and West Germany.*

gi•gan•tic /jī găn' tĭk/ *adj.* extremely large. *Elephants and whales are gigantic.*

gig•gle /gĭg' əl/ *v.* (**gig•gles, gig•gled, gig•gling**) to give repeated high-pitched laughs. *The children giggle when they watch cartoons.*

glow¹ /glō/ *v.* to give off light; to shine. *Fireflies glow in the dark.*

glow² /glō/ *n.* a soft light. *You can see the glow of the lamp through the window.*

glue /glōō/ *n.* a sticky liquid that hardens to hold things together. *Broken toys can be mended with glue.*

goal /gōl/ *n.* a purpose; an aim. *Mark's goal is to play the double bass in a symphony orchestra.*

gov•ern /gŭv' ərn/ *v.* to direct; to rule. *The mayor and the council govern the city.*

Spelling Dictionary

grab /grăb/ *v.* (**grabs, grabbed, grab•bing**) to take or grasp suddenly. *If you grab the cat's tail, he may scratch you.*

grass•hop•per /grăs′ hŏp′ ər/ *n.* a jumping insect with wings and powerful rear legs. *Grasshoppers feed on plants.*

Greece /grēs/ *n.* a country in southeastern Europe that borders on the Mediterranean Sea. *Corinth and Athens are cities in Greece.*

Greek¹ /grēk/ *n.* **a.** one born or living in Greece. *The ancient Greeks were the first people to stage plays.* **b.** the language of Greece. *Greek uses a different alphabet from English.*

Greek² /grēk/ *adj.* of or from Greece. *We saw Greek sculpture at the museum.*

greet•ing /grē′ tĭng/ *n.* the words in a letter used to address someone. *The greeting in a friendly letter is followed by a comma.*

group /grōōp/ *n.* a gathering or arranging of people or objects. *There is a large group of people in the hotel lobby.*

grow /grō/ *v.* (**grows, grew, grown, grow•ing**) to expand or increase in size. *Trees grow slowly.*

grown /grōn/ *v.* a form of **grow**.

gym /jĭm/ *n.* a gymnasium. *The teams practice in the gym.*

gym

had•dock /hăd′ ək/ *n.* (**had•dock** or **had•docks** *pl.*) a food fish of the cod family. *Haddock are found in the North Atlantic.*

had•n't /hăd′ nt/ had not.

ha•lo /hā′ lō/ *n.* a circle of light around the sun or moon. *A halo is caused by light reflected by ice crystals in the sky.*

hand•made /hănd′ mād′/ *adj.* not made by a machine. *The handmade quilt was beautiful.*

hand•writ•ing /hănd′ rī tĭng/ *n.* writing done by hand with a pen or a pencil. *Neat handwriting always makes a good impression.*

hap•py /hăp′ ē/ *adj.* (**hap•pi•er, hap•pi•est; hap•pi•ly** *adv.*) feeling or showing pleasure; joyful. *The happy man whistled as he worked.*

hard•en /här′ dn/ *v.* to make or become hard. *The ground hardens during cold weather.*

harp /härp/ *n.* a tall musical instrument having many strings that are plucked by hand. *A harp can make rippling patterns of notes.*

has•n't /hăz′ ənt/ has not.

haul /hôl/ *v.* to pull with force; to drag. *The girls hauled their rowboat out of the water.*

have•n't /hăv′ ənt/ have not.

head•ache /hěd′ āk′/ *n.* a pain in the head. *Too much noise gives some people a headache.*

head•ing /hěd′ ĭng/ *n.* the address and date at the top of a letter. *Be sure to give your complete address and ZIP code in the heading.*

heav•y /hěv′ ē/ *adj.* (**heav•i•er, heav•i•est; heav•i•ly** *adv.*) hard to move because of its weight; not light. *This heavy trunk will need two people to lift it.*

he'd /hēd/ he had, he would.

hedge /hĕj/ *n.* a thick row of bushes planted as a fence or boundary. *A hedge should be trimmed evenly.*

height /hīt/ *n.* tallness. *The height of that mountain is 15,000 feet.*

held /hĕld/ *v.* past tense of **hold**.

he•li•um /hē′ lē əm/ *n.* a chemical element that is one of the lightest gases known. *Filling balloons with helium will make them float to the ceiling.*

he'll /hēl/ he will; he shall.

hel•lo /hĕ lō′/ *interj.* something said to express greeting. *The crossing guard always says "Hello" as we go by.*

help•ful /hĕlp′ fəl/ *adj.* giving aid; useful. *It was really helpful of you to do the dishes for me.*

help•less /hĕlp′ lĭs/ *adj.* not able to help oneself or others. *We felt helpless to stop the school's litter problem until we planned a recycling program.*

herd /hûrd/ *n.* a number of animals that feed and move about together. *The herd of deer was hard to spot in the dim forest.*

he•ro /hîr′ ō/ *n.* (**he•ros** or **he•roes** *pl.*) a man or boy admired for his bravery or fine qualities. *Abraham Lincoln is a national hero.*

high /hī/ *adj.* tall; far above the ground. *Eagles build nests on high cliffs.*

high school /hī′ skōōl′/ *n.* a level of school that follows elementary school; secondary school. *High school usually includes grades nine through twelve.*

high•way /hī′ wā′/ *n.* a main road. *Highways are usually numbered to simplify maps and road signs.*

hike /hīk/ *v.* (**hikes, hiked, hik•ing**) to take a long walk for exercise or pleasure. *We sang marching songs as we hiked up the trail.*

hik•er /hī′ kər/ *n.* one who hikes. *Sturdy, comfortable shoes are a must for every hiker.*

hikers

hinge /hĭnj/ *n.* a joint that allows a part to move or bend. *The door swung on one hinge.*

hire /hīr/ *v.* (**hires, hired, hir•ing**) to employ; to pay a person for working. *Because of good business, the store hired three more clerks.*

hold /hōld/ *v.* (**holds, held, hold•ing**) to have or take and keep; to grasp. *Hold tightly to the dog's leash.*

hol•i•day /hŏl′ ĭ dā′/ *n.* a day on which a special event is celebrated. *Independence Day is the favorite holiday of many people.* [Middle English *holidai,* holy day]

hon•est /ŏn′ ĭst/ *adj.* tending not to lie, cheat, or steal; able to be trusted. *An honest person always tells the truth.*

hon•or¹ /ŏn′ ər/ *n.* **a.** respect or esteem. *A medal is a mark of honor.* **b.** a sense of what is good or right. *Her honor would not permit her to cheat.*

hon•or² /ŏn′ ər/ *v.* to show respect for. *We say the pledge of allegiance to honor our country's flag.*

hope•less /hōp′ lĭs/ *adj.* having very little chance of working out right. *After darkness fell, they decided the search for the ball was hopeless.*

hos•pi•tal /hŏs′ pĭ tl/ *n.* a place where persons who are sick or injured are cared for. *Patients who have an operation may stay in the hospital for a few days.*

ho•tel /hō tĕl′/ *n.* a place that provides guests with lodging and usually meals and other services. *Our grandparents stayed in a hotel near the beach in Florida.*

how•ev•er /hou ĕv′ ər/ *conj.* nevertheless. *I've never tasted eggplant before; however, it looks delicious.*

huge /hyōōj/ *adj.* very large. *A skyscraper is a huge building.*

hu•man /hyōō′ mən/ *adj.* of or relating to persons. *It is a human weakness to put things off.*

hunt•er /hŭn′ tər/ *n.* a person or animal who hunts. *The hawk's keen eyesight makes it a good hunter.*

hur•ry /hûr′ ē/ or /hŭr′-/ *v.* (**hur•ries, hur•ried, hur•ry•ing**) to act quickly or with haste; to rush. *If we hurry, we may still catch the bus.*

ice • berg /īs′ bûrg′/ *n.* a big piece of ice that floats in the ocean. *The biggest part of an iceberg is underwater.*

i • ci • cle /ī′ sĭ kəl/ *n.* a pointed, hanging piece of ice, formed by the freezing of dripping water. *Icicles hung from the roof of the house.*

I'd /īd/ I would; I should; I had.

i • de • a /ī dē′ ə/ *n.* a thought; a plan. *Bringing plants to decorate the room was Kristin's idea.*

ill • ness /ĭl′ nĭs/ *n.* poor health; a disease. *Craig went home from school because of illness.*

im • mune /ĭ myōōn′/ *adj.* able to resist disease. *Being vaccinated against measles makes you immune to that disease.*

In • di • a /ĭn′ dē ə/ *n.* a large country in southern Asia. *Only China has more people than India.*

In • di • an[1] /ĭn′ dē ən/ *n.* one born or living in India. *He met an Indian from Bombay.*

In • di • an[2] /ĭn′ dē ən/ *adj.* of or from India. *She was wearing an Indian sari.*

in • fect /ĭn fĕkt′/ *v.* to make ill by the introduction of germs. *A wound can become infected if it is not kept clean.*

in • jure /ĭn′ jər/ *v.* (in•jures, in•jured, in•jur•ing) to harm. *No one was injured when the tree fell down.*

in • let /ĭn′ lĕt′/ *n.* a recess in the land along a coast; a bay or cove. *The inlet was a perfect place for sailing.*

in • sect /ĭn′ sĕkt′/ *n.* a small animal with six legs and a body that has three sections. *A beetle is an insect.*

insect

in • stead /ĭn stĕd′/ *adv.* in place of. *Since the manager wasn't in, we talked to her assistant instead.*

in • vite /ĭn vīt′/ *v.* (in•vites, in•vit•ed, in•vit•ing) to ask a person to go somewhere or do something. *My mother invited my friends to lunch.*

Ire • land /īr′ lənd/ *n.* the island country west of Britain. *The shamrock is an emblem of Ireland.*

I • rish[1] /ī′ rĭsh/ *n.* the people of Ireland. *The Irish are known for their lilting accent.*

I • rish[2] /ī′ rĭsh/ *adj.* of or from Ireland. *The Irish countryside is green and beautiful.*

i • ron /ī′ ərn/ *v.* to press with an iron to remove wrinkles. *Most fabrics today do not need to be ironed.*

is • land /ī′ lənd/ *n.* a piece of land with water all around it. *People must take a boat or an airplane to get to an island.*

I • tal • ian[1] /ĭ tăl′ yən/ *adj.* of or from Italy. *"Pizza" is an Italian word.*

I • tal • ian[2] /ĭ tăl′ yən/ *n.* **a.** one born or living in Italy. *Many Italians live in Rome.* **b.** the language of Italy. *Many operas are sung in Italian.*

It • a • ly /ĭt′ ə lē/ *n.* a country in southern Europe bordering on the Mediterranean. *Italy is shaped like a boot.*

itch /ĭch/ *v.* to have or cause tickly irritation on the skin. *A poison ivy rash itches.*

I've /īv/ I have.

Spelling Dictionary

Spelling Dictionary

Jan. January.

Jan•u•ar•y /jăn′ yoo ĕr′ ē/ n. the first month of the year. *January has thirty-one days.*

Ja•pan /jə păn′/ n. a small country of islands to the east of China. *Tokyo is the capital of Japan.*

Ja•pan•ese¹ /jăp′ ə nēz′/ adj. of or from Japan. *Japanese writing is very different from ours.*

Ja•pan•ese² /jăp′ ə nēz′/ n. **a.** the people of Japan. *Many Japanese live in apartments.* **b.** the language of Japan. *Japanese is an interesting language to learn.*

jog /jŏg/ v. (**jogs, jogged, jog•ging**) to run at a slow, regular pace. *She likes to jog early in the morning.*

joint /joint/ n. a place where two bones are connected, allowing motion. *Your leg bends at the knee joint.*

joy /joi/ n. a feeling of happiness or pleasure. *Imagine my joy when I received Sandy's letter.*

joy•ful /joi′ fəl/ adj. full of joy. *The first and last days of school are always joyful.*

judge /jŭj/ n. one who presides over a court of law by hearing cases and making decisions. *A judge must be completely fair.*

juice /joos/ n. the liquid that can be squeezed out of fruits, meat, or vegetables. *He has a glass of orange juice every morning.*

Ju•ly /joo lī′/ n. the seventh month of the year. *July is usually hot in Texas.*

jum•ble /jŭm′ bəl/ v. (**jum•bles, jum•bled, jum•bling**) to mix up. *The letters of the word were jumbled in the puzzle.*

June /joon/ n. the sixth month of the year. *June has thirty days.*

jun•gle /jŭng′ gəl/ n. wild land near the equator with thickly grown tropical plants. *Parrots and monkeys live in the jungle.*

ju•ror /joor′ ər/ n. one who serves on the jury of a court. *Many adult citizens take turns serving as jurors.*

284

ju•ry /joor′ ē/ n. (**ju•ries** pl.) a group of persons selected to listen to the evidence in a court case. *Robert served on a jury of twelve members.*

jus•tice /jŭs′ tĭs/ n. fairness. *Justice demands that you tell the truth.*

keep /kēp/ v. (**keeps, kept, keep•ing**) **a.** to store; to put away; to save. *I keep all my old homework.* **b.** to continue. *Let's keep looking until we find it.*

kept /kĕpt/ v. past tense of **keep**.

ket•tle /kĕt′ l/ n. a pot used for heating liquids. *Put the kettle on the stove.*

kil•o•gram /kĭl′ ə grăm/ n. a measure of weight equal to 1,000 grams. *A kilogram is a little over two pounds.*

kil•o•me•ter /kĭl′ ə mē′ tər/ or /kĭ lŏm′ ĭ tər/ n. a measure of length equal to 1,000 meters. *A kilometer is almost two-thirds of a mile.*

kind /kīnd/ adj. friendly; thoughtful of others. *Everyone likes kind persons.*

kind•ness /kīnd′ nĭs/ n. friendly or helpful behavior. *His kindness earned him the respect of the whole class.*

knee /nē/ n. the joint in the middle of the leg. *You bend your knees when you walk.*

knife /nīf/ n. (**knives** pl.) a flat cutting instrument with a sharp blade. *Jean sliced the carrots with a knife.*

knit /nĭt/ v. (**knits, knit** or **knit•ted, knit•ting**) to make by weaving yarn with long needles. *My father will knit a sweater for me.*

knock /nŏk/ v. to strike with the fist or with a hard object. *I knocked on the door but no one answered.*

knot /nŏt/ n. a fastening made by tying. *We joined the two ropes with a square knot.*

knot

know /nō/ *v.* (**knows, knew, known,
know•ing**) **a.** to have the facts about; to
understand. *Do you know how hail is
formed?* **b.** to be acquainted with. *I know
the Bakers but not where they live.*

known /nōn/ *v.* a form of **know**.

la • dy /lā′ dē/ *n.* (**la•dies** *pl.*) a polite term
for a woman. *Ladies and gentlemen, may I
have your attention?*

lamb /lăm/ *n.* a young sheep. *The lambs ran
playfully in the field.*

land • scape /lănd′ skāp′/ *n.* a picture of a
view of the countryside. *Some artists paint
landscapes.*

laugh /lăf/ *v.* to make sounds with the voice
that show amusement. *Everyone laughed at
the funny movie.*

laugh • ter /lăf′ tər/ *n.* the noise of laugh-
ing. *Laughter filled the classroom during
the puppet show.*

la • va /lä′ və/ *n.* the hot, melted rock that
comes from a volcano. *The lava flowed
down the mountain.*

la • zy /lā′ zē/ *adj.* not wanting to work. *He
was too lazy to help us.*

lead¹ /lēd / *v.* (**leads, led, lead•ing**) to direct
or show the way. *She will lead the hikers
home.*

lead² /lĕd/ *n.* **a.** a soft mineral used in some
pipes. *He put a weight made of lead on the
fishing line.* **b.** graphite used to make the
writing substance in a pencil. *My fingers
had black smudges from the pencil lead.*

lead • er /lē′ dər/ *n.* one who leads. *The
Scout troop needs a new leader.*

learn • er /lûr′ nər/ *n.* one who learns; a
student. *A good learner listens carefully.*

least /lēst/ *adj.* smallest in size or amount.
Which game costs the least money?

length /lĕngkth/ *n.* the distance from end to
end. *The length of the boat is forty feet.*

-less a suffix that means "without," used to
form adjectives: *endless.*

let's /lĕts/ let us.

Pronunciation Key

ă	pat	ŏ	pot	th	thin
ā	pay	ō	toe	*th*	this
âr	care	ô	paw, for	hw	which
ä	father	oi	noise	zh	vision
ĕ	pet	ou	out	ə	about,
ē	be	ŏŏ	took		item,
ĭ	pit	ōō	boot		pencil,
ī	pie	ŭ	cut		gallop,
îr	pier	ûr	urge		circus

let • ter /lĕt′ ər/ *n.* **a.** a single character in an
alphabet. *The letter **k** was missing from the
word.* **b.** a written note or message. *I got a
letter in today's mail.*

lev • el /lĕv′ əl/ *adj.* flat and even. *Most
floors are level.*

li • brar • y /lī′ brĕr′ ē/ *n.* a room or building
containing books that may be read or borrowed. *A library is also used for research
and studying.*

light • en /līt′ n/ *v.* **a.** to make brighter; to
add light to. *The new paint lightens the
room.* **b.** to make less heavy. *Taking out the
books lightened my suitcase.*

limb /lĭm/ *n.* a branch of a tree. *We hung the
swing from a strong limb.*

liq • uid /lĭk′ wĭd/ *n.* a flowing substance that
is neither a solid nor a gas. *Water is a liquid.*

lis • ten /lĭs′ n/ *v.* to pay attention; to try to
hear. *The audience listened closely to the
speaker.*

lis • ten • er /lĭs′ ə nər/ *n.* one who listens.
A good listener remembers what is said.

live • stock /līv′ stŏk′/ *n.* animals kept on
a farm, such as horses, cattle, or sheep. *The
farmer will sell some of his livestock.*

liz • ard /lĭz′ ərd/ *n.* a reptile with a long
body and tail, usually having four legs and
scaly skin. *Iguanas are lizards that live in a
dry, desert climate.*

lizard

285

loan /lōn/ *n.* an amount of money lent or borrowed. *Banks charge interest on loans.*

▶ **Loan** sounds like **lone**.

lone /lōn/ *adj.* alone; single. *A lone cloud floated in the blue sky.*

▶ **Lone** sounds like **loan**.

loop /lo͞op/ *n.* the curved shape of a line that dips and crosses itself. *We hung the crepe paper in loops.*

lose /lo͞oz/ *v.* (**los•es, lost, los•ing**) **a.** to be unable to find; to misplace. *Put the key in your pocket so you won't lose it.* **b.** to fail to win. *She lost the race by less than a second.*

lunch /lŭnch/ *n.* (**lunch•es** *pl.*) a light meal usually eaten around the middle of the day. *We have lunch at noon.*

lung /lŭng/ *n.* one of the organs in the chest that are used in breathing. *The lungs take in fresh air.*

-ly a suffix, used to form adverbs, that means: **a.** like; in the manner of: *finally.* **b.** at certain intervals: *weekly.*

mag • ma /măg′ mə/ *n.* the very hot melted rock inside the earth's crust. *When magma cools, it forms igneous rock.*

mail • box /māl′ bŏks′/ *n.* **a.** a public box into which people put items to be delivered by mail. *The contents of a mailbox are taken to the post office.* **b.** a private box for a home or business to which mail is delivered. *Check the mailbox to see if you got a letter.*

ma • jor /mā′ jər/ *adj.* larger; greater; primary. *He played a major role in the project's success.*

march /märch/ *v.* (**march•es, marched, march•ing**) to walk with even, steady steps. *The band marched in the parade.*

Mar. March.

March /märch/ *n.* the third month of the year. *The weather begins to warm up in March.*

mark /märk/ *v.* to make a visible sign on or by. *Mark the wrong answers with an "x."*

mar • ket /mär′ kĭt/ *n.* a place where things can be bought and sold. *A supermarket is a large, modern market.*

mas • ter /măs′ tər/ *v.* to become skilled in. *It takes time and practice to master a foreign language.*

mat • ter /măt′ ər/ *n.* all physical or material substance; concrete objects. *Matter has weight and occupies space.*

may /mā/ *v.* (**might**) **a.** to be allowed to. *May I be excused from the table?* **b.** to be possible that. *The package may arrive today.*

May /mā/ *n.* the fifth month of the year. *Flowers bloom in May.*

mean /mēn/ *v.* (**means, meant, mean•ing**) **a.** to intend. *I didn't mean to hurt her feelings.* **b.** to signify; to carry the meaning of. *The sign "+" means "plus."*

meant /mĕnt/ past tense of **mean**.

mea • sles /mē′ zəlz/ *n.* a disease marked by red spots on the skin. *Most children have been vaccinated against measles.*

mem • ber /mĕm′ bər/ *n.* a person who belongs to a group. *Members of the club voted to have a picnic.*

-ment a suffix that means "the result of an action or process," used to form nouns: *amusement.*

met • al¹ /mĕt′ l/ *n.* any of a number of substances that shine when polished and that can conduct electricity and heat. *Most metals are found in solid form.*

met • al² /mĕt′ l/ *adj.* made of or containing metal. *Many foods are packed in metal cans.*

me • te • or /mē′ tē ər/ *n.* a solid fragment from space that falls into the earth's atmosphere and burns. *Meteors are sometimes called shooting stars.*

meteor

Mex • i • can¹ /mĕk′ sĭ kən/ *adj.* of or from Mexico. *A sombrero is a Mexican hat.*

Spelling Dictionary

Mex•i•can² /mĕk′ sĭ kən/ *n.* one born or living in Mexico. *Many Mexicans visit the United States each year.*

Mex•i•co /mĕk′ sĭ kō/ *n.* a large country located between the United States and Central America. *The capital of Mexico is Mexico City.*

mid•dle¹ /mĭd′ l/ *n.* the point or part located at the same distance from each side or end; the center. *Your nose is in the middle of your face.*

mid•dle² /mĭd′ l/ *adj.* occupying a central position. *His middle name is Michael.*

might /mīt/ past tense of **may.**

mi•grate /mī′ grāt/ *v.* (**mi•grates, mi•grat•ed, mi•grat•ing**) to travel from place to place, especially as the seasons change. *Many birds migrate south for the winter.*

mil•li•lit•er /mĭl′ ə lē′ tər/ *n.* a measure of volume equal to 1/1000 of a liter. *Chemical solutions are often measured in milliliters.*

mind¹ /mīnd/ *v.* to object to. *Would you mind holding my books for a minute?*

mind² /mīnd/ *n.* the part of a person that thinks and remembers. *Your mind directs all your conscious actions.*

mi•nor /mī′ nər/ *adj.* smaller; lesser; secondary. *Brian played a minor role, so he didn't have to learn many lines.*

mix /mĭks/ *v.* (**mix•es, mixed, mix•ing**) to form by combining unlike items. *Will you mix the salad?*

mixed /mĭkst/ *adj.* made up of different kinds. *A bowl of mixed fruit sat on the table.*

mod•el¹ /mŏd′ l/ *n.* a small, exact copy or pattern. *She built several models of old automobiles.*

mod•el² /mŏd′ l/ *v.* to make or shape something. *Let's model animals out of clay.*

moist /moist/ *adj.* somewhat wet; damp. *The grass was still moist from the rain this morning.*

mois•ten /moi′ sən/ *v.* to make or become damp; to wet. *Moisten this cloth and use it to wipe the table clean.*

Pronunciation Key

ă	pat	ŏ	pot	th	thin
ā	pay	ō	toe	*th*	this
âr	care	ô	paw, for	hw	which
ä	father	oi	noise	zh	vision
ĕ	pet	ou	out	ə	about,
ē	be	o͝o	took		item,
ĭ	pit	o͞o	boot		pencil,
ī	pie	ŭ	cut		gallop,
îr	pier	ûr	urge		circus

mo•ment /mō′ mənt/ *n.* **a.** an instant; a very brief period. *I saw him for a moment, but I lost sight of him in the crowd.* **b.** a specific point in time. *I called the moment I heard you were sick.*

Mon. Monday.

Mon•day /mŭn′ dē/ or /-dā′/ *n.* the second day of the week, coming after Sunday and before Tuesday. *Monday is the first school day in the week.* [Old English *monandæg,* the moon's day.]

mon•key /mŭng′ kē/ *n.* a small, furry animal with hands, thumbs, and a long tail. *Monkeys have long tails, but apes have no tails at all.*

monkey

month /mŭnth/ *n.* one of the twelve parts into which a year is divided. *We go to school for nine months of the year.*

mood /mo͞od/ *n.* a state of mind; a feeling. *The sunny morning put me in a happy mood.*

mo•tel /mō tĕl′/ *n.* a hotel near a highway for people who are traveling by car. *We spent the night in a motel on our way to visit our cousins.*

moth•er /mŭ*th*′ ər/ *n.* the female parent. *My mother likes to listen to me read.*

mount /mount/ *v.* to climb onto; to get up on. *The rider mounted his horse and galloped away.*

mouth /mouth/ *n.* the opening in the head that contains the tongue and teeth and is used for taking in food and making sounds. *When you yawn, your mouth opens wide.*

move • ment /mo͞ov′ mənt/ *n.* action; a change in position or location. *The children watched the slow movement of the snail across the sidewalk.*

mul • ti • pli • ca • tion /mŭl′ tə plĭ kā′ shən/ *n.* the adding of a number a certain number of times. *Knowing your times tables will help you solve problems in multiplication.*

mum • ble /mŭm′ bəl/ *v.* (**mum•bles, mum•bled, mum•bling**) to speak unclearly so that you are hard to understand. *If you mumble, no one will understand you.*

mu • sic /myo͞o′ zĭk/ *n.* **a.** the art of making and combining sounds using rhythm, melody, and harmony. *Music is one of the fine arts.* **b.** the sounds made and combined in this way. *We can hear many kinds of music on the radio.*

na • tion /nā′ shən/ *n.* a group of people living together under one government, who usually have many of the same customs and speak the same language. *The United States, Japan, and Sweden are nations.*

near[1] /nîr/ *adv.* not far away in time or distance. *The train drew near.*

near[2] /nîr/ *prep.* not far from. *The school is near my house, only a block away.*

near • by /nîr′ bī/ *adj.* not far off. *They live in a nearby town.*

nec • tar /nĕk′ tər/ *n.* a sweet liquid in the blossoms of flowers, used by bees to make honey. *Bees go from flower to flower to collect nectar.*

nei • ther[1] /nē′ thər/ or /nī′-/ *pron.* not the one and not the other. *Neither of us was invited.*

nei • ther[2] /nē′ thər/ or /nī′-/ *conj.* also not. *If you're not going to the park, neither am I.*

nei • ther[3] /nē′ thər/ or /nī′-/ *adj.* not either. *Neither girl was tall enough for the part in the play.*

-ness a suffix that means "a state or quality," used to form nouns: *softness.*

news • pa • per /no͞oz′ pā pər/ or /nyo͞oz′-/ *n.* a printed paper that contains news, advertisements, cartoons, etc. *My grandfather likes to work the crossword puzzles in the newspaper.*

newspaper

nine • teen /nīn tēn′/ *n.* one more than eighteen; 19. *Ten plus nine is nineteen.*

nine • ty /nīn′ tē/ *n.* one more than eighty-nine; 90. *The temperature was over ninety degrees for several days this summer.*

ninth[1] /nīnth/ *adj.* next after the eighth; 9th. *Marty sat in the ninth chair.*

ninth[2] /nīnth/ *n.* one of nine equal parts. *We divided the cake into ninths.*

noise /noiz/ *n.* a sound, especially one that is loud and harsh. *The noise of the alarm clock startled me.*

no • mad /nō′ măd′/ *n.* a wanderer; someone without a permanent home. *In prehistoric times, tribes of nomads followed herds of animals in search of food.*

nor /nôr/ *conj.* and not; not either. *There was neither milk nor fruit juice in the refrigerator.*

noun /noun/ *n.* a word used to name a person, place, thing, or quality. *Words like **girl, Illinois, state, tree,** and **honor** are nouns.*

Nov. November.

No • vem • ber /nō vĕm′ bər/ *n.* the eleventh month of the year. *November has thirty days.*

nu • mer • al /no͞o′ mər əl/ or /nyo͞o′-/ *n.* a figure or other symbol that represents a number. *"VI" is the Roman numeral for six.*

nu • mer • a • tor /no͞o′ mə rā′ tər/ or /nyo͞o′-/ *n.* the part of a fraction written above the line. *In the fraction $\frac{3}{4}$, the numerator is 3.*

Spelling Dictionary

o•bey /ō bā′/ *v.* **a.** to follow the orders of. *Children obey their parents.* **b.** to act in agreement with; to carry out. *Good citizens obey the law.*

o•boe /ō′ bō/ *n.* a woodwind instrument played by blowing into a double reed. *The oboe's smooth, penetrating tone carries easily above an orchestra.*

Oct. October.

Oc•to•ber /ŏk tō′ bər/ *n.* the tenth month of the year. *Many leaves change color in October.*

of•ten /ô′ fən/ or /ŏf′ ən/ *adv.* many times; frequently. *We often see our relatives during the holidays.*

or•bit¹ /ôr′ bĭt/ *n.* the path of one body going around another. *It takes one year for the earth to travel in its orbit around the sun.*

or•bit² /ôr′ bĭt/ *v.* to move in an orbit around; to circle. *The moon orbits the earth.*

or•chard /ôr′ chərd/ *n.* a piece of land on which fruit trees are grown. *The apple orchard was two miles long.*

ought /ôt/ *v.* should. *You ought to wear a coat on a cold day like this.*

out•doors¹ /out dôrz′/ or /-dōrz′/ *n.* the area outside a house or building; the open air. *Campers enjoy the outdoors.*

out•doors² /out dôrz′/ or /-dōrz′/ *adv.* outside a building; out in the open air. *We played outdoors on the first sunny day of spring.*

out•rage /out′ rāj/ *n.* anger at an offensive act. *The community expressed outrage at the bribery scandal.*

own•er /ō′ nər/ *n.* one who owns or possesses something. *Who is the owner of this plaid jacket?*

Pronunciation Key

ă	pat	ŏ	pot	th	thin
ā	pay	ō	toe	*th*	this
âr	care	ô	paw, for	hw	which
ä	father	oi	noise	zh	vision
ĕ	pet	ou	out	ə	about,
ē	be	ŏŏ	took		item,
ĭ	pit	ōō	boot		pencil,
ī	pie	ŭ	cut		gallop,
îr	pier	ûr	urge		circus

pack•age /păk′ ĭj/ *n.* a wrapped box; a parcel. *How much will it cost to mail this package?*

pain•ful /pān′ fəl/ *adj.* causing or having pain; hurting. *The blister on my heel was painful.*

paint•er /pān′ tər/ *n.* **a.** a person who paints pictures; an artist. *Some painters make abstract designs.* **b.** a person whose job is painting buildings or furniture. *The painter stood on a ladder to paint the house.*

paint•ing /pān′ tĭng/ *n.* a painted picture. *We saw many paintings in the art museum.*

pa•per /pā′ pər/ *n.* **a.** a material made in thin sheets of pulp, from wood or rags. *The pages of this book are made of paper.* **b.** a newspaper. *Have you seen the comics in today's paper?* **c.** a written article; a report. *The teacher asked us to write a paper about the moon.*

pa•per•back /pā′ pər băk′/ *n.* a book bound with a flexible paper cover and binding. *Paperbacks usually cost less than hardcover books.*

par•ent /păr′ ənt/ *n.* a father or a mother. *Either parent may write a note excusing an absence.*

par•rot /pâr′ ət/ *n.* a tropical bird with a short, curved beak and brightly colored feathers. *A parrot can learn to repeat words.*

parrot

289

Spelling Dictionary

pass¹ /păs/ *v.* **a.** to go by. *They pass the fire station on the way to school.* **b.** to hand over; to give; to send. *Please pass the salad.* **c.** to succeed in. *The entire fourth grade passed the test.*

pass² /păs/ *n.* **a.** a written note; a permit. *Did the teacher sign your pass?* **b.** a narrow road through mountains. *We saw snow at the top of the pass.*

passed /păst/ *v.* past tense of **pass**.

▶ **Passed** sounds like **past**.

past¹ /păst/ *n.* the time that has gone by. *In the distant past, dinosaurs lived on the earth.*

▶ **Past** sounds like **passed**.

past² /păst/ *adj.* gone by; previous. *In the past month we had three inches of rain.*

▶ **Past** sounds like **passed**.

pas • tel /pă stěl′/ *n.* **a.** a chalklike crayon. *Pastels smudge easily.* **b.** a light, soft color. *The pale pink roses matched the pastels of the room.*

patch¹ /păch/ *n.* (**patch•es** *pl.*) a piece of cloth sewn over a hole or a tear. *My old pants have patches on them.*

patch² /păch/ *v.* (**patch•es, patched, patch•ing**) to cover with a patch; to repair. *Can you patch this up?*

pave • ment /pāv′ mənt/ *n.* the surface of a road or a street made by paving. *Some pavement is made with crushed rock, clay, and tar.*

pay • ment /pā′ mənt/ *n.* an amount of money paid. *Most people who rent a house or an apartment make a monthly payment to the landlord.*

peace • ful /pēs′ fəl/ *adj.* **a.** calm; quiet. *Early morning hours are peaceful.* **b.** not liking arguments or quarrels; liking peace. *Neutral nations are peaceful.*

peach /pēch/ *n.* (**peach•es** *pl.*) a sweet, juicy fruit with a large, rough stone in the center. *When ripe, a peach has a fuzzy, pinkish-yellow skin.*

peach

peb • ble /pĕb′ əl/ *n.* a small stone. *Pebbles have been worn smooth by water running over them.*

pelt /pĕlt/ *n.* the skin of an animal with fur or hair on it. *The early settlers bartered animal pelts for food and supplies.*

pen • ny /pĕn′ ē/ *n.* (**pen•nies** *pl.*) a coin worth one cent. *Ten pennies equal one dime.*

per • fect /pûr′ fĭkt/ *adj.* **a.** having no flaws or errors; exactly right. *Charlene turned in a perfect paper in science.* **b.** excellent; unusually good. *Today is a perfect day for swimming.*

pe • ri • od /pîr′ ē əd/ *n.* **a.** a dot (.) used in printing and in writing. *Most sentences end in a period.* **b.** a length of time. *We had a period of twenty days with no rainfall.*

per • son /pûr′ sən/ *n.* a human being; a man, woman, boy, or girl. *This elevator can hold six persons.*

pet • al /pĕt′ l/ *n.* the leaflike part of a flower. *Dried rose petals have a lovely fragrance.*

pic • co • lo /pĭk′ ə lō/ *n.* a small, high-pitched flute. *Many marching bands feature a piccolo.*

piece /pēs/ *n.* a part; a segment. *Would you like a piece of my orange?*

pil • grim /pĭl′ grəm/ *n.* **a.** a person who travels to a holy place. *Pilgrims in the Middle Ages journeyed to shrines or cathedrals.* **b.** **Pilgrim** one of the English Puritans who founded the American colony of Plymouth in 1620. *The Pilgrims came on the Mayflower.*

pil • low /pĭl′ ō/ *n.* a support used for the head in resting or sleeping; a cushion. *Do you like to sleep on a feather pillow?*

pit • y /pĭt′ ē/ *n.* sympathy or sorrow for the suffering of another. *We felt pity for her because she looked so unhappy.*

piv • ot /pĭv′ ət/ *v.* to turn around a fixed point. *The basketball player pivoted with one foot on the floor.*

place • ment /plās′ mənt/ *n.* location; arrangement. *The placement of the flowers added the perfect touch to the dinner table.*

plan • et /plăn′ ĭt/ *n.* a large body that rotates around the sun and reflects its light. *Earth is one of nine planets in our solar system.*

290

T290

play•er /plā′ ər/ *n.* **a.** a person who plays a game. *Beth is the shortest player on her soccer team.* **b.** a person who plays a musical instrument. *A guitar player is called a guitarist.*

play•ful /plā′ fəl/ *adj.* full of fun and enjoyment. *The baby was playful in his bath.*

plow¹ /plou/ *n.* a tool used in farming for turning up soil. *Plows have sharp blades and are pulled by horses, oxen, or tractors.*

plow² /plou/ *v.* to work with a plow; to till. *Fields are plowed before crops are planted.*

plum•age /pl‾oo′ mĭj/ *n.* the feathers of a bird. *Male birds have bright plumage.*

po•em /pō′ əm/ *n.* a verbal composition arranged so that it has rhythm and appeals to the imagination. *Not all poems rhyme.*

po•et /pō′ ĭt/ *n.* a person who writes poems. *Emily Dickinson was a famous American poet.*

po•lar /pō′ lər/ *adj.* having to do with the North Pole or the South Pole. *Polar weather is cold.*

pol•len /pŏl′ ən/ *n.* the yellow powder inside a flower. *Bees carry pollen from plant to plant.*

pol•y•gon /pŏl′ ē gŏn′/ *n.* a geometric figure that has three or more angles and sides. *A pentagon is a five-sided polygon.*

po•ny /pō′ nē/ *n.* (po•nies *pl.*) a kind of horse that is small in size when fully grown. *Children ride a pony at an amusement park.*

pony

port /pôrt/ or /pōrt/ *n.* **a.** a town with a harbor where ships may dock. *Boston and New York are Atlantic ports.* **b.** the left-hand side of a ship, boat, or airplane as one faces forward. *Ships show a red light toward port at night.*

post•er /pō′ stər/ *n.* a sign. *The poster in the restaurant window advertised the school play.*

pow•der /pou′ dər/ *n.* a substance made of fine grains. *It's easy to grind chalk into a powder.*

---

pow•er¹ /pou′ ər/ *n.* great strength, force, or control. *The police have power to enforce the law.*

pow•er² /pou′ ər/ *v.* to supply with power. *The boat is powered by an engine.*

pow•er•ful /pou′ ər fəl/ *adj.* having great power; strong. *The king was a powerful ruler.*

pow•er•less /pou′ ər lĭs/ *adj.* having no strength or power; helpless. *The farmers were helpless against the drought.*

prai•rie /prâr′ ē/ *n.* a large, flat area of land with much grass but few trees. *Buffalo once grazed on the western prairies.*

pre- a prefix that means **a.** before: *preschool.* **b.** in advance: *prepay.*

pre•heat /prē hēt′/ *v.* to heat beforehand. *Please preheat the oven before you put the potatoes in to bake.*

pre•pay /prē pā′/ *v.* to pay beforehand. *The company will prepay the postage.*

pre•school /prē′ skool′/ *n.* a place of learning before elementary school. *Children aged three to five may attend preschool.*

pre•test /prē′ tĕst′/ *n.* a test given beforehand to determine readiness. *If you already know the spelling words, you'll do well on the pretest.*

pre•view /prē′ vyōō′/ *v.* to view or watch in advance. *We were invited to preview the art show.*

print /prĭnt/ *n.* **a.** letters and words made on paper. *Some books use large print.* **b.** a picture or design made by printing. *The magazine article showed a print made with a wood block.*

prob • lem /prŏb' ləm/ *n.* a question to be worked out and answered. *Careful, step-by-step reasoning is the key to solving a math problem.*

prod • uct /prŏd' əkt/ *n.* a number produced by multiplying two or more numbers together. *The product of 3 and 5 is 15.*

pro • noun /prō' noun/ *n.* a word used in place of a noun. *"I," "them," and "its" are common pronouns.*

pro • vide /prə vīd'/ *v.* (**pro•vides, pro•vid•ed, pro•vid•ing**) to supply; to furnish. *The school provides hot lunches for students.*

pulse /pŭls/ *n.* the rhythm of blood in arteries, produced by regular contractions of the heart. *The nurse checked the patient's pulse.*

pump • kin /pŭmp' kĭn/ *n.* a large yellow-orange fruit that grows on a vine. *Cooks use pumpkin in pies and breads.*

pun /pŭn/ *n.* a play on words. *A pun involves two words that sound alike.*

quake /kwāk/ *v.* (**quakes, quaked, quak•ing**) to vibrate or shake. *The ground quaked beneath us during the mild earthquake.*

quar • rel[1] /kwôr' əl/ or /kwŏr'-/ *n.* an argument; a dispute. *The children had a quarrel about which program to watch.*

quar • rel[2] /kwôr' əl/ or /kwŏr'-/ *v.* to fight; to disagree, using angry words. *They quarreled about whose turn it was to bat.*

quart /kwôrt/ *n.* a liquid measure equal to two pints; one-quarter of a gallon. *My mother sent me to the store for a quart of milk.*

quar • ter /kwôr' tər/ *n.* a coin worth one fourth of a dollar, or twenty-five cents. *Two dimes and a nickel equal a quarter.*

quarter

quar • tet /kwôr tĕt'/ *n.* a group of four musicians performing together. *A string quartet consists of two violinists, one violist, and one cellist.*

queen /kwēn/ *n.* **a.** a female ruler. *The queen issued a proclamation.* **b.** the wife of a king. *When she married the king, she became his queen.*

ques • tion /kwĕs' chən/ *n.* **a.** a sentence that asks something. *"What time is it?" is a question.* **b.** a problem. *The litter question will be discussed tonight.*

quick /kwĭk/ *adj.* fast; swift. *The rabbit made a quick leap into the bushes.*

qui • et /kwī' ĭt/ *adj.* **a.** silent; still; having little noise. *The hum of the airplane was the only sound in the quiet night.* **b.** peaceful; calm. *Alice spent a quiet afternoon reading.*

quill /kwĭl/ *n.* a large, stiff feather or its hollow stem. *Quills were once used to make pens.*

quilt /kwĭlt/ *n.* a bed cover made of layers of cloth and padding sewn together. *Grandma told me how she made the patchwork quilt.*

quit /kwĭt/ *v.* (**quits, quit** or **quit•ted, quit•ting**) **a.** to stop. *We'll quit raking leaves when it gets dark.* **b.** to leave; to give up. *Mr. Walters quit his job to start his own business.*

quite /kwīt/ *adv.* **a.** completely; entirely. *I haven't quite finished eating.* **b.** really; truly. *His drawings are quite good.*

quiz /kwĭz/ *n.* (**quiz•zes** *pl.*) a brief test. *I missed two questions on the science quiz.*

quote[1] /kwōt/ *v.* (**quotes, quot•ed, quot•ing**) to repeat or refer to a passage from a story or poem. *Justin quoted a line from the poem in his essay.*

quote[2] /kwōt/ *n.* a quotation; a passage repeated from a story or a poem. *Quotes usually appear inside quotation marks.*

quo • tient /kwō' shənt/ *n.* the result obtained when one number is divided by another. *If you divide 16 by 2, the quotient is 8.*

Spelling Dictionary

ra•di•o /rā′ dē ō/ *n.* **a.** a way of sending sounds from one place to another by electromagnetic waves. *Before radio was discovered, messages were sent over wires.* **b.** a device for receiving such sounds. *Rita heard the election results on her radio.*

radio

rail /rāl/ *n.* **a.** a bar of wood or metal. *She sat on the top rail of the fence.* **b.** railroad. *Send this package by rail.*

rail•road /rāl′ rōd′/ *n.* a track made of two parallel steel rails on which trains travel. *The railroad goes through the middle of the town.*

rail•way /rāl′ wā′/ *n.* a railroad. *Many people travel to work each day by railway.*

ranch /rănch/ *n.* (ranch•es *pl.*) a large farm where cattle, horses, or sheep are raised. *Some fences on their ranch are made of barbed wire.*

range /rānj/ *v.* (rang•es, ranged, rang•ing) **a.** to extend or vary within certain limits. *The stories in this book range from sad to funny.* **b.** to travel over; to wander through. *Giraffes range the plains of Africa.*

rare /râr/ *adj.* not often found or seen. *My uncle saves rare postage stamps.*

rate /rāt/ *n.* **a.** the amount or degree of something measured in relation to something else. *We traveled at a rate of 40 miles per hour.* **b.** a price. *The plumber's rates are high.*

rath•er /răth′ ər/ *adv.* **a.** somewhat. *The baby is rather tired after the long ride.* **b.** more readily; more gladly. *The dog would rather stay inside on cold days than go out.*

rat•tle /răt′ l/ *v.* (rat•tles, rat•tled, rat•tling) **a.** to make a number of short, sharp sounds. *The windows rattle when the wind blows.* **b.** to move with short, sharp sounds. *The old car rattled over the bumpy road.*

Pronunciation Key

ă	pat	ŏ	pot	th	thin
ā	pay	ō	toe	*th*	this
âr	care	ô	paw, for	hw	which
ä	father	oi	noise	zh	vision
ĕ	pet	ou	out	ə	about,
ē	be	ŏŏ	took		item,
ĭ	pit	ōō	boot		pencil,
ī	pie	ŭ	cut		gallop,
îr	pier	ûr	urge		circus

reach /rēch/ *v.* **a.** to stretch out one's hand or arm. *Joel reached for the book on the top shelf.* **b.** to extend to. *The old road reaches the river and stops.*

read•er /rē′ dər/ *n.* a person who reads. *The teacher chose Kathy to be the reader of our lunchtime story this week.*

read•y /rĕd′ ē/ *adj.* (read•i•er, read•i•est; read•i•ly *adv.*) **a.** prepared. *We are ready for school.* **b.** willing. *My older brother is always ready to help me with my homework.*

reap•er /rē′ pər/ *n.* a machine that cuts and gathers grain. *The farmer used a new reaper for the harvest.*

rear¹ /rîr/ *n.* the back part. *We stood in the rear of the room.*

rear² /rîr/ *adj.* at or of the back. *Use the rear entrance.*

rear³ /rîr/ *v.* to rise on the hind legs. *The horse reared suddenly and the rider fell off.*

rea•son¹ /rē′ zən/ *n.* **a.** a cause or explanation. *Your parents will write the reason for your absence.* **b.** logic; the power to think. *Use reason to solve the problem.*

rea•son² /rē′ zən/ *v.* to think in a sensible way; to use logic. *See if you can reason out the meaning of the word.*

re•build /rē bĭld′/ *v.* (re•builds, re•built, re•build•ing) to build again. *They are planning to rebuild the old school.*

re•check /rē chĕk′/ *v.* to check again. *After he finished the test, Pedro went back and rechecked his answers.*

293

re•cord¹ /rĭ kôrd′/ *v.* **a.** to keep an account of. *The story of our country's beginning is recorded in history.* **b.** to put sounds on a magnetic tape, phonograph record, or compact disc. *The singer recorded two new songs.*

re•cord² /rĕk′ ərd/ *n.* **a.** an account of facts or events. *The secretary keeps the club's records.* **b.** the best performance. *Who holds the record for the race?* **c.** a thin disc used on a phonograph to produce sound. *We listened to the singer's new record.*

re•cov•er /rĭ kŭv′ ər/ *v.* **a.** to get back. *The police recovered the stolen goods.* **b.** to regain health. *Tracy recovered quickly after her illness.*

rec•tan•gle /rĕk′ tăng′ gəl/ *n.* a parallelogram that has four right angles. *A square is a rectangle.*

reef /rēf/ *n.* an underwater ridge of rocks, sand, or coral in a shallow area. *The boat's bottom scraped against the reef.*

re- a prefix that means: **a.** again: *rebuild.* **b.** back: *recall.*

re•heat /rē hēt′/ *v.* to heat again. *Dad reheated some leftovers for dinner.*

re•lay /rē′ lā/ or /rĭ lā′/ *v.* to take and pass along to another person or place. *Will you relay a message to Joan when you see her?*

re•main /rĭ mān′/ *v.* **a.** to continue without change; to stay. *The nurse reported that the patient's condition remained good.* **b.** to be left over. *After the picnic only a few sandwiches remained.*

re•main•der /rĭ mān′ dər/ *n.* a part or amount left over. *When you divide 15 by 6, the quotient is 2 and the remainder is 3.*

re•peat /rĭ pēt′/ *v.* **a.** to say again. *Will you repeat the question, please?* **b.** to say from memory. *Tomorrow each of you will be asked to repeat this poem.*

re•ply¹ /rĭ plī′/ *n.* (**re•plies** *pl.*) an answer. *I did not hear his reply because he spoke so softly.*

re•ply² /rĭ plī′/ *v.* (**re•plies, re•plied, re•ply•ing**) to give an answer; to respond. *She replied to my letter immediately.*

re•port¹ /rĭ pôrt′/ or /-pōrt′/ *n.* a detailed written or spoken account. *The newspaper report of the election listed the winners.*

re•port² /rĭ pôrt′/ or /-pōrt′/ *v.* to give an account or statement of. *The president of the company reported that sales had increased.*

re•port•er /rĭ pôr′ tər/ or /-pōr′-/ *n.* a person who gathers news for radio, television, or newspapers. *A reporter interviewed the candidates.*

rep•tile /rĕp′ tĭl/ or /-tīl/ *n.* any of the group of cold-blooded animals whose bodies are covered with plates or scales. *Snakes, turtles, and alligators are reptiles.*

reptile

re•read /rē rēd′/ *v.* (**re•reads, re•read, re•read•ing**) to read again. *I often reread my favorite books.*

rest•ful /rĕst′ fəl/ *adj.* offering rest, peace, or quiet. *My aunt finds sewing restful after a busy day.*

rest•less /rĕst′ lĭs/ *adj.* impatient; unable to be still. *The small children grew restless after the long delay.*

re•turn /rĭ tûrn′/ *v.* **a.** to come or go back. *We will return after the game is over.* **b.** to bring, send, or give back. *Return the book when you have finished reading it.*

re•view /rĭ vyōō′/ *v.* to study again; to go over. *She reviewed the chapter before she took the test.*

re•write /rē rīt′/ *v.* (**re•writes, re•wrote, re•writ•ten, re•writ•ing**) to write again. *The teacher asked us to rewrite our book reports, after correcting the spelling and punctuation.*

ridge /rĭj/ *n.* **a.** a narrow, raised line or strip; a crest. *Corduroy is a type of cloth that has ridges.* **b.** a long, narrow hill or mountain. *The sun sank behind the ridge.*

rig•id /rĭj′ ĭd/ *adj.* very stiff; not able to be bent. *A cast holds a broken arm in a rigid position so it can heal.*

rise¹ /rīz/ *v.* (ris•es, rose, ris•en, ris•ing) **a.** to get up. *He rose from his chair to greet us.* **b.** to move upward; to ascend. *We saw the balloon rise over the heads of the crowd.*

rise² /rīz/ *n.* an increase in height or amount. *The store announced a rise in prices.*

risk¹ /rĭsk/ *n.* a chance of loss or harm. *If you don't study, you run the risk of making a low grade.*

risk² /rĭsk/ *v.* to take the risk of; to venture. *You must risk making mistakes in order to learn.*

ri•ver /rĭv′ ər/ *n.* a large natural stream of water that flows into an ocean, a lake, or a sea. *The Mississippi is a large river that flows into the Gulf of Mexico.*

role /rōl/ *n.* a part or a character in a play. *Who will play the role of Peter Pan?*
► **Role** sounds like **roll**.

roll /rōl/ *v.* **a.** to move by turning over and over. *The ball rolled down the hill.* **b.** to wrap something around itself. *She rolled the yarn into a ball and put it in a drawer.*
► **Roll** sounds like **role**.

rough /rŭf/ *adj.* **a.** not smooth or even. *The car bounced and rattled over the rough road.* **b.** harsh; violent; not gentle. *The apples were bruised by rough handling.*

roy•al /roi′ əl/ *adj.* having to do with kings and queens. *The king and queen live in the royal palace.*

rule /rool/ *n.* **a.** a law; a regulation. *Always obey the school safety rules.* **b.** an instruction; a direction. *The rules describe how to play the game.*

Rus•sia /rŭsh′ ə/ *n.* a large country in eastern Europe and northern Asia. *Russia was the largest republic in the former U.S.S.R.*

Rus•sian¹ /rŭsh′ ən/ *adj.* of or from Russia. *Borscht is a Russian soup.*

Rus•sian² /rŭsh′ ən/ *n.* **a.** one born or living in Russia. *Russians must dress warmly in winter.* **b.** the language of Russia. *Russian uses a different alphabet from English.*

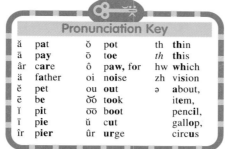

Pronunciation Key

ă	pat	ŏ	pot	th	thin
ā	pay	ō	toe	th	this
âr	care	ô	paw, for	hw	which
ä	father	oi	noise	zh	vision
ĕ	pet	ou	out	ə	about,
ē	be	ŏŏ	took		item,
ĭ	pit	ōō	boot		pencil,
ī	pie	ŭ	cut		gallop,
îr	pier	ûr	urge		circus

sad•ness /săd′ nĭs/ *n.* sorrow; grief. *Tears can be an expression of sadness.*

safe /sāf/ *adj.* free from risk or harm. *The sidewalk is a safe place to walk.*

sail•boat /sāl′ bōt′/ *n.* a boat moved by sails that catch wind. *The sailboat glided across the lake.*

sailboat

sam•ple¹ /săm′ pəl/ *n.* a part that shows what the rest is like. *The store gave away free samples of the new soap.*

sam•ple² /săm′ pəl/ *v.* (sam•ples, sam•pled, sam•pling) to test; to try. *We sampled the cookies we had baked for the party.*

sand•wich /sănd′ wĭch/ *n.* (sand•wich•es pl.) two or more slices of bread, with a layer of meat, cheese, or other food placed between them. *I like a sandwich made of peanut butter and bananas.*

Sat. Saturday.

Sat•ur•day /săt′ ər dē/ or /-dā′/ *n.* the seventh day of the week, coming after Friday. *We have no school on Saturday.* [Old English Sæternesdæg, translated from Latin *dies Saturni*, Saturn's day.]

scale¹ /skāl/ *n.* a device or machine for weighing things. *According to the scale in the doctor's office, she weighed seventy pounds.* [Old Norse *skāl*]

scale² /skāl/ *v.* to climb up or over. *The climbers used ropes to scale the cliff.*

scare /skâr/ *v.* (**scares, scared, scar•ing**) to frighten. *The sudden loud noise scared me.*

scene /sēn/ *n.* **a.** the place where a thing happens. *Gettysburg was the scene of a famous battle.* **b.** the time and place of a story or play. *The scene of the play is a mining town in the old West.* **c.** a division of an act of a play. *I appear in the second scene of the first act of the play.*

schoon•er /skoo′ nər/ *n.* a sailing ship with two or more masts. *Schooners are sometimes used as fishing vessels.*

sci•ence /sī′ əns/ *n.* knowledge made up of observed facts and arranged in an ordered system. *Science helps us understand the world we live in.*

scrape¹ /skrāp/ *v.* to scratch the surface of. *The basketball player scraped his knee when he fell.*

scrape² /skrāp/ *n.* a difficulty; an unpleasant situation. *Kevin was in a scrape when he couldn't find his homework.*

scratch¹ /skrăch/ *v.* to cut or scrape a surface. *You can tell that a diamond is genuine if it scratches glass.*

scratch² /skrăch/ *n.* (**scratch•es** *pl.*) a thin cut or mark. *The top of this old desk has many scratches.*

sea•son /sē′ zən/ *n.* one of the four parts into which a year is divided. *Spring is my favorite season.*

seat belt /sēt′ bĕlt′/ *n.* a safety strap designed to hold a person securely in a seat. *The flight attendant asked the passengers to fasten their seat belts.*

see /sē/ *v.* (**sees, saw, seen, see•ing**) **a.** to perceive with the eyes. *She could see the light shining in the distance.* **b.** to understand; to comprehend. *She will see the meaning of the story right away.*

sell•er /sĕl′ ər/ *n.* a person who sells; a vendor. *The flower seller had a stand on the street corner.*

▶ **Seller** sounds like **cellar**.

sen•tence /sĕn′ təns/ *n.* a group of words that expresses a complete thought. *"Will you come to my party?" is a sentence.*

Sept. September.

Sep•tem•ber /sĕp tĕm′ bər/ *n.* the ninth month of the year. *Many schools start in September.*

serve /sûrv/ *v.* **a.** to prepare and offer food. *We were served a delicious dinner.* **b.** to help others by performing a task. *Sarah will serve as club treasurer.*

set•tle /sĕt′ l/ *v.* **a.** to agree; to decide. *The class settled on Saturday as the day of the picnic.* **b.** to establish residence. *Their family settled in California years ago.*

sev•en•ty /sĕv′ ən tē/ *n.* the next number after sixty-nine; seven times ten; 70. *She will turn seventy next week.*

sew /sō/ *v.* (**sews, sewed, sewn** or **sewed, sew•ing**) to make by fastening with a needle and thread. *Can you sew on a sewing machine?*

share¹ /shâr/ *n.* a part; a portion. *Todd always does his share of work.*

share² /shâr/ *v.* (**shares, shared, shar•ing**) to use together. *The brothers share the same room.*

she'd /shēd/ she had; she would.

she'll /shēl/ she will; she shall.

shell /shĕl/ *n.* the hard outer covering of certain animals. *Snails, turtles, and clams have shells.*

shell

ship•ment /shĭp′ mənt/ *n.* goods sent or delivered to a certain place. *The store received a shipment of clothing from the manufacturer.*

show /shō/ *v.* (**shows, showed, shown** or **showed, show•ing**) to point out; to cause to be seen. *Show me the picture you liked.*

show•er /shou′ ər/ *n.* **a.** a short fall of rain. *During the afternoon there were three showers.* **b.** a bath in which water comes down in a spray. *I take a shower every morning.*

shown /shōn/ *v.* a form of **show**.

shy /shī/ *adj.* **a.** reserved; quiet. *After Josh made friends at his new school, he was no longer shy.* **b.** easily frightened. *A deer is shy.*

sig•na•ture /sĭg′ nə chər/ *n.* a person's name written by himself or herself. *In a letter, the signature goes immediately under the closing.*

sil•ly /sĭl′ ē/ *adj.* (**sil•li•er, sil•li•est**) foolish; not sensible. *It's silly to go out in the cold without a coat.*

sil•ver /sĭl′ vər/ *n.* a whitish precious metal. *Silver is used in making coins such as dimes and quarters.*

sim•ple /sĭm′ pəl/ *adj.* **a.** easy to understand. *The simple questions did not take long to answer.* **b.** plain; bare; with nothing fancy added. *She chose a simple red dress.*

sing•er /sĭng′ ər/ *n.* one who sings. *A choir is a group of singers.*

sin•gle /sĭng′ gəl/ *adj.* one alone; only one. *A single orange was left in the box.*

sis•ter /sĭs′ tər/ *n.* a girl or woman having the same parents as another person. *The two sisters were planning a surprise party for their parents' anniversary.*

skat•er /skā′ tər/ *n.* a person who skates. *The skaters checked the ice before skating on the pond.*

skiff /skĭf/ *n.* a flat-bottomed, shallow rowboat. *A skiff can be used with oars, sails, or a motor.*

skill /skĭl/ *n.* the ability to do something well as a result of practice. *His skill in playing the violin may someday make him famous.*

sky•line /skī′ līn′/ *n.* the outline of a group of buildings seen against the sky. *New York City's tall buildings give it an uneven skyline.*

skyline

slight /slīt/ *adj.* not big; small; slender. *Although it looks sunny, there's a slight chance it will rain later today.*

slip•per /slĭp′ ər/ *n.* a low, comfortable shoe that can be slipped on and off easily. *Slippers keep your feet warm on cool nights.*

Pronunciation Key

ă	pat	ŏ	pot	th	**th**in
ā	pay	ō	toe	*th*	**th**is
âr	care	ô	**paw, for**	hw	**wh**ich
ä	father	oi	n**oi**se	zh	vi**si**on
ĕ	pet	ou	**ou**t	ə	**a**bout,
ē	be	ŏŏ	t**oo**k		it**e**m,
ĭ	pit	ōō	b**oo**t		penc**i**l,
ī	pie	ŭ	c**u**t		gall**o**p,
îr	pier	ûr	**ur**ge		circ**u**s

smart /smärt/ *adj.* intelligent; clever; quick in mind. *A smart dog can learn many tricks.*

smell[1] /smĕl/ *v.* to get the odor or scent of through the nose. *We could smell dinner cooking as we came in.*

smell[2] /smĕl/ *n.* an odor; a scent. *The smell of orange blossoms filled the air.*

smog /smŏg/ *n.* fog that has become polluted with smoke. *In some cities smog makes it difficult to breathe.*

snug•gle /snŭg′ əl/ *v.* (**snug•gles, snug•gled, snug•gling**) to lie or press together; to cuddle. *The puppies snuggled close to their mother to keep warm.*

soar /sôr/ or /sōr/ *v.* to rise or fly high; to glide. *Eagles soar gracefully in the sky.*
▶ **Soar** sounds like **sore**.

sock•et /sŏk′ ĭt/ *n.* a hollow opening into which something fits. *The lamp flickered because the bulb was loose in the socket.*

soft•en /sô′ fən/ or /sŏf′ ən/ *v.* to make or become soft. *Ice cream softens in the heat.*

soft•ness /sôft′ nĭs/ or /sŏft′-/ *n.* the state or condition of being soft. *The softness of the wool blanket made it pleasant to use.*

so•lar /sō′ lər/ *adj.* of or having to do with the sun. *Solar rays can be harmful to the skin.*

sol•id /sŏl′ ĭd/ *n.* a substance with a definite shape that is neither a liquid nor a gas. *Wood, stone, and coal are solids.*

so•lo /sō′ lō/ *n.* a piece of music performed by one person. *Jim played a trumpet solo at the concert.*

some•times /sŭm′ tīmz/ *adv.* once in a while; now and then. *The sun sometimes shines when it is raining.*

son /sŭn/ *n.* a male child. *The mother took her son to a baseball game.*

sore /sôr/ or /sōr/ *adj.* painful; tender when touched. *His foot was sore after he stubbed his toe.*

► **Sore** sounds like **soar**.

sort /sôrt/ *v.* to separate things into like groups. *The baby can sort the blocks into two piles by color.*

sow /sō/ *v.* (**sows, sowed, sown** or **sowed, sow•ing**) to scatter seed over the ground for growing. *The farm workers were busy sowing the corn in the field.*

Spain /spān/ *n.* a country in southwestern Europe that borders on France and Portugal. *Spain and Portugal are located on the Iberian peninsula.*

Spain

Span•ish[1] /spăn′ ĭsh/ *adj.* of or from Spain. *The flamenco is a Spanish dance.*

Span•ish[2] /spăn′ ĭsh/ *n.* the language of Spain, Mexico, Central America, and most of South America. *Spanish is taught in many schools.*

spare /spâr/ *adj.* extra. *Every automobile should have a spare tire.*

spark /spärk/ *n.* **a.** a tiny particle of fire. *As the wood burned, it gave off bright sparks.* **b.** a brief, bright flash of light. *We saw the sparks of fireflies in the night.*

speak /spēk/ *v.* (**speaks, spoke, spo•ken, speak•ing**) to talk; to say words. *Speak clearly so that we can understand you!*

speak•er /spē′ kər/ *n.* **a.** a person who speaks or delivers public speeches. *The speaker at tonight's meeting will discuss the election.* **b.** a device that transmits sound. *These speakers will help everyone hear the music.*

speed[1] /spēd/ *n.* **a.** swiftness; quickness. *An antelope has great speed.* **b.** the rate of movement. *The airplane flies at a speed of six hundred miles an hour.*

speed[2] /spēd/ *v.* (**speeds, sped** or **speed•ed, speed•ing**) to go fast. *We watched the train speed past.*

spill[1] /spĭl/ *v.* to run out; to flow over. *The juice spilled on the tablecloth.*

spill[2] /spĭl/ *n.* an act of spilling: *an oil spill.*

spin•ach /spĭn′ ĭch/ *n.* a leafy green vegetable. *Spinach provides iron, which a healthy body needs.*

spoil /spoil/ *v.* **a.** to ruin; to damage; to destroy. *The stain will spoil your shirt if you don't wash it out quickly.* **b.** to become rotten or not fit for use. *The meat spoiled when it was left in the hot sun.*

spoke /spōk/ *v.* past tense of **speak**.

sport /spôrt/ or /spōrt/ *n.* any game involving exercise; recreation. *Swimming is a common summer sport.*

spread /sprĕd/ *v.* (**spreads, spread, spread•ing**) **a.** to open out; to unfold. *Spread out the map on the table.* **b.** to stretch out. *The bird spread its wings and flew away.*

square[1] /skwâr/ *n.* a rectangle with four equal sides. *A checkerboard is made up of squares.*

square[2] /skwâr/ *adj.* having four equal sides. *This room is square.*

squash /skwŏsh/ *n.* a vegetable with a hard rind and edible flesh. *Zucchini is a type of squash.* [Narragansett *askútasquash.*]

squeal[1] /skwēl/ *n.* a sharp, high-pitched cry. *The squeals of the pigs got louder as they saw the farmer bringing their food.*

squeal[2] /skwēl/ *v.* to make this sharp, high-pitched cry. *The baby squealed with delight.*

squeeze /skwēz/ *v.* (**squeez•es, squeezed, squeez•ing**) to press together hard; to compress. *Squeeze the sponge so that all the water comes out.*

squint /skwĭnt/ *v.* to look at with partly opened eyes. *The sun was so bright we had to squint to see.*

squirm /skwûrm/ *v.* to turn and twist the body. *We laughed to see the puppy squirm in the child's arms.*

stage /stāj/ *n.* the raised platform on which plays are presented. *When the lights came on, the actors were all on the stage.*

Spelling Dictionary

stake /stāk/ *n.* a stick or post with a pointed end that can be pounded into the ground. *The tent will stand straight when we tie it to these stakes.*

▶ **Stake** sounds like **steak**.

stare /stâr/ *v.* (**stares, stared, star•ing**) to look at with a steady gaze. *Mei Li stared at the painting, fascinated by the bright colors.*

state•hood /stāt' hŏod'/ *n.* the condition of being a state of the United States. *Alaska and Hawaii were the last states to gain statehood.*

state•ment /stāt' mənt/ *n.* a sentence that gives information. *Be sure your statement is accurate before you call it a fact.*

sta•tion /stā' shən/ *n.* the place from which a service is provided or operations are directed. *The local radio station will broadcast the game.*

steak /stāk/ *n.* a slice of meat or fish for cooking. *For dinner he ordered a steak, a baked potato, a salad, and a roll with butter.*

steak

▶ **Steak** sounds like **stake**.

steal /stēl/ *v.* (**steals, stole, sto•len, steal•ing**) **a.** to take without permission. *Theft is another word for stealing.* **b.** to move quietly and secretly. *We decided to steal away before the play was over.*

▶ **Steal** sounds like **steel**.

steam /stēm/ *n.* the vapor into which water is changed by heating. *We could see steam rising from the iron.*

steel /stēl/ *n.* a strong metal made from iron by mixing it with carbon. *Steel is used for making strong tools.*

▶ **Steel** sounds like **steal**.

steer¹ /stîr/ *v.* to cause to move in the correct direction. *Use the handlebars to steer the bike.*

steer² /stîr/ *n.* a male of domestic cattle that is raised especially for beef. *They herded the steers into the corral.*

still•ness /stĭl' nĭs/ *n.* quiet; silence. *After the city noise, the stillness of the country was a relief.*

Pronunciation Key

ă	pat	ŏ	pot	th	thin
ā	pay	ō	toe	th	this
âr	care	ô	paw, for	hw	which
ä	father	oi	noise	zh	vision
ĕ	pet	ou	out	ə	about,
ē	be	ŏŏ	took		item,
ĭ	pit	ōō	boot		pencil,
ī	pie	ŭ	cut		gallop,
îr	pier	ûr	urge		circus

---

stitch /stĭch/ *n.* (**stitch•es** *pl.*) one complete movement of a threaded needle through cloth or other material. *It took ten stitches to repair the rip in Diane's dress.*

stock /stŏk/ *n.* **a.** an amount of things to sell or to use; a supply. *For its big sale, the store ordered a large stock of clothes.* **b.** farm animals; livestock. *Some of the farmer's stock won prizes at the state fair.*

strain /strān/ *v.* **a.** to stretch; to pull tight. *The dog is straining at his rope.* **b.** to weaken; to injure; to hurt. *The pitcher strained a muscle in his arm at baseball practice.*

strait /strāt/ *n.* a narrow passage of water connecting two larger bodies of water. *Many ships sailed through the strait.*

strange /strānj/ *adj.* unusual; odd. *We were startled by the strange noise.*

strength /strĕngkth/ *n.* the quality of being strong. *He lost some of the strength in his muscles when he stopped exercising.*

stretch /strĕch/ *v.* (**stretch•es, stretched, stretch•ing**) **a.** to hold or put out; to extend. *She stretched her hand across the table.* **b.** to flex one's muscles. *Grandfather always stretches before he goes jogging.*

string /strĭng/ *n.* **a.** a thin cord or wire. *I tied a knot in the string.* **b.** **strings** the musical instruments with strings that are usually played by using a bow. *The strings form the largest section in an orchestra.*

stroke /strōk/ *n.* **a.** a complete movement that is repeated in an activity. *Swimmers practice their strokes.* **b.** a mark or movement made with a pen, pencil, or brush. *With a few strokes of the pen, the President approved the new law.*

Spelling Dictionary

299

stroll[1] /strōl/ v. to walk slowly and easily. *We strolled through the park.*

stroll[2] /strōl/ n. a slow walk for pleasure. *Our stroll in the garden was pleasant.*

stu·dent /stōōd' nt/ or /styōōd'-/ n. a person who studies or goes to school. *There are three hundred students in our school.*

stum·ble /stŭm' bəl/ v. to trip and almost fall. *Carlos stumbled over his sister's foot.*

sub·trac·tion /səb trăk' shən/ n. the taking away of one number or part from another. *25 − 8 = 17 is an example of subtraction.*

sum·mit /sŭm' ĭt/ n. **a.** the top of a mountain. *The climbers hope to reach the summit.* **b.** a high-level government conference. *The two nations discussed trade at the summit.*

Sun. Sunday.

Sun·day /sŭn' dē/ or /-dā'/ n. the first day of the week. *Sunday comes before Monday.* [Old English *sunnerdæg,* translated from Latin *dies solis,* day of the sun.]

sun·spot /sŭn' spŏt'/ n. any of the dark spots that appear on the surface of the sun. *Astronomers do not know exactly why sunspots appear.*

surf[1] /sûrf/ n. the waves of the sea as they break upon the shore. *After a rainstorm the surf is high.*

surf[2] /sûrf/ v. to ride breaking waves on a surfboard. *Mark learned to surf at the beach last summer.*

sur·prise[1] /sər prīz'/ v. (**sur·pris·es, sur·prised, sur·pris·ing**) to cause to feel wonder or delight; to astonish. *They surprised us by singing the song they had written.*

sur·prise[2] /sər prīz'/ n. something unexpected. *The flowers from Aunt Laura were a nice surprise.*

sweat·er /swĕt' ər/ n. a knitted garment worn on the upper part of the body. *A cardigan is a sweater that opens down the front.*

sweater

swell /swĕl/ v. (**swells, swelled, swelled** or **swol·len, swel·ling**) to increase in size or volume; to expand. *Wood swells in damp weather.*

swol·len /swōl' lən/ adj. a form of **swell.**

ta·ble /tā' bəl/ n. a piece of furniture that has legs and a smooth, flat top. *We eat supper at the kitchen table.*

ta·ble·cloth /tā' bəl klôth'/ or /-klŏth'/ n. a cloth used for covering a table. *Tony wiped the crumbs off the tablecloth.*

taste /tāst/ v. (**tastes, tast·ed, tast·ing**) to find or test the flavor of something. *Taste the sauce to see if it needs more garlic.*

taught /tôt/ v. past tense of **teach.**

tax[1] /tăks/ n. (**tax·es** pl.) money that citizens must pay to support the government. *Most of our city taxes are used to improve the schools.*

tax[2] /tăks/ v. to put a tax on. *The government taxes property.*

tax·i·cab /tăk' sē kăb'/ n. an automobile that people hire to carry them short distances. *The meter in a taxicab keeps track of the money owed for the ride.*

teach /tēch/ v. (**teach·es, taught, teach·ing**) to help to learn; to instruct. *Will you teach me how to play this game?*

team /tēm/ n. **a.** a group of players on the same side in a game. *The gym class divided into two teams to play kickball.* **b.** a group of people working together: *a team of lawyers.*

tear[1] /târ/ v. (**tears, tore, torn, tear·ing**) to pull apart or into pieces. *Be careful not to tear the letter as you open the envelope.*

tear[2] /tîr/ n. a drop of liquid from the eye. *She stopped crying and wiped the tears from her face.*

tem·per /tĕm' pər/ n. mood; state of mind. *Pam is always in a good temper on Fridays.*

tem·ple /tĕm' pəl/ n. a building for religious worship. *The ancient Greeks built many temples.*

ten•don /tĕn′ dən/ *n.* the tough tissue that connects muscle and a bone. *Scott strained a tendon in his leg and couldn't finish the race.*

ten•or /tĕn′ ər/ *n.* **a.** the musical part for a high male voice. *My dad sings tenor.* **b.** a man who sings a high part. *Our choir has more basses than tenors.*

term /tûrm/ *n.* a period of time. *The winter school term seems long because there aren't many holidays.*

ter•ror /tĕr′ ər/ *n.* very strong fear. *The actor showed terror by trembling.*

thank•ful /thăngk′ fəl/ *adj.* feeling or showing gratitude; grateful. *She was thankful when I returned her lost purse.*

thank•less /thăngk′ lĭs/ *adj.* not showing appreciation; ungrateful. *Be sure to write Uncle Jeff a thank-you note for his gift so you won't seem like a thankless person.*

they'd /thād/ they had; they would.

they'll /thāl/ they will; they shall.

thick•en /thĭk′ ən/ *v.* to make heavier or thicker. *You can use flour to thicken gravy.*

thick•ness /thĭk′ nĭs/ *n.* the condition of being heavy or thick. *The thickness of the paint made it difficult to apply.*

thin /thĭn/ *adj.* (**thin•ner, thin•nest**) slender; not thick. *A sheet of paper is thin.*

thirst /thûrst/ *n.* a desire for something to drink caused by a dry feeling in the mouth or throat. *The horses satisfied their thirst by drinking from a stream.*

thir•teenth[1] /thûr tēnth′/ *adj.* next after the twelfth. *We rode in the thirteenth car on the train.*

thir•teenth[2] /thûr tēnth′/ *n.* one of thirteen equal parts. *A baker's dozen can easily be divided into thirteenths.*

though[1] /thō/ *adv.* however. *You must admit, though, that she was partly right.*

though[2] /thō/ *conj.* in spite of the fact that; although. *Though it was getting late, we kept playing for a while longer.*

thought[1] /thôt/ *v.* past tense of **think**.

thought[2] /thôt/ *n.* **a.** the act or process of thinking. *She spent many hours in thought about the problem.* **b.** an idea, opinion, or belief. *Do you have any thoughts about how to improve our school?*

Pronunciation Key

ă	pat	ŏ	pot	th	thin
ā	pay	ō	toe	*th*	this
âr	care	ô	paw, for	hw	which
ä	father	oi	noise	zh	vision
ĕ	pet	ou	out	ə	about,
ē	be	ŏŏ	took		item,
ĭ	pit	ōō	boot		pencil,
ī	pie	ŭ	cut		gallop,
îr	pier	ûr	urge		circus

thought•ful /thôt′ fəl/ *adj.* **a.** engaged in thought; serious; meditative: *a thoughtful mood.* **b.** having consideration for others. *She is thoughtful of her friends and never hurts their feelings.*

thou•sand /thou′ zənd/ *n.* the next number after 999; 10 x 100; 1,000. *The figure for one thousand has four numerals.*

thun•der[1] /thŭn′ dər/ *n.* the loud noise caused by the violent expansion of air heated by lightning. *Thunder often comes before rain.*

thun•der[2] /thŭn′ dər/ *v.* to make this noise. *When it began to thunder, we headed for home.*

Thurs. Thursday.

Thurs•day /thûrz′ dē/ or /-dā/ *n.* the fifth day of the week, coming between Wednesday and Friday. *Our spring vacation begins on Thursday.* [Old English *dunresdæg,* Thor's day.]

tick•le /tĭk′ əl/ *v.* (**tick•les, tick•led, tick•ling**) **a.** to touch lightly to produce a shivering feeling and laughter. *She tickled me until I laughed.* **b.** to have this feeling. *His nose tickles when he has to sneeze.*

tight /tīt/ *adj.* **a.** not loose; firm. *The knot was so tight that we couldn't untie it.* **b.** fitting very closely. *My old shoes are too tight.*

tight•en /tīt′ n/ *v.* to make or become tighter. *Mother tightened her seat belt before driving away.*

tim•ber /tĭm′ bər/ *n.* trees; wooded land. *There was no timber on the mountaintop, only grasses and low shrubs.*

timber

Spelling Dictionary

times /tīmz/ *prep.* multiplied by. *Six times four is twenty-four.*

ti • ny /tī′ nē/ *adj.* (**ti•ni•er, ti•ni•est**) very small; wee. *An ant is a tiny animal.*

tire¹ /tīr/ *v.* to make weary or exhausted. *Exercising for a long time tires me.*

tire² /tīr/ *n.* an outer rim of rubber, often filled with air, that is fitted around the rim of a wheel. *I pumped air into my bicycle tire.* [Middle English, *tyre,* covering for a wheel, from *tyr,* attire.]

ti • tle /tīt′ l/ *n.* the name of a book, movie, painting, etc. *When I had finished reading the story, I couldn't remember its title.*

to • geth • er /tə gĕth′ ər/ *adv.* with each other; in one group. *We all walked to the game together.*

toot¹ /to͞ot/ *n.* a short, sharp sound made by a horn or whistle. *They heard the toot of the tugboat whistle.*

toot² /to͞ot/ *v.* to make this sound. *The engineer tooted the horn as the train entered the tunnel.*

to • tal¹ /tōt′ l/ *adj.* whole; entire. *The total price includes tax.*

to • tal² /tōt′ l/ *n.* an entire amount; a sum. *He added the numbers to find the total.*

tot • ter /tŏt′ ər/ *v.* to sway as if about to fall. *The child tottered as he was learning to walk.*

touch /tŭch/ *v.* to feel with the hand or other part of the body. *The builder touched the cement to see if it was still soft.*

tough /tŭf/ *adj.* strong; not easily torn or broken. *The rug is made of very tough materials.*

tour /to͝or/ *n.* **a.** a journey or trip with several visits. *The Friedmans made a driving tour of the New England states.* **b.** a brief trip of inspection. *Ms. Wright gave us a tour of her office.*

trac • tor /trăk′ tər/ *n.* a large machine on wheels, used for pulling trucks or farm equipment. *The farmer drove the tractor into the barn.*

trail • er /trā′ lər/ *n.* a large vehicle pulled or hauled by a car, truck, or tractor. *We used a trailer attached to our car to move our furniture.*

trap /trăp/ *n.* a device used to capture animals. *The tiger fell into a deep trap that the hunter had set.*

trav • el /trăv′ əl/ *v.* to go from place to place on a trip or journey. *We traveled to San Diego on our vacation.*

trawl • er /trô′ lər/ *n.* a boat used to catch fish by towing a net or line. *The trawler returned loaded with fish.*

tray /trā/ *n.* a flat, shallow holder with a low rim. *A waiter carries dishes on a tray.*

tray

treat • ment /trēt′ mənt/ *n.* **a.** a way of handling. *Baby animals receive special treatment at the zoo.* **b.** anything used to treat something. *The doctor said that ice was the best treatment for my sprain.*

trem • ble /trĕm′ bəl/ *v.* (**trem•bles, trem•bled, trem•bling**) to shake or quiver. *I was so nervous that my hands trembled.*

trick /trĭk/ *n.* **a.** something done to deceive. *The phone call was just a trick to get me out of the room while they planned the surprise party.* **b.** an act that requires a special skill. *Seth taught his dog the trick of rolling over.*

tri • o /trē′ ō/ *n.* a group of three performers. *Peter, Paul, and Mary were a famous singing trio.*

tri • ple /trĭp′ əl/ *v.* (**tri•ples, tri•pled, tri•pling**) to make three times as much or as many. *Three tripled is nine.*

trou • ble /trŭb′ əl/ *n.* **a.** something that causes worry or distress; difficulty. *The trouble with our car is that the motor won't run.* **b.** a bother; an extra effort. *It was no trouble to help her clean her room.*

true /tro͞o/ *adj.* right; accurate; not false. *It is true that ostriches cannot fly.*

trust /trŭst/ *v.* **a.** to believe in; to depend or rely on. *We trust the doctor to do what is best for us.* **b.** to expect; to assume. *I trust you have finished your homework.*

truth /tro͞oth/ *n.* **a.** that which agrees with the facts. *The truth is that we were wrong.* **b.** honesty. *Her apology had a feeling of truth.*

tube /to͞ob/ or /tyo͞ob/ *n.* a long, hollow cylinder used to carry or hold liquids and gases. *A drinking straw is a tube.*

Tues. Tuesday.

Tues • day /tooz′ dē/ or /-dā′/ or /tyooz′-/
n. the third day of the week, coming after
Monday. *Elections are usually held on a
Tuesday.* [Old English *Tiwesdæg,* Tiu's
day.]

tug • boat /tŭg′ bōt′/ *n.* a powerful small
boat used for towing larger vessels. *The
tugboat towed the ship into the harbor.*

tu • lip /too′ lĭp/ or /tyoo′-/ *n.* a
plant of the lily family that
grows from a bulb and blooms
in the spring. *Tulips have
large cup-shaped flowers.*

tur • key /tûr′ kē/ *n.* a large
North American bird covered
with thick feathers. *Turkeys
can weigh more than thirty
pounds.*

tulip

twelfth¹ /twĕlfth/ *adj.* next
after the eleventh. *Mary Beth celebrated her
twelfth birthday.*

twelfth² /twĕlfth/ *n.* one of twelve equal
parts. *Three twelfths make one fourth.*

twice /twīs/ *adv.* two times. *We liked the
song so much we sang it twice.*

U

um • pire /ŭm′ pīr′/ *n.* a person who rules
on the play of a game. *In baseball, the
umpire calls the balls and strikes.*

un- a prefix that means "not" or "the opposite of": *unafraid.*

un • cov • er /ŭn kŭv′ ər/ *v.* **a.** to remove the
cover from. *Steam rose from the hot dish as
Dad uncovered it.* **b.** to reveal or expose.
The truth was uncovered during the trial.

un • fair /ŭn fâr′/ *adj.* not fair; not honest or
just. *Cheating is unfair.*

un • hap • py /ŭn hăp′ ē/ *adj.*
(un•hap•pi•er, un•hap•pi•est;
un•hap•pi•ly *adv.*) not happy; sad; full of
sorrow. *When Maria was unhappy, we tried
to cheer her up.*

un • lock /ŭn lŏk′/ *v.* to undo a lock by turning a key. *Mr. Hughes unlocked the door
and let us in.*

un • luck • y /ŭn lŭk′ ē/ *adj.* (un•luck•i•er,
un•luck•i•est; un•luck•i•ly *adv.*) not lucky;
disappointing. *It was unlucky that we
missed the bus.*

un • pack /ŭn păk′/ *v.* to remove the contents of a suitcase or a package. *After we
moved, it took a week to unpack all the
boxes.*

un • safe /ŭn sāf′/ *adj.* not safe; dangerous.
Running into a crowded hallway is unsafe.

un • tie /ŭn tī′/ *v.* (un•ties, un•tied,
un•ty•ing) to loosen something that has
been tied. *She untied the ribbon and opened
the gift.*

up • stairs¹ /ŭp′ stârz′/ *adv.* up the stairs;
to a higher floor. *I went upstairs to bed.*

up • stairs² /ŭp′ stârz′/ *adj.* on a higher
floor. *Did you clean the upstairs hall?*

use /yooz/ *v.* (us•es, used, us•ing) to put into
service. *Use the cloth to dust the shelf.*

used¹ /yoozd/ *v.* past tense of **use.**

used² /yoozd/ *adj.* not new; owned by
another person in the past. *A used bike
costs less than a new one.*

use • ful /yoos′ fəl/ *adj.* of use; helpful. *She
gave me some useful advice about studying
for the test.*

use • less /yoos′ lĭs/ *adj.* of no use; serving
no purpose. *My sled is useless in the summer.*

303

Spelling Dictionary

verb /vûrb/ *n.* a word that expresses action or a state of being. *In the sentences "Go to the store" and "His dog is brown," the verbs are "go" and "is."*

view /vyo͞o/ *n.* **a.** what is seen; scene. *The view from the window by the beach is breathtaking.* **b.** opinion; idea. *His view was that we should change our plans.*

vil•lage /vĭl′ ĭj/ *n.* a number of houses and buildings in an area that is smaller than a town. *Everyone knows everyone else in our village.*

vi•o•la /vē ō′ lə/ *n.* a stringed instrument of the violin family. *A viola is slightly larger than a violin and has a deeper tone.*

vi•o•lin /vī ə lĭn′/ *n.* a musical instrument that has four strings and is played with a bow. *The violin is held under the chin when played.*

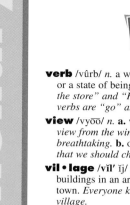

violin

vi•rus /vī′ rəs/ *n.* (vi•rus•es *pl.*) a tiny substance that causes certain diseases. *Mumps and measles are caused by viruses.*

vis•it /vĭz′ ĭt/ *v.* to go or come to see. *We visited Mrs. Gomez and her new baby after they came home from the hospital.*

vol•ca•no /vŏl kā′ nō/ *n.* (vol•ca•noes or vol•ca•nos *pl.*) a mountain formed by lava pushed out through an opening in the earth's surface. *Some islands are formed from volcanoes.*

vote /vōt/ *v.* (votes, vot•ed, vot•ing) to choose or decide in an election. *Our class voted to accept Joy's plan.*

vow•el /vou′ əl/ *n.* **a.** a sound made with the voice when the breath is allowed to pass out of the mouth freely. *The sound of "o" in "go" is a vowel.* **b.** any of the letters that stand for such a sound. *The most common vowels are a, e, i, o, and u.*

waist /wāst/ *n.* the narrow part of the body between the ribs and the hips. *Belts are worn around the waist.*

▶ Waist sounds like **waste**.

wan•der /wŏn′ dər/ *v.* to go without purpose or aim; to roam. *I wandered from room to room looking for something to do.*

was•n't /wŏz′ ənt/ or /wŭz′-/ was not.

waste /wāst/ *v.* (wastes, wast•ed, wast•ing) to use up carelessly or foolishly. *He wasted his money on toys he didn't need.*

▶ Waste sounds like **waist**.

waste•ful /wāst′ fəl/ *adj.* tending to waste; using or spending too much. *Taking more food than you can eat is wasteful.*

watch /wŏch/ *n.* (watch•es *pl.*) a small clock worn on the wrist or carried in a pocket. *I checked my watch to be sure I had the correct time.*

wa•ter[1] /wô′ tər/ or /wŏt′ ər/ *n.* the clear liquid that falls as rain. *Water becomes ice when it freezes.*

wa•ter[2] /wô′ tər/ or /wŏt′ ər/ *v.* to put water on. *Did you water the flowers today?*

wa•ter•fall /wô′ tər fôl/ or /wŏt′ ər-/ *n.* a flow of water falling from a high place. *In the spring, melting snow feeds waterfalls in the mountains.*

weak•en /wē′ kən/ *v.* to make weak; to become weak. *His legs weakened as he climbed up the mountain.*

weak•ness /wēk′ nĭs/ *n.* (weak•ness•es *pl.*) **a.** lack of strength or power. *An illness can cause weakness.* **b.** a weak point; a fault. *Poor fielding is the baseball team's only weakness.*

weave /wēv/ *v.* (weaves, wove, wo•ven, weav•ing) to make by lacing threads, yarns, or strips under and over each other. *She is weaving a basket out of straw.*

Wed. Wednesday.

Wednes • day /wĕnz′ dē/ or /-dā′/ *n.* the fourth day of the week. *Wednesday is the day after Tuesday.* [Old English *Wodnesdæg,* Woden's day.]

week • end /wēk′ ĕnd′/ *n.* Saturday and Sunday, as a time for rest, play, visiting, etc. *We are going bowling this weekend.*

we'll /wēl/ we will; we shall.

well-be • ing /wĕl′ bē′ ĭng/ *n.* the state of being healthy and happy; welfare. *Having friends is good for your well-being.*

we've /wēv/ we have.

when • ev • er /hwĕn ĕv′ ər/ *conj.* at any time that. *I'm ready whenever you are.*

wheth • er /hwĕ*th*′ ər/ *conj.* if. *He didn't know whether he should laugh or cry.*

whose /hōōz/ *pron.* of whom; of which. *Whose jacket did you borrow?*

width /wĭdth/ *n.* the distance from side to side. *The width of my room is ten feet.*

wife /wīf/ *n.* (**wives** *pl.*) the woman a man is married to. *He brought flowers to his wife on her birthday.*

win • ter[1] /wĭn′ tər/ *n.* the coldest season of the year. *Winter comes between autumn and spring.*

win • ter[2] /wĭn′ tər/ *adj.* of or for the winter. *Ice skating is a winter sport.*

wire /wīr/ *n.* a thread or strand of metal. *Electricity travels through wires.*

wise /wīz/ *adj.* **a.** having good sense; showing good judgment. *She made a wise decision.* **b.** having much knowledge or information. *Scientists and professors are wise.*

wit /wĭt/ *n.* **a.** cleverness; intelligence. *It took wit to think of such a good plan.* **b.** humor. *His wit kept us all chuckling.*

wit • ty /wĭt′ ē/ *adj.* (**wit•ti•er, wit•ti•est; wit•ti•ly** *adv.*) showing wit; clever and amusing. *The witty speaker made the audience laugh.*

wives /wīvz/ *n.* plural of **wife.**

wob • ble /wŏb′ əl/ *v.* (**wob•bles, wob•bled, wob•bling**) to move in a shaky way from side to side. *The baby's legs wobbled when she tried to walk.*

won • der /wŭn′ dər/ *v.* to be curious to know. *I wonder how the story will end.*

wring /rĭng/ *v.* (**wrings, wrung, wring•ing**) to twist and squeeze. *Wring out that wet cloth before you wipe the table.*

wrin • kle[1] /rĭng′ kəl/ *n.* a small crease or fold. *Rosa ironed the wrinkles out of her skirt.*

wrin • kle[2] /rĭng′ kəl/ *v.* to crease or crumple. *Your forehead wrinkles when you frown.*

writ • ten /rĭt′ n/ *v.* a form of **write.**

wrong /rông/ or /rŏng/ *adj.* **a.** not right; bad; wicked. *Telling lies is wrong.* **b.** not correct; not true. *Your answer was wrong.* **c.** out of order. *Do you know what's wrong with the phone?*

year /yîr/ *n.* a period of 365 days or 12 months. *The calendar year begins on January 1.*

you'd /yōōd/ you had; you would.

you'll /yōōl/ or /yŏŏl/ you will; you shall.

you're /yŏŏr/ you are.

you've /yōōv/ you have.

young /yŭng/ *adj.* not old or fully grown. *A fawn is a young deer.*

Spelling Dictionary

ze•ro /zîr′ ō/ or /zē′ rō/ *n.* (**ze•ros** or **ze•roes** *pl.*) the numeral 0; nothing. *If you multiply any number by zero, the product will also be zero.*

zip•per /zĭp′ ər/ *n.* a fastening device with two rows of tiny teeth that can be closed together by a sliding tab. *My boots close with a zipper.*

zipper

306

USING THE Thesaurus

The **Writing Thesaurus** provides synonyms—words that mean the same or nearly the same—and antonyms—words that mean the opposite—for your spelling words. Use this sample to identify the various parts of each thesaurus entry.

- **Entry words** are listed in alphabetical order and are printed in boldface type.
- The abbreviation for the **part of speech** of each entry word follows the boldface entry word.
- The **definition** of the entry word matches the definition of the word in your **Spelling Dictionary**. A **sample sentence** shows the correct use of the word in context.
- Each **synonym** for the entry word is listed under the entry word. Again, a sample sentence shows the correct use of the synonym in context.
- Where appropriate, **antonyms** for the entry word are listed at the end of the entry.

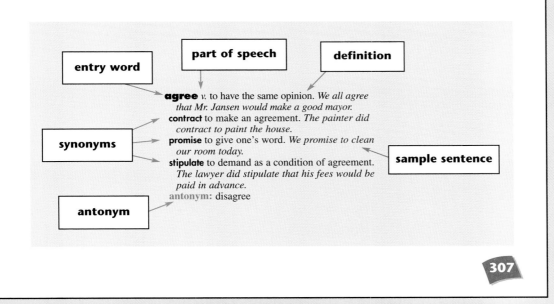

entry word

part of speech

definition

agree *v.* to have the same opinion. *We all agree that Mr. Jansen would make a good mayor.*
contract to make an agreement. *The painter did contract to paint the house.*
promise to give one's word. *We promise to clean our room today.*
stipulate to demand as a condition of agreement. *The lawyer did stipulate that his fees would be paid in advance.*
antonym: disagree

synonyms

sample sentence

antonym

307

able *adj.* having power, skill, or talent. *With practice you will be able to play the piano.*
competent able; qualified. *The meal was prepared by a very competent chef.*
skillful having skill. *The skillful player won the tennis game.*
talented gifted; having natural ability. *The talented musician played the piano for us.*
antonym: unable

adult *n.* a grown person. *You may vote when you are an adult.*
grown-up an adult. *The young child dressed up like a grown-up.*
human being human; person. *Every human being should exercise for good health.*
person man, woman, or child. *Each person registered to vote during the election.*

agree *v.* to have the same opinion. *We all agree that Mr. Jansen would make a good mayor.*
contract to make an agreement. *The painter did contract to paint the house.*
promise to give one's word. *We promise to clean our room today.*
stipulate to demand as a condition of agreement. *The lawyer did stipulate that his fees would be paid in advance.*
antonym: disagree

agreement *n.* an arrangement or understanding between two persons or groups. *The students came to an agreement about the best day for the litter cleanup.*
arrangement settlement; agreement. *The new arrangement satisfied everyone.*
contract an agreement. *The contract had specific terms for the car loan.*
settlement an arrangement; agreement. *The president worked for a quick settlement on wages for post office employees.*
understanding an agreement or arrangement. *We have an understanding about the terms for buying the house.*

ahead *adv.* in advance; in front. *Dad walked ahead to look for a campsite.*

before in front; ahead. *He walked before us to see that the path was clear.*
forward in front; ahead. *Once the line started to move, we all stepped forward.*
antonym: behind

aim *v.* to point at; direct toward. *Aim the arrow at the center of the target.*
beam to send out; direct. *The machine will beam the light at the sign.*
direct to point or aim. *He will direct the traffic away from the parade route.*
level to keep even. *The police officer will level his rifle at the target.*
point to aim; direct. *Ask John to point at the deer standing behind the bush.*
train to point; aim. *She will train the spotlight on the actor.*

alarm *n.* a signal warning that danger is near. *The alarm went off moments after the fire started.*
beacon light or fire used to warn. *The beacon was placed on the shoreline.*
bell anything that makes a ringing sound. *The bell rang to warn the ships in the fog.*
signal a sign of warning or notice. *A red light was the signal to indicate danger.*
siren a loud whistle. *The fire siren warned us that a fire truck was coming.*

alive *adj.* living; not dead. *People sometimes forget that trees are alive.*
existing living; having life. *The existing animals were saved from starvation.*
living being alive; having life. *The artificial plants looked like living ones.*
antonym: dead

alone *adv.* without anyone else. *The box was too heavy for one person to lift alone.*
singly by itself; separately. *Let us review each person singly to see how well his or her job is done.*
solely alone; the only one or ones. *I am solely responsible for the picnic plans.*

also *adv.* too; in addition; likewise. *Geraniums grow well not only in flowerpots but also in gardens.*
besides in addition; also. *Many people besides the parents came to the play.*

likewise also; too. *I will be there on time, and she will likewise.*

too also; besides. *The cats and dogs are hungry, too.*

amount *n.* the total or sum. *We raised the amount of money needed for the books.*

figure price; amount. *The figure for the car was less because of the rebates.*

number amount; total. *A number of people were invited to the party.*

sum amount; total. *We paid a large sum for the new house.*

total amount; sum. *A total of 100 tickets were sold for the community play.*

answer *n.* a reply. *I must send my answer to her letter quickly.*

acknowledgment something done to let one know that a service or gift was received. *An acknowledgment was sent to thank us for the gift.*

reply response; answer. *Your reply was very easy to understand.*

response an answer. *The response she gave was very prompt.*

apart *adv.* to pieces; in separate pieces. *The puzzle fell apart when it slipped off the table.*

independently on one's own. *The class members selected projects independently.*

separately individually; one at a time. *We worked separately on the project.*
antonym: together

apartment *n.* a group of rooms to live in, generally in a building housing more than one family. *They live in an apartment on the second floor.*

flat apartment or set of rooms. *We lived in a flat above the store.*

room a part of a building with walls of its own. *The hotel rented us a room for the night.*

suite set of rooms connected to each other. *The hotel suite had five rooms.*

army *n.* a large group of people who are organized and trained to serve as soldiers. *The United States Army fought in Europe during World War II.*

armed forces the army, navy, and air force of a country. *The armed forces took part in the Fourth of July parade.*

soldiers men or women in the army. *The soldiers were trained in Louisiana.*

troops soldiers. *The troops helped to rescue people after the earthquake.*

baby *n.* a very young child; an infant. *The baby had not learned to stand up yet.*

babe a baby. *The word babe is another word for baby.*

infant a very young child. *The new mother wrapped the infant in a soft blanket.*

young child a young boy or girl. *The young child was learning to walk.*

baby sitter *n.* one who takes care of young children. *John's mother called a baby sitter to stay with him for the afternoon.*

nanny a woman who takes care of children. *The nanny took the children to the park.*

nursemaid girl or woman who takes care of children. *The nursemaid knew how to prepare the baby's food.*

badge *n.* something worn to show that a person is a member of a group or organization. *Each firefighter wore a badge.*

emblem a badge or sign. *The police officer had an emblem on her uniform.*

name tag a badge worn that gives a name. *Everyone at the meeting wore a name tag to help people learn names.*

baggage *n.* suitcases; luggage. *Airline passengers may pick up their baggage inside the terminal.*

luggage baggage. *The passengers checked their luggage at the ticket counter.*

suitcase a flat, rectangular-shaped bag for traveling. *We packed our clothes in the suitcase.*

battle *n.* a fight between armies, navies, etc. during a war. *That battle was the turning point of the war.*
combat a fight or struggle. *The argument was settled without any combat.*
conflict a fight or struggle. *The conflict over wages lasted for years.*
encounter a meeting of enemies; battle; fight. *The peaceful encounter between the two groups led to a settlement.*
war a fight or conflict. *The war between the two groups lasted only a few days.*

because *conj.* for the reason that. *I study because I want to learn.*
as because. *As she knew how to act better than anyone else, she became the star of the show.*
for because. *We can't stay outside, for it is raining.*
since because. *Since you want a new toy, you should save your money.*

begin *v.* to start. *We will begin our school day with an arithmetic lesson.*
commence to begin; start. *The play will commence when the curtain opens.*
open to start or set up. *They will open a new store in the shopping center.*
start to begin. *We will start reading at the beginning of the chapter.*
undertake to try; to attempt. *We will undertake the new assignment as soon as we get to work this morning.*
antonyms: end, finish

believe *v.* to accept something as true or real. *Do you believe that cats have nine lives?*
assume to suppose; to believe something to be true or real. *We could assume that the bus driver knew the correct route.*
suppose to believe, think, or imagine. *I suppose we could try to fix the toy.*
think to believe; to have an opinion. *I think it will rain today.*
trust to have faith; believe. *I trust you know how to solve the math problem.*

beside *prep.* at the side of; near to. *The carton was left beside the trash cans.*
abreast side by side. *In the parade the Boy Scouts marched four abreast.*
alongside by the side of; side by side. *The trees were alongside the building.*

between *prep.* in the space that separates two things. *There were four people between me and the door.*
in the midst in the middle of. *The toys were put in the midst of the children.*

bitter *adj.* tasting sharp and unpleasant. *Do you think black walnuts have a bitter taste?*
sharp strongly affecting the senses. *The lemon drops had a very sharp taste.*
sour having a sharp, bitter taste. *The sour lemon juice was used in the tea.*

boast *v.* to brag; to talk too much about oneself and about what one can do. *Judy likes to boast about how fast she can run.*
bluster to talk in a noisy manner. *The man tried to complain and bluster at the clerk.*
brag to boast; praise oneself. *Tom always seems to brag about his bicycle.*
crow to show one's pride; boast. *We listened to the winners crow about how well they ran.*

bold *adj.* not afraid to face danger; brave and daring. *The bold gymnast attempted a difficult vault.*
brave showing courage; without fear. *The brave firefighter saved the people in the burning house.*
courageous brave; fearless. *The courageous child saved the animals from the cold winter storm.*
fearless without fear. *The fearless woman raced to catch the falling child.*
antonyms: cowardly, afraid, weak

break *v.* to come apart; separate into pieces. *The dish will break if it falls on the floor.*
crack to break without separating into parts. *The dish might crack when it lands on the floor.*
shatter to break into pieces. *The glass will shatter when it hits the floor.*
snap to break suddenly. *The rope did snap when we pulled on it.*
split to separate into pieces. *The seam split as he pulled on his jacket.*

brief *adj.* short; quick; direct. *Our meeting was brief.*
concise short; brief. *He gave a concise report to the group.*
little not long in time; short. *Please wait a little while before you go.*

short not long. *It took only a few minutes to read the short story.*

succinct brief; short. *The succinct comments really told the whole story.*

terse brief; to the point. *A one-word answer is a terse reply.*

brighten *v.* to lighten; make or become bright. *The lamp will brighten the living room.*

illuminate to light up; make bright. *The lights will illuminate the sky.*

lighten to make brighter; to add light to. *The new paint does lighten the room.*

antonym: darken

bubble *n.* a thin, round film of liquid that forms a ball around a pocket of gas or air. *The slightest touch can pop a bubble.*

bead any small, round object like a bubble. *A bead of water formed on the newly waxed car.*

blob a small drop. *A blob of jelly fell on the floor.*

build *v.* to make; put together. *Doug wants to build a model house out of toothpicks.*

construct to build; to fit together. *The builders will construct a new office tower.*

erect to put up; to build. *The highway crew can erect a new flag pole.*

make to build; put together. *We will make a tree house in the backyard.*

put up to build. *We followed the directions when we put up the tent.*

burst *v.* to break open suddenly. *The balloon will burst if it touches the light bulb.*

blow up to explode. *The balloon will blow up when Horace jumps on it.*

explode to burst with a loud noise. *The fireworks explode high in the sky.*

rupture to break; burst. *Where did the water main rupture?*

buy *v.* to purchase. *Sally had to buy a new pair of shoes before winter.*

purchase to buy. *He can purchase the jewelry at the shop by our house.*

shop to go to stores to look at or buy things. *We plan to shop for a new coat.*

antonyms: sell, market

calm *adj.* quiet; peaceful; motionless. *There wasn't even a breeze on that calm evening.*

composed quiet; calm. *The composed officer came forward to receive the award.*

cool calm; not excited. *The people kept cool and walked to the nearest exit.*

serene calm; peaceful. *A serene smile could be seen on her face.*

tranquil peaceful; quiet; calm. *The tranquil night air was very relaxing.*

antonyms: nervous, anxious

careful *adj.* cautious; full of care. *Be careful when you cross the busy street.*

cautious very careful. *The cautious player watched the ball at all times.*

considered carefully thought out. *His considered opinion was respected by everyone.*

diligent careful; steady. *He is a diligent worker.*

antonym: careless

careless *adj.* reckless; not cautious. *You can't afford to be careless with matches.*

negligent careless. *No one liked the negligent way Pat drove.*

thoughtless without thought. *Her thoughtless behavior made me angry.*

antonym: careful

cart *n.* a two-wheeled vehicle pulled by a horse or another animal. *The pony pulled a cart in the parade.*

buggy a small carriage pulled by a horse. *We rode in a buggy around the park.*

wagon a four-wheeled vehicle. *The wagon was pulled by a horse.*

case *n.* a large box; container. *Our music teacher carries her violin in a case.*

bin a box or container. *The grain was stored in a large bin.*

box container with four sides, a bottom, and a lid. *We packed the dishes in a box.*

carton a box made of cardboard. *The books were packed in a carton.*

container a box, can, etc. used to hold things. *She put the paper clips in a small container.*

certain *adj.* confident; sure; convinced. *She was certain you would win.*
decided definite; clear. *There is a decided difference between the two books on hamsters.*
definite clear; exact. *I want a definite answer to my question.*
sure certain; positive. *I am sure that is the right way to go.*
antonym: uncertain

charge *n.* an amount asked or made as payment. *There is no charge for this service.*
amount the total or sum. *We raised the amount of money needed to buy the books for our new library.*
cost price paid. *The cost of the shirt was more than I was willing to pay.*
price the amount charged for something. *The price of cars goes up every year.*

charm *v.* to delight; please. *The child's smile did charm the audience.*
delight to please greatly. *The pony rides will delight the children.*
enchant to delight. *The magician can enchant the audience with his tricks.*
fascinate to attract; enchant. *The music will fascinate all of us.*

chart *v.* to make a map or a diagram of. *My job is to chart our class's spelling progress.*
diagram to put a sketch on paper. *The builder will diagram the house plan for us.*
map to plan; arrange. *We will map out our work.*
outline to sketch; make a plan. *She tried to outline the entire trip for us.*
plot to plan secretly. *The pirate will plot a way to get the treasure.*

cheer *v.* to shout words of approval; to encourage by yelling. *We all cheer for our star player as he comes on the field.*
encourage to give courage. *The coach tried to encourage the players to do their best.*
shout to say loudly. *We shout encouragement to the runners.*
yell to shout loudly. *The fans yell cheers to the home team.*

cheerful *adj.* happy; joyful. *Kari gave a cheerful smile.*
good-humored cheerful; pleasant. *The good-humored clown entertained everyone.*

joyful full of joy. *The first and last days of school are always joyful.*
rosy bright; cheerful. *The good news meant there would be a rosy future.*
sunny happy, cheerful; bright. *May had a sunny personality that cheered everyone around her.*
antonyms: cheerless, sad, gloomy

chief *n.* a leader; a head of a tribe or group. *The chief leads the tribal council.*
captain head of a group; chief; leader. *John is the captain of the football team.*
head leader; chief person. *The head of the school was Mr. Smith.*
leader person who leads. *Jan was the leader of the debate team.*
officer person who holds an office in a club or organization. *The president is the top officer of the business.*

choice *n.* a decision; selection. *For dinner we will go to the restaurant of your choice.*
decision a choice. *I have made a decision about the theme for the food, costumes, and invitations for the big Fourth of July party.*
option choice; a choosing. *We have the option of taking a car, a bus, or a train to get to work.*
selection choice; act of selecting. *The store had a good selection of clothes for children.*

clear *adj.* having no clouds; bright. *The sun shone in the clear sky.*
bright very light or clear. *The bright day convinced us it would be a good day for a picnic.*
light clear; bright. *The lamp makes the room as light as day.*
sunny having much sunlight. *We wanted a sunny day for the parade.*

climb *v.* to go up, often using both hands and feet; to move on a steep slope. *The club members climb mountains all over the state.*
mount to go up. *We tried to mount the stairs as fast as we could.*
scale to climb. *We used ropes and hooks to scale the mountainside.*

clothes *n.* garments; articles of dress; clothing. *Some people order all of their clothes through a catalog.*
apparel clothing; dress. *This store sells very expensive women's apparel.*

dress clothing. *We studied about the dress of people from years ago.*
garments articles of clothing. *The queen's garments were made of velvet.*

clue *n.* a piece of information that helps solve a problem or mystery. *In this game we use a word clue to solve the puzzle.*
hint a sign; a suggestion. *The hint he gave us did not help us find the treasure.*
suggestion something suggested. *They gave us a suggestion to help us solve the problem.*

coach *n.* a person who trains athletes; person who teaches. *The basketball coach is happy when the team plays well.*
teacher a person who teaches. *We asked our teacher to help us with the report.*
trainer a person who trains others. *The trainer made the team practice throwing and catching.*
tutor a private teacher. *The tutor helped me learn how to do multiplication.*

coast *n.* the seashore; land along the sea or ocean. *There are many beaches along the coast of the Pacific Ocean.*
seacoast coast; land by the sea. *Maine has a beautiful seacoast.*
shore land along the sea, ocean, lake, etc. *We walked along the shore until we reached the path.*
shoreline place where water and shore meet. *The rising water changed the shoreline.*

compare *v.* to examine things for similarities or differences. *If you compare prices, you can save money when you shop.*
contrast to compare to show differences. *A list was made to contrast city living with country living.*
liken to compare. *The art collector did liken my painting to one hanging in the museum.*
match to fit together; be alike. *The curtains almost match the colors in the couch.*

cottage *n.* a small house. *We spent our vacation in a cottage on the beach.*
bungalow a small, one-floor house. *The family lived in a bungalow.*
cabin a small house, roughly built. *The mountain cabin was made of logs.*

crowd *v.* to push or squeeze together in a small space. *Many people tried to crowd into the small room.*

cram to put too many into a space. *Twenty people tried to cram into the small waiting room.*
jam to squeeze things or people together. *The riders tried to jam onto the train.*
swarm to crowd. *Hundreds of fans might swarm onto the field after the game.*

cute *adj.* delightfully attractive or appealing. *The child looked cute in her rabbit costume.*
attractive pretty; pleasing. *The attractive lady wore a black suit.*
charming attractive; very pleasing. *The children had charming roles in the play.*
pretty pleasing; attractive. *The pretty pictures decorated the walls.*
antonym: ugly

dampen *v.* to make moist or wet. *Dampen the cloth before you begin cleaning.*
moisten to make or become moist. *We will moisten the towel with water and clean up the mess.*
wet to make or become moist. *He can wet the soap to get lather.*

danger *n.* peril; chance of injury or harm. *Learning safety rules can help you avoid danger.*
hazard chance or harm. *The railroad crossing has been a serious safety hazard.*
peril chance of danger or harm. *The storm put the city in peril.*

darkness *n.* the state or quality of being without light or brightness. *The darkness of the sky warned of a coming storm.*
blackout a lack of light in a city or place due to loss of power. *The blackout lasted for two hours.*
dusk the time just before dark. *We got home at dusk.*
gloom darkness. *The gloom spread over the city as the sun set.*

deal *v.* to handle in a certain way; cope. *It is important to know how to deal with emergencies.*
cope to handle. *We will cope with the problem when it arises.*
handle to deal with. *The director will handle all of the problems.*

dew *n.* water droplets that form at night on cool surfaces. *In the morning you may see dew on the leaves.*
mist fine drops of water in the air. *We can see the mist out in the yard.*
moisture small drops of water in the air. *The moisture in the air made the car wet.*
vapor moisture in the air. *The water vapor in the air made the windows steam up.*

dodge *v.* to try to avoid; stay away from. *The batter stepped back from the plate to dodge the wild pitch.*
duck to move suddenly to keep from being hit. *She had to duck quickly to avoid the ball.*
lurch to lean or stagger. *The man began to lurch forward when he lost his balance.*
sidestep to step aside. *The pitcher had to sidestep to avoid being hit by the line drive.*

doubt *v.* to be unsure or uncertain. *I doubt that the Cortez family is home from vacation.*
question to doubt. *I question the report of rainy weather since the sun is shining brightly.*
suspect to doubt. *We suspect that he is not telling the whole story.*

drag *v.* to pull slowly along the ground; haul. *They drag the sled to the top of the hill and then slide down.*
pull to move; drag. *We can pull the wagon up the hill.*
tow to pull. *The truck will tow the car to the garage.*
tug to pull hard. *He must tug on the rope to lead the horse to the barn.*

eager *adj.* excitedly or impatiently wanting or expecting something. *We were eager for school to begin that day.*
avid very eager. *The avid fans cheered their team to victory.*
enthusiastic eager; interested. *The class was very enthusiastic about the field trip.*
zealous enthusiastic; eager. *The zealous efforts of the players made us feel we could win.*

easy *adj.* not hard or difficult. *The quiz was easy for me.*

effortless easy; using little effort. *Because the work was so easy, it was an effortless job.*
elementary basic; simple. *The computer instructor showed us the elementary steps for using the computer.*
simple not hard; easy. *The simple problems were the best part of the test we had today.*
antonyms: hard, difficult

echo *v.* to send back a sound. *Our shouts can echo throughout the canyon.*
reverberate to echo back. *Our voices reverberate off the walls of the cave.*
vibrate to resound; echo. *The clanging of the bells would vibrate in our ears.*

edge *n.* border; side. *The cup fell off the edge of the table.*
border side or edge of something. *We crossed the state border at noon.*
boundary a border or limit. *The river is the western boundary of our county.*
brim edge or border. *The cup was filled to the brim.*

enjoy *v.* to get pleasure from. *Did you enjoy the movie last night?*
delight to please greatly. *The clowns will delight the children.*
like to wish for; enjoy. *The children like the new game a lot.*

enough *adj.* as much or as many as needed. *The backpackers had enough food and water for three days.*
adequate enough; sufficient. *The food supply was adequate for a family of four.*
ample as much as is needed; enough. *My ample allowance easily covers lunches and supplies.*
sufficient as much as is needed. *We took sufficient food for the long trip.*

everyday *adj.* ordinary; all right for the usual day or event. *You should wear your everyday clothes to play outside.*
common usual; ordinary. *Having a lot of rain is common in this area.*
familiar common; well-known. *Coloring is a familiar activity for young children.*
ordinary everyday; common. *Today is a very ordinary day.*

example *n.* a sample; model; something that may be imitated. *If you don't under-stand how to do the problems, look at the example.*

case a special condition; example. *The doctor treated a bad case of measles.*

model something to be copied or imitated. *Use the pattern as the model for your drawing.*

sample something to show what the rest are like. *The sample gave us a taste of various French foods.*

eye *v.* to look at or watch. *We wanted to eye the visitors to see if we knew any of them.*

observe to see; notice. *We tried to observe the workers to discover ways to improve production.*

peer at to look closely. *She likes to peer at the people in the cars on the street below.*

view to look at; see. *We can view the craters on the moon with our new telescope.*

watch to look at; observe. *The class will watch the movie about space travel.*

factory *n.* a plant where goods are manufactured. *Much of the work in a factory is done by machines.*

mill a building where goods are made or manufactured. *At the cotton mill they make very fine cotton cloth.*

plant a building and equipment for making something. *The printing plant has huge presses for printing books.*

shop a place where specific work is done. *At the shoe shop they can repair your boots.*

fame *n.* the state of being well-known; respect; recognition. *George Washington was a man of great fame.*

dignity position of honor; rank; title. *The dignity of the office of President is upheld through traditions.*

majesty nobility. *The majesty of the queen impressed all the guests.*

nobility people of noble title. *The nobility ruled the country until the revolution.*

fasten *v.* to join; attach. *We can fasten this lamp to the wall over my desk.*

attach to fasten; fix in place. *Attach the rope to the front of the sled.*

bind to hold together. *We can bind sticks together as a bundle.*

join to put together. *Let's join hands and walk in a circle.*

tie to fasten; bind. *I will tie the packages together with string.*

fear *n.* a feeling of fright or alarm. *A dog shows fear by putting its tail between its legs.*

fright fear; alarm. *The screeching brakes gave us a fright.*

panic fear in many people. *The earthquake caused a panic in our city.*

scare fright. *The loud noises sent a scare through all of us.*

terror great fear; fright. *The sound of thunder caused terror in the child.*

feel *v.* to sense by touch. *Feel how soft this cloth is!*

handle to touch, feel, or use with the hands. *We must handle the stuffed toy to learn how soft it is.*

sense to feel; understand. *She seemed to sense that the dog's bark was a warning.*

touch to put a hand on something. *We wanted to touch the soft pillow.*

few *adj.* not many. *There are few copies of this rare book available.*

scant not enough. *The scant supplies worried the captain of the ship.*

scarce hard to get. *Some coins have become very scarce.*

sparse meager; scant. *The lack of food put everyone on a very sparse diet.*

antonym: many

firm *adj.* hard; solid. *They left the muddy road and walked on firm ground.*

solid hard; firm. *The solid ground turned to mud because of the rain.*

stable firm; steady. *The steel construction made the building very stable.*

steady firm; solid. *He used a steady hand to guide the animal to safety.*

antonym: soft

flavor *n.* a particular taste. *Lemonade can have a sweet or tart flavor.*

tang a strong flavor. *The chili powder gave the stew a zesty tang.*

taste the special flavor of food. *The meat left a strange taste in my mouth.*

flood *n.* water that flows over normally dry land. *The low bridge was underwater for an hour after the flash flood.*
deluge a great flood. *The deluge washed the bridge away.*
downpour a very heavy rain. *The downpour caused flooding in the streets.*

flour *n.* a fine powder of ground grain, usually wheat. *Flour is used in breads.*
bran the covering of grains of wheat, rye, etc. *The cereal contained bran.*
meal anything ground to a powder. *The corn meal was ground to a fine powder.*

flower *n.* the blossom of a plant. *Tulips are flowers that bloom in the spring.*
bloom a blossom; flower. *There was one perfect rose bloom in the vase.*
blossom the flower of a seed plant. *The peach blossom smells beautiful.*
bud a partly opened flower. *The bud will soon open into a lovely flower.*
floret a small flower. *The floret was purple and pink.*

fold *v.* to close or bend parts of something together in order to fit it into a smaller space. *When we take down the flag, we fold it into the shape of a triangle.*
bend to curve; to be crooked. *Bend the paper around the edges of the box.*
crease to make a fold. *She will crease the paper as she wraps the package.*
crinkle to wrinkle. *The paper will crinkle when it is crushed.*

forth *adv.* forward; onward. *From that day forth they were good friends.*
ahead in the front; forward. *We will go ahead with the project.*
forward toward the front. *Come forward and get your prize.*
onward toward the front. *We will move onward to see the monument.*

friend *n.* a person one knows and likes. *Erin is my good friend.*
acquaintance a person one knows but not as a close friend. *Almost every day I made a new acquaintance.*
classmate member of the same class. *Our new classmate studied with us for the test.*
companion a comrade; friend. *Jane and her companion worked and played together.*

comrade a close friend; companion. *The police officer and her comrade directed traffic.*
mate companion; friend. *My mate and I will try to go to a movie.*
antonym: enemy

funny *adj.* causing laughter or amusement. *The joke was funny.*
amusing entertaining; funny. *The author wrote many amusing stories.*
humorous amusing; funny. *I like the humorous stories he tells.*
witty showing wit; clever and amusing. *The witty speaker made the audience laugh.*

gather *v.* to bring or come together. *When clouds gather it often means rain.*
accumulate to gather little by little. *Dust can accumulate under the sofa.*
assemble to gather or bring together. *The students will assemble outside the museum.*
collect to gather together. *The students want to collect aluminum cans for recycling.*

gentle *adj.* light; soft. *The gentle breeze rustled the leaves.*
easy smooth and pleasant. *His quiet, easy way made everyone around him feel relaxed.*
mild not harsh; not severe. *She had a very mild manner.*
soft quiet; gentle; mild. *She has a soft voice.*
antonym: harsh

gigantic *adj.* extremely large. *Elephants and whales are gigantic.*
huge very big; extremely large. *The huge truck was loaded with steel rails.*
stupendous immense; extremely large. *The stupendous mountains were a beautiful sight to see.*

glow *v.* to give off light; to shine. *Fireflies glow in the dark.*
gleam to give off light. *The little lamp will gleam in the darkness.*
glitter to shine with sparkling light. *The beads on the costumes seemed to glitter.*
shine to send out light; glow. *Please shine your flashlight over here.*

twinkle to shine and glitter. *Stars twinkle in the night sky.*

glue *n.* a sticky liquid that hardens to hold things together. *Broken toys can be mended with glue.*
cement something that hardens to hold things together. *Rubber cement is used to hold the pictures in the album.*
paste mixture used to hold things together. *We used white paste to make the paper chains.*

goal *n.* a purpose; aim. *Mark's goal is to play the double bass in a symphony orchestra.*
aim a purpose; goal. *The aim of the exercise is to build up leg muscles.*
objective a goal; aim. *We each wrote an objective for our science project.*
purpose an aim; plan. *The purpose of the game is to find all the numbers.*
target a goal; objective. *Our target was to walk a mile in eight minutes.*

group *n.* a gathering or arrangement of people or objects. *There is a large group of people in the hotel lobby.*
branch a part; division; local office. *That branch of the company is located in Sweden.*
division one part of a whole; group; section. *This division of the company handles the manufacturing of our product.*
section part of a city, region, etc. *The city offices are in this section of town.*

happy *adj.* feeling or showing pleasure; joyful. *The happy man whistled as he worked.*
cheerful happy; joyful. *Kari gave us a cheerful smile.*
contented pleased; satisfied. *The contented cat lay by the fire and purred.*
delighted very glad; very pleased. *I am delighted that you came to visit.*
ecstatic very happy; joyful. *The winner had an ecstatic look on her face.*
glad happy; pleased. *We are glad that you won the prize.*
antonym: sad

harden *v.* to make or become hard. *The ground does harden during the cold weather.*
temper to bring to a proper condition of hardness. *A special process of heating and cooling will temper the steel.*
toughen to make or become tough. *The hard work will toughen our hands and our bodies.*

haul *v.* to pull with force, drag. *We tried to haul the rowboat out of the water.*
lug to drag or pull along. *We must lug the boxes down the stairs.*
pull to move; drag. *We can pull the wagon up the hill.*
tug to pull hard. *He must tug on the rope to lead the horse to the barn.*

heavy *adj.* hard to move because of its weight; not light. *We will need two people to lift this heavy trunk.*
hefty weighty; heavy. *The hefty man easily picked up the big boxes.*
husky big and strong. *The job required a husky person to lift the crates.*
ponderous very heavy. *An elephant is a ponderous animal.*
weighty heavy. *The hasty decisions caused weighty problems for the city.*
antonym: light

hedge *n.* a thick row of bushes planted as a fence or boundary. *A hedge should be trimmed evenly.*
fence a wall put around a yard or field. *The bushes made a fence around the yard.*
wall a structure built around an area. *The plants made a wall of flowers around the patio.*

helpless *adj.* not able to help oneself or others. *We felt helpless to stop the school's litter problem.*
incapable lacking ability. *He is incapable of performing that complicated task.*
incompetent lacking power or ability. *She is incompetent when it comes to flying a helicopter.*
powerless without power; helpless. *The powerless leader was finally removed from office.*
useless of no use. *The old motor is useless.*
antonym: capable

Writing Thesaurus

317

hero *n.* a man or boy admired for his bravery or fine qualities. *Abraham Lincoln is a national hero.* [heroine (female)]
adventurer person who seeks adventure. *The adventurer set out to explore the jungle.*
star a person with exceptional qualities. *The little child was the star of the show.*

high *adj.* tall; far above the ground. *Eagles build nests on high cliffs.*
alpine like high mountains. *The alpine trees rise high into the sky.*
tall having great height. *The tall building could be seen for miles.*
towering very high. *They climbed up the towering mountain.*
antonym: low

highway *n.* a main road. *A highway is usually numbered to simplify maps and road signs.*
boulevard a broad street. *The boulevard was named after a president.*
interstate a highway that connects two or more states. *Hundreds of cars, trucks, and buses use the interstate.*
road a way for cars, trucks, etc. to travel. *The road went from town to the farm in the country.*
thoroughfare a main road; highway. *Route 66 was a main thoroughfare in years past.*

hire *v.* to employ; pay a person for working. *Because business is good, the store can hire three more clerks.*
employ to hire or give work to. *The company does employ many people.*
engage to hire. *We must engage a crew to rake the leaves and mow the lawn.*
antonym: fire

holiday *n.* a day on which a special event is celebrated. *The family went to Grandmother's house for the holiday.*
fiesta a holiday or festival. *The community planned a summer fiesta.*
vacation a time with no school, work, or other duties. *The summer vacation gave us time to swim and play.*

honest *adj.* tending not to lie, cheat, or steal; able to be trusted. *An honest person always tells the truth.*

conscientious taking care to do what is right. *The children were conscientious workers in school.*
honorable showing a sense of what is right. *The honorable man was elected to the city council.*
sincere real; honest. *His sincere efforts showed how much he cared about his work.*
trustworthy reliable; dependable. *The bank employees were trustworthy.*
truthful telling the truth. *The witness gave a truthful account of the accident.*
upstanding honorable. *The upstanding judge was respected by the townspeople.*
antonym: dishonest

hopeless *adj.* having very little chance of working out right. *After darkness fell, they decided the search for the ball was hopeless.*
desperate not caring; without hope. *After the tornado, they made a desperate search for the mailbox.*
despondent having lost hope; discouraged. *The helpers were despondent over the conditions left by the storm.*
discouraged lacking in courage. *The discouraged partners tried to sell the business.*
dismayed greatly troubled. *She was dismayed that she failed to get to school on time.*
antonym: hopeful

hotel *n.* a place that provides guests with lodging, meals, and other services. *Our grandparents stayed in a hotel near the beach.*
inn a place where travelers can get food and rooms. *The inn was built near a major highway.*
lodge a place to live in. *The ski lodge was located in Aspen, Colorado.*
resort a place people go to vacation. *The resort by the ocean had water sports and many other things to do.*

however *conj.* nevertheless. *I've never tasted eggplant before; however, it looks delicious.*
nevertheless however; nonetheless. *We knew what to do; nevertheless, we waited.*
yet nevertheless; however. *The game was well played, yet it would have been better if we had won.*

huge *adj.* very large. *A skyscraper is a huge building.*
enormous extremely large. *The enormous hippopotamus wandered down to the river.*
immense very large; huge. *The immense shopping center was the largest in the United States.*
tremendous very large; enormous. *The tremendous whale slowly swam in front of the ship.*
antonyms: tiny, little, small

idea *n.* a thought; a plan. *Bringing plants to decorate the room was Kristin's idea.*
impression idea; notion. *My impression of him changed when I saw how hard he worked.*
inspiration brilliant idea. *My inspiration for the design came from the patterns in the wallpaper.*
notion idea or understanding. *I don't think he has any notion of what I said.*
thought idea; what one thinks. *My thought on the topic was written in my report.*
view an idea; picture. *The outline will give you a general view of the story.*

illness *n.* poor health; a disease. *Craig went home from school because of illness.*
ailment sickness; illness. *The ailment caused her to be very tired.*
malady a disease or deep-seated illness. *Cancer is a very serious malady.*
sickness an illness. *The fever was caused by the sickness.*

invite *v.* to ask a person to go somewhere or do something. *My mother will invite my friend to lunch.*
ask to invite. *We must ask everyone to come to the school party.*
request to ask. *She did request that we go to hear the speech on safety.*

island *n.* a piece of land with water all around it. *People must take a boat or an airplane to get to an island.*
cay a low island; reef. *The cay was to the north of our hotel.*
isle a small island. *Only the lighthouse was left on the isle.*

joyful *adj.* full of joy. *The first and last days of school are always joyful.*
enjoyable giving joy. *We had a very enjoyable day at the zoo.*
pleasurable pleasant; enjoyable. *The trip was a pleasurable time for all of us.*

judge *n.* one who presides over a court of law by hearing cases and making decisions. *A judge must be completely fair.*
justice of the peace a local official who handles small cases and other minor duties. *The justice of the peace performed the wedding ceremony.*
magistrate a judge in a court. *The court magistrate asked the jury to give its verdict.*

jumble *v.* to mix up. *We had to jumble the letters of the word for the puzzle.*
muddle to make a mess of. *He did muddle his speech because he lost his notes.*
snarl to tangle. *As it ran around the room, the cat managed to snarl the yarn.*
tangle to twist together. *The rope might tangle around the post.*

jungle *n.* wild land near the equator with thickly grown tropical plants. *Parrots and monkeys live in a jungle.*
bush wild, unsettled land. *The explorers roamed the bush of Australia.*
chaparral an area of thick shrubs and small trees. *Animals live in the chaparral of the southwestern United States.*

keep *v.* to store; put away; save. I *keep all my old homework.*
hold to keep. *Please hold my book while I play on the slide.*
retain to keep; continue to have or hold. *I will retain the receipts for my income tax records.*
save to store up. *I will save the tickets to use next week.*
store to put away; save. *Squirrels store nuts for the winter.*

kettle *n.* a pot used for heating liquids. *Put the kettle on the stove.*
boiler large container. *The water was heated in the boiler.*
caldron a large kettle. *We made soup in the old, black caldron.*

kind *adj.* friendly; thoughtful of others. *Everyone likes kind people.*
friendly like a friend. *The friendly salesperson helped us with our problem.*
good-hearted caring; generous. *The good-hearted neighbor helped everyone.*
gracious kindly; pleasant. *The gracious hostess tried to make sure that her guests had a good time.*
hospitable kind and friendly. *The town was hospitable to newcomers.*
thoughtful considerate; kind. *The mayor was always thoughtful of our wishes.*
antonyms: cruel, mean

knock *v.* to strike with the fist or with a hard object. *I did knock on the door but no one answered.*
hit to strike; knock. *The stick hit the ground with great force.*
punch to hit with the fist. *He continued to punch the bag until it ripped.*
slap to strike with an open hand. *She thought she had to slap the horse to make it move.*

know *v.* to have the facts about; understand. *Do you know how hail is formed?*
comprehend to understand the meaning of. *I can comprehend that scientific term.*
recognize to know again. *I did recognize that the story was similar to one I already knew.*
understand to get the meaning of. *I understand how to bake chicken pie.*

lady *n.* a polite term for a woman. *We knew by her manners that she was a real lady.*
female woman; girl. *Is the new student a female or a male?*
woman a grown female person. *Do you know the woman in the blue gown?*

laugh *v.* to make sounds with the voice that show amusement. *Everyone seemed to laugh at the funny movie.*

giggle to give high-pitched laughs. *The little children tried not to giggle at the cartoons.*
snicker to make a sly or silly laugh. *The teens liked to snicker at the old movie.*

lead *v.* to direct or show the way. *She will lead the hikers home.*
direct to tell or show the way. *Please direct me to the registration desk.*
guide to direct; lead. *The ranger did guide the tourists through the forest preserve.*
show to guide; direct. *I will show you the way to the museum.*

leader *n.* one who leads. *The Scout troop needs a new leader.*
captain head of a group; chief; leader. *John is the captain of the football team.*
chief a leader; a head of a tribe or group. *The chief of the tribe wore a headdress of feathers and beads.*
director person who manages or directs. *The director told the actors where to stand.*
guide person who leads or directs. *The guide showed us the way to the campsite.*
manager a person who manages. *Have you met the new store manager?*
master one who has power over others. *The master of the house made the rules.*

learner *n.* one who learns; student. *A good learner listens carefully.*
pupil a person who is learning. *He is the new pupil in the dance class.*
scholar a person in school; a learner. *The scholar studies her lessons every day.*
student a person who studies. *Which student is doing the spelling assignment?*
trainee a person who is being trained. *She is a trainee at the hospital.*

least *adj.* smallest in size or amount. *Which game costs the least money?*
lowest not tall; not high. *This is the lowest score on the test.*
slightest smallest of its kind. *The slightest one is four feet tall.*
smallest littler than others. *This is the smallest doll I have ever seen.*
antonym: most

lighten *v.* to make brighter; to add light to. *The new paint does lighten the room.*
brighten to lighten; make or become brighter. *The lamp will brighten the living room.*

illuminate to light up; make bright. *The lights seem to illuminate the sky.*
antonym: darken

listen *v.* to pay attention; try to hear. *The audience did listen closely to the speaker.*
eavesdrop to listen secretly. *You can eavesdrop by putting your ear against the wall.*
hear to listen; to take in sounds. *We could hear everything that she said.*
heed to give attention to. *We must heed the advice we were given.*

lose *v.* to be unable to find; misplace. *Put the key in your pocket so you won't lose it.*
mislay to put away and forget where. *Where did you mislay your science book?*
misplace to put in the wrong place. *I always seem to misplace my gloves.*
antonym: find

major *adj.* larger; greater; primary. *We spent the major part of the day at the beach.*
greater better; larger. *The greater part of the afternoon was devoted to studying.*
larger bigger; greater. *The larger section of the office was used for the accounting division.*
superior better; greater. *This clothing is of superior quality.*

mark *v.* to make a visible sign on or by. *Mark the wrong answers with an "X."*
initial to mark or sign with initials. *Each member of the family needed to initial the document.*
inscribe to mark with letters, words, etc. *The jeweler will inscribe her initials on the bracelet.*
stamp to mark with some tool. *She needed to stamp the date on each letter.*

market *n.* a place where things can be bought and sold. *A supermarket is a large, modern market.*
emporium a large store selling many kinds of things. *At the emporium you can buy clothes, shoes, and things for the home.*
shop a place where things are sold. *The dress shop had an assortment of clothes to sell.*

store a place where things are kept for sale. *The store was located near my house.*

master *v.* to become skilled in. *It takes time and practice to master a foreign language.*
conquer to overcome; to get the better of. *If we want to conquer a difficult task, first divide it into small parts.*
learn to gain skill or knowledge. *We will learn about Africa in Social Studies.*

middle *n.* the point or part located at the same distance from each side or end; center. *Your nose is in the middle of your face.*
center the middle point. *The table is in the center of the room.*
midst the center. *The child is in the midst of the group.*

moment *n.* an instant; a very brief period. *I saw him for a moment, but lost sight of him in the crowd.*
instant a moment in time. *The horse stopped for an instant and then raced away.*
second instant; moment. *He paused for a second before turning the key.*

mount *v.* to climb onto; to get up on. *The rider wants to mount his horse and gallop away.*
ascend to go up. *The group can ascend the steps to the platform.*
climb to go up; ascend. *We tried to climb to the top of the tower.*
vault to leap or jump. *She could vault over the hedge.*

movement *n.* action; change in position or location. *The children watched the slow movement of the snail across the sidewalk.*
action movement; way of moving. *She enjoys the action of a hockey game.*
gesture movement of the body to give an idea. *Waving her hand was a gesture to say she did not want to be disturbed.*

mumble *v.* to speak unclearly so that you are hard to understand. *If you mumble, no one will understand you.*
murmur to say softly. *We told her not to murmur her thanks, so everyone can hear her.*
mutter to speak unclearly. *He always seems to mutter when he gets tired.*
whisper to speak softly. *I like to whisper secrets to my closest friend.*

near *adv.* not far away in time or distance. *The train drew near.*

alongside by the side of. *The big car pulled up and parked alongside our car.*

closely near; next to. *The books are stacked closely together.*

antonym: far

nearby *adj.* not far off. *They live in a nearby town.*

adjacent near or close. *The new store will be on the adjacent lot.*

adjoining next to; bordering. *The adjoining lakes were connected by a stream.*

close near; together. *The buildings are very close to each other.*

newspaper *n.* a printed paper that contains news, advertisements, cartoons, etc. *My grandfather likes to work the crossword puzzles in the newspaper.*

daily a newspaper printed every day. *The article appeared in the daily.*

paper a newspaper. *Have you seen the comics in today's paper?*

obey *v.* to follow the orders of. *Children are taught to obey their parents.*

comply to follow a request. *I will comply with the captain's orders.*

conform to follow a law or rule. *She didn't like to conform to the rules of the tennis club.*

observe to keep; follow. *We always try to observe the rules about being quiet in the library.*

antonym: disobey

often *adv.* many times; frequently. *We often see our relatives during the holidays.*

frequently often; repeatedly. *We frequently shop at the grocery store in our neighborhood.*

recurrently repeatedly. *He had to cough recurrently.*

repeatedly more than once. *She repeatedly asked for news of her lost puppy.*

owner *n.* one who owns or possesses something. *Who is the owner of this plaid jacket?*

landlord person who owns a building. *We paid the rent to the landlord.*

partner one of a group who owns a company. *Each partner invested a lot of money in the new business.*

proprietor owner. *The proprietor of the store was very helpful to every customer.*

package *n.* a wrapped box; parcel. *How much will it cost to mail this package?*

bundle things tied or wrapped together; package. *The bundle of gifts contained many games and toys.*

parcel a package. *The driver delivered the parcel this morning.*

paper *n.* a written article; a report. *The teacher asked us to write a paper about the moon.*

article a written report; composition. *The article contained factual information about air pollution.*

document written information; report. *The lawyer found the document she wanted to use in court.*

report a written account of something. *The report was prepared by a committee.*

pass *v.* to hand over; give; send. *Please pass the salad.*

deliver to hand over; give out. *The postal carrier will deliver the mail in the morning.*

hand to pass; give. *Please hand me the jar of jam.*

transfer to move from one place to another; to hand over. *We had to transfer the order to the New York office.*

past *adj.* gone by; previous. *This past month we had three inches of rain.*

earlier previous; coming before. *The earlier report said the president would arrive on Tuesday.*

previous coming before; earlier. *The previous lesson showed us how to multiply.*

322

prior earlier; coming before. *The job did not require prior experience.*

payment *n.* an amount of money paid. *Most people who rent a house or apartment make a monthly payment to the landlord.*
compensation an amount paid. *We were given compensation for our work.*
installment part of a payment. *The loan was to be paid back in twelve monthly installments.*
settlement payment. *The court settlement helped her pay the legal fees.*

perfect *adj.* having no flaws or errors; exactly right. *Charlene turned in a perfect paper in science.*
flawless perfect; without flaw. *The flawless diamond was very valuable.*
ideal perfect; having no flaws. *This is an ideal day to go to the beach.*
impeccable perfect; faultless. *The group had impeccable manners.*

piece *n.* a part; a segment. *Would you like a piece of my orange?*
fragment a piece broken off. *We found a fragment of the broken dish near the sink.*
part a piece; less than the whole. *The best part of the dinner was the dessert.*
portion a part; share. *One portion of the work was already completed.*
segment piece or part of a whole. *She picked the shortest segment of the straw.*

placement *n.* location; arrangement. *The placement of the flowers added the perfect touch to the dinner table.*
arrangement items in proper order. *The arrangement of pictures told the story of the Little Red Hen.*
location place; position. *The store's location was ideal because it was on a corner of a busy street.*

playful *adj.* full of fun and enjoyment. *The baby was playful in his bath.*
frisky lively; playful. *The frisky puppy ran all around the yard.*
frivolous silly; full of fun. *Her frivolous behavior made us laugh.*
mischievous teasing; full of fun. *The mischievous kitten unraveled the yarn.*

port *n.* a town with a harbor where ships may dock. *Boston is an Atlantic port.*
dock platform built over water. *The ship unloaded at the dock.*
harbor a place to dock ships and boats. *The steamship docked at the harbor.*
wharf a dock; platform built out from shore. *The huge ship was tied at the wharf.*

powder *n.* a substance made of fine grains. *It's easy to grind chalk into a powder.*
dust fine, dry earth. *The dust settled all over the road.*
grit fine bits of sand or gravel. *The boat was covered with grit.*
sand tiny bits of stone in large amounts, found in the deserts and on shores along oceans, lakes, and rivers. *This beach has smooth sand.*

power *n.* great strength, force, or control. *The police have power to enforce the law.*
control power to direct. *The police have control over the traffic.*
force power; strength. *The force of the wind blew the door open.*
strength power; force. *He had the strength of a giant.*

powerful *adj.* having great power; strong. *The king was a powerful leader.*
able having power, skill, or talent. *He is an able warrior.*
forceful having much force or strength. *The forceful leader told everyone what to do.*
mighty showing strength. *The mighty ruler rode off to battle.*
strong having much force or power. *The strong woman lifted weights every day.*
antonym: powerless

powerless *adj.* having no strength or power; helpless. *The farmers were powerless against the drought.*
helpless not able to help oneself. *The helpless child needed his parents.*
sickly not strong. *A sickly person should not go hiking in the mountains.*
unable not able. *I would like to help you, but I am unable.*
antonym: powerful

Writing Thesaurus

323

preschool *n.* a place of learning before elementary school. *Children aged three to five may attend preschool.*

day-care center a place where young children are cared for while parents work. *Our community has a new day-care center.*

nursery school a place for children under the age of five. *The nursery school helps the young children learn about numbers and letters.*

quake *v.* to vibrate or shake. *The ground did quake beneath us during the mild earthquake.*

quaver tremble; shake. *The old house seemed to quaver as the strong winds blew.*

shake to move quickly. *Please shake the dirt off your boots.*

tremble to shake from fear, cold, etc. *We started to tremble when we heard the storm was near.*

vibrate to move rapidly. *The strings of the violin vibrate as he plays.*

quarrel *v.* to fight; to disagree, using angry words. *They always quarrel about whose turn it is to bat.*

argue to give reasons for and against an issue. *The students argued about the playground rules.*

bicker to quarrel. *The children started to bicker over whose turn was next.*

brawl to quarrel in a loud manner. *Two players started to brawl during the hockey game.*

wrangle to argue or quarrel. *The group seemed to wrangle over every topic that was brought up at the meeting.*

queen *n.* a female ruler. *The queen issued a proclamation.*

czarina a Russian empress. *The czarina wore beautiful clothes.*

empress a woman who rules an empire. *The empress was admired by everyone.*

question *n.* a problem. *The litter question will be discussed tonight.*

issue a problem; a point or topic. *The tax issue was always hotly debated.*

problem a difficult question. *The new economic problem troubled the country.*

topic subject that people write or talk about. *The topic of my report is health.*

antonym: answer

quick *adj.* fast; swift. *The rabbit made a quick leap into the bushes.*

fast moving with speed; quick. *The fast runner took the lead and won the race.*

rapid fast; quick. *They keep up a rapid pace on the assembly line.*

speedy fast; rapid; quick. *The speedy messenger delivered the package on time.*

swift very fast; rapid. *He gave a swift response to every test question.*

antonym: slow

quit *v.* to stop. *We'll quit raking leaves when it gets dark.*

cease to stop; put to an end. *The noise will cease when the speaker begins.*

stop to halt; to keep from doing something. *We couldn't stop them from winning.*

quiz *n.* a brief test. *I missed only two questions on the science quiz.*

checkup an examination; inspection. *I saw my doctor for a checkup yesterday.*

examination a test; set of questions. *We were given an examination by our teacher.*

test an examination, often consisting of a series of questions or problems. *There were twenty items on the test.*

quote *v.* to repeat or refer to a passage from a story or poem. *Justin wanted to quote a line from the poem in his essay.*

recite to say from memory. *We had to choose a poem to recite in class.*

repeat to say again. *Please repeat what you said about using the dictionary.*

range *v.* to extend or vary within certain limits. *The stories in this book range from sad to funny.*

encompass to include; contain. *The article will encompass a lot of information.*

span to extend. *The new bridge will span the rocky canyon.*

vary to change; be different. *The colors may vary in shades from light to dark.*

rare *adj.* not often found or seen. *My uncle saves rare postage stamps.*

scarce rare; hard to get. *Some jungle animals have become very scarce.*

324

uncommon rare; unusual. *Hummingbirds are uncommon in this state.*

unusual not common; rare. *This unusual flower only grows in the desert.*

rattle *v.* to make a number of short, sharp sounds. *The windows rattle when the wind blows.*

bang to make a loud noise. *The wind caused the shutters to bang against the house.*

clang to make a loud, harsh sound. *The bells began to clang as the wind blew.*

clatter to make a loud noise. *The dishes clatter as we stack them in the kitchen sink.*

reader *n.* a person who reads. *The teacher chose Kathy to be the reader of our lunchtime story this week.*

bookworm a person who loves to read. *Karl is a bookworm; he reads all the time.*

browser a person who looks through materials. *Robert is only a browser; he seldom reads a whole book.*

ready *adj.* prepared. *We are ready for school.*

available able to be used. *She is available to start work tomorrow.*

prepared ready. *The prepared lessons were put on tape.*

reason *n.* a cause or explanation. *Your parents will write the reason for your absence.*

cause reason for action. *What was the cause of the accident?*

explanation something that explains. *He didn't give an explanation for his absence.*

motive reason; thought or feeling. *My motive for the trip was to hike farther than any of my friends had.*

purpose reason for which something is done. *The major purpose of the lesson was to learn how to divide.*

rebuild *v.* to build again. *They are planning to rebuild the old school.*

reconstruct to construct again. *The townspeople wanted to reconstruct the library after the fire.*

restore to put back; establish again. *My uncle likes to restore old furniture.*

record *n.* an account of facts or events. *The secretary keeps the record of the club's activities.*

diary a personal record of daily events. *Her diary told about the events of her life.*

memo a short written statement. *The memo announced a special company picnic.*

remain *v.* to continue without change; stay. *The nurse reported that the patient's condition did remain good.*

continued to stay; remain. *The weather will continue to be sunny and nice.*

linger to stay on. *He could linger for hours in the library.*

loiter to linger. *We liked to loiter along the way and to look in the store windows.*

stay to continue; remain. *She decided to stay near the child until he fell asleep.*

report *v.* to give an account or statement. *The president of the company did report that sales had increased.*

disclose to tell; to make known. *I will never disclose my friend's secret.*

reveal to make known. *I will reveal my findings to the press next week.*

tell to say; put in words. *The travel agent will tell us about France and Italy.*

restful *adj.* offering rest, peace, or quiet. *My aunt finds sewing restful after a busy day.*

calm quiet; peaceful; motionless. *There wasn't even a breeze on that calm evening.*

cozy warm; comfortable. *The cozy cottage was difficult to leave.*

peaceful calm; quiet. *Early morning hours are peaceful.*

quiet stillness; peace. *The quiet library was a good place to study.*

snug warm; comfortable. *I felt snug in a warm coat.*

tranquil peaceful; quiet; calm. *The tranquil night air was very relaxing.*

antonym: restless

restless *adj.* impatient; unable to be still. *The small children grew restless after the long delay.*

agitated restless; impatient. *The agitated crowd began to yell at the speaker.*

impatient not patient; restless. *We became impatient while waiting in line.*

nervous upset; excited. *A nervous person tends to fidget a lot.*

uneasy restless; disturbed. *The tornado warnings gave us an uneasy feeling.*

antonym: restful

325

return *v.* to come or go back. *We will return after the game is over.*

reappear to appear again. *After the clouds pass, the stars will reappear in the night sky.*

recur to occur again. *The problem will recur if we don't make any changes.*

review *v.* to study again; go over. *She did review the chapter before she took the test.*

critique to review critically. *He had to critique the play and analyze the plot.*

examine to look closely at. *I will examine all of the information before I decide what to do.*

study to try to learn. *I will study my spelling words tonight.*

survey to examine; look over. *She will survey the situation before she decides what to do.*

rigid *adj.* very stiff; not able to be bent. *A cast holds a broken arm in a rigid position so it can heal.*

firm solid; hard. *The sailors were glad to set foot on firm ground.*

hard not soft; firm. *We couldn't pound the stakes into the hard ground.*

stiff rigid; not able to bend. *The stiff paper could not be bent around the package.*

tense stiff; stretched tight. *The tent was held up by the tense ropes.*

rise *n.* an increase in height or amount. *The store announced a rise in prices.*

boost an increase in price, amount, etc. *The boost in prices made food cost more this year.*

growth an increase; amount grown. *This year's growth has made the company very successful.*

raise an increase in amount. *The workers were given a yearly raise in pay.*

swell an increase in amount. *The swell of shoppers made the store owners happy.*

role *n.* a part or character in a play. *Who will play the role of Peter Pan?*

character a person or animal in a book, play, etc. *The main character was a big monster from outer space.*

impersonation a representation. *The woman gave an impersonation of a movie star.*

part a role; character in a play. *The students will try out for each part in the school play.*

roll *v.* to move by turning over and over. *The ball started to roll down the hill.*

revolve to move in a circle. *The planets revolve around the sun.*

rotate to turn about a center. *Earth does rotate on its axis.*

turn to rotate; move around. *The wheels will turn as the horse pulls the wagon.*

whirl to spin; turn round and round. *The dancers whirl around the stage.*

rough *adj.* not smooth or even. *The car bounced and rattled over the rough road.*

bumpy full of bumps. *We took a bumpy ride in an old wagon.*

rocky bumpy; full of rocks. *The car made lots of noise as it bounced over the rocky mountain road.*

uneven not level or flat. *The uneven ground made it hard to walk.*

royal *adj.* having to do with kings and queens. *The king and queen live in a royal palace.*

regal belonging to royalty. *The regal party was held in the palace of the king.*

sovereign having the power of a ruler. *The queen was the sovereign leader of the British Commonwealth.*

rule *n.* a law; regulation. *Always obey each and every school safety rule.*

fundamental a basic principle. *You can't learn a sport one fundamental at a time.*

law a rule or regulation made by a state, country, etc. *Each law was made by the state government.*

principle a basic law or assumption. *It is a scientific principle that what goes up must come down.*

regulation rule; law. *This regulation controls flights to all airports.*

sadness *n.* sorrow; grief. *Tears can be an expression of sadness.*

grief sadness; sorrow. *His grief made him a very quiet person.*

melancholy sadness; low spirits. *Her melancholy was caused by several painful events.*

sorrow grief; sadness. *Her sorrow was caused by the loss of her pet.*

unhappiness sorrow; sadness. *His illness caused his family much unhappiness.*
antonym: happiness

safe *adj.* free from risk or harm. *This sidewalk is a safe place to walk.*
armored protected with armor. *An armored car is a safe way to transport money.*
protected guarded; safe. *He led a very protected life.*
secure safe. *They built a secure fence all around the farm.*

sample *n.* a part that shows what the rest are like. *The store gave away a free sample of the new soap.*
example one thing that shows what others are like. *He used Dallas as an example of a Texas city.*
specimen one of a group used to show what others are like. *Janet collected a new rock specimen from her world travels.*

scale *v.* to climb up or over. *The climbers used ropes to scale the cliff.*
climb to go up; ascend. *We tried to climb to the top of the tower.*
mount to climb onto; to get up on. *The rider wanted to mount his horse and gallop away.*
vault to leap or jump. *She could vault over the hedge.*

scare *v.* to frighten. *The sudden loud noise did scare me.*
alarm to frighten; fill with fear. *The loud whistle and siren seemed to alarm everyone.*
frighten to scare; fill with fright. *The thunder did frighten us.*
startle to frighten suddenly. *He made a loud noise to startle the birds out of the tree.*

scratch *v.* to cut or scrape a surface. *You can tell that a diamond is genuine if it can scratch glass.*
claw to scratch or pull apart. *The cat will claw the chair until the stuffing comes out.*
scrape to scratch the surface of. *The basketball player did scrape his knee when he fell on the basketball court.*

season *v.* to improve the taste. *The chef will season the soup with herbs.*
flavor to season. *The spices flavor the pot of stew.*

salt to sprinkle with salt. *He always seems to salt his food more than anyone else does.*
spice to season; add spice. *She decided to spice the pie with nutmeg and cloves.*

seller *n.* a person who sells; a vendor. *The flower seller had a stand on the street corner.*
merchant a person who buys and sells. *The merchant in the shopping center is having a special sale.*
vendor a seller; peddler. *The vendor services the candy machines once a week.*

serve *v.* to help others by performing a task. *Sarah will serve as club treasurer.*
administer to be helpful; contribute. *Their job is to administer to the elderly.*
help to do what is needed. *I can help you fix up the old house.*
perform to do. *She did perform many duties as an officer of the company.*

settle *v.* to establish residence. *Their family did settle in California years ago.*
locate to establish in a place. *She will locate her business near San Francisco.*
place to put. *We will place the sign near the busy intersection.*
reside to occupy a home or place. *The decision to reside at this address was made years ago.*

share *n.* a part; a portion. *Todd always does his share of work.*
allotment a part; share. *The largest allotment was for food and housing.*
part a share. *We only wanted the part of the reward that belonged to us.*
portion a share; part. *A portion of time at the end of the day is set aside for storytime and cleanup.*

shipment *n.* the goods sent or delivered to a certain place. *The store received a clothing shipment from the manufacturer.*
cargo the freight carried on a ship or other vehicle. *The barge carried a cargo of lumber to the mill.*
freight goods carried by plane, truck, ship, or train. *The dockworker sent the freight by truck.*
load something that is carried. *The load was too heavy for the small car.*

shower *n.* a short fall of rain. *During the afternoon there was a thunder shower.*

cloudburst a sudden rain; violent rainstorm. *We were caught in the cloudburst and got very wet.*

downpour a very heavy rain. *The downpour started while we were at a picnic.*

rain water falling from the clouds in drops. *The rain came down all morning.*

torrent an outpouring. *A torrent of rain caused the river to flood the whole valley.*

shy *adj.* reserved; quiet. *After Josh made friends at his new school, he was no longer shy.*

bashful reserved; shy; easily embarrassed. *As a bashful child, she did not like to be with groups of people.*

quiet peaceful; calm. *Alice spent a quiet afternoon reading.*

reserved quiet; keeping to oneself. *The reserved child seldom spoke to anyone in his class at school.*

unsociable reserved; bashful. *Ann was an unsociable child and often kept away from other people.*

simple *adj.* easy to understand. *The simple questions did not take long to answer.*

easy not hard to do. *The science experiment was easy.*

effortless requiring little effort. *Typing is an effortless task for him.*

elementary simple; easy to learn first. *When learning a new sport, begin with the elementary principles.*

singer *n.* one who sings. *The singer joined a choir.*

artist one skilled in the performance of an art. *The opera singer was a talented artist.*

crooner a person who sings in a soft, sentimental style. *Crooners were popular in the forties.*

songster a singer. *The songster sang everyone's favorite songs.*

vocalist a singer. *The vocalist had an excellent soprano voice.*

single *adj.* one alone; only one. *A single orange was left in the box.*

lone alone; single. *A lone cloud floated in the blue sky.*

one a single unit. *One apple fell from the tree.*

only single; sole. *Rose was the only child to win two races.*

sole single; only one. *The pilot was the sole survivor of the plane crash.*

skill *n.* the ability to do something well as a result of practice. *His skill in playing the violin may someday make him famous.*

ability skill; power to do something. *She has unusual ability in mathematics.*

knowledge ability; what one knows. *His knowledge of World War II was outstanding.*

talent a natural ability. *John had a special talent for building birdhouses.*

slight *adj.* not big; small; slender. *Although it looks sunny, there is a slight chance of rain later today.*

delicate thin; of fine quality. *The blouse was trimmed with a delicate lace collar.*

faint weak. *The faint colors hardly showed on the dark paper.*

little not big; small. *The little problems could easily be solved.*

slim slender; small. *We had a slim chance of winning the game.*

small not large; little. *The picture had a small, decorated frame.*

tender not strong; delicate. *The tender flowers were hurt by the heavy rain.*

smart *adj.* intelligent; clever; quick in mind. *A smart dog can learn many tricks.*

bright clever; quick-witted. *The bright girl was the leader of the debate team.*

brilliant having great ability or skill. *The brilliant boy won a scholarship to an engineering school.*

clever bright; brilliant; quick-witted. *The clever student solved the math problem.*

intelligent having intelligence. *The intelligent animals knew when it was feeding time.*

resourceful quick-witted; able to think of ways to do things. *The resourceful team quickly scored the points they needed to win the football game.*

smell *n.* an odor; a scent. *The smell of orange blossoms filled the air.*

fragrance pleasant odor or smell. *The new fragrance smelled like fresh flowers.*

odor a smell; scent. *The odor from the bouquet of flowers made the whole room smell good.*

perfume a sweet smell. *The perfume of the roses filled the air.*
scent an odor; a smell. *The dogs followed the scent of the wolf.*

snuggle *v.* to lie or press together; cuddle. *The puppies need to snuggle close to their mother to keep warm.*
cuddle to lie closely. *The kittens like to cuddle next to each other in the blanket.*
curl up to roll up; draw up. *He wanted to curl up in his favorite chair with a blanket and a good book.*
nestle to snuggle cozily or comfortably. *She will nestle her head in the pillow.*

soar *v.* to rise or fly high; glide. *Eagles soar gracefully in the sky.*
fly to move through the air. *The planes fly high in the sky above the clouds.*
glide to move along smoothly. *The birds glide across the sky.*
sail to move smoothly. *The kite did sail high above the trees.*

soften *v.* to make or become soft. *Ice cream will soften in the heat.*
dissolve to change to a liquid. *Sugar will dissolve when mixed with water.*
melt to warm to turn into liquid. *We will melt the butter to use in the recipe.*

son *n.* a male child. *The mother took her son to a baseball game.*
boy a male child. *The boy was ten years old today.*
child a young boy or girl. *The child is the son of Mrs. James.*
descendant offspring; person born of a certain group. *He thought he was a descendant of King Henry VIII.*
offspring the young of a person or animal. *John is the only offspring of Mr. and Mrs. Smith.*
antonym: daughter

sore *adj.* painful; tender when touched. *His foot was sore after he stubbed his toe.*
aching dull, continuously painful. *The aching arm was put in a sling.*
painful full of pain; hurting. *The painful cut was bandaged by the nurse.*
tender painful; sensitive. *The bump on my arm was tender to the touch.*

sort *v.* to separate things into groups. *The baby can sort the blocks into two piles by color.*
arrange to put in order. *We can arrange the books by content.*
assort to arrange by kinds. *We tried to assort the magazines in alphabetical order.*
classify to arrange in groups or classes. *The team decided to classify the papers according to the student's last name.*

spare *adj.* extra. *Every automobile should have a spare tire.*
additional extra; more. *We can get additional tickets if we need them.*
extra additional; beyond what is needed. *The extra food makes another meal.*
reserve extra; kept back. *The reserve stock will be sold at the annual meeting.*
supplementary additional. *The supplementary books had more sports stories.*

spark *n.* a brief, bright flash of light. *We saw the spark of a firefly in the night.*
beam a ray of light. *The beam from the flashlight was seen across the road.*
flicker an unsteady light. *The flicker of the lamp was not enough light to cook by.*
gleam a beam of light. *The gleam of the spotlight was seen for miles.*
ray a beam of light. *The ray of light shone through the trees.*

speak *v.* to talk; to say words. *Speak clearly so that we can understand you.*
pronounce to speak; to make sounds. *I will pronounce each spelling word for you.*
state to express; to tell. *He will state the conditions of the agreement.*
talk to speak; use words to give ideas or feelings. *I often talk about safety.*
utter to speak; make known. *She meant to utter her opinion loudly so that everyone could hear.*

speaker *n.* a person who speaks or delivers public speeches. *The speaker at tonight's meeting will discuss the election.*
lecturer person who lectures. *The lecturer spoke to the group on the subjects of health and fitness.*
spokesperson person who speaks for others. *The group elected her as the spokesperson.*

Writing Thesaurus

329

speed *n.* swiftness; quickness. *An antelope has great speed.*

haste a hurry; trying to be fast. *He did everything in haste.*

hurry rushed movement or action. *She was in a hurry to get to the airport.*

rush a hurry. *The rush of the work schedule made everyone tired.*

spill *v.* to run out; to flow over. *He tried not to spill juice on the tablecloth.*

flow to pour out. *The water started to flow over the riverbanks.*

pour to flow steadily. *The water will pour out of the broken pipe.*

run to flow. *Water will run through the streets when it rains hard.*

stream to flow; pour out. *The light seemed to stream down from the sky.*

spoil *v.* to ruin; damage; destroy. *The stain will spoil your shirt if you don't wash it out quickly.*

damage to ruin; spoil. *The cold weather can damage the fruit.*

destroy to break into pieces. *The wind might destroy the old, wooden fence.*

ruin to spoil; destroy. *The spilled paint will ruin the carpet.*

smash to destroy; ruin. *The car did smash the bicycle that was left in the driveway.*

squeal *v.* to make a sharp, high-pitched cry. *The baby did squeal with delight.*

cheep to make a little, sharp sound. *We heard the baby birds cheep in the nest.*

cry to make an animal noise. *The wolf seemed to cry at the moon in the night sky.*

peep to make a sound like a chirp. *We heard the little chick peep for its mother.*

stillness *n.* quiet; silence. *After the city noise, the stillness of the country was a relief.*

hush silence; quiet. *A hush in the room made us wonder what was wrong.*

quiet state of rest. *The quiet of the night was perfect for sleeping.*

silence an absence of noise. *The teacher asked for silence while we read the directions for the activity.*

strange *adj.* unusual; odd. *We were startled by the strange noise.*

bizarre odd or queer in appearance. *The bizarre picture had very unusual colors.*

extraordinary very unusual; strange. *The extraordinary size of the elephants made us stop and stare.*

fantastic unusual; odd. *The fantastic shadows were caused by the huge lights.*

student *n.* a person who studies or goes to school. *Kia is a student at the new high school.*

pupil a person who goes to school. *Each pupil in the class is learning about the Civil War.*

scholar a very well-educated person. *Do you know that famous scholar?*

schoolchild a boy or girl attending school. *One schoolchild will receive an award for perfect attendance.*

surprise *v.* to cause to feel wonder or delight; to astonish. *They wanted to surprise us by singing the song they had written.*

amaze to surprise. *It did amaze me to see so many people at the parade.*

astonish to amaze; surprise. *The magic trick will astonish all of us.*

astound to surprise. *The news of winning the prize did astound all of us.*

shock to surprise; amaze. *It will shock us to hear we had won the contest.*

startle to surprise suddenly. *The loud noise certainly did startle us.*

taste *v.* to find or test the flavor of something. *Taste the sauce to see if it needs more garlic.*

sample to take part of. *We tried to sample the various foods to see what we liked best.*

savor to enjoy the taste or smell. *We did savor the spicy flavor of the chili.*

try to test. *Please try the soup to see if it has enough seasoning.*

team *n.* a group of people working together. *We hired a team of lawyers.*

crew a group working together. *The flight crew handled the passengers on the plane.*

gang a group of people working together. *The road gang was busy repairing the holes in the road.*

workers people who work. *The farm workers were hired to plant corn.*

tear *v.* to pull apart or into pieces. *Be careful not to tear the letter as you open the envelope.*
fray to become worn. *This cloth might fray along the edges.*
rip to tear apart. *I hurried to rip open the package to see what was inside.*
shred to tear or cut into pieces. *We shred the paper and make decorations out of it.*

term *n.* a period of time. *The winter school term seems long because there aren't many holidays.*
interval space in time. *We were busy during the interval between noon and three o'clock.*
period a portion of time. *Several battles were fought during the period of British rule.*
time a span for a certain activity. *The time was spent working on our science projects.*

thankless *adj.* not showing appreciation; ungrateful. *Be sure to write Uncle Jeff a thank-you note so you won't seem thankless for his gift.*
unappreciative not showing appreciation. *The unappreciative boy did not pretend to enjoy his gift.*
ungrateful not thankful. *The ungrateful citizens picketed the statehouse.*
antonym: thankful

thicken *v.* to make heavier or thicker. *You can use flour to thicken gravy.*
congeal to become solid by cooling. *The sauce will congeal as it cools.*
jell to thicken; congeal. *The fruit juice will jell if you put it in the refrigerator.*

thin *adj.* slender; not thick. *A sheet of paper is thin.*
slender slim; long and thin. *The diet helped him maintain a slender body.*
slight slender; not big. *His slight body made him a quick runner.*
slim thin; slender. *She had a slim figure because she exercised regularly.*
antonym: thick

thought *n.* the act or process of thinking. *She spent many hours in thought about the problem.*
consideration thinking about events to make a decision. *We gave careful consideration to the request.*
reflection thinking carefully, thoughtfully. *Our reflection on the game helped us understand why our team lost.*

study reading and thinking to learn. *My study of chemistry involved learning a lot of formulas.*

thoughtful *adj.* having consideration for others. *She is thoughtful of her friends and never hurts their feelings.*
considerate thoughtful of others. *A considerate person will often lend a hand to help others.*
diplomatic having skills in dealing with others. *His friends said he was diplomatic when faced with a conflict.*
tactful able to say and do the right thing. *Everyone likes a tactful person for a friend.*
antonym: thoughtless

thunder *v.* to make a sound like thunder. *When it began to thunder, we headed for home.*
boom to make a deep sound. *The announcer's voice can boom across the stadium.*
drum to tap again and again. *He likes to drum his fingers loudly.*
roar to make a loud noise. *The lions roar when it is time to eat.*
rumble to make a deep sound; make a continuous sound. *Thunder seemed to rumble in the distance.*

tiny *adj.* very small; wee. *An ant is a tiny animal.*
little small; not big. *The little car was a perfect toy for the young child.*
small little. *The small child seemed to be lost.*
wee tiny; very small. *The story was about a wee person who lived in the woods.*
antonym: huge

tire *v.* to make weary or exhausted. *Exercising for a long time does tire me.*
exhaust to tire. *The long hike over the hills did exhaust the campers.*
fatigue to make weary or tired. *The hard work will fatigue the road crew.*
weary to become tired. *The long walk will weary all of us.*

touch *v.* to feel with the hand or other part of the body. *The builder wanted to touch the cement to see if it was still soft.*
feel to touch. *Mike did feel the wood to see if it needed to be sanded more.*
handle to touch; hold. *She must handle the glass statues very carefully.*
stroke to move the hand gently. *She liked to stroke the pet kitten.*

tough *adj.* strong; not easily torn or broken. *The rug is made of very tough materials.*
hard not soft. *The ice on the lake was frozen as hard as a rock.*
rugged uneven; rough. *It was difficult to walk over the rugged countryside.*
strong having power and force. *The strong workers lifted many boxes on and off the trucks every day.*
antonym: weak

tremble *v.* to shake or quiver. *I was so nervous that my hands began to tremble.*
flutter to wave quickly. *The flag will flutter in the wind.*
quake to vibrate or shake. *She said that she began to quake every time she heard her name called.*
quaver to tremble or shake. *My voice would quaver when I tried to speak.*
shudder to tremble. *The cold winter wind made us shudder.*

trick *n.* something done to deceive. *The phone call was just a trick to get me out of the room while they planned the surprise party.*
joke something funny and clever. *Bob likes to play this joke on his friends.*
lark something that is fun. *Our trip to the house of mirrors was an interesting and exciting lark.*
prank a playful trick. *The phony message was only a prank.*

true *adj.* right; accurate; not false. *It is true that ostriches cannot fly.*
accurate without errors. *She kept accurate accounts of the company's business.*
actual real. *The actual events of the day were recorded in the newspaper.*
correct not wrong; free of mistakes. *He had the most correct answers on the test.*
factual consisting of facts. *We keep factual accounts of each experiment.*
antonym: false

truth *n.* that which agrees with the facts. *You can trust her because she always tells the truth.*
fact something true. *This fact of the case was presented in court.*
reality true state or existence. *The reality may be that these space creatures do not exist.*

uncover *v.* to reveal or expose. *They will uncover the truth during the trial.*
expose to uncover. *We will expose the truth to the television news reporter.*
reveal to make known. *We knew she would not reveal our secret to anyone.*
unearth to find out; discover. *The investigator finally was able to unearth the truth about the accident.*

unhappy *adj.* not happy, sad; full of sorrow. *When Maria was unhappy, we tried to cheer her up.*
sad not happy. *Losing the game made the team feel sad.*
sorrowful full of sorrow. *The death of a pet is a sorrowful occasion.*
unfortunate not lucky. *Losing your money for the show was an unfortunate event.*
unlucky not lucky. *With everything that has happened, he is a very unlucky person.*
antonyms: happy, glad

unlock *v.* to undo a lock by turning a key. *Mr. Hughes can unlock the door and let us in.*
unbolt to undo the bolts. *He will unbolt the door to let us into the house.*
unfasten to untie; undo. *We tried to unfasten the rope that was tied to the fence.*
unlatch to undo a latch. *The farmer was able to unlatch the door to the shed.*
antonym: lock

unsafe *adj.* not safe; dangerous. *Running in a crowded hallway is unsafe.*
dangerous risky; not safe. *The old road through the hills is a dangerous route.*
hazardous dangerous; full of risk. *The hazardous waste was to be buried in a cave.*

useful *adj.* of use; helpful. *She gave me some useful advice about studying for the test.*
helpful giving aid; useful. *My assistant is especially helpful when things get busy.*
serviceable useful. *The mixer has been serviceable for many years.*
worthy having worth. *The plan to restore the old buildings is a worthy cause.*
antonym: useless

view *n.* opinion; idea. *His view was that we should change our plans.*
  idea plan or belief. *The class chose one idea about the scenery for the play.*
  opinion what one thinks. *She asked my opinion on the color of dress to buy.*
  outlook a view. *He has an interesting outlook on the future of the city government.*

village *n.* a number of houses and buildings in an area that is smaller than a town. *Everyone knows everyone else in our village.*
  hamlet a small village. *The little hamlet was nestled in the Swiss mountains.*
  suburb town or village near a city. *We live in a suburb of Chicago.*
  township part of a county. *The township has police and fire departments.*

wasteful *adj.* tending to waste; using or spending too much. *Taking more food than you can eat is wasteful.*
  extravagant wasteful; spending too much. *Extravagant persons often spend more than they need to.*
  lavish giving or spending very generously. *The lavish gifts were too fancy to be used by anyone.*

wise *adj.* having much knowledge or information. *Scientists and professors are wise.*
  knowing well-informed; having much knowledge. *My aunt had a knowing smile on her face when I explained the problem.*
  profound showing great knowledge. *Robert says profound things about the future.*
  sage wise. *You should listen to her sage advice.*
  tactful having tact. *Beth is kind and tactful when she deals with difficult people.*

wonder *v.* to be curious to know. *I wonder how the song will end.*
  disbelieve to refuse to believe. *Marie seemed to disbelieve the story about how the vase was broken.*
  doubt to have difficulty believing. *I doubt if we will ever know the cause of the fire.*
  question to doubt. *I still question the motives of the city officials.*

wring *v.* to twist and squeeze. *Wring out the wet cloth before you wipe the table.*
  squeeze to press hard. *I will squeeze the grapefruit to get all the juice out.*
  twist to wind or turn. *He should twist the rag to get out the water.*

wrinkle *n.* a small crease or fold. *Rosa ironed the wrinkle out of her skirt.*
  crease a wrinkle. *The crease in his forehead showed us he was very worried.*
  crinkle a wrinkle or crease. *The crinkle in the wrapping paper spoiled the package.*
  rumple a wrinkle. *They pressed every rumple from the tablecloths.*

wrong *adj.* not correct; not true. *Your answer was wrong.*
  false not correct; not true. *We were given false information about the crime.*
  inaccurate not accurate. *Our cost estimates were wrong because we were given inaccurate information.*
  incorrect not correct; wrong. *The incorrect directions caused us to get lost.*
  antonym: right

young *adj.* not old or fully grown. *A fawn is a young deer.*
  juvenile young; youthful. *I enjoy reading juvenile books.*
  youngish rather young. *The youngish group was the first to the top of the mountain.*
  youthful young; looking or acting young. *The group had very youthful spirits.*

Writing Thesaurus

333

NOTES

NOTES

NOTES

ANNUAL PRETEST/POSTTEST*
Form A

Word	Dictation Sentences
1. **icicle**	When the dripping water froze, an **icicle** was formed.
2. **title**	The **title** of the song is written on the cassette.
3. **poet**	A person who writes a poem is called a **poet**.
4. **fold**	After the bath towels are washed, I often **fold** them.
5. **glue**	Lee repaired the book cover with **glue**.
6. **rule**	Staying quiet during a fire drill is a good **rule**.
7. **moist**	Many plants grow well in **moist** soil.
8. **choice**	You can have your **choice** of cereal.
9. **sort**	Please **sort** the clothes before you wash them.
10. **forth**	The swing moved back and **forth**.
11. **rear**	If you are at the end of the line, you are in the **rear**.
12. **fear**	When the lion at the zoo roared, I was filled with **fear**.
13. **mark**	Before the race began, we had to **mark** the starting point.
14. **smart**	Kim thought Jonathan was **smart** to study.
15. **spread**	Jill will **spread** cream cheese on a roll.
16. **meant**	I may have said yes, but I **meant** to say no.
17. **knee**	As she climbed the stairs, Tonya hurt her **knee**.
18. **wring**	I twisted the towel to **wring** out the water.
19. **quite**	I was **quite** surprised to see Anne.
20. **quilt**	She used bright colors in the **quilt**.
21. **gym**	During the winter, we play basketball in the **gym**.
22. **strange**	When I travel to another country, many things seem different and **strange**.
23. **battle**	We walked because we did not want to **battle** the traffic.
24. **settle**	Sand in the water will **settle** to the bottom.
25. **stumble**	You must take care not to **stumble** on the rough ground.
26. **double**	I had to **double** the ingredients in the recipe.
27. **winter**	The coldest season of the year is **winter**.
28. **danger**	Because of his skill, the lion tamer was in little **danger**.
29. **nearer**	The light will become brighter as you get **nearer**.
30. **quietest**	The library is the **quietest** room in the school.
31. **loan**	Will you please **loan** your pencil to me?
32. **sore**	After I ran, my muscles were **sore**.
33. **she'd**	Now **she'd** like to have some spinach.
34. **he'll**	If I ask Curtis to come with me, I know **he'll** agree.
35. **unsafe**	Crossing the street without looking both ways can be very **unsafe**.
36. **uncover**	Each morning Joe will **uncover** his canary's cage.
37. **farmer**	Grandma has worked hard as a **farmer** for many years.
38. **climber**	A mountain **climber** is very careful.
39. **thankful**	I was **thankful** for the lovely gift.
40. **playful**	The kittens were in a **playful** mood.
41. **Monday**	Most people go to school or work on **Monday**.
42. **Thursday**	**Thursday** is named after Thor, the Viking god of thunder.
43. **adults**	People who are eighteen years old are often considered **adults**.
44. **monkeys**	We watched the playful **monkeys** at the zoo.
45. **poem's**	Please underline the **poem's** title.
46. **mother's**	I think your **mother's** job is interesting.
47. **sadness**	When her best friend moved away, Sherry was left with a feeling of **sadness**.
48. **softness**	You could feel the **softness** of the cotton.
49. **everyday**	I do my **everyday** chores after school.
50. **whenever**	Please visit us **whenever** you can.

*For more information on using these tests, please see pages Z10–Z11.

ANNUAL PRETEST/POSTTEST*
Form B

Word	Dictation Sentences
1. **climb**	John likes to **climb** the knotted rope at the gym.
2. **tiny**	The baby is so **tiny** you can hold him in one arm.
3. **obey**	I try to **obey** my parents' instructions.
4. **bold**	His handwriting was **bold** and easy to read.
5. **true**	The story I read was **true**.
6. **tube**	Water will flow through the **tube**.
7. **joint**	The part of the arm that allows it to bend is called the **joint**.
8. **spoil**	Some salads **spoil** quickly if they are not kept cold.
9. **sport**	Basketball is my favorite **sport**.
10. **forty**	Of all the books, only **forty** are new.
11. **tear**	That doll can cry a real **tear**.
12. **year**	She will go to school next **year**.
13. **march**	Everyone was asked to **march** in the parade.
14. **market**	My sister bought fresh vegetables at the **market**.
15. **ready**	Randy will be **ready** soon.
16. **already**	I have **already** done my homework.
17. **knife**	Please be careful when using a **knife**.
18. **known**	I have **known** Pete all my life.
19. **quick**	During the debate, Ben was **quick** to answer.
20. **quill**	We found a porcupine **quill**.
21. **gigantic**	Dinosaurs were **gigantic** creatures.
22. **range**	It is hot in the kitchen because Grandmother is cooking on an electric **range**.
23. **bottle**	You can buy juice in a **bottle** or can.
24. **kettle**	Grandmother cooks soup in a large iron **kettle**.
25. **tremble**	I began to **tremble** at the thought of singing a solo.
26. **wrinkle**	I will iron the **wrinkle** out of this dress.
27. **silver**	Native American jewelry is sometimes made from **silver**.
28. **shower**	This afternoon we had a brief rain **shower**.
29. **nearest**	The **nearest** town is a mile away.
30. **quieter**	He speaks softly and is **quieter** than Pat.
31. **lone**	In our front yard stood a **lone** pine tree.
32. **soar**	The eagle was able to **soar** above the treetops.
33. **you'd**	I invited you to the game because I thought **you'd** enjoy it.
34. **they'd**	When I found my friends, **they'd** already eaten lunch.
35. **unfair**	No one likes an **unfair** rule.
36. **unlock**	She has a key to **unlock** the door.
37. **player**	Sam is the tallest **player** on the basketball team.
38. **leader**	The captain of the team is our **leader**.
39. **joyful**	The wedding celebration was a **joyful** one.
40. **careful**	Please be **careful**.
41. **Tuesday**	Mother went shopping on **Tuesday**.
42. **Wednesday**	We went to the dentist on **Wednesday**.
43. **members**	Gail and Tommy are **members** of the band.
44. **slippers**	Kathy has fluffy white **slippers**.
45. **child's**	He was proud of his **child's** honesty.
46. **farmer's**	Mrs. Lee bought the **farmer's** apples.
47. **kindness**	John was thankful for Lynn's **kindness**.
48. **weakness**	The x-ray showed no **weakness** in the steel beam.
49. **sometimes**	Pat and I **sometimes** play tennis.
50. **everyone**	We will begin when **everyone** is here.

*For more information on using these tests, please see pages Z10–Z11.

Scope and Sequence

	GRADE 3	GRADE 4	GRADE 5
Spelling and Phonics			
Auditory/Visual Discrimination		T27, T45, 62–67, T69, T81, 86, T87, 104, T105, T117, 140–145, T177, T189, 194–199, T213	
Sound-Letter Association		T9, T15, T21, 33, T45, T63, T105, T177, T213	
Beginning and Ending Sounds	9, 15, 21, 45, 51, 57, 63, 171, 201	15, 33, 51, T57, 87, T93, 105, 117, T123, T135, 135, 213	
Rhyming Words	27, 33, 45, 51, 63, 69, 82, 99, 117, 129, 135, 141, 165, 189	9, T33, 99, 106, 130, 141	16, 70, 100
Word Analysis	9, 15, 21, 33, 51, 57, 63, 81, 87, 93, 99, 105, 117, 123, 129, 135, 141, 153, 159, 165, 177, 189, 195, 201, 207, 213	9, 15, 33, 45, 51, 69, 105, 123, 135, 141	
Developing Oral Language Skills			
	T9, T15, T21, T27, T33, T45, T51, T57, T63, T69, T81, T87, T93, T99, T105, T117, T123, T129, T135, T141, T153, T159, T165, T171, T177, T189, T195, T201, T207, T213	T9, T15, T21, T27, T33, T45, T51, T57, T63, T69, T81, T87, T93, T99, T105, T117, T123, T129, T135, T141, T153, T159, T165, T171, T177, T189, T195, T201, T207, T213	T9, T15, T21, T27, T33, T45, T51, T57, T63, T69, T81, T87, T93, T99, T105, T117, T123, T129, T135, T141, T153, T159, T165, T171, T177, T189, T195, T201, T207, T213
Spelling and Thinking/Word Sorting			
Sound and Letter Correspondence			
Short Vowels	8, 12, 14, 18, 20, 24, 38–40, 152, 156, 158, 162, 224–226	8, 12, 38–39, T87, 224	32, 36, 38, 41, 228
Long Vowels	44, 48, 50, 54, 56, 60, 62, 66, 68, 72, 74–77, 182, 229–233, 245	14, 18, 20, 24, 26, 30, 32, 36, 38–41, 44, 48, 50, 54, 74–75, 225–230	8, 12, 14, 18, 20, 24, 38–40, 224–226

Scope *and* Sequence

	GRADE 3	GRADE 4	GRADE 5
Spelling and Thinking/Word Sorting (cont.)			
Vowel Digraphs and Diphthongs	26, 30, 32, 36, 38, 40–41, 68, 72, 77, 116, 120, 146–147, 239	50, 54, 56, 60, 62, 66, 74–76, 230–232	20, 24, 26, 30, 38, 40, 86, 90, 110–111, 226–227, 235
r-Controlled Vowels	122, 126, 128, 132, 134, 138, 146–148, 240, 241, 242	62, 66, 68, 72, 74, 77, 80, 84, 110–111, 128, 132, 146, 148, 164, 168, 232–234, 241	62, 66, 68, 72, 74, 76–77, 80, 84, 110–111, 232–234
Consonants, Clusters, and Digraphs	80, 84, 86, 90, 92, 96, 110–112, 152, 156, 158, 162, 182–183, 234–236, 244–245	92, 96, 98, T99, 102, 104, 108, 110, 112–113, 237–238	44, 48, 74–75, 104, 108, 110, 113, 170, 174, 182, 184, 229, 238, 247
Homophones	140, 144, 146, 149, 243	140–141, T141, 142, 143, 144, 146	
High Frequency Words (Words Writers Use)	104, 108, 112, 238		188, 192, 218–219, 249
Unstressed Endings		116, 120, 122, T123, 146–147, 165, 239–240	50, 54, 56, 60, 74–76, 230–231
Special Spellings	98, 102, 110, 112, 152, 156, 162, 176, 180, 182–183, 237	86, 90, 92, 96, 110–112, 235–236	140, 144, 146, 149, 200, 204, 206, 210, 212, 216, 218, 220–221, 243, 251, 253
Structural Patterns			
Plurals	188, 192, 194, 198, 218–219, 249–250	188–189, 192, 218–219, 249	158, 162, 182–183, 245
Inflectional Endings	164, 168, 170, 174, 182, 184, 236, 246–247		128, 132, 146, 148, 241
Contractions	176, 180, 182, 185, 248	152, T153, 156, 182–183, 244	
Compounds	212, 216, 218, 221, 253	206, T207, 210, 218, 220, 252	134, 138, 146, 148, 242
Possessives		194, T195, 198, 218–219, 250	
Prefixes and Suffixes	164, 170, 174, 200, 204, 206, 210, 218, 220, 251–252	134, 135, 138, 146, 148, 158, T159, 162, 164, 168, 170, T171, 174, 182–184, 200, T201, 204, 218, 220, 242, 245–247, 251	92, 96, 98, 102, 110, 112, 122, 126, 146–147, 152, 156, 164, 168, 176, 180, 182–185, 194, 198, 218–219, 236–237, 240, 244, 246, 248, 250
Content Words		176, 180, 182, 185, 212, 216, 218, 221, 248, 253	116, 120, 146–147, 239

T340

	GRADE 3	GRADE 4	GRADE 5
Spelling and Vocabulary			
Word Meaning	123, 135, 141, 160	9, 21, 27, 33, 45, 51, 57, 63–64, 69, 81, 87, 93, 99, 105, 117, 123, 129, 135, 141, 153, 159, 165, 171, 177, 189, 195, 201, 207, 213	9, 15, 21, 27, 33, 69, 81, 87, 93, 99, 105, 123, 129, 141, 153, 159, 165, 171, 177, 189, 195, 201, 207, 213
Word Structure	9, 15, 21, 27, 33, 51, 69, 93, 117, 123, 129, 135, 153, 159, 171, 177, 195, 201, 207, 213	9, 15, 21, 27, 33, 45, 69, 105, 123, 177, 189, 195, 201, 213	9, 33, 81, 87, 93, 99, 105, 117, 123, 135, 141, 153, 159, 165, 177, 189, 195, 201, 207, 213
Word Clues	9, 15, 81, 99, 105, 117, 129	10, 64, 81, 94, 105, 166	15, 51, 117, 135, 171
Related Meanings	105	T29, 57, 189, 195	27, 33, 45, 63, 129
Words With Similar Meanings	93, 207–208	27, 117, 171, 201, 209	21, 27, 88, 142, 160
Synonyms and Antonyms	70, 87, 106, 117–118, 123, 160, 207–208	15, 63, 87–88, 94, 135, 153, 159, 171–172, 202, 207	10, 28, 45, 51, 57, 63, 69, 88, 123, 142, 160, 177, 195, 201
Spelling and Reading			
Context Clues	10, 16, 22, 28, 34, 46, 52, 58, 64, 70, 82, 94, 100, 106, 118, 124, 130, 136, 142, 154, 160, 166, 172, 178, 190, 196, 202, 208, 214	10, 22, 28, 34, 46, 52, 58, 64, 70, 82, 88, 100, 106, 118, 124, 130, 136, 142, 154, 160, 166, 172, 178, 190, 196, 202, 208, 214	10, 16, 22, 28, 34, 46, 52, 58, 64, 70, 82, 88, 94, 100, 106, 118, 124, 130, 136, 142, 154, 160, 166, 172, 178, 190, 196, 202, 208
Analogies	10, 22, 28, 34, 46, 94, 118, 166, 178, 214	10, 16, 22, 28, 34, 52, 70, 82, 94, 118, 130, 208	10, 16, 22, 34, 52, 58, 82, 94, 124, 130, 154, 172, 178, 196
Classification	52, 124, 130, 142, 154, 172, 190, 196, 202	70, 88, 190, 214	10, 46, 94
Other Strategies	16, 28, 46, 58, 64, 70, 82, 88, 130, 202, 208	34, 46, 64, 94, 100, 118, 136, 160, 166, 178, 196	10, 16, 21, 27, 70, 88, 94, 100, 142, 160, 166, 190, 214
Spelling and Writing			
Expository Writing	29, 47, 59, 71, 101, T114, 131, 143, 161, 191, 209, T222	47, 83, 95, T114, 137, 179, 203, 209, T222	17, 29, 65, 95, T114, 119, 143, 161, 191, 197, 203, 209, 215

Scope and Sequence

	GRADE 3	GRADE 4	GRADE 5
Spelling and Writing (continued)			
Narrative Writing	17, 23, 35, T42, 65, T78, 107, 125, 167, T186, 197, 215	11, 17, 23, 53, 65, 71, T78, 101, 125, 143, 161, 173, T186, 191	11, 23, 47, 71, T78, 83, 101, 125, 131, 167, T186, 191
Descriptive Writing	53, 83, 95, 137, 173, 179	42, 53, T42, 71, 117, 131, 167	T42, 53, 89, 137, 179, T222
Persuasive Writing	11, 89, 119, T150, 155, 203	29, 35, 59, 89, 107, 119, T150, 155, 197, 215	35, 59, 107, T150, 155, 173
The Writing Process	11, 17, 23, 29, 35, T42, 47, 53, 59, 65, 71, T78, 83, 89, 95, 101, 107, T114, 119, 125, 131, 137, 143, T150, 155, 161, 167, 173, 179, T186, 191, 197, 203, 209, 215, T222, 258–259	11, 17, 23, 29, 35, 42, T42, 47, 53, 59, 65, 71, T78, 83, 89, 95, 101, 107, T114, 117, 119, 125, 131, 137, 143, T150, 155, 161, 167, 173, 179, T186, 191, 197, 203, 209, 215, 222, T222, 258	11, 17, 23, 29, 35, T42, 47, 53, 59, 65, 71, T78, 83, 89, 95, 101, 107, T114, 119, 125, 131, 137, 143, T150, 155, 161, 167, 173, 179, T186, 191, 197, 203, 209, 215, T222, 258
Graphic Organizers	T42, T78, T114, T150, T186, T222	T42, T78, T114, T150, T186, T222	T42, T78, T114, T150, T186, T222
Proofreading	11, 17, 23, 29, 35, 43, 47, 53, 59, 65, 71, 79, 83, 89, 95, 101, 107, 115, 119, 125, 131, 137, 143, 151, 155, 161, 167, 173, 179, 187, 191, 197, 203, 209, 215, 223	11, 17, 23, 29, 35, 43, 47, 53, 59, 65, 71, 79, 83, 89, 95, 101, 107, 115, 119, 125, 131, 137, 143, 151, 155, 161, 167, 173, 179, 187, 191, 197, 203, 209, 215, 223	11, 17, 23, 29, 35, 43, 47, 53, 59, 65, 71, 79, 83, 89, 95, 101, 107, 115, 119, 125, 131, 137, 143, 151, 155, 161, 167, 173, 179, 187, 191, 197, 203, 209, 215, 223
Content Connections			
Language Arts	19, 25, 103, 109, 121, 145, 169, 175, 193, 199, 217	37, 61, 109, 121, 139, 145, 157, 163, 181, 205	13, 19, 31, 37, 67, 97, 127, 133, 157
Science	13, 19, 25, 31, 37, 49, 55, 85, 91, 97, 103, 127, 139, 145, 157, 163, 199	13, 31, 55, 67, 103, 127, 169, 193, 199, 211	13, 25, 55, 85, 91, 121, 145, 163, 181, 193, 199, 205, 211, 217
Social Studies	55, 61, 67, 73, 85, 109, 157, 169, 175, 181, 205, 211	13, 25, 49, 55, 67, 73, 85, 97, 127, 133, 139, 157, 169, 175, 181, 205, 217	19, 49, 61, 97, 103, 121, 127, 139, 175, 181, 199, 205
Fine Arts	49	25, 49, 61, 103, 145	31, 73, 85, 109, 157, 193, 211

	GRADE 3	GRADE 4	GRADE 5
Content Connections (continued)			
Math	13, 31, 37, 67, 73, 91, 97, 127, 133, 181, 193, 205	19, 85, 97, 109, 121, 133, 163, 193, 217	37, 61, 91, 103, 109, 163, 169, 175, 217
Health	61, 121, 133, 139, 163, 211, 217	19, 31, 73, 91, 175, 199	55, 73, 139, 145
Grammar, Usage, and Mechanics			
Nouns	78	57, 69, 78, T165, 207	114
Pronouns	222	150	114, 150
Possessives		42	150
Verbs	114, 150	57, 69, 114, T165	42, 78
Adjectives	186	186, 207	186
Adverbs		207, 222	222
Conjunctions		93, 207	
Types of Sentences	42		
Parts of a Sentence			42, 78
Dictionary/Thesaurus			
Alphabetical Order	9, 21, 27, 33, 81, 93, 105, 117, 153, 169, 213	9, 21, 81, 105, 129, 159, 213	
Definitions	15, 63, 207	15, 69, 189, 195, 201	51, 63, 69, 81, 87, 123, 141, 207
Phonetic Spellings	45, 57, 99, 129, 135, 141, 159, 177	33, 63, 123, 141, 153, 165	9, 21, 27, 57, 105, 129, 135, 141, 159, 171, 189
Parts of Speech and Inflected Forms	51, 123, 165, 171, 195, 201	15, 45, 57, 69, 93, 135, 195, 207	15, 57, 99, 123
Guide Words	87, 105, 117, 189, 213	105, 129, 159	93, 153, 165
Syllabication	69	T9, 51, 63, 123	21, 27
Etymologies and Homographs		27, 69, 177	45, 117, 213
Using a Thesaurus/Synonyms		87, 99, 117, 171, 201	33, 177, 195, 201

Scope and Sequence

	GRADE 3	GRADE 4	GRADE 5
Electronic Spelling			
Computer Terms	79	79	79, 151, 223
Search Engines	187	43	43
Spell Checker	115	115, 151	115
Graphics		187	187
Internet	223	223	
File Names	43		
E-Mail	101, 151, 191		
Handwriting			
One-Minute Handwriting Hints	T10, T16, T22, T28, T34, T46, T52, T58, T64, T70, T82, T88, T94, T100, T106, T118, T124, T130, T136, T142, T154, T160, T166, T172, T178, T190, T196, T202, T208, T214	T10, T16, T22, T28, T34, T46, T52, T58, T64, T70, T82, T88, T94, T100, T106, T118, T124, T130, T136, T142, T154, T160, T166, T172, T178, T190, T196, T202, T208, T214	T10, T16, T22, T28, T34, T46, T52, T58, T64, T70, T82, T88, T94, T100, T106, T118, T124, T130, T136, T142, T154, T160, T166, T172, T178, T190, T196, T202, T208, T214

Spelling Connections Word List
Grades 1–6

Note: Each word is identified by grade level, unit number, and list designation. Words may be featured more than once per grade or in more than one grade. Words in the targeted grade level are printed in blue.

C	Core List
A	Assessment
LA	Language Arts
SS	Social Studies
S	Science
H	Health
M	Math
FA	Fine Arts
CH	Challenge
P	Preview
R	Review
WW	Writer's Words

A

a 1-14-C
abbreviation 6-29-LA
ability 5-29-C
able 4-3-C
abolish .5-33-SS
about 3-16-C; 4-9-R
above 3-16-C
absence .6-32-C
absent 6-10-C
accent 6-1-C
accept 5-23-C
acceptable 6-19-C
accident .6-17-C
accord .6-11-SS
accountant 6-36-A
accurate .6-25-C
accurately 6-11-P
accuse 6-5-C
ache 4-28-H
achieve 6-8-C
achieving .6-8-P
acid 4-32-S
acorn 2-31-CH
acquire .5-31-CH
acre 6-35-P
acreage 6-21-P
across 3-19-C
act 3-1-C
action 6-29-C
active 5-5-C

actively 6-11-CH
activities 6-2-P
activity 5-29-C
actor 4-32-P; 5-25-C
acute 6-5-C
add 2-2-M
addend 4-26-M
addition 4-26-M
additional 5-8-CH
additionally 6-11-C
address 5-31-C
adequate 6-1-CH
adj. 5-35-CH
adjective 4-9-LA
admirable 6-19-P
admire .6-3-P
admit 6-1-C
admittance 6-32-CH
admitted 5-16-P; 6-15-C
admitting 6-15-C
adobe .3-9-SS
adorable 6-19-C
adore 6-9-C
adults .4-31-C
adv. 5-35-CH
advance 6-1-C
advancement 6-21-C
advantage 6-21-C
adventure 5-1-LA
adventurer 4-30-A; 5-25-CH
adventuresome 6-22-P
adventurous 5-32-C
adverb .4-9-LA
affectionate 6-30-A
affinity 6-13-P
affirm 6-9-P
afford .6-17-P
afraid .3-16-C
Africa 4-35-C; 5-19-R
after 3-17-C
afternoon 3-35-C
aftershock 4-34-S
afterward 6-11-C
again .3-16-C
against 5-10-LA
age 3-14-C; 4-17-R
aged 6-33-C
agent 5-28-P; 6-31-C
ago 1-14-WW; 2-16-R
agree 3-16-P; 4-4-C
agreement 4-33-C; 5-29-R
agriculture 6-19-SS
ahead .4-14-C

aid 3-8-C
ailment 6-24-A
aim 4-3-C
air 3-22-C
aircraft 5-12-A
airless .4-28-R
air mail 3-32-P; 4-34-C
airplane 3-35-C
airport 4-10-SS
airy 4-16-S
aisle 4-24-A; 6-16-C
Alabama (AL) 5-19-C
alarm 3-16-P; 4-13-C
alarm clock 4-34-C
Alaska (AK) 5-19-C
Albany, NY 5-19-CH
album 6-1-C
alert 5-10-C
alike 2-15-P; 3-28-LA
alive 3-7-P; 4-2-C; 5-31-R
all 2-7-C
alley 5-24-A
alliance .6-3-P
alligator 4-21-P; 5-34-C
allow 5-14-C
allowance 4-9-P; 5-14-C; 6-32-R
all right 5-31-P; 6-23-C
ally 5-24-A; 6-11-SS
almanac 6-28-LA
almond 6-16-C
almost 2-7-P; 3-11-C
alone 4-2-C
along 5-10-LA
aloud 3-4-P; 4-23-CH
alphabet 4-26-LA
already .4-14-C
also 4-7-C
alternate 5-4-CH; 6-33-R
although 5-31-C
altimeter 6-34-CH
altitude 4-21-SS
alto 5-31-FA
always 2-13-P; 3-8-C
am 1-2-C; 2-7-R
A.M. 5-35-P; 6-35-C
amateur 6-28-C
amaze .6-14-C
amazement 6-21-P
ambitious 6-27-P
ambulance 6-32-C
amendment 6-13-SS
America 4-35-C; 5-19-R
American 4-35-C

C

T352

T358

T375